NO
GIFTS
FROM
CHANCE

No
GIFTS
FROM
CHANCE

*A Biography of
Edith Wharton*

W

SHARI BENSTOCK

CHARLES SCRIBNER'S SONS • NEW YORK

MAXWELL MACMILLAN CANADA • TORONTO
MAXWELL MACMILLAN INTERNATIONAL
NEW YORK   OXFORD   SINGAPORE   SYDNEY

FOR B.B.

Charles Scribner's Sons
Macmillan Publishing Company
866 Third Avenue
New York, NY 10022

Maxwell Macmillan Canada, Inc.
1200 Eglinton Avenue East
Suite 200
Don Mills, Ontario M3C 3N1

Macmillan Publishing Company is part of the Maxwell Communication Group
of Companies.
Library of Congress Cataloging-in-Publication Data
Benstock, Shari.
No gifts from chance: a biography of Edith Wharton/by Shari
Benstock.
p.   cm.
Includes bibliographical references and index.
ISBN 0-684-19276-4
1. Wharton, Edith, 1862–1937—Biography.   2. Women authors,
American—20th century—Biography.   I. Title.
PS3545.H16Z595   1994
813'.52—dc20   93-33704
[B]
Macmillan books are available at special discounts for bulk purchases for sales
promotions, premiums, fund-raising, or educational use. For details, contact:
Special Sales Director
Macmillan Publishing Company
866 Third Avenue
New York, NY 10022
10 9 8 7 6 5 4 3 2 1
Printed in the United States of America

Contents

Book III   Rewards

Preface

W

"THIS BRAVE AND SUBTLE SPIRIT"

I magine, for a moment, a young woman born to wealth and privilege in the leisured society of nineteenth-century Old New York. Fitted into brocade and velvet, her red-gold hair caught in a ringlet of curls, she is expected to become a society matron. But another calling—born of her love for words and a gift for storytelling—intervenes against these well-laid plans. Entering the ballroom of Mrs. Levi Morton's Fifth Avenue mansion as a seventeen-year-old debutante, she has already lived a third of her life in Europe, written a novel and several short stories, and published (under her pastor's name) a translation of a German poem, receiving for it an honorarium of $50, her first literary earnings. Before the assembled guests, representatives of a society that was hers by birth and where she was expected to take her rightful place, she stood paralyzed with fear.

In retrospect, the compelling question about Edith Newbold Jones on that cold January evening in 1879 is one Edith Wharton asked about George Sand and George Eliot. It concerns self-transformation: How did the frightened debutante become the social chronicler of her age, an internationally acclaimed author of forty-seven books, a woman of firm opinions and independent mind? Loosening the social bonds that immobilized her in Mrs. Morton's ballroom required courage, audacity, and a willingness to risk censure—qualities inimical to New York's "age of innocence."

Nothing in Edith Jones's background heralded her diverse creativity and abounding energy, nor was she encouraged to develop her "gift." Her imaginative powers worried her parents and "positively frightened" her husband. Her talents might well have lain dormant or been cut to the measure of drawing room conversation and dinner table dialogue (at which she was expert). Instead, she began a long literary apprenticeship, working alone and without mentors. At age thirty-seven, she emerged on the American and English literary scene as author of *The Greater Inclination* (1899), a book of short stories. Reviewers proclaimed her a writer with "that rare creative power called literary genius." Many years later, she told an aspiring writer, "I do not regret having written and re-written for so many years before I published." An anomalous figure, the last literary descendant of the Anglo-Dutch merchants who had founded New York, she had little in common with her literary contemporaries. Born into the middle class, they looked westward for inspiration and subject matter. Alienated by the grasping materialism of industrial America, she returned to Europe, where she had lived as a child, and spent the last thirty years of her life in France. In the postwar period of Jazz Age excess, she found her way back to Old New York. Retracing its faded outlines in memory and imagination, she resurrected her own past—not as nostalgia, but as social critique. In *The Age of Innocence* and *Old New York*, the twin gods of graciousness and respectability once again thwart the ambitions and dreams of young women and men.

Disciplined to the daily task, she wrote every day until the last weeks of her life. In a 1937 obituary, the *New York Herald* remarked that Edith Wharton's "determination to write novels constituted a defiance of tradition difficult to comprehend today." More than fifty years after her death, her determination and defiance and the extraordinary range of her accomplishments seem all the more remarkable. She might have spent her afternoons reading novels (as her mother did); instead, she spent her mornings writing them. Drawn to the scenes of her self-transformation—recorded in fiction, poetry, and memoirs—we watch her conquer fate through the act of writing. Awaiting "no gifts from chance," she fashioned life to her own desires.

Acknowledgments

I am indebted to the libraries whose archives of Edith Wharton's correspondence, manuscripts, diaries, and photographs constitute the primary resources for this biography (see Archives) and to the generous assistance of staff members at these institutions, who have assisted me during the past six years. My investigations outside library reading rooms led to unexpected discoveries. I am deeply indebted to dozens of government officials in the United States and France who assisted my search for birth, death, tax, divorce, estate, church, cemetery, medical, and military records. Their invaluable work has helped establish a fuller, more accurate, record of Edith Wharton's life that sheds light on her family relationships and discounts several prominent myths. In France, I was assisted by: United States Embassy (Paris) and U.S. Consular Agency (Nice); Mayor's Office, City of Paris; Church of the Holy Trinity (Paris); Mayor's Office, City of Cannes; Cimetière du Grand Jas (Cannes). In the United States, the National Archives and Records Administration facilitated my work on census records, immigration and naturalization procedures, and boat passenger lists. I am particularly indebted to staff members at the Military Reference Division, Washington, D.C., and assistance from the New England and Northeast regional centers of the National Archives. The following archives and organizations aided my work. New York: New

York City Department of Records and Information Services, Municipal Archives Division; New York Public Library Microfilm Division, Genealogical Division, and NYPL theater archives at Lincoln Center; New-York Historical Society; New York Society Library; Columbia University, Columbiana Collection; Columbia County Historical Society. Massachusetts: Massachusetts State Archives, New England Historic Genealogical Society, Edith Wharton Restoration (Lenox), Lenox Public Library, Ashfield Historical Society. Pennsylvania: College of Physicians (Philadelphia), University of Pennsylvania Archives, Episcopal Diocese of Pennsylvania. Rhode Island: Newport Historical Society and the Redwood Library (Newport).

This book was supported by sabbatical leave (1992–1993) and a Max Orovitz Summer Research Grant from the University of Miami. A Ball Brothers Foundation Visiting Fellowship in summer 1991 underwrote my work at the Lilly Library, Indiana University. My research on Edith Wharton (conducted while teaching full-time and without graduate student research assistance) was substantially aided by my husband, Bernard Benstock, to whom this book is dedicated. He proved a patient reader of microfilm, an indefatigable archivist, a literary detective *par excellence*, and a superb proofreader—not to mention his talents as chef and travel companion. My thanks to Belinda Ghitis for her efficient assistance on a variety of research problems.

I am indebted to the Edith Wharton Estate for access to unpublished materials, and I am especially grateful to William R. Tyler, residuary legatee of the estate, who graciously aided my work, sharing his memories of Edith Wharton and answering my many questions. My thanks, as well, to attorney Herbert A. Fierst and literary agent Gloria Loomis for facilitating permissions. Elaine Markson, my literary agent, and Barbara Grossman, my editor at Scribners, provided the impetus for this book: Elaine asked me to write it, and Barbara arranged to publish it. They took in stride every unexpected turn on the long road from research to writing, and encouraged me to do the same. At Elaine Markson Literary Agency, Stephanie Hawkins and Sally Wofford kept me on schedule and solved problems before I had a chance to worry about them. At Scribners, Jennie Sharf facilitated the editorial process with patience and good humor.

I am fortunate to have as friends several biographers who shared their thoughts on biography and let me peek at their biographies-in-process: Beth Brombert, Isabelle de Courtivron, Janet and Gareth

Dunleavy, Noel Riley Fitch, Fred Kaplan, Brenda Maddox, Linda Wagner-Martin, and Susan Williams.

My greatest debts are to stalwart friends and colleagues who read the manuscript in draft, offering helpful suggestions and invaluable insights. The mistakes are my own, the credit is theirs: Steven Alford, Suzanne Ferriss, Barbara Grossman, Scott Marshall, Linda Wagner-Martin, Alan Price, Nancy Walker, and Susan Williams. With special thanks to Tom Hayes, Fred Kaplan, Scott Marshall, Alan Price, and Jacques Fosse for sharing their research finds.

Author's Note

This is the first full-life biography of Edith Wharton to document published and unpublished sources. Approximately 80 percent of the material included in endnotes to this book is drawn from unpublished letters and manuscripts and difficult-to-find items. The notes provide students and scholars of Edith Wharton's work a map to the rich resources housed in research libraries (see Archives).

Because her novels and novellas exist in many editions, I have not provided page numbers for quotations from these sources. Short story references are to the *Collected Short Stories of Edith Wharton* (see Chronology). Page numbers are provided for nonfiction works. Speculative datings for unpublished letters are bracketed. Quoting from her published and unpublished letters, I have silently emended abbreviations ("which," "should," "could") and eliminated the ampersand.

They, believe me, who await
No gifts from chance, have conquered fate.

> —*Matthew Arnold, "Resignation: To Fausta," 1853 (Edith
> Wharton, Commonplace Book, 1908)*

Literature was the center of her life—indeed her life itself was literature, for the habit of transposing everything into terms of her art, extended to herself. She saw herself, I am convinced, in "situations" even while she was dealing with them. An experience that in the living of it had been a series of contretemps, she would reset as she would have wished it and was thereafter convinced that it had happened so.

> —*Robert Norton, "Memoir," 1937*

Her whole attitude in life bore the stamp of two fearless virtues, courage and simplicity. I mean, the quest for an inmost reality in all psychological situations, as they appeared before her at the bidding of her imaginative power.

> —*Elisina Tyler to Frederic R. King, May 20, 1949*

Book One

THE
OLD ORDER

Chapter 1

A QUESTION OF HERITAGE

EDITH NEWBOLD JONES, WHO GREW UP TO BECOME THE writer Edith Wharton, was born on January 24, 1862, in her parents' spacious brownstone at 14 West Twenty-third Street, just off Fifth Avenue and the fashionable Madison Square. At her daughter's birth, Lucretia Stevens Rhinelander Jones, a society matron in her late thirties, had been married for eighteen years to George Frederic Jones, a gentleman of leisure. They had two sons—Frederic, aged sixteen, who in autumn 1862 would enter Columbia College, and Henry, aged eleven, known to his friends as "Harry." A handsome, worldly woman very certain of her social place as *the* Mrs. Jones among an extended family of Knickerbocker descendants, Lucretia had long since left behind nursery duties. Indeed, the Twenty-third Street house had no nursery and one had to be improvised. We know nothing of Lucretia's feelings about her third pregnancy, but it broke the pattern of an otherwise predictable existence. Late and unexpected, the pregnancy also betrayed her active sexuality, a possible embarrassment for a woman who could be priggish about such matters. The baby's birth gave rise to gossip about Lucretia's private life and speculation about Edith's paternity.

EDITH'S BIRTHPLACE, a five-story, chocolate-brown town house, so marked her childish imagination that years later, she could recall every detail of its setting and furnishings—the low steps leading to a front vestibule painted in Pompeian red and trimmed with a frieze of stenciled lotus leaves; the heavily draped white-and-gold drawing rooms where straight-backed chairs cushioned in purple brocade stood at attention like sentinels along the walls; the central staircase, carpeted in red velvet, spiraling toward the upper regions of the tall house. From this vantage point, Edith observed the comings and goings of her parents and their friends. She watched her mother, a figure of best-dressed womanhood, welcome dinner guests or sweep down the staircase to her waiting carriage, "resplendent in train, aigrette and opera cloak."[1]

The 1860 national census gives an interior view of this household prior to Edith's arrival. Of more than twenty George Joneses living in the borough of Manhattan, only one is listed as a "gentleman"— George Frederic Jones, owner of a town house valued at $20,000 and personal property at $6,000. (He spent far more money on his Newport cottage, built in 1861 and valued at $60,000.) Like similar establishments, the house was staffed primarily by Irish immigrant women, hired cheaply, as were the black cook and coachman. The comparative understatement of the Joneses' style of living marked them as "Society of Birth" with inherited social standing, people who kept to their circle of peers and shunned nouveau riche pretentiousness. Although Lucretia strictly adhered to rules of correct speech and behavior, she did not adopt the formal English model of house management (as her daughter would), perhaps because she was not as fastidious as she expected others to be. A perfectly regulated household required a good deal of discipline on the part of its mistress, and Lucretia was indolent by nature. A woman settled comfortably into her worldly security, she did not put herself out for others. Following the customs of her class, she chose inertia over activity, except when it came to shopping, for which she had an inexhaustible reserve of energy. Edith later recalled that her mother expected much of her servants but gave them no consideration.[2]

The most important and imposing figure among the seven-member staff was Maryland-born Mary Johnson, aged forty-two in 1860, an extraordinarily talented cook who prepared delicious southern fare. Edith remembered her as a "gaunt towering woman of a rich bronzy black," with golden loops in her ears and brightly colored kerchiefs on her head. Illiterate, she cooked from memory and inspiration. Lucretia Jones, writing in a "script of ethereal elegance," recorded Mary's special dishes alongside Rhinelander-Stevens family recipes. George Frederic, a gastronome whose mother, Elizabeth Schermerhorn, was reputed to have been the best cook in New York, presided proudly over his table and served excellent wines from the family cellar. Three Irish domestics—Mary Kiernan and two young sisters, Margaret and Ann Flood—kept the house in order. George Watts, a thirty-year-old black man from New York, served as coachman, and William Strong, aged twenty, was warder. Also listed on the census roll was a James Blake, possibly the tutor to Frederic and Henry Jones. Although their friends used students from Columbia College or called into service elder bachelor cousins to tutor their children, the Joneses—who placed a high priority on the quality of their sons' education—engaged an Englishman as tutor. He may have resided in the Jones household; in any case, his name was linked amorously with that of Lucretia Jones.

The central figure in Edith's infant world was Hannah Doyle ("Doyley"), her red-cheeked and humorous Irish nurse. Formerly Harry's nursemaid, Doyley had been kept on in the household as a seamstress. Called back into nursery service at age forty-two, she lovingly tended red-haired, blue-eyed Edith through those first winter months. When spring arrived, Doyley wheeled the baby in a high-framed black carriage to Madison Square Park for afternoon outings. She was the "warm cocoon," the "rich all-permeating presence" in which infant Edith lived "safe and sheltered." "How I pity all children who have not had a Doyley," Edith wrote some seventy years later, "a nurse who has always been there, who is as established as the sky and as warm as the sun, who understands everything, feels everything, can arrange everything, and combines all the powers of the Divinity with the compassion of a mortal heart like one's own!" Doyley's loving smile was the one constant in a childhood world that for all its comforts was sometimes lonely and darkened by illness.[3]

MYSTERIES OF LOVE AND WAR

Edith entered a world divided by the Civil War, its rancor and deadly slaughter forming the distant background of her first three years of life.

On the raw and bleak Friday of her birth, New Yorkers looked south to Cincinnati, Ohio, where Federal army troops, shin-deep in mud after days of rain, attempted to break the Confederate line. "Our Artillery Operating Within Sixty Yards of Enemy's Lines," proclaimed the *New York Times*, its front pages filled with special reports and regional dispatches of some half-dozen battles. Three months later, on Easter Sunday, Union forces were engaged in the most dramatic naval engagement yet in the war, the battle for New Orleans, which would secure the Federal naval blockade of southern ports. Bursts of shellfire filled the sky with black smoke, and before the week was out, the city was in Union hands.

In New York that spring morning, Easter Sunday, the Joneses prepared for their daughter's baptism. Swaddled in white lace and christening cap, Edith squinted in the sun as the family brougham made its way south to Grace Church, the white marble Gothic Revival structure on the corner of Broadway and Eleventh Street. George Frederic and Lucretia were not members of this congregation, nor would Edith ever be, but entering its baptismal rolls guaranteed one's place in the social hierarchy of the city. Edith was duly enrolled, the only official notice of her birth. (No record exists in the New York City Department of Records.) In the church registry, her name appears on the same page as a child born to George Frederic Jones's cousin Caroline Schermerhorn Astor, wife of William Backhouse Astor; *the* Mrs. Astor, she was the acknowledged leader of New York society. Entered just beneath the name "Edith Newbold Jones" is that of a baby girl born to Thomas House Taylor, fourth rector of the church, who baptized all three of the Jones children.

Standing before Dr. Taylor on April 20, 1862, were Edith's parents and her sponsors—Lucretia Jones's favorite sister, Mary Elizabeth Rhinelander, and her husband, Thomas H. Newbold (for whom Edith was named), and a cousin, Miss Caroline King. No sponsor represented the Joneses, although members of George Frederic's family had sponsored Edith's brothers. Following the name "Jones" on the registry pages for each child is the notation "George F. & ————." On Edith's record, a clerk later penciled in the name "Lucretia Rhinelander." These clerical oversights (unique in the Grace Church baptismal registry) might be explained as a too strict enforcement of the code of feminine propriety by which a woman's name was to appear in print only three times—at birth, marriage, and death—were it not that Edith seemed to suffer from a lack of mother love. The paid guardianship of nurses and governesses covered over this absence of the maternal. The father's name, properly recorded in the official book, covers over another gap—the mystery of paternity.[4]

Two rumors circulated about the circumstances of Edith's birth. One version claimed that she was the daughter of her brothers' tutor; in the other, she was the daughter of a Scottish lord. The first story was by far the better-known tale; Edith heard it long after the principals were dead. Cultivated in the hothouse climate of a narrow and inbred society, these tales emerge against the backdrop of two highly publicized scandals in the Jones and Stevens families in the 1860s and 1870s. The events that befell Lucretia's cousin Mary Stevens Strong and George Alfred Jones (George Frederic's cousin) mixed tragedy and farce as they exposed the "sins of society," passionate intrigue enacted behind heavily draped windows of Manhattan brownstones.[5]

Mary Stevens Strong, daughter of a prominent banker and littérateur, made the front pages of New York newspapers when in the early 1860s, her husband, Peter Remson Strong, sued her for divorce. Married in 1853, they had three children and apparently lived together happily until Peter's brother came to live with them after his wife's death. He and Mary entered into an "illicit intimacy" that, "in a fit of remorse," she confessed to her husband in January 1862. Word of the couple's separation spread through New York society the week of Edith Jones's birth, but three years passed before the spectacular divorce and child custody trial opened in Superior Court on November 25, 1865. Key testimony came from the children's governess, who provided "damaging revelations" about her mistress. City newspapers offered editorial opinions, the *New York Herald* claiming that the tragedy indicated "deep social demoralization . . . due to the influence of the Academy of Music and theaters."[6]

The second scandal broke in October 1872, when the financial misdealings of George Alfred Jones became public. To support a mistress, he had defrauded some of the most revered society families—the Auchmutys, Chadwicks, and Costers, among others. Under threat of criminal proceedings, he and his wife were forced to surrender their real estate and personal property, raising a sum covering about 40 percent of his defalcations. They then retired to Bristol, Connecticut, where he manufactured clocks, lamp parts, and dolls to pay off his liability. New York diarist George Templeton Strong noted that Jones had earlier been led into "evil courses" by losing some $60,000 (almost $1,000,000 at today's rates) in a mechanized "walking-doll" enterprise.[7]

These were not isolated instances of immoral behavior in old society, but newspaper accounts of the court trials made them difficult to ignore. We do not know Lucretia's feelings about her cousin, Mary Stevens Strong, but Edith remembered that her mother "always darted away from George Alfred's name after pronouncing it." When, as a married woman, Edith at last found the courage to ask what he had done, her mother's "muttered" response combined scorn with "excited curiosity." "Some woman," she answered. "Thank heaven *she* was not responsible for him—he belonged to my father's side of the family!" The family washed its hands of George Alfred; except as a "nursery hobgoblin" to scare children, he ceased to exist.[8]

In Edith's opinion, Lucretia maintained an "incurably prosaic" view of life, yet the two stories that circulated about her were anything but commonplace. In their tragicomic eccentricity, these tales exceeded anything Lucretia might have discovered in the popular novels she read on afternoons when her husband attended services at Calvary Church or strolled along the avenues. The English tutor was said to have gone West subsequently and been killed by Indians in the Badlands, or perhaps with General Custer in the battle of the Little Big Horn. If pedantic and proper Lucretia seemed an unlikely adulteress, even less does Edith's brief mention of her brothers' "extremely cultivated English tutor" fit a frontiersman felled by Indians. Yet, the rumor, which persisted beyond Edith Wharton's death, joined illicit love to frontier adventure.[9]

Many foreigners went West in the late 1860s, and some joined Custer to fight Indians and secure lands in the westward expansion. But these men were usually immigrants with little or no education, not English public school graduates who could work for private wages. The Civil War created Custer, making him a major general while still in his mid-twenties. After the war, he became the darling of East Coast society and gained financial support from captains of industry and financiers such as August Belmont, who invested in frontier exploration. Custer may have met the tutor through New York society connections; in autumn 1866, the tutor would have been looking for work, the Joneses having left for Europe to wait out the postwar economic depression. Boat passenger and visa records reveal no "James Blake," or anyone else serving as teacher for Harry Jones (then sixteen years old), among the George Frederic Jones entourage.[10]

The tutor might also have been among the Civil War veterans who comprised Custer's first troops of Indian fighters. War experience would explain his fighting capabilities; if he did father a child by the wife of his employer and thus needed to disappear from New York society, the Union forces would have offered a ready answer to his problem. According to the rumor, the tutor paid for his Indian adventures with his life. But his name is not included on the roll call of 262 men who died with General Custer on June 26, 1876, at the Little Big Horn River in Montana, in a battle with Lakotas led by Crazy Horse, Sitting Bull, and Rain in the Face that lasted but twenty minutes.[11]

A second, and in some ways more intriguing, story about Edith Wharton's birth combines May-December romance with society high life. In this whispered tale, she was said to be the daughter of Henry Peter Brougham, who gave his name to the elegant horse-drawn carriage. The first baron of Brougham and Vaux, redheaded Henry Peter was a learned, high-strung, passionate, and witty Scotsman who was appointed to high positions in the British government, first as attorney general and later as lord chancellor. An erudite and fiery lawyer, a political liberal who abhorred slavery and fought for educational and legal reform, he was also a lifelong student of the physical sciences, founder of the famed Edinburgh Speculative Society, and regular contributor to the *Edinburgh Review*.

When, in 1820, he successfully defended Queen Caroline against her husband's accusation of infidelity, Brougham became the most popular man in England, his portrait appearing on pub signs and in shop windows. Endowed with an excellent memory and a seemingly boundless command of language, he loved literature and good conversation and was a facile writer and powerful orator who accented his speech with angular motions of his arms. His oversized hands and awkward movements made him a frequent subject of caricature, but he was known for his strong "animal spirits" and said to have been a womanizer even in late old age. Restless and easily excited, he had a broad sense of humor and a keen grasp of the ludicrous. His qualities of mind and shared physical and psychological traits with his presumed daughter give the tale a certain comic truth value.

By 1860, when he was appointed chancellor of Edinburgh University, Lord Brougham lived most of the year in Cannes. Entertaining lavishly at his Villa Eléanore, he succeeded in transforming the little fishing village into a society capital. Like other wealthy Americans, George Frederic and Lucretia Jones often wintered in Cannes and were probably there in spring of 1861, when Lucretia became pregnant with Edith. The most improbable element of the paternity story, however, was Lord Brougham's age: when he was supposed to have bedded Lucretia and fathered Edith, he was nearly eighty-two years old.[12]

That two such stories (and perhaps others we do not know of) circulated about Edith's birth suggests that neither was true, or at least not provable. They were efforts to explain a late pregnancy and the birth of a child so unlike other offspring of New York society as to seem a changeling. But each tale strikes a blow at Lucretia Jones's carefully guarded respectability. The first rumor cuts her down to size; in her womanly desires, she is weak, silly, even pitiable, taking whatever is closest at hand to satisfy herself. In the second tale, she is an object of outright ridicule. That haughty Mrs. Jones should have given herself to an ancient Scottish lord! The whispered tales speak volumes about the feelings Lucretia engendered in New York–Newport society—jealousy, resentment, envy, bitterness. They also support Edith's views of her mother as a closed and clannish woman who held to the narrowest definitions of "nice people" and "polite society," but who took for herself all the privileges of her social standing. An acknowledged *mondaine*, she may have given herself a margin of indiscretion she would not have allowed others. In both stories, George Frederic Jones plays the foolish cuckold, pretending not to notice his wife's infidelity, thus avoiding scandal.

If high society resented Lucretia's aloofness, it was openly curious about Edith, whose difference from young women of her circle and others of her family soon revealed itself. She was too precocious, too well read, too introspective, too firm in her opinions. The rumors purported to explain the source of Edith's talent while also undercutting her social status (the tutor story) and mocking aspects of her temperament and demeanor (the Lord Brougham story).

Edith did not learn of the rumors about her birth until later in life, but her fiction—especially during the extraordinarily prolific period of the 1920s—contains many tales of illegitimacy and secret love affairs, children given away or hidden away to avoid social scandal, and marriages of pretense. Two close women friends of Edith provided anecdotal evidence about the first rumor of her parentage and her reactions to it. Matilda Travers Gay, daughter of a prominent New York lawyer and man-about-town, William R. Travers, knew Edith as a child and maintained that she was the "image" of the tutor. George Frederic knew the circumstances of his wife's pregnancy, she said, and had agreed to love and care for Edith as though she were his own, even providing a substantial legacy for her in his will. Another friend, Margaret Terry Chanler, said that Edith not only had reason to believe she was the tutor's daughter, but also had once tried to trace him, only to learn that he was long dead.[13]

Prior to World War I, when Edith was in her late forties, she had an extramarital affair hidden from her husband and their closest friends, and even from her servants, whose respect she did not want to lose. Her brothers, Frederic and Harry, had fewer scruples in this regard. When in the early 1890s Frederic was caught in an affair with a New York nouveau riche, he left the United States for France, where he lived with the woman for a time under an assumed identity. Late in life, Harry fell in love with a European woman who pretended to be a countess but was in reality a gold digger. He may have fathered a child by her, his "niece," a young woman he supported financially. To provide for his "niece" and the countess (whom he married just before his death), he disinherited both his sister, Edith, and Frederic's daughter, Beatrix Jones.[14]

EDITH NEWBOLD JONES was born into a family rife with secrets and fearing scandal. Except for one, their secrets were sexual in nature. In 1863, Congress passed the National Conscription Act, declaring that all men between ages twenty and forty-five were eligible to serve in the "national forces." George Frederic Jones, forty-two years old, was required to register for the draft. In general, men of his class did register. They then paid commutation fees to keep their names out of the draft pool. (In the first year of the draft act, the U.S. Treasury collected nearly $12,000,000 in fees.) Others hired substitutes, usually bounders and fugitives, to take their places in the Union ranks. Grover Cleveland, future president of the United States, and Theodore Roosevelt, Sr., a member of the Joneses' social set, bought substitutes. Roosevelt suffered lifelong guilt for his action, guilt that his son Theodore, Edith's friend in adulthood, also felt. The New York City draft riots in July 1863 dramatized the rage against social and economic prejudice legalized under the draft act. George Frederic and his family were in Newport on Saturday, July 11, when violence erupted at 766 Third Avenue, the registry office where officials drew the first names for the draft. George Frederic had nothing to fear—he had not registered for the draft. For a gentleman, the risks of skirting the draft law were minimal; if caught, George Frederic would have paid a fine. He was not caught, and he apparently never revealed to anyone what he had done.[15]

Edith was three years old when Robert E. Lee surrendered to Ulysses S. Grant at Appomattox Court House. Grant would later become one of her great heroes, and among her favorite sayings was his answer when Lee asked if the Confederate cavalry should hand over its horses to Union forces: "No, you will need them for autumn ploughing," Grant said. These words, she told a friend years later, "are the expression of a whole world of feeling." In adulthood, she read widely on this period of American history, yet the war itself merits only a single mention in her autobiography, *A Backward Glance* (1934): the war resulted in an economic depression that forced her father to economize by taking his family to Europe, where they could live more cheaply. This "happy misfortune" gave Edith six years in Europe during a formative period of her youth. The Civil War figures in only two of her fictional works, but they provide revealing glimpses into the social climate of that time. "The Spark," one of the *Old New York* tales (1924), describes New York's Seventh Regiment marching off to battle in the glory days of 1861 to the sounds of marching bands and cheering crowds of bystanders on Broadway, soldiers' pockets stuffed with sandwiches made by Charley Delmonico, the society restaurateur.[16]

"The Lamp of Psyche," written in 1893, the thirtieth anniversary of the draft act, is usually read as a tale of love inspired by the myth of Cupid and Psyche. It concerns a Boston gentleman who cannot explain how he avoided going to war. Edith projects a version of herself onto Delia, his wife, described as a "much-indulged" daughter of "incredibly frivolous" parents, a woman who "had never been very pretty" and who took herself with "a dash of contemptuous pity." When she asks her husband why he did not serve in the Union army, he first says, "I don't know," and then admits "the truth": "I've completely forgotten the excellent reasons that I doubtless had at the time for remaining at home." His response destroys his wife's "ideal" of him. She sees that the "long-past action was still a part of his actual being; he had not outlived or disowned it; he had not even seen that it needed defending."

This statement captures the attitude of many society gentlemen who found ways to avoid military service, and it might be read as Edith's belated commentary on her father, a member of the Republican party but someone who had little sense of civic responsibility and felt no call toward political activism. "The Lamp of Psyche" suggests that she had pondered (although perhaps never openly inquired about) his activities during the Civil War.

Among Edith's forebears was a military hero, her maternal great-grandfather, Major General Ebenezer Stevens. Drafted into the artillery during the Revolution, he captained a regiment that besieged Quebec and later fought under General John Burgoyne at Ticonderoga and Saratoga. On a trip to Washington, D.C., as a girl, Edith visited the Capitol Rotunda and saw her great-grandfather portrayed in John Trumbull's Revolutionary War paintings. She had a "secret partiality" for him, admiring his "abounding energy and *joie de vivre*" (known as the "Great Progenitor," he fathered fourteen children). More importantly, she considered him a "model citizen," a man who lived a life of purpose. In his courage and resolve, he stood quite alone among her ancestors, and she proudly took him as a guide for her own behavior.[17]

BEGINNINGS

Our first glimpse of Edith is a miniature by an unknown artist made when she was three years old. Pale blue eyes peer wide-eyed from a squarish, chubby-cheeked face. Her lips are drawn in a bow, eyebrows sketched by two curved lines, the red hair pulled into big sausage curls at the temples. Later pictures emphasize her high, wide forehead and undershot jaw. In only one portrait, made in Europe by Edward Harrison May when she was five years old, could she be called beautiful. Posed in half-profile in a pale-blue taffeta dress trimmed in gray fur, her hands clasping a vase of flowers and her red-gold hair cascading gloriously down her back, she appears as a Renaissance child whose soft eyes and gentle smile might have engaged a court painter.

This is a rare view of Edith Jones, who more often is shown behatted and beribboned, a young lady of fashion frozen in place, devoid of spontaneity or personality. In stylized studio portraits of her adolescence, she tries to meet the camera's expectations, rarely smiling and often staring sad-eyed into the distance. By contrast, a little-known childhood photograph shows her dressed in a plain pinafore, her hair uncurled and bangs badly cut. No Renaissance princess or fashion mannequin, she looks tired and somewhat forlorn—but recognizably a real child. These visual images of young Edith dramatically expose the contradictions between the "safe, guarded, monotonous" little-girl world described in her memoirs and the lived experience of an impulsive tomboy who grew into a "self-conscious child."[18]

"Much governessed and guarded," Edith said she had little awareness of her parents' activities. Yet, she sensed that her mother felt burdened by George Frederic's taste for New York and Newport society and by the responsibility of overseeing two large houses. "Society is completely changed nowadays," Lucretia would say. "When I was first married we knew everyone who kept a carriage." If a carriage signified social status in the 1840s, by the 1870s—when Edith heard her mother sigh over the changed standards—men with new, industrial wealth provided carriages for their "fashionable hetaera." Lucretia Jones was shocked by this open defiance of social propriety and embarrassed when her young daughter impertinently pointed out on Fifth Avenue a smart canary-yellow brougham with a coachman and high-stepping bays. Edith should turn her head when the dark-blue Jones carriage passed the yellow one, her mother said. The shiny carriage that caught Edith's eye belonged to financier August Belmont, purchased for his lover, a woman he "kept" in a Madison Avenue apartment.

By the standards of the later Gilded Age, the Joneses lived a simple life centered on social and church activities. They entertained at small dinners and luncheons with close friends and relatives—except on January l, the official opening of the winter season, when Lucretia gave an open house. In the Dutch tradition, the master of the house prepared a special punch from the family Madeira (which had "gone round the Cape") and then joined his men friends in making New Year's morning calls. At each house, they drank "bumpers of Madeira" and tasted baked goods and other delicacies served by the mistress of the house. Diarist George Templeton Strong recalled that Lucretia Jones's open house on New Year's Day 1860 was particularly festive.[19]

George Frederic enjoyed strolling along New York streets, and by the time she was four, Edith regularly accompanied him. She dated the birth of her identity from a promenade up Fifth Avenue on a bright, sunny midwinter day in 1866. Dressed in a warm wool coat and pretty satin bonnet trimmed in tartan plaid, she looked out on the world through a filigreed veil of Shetland wool covering her eyes and cheeks, her small, mittened hand lying inside the "large safe hollow" of her father's warm hand. Along the way, they met her cousin Daniel Fearing. An outgoing little boy, he lifted her veil and planted a bold kiss on her cheek. She was thus "wakened to conscious life by the two tremendous forces of love and vanity." A web of sensations formed around this event—the feel of winter cold, the slanting sunlight seen through the filigreed veil, the little boy's kiss, her father's large, warm hand, and the wide avenue lined with brownstones. Possessing an acute visual memory and a delicate sensitivity to customs, manners, and emotional atmospheres, Edith later re-created Old New York in stories and novels by drawing on her earliest experiences. Walking with her father up Fifth Avenue that winter morning, she was already seeing the world through the eyes of a storyteller.[20]

Edith descended from prosperous English and Dutch merchants, bankers, and lawyers: on her mother's side, the Stevenses, Ledyards, and Rhinelanders; on her father's, the Schermerhorns, Pendletons, and Joneses. George Frederic and Lucretia were distant cousins (related through the Gallatins), and although theirs were not aristocratic colonial families, they traced their New World roots back nearly three hundred years. When young George Frederic and "Lu" met in the early 1840s, they had everything in common but wealth. Edith recounted her parents' courtship and the first years of their marriage as a romantic tale of a tall, handsome young man born of a prestigious and wealthy family who at age twenty fell in love with the eldest (and least pretty) of the "poor Rhinelander girls," whose father had died young, leaving his wife, daughters, and son in diminished circumstances.[21]

Although Rhinelander men were renowned for business enterprise, Frederick William Rhinelander (Lucretia's father) preferred literature to his account books. The family fortunes fell further after his death, when his brother, charged with managing the properties, made himself rich at the expense of the widow and children. The theme of indolent men with inherited wealth and little business sense who died young and left their wives and children without adequate support would become a staple of Edith Wharton's fiction. She herself was victimized by cousins who managed her trusts ineptly; she fought her brother Frederic, who profited through inheritances meant for Edith and Harry, and she provided financial support for her disadvantaged sister-in-law and niece.[22]

Wishing a better match for their son, and thinking him too young to marry, George Frederic Jones's parents forbade him to see "Miss Rhinelander of Hell Gate." His father even denied him the sailing boat that would have carried him easily from what is now East Eighty-first Street up Long Island Sound to the "pretty country house with classic pilasters and balustraded roof" where Lucretia lived. Wily as Odysseus, George Frederic early one morning turned the oar of his rowboat into a mast and made his bed quilt into a sail. Thus rigged out, he hurried to his lady love. Devotion eventually overcame parental objection, and in 1844, George married Lu. Like other fashionable young couples, they honeymooned in Cuba, traveling in *volantes* to visit plantations. Returning to New York, they set up housekeeping at 80 East Twenty-first Street in Gramercy Park.[23]

A graduate of Columbia College, George Frederic had received an "Honorary Testimonial" degree in 1841, one of only two graduates in the first class of the "Literary and Scientific Course." His studies prepared him for the career of gentleman of leisure that he pursued for the rest of his life. His bride, who with her sisters had learned needlework, music, drawing, and "languages" (drawing room French, Italian, and German), took her place among the young society matrons of the day. She looked forward to a life of hospitality and foreign travel, and in these ways "avenged" the indignities of her social debut two seasons earlier in 1842. The reduced family fortunes and her position as the eldest and least beautiful of the Rhinelander daughters had meant that Lucretia appeared at her coming-out ball dressed in a homemade white tarlatan gown and her mother's hand-me-down satin slippers. Suffering martyrdom in pinched shoes that impeded her dancing, she "never ceased to resent the indignity inflicted on her." As Mrs. George Frederic Jones, she adorned herself in furs, feathers, and satin bonnets; her ball gowns came from the rue de la Paix and her jewels from Cartier. She discovered the capital of fashion on her first trip to the Continent in 1847, three years after her marriage, when she and George Frederic traveled for a year in Europe with their infant son, Frederic.[24]

Paris was the *pièce de résistance* of that long voyage by boat, train, and diligence from England to France, Holland and Belgium, Germany, Switzerland, Austria, and Italy. George Frederic loved Paris—a city of theater, opera, flower markets, museums, and restaurants—and he and Lucretia made two visits on this tour, first in spring 1847 and again in winter 1848. It was an adventuresome undertaking for a young couple, and "a very strenuous journey for people with a small child," as George Frederic remarked in his travel diary. Lucretia and the baby were often ill.

The trip came to an unexpected end in spring 1848, when revolution broke out in Paris and the monarchy fell. Riots began on February 22, and two days later, from the balcony of their rue de Rivoli hotel, the Joneses witnessed the abdicated King Louis Philippe and Queen Marie Amélie escape across the Tuileries Gardens. (Lucretia, with her "inexhaustible memory" for fashion details, noted in the royal family's brief and dramatic passage the special features of their court dress.) George Frederic recorded in his diary that mobs then "pillaged the palace," throwing from its windows furniture and clothing that were later burned in the garden.[25]

Despite such scenes, and the presence of 100,000 troops in the city, the Joneses did not leave Paris immediately. For three more months, they kept up their daily routine: while Lucretia was fitted for her first Paris wardrobe, George Frederic took afternoon strolls. Four weeks to the day after the riots began, while walking with his two-year-old son, Frederic, in the Tuileries, George Frederic noted that the gardens were now "too democratic to be pleasant." By March, the spirit of revolution had spread to Vienna and Berlin, cities they had visited the previous year. Although worried about general unrest, George Frederic and Lucretia maintained their rounds of theater and opera until they encountered serious difficulties getting money through letters of credit. On May 25, after weeks of Paris street demonstrations that ended in the dissolution of the National Assembly, they left for England. George Frederic detested London ("certainly the most wretched place under heaven"), and within days of their arrival he fell into a deep depression. "All the style in London [is] to be found in the horses and carriages," he noted in his diary, "the men and women have certainly very little of it." He admitted to being desperately homesick, and by June 1, 1848, he and his family were on their way back to New York.[26]

George Frederic had enjoyed introducing his bride to places he had seen on his Grand Tour in 1838, when he crossed the ocean with his father on one of the last sailing passenger ships. Edith, who made the transatlantic voyage by steamship some sixty times in her life (despite her fear of the ocean), and who traveled extensively in Europe and North Africa, caught the romance of travel from her father's stories. George Frederic's Grand Tour abroad, however, was his father's last journey. Edward Renshaw Jones died in 1839, leaving his son a small fortune in Manhattan and Brooklyn real estate that supported Lucretia and her three children long after George Frederic's death in 1882.[27]

The answer to many problems in Old New York, whether the threat of social scandal or a drop in the family fortunes, was travel abroad. Thus, in 1866, with property values falling, the Jones family rented out their New York and Newport houses and booked passage for France, where Edith (nearing her fifth birthday) caught her first glimpses of the "background of beauty and old-established order" that would define her aesthetic tastes and sensibilities. On November 17, 1866, as the country struggled with the social, political, and economic realities of Reconstruction, George Frederic Jones swore his allegiance to the Constitution and government of the United States of America, paid $5, and received a passport to travel abroad.

He sailed to Europe with his wife, daughter, and two sons, accompanied by Hannah Doyle, who doubled as Edith's nurse and Lucretia's personal maid. Except for Frederic, who had graduated from Columbia College in 1865 with a "gentleman's degree" in beaux-arts and later completed a master of arts degree, the Jones family remained in Europe until June 1872. During their first two years abroad, Harry finished his preparations for university, and on April 10, 1868, was admitted as a pensioner to Trinity Hall, Cambridge University. Monseigneur Gardiner, chaplain of Paris, sponsored him and certified his private studies. In 1872, Harry received his bachelor of arts degree. In these same years, George Frederic taught Edith to read, and she gained fluency in French and Italian, and began to study German.[28]

EUROPEAN AWAKENINGS

Edith's love of Europe, and especially of Italy, began in the family's first year abroad, which they spent in Rome. Bathed in spring sunshine, the city of romantic ruins awakened her senses to the perfume of violets and daffodils heaped on the Spanish Steps, the sounds of locanda music echoing from Trastevere, and the feel of "springy turf" underfoot on the grounds of great Roman villas, where she walked with her mother among statues and stone pines. Relieved of entertaining and household management duties, Lucretia spent time with her daughter. Together they searched the Palatine slopes for porphyry and lapis lazuli frag-

ments, relics of the palace of the Caesars that Lucretia turned into pa-
perweights and inkstands. In good weather, Hannah Doyle accompanied Edith to the Monte Pincio high above the city and watched as
Edith rolled hoops and skipped rope with one of her earliest childhood
playmates, Margaret Terry ("Daisy") and her little brother, Arthur.
They were the children of Louisa Ward (sister of writer Julia Ward
Howe) and Luther Terry, an expatriate American artist who made his
living painting portraits of his compatriots. The two girls would not
become real friends until many years later, after they both were married, but in her mind's eye, Daisy recalled "Pussy" Jones's "quantity of
long red-gold hair" and her "smart little sealskin coat, the first I ever
saw."[29]

Although adventurous in few other ways, Edith's parents next took
her on an arduous (some would say foolhardy) journey across central
Spain to the southern cities of Córdoba and Seville. Under the spell of
Washington Irving's *Alhambra*, George Frederic wished to see the
Moorish courtyards and fountains of Granada's ancient palace fortress.
Of her months in Rome, Edith recalled the scent of box hedges and the
texture of "weather-worn sun-gilt stone," but the Spanish trip produced in her jumbled sensations—jingling diligence bells, cracking
whips and yelling muleteers, jabbering beggars, squalid posadas, a
breakdown on a windswept sierra, and the taste of chocolate and olives.
"From that wild early pilgrimage," she wrote years later, "I brought
back an incurable passion for the road." Letting her passion take its
lead, as an adult she crisscrossed Europe in chauffeur-driven luxury
cars, accompanied by friends, members of her household staff, and
pampered lapdogs. Spain, which changed less during a half-century
than any other of the European countries that Edith knew well, drew
her back four more times, three of the trips taking place in the final
decade of her life. Although the extremes of temperature and the dirt
and noisy confusion of Spain did not hold the same charm for her then
as they had in her early childhood, she loved the country in her last
years primarily for its links to the Middle Ages—the period in art, architecture, and literature that she loved best. Still searching for her
spiritual roots, she was twice willing in the last years of her life to brave
foul weather, bad roads, questionable food and lodging to visit Santia-
go de Compostela.[30]

Edith's parents eventually tired of traveling and settled in Paris for
two years (1868–1870), taking an apartment at 61 avenue Joséphine on

the Right Bank. A member of the international Paris community, George Frederic was well known to the American Legation and to local religious and government offices, whose combined services he used to establish credit, arrange housing, and find doctors, dentists, and legal assistance. A founding member of the Anglican Holy Trinity parish, he cultivated the society of transplanted New Yorkers and Newporters, and joined in the rounds of dinners and evenings at the opera and theater.[31]

Two events of this period directed Edith toward literature. She discovered "making up," a form of storytelling that combined intense imaginative and sensual pleasures, and she learned the alphabet. Henry Bedlow, a mustached elderly family friend from Newport, shared her "secret story-world." After Sunday dinner, he would draw her onto his knee and tell her tales of the Greek gods and goddesses. Edith recast these mythic figures, envisioning them as the ladies and gentlemen she saw riding in the Bois de Boulogne or along the Champs Elysées, the ladies in flounced taffetas lounging indolently in open *daumont* carriages flanked by escorts of handsome outriders. Telling these stories out loud to herself, she experienced a rush of pleasure at the sounds of her words.[32]

She discovered other pleasures in the physical properties of certain books. The Galignani Press edition of Washington Irving's *Alhambra*—with its closely printed pages, heavy black type, narrow margins, and rough-edged yellow sheets—made her fancy swell, burst, and overflow, sweeping her off "full sail on the sea of dreams." (Books sometimes produced in her powerfully erotic, even frightening, responses that only later in life did she recognize as sexual.) When overcome by the urge to "make up," Edith shut herself in her mother's bedroom and paced the floor, *Alhambra* in hand (often upside down, as she did not yet know how to read), turning its pages in rhythm to her own voice. Curious about her activities, nurses and parents spied through cracks and keyholes. Lucretia tried to copy down Edith's words, but they flowed so quickly she could not capture them. At first amused by this strange ritual, the Joneses became increasingly concerned about the compelling power the imagined world exerted over their daughter, a power she later called a "devastating passion" and a "perilous obsession."[33]

To "make up," Edith had to move about and pace the floor. Reading, however, required that she sit immobile. Telling stories triggered physical urges, movement and speech, but reading induced a motionless and fixed concentration. Finding her in this trancelike pose one day, her parents discovered she was reading Ludovic Halévy's *Fanny Lear*, a play about a prostitute that was having a *succès de scandale* in the late 1860s. Edith, age six, now divided her time between improvising tales and reading books that her mother judged appropriate for her. When her maternal grandmother, Mary Stevens Rhinelander, came for an extended visit, Edith read Tennyson's *Idylls of the King* aloud to her. Lace-capped and wrapped in black moiré silk, Grandmamma was very deaf, but she dutifully held up a japanned ear trumpet as her granddaughter shouted out the verses. Edith felt her body tingle in "rhythmic raptures" at words she did not understand.[34]

Discovery of this sensual and dramatic "other" world separated Edith from children who did not know how to enter her "labyrinth." Her parents worried about her self-absorption. Reflecting on these events many years later, Edith dismissed their concerns. In her external life, she said, she had all the "normal instincts" of her sex—enjoying pretty dresses, puppies, and romps with little boys in the tree-lined *allées* of the Champs Elysées. Girls did not interest her, nor did she like to play with dolls, and she reluctantly (but obediently) attended parties and dancing classes, such as the one conducted by Mlle Michelet, a stern, mustached ex-ballerina. Although a tomboy, Edith was already familiar with feminine arts, and she displayed her gifts to best advantage. Playing ball or skipping rope with the Harrys, Willies, and Georgies, she shook out her long red hair "so that it caught in the sun!" A few years later, she amused herself by stealing the handsome German fiancé of a daughter of the Livingston family. He was attracted to her "sense of fun," and she enjoyed keeping his "poor fiancée on the rack for a few weeks." It was, she admitted, the only adventure she ever embarked on with "malice prepense."[35]

Edith's account of her awakening to written and spoken words leaves no doubt that they produced in her ecstatic, almost orgasmic, responses. Possessed by a "furious Muse," a "Pythoness-fury," she answered their call with "accumulated floods of . . . pent-up eloquence." Such moments transported her "body and soul" into a state of exultation, and she experienced "exquisite relief" from her struggle to "be like other children." Her desire for language—whether Holy Writ, Renaissance sonnets, or everyday vernacular—transgressed the boundaries of convention. Even at this early age, she was pulled between conforming to social codes and giving free rein to her powers of expression.[36]

Edith noticed that her father was also moved by language, especially the King James Bible and the long sweep and strong beat of Tennyson's verse. "I imagine there was a time," she wrote, "when his rather rudimentary love of verse might have been developed had he had any one with whom to share it." But his wife's matter-of-factness "shrivelled up any such buds of fancy" in him. Edith wondered what kind of man her father was meant to be, what desires had been stifled in him. She first pictured him in her mind's eye as the "tall splendid father who was always so kind." Later, she saw him in his ground-floor study in the West Twenty-third Street house, bent over his household account books, diminished by economic worries and marital strains into "my poor father." At the end of his life, he stared mutely from his deathbed, a victim of paralytic stroke, who struggled in vain to convey a good-bye message to his twenty-year-old daughter, who sat at his bedside.[37]

Edith sensed that her father was "lonely" and "haunted by something always unexpressed and unattained." She hinted that nearly forty years of marriage to Lucretia had reduced George Frederic, the handsome, blue-eyed suitor, into a broken and disappointed man. He had sailed up Long Island Sound to meet his beloved at dawn on a summer's day. But it was a "false dawn," as his beloved apparently had no poetry in her soul.[38]

As an adolescent, Lucretia Rhinelander read and copied out into a black notebook sentimental Victorian verse by John-Jacob Guerney and the moral inspirations of Lydia Sigourney. Except for William Wordsworth's "A perfect creature nobly planned," Lucretia's choices were ones that her daughter—into whose hands the notebook eventually came—would hardly call poetry. A typical example is Rosa Patience McNevan's "My Childhood's Hours," copied by Lucretia in 1838, when she was fourteen. It describes an ideal mother's love, one that in Lucretia's upbringing was perhaps more longed for than achieved.

> My childhood's hours! my childhood's hours!
> How oft my thoughts fly back
> To that sweet time when brightest flowers,
> Seem'd strew'd on Life's dull track. . . .
>
> And when a teardrop filled my eyes
> Caused by my infant woes
> A mother's voice would calm my sighs
> And still me to repose.

Brimming with nostalgia and regret, composed in singsong rhythms and banal images, the poem is maudlin Victoriana. It illuminates a vulnerable, pathetic side of the young Lucretia Rhinelander that by adulthood had hardened into orthodoxy. Spontaneity and girlish enthusiasms had, apparently, been early killed. She was only twelve years old when her father died in 1836, aged forty. As the eldest child, Lucretia would have felt the loss more keenly than did her siblings, not only the economic deprivations that required her to wear her mother's hand-me-downs at her debutante ball, but also in bearing the emotional demands of her mother and in assuming greater responsibility for her younger sisters and brother. As an adult, Lucretia attended to her widowed mother out of filial duty (as Edith would do for Lucretia), but she never forgave Mrs. Rhinelander for the indignity of her "coming out." Edith never forgave Lucretia for failing to give her the love and affection she showered on her sons.[39]

TRUTH, FICTION, AND TERROR

Lucretia ruled that her children should be polite; George Frederic, that they be kind. Between these two forms of social conduct lay a vast uncharted territory of moral conscience that Edith and her brothers had to map for themselves. Sensitive, responsive, and desiring to please her parents, she developed a severe code of truth-telling and moral probity far more demanding than her nurse, governess, or parents would ever have imposed on her. Moral self-discipline, joined to the word, empowered her imagination, and her heightened sensitivity to visual impressions caused her to suffer intensely from ugliness. These elements conjoined in a humiliating incident that Edith recalled from her Paris dance classes with Mlle Michelet, whose "shrivelled, bearded" mother accompanied the children on the piano.

Edith confided to a little boy she was then in love with that the old lady looked like *une vieille chèvre* (an old goat). The image was no doubt all too appropriate, but having said something *about* the old woman that she would not have said *to* her, Edith felt compelled to confess openly her indiscretion to avoid punishment by the "dark Power" she called God. Gathering her courage, she confessed in front of the dancing class; instead of praising her honesty, Mlle Michelet rebuked her "impertinence." This response left Edith in a state of "moral bewilderment"; she also knew that Lucretia would have disapproved of her indiscretion and her method of making amends for it.[40]

Transgression and confession were indissolubly linked in Edith's mind. When she wanted to be a very bad child, she would upset Doyley's workbasket and then run to her to confess. One afternoon in 1871, while the Joneses were living in Florence, Lucretia went out shopping, leaving instructions that Edith should not eat any of the apricots from a dish on the table. Disobeying, Edith ate three of them. When her mother returned, she ran to confess what she had done. Lucretia replied, "I did not expect it of you." Lying on her deathbed almost seventy years later, Edith exclaimed, "Oh, the shame of it! I feel it still."[41]

The great divide between Edith's self-evolved standard of truth-telling (which she ascribed to "God") and the code of politeness demanded by her mother induced in her a painful moral confusion she could not admit to anyone—certainly not to her mother, who, of the two "absolutely inscrutable beings" that she tried to please, was by far the more unfathomable. From Edith's childhood perspective, Lucretia was illogical and capricious. Could God also be inconsequent? Perplexed, she tried to calm her fears by applying reason: "If the servants did anything to annoy Mamma, it would be no satisfaction to her to kill Harry or me." The cause of Lucretia's anger might be her servants, but her potential victims were her children—or so Edith feared. Alone, bewildered, desiring to understand "what it was all about," she saw God and her mother as "dark fatalities." In a notebook from her adolescent years, she wrote, "If I ever have children I shall deprive them of *every pleasure* in order to prepare them for the inevitable unhappiness of life!"[42]

Sometime after the Mlle Michelet incident, Edith underwent another kind of psychic torment that left her prey to new terrors. The Joneses concluded their Paris visit in summer 1870, and by July 15, the day France declared war on Prussia, they were at Bad Wildbad, a "primitive watering-place" in the Black Forest where George Frederic and Lucretia took a cure. At age eight and a half, Edith was no longer cared for only by her beloved Doyley, but she also had a German governess, who taught her German using the New Testament and instructed her in the arts of knitting, tatting, and making wildflower garlands from blossoms they gathered on woodland walks. On one such walk, Edith was suddenly seized with terrible pain and collapsed with what was eventually diagnosed as typhoid fever. She was near death by the time her parents found a physician, the czar of Russia's doctor, who correctly identified her illness. The long siege of typhoid fever, with its high temperatures and chills, became the dividing line between Edith's "little childhood" and the next stage of life.

She begged for books to help pass the long weeks of her convalescence, but finding something appropriate for her proved a difficult problem. Edith disliked children's stories, her attitude doubtless a relief to Lucretia, who worried that the authors of children's books might unknowingly use "bad English." Although Lucretia herself apparently only read novels and horticulture publications, she prized well-spoken English, having grown up in a family that prided itself on speaking the language flexibly but fastidiously. Moreover, in a world governed by codes of politeness, speaking English poorly was a "supreme offense" of "bad manners." Edith later admitted that by monitoring her reading, Lucretia had kept her from "wasting . . . time over ephemeral rubbish" and indirectly led her to the "great classics," which gave her mind a "temper which my too-easy studies could not have produced."[43]

From a contemporary perspective, Lucretia's attitudes seem to verge on pedantry, if not undue exercise of parental authority. But they were based on European practices intended to maintain the cultural system by molding children to the expectations of society. Monitoring children's reading both for the appropriateness of subject matter and reading level was a responsibility French parents, for example, took very seriously. French children were not given free run of the family library (as in America), and young ladies especially were to be shielded from harsh realities and crude forms of expression. Preparing her daughter to become a matron in old guard New York, Lucretia Jones unwittingly directed Edith's steps toward Europe and French ways. Appreciating long-held traditions and regularized habits, Edith was drawn (even in childhood) to cultural conservatism that valued preservation over innovation.[44]

A crisis in Edith's convalescence from typhoid fever was occasioned by a book—a children's tale brought by two friends as a get-well token. The "robber story" so affected her fevered imagination that she relapsed and again came close to death. When she emerged from the ensuing fever, it was to a world "haunted by formless horrors" in which for several years a "dark undefinable menace" dogged her steps, "lurking and threatening." She feared daylight and darkness, houses and open streets, and suffered hallucinations. Returning home from walks in the company of her maid or governess, she felt the unnameable thing following at her heels, pressing on her. Waiting on the doorstep to be let into the house, she was seized with a "choking agony of terror" followed by a "rapture of relief" once she was safe on the other side of the threshold. These events, she later claimed, obliterated the "torturing moral scruples" of her early childhood, but transformed her from a fearless child to one who lived in a chronic state of anxiety, prey to a "physical timidity."[45]

Although she believed herself to have been a fearless child before the bout with typhoid fever, she had already demonstrated extreme sensitivity to words and environments. Behind the "menace" was a previous incident associated with a certain book, a particular house, and visual impressions of ugliness. Sometime before she was three years old, Edith visited her father's stern, unmarried sister, Elizabeth Schermerhorn Jones, at Wyndcliffe, her eighty-acre estate on the Hudson River. Elizabeth, too, had suffered a terrible illness in childhood, but her parents saved her from the tuberculosis that had killed two of her siblings by shutting her away for nine months in the Mercer Street family house in Lower Manhattan. They sealed the windows of her bedroom and kept the fireplace lit; by these drastic measures, Elizabeth Jones survived into hardy adulthood and became a "ramrod-backed old lady compounded of steel and granite." In 1852, she built a twenty-four-room turreted villa, the most expensive house ever before built in Rhinecliff, New York. Such display of wealth, it was said, gave rise to the expression "keeping up with the Joneses."[46]

Edith found the Victorian-Italian villa dark, immense, and intolerably ugly. Overcome with "inarticulate misery," she envisioned stern Aunt Elizabeth *as* the house: her "battlemented caps" were the turrets of the mansion, her "granite exterior" was like the "grimly comfortable home." She also became convinced that a wolf was under her bed. This was the first of several terrifying childhood events Edith later described as "hauntings by tribal animals." From this moment on, she could not be alone while looking at pictures in her "Little Red Riding Hood" storybook. Dragging her nursery stool behind her, she sought out Doyley or her mother.[47]

Ugly houses and scary books, their terrors exacerbated by life-threatening childhood illnesses, produced in Edith fears and phobias that haunted her for years. She survived the typhoid fever with a weakened immune system. Her lifelong battle against "chronic tonsillitis" and bronchial illnesses began in this second stage of childhood. When the weakness and fever that accompanied each attack passed off, she usually experienced a sense of *bien-être*—well-being and renewed energy.

In these same years, young Teddy Roosevelt suffered severe asthma attacks, describing their aftereffect as a strong sense of well-being. Teddy's childhood diary reveals that his acute attacks were often preceded by the fear of being scolded or by depression (feeling "doleful"). Like Edith, who was four years younger, he was especially sensitive to language, and his fear of certain words could induce an asthma attack. Her fears of certain words and stories had brought her to the threshold of death during her fight against typhoid fever. Trying to disperse the ghosts and goblins that haunted her late childhood by turning them into fiction, she came to believe that her creative animus was aligned with these dark powers. To exorcise them (had she been able) might have meant sacrificing her talent and the emotional pleasures that storytelling and writing gave her. Mastering the art of writing through long years of apprenticeship became a means of conquering her fears. She could call up ghosts at will, rather than being surprised by them at the doorstep.[48]

Yet the woman who would become a renowned writer of ghost stories could not, until she was twenty-seven years old, sleep in a room that contained such a tale. She admitted even to burning books: "It frightened me to know that they were downstairs in the library!" One cannot pass lightly over such acts or discount the extremity of suffering that brought her to destroy what she loved best. The psychological effects of the typhoid fever and the attendant illnesses that followed it lasted for years. During the months of her physical recovery and through all the nightmare fears of childhood, her parents, she recalled, were indulgent and understanding. They did not scold or ridicule or try to "harden" her by making her sleep in the dark. Their kindness, she later averred, allowed her to grow into "a woman hardly conscious of physical fear." In her childhood, however, irrational powers laid claim to her imagination: "Fear of *what*? I cannot say—and even at the time, I was never able to formulate my terror."[49]

Retrospectively, Edith described these dramatic incidents as the experiences of a highly imaginative child susceptible to images and words whose "fancy" held the power both to frighten and elate her. Her experiences reveal the cost of striving to preserve an equilibrium between "sociable instincts" and "solitary intellectual sympathies." She was governed by two "ruling sentiments": "the desire to learn and the desire to look pretty." Neither of these, she claimed, received encouragement from her parents. The world of learning beyond the usual drawing room accomplishments of young ladies was culturally marked "for men only," a message that resounded all the louder for Edith because she was given, almost, free access to her father's library. It was unlike any other room in the house, a retreat for George Frederic from the excesses of the French Second Empire that dominated the West Twenty-third Street brownstone. The sixteen-foot-square ground-floor study housed his gentleman's library, a younger son's "meager portion" of a much larger family collection. Hung in handsome dark green damask, the room had a medieval motif, its crowning ornament a huge mantelpiece supported by visored knights. She spent many childhood hours in a "secret ecstasy of communion" in this room, stretched out on the rug, her chin resting on cupped hands, reading her father's books and watched over by the visored knights, guardians of a man's world.[50]

In later life, she resented her parents for failing to give her an education that challenged and directed her natural interests. She described her childhood and youth as an "intellectual desert" (something of an overstatement, as we shall see), but the feminine world also held dangers. To "look pretty" and thus achieve the goal of being "adored" was to court vanity and place herself in direct competition with Mamma. Edith knew she was no match for her mother. Feeling not only "different" from her family but also lesser than they, she was "humiliated":

> I was laughed at by my brothers for my red hair, and for the supposed abnormal size of my hands and feet; and as I was much the least good-looking of the family, the consciousness of my physical short-comings was heightened by the beauty of the persons about me. My parents— or at least my mother—laughed at me for using "long words," and for caring for dress (in which heaven knows she set me the example!); and under this perpetual cross-fire of criticism I became a painfully shy self-conscious child.

By age ten, Edith began to withdraw within herself, seeking relief from "outward miseries," the shame and confusion of her failures as daughter and sister.[51]

THE RETURN

When the steamer docked in New York in June 1872, Edith's American exile from the European scenes of her early childhood was at hand. "How ugly it is!" she thought. Dreaming that her family was on their way back to Europe, she would awake in a state of exhilaration that turned to "deep depression." As time passed and her longing for Europe increased, she asked her father when they might return—"Whenever we can afford it," he answered. Six years of "economizing" abroad had not solved George Frederic's financial problems, which were caused in part by mismanagement of his inherited properties. On September 19, 1873, "Black Friday," a panic hit Wall Street: forty banks and brokerage houses in New York City went bankrupt. This disaster was part of a Euro-American economic depression, the worst the century had yet experienced. In America, its causes included easy credit and international inflation, leftover debt from the Civil War, the costs of rebuilding Chicago after the 1871 fire, overspeculation in railroads, and trade dislocations. The post–Civil War boom was over, although Chemical Bank—in which George Frederic held stock; his forebear Joshua Jones had co-founded the institution—survived this prolonged depression intact. But the return on George Frederic's safe investments and rents from his real estate could not keep up with rising inflation.[52]

Edith spent her first summer back in America, like all those to follow, in Newport. She retained no memories of her first visits there as a baby, and she saw it now as for the first time. After six years of hotel and apartment life, she delighted in the spacious family home on Harrison Avenue with its honeysuckled veranda, clover and daisy meadows to run in, cove to swim in, and kitchen garden full of pears and strawberries. She romped with her dogs, climbed trees, and fished for "scuppers" and "porgies" from the landing pier. Lucretia and George Frederic reestablished their American life, seeing old friends and accustoming themselves to Newport's new faces and new wealth. Newport was coming into its own as the most fashionable seaside resort in America, a place with few lodging houses. Visitors came on invitation only, and usually stayed with friends who owned the towering, sprawling "cottages" dotted around the rocky coastline.[53]

The entire Jones family gathered at Newport that summer. Harry, home from England with his degree from Cambridge, courted a young woman named Caroline Hunter, who lived with her family on K Street.

They became engaged a year later, but their marriage plans ended in tragedy on November 22, 1873, when Caroline and her parents, en route to France, died when the ship on which they were traveling, the *Ville de Havre*, was struck by a sailing vessel and sank. Also drowned were Lucretia's youngest sister, Eliza Edgar, and her daughter. A popular bachelor and man-about-town, Harry did not fall in love again for many years.

In 1872, Frederic, established in New York as a bookbinder, was married and the father of a newborn baby. On March 24, 1870, in a ceremony performed by the Right Reverend William H. Odenheimer, Episcopal bishop of the diocese of New Jersey, he had wed Mary Cadwalader Rawle ("Minnie"). A slim, spirited, dark-haired young woman with dramatic looks, a quick wit, and laughing voice, she was the daughter of William Henry and Mary Binney Rawle of Philadelphia and a descendant of prestigious colonial families. The newlyweds spent their honeymoon in Europe, where they visited the Joneses, and on their return to New York, Frederic and Minnie moved into a small house. In summer 1872, they were established with their newborn daughter, Beatrix, at Pencraig Cottage, a two-story dwelling opposite the winding drive that led to the "friendly gables" of Pencraig, the Jones estate. Lucretia and George Frederic, only a decade earlier new parents themselves, were accustoming themselves to being grandparents.[54]

In the sunshine of these Newport summers, Edith was a child of "shouts and laughter" and constant physical activity. The morbid, self-scrutinizing, and sometimes unhappy child who had appeared with the onset of typhoid fever retreated to the shadows. A little girl who could hear in her imagination the "choiring of spheres" now came alive to rocky landscapes and ocean breezes. She trembled at the sight of "wind-warped fern" and brier rose and began to experience her body in new ways. Life rang in her ears and hummed in her blood, its messages felt in "vague tremors" when she rode her pony, swam in the bay, or danced and tumbled with the boys from next door, the sons of astronomer Lewis Rutherfurd—one of whom was in love with her, while she had fallen in love with his brother. Puzzled by these new, strangely pleasant sensations, she asked her mother one day what they meant. Lucretia had two answers ready for such questions—"You're too little to understand" and "It's not nice to ask about such things." The presence of adored baby Trix may have contributed to Edith's curiosity about girls' bodies and babies, but when an older cousin volunteered the information that babies come from people, not flowers, Edith felt a vague sense of "contamination." She ran to tell her mother the news and to confess that she had come by the information accidentally. She received a severe scolding: "I was left with a penetrating sense of 'not-niceness,'" she later wrote, "which effectively kept me from pursuing my investigations farther."[55]

Soon after returning to America, the Joneses sent back the German governess they had engaged to educate Edith; she had proved "unsympathetic and unsatisfied." She was replaced by Anna Bahlmann, a nineteen-year-old German girl who had taught the Rutherfurd daughters prior to their entrance into society. Like Doyley, Anna would become Edith's lifelong friend. When Edith married, Anna came to live with her and work as her secretary, serving in this position until her death in 1916. As a "finishing governess," she took seriously her duties to prepare Edith for the life of a society matron and preserve her from corrupting influences. Never marrying, she retained a virginal air. When Edith once asked her about the "passion of love," Anna responded, "Why, my dear, there's *nothing* in it," adding, "All my married friends tell me so." Anna also restricted Edith's intellectual curiosity. She refused to read Johann Wolfgang von Goethe with her, even though the poet-scientist was one of the great stylists of the German language. Indeed, he was a controversial figure: his writings on natural science and the theory of evolution (which presaged the work of Charles Darwin) were considered by some as irreligious, his lyric poetry and dramas too impassioned and too dangerously under the spell of German Romanticism.[56]

Emelyn Washburn, daughter of the scholarly rector at the fashionable New York Calvary Episcopal Church, where the Joneses attended services, was a student of German literature and an avid reader of Goethe. She asked Lucretia to allow Edith, then thirteen years old, to read the German poet. Lucretia agreed, and Edith discovered in his writings a mind whose sensibilities matched her own. From poetry, drama, and autobiography to natural science and philosophic inquiry, Goethe had a greater influence on her than any other thinker. She later ordered a set of his complete works, had them bound in leather, and read everything but his enormously popular novel *The Sorrows of Young Werther*. Lucretia had made her daughter promise never to read a novel without first asking permission. In exacting this pledge, she repeated her own mother's injunction. Apart from the first volume of Sir Walter

Scott's *Waverley*, Lucretia had never read a novel until after her marriage, when, following the example of her mother and sisters, she began to "devour" fiction.[57]

Edith later condemned Lucretia for denying her knowledge about essential but "forbidden" topics, like human sexuality. Hungry for knowledge and longing to escape childhood ignorance, Edith turned to Anna, whom she loved but who never "struck a spark" from her, she said. She claimed never to have known in these years anyone who cared for "les choses de l'esprit" (intellectual things) and wondered whether "any child possessed of that 'other side' was ever so alone in it as I." Not until she was past twenty did she "exchange a word with a really intelligent human being." Had she forgotten Professor Lewis Rutherfurd, the renowned astronomer, who led her and other neighborhood children on hikes along the Newport cliffs, entertaining them with lively commentaries on the natural world? Certainly, Edith's lifelong interest in astronomy developed from his early teachings. Dr. Washburn and Emelyn also fostered her intellectual and artistic development. But these people were exceptional among the Joneses' friends.[58]

For American women of Edith's social class, education reined in rather than expanded their natural curiosity, cultivating in them a charming, but false, naïveté. A metaphor for shrouded innocence appears in her account of archery club contests in Newport, a town given to an almost "pagan worship of physical beauty." Lovely young women like Margaret and Louisa Rutherfurd displayed their archery skills before an audience of family and friends. Dressed in floating silk or muslin, their faces hidden from sun and sea air by veils as thick as curtains, they glided slowly across the August Belmont lawn, unable to see clearly where their steps led them. Poised before the target and ready to take aim, they threw back the veils and revealed their identities. The onlookers thrilled to this moment, and even to Edith's childish eyes "the effect was dazzling when the curtain was drawn, and young beauty shone forth"—a beauty untouched by paint or powder.[59]

The idea that physical beauty could spoil, like an apple too long in the sun, had its intellectual counterpart. A young lady might destroy her health and mental well-being by learning too much. Edith's bout with typhoid had frightened her parents; anxious about her health and afraid of fatiguing her brain, they forbade her learning anything that required mental effort. She reasoned that their solicitousness was due, in part, to her being a late-born child and was also a reaction against the severity of their own early training. But parental solicitude prevented Edith from concentrating even on subjects in which she had a "restless" interest. There was no danger of overworking her brain, because the subjects that might have disciplined her mental faculties— Greek, Latin, logic, philosophy, mathematics, and natural science—were not on the menu of courses served up to young girls.[60]

In 1875, when Edith was on the threshold of adolescence, she met Emelyn Washburn, a young woman six years her senior, who both befriended and tutored her. Studious, religious, and musically gifted, Emelyn was a rather odd person who suffered from a variety of illnesses, including weak eyesight. (Edith later described her as a "queer, shy invalid" in whom she suspected "strong traces of degeneracy"—meaning, apparently, latent lesbianism.) Emelyn quickly recognized that Edith, a "nervous child," was "starving for mental nourishment" and had not been taught proper study habits. The Washburn family first learned of Edith when she sent them a handmade outfit intended for the young daughter of an Episcopal missionary. The workmanship of the clothing was so remarkable that Mrs. Washburn sent a note to thank her, not realizing that "Miss E. N. Jones" was a girl of thirteen.

The two families began to exchange visits, and from 1875 to 1879, Edith sat beside Emelyn on Sunday mornings in the rector's pew. His richly modulated voice and dramatic delivery cast a spell over her, and, unaware of her restlessness, she picked at the fabric of Emelyn's camel hair coat. Recognizing that Edith needed to occupy her hands, Emelyn gave her a large pearl button that she had sewn onto a string. Edith pulled the button back and forth through her fingers as she listened to Dr. Washburn. She never outgrew this physical restiveness; in adulthood, she knitted, tatted, or fussed with a cigarette while others talked.[61]

Edith's days now followed a predictable routine, divided between morning study with Anna (she prepared her lessons while Doyley brushed her hair) and afternoons spent driving with Lucretia in Central Park or accompanying her father to church services. Sometimes she joined Emelyn in the rector's library, where she wrote notes to the Rutherfurd boys and her brother Harry's friends on Dr. Washburn's new typewriter. A cousin of Ralph Waldo Emerson's, Dr. Washburn had since his youth participated in the New England intellectual group that included Bronson Alcott, Henry David Thoreau, and Margaret Fuller. Although he had a marked dislike of clever women, especially those like Fuller who he felt talked too much, he encouraged his daughter's intellectual interests and hired a German tutor to give her a "gentleman's" education. In these years, Emelyn studied Anglo-Saxon, Icelandic, Old Norse, and Old and Middle High German. She encouraged Edith's interest in ancient sagas and tutored her in languages. On warm spring days, they sat on the library roof reading Dante's *Divine Comedy* or Goethe's poetry.[62]

Enjoying Emelyn's companionship, Edith did not share all her interests. She was not musical and only occasionally attended concerts, nor did she wander about the city, as Emelyn did. In a vain effort to cure her eyes, Emelyn rode ferries around the island, gazed at the tall ships at South Street pier, and observed Italian life on Mulberry Street. She regretted that Edith knew only one portion of the city and only one side of society. "I wish Edith had had some streetlife," she wrote years later, "and known all sorts and conditions of men as I did—and learned to love New York." But Edith was not allowed on the streets alone, nor can one imagine her holding conversations with deckhands and sailors as Emelyn did. Doyley chaperoned her even the five short blocks from West Twenty-third Street to the rectory.[63]

Emelyn took great interest in younger friends, and on one occasion organized a Christmas party, just so that Edith (age fourteen) could have a Christmas tree of her own. "I should like to have a tree once in my life!" Edith had exclaimed. Delighted by the idea, Lucretia went with the girls to choose decorations and share the expenses. When the day of the party arrived, four-year-old Trix Jones was ill with scarlatina. To cheer her, Emelyn and Edith decorated a little tree and placed a doll under it that Trix named "Emelyn Christmas." Edith loved entertaining small children and making them laugh at her invented stories, Emelyn recalled, just as she loved listening to adult conversation and contributing weighty or witty remarks. "Sometimes she looked like a little, most loveable child," Emelyn said, "and again she seemed years older." Edith's various nicknames reveal something of her mercurial character. The servants and Anna Bahlmann addressed her as "Edith." Doyley called her "Sweet" (Harry was "Darling"). Harry referred to Edith as "John," as did his friend Teddy Wharton, whom Edith would later marry. She was "Lily" to the Rutherfurds and "Puss" to Lucretia. Others called her "Pussey," but Emelyn referred to her as "the child" and addressed her in writing as "E.N.J."[64]

That same year, 1876, Edith wrote a thirty-thousand-word novella entitled *Fast and Loose*, its title taken from the popular English novelist Robert Lytton's *Lucile:* "Let woman beware/How she plays fast and loose thus with human despair/And the storm in man's heart." Signed "David Olivieri," it was a comic send-up of English romances. Edith kept it secret from all but Emelyn, who enjoyed its satire of contrived plots and stylized narrative modes. She was especially amused by the mock reviews Edith appended to the text, which recounted the author's failures, parodying the language and attitudes of contemporary critics. A "review" from the *Nation* mimicked the authoritative, judgmental tone adopted by critics: "Every character is a failure, the plot a vacuum, the style spiritless, the dialogue vague, the sentiment weak, and the whole thing a fiasco." Edith had developed an acute sense of self-judgment, and although the reviews were meant as a joke, they played on her fear of failure.

Fast and Loose was her second effort at writing a long narrative. The first, begun in 1873, when she was eleven, was derided by her mother. A novel of social observation, it belonged to the genre that would become Edith's special provenance, and its domestic subject matter and opening dialogue suggest the influence of stories from local newspapers, such as the *Newport Mercury*:

> "Oh, how do you do Mrs. Brown?" said Mrs. Tomkins. "If only I had known you were going to call I should have tidied up the drawing-room."

On hearing these sentences, Lucretia remarked, "Drawing rooms are always tidy." With this acerbic comment ringing in her ears, Edith turned from fiction to poetry.[65]

When she confessed to Emelyn in 1877 her desire to write professionally, her friend suggested she begin with translation, an idea Dr. Washburn supported. They chose *"Was die Steine Erzahelen"* (What the Stones Tell) by German poet Heinrich Karl Brugsch, who sometimes signed himself "Brugsch Bey," adding the Turkish title of honor, as he did on this poem. Emelyn supervised the work, Dr. Washburn looked it over and made slight changes, and they sent it off to a new magazine. Edith's parents did not want her name to appear in print, so the translation was signed with Emelyn's initials, "E. W. Washburn," but published over the signature of Emelyn's father, "E. A. Washburn," who was well known in New York literary circles. The magazine sent a check for $50, which Dr. Washburn gave to Edith, who was very proud of having earned money for her first publication. Soon, her father arranged to publish some of her poetry in a "little booklet" that appeared before Christmas 1878.[66]

The chapbook of two dozen original poems and five translations from German poets—three songs by Emanuel Geibel, "Longing" from Friedrich Schiller, and "A Song" from Friedrich Rückert—was privately printed by C. E. Hammett, Jr., of Thames Street in Newport. Unsigned, and printed under the generic title *Verses*, its frontispiece carried a quotation from Bettine Brentano, a friend of Goethe's: "Be friendly, pray, to these fancies of mine." This book is a rare and valuable item (only nine copies exist); its poems date from 1875, when Edith was thirteen years old, to late 1878. Composed on narrow sheets of vellum, the writing crabbed and childish and wandering across the pages, the poems' subject matter and diction belie the youth of their author.[67]

Among songs in honor of spring and summer, nightingales and daisy chains, and alongside a ballad entitled "May Marian," a remembrance of a fancy-dress ball danced on the lawn of Swanhurst at Newport in August 1878, are dark poems about death, old age, and lost "first love"— "That dreamflower rare and white,/That puts its magic blossom forth/ And dies in a single night." A dramatic monologue entitled "The Last Token—A.D. 107" tells of a Christian maiden facing death in an amphitheater filled with lions, her Roman lover looking on from the stands, his face "aquiver" for her sake. Some poems suggest that Edith had already suffered the pain of broken romance, and several mourn a lost, happier past. An undated poem called "October" invokes:

> A cold grey sea, a cold grey sky
> And leafless swaying boughs.
> A wind that wanders sadly by,
> And moans about the house.
>
> And in my lonely heart a cry
> For days that went before;
> For joys that fly, and hopes that die,
> And the past that comes no more.

Some manuscript sheets include marginal doodles. "Raffaelle to the Fornarina," about a woman who sat for one of Raphael's Madonna portraits, begins: "Knot up the filmy strands of golden hair,/That veil your breast, yet leave its beauties bare." On the backside of the sheet, Edith drew heads of ladies, their hair pulled into buns, and pairs of dancing shoes grouped together below the heads; she sketched a sailing ship and wrote "Him" above it, the letters drawn to resemble sailors' knots.

The occasion of *Verses* is less life than literature and art; except in one or two cases, the lyrics either parody or copy standard subjects and poetic forms. Her next publication, however, was drawn from a real incident, which she read about in the newspaper. The seventy-two-line poem, "Only a Child," appeared in the *New York World* newspaper on May 30, 1879. Signed with the pseudonym "Eadgyth," it was accompanied by an explanatory editorial: "The *Press* of May 27 published an account of a suicide in the House of Refuge at Philadelphia of a boy who was only twelve years old. He was locked up in solitary confinement. They found him hanging by the neck dead and cold. Tired of waiting for a release that never came, he had at last escaped—from the House of Refuge!" (The subject appealed to a "morbid strain" in her nature, Edith later admitted.) Composed in rhymed couplets that repeat the refrain "poor little hands," the poem tells the story of the boy's last hours, inculpating the religious and social institutions Edith considered responsible for the child's death. The poem's high moral tone screens Edith's compassion for innocent beings, children and animals, that she retained throughout her life.[68]

Death was often the occasion of her early poetry, and she excelled in writing religious elegies. On April 4, 1876, she composed a poem commemorating the death of Pauline Foster Du Pont's daughter. A meditation on lines from St. Mark ("She is not dead, but sleepeth"), it uses a fixed stanzaic form and in sentiment and style gives the impression of having been written by someone far older than a fourteen-year-old. From childhood on, Edith employed elevated poetic diction and spoke in an arch conversational style that changed little as she matured. The temperament of her fiction also remained stable, although she later modulated the third-person omniscient mode by eliminating adjectives that overstated satiric or dramatic effects.

As a child, Edith spoke like an adult, as do the children in her stories; her letters resemble eighteenth-century fiction in the mode of Samuel Richardson or Henry Fielding. The earliest known letter in her hand, written to Pauline Du Pont in 1874, is a breathless account of life at Pencraig during the week that Pauline's younger sister Anna became engaged to Dr. Beverley Robinson, the Jones family physician.

"My dear Pauley, Feeling myself bound to report the exact mental and moral condition of Anna, since Doctor Robinson's flying visit last Saturday, as well as everything which occurred during that eventful period of her existence, I think I can do no better than write to you, for I am the only good correspondent of our family and you really ought to know something about the general excitement, besides what Anna writes to you." These lines reveal a recognizable Edithian verve. But little wonder that a curator of manuscripts in the library that houses this letter thought "Edith Newbold Jones" may have been a paternal aunt rather than a twelve-year-old girl.[69]

In spring 1880, five of her poems appeared anonymously in the *Atlantic Monthly*, having found their way to this most revered of American literary magazines by a circuitous route. A Newport neighbor and close friend of Harry Jones's, Allen Thorndike Rice (later owner and editor of the *North American Review*), read *Verses* and asked to see other examples of Edith's writing. Impressed, he sent some of the poems to the venerable Henry Wadsworth Longfellow. His letter to the aging poet describes the poems as remarkable for a young woman of "a most estimable New York family," who had been "brought up in fashionable surroundings little calculated to feed her taste for the Muses." Longfellow enclosed the poems with a letter of praise to William Dean Howells, editor of the *Atlantic*.[70]

The poems disclose several sides of Edith's authorial persona. In one, the poet learns patience, personified as a mother whose "strong arms/ Uphold my footsteps on the path of pain." The speaker experiences deep suffering ("I long to cry . . . I seek to fly"), caused apparently by her lost lover:

> *O my Beloved, life's golden visions fade,*
> *And one by one, life's phantom joys depart;*
> *They leave a sudden darkness in the heart,*
> *And patience fills their empty place instead.*

A poem entitled "Wants" rehearses the stages of women's lives, from early loves to the desire for children ("And when they go, we're fain to love/Some other woman's for their sake"), to duty as a balm for failed love and friendship, to the final desire for the sleep of death. The dramatic monologue "A Failure," however, reveals something of Edith's psychic situation in this period. One might read it as an address to a lost lover; more likely, it addresses a mentor figure, whom the young woman strives to please but fails.

I meant to be so strong and true!
The world may smile and question, When?
But what I might have been to you,
I cannot be to other men.
Just one in twenty to the rest,
And all in all to you alone, —
This was my dream; perchance 'tis best
That this, like other dreams, is flown.

For you, I should have been so kind,
So prompt my spirit to control,
To win fresh vigor for my mind,
And purer beauties for my soul.
Beneath your eyes, I might have grown
To that divine, ideal height,
Which, mating wholly with your own,
Our equal spirits should unite.

To others I am less than naught;
To you I might have been so much,
Could but your calm, discerning thought
Have put my powers to the touch!
Your wisdom made me thrice as wise,
And read new meanings in my eyes.

Ah, yes, to you I might have been
That happy being, past recall,
The slave, the helpmeet, and the queen—
All these in one, and one in all,
But that which I had dreamed to do
I learned too late was dreamed in vain,
For what I might have been to you,
I cannot be to other men.

Reverend Washburn was Edith's primary mentor in these years, and soon after her poems were published, she was asked to dine at his house. She brought all her poetry. After reading it, he advised her to continue writing but not to publish anything "for a while more." Perhaps hurt by his advice, seeing it as rejection or failure (Dr. Washburn may be the "you" of her poem), she took it too much to heart. Nine years passed before another poem, "The Last Giustiniani," appeared in the October 1889 issue of *Scribner's Magazine*.[71]

MOTHERS AND FATHERS

In *Life and I*, Edith explains that she made her debut into New York–Newport society prematurely (at age seventeen) because her parents were "alarmed at my growing shyness, at my passion for study, and my indifference to the companionship of young people of my own age." This may have been their stated reason (if so, it signaled their worry about her solitary intellectual habits), but Lucretia confided to Emelyn Washburn that Edith's early launch into the social whirl was occasioned by the precipitous decline of George Frederic's health— brought on, in part, by financial worries. Emelyn "learned to love" Lucretia Jones "very dearly" and served as her confidante; the years 1879 and 1880 were anxious ones for her, Emelyn later recalled, but Edith was never aware of her mother's worry. The economic boom that followed the post–Civil War depression had changed New York. The old families were eclipsed financially by the industrialists and stock market speculators who had invaded Wall Street. Called "bouncers," "silver gilts," and "climbers," they were scaling the walls of the Fifth Avenue society fortress: the Gilded Age was at hand.[72]

While Old New York registered its horror at the excesses of the nouveau riche, patriarchs also felt a certain pressure to keep up. In the winter of 1872–1873, Ward McAllister organized the Patriarchs Ball patrons, twenty-four men of unquestioned rank, in an effort to fix the limits of society. But some of the oldest families thought McAllister and Mrs. William Backhouse Astor, his partner in this enterprise, had cast their social net too far. The Assembly Balls, an even more exclusive group, began a few years later, the membership of its nominating committee shrouded in secrecy. Minnie Jones served on the Committee of Management and recalled that they kept Alice Gwynne Vanderbilt (wife of Cornelius Vanderbilt II) waiting two years for admission. By the time Edith made her debut in 1879, the Astors and the Vanderbilts outnumbered the old guard and were among the most powerful members of society.[73]

George Frederic Jones had nothing like the wealth of these newcomers; suffering economic losses from the real estate depression, the Joneses tried to keep up appearances. Lucretia confided to Emelyn that she feared losing the West Twenty-third Street house (which was mortgaged); and Edith later recalled that the conservatory next to the billiard room had been left unfurnished: "the money gave out with the furnishing of the billiard-room." Lucretia hoped that "Puss" would have one social summer in Newport and one winter in New York society before they were forced to alter their living style—a change that would affect Edith's chances on the marriage market, as Lucretia remembered from her own experience.[74]

Declaring the absurdity of the usual debutante entertainments, a huge "tea" and expensive ball, Lucretia arranged an understated, elegant party, choosing guests from the extended Rhinelander-Jones families. She counted on her practice of keeping open house and Harry's popularity to help Edith make wider social connections. Renting the ballroom at Delmonico's, as other mothers might have done, was out of the question: "My mother would never have consented to my making my first appearance in a public room," Edith recalled. (Snobbery may have accommodated economy in this decision.) Instead, Lucretia turned to her friend Mrs. Levi Morton, the former Anna Livingston Read, wife of Levi Parsons Morton, a leader in New York society and a cosmopolitan with a wide experience of Europe. At age forty-five, he was a recognized financier of great genius and a man with a political future, who became vice president under President Benjamin Harrison (when Edith's brother-in-law, William Wharton, was assistant secretary of state). He later served as minister to France and governor of New York. The choice of the Mortons' Fifth Avenue mansion for Edith's debutante ball perfectly suited Lucretia's desire to situate her daughter within the prestigious family network that was Edith's by birth and to suggest that by experience and association, Edith Newbold Jones had an affinity with Europe.[75]

Edith might have resented the calculated restraint of these proceedings, feeling that she had not gotten her due. More likely, she felt relief at not having to face a room filled with several hundred people. Dressed in a pale green brocade décolleté gown with dropped shoulders and a white muslin skirt trimmed in rows of ruffled Valenciennes, her red-gold hair piled high on her head, she clasped a large bouquet of lilies of the valley. Edith wrote two accounts of the evening, and they vary widely from each other. In *A Backward Glance*, she portrays the evening as a "long cold agony of shyness" in which she "cowered" beside her mother in "speechless misery." But in *Life and I*, the draft version of her autobiography (first published in 1990), she describes the ball as a "pink blur of emotion" in which—after her initial hesitation—she danced both with her brother Harry's friends (all of whom were ten to twelve years older than she) and also with young men her own age. In both versions, she admits that the weeks following that ball were happy ones. She gives a rather flat summary of this time in *A Backward Glance*, whereas *Life and I* captures her emotional state in breathless, almost rhapsodic prose: "Oh, how I loved it all—my pretty frocks, the flowers, the music, the sense that everybody 'liked' me, and wanted to talk to me and dance with me!" Lucretia's hope that Edith would have at least one gay "season" in New York was fulfilled.[76]

Harry's social connections served her well, as did Minnie and Frederic Jones's hospitality. She attended dinners, Sunday lunches, and after-theater parties with the "older girls" and young married women, soon finding herself at ease in a "charmed circle" of people ranging in age from eighteen to fifty. That summer, Pencraig filled up with friends who swam, fished, raced boats, and took excursions on steam yachts. This group lacked intellectual interests, but Edith responded to their good humor and gaiety. She wanted "brilliant adventures," however, and none came her way. "I led, I dominated," she later recalled. "I was conscious of 'counting' wherever I went—but I inspired no romantic passions!"

A year passed, and in summer 1880, Edith tasted romance with Harry Leyden Stevens, a handsome, sociable, and clever young man of twenty educated at St. Mark's School and in Europe, where he had taken a mountain cure for incipient tuberculosis. His mother was a widowed socialite, Mrs. Paran Stevens, who had recently made a brilliant match for her daughter, Mary Fisk, with Arthur Paget, son of Lord Clarence Paget. Their marriage scandalized the English aristocracy because neither the late Paran Stevens nor his wife had social credentials, but it gave Mrs. Stevens entrée into Newport and New York society through the Court of St. James's.[77]

"Auntie" Stevens, as she came to be known, was born Marietta Reed, daughter of a greengrocer in Lowell, Massachusetts. She grew up to be a schoolteacher, and at nineteen married Paran Stevens, a man more than twice her age. A successful Boston businessman, he owned the Parker House and Tremont hotels and, later, the Fifth Avenue Hotel in New York City. He preferred breeding racehorses to hobnobbing with society, but after his death in 1872, his widow moved to New York and set out to establish herself as a society hostess at her home at 244 Fifth Avenue. In 1880, when the Joneses traveled to Bar Harbor to visit Frederic and Minnie, who were busy designing their cottage on Mount Desert Island, Harry Stevens came along. He was Edith's "shadow," Louisa Rutherfurd reported to her sister, Margaret, who was in Paris on her honeymoon. Louisa pondered whether "Lily" Jones would actually marry young Stevens. She did not think so, although "they are perpetually together." "Lily" was drawn, pale, and looking "wretched," she said, yet she still had success with handsome young men. A rumor circulated that Miss Jones "let men take liberties with her." Edith recovered her health during her weeks in the invigorating air of Bar Harbor, a suggestion that Newport dampness aggravated her bronchitis and asthma. Her father's health, however, did not improve. In autumn, the Jones family closed up Pencraig and went to Cannes, where they hoped the mild Riviera climate would aid George Frederic's recovery.[78]

EDITH JONES and Emelyn Washburn lost their fathers within a year of each other, both men dying of strokes. In Fontainebleau in spring 1881, Emelyn received the message that her father had died in New York. On hearing the news, Edith sent Emelyn several memorial verses. Only one of these now exists, an untitled poem comprised of two sonnets based on a prayer of St. Chrysostom's: "In this world the knowledge of Thy Truth, and in the world to come Life Everlasting." Edith must have recognized by this time that her own father was extremely ill. Aged beyond his years, George Frederic was gaunt and bent over, his illness manifesting itself in extreme nervousness. Stricken in early spring 1882, he died at the Bellevue Hotel in Cannes on March 15, at age sixty-one, and was buried in the Jones family vault in Cannes. In early summer, Edith, Harry, and Lucretia returned to Newport.[79]

George Frederic's death radically changed Lucretia's life. She never again lived in the house on West Twenty-third Street, which was rented out when they left for Cannes, nor did she return to Calvary Church, where she and George Frederic had attended services for thirty-eight years. In winter 1882, Lucretia took a house on Washington Square. A short time later, she inherited a large property, her portion of a Rhinelander estate, and was suddenly freed of the financial worries she had carried for so long and that had contributed to her husband's illness and death. Keeping the West Twenty-third Street house as a rental property, she purchased another at 28 West Twenty-fifth Street, which she set about remodeling.

Lucretia Jones no longer entertained or went out into society. Her name never appeared in a New York City directory, although she was listed as "Mrs. George Frederic Jones" in the *Social Register.* Frederic lived nearby at 312 East Eighteenth Street, and visited his mother daily. His daughter, Trix, now ten years old, remained devoted to her grandmother. Pencraig in Newport, which had been so full of friends and laughter only two summers earlier, was now silent.[80]

DAUGHTERS AND SONS

When the George Frederic Jones family left for Cannes by way of London in November 1880, gossips conjectured that Edith and Harry Stevens were already engaged. They were not. During her first Riviera winter, Edith made friends with Americans who had married into European aristocracy, including daughters of Lucretia's childhood acquaintances. Joining them in picnics, tennis parties, and dinners, she also explored the scented pine forests high above the coastline, a pleasure she retained into late old age. As Mrs. Stevens regularly wintered on the south coast of France, Harry and Edith may have been together again that first winter, but they apparently met up in Venice in late summer 1881. Her poetic satire, "Intense Love's Utterance," recorded her reading during these months—John Ruskin's *The Stones of Venice* and Walter Pater's *Renaissance Studies* (gifts from her father)—and ends by according art a higher place than love's temporal pleasures. The unpublished lyric testifies to Edith's priorities and provides clues to the directions the romance with Harry would take.[81]

Harry followed the Joneses back to Cannes and stayed on through George Frederic's final illness and death. Lucretia noted in a letter to Emelyn Washburn that his devotion to Edith was a comfort to her. A few months later in Newport, he was still earnestly courting Edith. On Thursday, August 19, the *Newport Daily News* reported several social notes in which Mrs. Paran Stevens figured prominently, and one that featured her son:

> The engagement of Mr. Harry Stevens, only son of Mrs. Paran Stevens, to Miss Edith Jones, daughter of the late George F. Jones, has been announced.

A similar notice appeared in the *Newport Journal and Weekly News*; the gossipy society weekly *Town Topics* also noted the engagement. Oddly worded, the notice announces the man's engagement rather than the future bride's; it was undoubtedly the work of Mrs. Paran Stevens—or her hired publicist. She missed no opportunity to have her name appear in newspapers and society columns, whereas Lucretia Jones abhorred the idea of her name appearing in a newspaper. Nonetheless, Lucretia should have announced the engagement, but the requirements of formal mourning may have prevented her from fulfilling this duty.[82]

The previous Sunday, August 15, she had sent Edith around to her uncle and godfather, Fred Rhinelander, with a handwritten note. Lucretia had wanted to come herself with "Pussie" to announce the engagement to Mr. Stevens, she wrote, but the heat had caused her to feel "wretchedly": "I shall hope soon to be able to tell you how pleased we all are, notwithstanding this other loss to me within these last months, which naturally is hard for she has always been so very, very dear to me in all the years we have had together, friend and loving child in one." This rather muddled expression of her sentiments hints that Lucretia was saddened by the prospect of her daughter's leaving the parental home. Her son Harry, now thirty-two years old, lived a quite independent life, and she would be alone.

Edith would not remember her mother as an affectionate person, nor recall their relationship as a particularly loving one. Her memories were colored, however, by events still in the future. What Lucretia really thought of her daughter's impending marriage, one can only guess. Although everyone agreed that Harry Stevens was charming, he had an ambitious, showy, and headstrong mother. Emelyn Washburn knew the family at Calvary Church, and she commented years later that Mrs. Stevens would have been an "impossible mother-in-law."[83]

Whatever Lucretia's worries or Edith's desires, the wedding was not fated to take place. Two months later, on Thursday, October 28, *Town Topics* reported: "The marriage of Mr. Henry Stevens, Mrs. Paran Stevens's son, to Miss Edith Jones, which was announced for the latter part of this month, has been postponed, it is said indefinitely." Again, one senses Marietta Stevens at work. Edith told Emelyn she had been forced to break her engagement, and Lucretia later said that Mrs. Stevens engineered the breakup. Gossip went round that Mrs. Stevens was angered because members of the Rhinelander-Jones families still refused to speak to her, even though she had gained social standing. But she may have had second thoughts about the timing of her son's marriage. By the terms of Paran Stevens's will, his wife had sole control of her son's property—an estate amounting to more than $1,000,000—until he married or reached the age of twenty-five. He was now twenty-three. Thus, his mother may have broken up the romance to protect her financial interests; she was known for her litigiousness, and had already sought legal means to divert part of her son's trust.[84]

Whatever the reasons for the broken engagement (and they are not self-evident), Edith was made to take public responsibility for it. *Town Topics* gave as "the only reason for the breaking of the engagement hitherto existing between Harry Stevens and Miss Edith Jones is an alleged preponderance of intellectuality on the part of the intended bride. Miss Jones is an ambitious authoress, and it is said that, in the eyes of Mr. Stevens, ambition is a grievous fault." This arrow, undoubtedly launched by Marietta Stevens, hit its mark—turning back on Old New Yorkers the very accusation of ambitiousness that had been used against her when she tried to secure a foothold among them. Her place in society now secure, and new industrial wealth in the ascendancy, she could afford to launch a dart or two. Other bright and ambitious daughters of Old New York society were not always condemned for their industry. The brilliant and energetic Margaret Rutherfurd, for example, worked tirelessly to further the diplomatic career of her husband, Henry White, and was praised for it. Furthering a husband's career and carving out a social place for oneself (as Mrs. Paran Stevens had done) were acceptable avenues for women. Literary ambitions, when combined with what appeared to be social and intellectual contempt, brought condemnation.

Lucretia was apparently kind to Edith at this difficult moment. Certainly, the younger matrons in New York and Newport, many of them friends of Minnie Jones, took Edith's part. ("Is it not sad about Pussy's engagement," a Rhinelander cousin wrote to her brother. "Mrs. S. is at the bottom of it all.") The trauma for Edith was not so much in losing Harry Stevens, especially if she did not really love him, but in being publicly shamed. Lucretia lost no time in removing Edith from the scene of her defeat. By the end of November, Mrs. Jones and her two unmarried children were once again in Paris, and Mrs. Stevens was on her way to Nice for the winter.[85]

A SEASON OF SUITORS

Harry Stevens disappeared from Edith's life apparently without a word, apart from later fictional references to his mother. Lucretia Jones could easily avoid comment on these events, as she was adhering to the strictest rules of family mourning—heavy veils, black-bordered stationery, mourning bands, and a virtual retreat from society. Edith went out very little, but on her return from the winter trip to Europe, she again took her place in the social set of young marriageables. Her fourth season "out," two of them had been spent in Europe. Thus, January 1883 constituted a sort of second debut as she returned to the scene she had so suddenly left in November 1880 by accompanying her parents to France. She entered the Patriarchs Ball on the arm of Julian Buckler, younger half brother of Henry White; Julian wrote to yet a third brother, Willie Buckler, of Edith's extreme nervousness as she faced the cold stares of the New York matrons whom she had scandalized by breaking off her engagement to an eminently eligible young man. They believed she had put her literary ambitions above her duty to marry. Edith admitted to suffering from an "inferiority complex" at this time. She had all but forgotten her "literary dreams," she later confessed. Rather than feeling superior, she felt her friends were "quicker and more amusing" than she.[86]

Edith was deeply discouraged. "I could not believe," she wrote in her memoirs, "that a girl like myself could ever write anything worth reading, and my friends would certainly have agreed with me." Lucretia's reproof of her first narrative effort ten years earlier had brought to a halt the "creative frenzy" of Edith's storytelling. Turning to poetry, she had had some success before Allen Rice—her patron of sorts—dashed her hopes: "You know," he said, "writing lyrics won't lead you any-where. What you want to do is write an epic. . . . Why don't you try your hand at something like 'Don Juan'?" At this advice, she "shrank back into [her] secret retreat," thinking herself unfit to be either poet or novelist. She still read widely, but her "dream of a literary career . . . faded into unreality." This remark casts a bright light on her desires: not content to write for herself, she wanted a literary *career*. She was in-deed an "ambitious authoress," as the columnist for *Town Topics* had noted.[87]

On January 24, 1883, Edith came into her majority, and the follow-ing day, Frederic and Henry Jones signed a revocation of power of at-torney. Of legal age, she could now sign contracts, undertake financial obligations, and act on her own behalf. Yet, she had no money of her own, despite a sizable inheritance from her father. She depended on her mother for a home, and her estate was in the hands of her brothers, the appointed trustees. By the terms of George Frederic Jones's will, Edith (in co-partnership with her brothers and their descendants) received about $600,000 in various real estate holdings, including seven proper-ties on the east side of Sixth Avenue and the north side of Fifty-fourth Street (one on the site of what is now the Warwick Hotel), four proper-ties on West Eighteenth Street, several commercial properties on lower Broadway, one in Brooklyn, and another on Long Island. Her interest and rental income amounted to about $10,000 a year, rising and falling with the real estate and stock markets. She lived primarily on the income from this and one other inheritance until she published her first novel in 1902. Her literary fortunes then began to rise faster than the interest on her trust funds, and by the final decades of her life, she was supported almost entirely by her literary earnings.[88]

Chapter 2

W

EXPLORATIONS

I N SUMMER 1883, LUCRETIA JONES DECIDED TO AVOID NEWPORT, with its painful memories of the previous year. Instead of going to Pencraig, she took Edith and Harry to Bar Harbor, Maine, where Frederic and Minnie had built their estate, "Reef Point." For many years a popular summer place for Philadelphians and Bostonians, Bar Harbor in the post–Civil War years had begun its transformation from a village of rough-and-ready fishermen, sailors, and hunters to an elegant and cultured resort. Two men who would play defining roles in Edith's future life came to Bar Harbor that summer: thirty-three-year-old Teddy Wharton, a friend of Harry Jones's and a man Edith had known for almost a decade; and Walter Van Rensselaer Berry, age twenty-four, who arrived in July to golf and play tennis. He would become, in Edith's words, "the love of all my life."[1]

Berry was related to Edith on Lucretia's side of the family through the Van Rensselaers. Proud of his mother's aristocratic heritage, he always signed himself "Walter V. R. Berry." Catharine Van Rensselaer descended from the original colonial "patroon" Killian Van Rensselaer; the family had been ceded vast land holdings in Upstate New York by the king of the Netherlands. After marrying Catharine, Nathaniel Berry moved from his native Connecticut to Albany, New York, and supervised his wife's property. They lived for some years in Paris, where their son Walter was born and spent the early years of his life. When he graduated from Harvard in 1881, Walter made a leisurely Grand Tour of Europe and then returned to the United States in 1883 to study law. He may have read law at Columbia College, but he did not take a degree. Desiring a career in international law and diplomacy, he opened a law firm in Washington, D.C., in 1885, and remained there until 1908.[2]

Although it would be some years before the arc of his life met and joined with Edith's, they were immediately drawn to each other that summer in Newport. Berry stood six foot three inches to Edith's five foot five, and in a white linen suit and summer boater, he was handsome, despite his large ears and thin frame. Humor played behind intelligent blue eyes, and his dry, crackling wit sparked her own.

Not everyone appreciated Berry, who preferred to stand aside from groups, observing human follies with cool regard. Aloof, some said superior, he seemed a dilettante. Women found him debonair. Most of Edith's men friends disliked him. Percy Lubbock would later characterize him as a "dry shadow" over her life, a shell of a man she took for the "flower of manhood." Yet, other discerning men—Henry James and Bernard Berenson, for example—genuinely cared for Berry and valued his friendship. Royal Cortissoz, art critic for the *New York Times*, wrote to Edith on hearing of Berry's death in 1927:

> He was so finely tempered and he had so much of what I call "margin." With so many men there is no margin at all. Everything that they have lies on the surface. He made me feel that there were all manner of deeper places in him—and they were all good. I loved that smile of his. Was there a trace of cynicism in it, of worldliness? Perhaps. But I felt only its gentleness and sweetness. He had a mind and a heart, and he was himself, not a cosmopolitan amalgam, though he was so much a man of the world.

This was Edith's "Walter," the man who read poetry aloud to her ("unforgettable . . . sensitive and moving"). Her imaginative powers failed when she tried to "picture what the life of the spirit" would have been without him. He nurtured her spiritually and intellectually, and she spoke of him as a savior: "He found me when my mind and soul were hungry and thirsty, and he fed them until our last hour together." A large photograph of him adorned her boudoir mantelpiece, placed alongside a portrait of Teddy.[3]

We have long thought that Edith Jones became Mrs. Edward R.

Wharton because Walter Berry did not ask her to marry him, but there is no evidence that she expected a proposal of marriage. She later described their meeting as a "communion of kindred intelligences" cut short when "chance separated us." In other remarks, she suggested that Berry's professional ambitions drew him away from her. In the last days of her life, she told her friend Elisina Tyler that he had once written her a "real love-letter." Fearing, perhaps, the "dreadful devouring quality in love," she did not take his lead. "I am glad I dealt with it as I did," she said. "I should never have had his precious friendship all my life if it had been otherwise." Even at age twenty-one, Edith showed a preference for the promise of long friendship to fleeting hours of romance. She and Walter would later have their romance, although it was not the conventional extramarital liaison of secret love trysts. When its "great days" were over, she reinvented the terms of their endearment.[4]

But what of Walter's desires? He was a perpetual bachelor, squiring beautiful women around Washington, New York, and Paris. In his midfifties, he reportedly had an affair with Mrs. Robert Goelet, a New York society matron half his age. She wanted to marry him, some said, but her husband refused a divorce and instead "forgave" her. Edith may not have known in summer 1883 that Walter had chronic health problems resulting from malaria contracted in childhood. This disease accounted for his battle against anemia and weight loss and his vulnerability to flu and respiratory problems caused by a bad lung. Always under a doctor's care, he took summer cures in the Adirondacks, visited Bar Harbor as much for its bracing air as for its society, and when in Europe sought out mountain retreats. Their susceptibility to respiratory ailments created a bond between Walter and Edith, a sympathetic understanding of both the physical and psychological effects of recurrent illness.

Although guarding his health, Walter had a highly successful career, first as a lawyer, later as a judge on the International Tribunal in Egypt (illness forced him to resign his appointment), and finally as president of the American Chamber of Commerce in Paris. He experienced recurrences of malaria in adulthood, and by his early forties, he stayed home in bed at least one day a week. These "rest cures," during which he reviewed legal briefs, wrote letters, read, and napped, allowed him to maintain his energy. He avoided marriage, with its possibility of parenthood, and his letters to Edith reveal depths of loneliness.[5]

In 1923, he wrote her a letter recalling the faraway summer of their first meeting, when they had canoed on a lake:

Dearest—The real dream—mine—was in the canoe and in the night afterwards,—for I lay awake wondering and wondering,—and then, when morning came, wondering how I could have wondered,—*I*, a $-less lawyer (not even *that*, yet) with just about enough cash for the canoe and for Rodick's [hotel] bill—

And then, later, in the little cottage [Pencraig] at Newport, I wondered why I *hadn't*—for it would have been *good*,—and then the slices of years slid by.

Well, my dear, I've never "wondered" about anyone else, and there wouldn't be much of me if you were cut out of it. Forty years of it is you, dear. W.

THE GENTLEMAN FROM BOSTON

When Lucretia Jones and her two children left Bar Harbor for Newport at the end of July 1883, Teddy Wharton traveled with them. Harry's longtime friend, he had for ten years been an annual visitor to Pencraig, first meeting "Pussy" when she was a girl of eleven. A well-built man of medium height, Edward Robbins Wharton had a gentle nature and an ability to see through pretense at a glance. Legend has it that in Newport, late for a luncheon engagement, he hailed a butcher's cart on fashionable Bellevue Avenue. A few days later, a nouveau riche who had heard of his ride in the butcher's cart remarked, "I would not do that if I were you." "No," Teddy answered, "if I were you, I would not do that either."

A gentleman of leisure, Teddy had no profession and desired none. He resided at 127 Beacon Street in Boston with his mother and spinster sister, Nannie, passing his days making the rounds of the Somerset and other men's clubs. A man very like his friend Harry Jones, he shared Edith's love of the outdoors and her fondness for animals, especially dogs and horses. He took great pleasure in society, and his playful sense of humor and youthful gaiety made him seem younger than his years. Edith felt comfortable with him, and Lucretia liked him for the same reasons she had liked Harry Stevens: he was "sunshine in the house."[6]

Teddy Wharton descended from Virginia landowners, but his paternal grandparents, John and Nancy Craig Wharton, came from Philadelphia. In 1843, his father, William Craig Wharton, then in his early thirties, married Nancy Willing Spring. Ten years younger than her husband, she was born in Amherst, Massachusetts, the granddaughter of a prominent physician. No record of William Wharton's educational and professional background has been found, nor do we know how he met Nancy Spring. They apparently lived in Jamaica Plain, Massachusetts, during the first seven years of their marriage, although no record of their residency exists in the state archives. By 1850, they had moved to Brookline, and according to the national census, Mr. Wharton owned an estate valued at $20,000. He had four children—Nancy (1844), Ann (1846; she later died), William (1847), and a new baby, Edward, born April 3, 1850.[7]

In 1869, when Edith and her parents were living in Paris, Teddy entered Harvard as a freshman. A year older than his classmates, he may have traveled abroad before beginning his studies. In his first year, he studied Greek, Latin, history, and ethics (his worst subject), and was often reported absent from class. More interested in socializing than studying, he passed the year's work with barely a 65 percent average. During his sophomore year (1870–1871), while Edith Jones, age eight, battled typhoid fever in Wildbad, Germany, Teddy added chemistry, physics, natural history (his best subject), German, and "themes" (writing) to his curriculum. But his grades fell further. By his junior year, he stood tenth from the bottom of his class of 128 students, earning only 45.4 percent of the year's total possible points. He improved his standing in his senior year and graduated in June 1873, ranking eighty-fifth in his class, at the top of the lower third. At the same Harvard ceremony, his brother William, who three years earlier received his B.A. with honors in Greek, Latin, and ancient history, took a degree in law. William became a successful Boston lawyer and a well-known political figure, first as a member of the Massachusetts House of Representatives and later as assistant secretary of state under President Benjamin Harrison.[8]

Teddy, unlike his rather dour brother Billy, had a sense of fun that attracted Edith. Lucretia encouraged his attentions to her daughter and honored him at Pencraig in the summer of 1883 with a gala dinner party—an entertainment so elaborate it drew the attention of *Town Topics*. If she had hoped Teddy would make a speedy proposal of marriage, then Lucretia was disappointed. A bachelor of many years and a man who apparently had never yet had a serious relationship with a woman, Teddy did not rush headlong into romance. Indeed, the word "romance" hardly seems suited to his casual, teasing, older-brother manner, the demeanor he assumed with all women, no matter their age. Six months passed without an announcement of an engagement, although in January 1884, he escorted Edith to the New York Patriarchs Ball at Delmonico's, where they danced waltzes and quadrilles.

No mention of his friendship with Edith appears in a letter to his favorite aunt, Sarah Cleveland, written later that spring, although he remarked that his "winter gaieties were telling on a constitution enfeebled by old age [he was thirty-four], and the cases of the beau monde." He spoke of literature, the only serious topic he broached in the letter. He preferred the writings of Ralph Waldo Emerson ("original always") to those of James Russell Lowell, whom he found "too fond of showing how much he had read." Edith's influence appears not only in the viewpoint of this pronouncement, but also in its wording: she frequently put the adverb after the adjective to add weight to her opinions. Employing a strategy of exaggerated self-deprecation, Teddy joked about his intellectual deficiences. He was not uncultured, but he had difficulty in spelling ("writting"): "My spelling is weak so don't look at each word but get the general sense. T.W."[9]

Some months later, Teddy asked Lucretia for her daughter's hand in marriage. The bride's mother and her future son-in-law arranged for Tiffany's to make a very special engagement ring. To the social worlds of New York, Newport, and Boston, news of the marriage came without warning. Announcement of Teddy and Edith's engagement in January 1885 appeared in the press barely one month before the April wedding. The Boston correspondent for *Town Topics* noted that the forthcoming marriage was a chief topic of conversation in that city because Miss Jones was not generally known there. In fact, the two families were not well known to each other. Teddy had a small allowance but as yet no inheritance. (He would not gain his legacy for another twenty-five years, at age sixty.) During the early years of their marriage, they lived primarily on interest from Edith's trust fund. Because they had no money to buy a home, Lucretia let them use Pencraig Cottage, the small house across the street from Pencraig. They moved into the house (which Edith had redecorated to her taste) in late summer 1885. During the first three months of their marriage, Edith and Teddy lived with Lucretia in Newport; when in New York, they stayed with her on Twenty-fifth Street.[10]

The marriage suited Lucretia's needs. Intent on keeping her children close at hand, she was not losing a daughter but gaining another son. What depth of feeling Edith held for her husband we do not know, although Emelyn Washburn believed she really loved him. Edith wanted to be a married woman and mistress of a house; these roles were inseparable, of course, but she was particularly drawn to the image of herself as homemaker and hostess, "busy" with her house and garden. At twenty-three, her 1879 debut six years in the past, Edith was running out of time, as she and Lucretia undoubtedly realized. In retrospect, her marriage to Teddy Wharton seemed "utterly inconceivable" (in Henry James's words), but at the time, it appeared a good match. Teddy's kindheartedness and good humor compensated for other qualities she might have hoped to discover in a mate—Walter Berry's wit and intelligence, for example.[11]

Only one cloud shadowed Edith's union with Teddy—a possible strain of inherited mental illness in the Wharton family. Teddy's father, then in his early seventies and suffering from "melancholia," had for some years resided intermittently at McLean Hospital in Somerville, a suburb of Boston. As his condition deteriorated, he could no longer return home for visits. Little direct testimony exists about William Craig Wharton's illness, but Ogden Codman, a Boston architect whose family knew the Whartons well, described him as a "trial" to his wife and children. In Codman's uncompromising assessment, they "never had a minutes [sic] peace till he was shut up." Many old Boston families had inherited strains of mental illness, and Mr. Wharton's disease fit a pattern evident among the Adamses, Bigelows, Hoopers, Jameses, and Sturgises. Observing similar signs of aggressivity and depression in Teddy Wharton when he entered his fifties, Codman and other Boston friends pressured Edith to commit her husband to McLean Hospital. The Wharton family stubbornly maintained that Teddy was mentally stable. "When I remember that the Drs. assured [Teddy's] family, before our marriage, that his father's insanity was not hereditary," Edith wrote a friend in 1928, "I wonder at the blindness that exists in that subject—still exists, probably."[12]

Mrs. Edward R. Wharton

Edith Jones's wedding was "a very quiet one," the *New York Times* reported. Indeed it was, but the *Times* incorrectly stated that the guest list was "limited to the immediate relatives of the two families." According to the *Newport Daily News*, many Newporters attended the wedding; Mrs. Wharton, the newspaper announced, would spend "a portion of the season here at the residence of Mrs. Jones on Harrison Avenue." Teddy merited only passing mention in Newport newspapers (referred to as "Alfred"), but his bride's name did not appear on the wedding invitation:

> Mrs. George Frederic Jones requests the honour of your presence at the marriage of her daughter to Mr. Edward R. Wharton, at Trinity chapel, on Wednesday April Twenty-ninth at twelve o'clock.

Some have taken this puzzling slip as proof of how little Lucretia cared for her daughter, yet the omission may have been made by Edith herself.

A clue to this strange document, which fails not only to mention the bride's name, but also to give the complete date of the ceremony, occurs in Edith's short story "The Last Asset," published in 1904. Hermione Newell, age twenty-three (as Edith was in 1885) and too long on the marriage market, is inclined to "good works and afternoon church, [has] a taste for the society of dull girls, and a clinging fidelity to old governesses and retired nursemaids." Living in the "glare" of her society mother (a woman more closely resembling Mrs. Paran Stevens than Lucretia Jones), Hermione serves as her mother's secretary–cum–lady's maid, writing notes and running errands. When Mrs. Newell arranges a marriage for her daughter with a scion of Paris Faubourg St. Germain nobility, Hermione herself writes out the marriage notice for the newspapers. It follows the standard formula: the bride is named as the daughter of Samuel C. Newell, Esq. (from whom her mother had long since separated); however, Mrs. Newell merits no mention. The tale turns on the necessity of Mr. Newell attending his daughter's wedding; when he appears at the service, it is as if from the dead, and father and daughter are reunited.[13]

A solitary and unattended figure, Edith no doubt wished her father were present at the wedding. The wedding party included four ushers, among them a Rhinelander cousin, and Teddy's best man, Percival Lowell, a friend from Boston. But Edith had no bridesmaids, a circumstance that did not go unnoticed by *Town Topics*, which commented that "many people expected" bridesmaids. But whom might she have chosen? The beautiful Louisa Rutherfurd, a Newport neighbor, might have upstaged her. Half-blind spinster Emelyn Washburn, her only long-standing friend, would have made an unlikely attendant. Edith apparently had no close friends among her Rhinelander-Jones cousins.

Beatrix Jones, age twelve, was too young, and Minnie, a matron of Teddy's age, too old.

Her wedding illuminates Edith's singular place in New York–Newport society. We can see her emerge through the door onto the low front steps of her mother's West Twenty-fifth Street house, facing Trinity Chapel. A small figure dressed in white satin, a cluster of lilies of the valley enclosed by lace and mull at her throat, she holds a hammered silver Book of Common Prayer, a gift of Teddy's best man, its cover decorated with an embossed art nouveau design in mother-of-pearl. On the arm of her godfather, Fred Rhinelander, her court train looped in her right hand, she crosses the street in the noonday sun. Behind her tulle veil, secured by a diamond tiara encrusted with gems worn by Lucretia at her wedding some four decades earlier, Edith was that morning as fearful and insecure as the adolescent girl who clung to her parents at her coming-out party in 1879 and who four years later shook with dread as she entered the Patriarchs Ball escorted by Julian White. She was unprepared for almost everything that marriage to Teddy Wharton would require of her.[14]

Several days earlier, "seized" with "dread of the whole dark mystery" of marriage, she had begged Lucretia, "with a heart beating to suffocation," to tell her "what being married was like." At first uncomprehending, Lucretia became embarrassed, then cruel. Edith's account, recorded in a draft of her autobiography, dramatizes a scene in which mother and daughter confront one another across the impasse of sexuality:

> Her handsome face at once took on the look of icy disapproval which I most dreaded. "I never heard such a ridiculous question!" she said impatiently; and I felt at once how vulgar she thought me.
>
> But in the extremity of my need I persisted. "I'm afraid, mamma—I want to know what will happen to me!"
>
> The coldness of her expression deepened to disgust. She was silent for a dreadful moment; then she said with an effort: "You've seen enough pictures and statues in your life. Haven't you noticed that men are— made differently from women?"
>
> "Yes," I faltered blankly.
>
> "Well, then—?"
>
> I was silent, from sheer inability to follow, and she brought out sharply: "Then for heaven's sake don't ask me any more silly questions. You can't be as stupid as you pretend!"

The force of Lucretia's anger and her blindness to her daughter's needs could only have increased Edith's terror of what would happen after marriage. Edith would learn about the "processes of generation" from Teddy, but not until several weeks after their wedding. As a new bride, she apparently knew little more about human reproduction than she had at age ten, when she ran to tell her mother that babies did not come from flowers and received a harsh reproof from Lucretia in response. She would not know for some years how the painful encounter with her mother would "falsify and misdirect" her life. When she at last recognized her sexual needs, she felt betrayed—not only by her mother (who by that time was dead), but also by the cultural system that kept young women in a state of false modesty and innocence. Until she was forty-seven years old, Edith puzzled over the mystery of marital relations, pondering what it was that other women knew that she did not.[15]

Teddy and Edith promised themselves to each other before the Reverend Morgan Dix, rector of Trinity Church, and sealed their vows in an exchange of wedding rings. No photograph exists of her wedding ring (probably a plain band that matched Teddy's), but a 1905 publicity photo shows her engagement ring, a hoop of diamonds (purchased by Teddy) joined to two other hoops, one of rubies and another of diamonds, both gifts from Lucretia. The interlocking rings suggest a symbolic union of mother-husband-daughter, as if in entrusting Edith to Teddy, Lucretia bound her daughter more closely to her. Lucretia showed affection for Edith not by kind words and confidences, but by gifts of jewels (virtually all of Edith's jewelry came from her mother) and beautiful clothes—the sort of adornments that Lucretia had wanted for herself when she was Edith's age.[16]

After the ceremony, the bride and groom, with their attendants and guests, crossed Twenty-fifth Street to Lucretia's house, where Pinard Brothers caterers served a wedding breakfast. Having no money for a trip to Cuba (still the favorite spot for fashionable honeymoons), they went directly to Pencraig. On May 1, the *Newport Daily News* announced in its "Local Events" column that "Mr. and Mrs. Alfred [sic] Wharton have arrived in Newport." A little more than two months later, Harry Stevens died from complications of tuberculosis, and his mother gained control of the fortune that would have been his. Gossips had it that he died of a broken heart for Pussy Jones. Edith's feelings on the death of her former fiancé are not known.[17]

For the next eight years (1885–1893), Edith and Teddy spent June until February at Pencraig Cottage, traveling each spring to Italy. We know little about the first years of Edith's marriage, apart from the brief view she provides in *A Backward Glance*, but it must have been a difficult period of adjustment—not only sexually, but intellectually and spiritually as well. Their European trips, carefully planned and eagerly awaited, constituted Edith's escape from a life that became increasingly wearisome and boring. "I was never very happy at Newport," she confessed. Photographs from these years, many of them taken at the Newport Casino, confirm Edith's unhappiness. She no longer had a youthful air: her mouth was drawn in a firm, straight line, her eyes dark and unsmiling. The damp climate induced bronchial infections, tonsillitis, and asthma attacks. In November and December, Newport was a lonely place, the summer crowd having returned to Boston and New York. When wet cold seeped through the uninsulated walls of Pencraig Cottage and bleak, impenetrable fogs rolled in off the Atlantic, Edith felt chilled both in body and spirit. Falling ill, she would improve just in time to board the boat for Europe: "It was then that I really felt alive."[18]

Her physical ailments produced the sense of being only half-awake; she lived in a kind of limbo, having as yet "no real personality" of her own. She would come into fully conscious selfhood with the publication of her first collection of short stories, *The Greater Inclination* (1899), some fourteen years in the future. She dreamed of having her own home, as though by taking possession of a house she could capture her own elusive self. The house as metaphor for woman became a dominant literary trope of her writing.

As a young matron, Edith took seriously her social and civic responsibilities, but chose carefully the people and projects she felt merited her attention. Pencraig Cottage was a model of efficiency, its domestic staff of cook and housemaids overseen by Catherine Gross, an Alsatian woman eleven years older than Edith, hired in 1884 as her companion. Rosy-cheeked and smiling, Gross embodied the warmheartedness that Edith wanted most in her domestic environment. In 1888, when their finances had improved, Teddy hired Alfred White (a man of twenty) to serve as his valet. In future years, Gross and White shared the responsibility of directing the Wharton household.[19]

Edith's sure sense of household management had no parallel in the private sphere of marriage. She must have cast aside many illusions about marital happiness in those first years, opting for a friendly regard with Teddy rather than passion. Had she hoped for children? Did she establish, and maintain, sexual relations with her husband, or were gossips correct in their speculation that the Whartons had a *mariage blanc*? According to the customs of their social class, they maintained separate bedrooms, a condition that did not necessarily inhibit sexual relations. Edith's frequent illnesses and breathing problems prevented her from sharing a bedroom, even when they traveled, and at home, her boudoir and bedroom suite were the setting for her literary work.

As the years passed, it became clear that Edith would produce books, not babies. Lucretia, whose sad widowhood was mitigated only by the presence of her family, must have hoped for more grandchildren. Yet, her wedding-eve mockery of Edith's naïveté about the physical intimacies of married life may have condemned her daughter to childlessness. Solicitous of his wife, Teddy was no authority on female sexuality, and he was surely unprepared to deal with the consequences of Edith's sexual ignorance and fear. These failures, never openly acknowledged, foreshadowed other failures of psychological and intellectual intimacy. In becoming "Mrs. Edward R. Wharton," Pussy Jones had not crossed the threshold into adult womanhood. Instead, the humming eroticism of her youth ("Life, real Life") turned back on itself, draining her energies and feeding self-doubt and unfilled longings. Rather than bringing her into the magic circle of feminine self-knowledge, marriage isolated her from women. In her Newport years, Edith appears to have had no close women friends.[20]

Bored by "watering-place mundanities" and disgusted by the show of new wealth apparent in the ostentatious mansions and mock châteaux that rose along Bellevue Avenue and Ocean Drive, Edith wilted and grew hollow-eyed. Teddy thrived and became pudgy. He enjoyed all the pleasures Newport offered, from riding and boating to croquet and tennis matches. Happy to have escaped the stuffy proprieties of Boston, a city he never cared for, he exchanged a narrow but comfortable life attended by his sister Nannie and his mother (whom he called "Duck") for the fashionable elegance of a seaside resort. Maintaining a fond, brotherly relation with Harry Jones, he teased and jollied Lucretia, just as he did his own mother. He shared Edith's enthusiasm for travel and followed her lead in cultural and artistic matters. As a couple, they were of one mind on finances, politics, and family relations. An attentive husband who tried to anticipate his wife's desires, Teddy was said to walk about with a $1,000 bill in his pocket, just in case "Puss" should want to buy something. He bore silently his own disappointment at the impasses of their intimate life.[21]

PORTALS OF DISCOVERY

Soon after her marriage, Edith began to study seriously the history of architecture, furniture design, and house decoration. Her Italian travels contributed to these studies by opening her eyes to the neoclassical order of the eighteenth century. But the major "Awakener"—her term for people or books that opened new worlds and extended her horizons—was James Fergusson's monumental *History of Architecture*. In a day when few such studies were available, this was to her an "amazing innovation." Historically and technically precise, it cleared the mists from her "haunting sense of the beauty of old buildings." Like William Hamilton's *History of Philosophy* and Henry Coppee's *Elements of Logic*, textbooks that her brother Harry had brought home from Cambridge and that she read as a teenager, Fergusson's work gave her not merely an intellectual perspective, but a vocabulary as well. She quickly learned the language of architecture and articulated with precision the relation of form, balance, and proportion. Rejecting the excesses of her mother's purple brocade Second Empire drawing rooms, she created light and airy spaces of elegant simplicity.[22]

Her house arranged and its gardens in order, Edith was ready to entertain. But whom should she invite? Desirous of good talk among a small circle of acquaintances, and with no interest in general "society," she turned to old family friends, among them Egerton Winthrop, another of her great "Awakeners." A longtime friend of her parents and a man of impeccable Anglo-Dutch heritage, he traced his family line to Governor Stuyvesant of New York and to John Winthrop, first colonial governor of Massachusetts. Widowed at an early age, he had lived for many years in Paris and returned to America in 1885 because his grown sons, who were only slightly younger than Edith, entered Harvard.

A bibliophile and art collector, Winthrop had refined tastes and an educated eye. Among people he did not know well or those with "commonplace" interests, he could be shy and stiff, sometimes tripping over footstools and knocking fragile objects to the floor. But in a congenial group, he relaxed and became a stimulating talker. Recognizing Edith's desire to learn, and spotting the gaps in her education, he systematized her reading, taught her the elements of literary analysis, and discussed French literature and history with her. Most important, he opened her eyes to the "wonder-world" of nineteenth-century science. Having read Goethe, she now read Charles Darwin's *Origin of Species*, Alfred Wallace's *Darwin and Darwinism*, and the works of Thomas Henry Huxley (whose grandson, writer Aldous Huxley, would later become a good friend), Herbert Spencer, and Jean Baptiste de Lamarck. These were "magic casements" onto her "little geocentric universe," and she never lost interest in the philosophic debates they engendered or forgot the thrill of her first discoveries.

Edith credited Winthrop with being the first person who "taught my mind to analyze and my eyes to see." He prepared an instruction sheet, entitled "Darwinism, etc. Suggestions," for mastering difficult scientific material. Read and reread slowly, he said, making marginal notes on important material, marking with an X everything she did not thoroughly understand. In the evenings, she should "think over" her daily reading and record her ideas about it. Notes should be systematized—terms and quotations listed on one page of the book and definitions of scientific words on another. Key words were to be learned "by heart—while your hair is being done!" If she needed a good dictionary, he promised to send her one. "Don't forget," he concluded, "that this sort of thing will make you able to do everything better."[23]

Edith enjoyed men like Winthrop—cultivated and quick-witted New York gentlemen who "lived in dilettantish leisure" much as her father had. As a group, she preferred them to "club men" and sports enthusiasts (like Teddy), but she also recognized their limitations. They appear in her fiction clinging tight to the ways of their small world, avoiding civic responsibility, and making little use of their talents. Every society needed such a cultivated leisure class, she believed, but the spirit of American democracy had caused the country to waste this valuable resource. (One recalls her father's comment that the Tuileries Gardens were "too democratic" after the fall of King Louis Philippe.) Whereas Europe successfully integrated the frivolous and the intellectual, *la vie mondaine* and *la vie de l'esprit*, New York aesthetes abhorred "society," while the fashionable could not live outside of their own conventions. "It is only in sophisticated societies that intellectuals recognize the uses of the frivolous," Edith concluded. She did not yet know how to join these two poles, but she would learn.[24]

In February 1886, on their first European trip together, Teddy arranged for his Boston friend Julian Story to paint Edith's portrait in his Paris studio. (This portrait of her face was later lost.) She endured with difficulty the long hours of posing. One day, bored and seeing that the portrait would be a failure, she spied in a corner of the studio a graceful little armchair that Story identified as eighteenth-century Venetian—as unlike the monstrously heavy Venetian pieces from her mother's drawing room as anything could be. Decrying the lack of attention to this later period of Italian furniture and architecture, Story commented that historians and art critics all acted "as if Italy had ceased to exist at the end of the Renaissance." The chance view of the "artlessly simple" armchair and Story's offhand comment occasioned an epiphany. Edith devoted the next twenty years of her life to the study of Italian art and architecture, with an emphasis on the eighteenth century. Making good use of her linguistic skills, she read in several languages, beginning with German works on the Italian Renaissance, peeling away layers of history to discover (she hoped) the bedrock of Western culture.[25]

Edith's early studies of the Renaissance and *settecento* led her back to the classical roots of Italian civilization. After two seasons of explorations in Italy with Winthrop, she wanted to see the classical world firsthand. "I would give everything I own to make a cruise in the Mediterranean!" she exclaimed one day to James Van Alen, a cultivated member of the New York leisured class who in his youth had explored the Peloponnesus. He immediately offered to take Edith and Teddy as his guests on a chartered yacht. Desiring to have their say in choosing the itinerary, they asked him to calculate the costs of a three-month cruise. Their portion—half the total expenses—consumed their combined incomes for an entire year, some $10,000 (equivalent to untaxed income of $150,000 today). The Wharton and Jones families objected to this plan, seeing it as a mad and dangerous scheme. After all, little more than a decade earlier, a party of Englishmen had been seized by brigands near Athens, only one escaping alive! Who had ever heard of such an idea—Mediterranean cruises were mere fads of the wealthy!

To the young couple, the primary problem was not brigands but finances. Teddy could contribute little to their expenses, and Edith did not control her money. They tried without success to secure a loan, and when it appeared that they must abandon their plans, Teddy asked Edith if she really wanted to go. She nodded a yes, and he replied, "All right. Come along, then." They decided to worry about finances later and embarked on what she called "the crowning wonder of my life."[26]

After delays in Paris due to icy fog, the three travelers departed by steamer from Marseilles on February 17, 1888, making port in Algiers the following evening. Setting down in a "sea of mud," they made their way to the Custom House encircled by Arabs, the first Edith and Teddy had ever seen, "startlingly picturesque in the flashes of lantern light, with their white burnouses and long white cloaks." A gig then took them to the *Vanadis*, moored under a star-studded sky. On board, they sat down to dinner in a lounge filled with welcoming roses and violets.

Van Alen had chartered and provisioned the yacht, but Edith chose the books for its library. She carried a current edition of Murray's tourist guide, but her preferred references were literary and philosophic writings on ancient lands—Goethe's *Travels in Italy*, Villiers de l'Isle-Adam's writings on Rhodes, and Théophile Gautier's aesthetic treatises and travel accounts of the journey from Constantinople to Athens. She had helped chart the itinerary, consulting atlases in advance of the trip; once on board the *Vanadis*, she often visited the captain's bridge to examine nautical charts. Edith was a modern pilgrim on the track of cultural and religious ruins—Greek and Roman amphitheaters, catacombs, temples, monasteries, hermitages, and burial grounds. Interested primarily in archaeology, she visited little-known shrines and ascended mountains perched sidesaddle on a donkey, holding her white parasol above her head. In the evening, as the men smoked cigars and sipped cognac, she read aloud from the Butcher and Lang translation of Homer's *Odyssey*, her book illumined by the yellow flame of a gas lamp.[27]

Until recently, Edith's journal of the voyage, *The Cruise of the Vanadis*, was assumed lost or destroyed. Typed and bound (but unsigned), it sat for many years on a back shelf in the municipal library of Hyères, France, where she wintered in the last decades of her life. Its seventeen chapters follow the *Vanadis* from its departure in Algiers to arrival at Ancona, Italy, some three months later, on May 7, 1888. The itinerary traces an elongated loop on the map of the Aegean and follows part of Odysseus's return voyage from Troy to Ithaca. They toured some forty islands and towns, traveling from Tunis to Malta and Sicily, then crossing the Ionian Sea to Corfu and Rhodes, moving north along the coast of Asia Minor before turning west to the Greek mainland, then northward along the Dalmatian coast.[28]

Her first experiment in travel writing, *The Cruise of the Vanadis* mixes the impersonal and the idiosyncratic, neither identifying the voyagers nor explaining how the narrative came to be written. It anticipates the richly detailed and colorful language of her later writings on Italy, France, and Morocco, however, and through the anonymous authorial voice, Edith Wharton revels in the otherness and exoticism of places distant in time and space from the "civilized" capitals of Europe and the industrialized West. She sees Africa, Asia Minor, and the Aegean islands through the eyes of a Westerner and expresses attitudes that today appear colonialistic, even imperialistic.

The native peoples appear simple, yet ancient, regarding her with eyes that sometimes fascinate, sometimes frighten. As if documenting an unknown species, she meticulously tracked details of manners, social customs, and religious rites (Roman Catholicism, Greek Orthodoxy, Judaism, and Islam), cataloged regional foods, and even prepared an encyclopedic glossary of local flora. Having mocked her mother's mania for collecting trinkets, she seems never to have missed an opportunity to bargain for faience, embroideries, rugs, and jewelry made of gold and silver coins. She returned to New York with Roman, Etruscan, Greek, Egyptian, Saracen, Anatolian, and Norman artifacts.

The desire to explore and plunder, trading silver for trinkets, belonged to her "archaeological ardours." Carried away by the experience of unearthing the ancient past, she averted her eyes from squalor, except in Ithaca, where she claimed never to have seen "greater appearances of misery and poverty." A few days later in Montenegro, however, the desolation was so complete that even the colorful and handsome national dress, which was expensive and required by the prince for holiday celebrations, could not distract her from the human suffering.[29]

In every setting, she sought out the quaint, the unusual and beautiful, perhaps not realizing that she herself was a wondrous and exotic object. Women stared openly at her, grasping her clothing and chattering to each other in her presence. Edith's recording eye captured their domestic habits and dress—"Jewesses with silk turbans over their plaited hair," Arab women in white burnouses "with black silk yashmaks over their faces," Corinthian women wearing "finely-plaited petticoats of shot silk" and "purple velvet jackets embroidered in gold." She made no comment, however, on living conditions in societies where women had no legal or civil rights. Thirty years later, visiting Morocco as a guest of the French government, her perspective was still Western, Christian, and colonialistic, but her attitudes had changed toward the circumstances in which Arab women and children lived. In 1888, starving babies and legless beggars were "local atrocities," but in 1917, they called to mind the ravages of World War I.[30]

Her chief object on the trip was Mount Athos, the sacred mountain on which, according to legend, Satan tempted Christ. She realized that the monastic prohibition against women would prevent her from seeing the mountain at close range. When Teddy and Van Alen went ashore with the ship's multilingual Maltese cook to find the Turkish governor and acquire clearance to the monasteries, Edith ordered the captain (a surly, unpleasant man) to bring the yacht close to the forbidden shores of Mount Athos. Seeing its approach, the black-haired, long-robed caloyers descended the hillside to prevent Edith from setting foot on land. Watching from the boat as Teddy and Van Alen climbed to the monastery at Vatopedi, she contemplated the unbroken chain of monasticism dating back to the tenth century, "a life unaffected by modern inventions, discoveries and revolutions, a life as primly mediaeval as when the hermit Athanasius laid the first stone of the Lavra."[31]

Edith's fascination with hermitism may date from this moment of exclusion and wonder. Later writings reveal her secret affinity with the solitary life, but at this juncture her travel narrative takes an odd turn: she summarizes what the men saw as though she had accompanied them. This secondhand report of jeweled icons and sacred treasures is noteworthy for its absence of emotion and evocative descriptions that characterize her larger narrative. Unable to provide her own "impression" of the monasteries, the central moment of her travelogue remains a mere parenthesis.

From Mount Athos, they traveled to Athens, where, on April 20, they collected mail that had accumulated in the two months since their departure from Marseilles. Learning that one of her dogs had died, grief-stricken Edith hardly noticed the letter saying that her father's second cousin, Joshua Jones, a man she had never met, was dead. A recluse living in an unheated room of the New York Hotel, he perished from pneumonia, leaving behind an immense fortune to be divided among the Jones cousins. Edith and her brothers each inherited outright $120,000 in real and personal estate. Frederic's wife, Minnie, commented dryly that what appeared to be the old man's miserliness was only "a wise economy."[32]

The legacy gave Edith unexpected financial independence. She settled her debt to Van Alen for the Aegean cruise and used the remaining sum as collateral for loans on properties she would soon purchase in Newport and New York. The unexpected windfall taught her a lesson she followed all her life: when something difficult and wonderful presented itself, she should measure the risk against the worth of the adventure and trust to her "star" to see it through. She and Teddy immediately decided to take another long trip, this time on a sailing vessel to the Canaries and Azores. They chose a schooner and drew up the charter, but canceled their reservations on learning that cholera had spread through the islands. Edith never made that trip, just as she never fulfilled her dream of cruising the Nile in Egypt or crossing India. But the gods foretold that she would sail the Aegean again. She paid for the second trip not from inherited money but from her literary royalties, which by 1926, at the height of her earning powers, were immense.[33]

FIRST STEPS

At the close of the 1880s, Edith focused her energies on writing and house decoration, activities that marched in tandem into the new century. Returning to New York for the winter season in December 1888, after several years of extended European travels, she and Teddy made a "first trial" of the city: they rented "the smallest of small houses" on Madison Avenue. Egerton Winthrop thought this a good occasion for Edith to enter fully into the role of society matron, but she showed no more inclination for large-scale society entertaining in New York than she had in Newport, nor did her tiny house lend itself to such purposes.[34]

During their first winter in New York, the Whartons searched for a pied-à-terre of their own, and in late 1889 chose a narrow five-story brownstone on Fourth Avenue at the corner of Seventy-eighth Street (renumbered 884 Park Avenue) in Lenox Hill. An unfashionable neighborhood, the area was a mix of apartment buildings and tenements. Vents from underground train tracks shot steam, smoke, and cinders into the air, and trains racketed under the sidewalks. Edith's decision has often been explained as an effort to distance herself from her mother on Twenty-fifth Street. Perhaps so, but the more likely explanation was the proximity to Central Park: "On account of the bicycling, I would rather be up there in a 'bicoque' [shanty] than downtown," she wrote Ogden Codman, Jr., who would be her Lenox Hill neighbor. Trying to strengthen Edith's resistance to colds and flu, her doctors encouraged outdoor exercise. Afflicted with nausea caused by drainage of her sinus and throat passages, Edith had begun to lose weight. Photographs of her in this period show a thin woman with shadowed, unhappy eyes.[35]

The purchase agreement for 884 Park Avenue was finalized in November 1891, two years after negotiations began. The Whartons apparently paid about $20,000 for the house (a high price, given the location). Berkeley Updike, a Boston friend of Teddy's and the printer who produced several of Edith's books, claimed that the house was partial settlement for a debt—probably owed to the late Joshua Jones, who had owned a large tract of real estate in that area of Manhattan. They rented out the house until 1896, when Edith asked Ogden Codman, Jr., the "clever young Boston architect" whom she had met in Newport twelve years earlier, to help her remodel and redecorate the "little shanty."[36]

In March 1893, two years after purchasing the New York house, Edith bought Land's End in Newport, paying an extraordinary price for an "ugly wooden house with half an acre of rock"—$80,000, almost $1,200,000 at today's rates. She commissioned Codman, whose uncle, John Hubbard Sturgis, had built the house some forty years earlier, to alter the existing structure, decorate the interior, and design gardens. A fruitful collaboration between architect and client, it led to their writing *The Decoration of Houses*, the first American handbook of interior decoration and Edith's first book publication.[37]

During the 1888–1889 season in the Madison Avenue house, Edith had three poems accepted for publication, one by the venerable *Atlantic Monthly* and two others by *Scribner's Magazine*, a new journal that quickly established its place among the top four literary periodicals in America. The others were *Harper's Monthly* and *Century Monthly Magazine* (which replaced the old *Scribner's Monthly*), edited by Richard Watson Gilder, the most powerful magazine editor in America. Edith would publish regularly in all of these journals, but her literary "home" was *Scribner's Magazine*. The three poems announced the emergence of "Edith Wharton," professional writer. She was twenty-seven years old.[38]

We know little about Edith's writing habits between 1880 and 1889. Although her desk held "a large collection of blank verse dramas and manuscript fiction," she had lost contact with the publishing world and claimed not to know how "authors communicated with editors." Sending her poems to the literary magazines, she had enclosed her engraved visiting card, "Mrs. Edward R. Wharton"—the signifier of her marital and social status. When the two letters of acceptance arrived in the same mail, she bounded "senselessly and incessantly" up and down the stairs of the little Madison Avenue house, trying to give her "excitement some muscular outlet!" Accepting two poems, Edward L. Burlingame, editor of *Scribner's Magazine*, asked to see other things she had written. His request sent her into further raptures. She gathered up her recent writing and made the first of many trips to the Scribners offices at 743 Broadway.[39]

BUYING AND REDECORATING houses, establishing an ever-more-elegant and complicated style of life, Edith reserved mornings for literary work. She wrote in bed, propping her inkpot precariously on an improvised writing board and using second sheets from her stationery box as manuscript paper. In childhood, she had written on wrapping paper saved for her by the Irish housemaids. In adolescence, she wrote on her mother's cream-colored vellum; late in life, she used pale-blue writing paper that was easy on her eyes. The quality and color of paper, the thickness of her pen nib and smooth flow of ink (she used black on the cream paper and blue for the pale-blue stationery), the snuggled comfort of her bed with one or another of her little dogs tucked up beside her, the piles of books and the latest reviews strewn across the rose-colored duvet—all of these were critical elements in her creative process.[40]

In contrast to the setting in which they were composed, her first stories explored the cramped lives of people with limited means and imagination who existed on the edge of poverty. Turning to subjects so anomalous to her own social setting and style of life, she discovered a central principle of her literary method: external conditions provide a window onto the inner life. Houses tell stories, stones carry the history of civilization, interior furnishings become metaphors of human experience. "Mrs. Manstey's View" (1891), Edith's first published short story, and *Bunner Sisters*, a novella written in 1893, reveal emotional worlds dominated by pain, loneliness, and a sense of otherness. How did a young society matron know about Mrs. Manstey, the elderly widow who, since her husband's death seventeen years earlier, has inhabited a third-floor back apartment of a boardinghouse? Where had she seen the pinched, middle-aged Bunner sisters, Ann Eliza and Evelina, whose goods shop occupies the basement of the last remaining private residence near Stuyvesant Square, on a side street that "rapidly fell from shabbiness to squalor"? We can only speculate on how Edith established the verisimilitude of these tales. She may have read about such people in newspapers, caught glimpses of the decaying urban terrain from her carriage while traveling about the city, or drawn on her recollections of upper Fourth Avenue and Lenox Hill. However she discovered these worlds, she re-created their reality with subtle accuracy.[41]

Writing in isolation and with no literary mentors to encourage and guide her, Edith relied on editors to evaluate her work. Hence, Edward Burlingame, her first editor at Scribners and a man with high artistic standards, played a key role in her literary development. Son of a diplomat, Burlingame was educated in Great Britain and the United States and gained his editorial experience in newspaper and book publishing. His comments on Edith's early writing had the power to lift her spirits or cast her into deepest depression, but he seemed unaware of her sensitivity and of the godlike position to which she had elevated him. He described "Mrs. Manstey's View," a powerful tale of some seven pages in print, as a "slight sketch." Published in the July 1891 issue of *Scribner's Magazine*, it was reprinted two years later in a Scribners volume, *Stories of New York*, a sign that her "sketch" had a value beyond its length. He praised the far more ambitious *Bunner Sisters* as full of "admirable detail and color," but sent it back to her, saying that its drama failed to "carry its great length." The thirteen-chapter novella was, he explained, too long to publish in one issue of the magazine and to divide it would destroy its effect. (This was Edith's first encounter with the contingencies of periodical publishing.)[42]

In November 1893, Burlingame suggested that she collect some stories for a volume. In response to this encouragement, she again offered *Bunner Sisters*, saying that although she was "not a good judge" of her work, she had concluded ("after several careful readings") that it was "up to the average" of her writing. Burlingame apparently did not agree, and the novella remained unpublished for twenty-three years— until 1916, when it finally appeared in *Scribner's Magazine*. The editors paid $2,000 for it, the highest price Edith had yet received for a novella. By this time, Burlingame had retired, she was an internationally famous writer, and Scribners was taking anything she was willing to give them.[43]

In summer 1891, just as "Mrs. Manstey's View" appeared in *Scribner's*, Edith examined marital relations (and her own conjugal disappointments) in a tale entitled "The Fullness of Life." Edith took the setting for this tale of the afterlife from an Easter-week visit with Teddy to Florence, part of their spring tour of Italy. A woman dies quietly, vaguely satisfied that she will never again hear the creaking of her husband's "horrible boots" or be bothered about the day's dinner or the butcher's bill. Meeting the Spirit of Life in Paradise, the woman admits to not having known "that fullness of life which we all feel ourselves capable of knowing." In response to the Spirit's question about her feelings toward her husband, she offers an elaborate image, the most famous in Edith Wharton's fiction:

> I have sometimes thought that a woman's nature is like a great house full of rooms: there is the hall, through which everyone passes going in and out; the drawing room, where one receives formal visits; the sitting room, where members of the family come and go as they list; but beyond that, far beyond, are other rooms, the handles of whose doors perhaps are never turned; no one knows the way to them, no one knows whither they lead; and in the innermost room, the holy of holies, the soul sits alone and waits for a footstep that never comes.[44]

The Spirit offers the dead woman the chance to spend eternity with a "kindred soul," but she chooses to wait for her husband, explaining that she would not "feel at home without him." Even in eternity, she is bound to the habit of his customary presence. The husband in the story is unmistakably a version of Teddy Wharton, a man of habit but lacking in discipline, a man with desires but no goals, a man who does not feel the need to enrich his inner life.

The scene Edith sets in the Church of Or San Michele gives a view of Teddy not, perhaps, as he was in spring 1891, but as he would become—withdrawn, dissatisfied, disappointed, and self-absorbed. An elaborately carved, Greek-influenced tabernacle of Orcagna stands (still today) in the center of the church. The woman sees in its ornate carvings the totality of civilization and is transported on "a mighty current" of "human passion and endeavor." (We glimpse Edith Wharton's spiritual nature in her character's responses.) She thinks the tabernacle holds a mystery that could be unveiled, if there were a kindred spirit with whom to share her feelings, and turns to her husband, who sits beside her "in an attitude of patient dejection, gazing into the bottom of his hat." Rising, he speaks "mildly" to her: "Hadn't we better be going? There doesn't seem to be much to see here, and you know the table d'hôte dinner is at half-past six o'clock."

The story puzzled Burlingame, who thought its idea a "capital conception" but its dialogue too "soulful." Returning the story, he suggested a few revisions, but Edith did not reply to his letter. Nor did she respond to his inquiries about the story. Finally, he requested that she send it back. She did so on August 26, 1893, more than two years after she wrote it, having deleted one sentence that seemed "over-done." She enclosed with the manuscript a note expressing "sincere regret that it is not better suited to your purposes." He published it in the December issue of the magazine.[45]

In 1898, nearly ten years after she submitted her first poems to Burlingame, she was preparing her first volume of short stories. He reminded her of the early stories, "Mrs. Manstey's View" and "The Fullness of Life," and she responded to him in the voice of an experienced, professional, and gracious author:

> As to the old stories of which you speak so kindly, I regard them as the excesses of youth. They were all written "at the top of my voice," and The Fulness [sic] of Life is one long shriek.—I may not write any better, but at least I hope that I write in a lower key, and I fear the voice of those early tales will drown all the others: it is for that reason that I prefer not to publish them.

She never allowed "The Fullness of Life" to be reprinted, and she refused Burlingame's persistent request to include in the volume "The Lamp of Psyche," the story of a woman's disillusionment in her husband, who evaded military service during the Civil War. Yet, Edith did include "The Journey," a far more chilling treatment of marriage. An invalid man dies on a cross-country train journey. His wife, who hates his irritability and chafes at never having the chance to "spread her wings," conceals his death. When the train reaches its destination and the porter offers to help her "ill" husband disembark, she can no longer conceal the reality. Fainting, she strikes her head against the berth, perhaps dying in the fall. This husband and wife are recognizable portraits of Teddy and Edith Wharton. On reading the story, Walter Berry commented that Edith had a "gruesome streak."[46]

ON MAY 22, 1891, while Edith and Teddy were in Europe, William Craig Wharton committed suicide at McLean Hospital, north of Boston. The death certificate gave the official cause of death as melancholia. Nine years later, when Teddy began to demonstrate "queer" behavior, Ogden Codman recalled the circumstances surrounding Mr. Wharton's breakdown and suicide in a letter to his mother, and drew the link between father and son: "You know they had to shut up old Mr. Wharton at about seven years before he died as he got so strange and irritable." Long before anyone else, Codman recognized that Teddy's childlike qualities were ill omens. Calling him a "chief *Bore* in waiting," he remarked that Teddy "never had any real occupation and was somehow like a sort of school boy in his tastes and in his mental development." To his mind, marrying Teddy had been Edith's "greatest mistake"; he thought her selfish and lacking in good judgment, but Codman pitied her during the last years of her marriage: "One cannot help feeling that her punishment has been awful—tied to a crazy person, who is only just sane enough not to be locked up." By 1910, Teddy was severely ill, and Codman took the position that he should "follow his father's example and kill himself."[47]

We know nothing of Teddy's grief at the news of his father's suicide, or whether he had sensed his father's suffering. Had Teddy visited his father during his confinement at McLean's? Did he return from Europe in time to attend the funeral? He went into formal mourning for his father, as did Edith, who probably had never met him. The old man's suicide (however he effected it) and the pain and loneliness of his last years surely played on her imagination. His demise mirrored, ironically, the suicide of the nameless little boy in the Philadelphia House of Refuge whom she had memorialized in her 1879 poem "Only a Child."

An 1892 poem, "Experience," may have been influenced by her father-in-law's death. Composed of double sonnets on themes of death and woe, the poem describes the alchemical process by which time turns grief into gold. It defines human experience as the sum of individual pain, which dies with each of us; every generation coins "new griefs again." Part II is an apostrophe to death:

> *O Death, we come full-handed to thy gate,*
> *Rich with strange burden of the mingled years,*
> *Gains and renunciations, mirth and tears,*
> *And love's oblivion, and remembering hate,*

> *Nor know we what compulsion laid such freight*
> *Upon our souls—and shall our hopes and fears*
> *Buy nothing of thee, Death? Behold our wares,*
> *And sell us the one joy for which we wait.*
> *Had we lived longer, life had such for sale,*
> *With the last coin of sorrow purchased cheap,*
> *But now we stand before thy shadowy pale,*
> *And all our longings lie within thy keep—*
> *Death, can it be the years shall naught avail?*
> *"Not so," Death answered, "they shall purchase sleep."*

Against the mental suffering of his old age, William Craig Wharton purchased "sleep."[48]

He made his will in 1875 (long before he first entered McLean's), and left everything to his wife. The estate, valued at about $500,000, was somewhat smaller than that of George Frederic Jones. After Nancy Wharton's death in 1909, each of her children received $143,513 in cash and securities; together, they held rights to several investment properties in Boston. By mutual agreement, Nannie Wharton (then sixty-five years old) retained the right to reside in the Beacon Street townhouse and use the country cottage, "Pine Acre," which her mother had purchased in Lenox in 1891.[49]

NEW VISTAS

By summer 1893, Edith and Teddy were established at Land's End, their Newport waterfront estate on a treeless expanse of cliff edge overlooking a seascape that stretched all the way to Ireland. Whether she chose this location because she loved to watch the "endlessly changing moods of the misty Atlantic" and hear the "night-long sound of the surges against the cliffs" or whether, as some have suggested, she meant to distance herself from her mother, who lived at the opposite side of the island, no one can say. Edith had not broken with Lucretia, nor would she.

Among the first luncheon guests at Land's End were Paul and Minnie Bourget, who arrived with a letter of introduction from one of Teddy's cousins in Paris. Ten years older than Edith, Bourget was an elegant stylist whose poems, novels of society, and essays on contemporary life had gained popular regard in Europe. His name was not yet well known in America, but *Outre-mer*, a collection of essays on America commissioned by the *New York Herald*, would gain him a popular audience. His editors suggested that Newport should serve as the model for an essay on a "fashionable watering-place." He stayed a month in the seaside resort.

Born in Antibes, the son of a provincial scholar, Charles-Joseph-Paul Bourget won a scholarship to the prestigious Louis le Grand lycée in Paris. He shed his country clothes and attitudes, proved himself in its competitive intellectual environment, and re-created himself as a dapper Parisian. In 1891, at age thirty-nine, he married a woman fifteen years his junior. Edith admired his *Sensations d'Italie*, the record of their honeymoon travels. As much as she came to respect "the brilliant and stimulating husband," she recognized his "quiet and exquisite companion" as the rarer being. Jewish, probably of Sephardic origin, Minnie had large dark eyes and sculptured features that recalled to Edith the "Tanagra Madonna," seen on her Aegean voyage. Although she appeared to be self-possessed, Minnie was an "attentive shadow" to her charming but affected husband. In Edith's words, Minnie adopted a posture of "voluntary invisibility," and from their first meeting, Edith worried about Minnie's submissiveness to her adoring husband.[50]

Talk at the luncheon table moved rapidly between French and English. Minnie knew English well, Teddy had virtually no French, Bourget spoke a rather comic and not entirely fluent English that led to hilarious misunderstandings, while Edith adopted a grammatically correct and rather stilted French. (Bourget claimed she spoke perfect Louis XIV.) We have long assumed that he used Edith as the model for the "intellectual tomboy," one of several "young-girl types" he discussed in *Outre-mer*:

> Though like all the others [this girl] gets her gowns from the best houses of the Rue de la Paix, there is not a book of Darwin, Huxley, Spencer, Renan, Taine, which she has not studied, not a painter or sculptor of whose works she could not compile a catalogue, not a school of poetry or romance of which she does not know the principles. She subscribes impartially to the *Revue des Deux Mondes* and the gazettes of the latest coteries of the Latin Quarter or Montmartre.

Only she does not distinguish between them. She has not an idea that is not exact, and yet she gives you the strange impression as if she had none. One would say that she had ordered her intellect somewhere, as we would order a piece of furniture, to measure, and with as many compartments as there are branches of human knowledge. She acquires them only that she may put them into these drawers. . . . Before the intellectual girl one longs to cry:—"Oh, for one ignorance, one error, just a single one. May she make a blunder, may she prove not to know!" In vain. A mind may be mistaken, a mind may be ignorant, but never a thinking machine!

This vision of intellectual womanhood is not a portrait of Edith Wharton. She was horrified by the "mail order" mentality captured in this sketch. She took pride in her ability to define, discriminate, and "distinguish"—indeed, these traits were the hallmark of both her conversation and writing. And they were traits that Bourget appreciated. He espoused the "gospel of work," and admired Edith not only for her literary productivity, but also because she worked "seriously" at her art, had a "literary conscience," and attended to every element of her *métier*, no matter how small or seemingly unimportant.[51]

Edith had every reason to feel that her first encounter with a European intellectual had gone well. Wanting to see more of their new friends, Edith and Teddy stopped off in Paris on their way to Italy in late 1893 and called on the "Minnie-Pauls" just after Christmas. Bourget gave Edith a letter of introduction to Violet Paget, an English-born art critic living outside Florence, who wrote on eighteenth-century Italian art, architecture, and gardens under a male pseudonym, Vernon Lee. A few years older than Edith, she would become a lifelong friend and a model for Edith of cultured intelligence and independence of spirit. Her writings had already served as "best-loved companions" on Edith's search for *settecento* Italy. In early spring 1894, Edith called on her at the Villa Il Palmerino in a village above Florence, where Lee lived with her parents and half-brother, poet Eugene Lee-Hamilton. Over tea, Edith sat in rapt silence as Vernon Lee talked, her quick speech accented by hand gestures and a darkening of her gray-green eyes. Edith later described her talk as having the "opalescent play of a northerly sky."[52]

Until now, Edith's few intellectual friendships had been with men, and she was pleased to meet a "highly cultivated and brilliant woman."

Vernon Lee projected a male persona, however, dressing in the style preferred by intellectual lesbians—a man's shirt, foulard, and velvet jacket over a long skirt. In her attention to Lee's conversation, Edith may have missed these clues to her sexual preference, or perhaps the dress style conveyed nothing. Edith's homophobia surfaced in her Paris years, directed at the lesbian community gathered around the American poet Natalie Barney. In her adult life, Edith had only one lesbian friend, Vernon Lee, and she either did not recognize Lee's sexuality or turned a blind eye to it.[53]

WHILE IN FLORENCE, Edith made a side trip into the country, ostensibly to escape the "over-civilized" Italy of guidebooks. Her real goal was to document some little-known religious art she had read about. An arduous trip over back roads and mountains in an "archaic little carriage," it resulted in a major discovery. Edith refuted the provenance of a group of life-sized terra cotta figures at the Franciscan monastery of San Vivaldo, some one hundred kilometers southwest of Florence. Thought to have been produced by an obscure seventeenth-century artist, they were fifteenth-century and the work of Giovanni della Robbia. Vernon Lee, an authority on Tuscan art, knew nothing of this group, nor did Enrico Ridolfi, the director of the Royal Museums at Florence.[54]

Edith recognized in the San Vivaldo figures aspects of Greek sculpture that she had seen on her Aegean voyage. Comparing them with figures in a high relief presepio at Florence's Bargello Museum, she arranged to have the sculptures photographed, sent the prints to Professor Ridolfi, and convinced him of her claims. Not only were the figures a rare find—hidden away for almost four hundred years—but it was even more unlikely that someone with no formal art training could make the attribution.

She recounted her discovery in her first travel essay, "A Tuscan Shrine," written in May and June 1894, while she and Teddy traveled in Italy. She urged Burlingame to publish it: "The article speaks for itself," she said, "the subject cannot fail to be of interest to the public." He agreed, and the essay appeared in the January 1895 issue of *Scribner's Magazine* and later in her book *Italian Backgrounds*. The essay reveals Edith's extensive knowledge of Renaissance Italian art and her discriminating eye as an art historian. She took her methods of investigation from Giovanni Morelli, whose techniques Bernard Berenson later refined and used with immense success. Even so, when Berenson heard the story some years later, he was unconvinced by Edith's evidence and doubted the accuracy of the attribution.[55]

Documenting her art discoveries, Edith was adventurous and assertive. She lacked self-assurance about her literary work, however. On March 26, she wrote Burlingame a confused and sad letter in answer to his rejection of "Something Exquisite," which she hoped to include in her short story volume. Asking that he "have no tender hearted compunctions" about criticizing her stories, she confessed to having "lost confidence." Hers was not the "wail of the rejected authoress" but "a cry for help and counsel." By July, when she wrote him of her San Vivaldo discoveries, he had rejected another story. Lacking a sufficient number of tales for the volume, she asked for a six-month extension to complete the book. Some seventeen months passed before she submitted a "waif," a set of ten aphoristic fables entitled "The Valley of Childish Things and Other Emblems." To a modern reader, these proverbs resemble the early modernist work of Djuna Barnes; not surprisingly, they perplexed Burlingame, and he rejected them. It was now December 1895, and Edith wrote to say that for the past year, she had been "very ill" and was "not yet allowed to do any real work."[56]

ECLIPSE

Because 1895 is a virtual blank in Edith's private history, it has long been assumed that she suffered a debilitating depression that prevented her from writing. She continued to appear in print, however: *Scribner's Magazine* published "A Tuscan Shrine" and "The Lamp of Psyche." The *Century* printed a poem ("Jade") in January 1895 and "The Valley of Childish Things" in July 1896. Nothing followed until January 1898.

Edith did suffer from repeated bouts of flu, bronchitis, and sinus problems in this period, but she was in good health most of the time and radiated *"bien-être."* Her many letters to Ogden Codman document a busy year of travel and house decoration. "The older I grow," she wrote from Italy in spring 1895, "the more I feel that I would rather live in Italy than anywhere. The very air is full of architecture—'la ligne' is everywhere. Everything else seems coarse or banal beside it. I never weary of driving through the streets and looking at the doorways and windows and wells and all the glimpses one gets. What an unerring sentiment for form! . . . it breaks my heart every time I have to leave it." Codman shared her sentiments, although he, too, would eventually choose France as his European home.[57]

A Bostonian born of an old and wealthy Beacon Street family, "Coddy," as Edith called him (creating for herself the character of "Mrs. Pusscod"), was a year younger than she. When he was a young child, his family had entered a self-imposed European exile owing to financial difficulties; they left America in 1872 for Brittany just as the George Frederic Jones family returned to New York after six years abroad. Schooling himself in architecture, Codman began his career by restoring historic eighteenth-century buildings. He believed that interior decoration should follow the order and balance of architectural lines and that rooms should be light and spacious.

He met Edith in Newport in 1884, when he returned from France. After first establishing himself as an interior decorator in Boston, he opened a Newport branch of his office in 1893. Later that year, and with Edith's help, he won his first Newport commission—to decorate ten bedrooms on the upper floors of The Breakers, the Cornelius Vanderbilt II mansion, which had burned to the ground the previous November. Legend has it that Edith and Teddy were guests of the Vanderbilts that fateful afternoon when a chimney fire destroyed the house.

In spring 1895, Codman worked for the Vanderbilts and also completed a new interior decoration project at Land's End while Edith and Teddy were traveling in Europe with Egerton Winthrop. Having decided to make a glass veranda out of a porch off the sitting room (an idea she later considered misconceived), Edith was searching for an Italian glass ceiling that could be dismantled and shipped back to the United States. As part of her research on eighteenth-century Italy, she visited palaces and villas that gave her house-decorating ideas. Gathering photographs and reporting her "finds" to Codman, she was not yet certain how she would use this information, but her understanding of Italian landscape and architecture would lead to three books—*The Decoration of Houses* (1897), *Italian Villas and Their Gardens* (1904), and *Italian Backgrounds* (1905).[58]

With her eyes full of Italian splendors and packing crates full of "pretty old noyer" furniture (but no glass ceiling), she was due to land in Newport on June 9. "I do hope you will be an angel and have the rooms ready, and the paint dry when we arrive," she wrote Codman. Should she find paint pots in the glass veranda, she would destroy his reputation by spreading the rumor that he had inspired the hall and billiard room in Frederick Vanderbilt's Newport mansion, no doubt one of those creations that, she said, "retard culture so very thoroughly." From Paris on May 24, Teddy underscored the importance of Coddy's finishing the work at Land's End in time. "If you have any kind feeling left for the little Wharton's [sic], *do, oh please do*, that glass veranda." He described Puss as "seedy," having just battled her fourth round of influenza.[59]

Little documentation exists for Edith's activities during the next eight months, but in spring 1896, she was a woman of enormous energy, stamina, and vision. We cannot assume, then, that she suffered a "total nervous collapse that endured . . . for more than two years," as R. W. B. Lewis has claimed. More likely, she returned to Newport in summer 1895 and continued her interior decorating work at Land's End and laid out its extensive gardens. By Christmas, Edith and Codman had decided to collaborate in writing a book on house decoration, a project that would consume her energies for the next two years.

Edith's December 1895 letter to her editors at Scribners saying that she had been very ill during the past year was in some measure disingenuous. She would employ this kind of subterfuge throughout her career as a professional writer, using illness to force accommodations on editorial deadlines and expectations. She did not invent illnesses or pretend to be ill when she was not, but she did dramatize her situation to editors who were far away and could not verify the state of her physical health. The psychic roots for this behavior lay (very probably) in her parents' reactions to her childhood bout with typhoid and her struggles with tonsillitis and bronchitis: when she was seriously ill, Lucretia and George Frederic had showered her with attention and affection and released her from the daily routine of lessons.

Despite frequent bouts of flu, Edith had kept up her demanding travel schedule all during spring 1895; although she may "not yet [have been] allowed to do any real work" in December, she was about to launch the book project with Codman. Because Burlingame had rejected several of her short stories in 1894 and 1895, she had stopped sending him fiction. Her December letter both rebuffed his attempt to push her forward on the short story volume and acted as a smokescreen to hide her lack of self-confidence. That she was passing through a period of self-doubt about her literary abilities would only later become apparent.[60]

During an eight-month European trip in 1896, when she crisscrossed France and Italy, Edith did exhaustive research for *The Decoration of Houses*, acquiring photographs and taking notes from which she composed early drafts of the manuscript. By April 17, the Whartons had already been to France, and made a first sweep across northern Italy, traveling from Milan to Parma, Modena, Bologna, and Ravenna. In May, they spent ten days in Venice and attended a Tiepolo exhibition; they then went to Paris before crossing the channel to England to stay with Codman's cousin, Howard Sturgis, at Windsor. In September, Edith and Teddy doubled back to Paris and Versailles.

Their greatest pleasure in these months was riding bicycles on back-country roads. Writing Codman from Ravenna in April, Edith noted that "the roads in this part of Italy are capital, and you can't fancy what fun it is to jump on one's bicycle at the railway station and fly about one of these quiet little towns." She bought "absurdly cheap" eighteenth-century Italian furniture and urged him to come around to her opinion that it was far preferable to the French. Searching out yet more villas and palaces for their book, she provided him with a detailed description of Stupingi, the royal hunting lodge in Turin built by Juvarra, and extended an invitation to join them. In the next breath, she asked about her "Park Avenue shanty," which she wanted him to remodel. Was the plumbing in good condition? Could the pantry be enlarged?[61]

Rather than sounding like someone physically ill or in the midst of a psychic breakdown, her letters from Europe display a greater than usual energy and enthusiasm. After the bouts of flu in 1895, she regained her strength and discovered that bicycling added immensely to her enjoyment of the French and Italian countryside. When they passed through Paris in late summer, Edith and Teddy stayed with Harry Jones, who had recently moved to an apartment at 146 avenue des Champs Elysées. Harry's move to Paris had been occasioned by events in New York earlier that spring.[62]

On March 16, 1896, the New York State Supreme Court granted Mary Cadwalader Jones a divorce from her husband, Frederic. Married for twenty-six years, they had been separated since 1892. According to New York law, Minnie had to bring her petition before the court within five years of first discovering her husband's adultery, and to declare that she had not voluntarily cohabited with him in that time. She had known he was an adulterer for almost ten years, having caught him in flagrante with another woman in their house at 21 East Eleventh Street in June 1887. She remained in the marriage because of Beatrix (then fifteen years old), but also perhaps for her own sake. Divorce was unacceptable in old society, and a divorced woman—however much the victim of her husband's deceit—often found the doors of familiar drawing rooms closed against her.[63]

Frederic had maintained a liaison with a Mrs. Elsie D. West, a woman twenty years younger. The affair, which probably began in 1891, was first documented in January 1892. Frederic met Mrs. West at her home on East Thirty-third Street during the afternoons. They also lived together for periods of time in France, where he was known as "Mr. West," even to friends visiting from New York. Receiving the court petition in Paris, he denied all the charges, waived his right to a trial by jury, and the general counsel at the American Legation took the necessary depositions. A former housemaid identified "Mr. West" as the man she knew in New York as "Mr. Jones" from a photograph of him made in Newport. At fifty, Frederic was the image of his father, a benign expression on his face, his eyes clear, his gray hair thinning across the forehead but his muttonchop whiskers thick along the jawline. From October 1894, Mrs. West and Frederic Jones lived as a married couple in France, the maid testified, and for two weeks in February 1895, they had occupied a room with only one bed at the Hotel Terminus in Paris. The Whartons were also in Paris during that period, Edith preoccupied in running errands for Codman, but they apparently did not see "Mr. West."[64]

The strangest element in the case was Frederic's masquerade; when he married Elsie West in France sometime later, she became "Mrs. Frederic Jones." His infidelities were undoubtedly known among his society friends, but the divorce took place under a thick shroud of secrecy, meant to protect Minnie and Beatrix. Frederic never returned to the United States. Minnie changed her name to "Mrs. Cadwalader Jones" and went about her life as usual. His sexual disloyalty carried over into financial matters, however, and she lost heavily in the divorce. Beatrix, who had opened an office as a landscape gardener a year earlier in the converted attic at 21 East Eleventh Street, provided financial support for her mother.[65]

Among the Joneses, Harry tried to remain neutral, while Edith sided with Minnie, refusing to receive the "disreputable" woman. Although there was no open break between Edith and her mother, Lucretia (age seventy-two) soon followed Frederic and Harry to Paris. By late 1897 or early 1898, she was in residence at 50 avenue du Bois de Boulogne on the Right Bank, where in September 1898, she became seriously ill and lingered on for almost three years. Her ill health was doubtless hastened by Frederic's divorce. In April 1899, Teddy saw to the disposal of furniture at Pencraig, and the Newport house was rented out. At that same moment, Edith urged Codman to devise a plan by which the neighboring house on Park Avenue, 882, could be joined to 884 to make a single dwelling—a necessity now that she had to find a place for some of her mother's things.[66]

DECORATING HOUSES

Edith and Teddy spent the autumn and early winter 1896 in Newport, while remodeling work continued at 884 Park Avenue. She drafted the opening sections of *The Decoration of Houses* and in January, after returning to New York, sent a copy of the manuscript to architect Charles McKim, founder of the American Academy in Rome and designer of the Boston Public Library. How she knew McKim, the foremost architectural authority of his day, we do not know—perhaps through her society connections. He praised the book, but his three pages of reading notes on the text convinced Edith to revise the opening chapter.

She also advised Codman on his business operation, having learned that clients resented his charges on furniture and antiques he purchased for them in Europe. He charged a 25 percent commission on each item, and even very wealthy clients thought him too expensive. Edith suggested a circular announcing a reduced rate of 15 percent. Proofreading the proposed circular on January 7, she realized that Codman had no facility with language. "You are a gentleman addressing yourself to gentlemen, and it is perfectly easy to be business-like in good English," she told him. He accepted her corrections and that evening was her guest at the opera: "We have Mr. [August] Belmont's box."[67]

In truth, Edith was having a difficult time writing the house decoration book. She "literally could not write out in simple and precise English the ideas which seemed so clear" in her mind, she said. And Codman, rambling in gossipy, run-on sentences, had a prose style "excusable in an architect, whose business it was to build in bricks, not words." Always a bit jealous of Edith's success, he later claimed to have written the book himself, saying that she merely polished his prose. But records show that Edith formulated the book's ideas and organization, searched out many of the photographs and drawings that document its claims, prepared the bibliography, handled negotiations with editors, printers, and publicists, and lined up reviews in leading journals prior to publication. *The Decoration of Houses* was the first test of Edith's skills as author, editor, book designer, agent, and businesswoman. She took away from the experience everything she needed to manage and promote her own writing career, having learned to deal resolutely with editors and publishers.[68]

Minnie Jones, now employed as a reader for the Macmillan publishing company, also reviewed the manuscript. She suggested that her employer might be interested in it, and offered to bring it to an editor in New York. In late February 1897, by what seemed a stroke of luck, Macmillan accepted the book, insisting that it go to press in spring. In early March, a Mr. Brett was at work on the photographs while Minnie read the manuscript for editorial corrections. But by mid-March, things stalled and the book's future was in question. A financial panic (the worst in a decade) unsettled Wall Street and caused Macmillan to worry about sales. Brett, presumably, had shown the book to an architect, who greeted it with "cries of derision," and the authors were summoned to meet with Mr. Brett. "I don't wish to seem peremptory," Edith wrote Codman, "but I think a good deal depends on the impression produced during that visit." The meeting did not go well, and the publisher canceled the contract. Angry, Edith wrote Codman on May 9, 1897: "Before we embark on any other experiments with the book, I am going to make it a condition that you leave the transactions entirely to me."[69]

Convincing her hesitant editors at Scribners to take the book, she saw it through to publication. Codman completed the library at Land's End during the spring and began work on a lodge for the Whartons' butler, Alfred White, and his wife. Once back in Newport, Edith gardened, revised the book (to which she hoped to add a chapter on formal gardens, a project never realized), entertained Nannie Wharton and "Duck," who fell ill with bronchitis, and did volunteer work for the Newport schools, choosing several plaster busts of classical and mythic figures for schoolrooms. Teddy sketched rough-hand designs for bathhouses at Bailey's Beach, the only Newport beach that high society considered suitable, and asked Codman to draw up elevations for the buildings.[70]

Edith's letters pursued Codman wherever he went. "I have finished *walls* (which will have to be a chapter by themselves preceding the Chps. on openings)," she announced, "and I should like you to read it at once." Soon after, she wrote, "I think I have mastered hall and stairs at last, and I should like to see all the French and English Renaissance house plans you have"; she hoped to include line drawings in the book, but in the end abandoned the idea. Advising him on handling clients, she commiserated with him about "stupid" people who did not know their own minds and made him tear out his own work. She repeatedly invited him to Newport to discuss the book. He promised to come, then canceled at the last minute, apparently too overworked to spare time. As the weeks wore on, in a summer of record heat, Edith lost patience with her so-called collaborator. At the end of July, she asked him to choose photographs for the book, but her request went unanswered.[71]

Three weeks later, Teddy wrote a pointed note to Codman, pleading with him to do his part on the book. His letter followed one that Edith had written earlier in the summer:

> Anytime in the last three months you could have made the whole bibliography in your office in an hour. . . . I regret very much that I undertook the book. I certainly should not have done so if I had not understood that you were willing to do half and that the illustrations and all the work that had to be done with the help of your books were to be included in your half. I hate to put my name to anything so badly turned out.

By the time Teddy mailed his letter, Edith was feeling somewhat better about things. Walter Berry had arrived at the end of July for a month-long visit and, in response to her request for help, provided practical guidance and encouragement. Under his supervision, she rewrote and reorganized sections of the manuscript, and at the end of August, he pronounced the book "fit for publication."[72]

With every letter to Codman, Edith sent another to William Crary Brownell, head of the book division at Scribners since 1888 and an important "taste-maker" and critic, who wrote extensively on nineteenth-century English and American prose fiction. A former newspaper reporter for the *New York World* and the *Philadelphia Press*, he was an acute judge of literature and a master stylist. At his death in 1928, Edith called him the "most discerning literary critic" of his time. In editorial matters, he preferred written communications rather than face-to-face discussions with authors. Like Edith, he had something of a "grand air" about him and did not suffer fools gladly. She knew that he was the man she had to please at Scribners, but Codman was no doubt unaware of the risk for her in having submitted their book to her own publisher, who had been awaiting her short story collection for almost four years.[73]

Like the senior editors at Macmillan, Brownell worried about the intended audience and expected sales of the house decoration book; Charles Scribner felt the project lacked potential. But a contract for a small edition was drawn up and signed in July, giving a 10 percent royalty (divided between the authors) on the copy price of $2.50, to be paid after the first 1,000 copies were sold. To the surprise of authors and publishers, the book sold very well and stayed in print for many years. Forty years later, on the day in June 1937 when Edith collapsed from a heart attack that marked the onset of her final illness, she was a guest at Codman's country house in France. They were working on a revised edition of *The Decoration of Houses*.

Inexperienced as she was at book preparation in 1897, Edith had firm opinions about how books should be manufactured and marketed. From cover to cover, she saw to every detail of the intellectual and material form of *The Decoration of Houses*. Scribners wanted thirty-two illustrative plates to accompany the text, and she argued for fifty-six halftone plates (primarily of French and Italian palaces), even meeting with Brownell, who was vacationing in Newport. She also convinced him to ask Berkeley Updike, founder of the Merrymount Press in Boston, to design the cover and title page. Updike, a friend and traveling companion of Codman's, was not yet well acquainted with Edith, but he would come to know her every mood and manner. She was a favorite topic of discussion between Coddy and "Upsy," who, although they sometimes saw themselves as victims of her constant pursuit of perfection, were initially captivated by her. While her friendship with Codman would pass through a long period of estrangement (during which time he tracked her every move and gossiped relentlessly about her), Updike later admitted that he cared for her deeply. Lanky and large-eared, he had been a little in love with her. She could be difficult, as Henry James would later say, but neither Codman nor Updike ever worked with a more discriminating writer. No printing or proofing error escaped her eye. She had a keen aesthetic sense as to typeface, width of margins, quality of paper, and the size of a book—its weight in the hand, the feel of its pages, the ease of print on the eye. As Messrs. Scribners were to learn, she was not often satisfied.[74]

By the end of September 1897, she had dispatched *The Decoration of Houses* to Scribners. Greeted as a handbook for the rich, it was intended to combat the tasteless excesses of Gilded Age decorating. Although its illustrative photographs are of villas, châteaux, and palaces, the principles that guide the work can be (and have been) applied to more humble dwellings than the palaces of Fontainebleau or Versailles. The book describes the historical relation of interior decoration to architecture that held sway until the second quarter of the nineteenth century, reminding readers of all that was lost when interior decoration no longer followed the structural principles of architecture.

Opening with a brief history of house design and decoration, the authors consider the general function of rooms, allotting a chapter to the primary architectural elements (walls and doors), and treating types of rooms (library, dining room, and so forth) in a chapter each. Practical directives—"Doors should always swing *into* a room"—are explained by the building's architectural order and function (doors are a "serviceable feature"), which mutually support a design for good living: "This facilitates entrance and gives the hospitable impression that everything is made easy to those who are coming in." In its logical and direct manner of presentation, *The Decoration of Houses* is gracious and charming. In every way, it is stamped with Edith Wharton's signature.[75]

As publication day neared, she was working harder than ever, her anxiety levels rising under the pressures of proofs and last-minute design decisions. She approached Minnie's young friend, playwright Edward Sheldon, to help her arrange a review in the *Nation* (which, to her chagrin, gave the book one of the few quibbling reviews it received, probably written by Russell Sturgis, a follower of the Paris Beaux-Arts school of "confectionary" design). Walter Berry reviewed it in the *Bookman*, describing it as a work of "large insight and appreciation" on a subject "generally misunderstood and mistreated." Edwin H. Blashfield, an in-law of Brownell's, gave a praiseworthy review in the *Book Buyer*. More important than these commentaries, however, was the attention the book received in architectural reviews. While Minnie read page proofs and Edith set the stage for the book's public reception, Codman faced lawsuits from clients who disputed his fees. Bad economic times had made 1897 a difficult year for him, but he also treated his clients peremptorily. Teddy Wharton, who a few years later would threaten to sue Codman, invited him to Land's End: "Bring yourself and a few portable troubles and law-suits with you."[76]

The Decoration of Houses appeared in bookstores on December 3, in time for the Christmas season. Five days later, Teddy wrote Codman from Newport, "in despair" about Edith's health. She was ill with flu and hadn't been well in more than a month. "I hate to think so but I believe this place does not agree with her, we have been here too long." Three years later, as she struggled to meet a deadline on *The Touchstone*, Walter Berry reminded her of December 1897 and her "close call on nervous prostration." Although she was still very ill on December 13, they moved back to New York City. By the seventeenth, she had regained something of her old spirit, writing Codman to complain about the *Nation* review: "Intelligent disagreement is helpful and stimulating, but such blind, stupid, total misapprehension makes me sick." She then proposed that they do another book "*together*": "Garden architecture" or "The Garden in relation to the House." This project became *Italian Villas and Their Gardens*, the fruit of her many travels in Italy. She wrote it alone.[77]

Scribners' London agent tried to find a British publisher for *The Decoration of Houses*, submitting it to Spencer Blackett, of the Kegan Paul firm. They sought an outside reading from a Mrs. Caroline Shaw, editor of *Art at Home*. She rejected the manuscript: "The entire book is taken up with prints from the books they mention with a few very 3rd rate remarks on their own account and it may go down in America but in this country *certainly not*. I never had such trash." Blackett forwarded this letter to the Scribners agent, commenting that "after the report she gives, I do not think you will blame me by declining Miss [sic] Wharton's book." The firm of Chapman and Hall also rejected it, but finally B. T. Batsford agreed to publish it in England from the Scribners plates, buying four hundred sets of unbound sheets. In America, *The Decoration of Houses* went into a second edition in 1901.[78]

DETOURS AND DELAYS

Four years had now passed since Edward Burlingame proposed that Edith gather stories for a volume. In accepting her story "That Good May Come," a tale of New York society gossip about illicit love affairs, he offered to take "everything else of the same quality you are willing to give me." In the years that followed, he rejected outright or asked for extensive revisions on six of eight stories Edith sent him. In December 1897—having had no literary contributions from her for two years—he asked her to translate three stories from Italian. She had no experience translating prose works and had never translated from Italian into English. Two months later, she wrote saying she had been "really ill" and her "matière grise" was so "soft and sloppy" she could not do much. Her discouraged letter to Burlingame gave no hint that she was on the threshold of her most productive period of writing in a decade.

By the end of March 1898, in spite of illness and fatigue, she had completed the Italian translations and written "The Pelican," a story that exposes the false compromises women with professional desires were forced to make in a society that privileged marriage and motherhood. A young widow gives lectures to support herself and her infant son. She is a poor speaker, and people come only out of sympathy for her situation, but she draws large crowds. Years later, her grown son discovers that his mother is still using him as the pretext for her career, saying that she needs the money to pay for his education. Confronting her angrily, he destroys the façade of maternal sacrifice that perpetuated her career, leaving her in tears. Mailing the story to Burlingame, Edith and Teddy boarded the train to Washington, D.C., to visit Walter Berry.[79]

This was their first excursion since returning from Europe in autumn 1896, eighteen months earlier. The first weeks of the stay were not a success. Hoping to "gain" from outdoor exercise, Edith found it too cold and snowy to walk, much less to ride a bicycle. She thought the White House beautiful, but its grounds were "forlorn" and the parks depressingly "neglected." The Capitol pleased her—"taken altogether, site, surroundings and architecture, it seems to me one of the finest public buildings in the world"—but she described the recently built National Library, an ornate Italian Renaissance–cum–Beaux-Arts confection as *navrant* (heartrending). Discouraged by bad weather and lack of things to do, she and Teddy thought of returning to New York.[80]

The frigid Washington air buzzed with talk of war, as it had since the February bombing of the battleship *Maine* in Havana Harbor. Many Americans blamed the Spanish for the explosion, an act of retaliation against American sympathy with the Cuban rebels, who since 1895 had been engaged in civil war against the Spanish governor.

Among politicians calling for war with Spain were first-term senator Henry Cabot Lodge and Teddy Roosevelt, now assistant secretary of the navy. President McKinley, meanwhile, offered assistance in arranging peace between the rebels and the government in Cuba. "McKinley has no more backbone than a chocolate eclair," Roosevelt was heard to say. "War is sure, I fancy," Edith wrote Codman in early April, agreeing with him that America had "entered upon a period of national disgrace" in taking arms against Spain. Berry joked about "what lots of work there will be for Coddy to do" if the Spaniards invaded Newport. Meanwhile, Henry James worried that the Spanish fleet might bombard Boston Harbor.

On April 21, the United States declared war on Spain, and within days, Teddy Roosevelt resigned his post to join the cavalry. Hearing the news, John Hay, American ambassador to the Court of St. James's in London, wrote his friend Henry Adams (then traveling in Constantinople on a two-year voyage from Egypt to the Levant) that in joining a "cowboy regiment," Roosevelt was renouncing a government post "where he had the chance of his life." Adams thought Roosevelt had gone mad, as did Winthrop Chanler, husband of Edith's friend Daisy: he was "wild to fight and hack and hew." Everyone agreed it would end his political career. Yet, events were to prove them wrong. Roosevelt returned a hero, and was chosen to be McKinley's running mate in the reelection campaign. In September 1901, after McKinley's assassination, Roosevelt became president of the United States. On a 1905 visit to Washington, Edith and Teddy were his luncheon guests at the White House.[81]

While war was brewing in spring 1898, the capital city came into bloom, the pale green of leafy trees hiding "hideous houses." Edith ventured forth on bicycle, enjoying the wide avenues and long, open vistas of Pierre L'Enfant's street plan. "That *is* composition!" she exclaimed. Freed of household responsibilities and away from her social calendar, she slept and ate well, indulged herself in the outdoor exercise she loved best, and enjoyed being a tourist. She even took an excursion to George Washington's home at Mount Vernon. She and Teddy had few acquaintances in the city, and although Berry wanted to bring her into his wide circle of friends, the only one with whom she would establish a deep affection was George Cabot Lodge, twenty-four-year-old son of Massachusetts senator Henry Cabot Lodge. "Bay" Lodge was acting as secretary to his father (and would soon serve with the U.S. Navy in

Cuba), but his real love was poetry, and it was literature that fueled his friendship with Edith. She later described him as "one of the satisfactory people who are the same colour all through, like linoleum. So many are just oil cloth!"[82]

By the end of her six-week stay in Washington, Edith seemed fully recovered from her winter ill health. The trip was such a success that she returned again in June for a week's stay. The city's main attraction for Edith was Walter Berry. They had seen little of each other in the years since first meeting in 1883 at Bar Harbor—or so we assume. (No extant letters document this fourteen-year gap in their friendship.) Berry's long visit to Land's End in summer 1897 marked a new phase of mutual support and trust that would deepen over the coming years, providing the basis for an emotional and intellectual intimacy that lasted until Berry's death in 1927. Edith's writing in the late 1890s revealed a growing restiveness in her marriage and a desire to loosen the bonds that kept her within the fold of society life. Her poetry, which cuts to the quick of her emotions, reveals sorrow and loneliness behind her social smile and graciousness. In "The One Grief," published in the July 1898 *Scribner's*, the newfound friend of her heart is not "young joy" but grief "That walks beside me in sunshine and in shade,/And hath in all my fortunes equal part." Once "Aghast to find it bending o'er my bed," the speaker has come to cherish the grief that "has been interpreter/For me in many a fierce and alien land." Yet, there was something in this private grief, "the helpmeet of my heart," that fed her creativity and gave expression to her desires.[83]

We know from Walter's letters to her in 1898 and ensuing years that he encouraged her to write and to make all necessary changes in her social schedule to accommodate literary work. He cheered her successes and gave her courage in times of despair, and his encouragement had immediate results. Back at Land's End in May 1898, Edith worked hard for several weeks, producing stories at such a rate that in July, she announced to Burlingame the long-awaited volume: it would be ready in autumn. She had written four new stories ("The Muse's Tragedy," "Souls Belated," "A Coward," and "The House of the Dead Hand") and revised two earlier ones, "The Twilight of the God" and "A Cup of Cold Water"—a story about a man dissuaded from his desire to commit suicide when he saves a woman attempting to kill herself with a revolver. Burlingame thought it "wildly improbable," and Walter Berry thought it morbid (his reaction hurt Edith deeply), but she included it in the story volume. Taken aback by her creativity, Burlingame counseled patience and advised a slow reintroduction of "Edith Wharton, fiction writer." His argument was "irrefutable," but she was confused and dismayed. Having waited all these years for the book, why didn't they want to publish it as soon as possible? she asked herself. The Spanish-American War had "crowded out" her stories and forced postponements in *Scribner's* fiction schedule. Burlingame wanted several more of her stories to appear in the magazine before he announced the collection.[84]

Frustrated, but unable to force a concession from her editors, Edith fell ill with hay fever and bronchial problems. Seeking better air than Newport could offer, she and Teddy went north in August to Bar Harbor. Bad weather mixed with good during their stay, but fair or foul, Edith flourished under the high skies of Mount Desert Island. She visited Minnie and Beatrix at Reef Point, and thought the home of Teddy's cousin, Mrs. Gardiner, an "ideal of a country-place." It gave her ideas for a real country house somewhere away from the seashore. Although Teddy loved Newport society, he was beginning to realize that the climate (social and meteorological) contributed to Edith's ill health. Before another year was out, they had found the perfect place.[85]

At Land's End in September, she renewed her efforts to hasten publication of her book, a volume still untitled. Burlingame did not care for any of the (decidedly uninspiring) titles she proposed: "The Ways of Men" (from Alexander Pope), "Mortals Mixed of Middle Clay" (Ralph Waldo Emerson), and "Motives." She repeated her arguments of late June about the book, adding a new element: "My reason for pressing the publication of the book is that my mother, who lives in Paris, has been ill lately, and that there is a strong probability of my having to go abroad in December or January for an indefinite time—I do want to see the book through before going." Burlingame, his patience wearing thin, called her "uncertain, coy, and hard to please." By September 18, she had apparently thought things through, or realized that her editors at Scribners would not budge. She apologized to Burlingame for having "troubled" him and to Brownell for having "bored" him with her request. "I see now that it would have been impossible for you to comply with it."

One month later, Edith sent W. C. Brownell a brief note: "Since I last wrote to you I have been seriously ill, and we have been obliged to give up our plan of going abroad." She asked that he send proofs of her book to the Stenton Hotel, Broad and Spruce streets, in Philadelphia. She did not mention her mother's illness (Edith knew Lucretia was not in imminent danger), nor did she specify her own ailment—a bronchial congestion so severe that it affected her heart. She needed rest and a change of climate, and on October 31, she and Teddy left Land's End.[86]

CITY OF BROTHERLY LOVE

When Edith traveled to Philadelphia in November 1898, it was rumored that she had suffered a nervous breakdown, an inaccurate explanation she let stand. On the face of it, her choice of Philadelphia seemed obvious: Silas Weir Mitchell, a prominent Philadelphia neurologist at the Orthopaedic Hospital (renamed in the 1870s as the "Orthopaedic Hospital and Infirmary for Nervous Diseases"), had developed a widely known "rest cure" for people suffering from nervous exhaustion (or neurasthenia), his method developed from treating Civil War soldiers who suffered what was once called shell shock and now is known as post-traumatic stress syndrome. Dr. Mitchell believed neurology was linked to orthopedics and that nervous exhaustion was related to anemia. Feeding patients high-fat diets, he elevated their red-blood level and thus made their "spirits" rise. His publications included an influential study of blood and his famous 1881 treatise *Lectures on the Diseases of the Nervous System, Especially in Women.*[87]

Demanding, severe, and in some sense brutal, the Weir Mitchell "cure" was not something one entered into casually. It required confinement, isolation, round-the-clock observation, rest, and regular feeding under supervision of a physician and specialist nurse. While the routine was adapted to individual needs, the basic terms of the cure were not negotiable. Away from the outside world, confined to bed for six to eight weeks, patients were forbidden to do anything for themselves except to brush their teeth; a nurse bathed them and gave daily massages, and assisted them in all activities, including feeding, urination, and bowel movements. Deprived of external stimulation or information about their condition, they quickly became dependent on their caretakers. Indeed, patient dependency and "infantilization" were central features of the cure. Charlotte Perkins Gilman described from personal experience the disturbing psychological effects of the cure in her story "The Yellow Wallpaper." Henry James, taking the cure in 1910 at home under the supervision of Weir Mitchell's former colleague Dr. William Osler, became so distressed that he threatened to jump out a second-story window. William Dean Howells's daughter Winifred died at age twenty-six after Mitchell subjected her to forced feeding; an autopsy revealed organic causes for her anorexia.[88]

Available evidence from 1898–1899 casts strong doubt on the popular belief that Edith underwent a formal rest cure of the kind administered by Dr. Weir Mitchell. She was not admitted to the Orthopaedic Hospital, nor did she visit the day clinic on Summer and Seventeenth streets. Instead, she took a suite of rooms at the Stenton Hotel; Teddy was with her much of the time, and Walter Berry wrote her frequently during her "Stenton-cure," as he called it. His letters open a window onto her Philadelphia activities, as does correspondence with her editors at Scribners. She wrote several times a week to Walter (he was also ill during this period) and sent him copies of Henry James's novels; he clipped humorous anecdotes from newspapers to spur her creativity. Between massages and hefty meals, she read and wrote fiction. She prepared the final version of *The Greater Inclination* and wrote "The Portrait," a story of a painter who purposely produces a portrait that disguises the vulgarity of a corrupt politician, who died as a suicide, to spare the feelings of his daughter. (Despite Burlingame's resistance, Edith substituted this story for "The Lamp of Psyche.") Meanwhile, Teddy, with Walter's help, searched for a house in Washington, D.C., where the Whartons hoped to be installed by Christmas.

The recently cataloged records of Dr. Mitchell's work on nervous disorders for the years 1890–1900, housed in the archives of the College of Physicians in Philadelphia, contain no references to Edith Wharton, nor do her own papers from this period reveal that she underwent the Mitchell treatment. Dr. Mitchell, nearing his seventieth birthday in 1898, was not in Philadelphia during these months. In January 1898, his twenty-two-year-old daughter, Maria, child of his second marriage, died of diphtheria. So grief-stricken was he that friends and colleagues feared for his own life. To recover from their loss, he and his wife took an extended voyage to the Near East, traveling in Turkey and Egypt. They were away from America for eighteen months, including October 1898 to January 1899. Despite Walter's joking reference to Dr. Mitchell ("how, in the name of Weir, the God of Restcures, did you manage to catch a cold under those Stenton duvets?"), Edith was not under his care, nor was she being treated by one of his deputies.[89]

Yet the rumor that she took the cure in autumn 1898 has become a "fact" of her personal history. The most popular psychological theory ascribes her suffering to an identity crisis occasioned by her literary productivity during the summer. This theory replaces a long-standing rumor that Weir Mitchell, himself a novelist, had advised Edith to write as a form of psychological therapy. The story was untrue, although Edmund Wilson claimed it as "authentic fact"; moreover, its premise ran counter to the philosophy of Mitchell's cure, where patients were forbidden any kind of intellectual or creative work. The cure purposely induced a vegetative state and reduced patients to childlike dependency as a means of curtailing their anxiety and supposedly overstimulated imaginations.[90]

The association of creativity and "fancy" with dark, subversive forces was a primary theme of nineteenth-century American and British literature, a theme Edith Wharton developed in several works (see *Tales of Men and Ghosts*, 1910). Psychological interpretations of her physical "breakdowns" and "rest cures" often overlook or discount the physiological sources of her ailments. Stress and overwork increased her vulnerability to sinus irritation, throat infections, flu, bronchitis, asthma, and lung congestion, but the primary determinant in these illnesses (as she herself acknowledged) was proximity to sea air, a daily feature of Newport life after she moved to Land's End.

In January 1899, Teddy reported to Walter that Edith's physician had at last discovered the cause of her trouble and had set about casting out the "real devil." The "devil" appears to have been physiological in origin, as the doctor also reported that her heart was doing "splendidly." Her physician was Dr. George McClellan, a medical researcher held in high regard and a nephew of the Union army general George B. McClellan; both his grandfather, the founder of Jefferson Medical College in Philadelphia, and his father were famous surgeons. An 1870 graduate of Jefferson and later a member of its faculty, Dr. McClellan specialized in the study of anatomy and the effects of surgical shock. The author of many books, he was a scholar and teacher, and never had a private practice. Although a faculty colleague of Weir Mitchell's, Dr. McClellan was not on staff at the Orthopaedic Hospital and Infirmary for Nervous Diseases, nor is there any evidence that he had expertise in the Mitchell cure.[91]

How Edith came under Dr. McClellan's care remains a mystery, although it is possible that Teddy's second cousin, Harry Redwood Wharton, a well-respected Philadelphia surgeon, teacher, and researcher, may have brought them together. However it happened, Dr. McClellan did not succeed in driving out the "real devil." Over the next four years, Edith consulted a variety of doctors and submitted to painful medical procedures in an effort to stop the cycle of flu and bronchitis. Her condition improved markedly in 1900, when she spent her first summer in the Berkshire mountains of western Massachusetts. In 1903, she discovered Salsomaggiore, a mineral spa in northern Italy, where she regularly took steam inhalations that reduced the frequency and severity of her bronchial illnesses.

Edith later gave two explanations for her ill health in the 1890s—one story cast her suffering in psychological terms, the other emphasized its physiological causes. In 1908, her friend Elizabeth (Lily) Norton, the daughter of Harvard professor Charles Eliot Norton, underwent a failed cure for her lifelong hay fever and asthma. Edith wrote to Elizabeth's older sister Sara:

> Tell Lily, if it's any comfort, that for *twelve* years I seldom knew what it
> was to be, for more than an hour or two of the twenty four, without an
> intense feeling of nausea, and such unutterable fatigue that when I got
> up I was always more tired than when I lay down. This form of neuras-
> thenia consumed the best years of my youth, and left, in some sort, an
> irreparable shade on my life. Mais quoi! [But what of it.] I worked
> through it, and came out on the other side, and so will she, in a much
> shorter time, I hope.

Four years later, in 1912, Edith described this same period of suffering to Bernard Berenson: "Some occult and un-get-at-able nausea was my constant companion for twelve years . . . and then disappeared suddenly when we moved from the seashore to the hills." In 1918, when her editor W. C. Brownell had a severe nervous breakdown, she commiserated with his suffering while denying any personal experience of neurasthenia: "I am not neurasthenic, or anything approaching it."

After her weeks in Philadelphia, she "recuperated" in Washington, D.C. Walter discovered a beautifully furnished, sunny house to rent at 1329 K Street, not far from his own residence at 1512 H Street. The Whartons rented the K Street house during the spring, having leased

884 Park Avenue. Teddy wanted the K Street plumbing tested and the stable put in order, and Edith objected to sleeping in an imitation Florentine bed. But these problems were soon solved. In his New Year's letter to her from Washington, written at midnight to the background noise of whistles and horns "clanging, shrieking and tootling," Walter wished her "Luck for '99, no more rest-cures, Pelicans galore [a reference to her story in the November *Scribner's*], and any other particular wish you are spinning donnees about!"

Teddy, just in from Philadelphia, brought word that Edith, newly outfitted in a black suit trimmed in fur, was so improved that he had ordered stationery engraved with her Washington address. Unless she wired to the contrary, the Italian bed was going into the garret, along "with all the carved pieces to match," to be replaced by a Louis XVI four-poster in which Walter envisioned her "beautifully installed." He closed with the plea "Do write, Edith, please."[92]

Chapter 3

ENDEAVORS

B Y THE END OF JANUARY 1899, EDITH WAS SETTLED IN frigid Washington, the city swept by snowstorms that froze the pipes in the K Street house and chilled her spirits. Housebound with flu, she continued reading about *settecento* Italy, Walter supplying her with books from his library and the Library of Congress. In February, they corrected proofs of *The Greater Inclination*, and he acted as her agent in selling the British rights to John Lane's Bodley Head Press in London. Her anxieties about the book increased as publication day neared, and she found fault with virtually every aspect of its production. At her urging, Scribners had hired printer Berkeley Updike, whose title-page design for *The Decoration of Houses* had pleased her, but she disliked his choice of typeface for the new book. Wanting to track reviews, she subscribed to Henry Romeike's press cutting bureau. Despite "very flattering" notices, the book disappeared from the pages of daily papers. Her comparative analysis showed that Scribners did not employ the "energetic and emphatic advertising" methods of Macmillan, Dodd and Mead, *McClure's,* and *Harper's.* In April, she wrote William Crary Brownell, head of the book department at Scribners: "I don't, of course, flatter myself that there is any hope of modifying the business methods of the firm, but I think myself justified in protesting them in my own case." The neglect of her book was "essentially unjust," and she was not tempted to offer her "wares a second time" to Scribners.

Edith's accusations had a factual basis: relying on their established name and on the circulation of *Scribner's Magazine*, the firm promoted its books less aggressively than did other publishers. Their advertising department adopted "energetic and emphatic" modern methods only after World War I, by which time Edith had taken her "wares" to Appleton, a company known for its enterprising business methods. Even without wide publicity, *The Greater Inclination* sold very well for a first volume of short stories. It appeared on March 25 in a stunning edition with gilt-edged endpapers and a gray-green cloth cover stamped with an ornate design in dark red. The 154-page volume of eight stories sold for $1.50 in a first edition of 1,250 copies, on which Edith received a 10 percent royalty. By June, the first edition had sold out. The next 1,000 copies, then in press, were already spoken for, and another 500 had been sent to John Lane in London. Scribners estimated the year's sales would top 5,000 copies, but final sales reached slightly over 3,000—about what one would expect today for a short story collection.[1]

The book impressed the reading public: from New York, Newport, and Boston to Baltimore, Toledo, and Chicago, it received praise. The *Academy* proclaimed the stories "distinguished and delightful," and Harry Thurston Peck, writing in the *Bookman*, declared Edith Wharton a "New Writer Who Counts." She possessed "that rare creative power called genius," he concluded: "We have seen nothing this year that has impressed us so much as Mrs. Wharton's book." Edith's secretary, Anna Bahlmann, pasted reviews into a scrapbook covered in paper designed to look like Italian watered silk. These first commentaries on her writing set the terms for discussion of her books for many years to come. The crystalline quality of her prose style and perfection of her narrative method would become hallmarks of critical response. Edith spoke and wrote the "Queen's English" rather than "American," using British spelling and punctuation. Uncertain of her nationality, the reviewer for the *Brooklyn Eagle* instructed her on American usage: "We telegraph to one another; we do not 'wire.'" One Baltimore reviewer found her style "a little too consciously clever at times" and a "little too sparkling for real life"; another thought it affected.[2]

Several critics observed that in style and subject matter her writing resembled Henry James's. These remarks forged the link between her literary reputation and his—a critical convention that exists even today.

John D. Barry, one of Edith's harshest critics, disparaged the "Jamesian" influence of her book. It so roused his anger that he discussed it twice in his "New York Letter" to the *Boston Literary World*. On April 1, he observed that she skillfully copied Henry James's method of developing character motive and mimicked his quirks of style—repeating words and "spoiling the formation of his sentences by inserting parenthetical clauses." Six weeks later, having learned that she did not "relish" references to her indebtedness to James, he devoted another column to her, advising her to not "so slavishly follow this questionable model" in her next book.

Acknowledging that *The Greater Inclination* had received favorable notices, he remarked that its author was well known in New York society, a place starved for "literary geniuses." Rather than facilitating her literary success, as Barry assumed, her social status had slowed her development and made her the object of curiosity.[3]

A personal assessment of a different sort appeared in the *Newport Daily News*. Taking pride in Edith's place in the community, the reviewer stressed the originality of her work and its "remarkable power of insight and imagination." He puzzled, however, over the apparent disjunction between her own life and the suffering revealed in the stories: "One would almost imagine . . . that the author must have suffered and gone deep into life in order to bring up from its depths such knowledge of the world as is disclosed in her pages. And yet this is far from being the case." To disprove Edith's personal knowledge of suffering, he cited her family background, her marriage to a member of a prominent Philadelphia family, her love of travel, and her work with the Rhode Island Society for the Prevention of Cruelty to Animals! Class and gender bias determines the reviewer's bemused praise of Edith Wharton's literary accomplishment just as it does John D. Barry's attack on it. The two reviewers ring changes on Allen Thorndike Rice's 1879 attempt to explain to the aged Henry Wadsworth Longfellow how adolescent Edith Jones, "brought up in fashionable surroundings little calculated to feed her taste for the Muses," had produced poetry worthy of serious consideration. Rice recognized her talent, but could not explain its social circumstances.[4]

When *The Greater Inclination* appeared in London, more praiseworthy reviews followed. Edith always maintained that British reviewers had greater insight into her work than did American critics, and she measured her artistic success (as opposed to her popularity as a novelist) by the British press. A comparative reading of reviews across her long literary career shows the accuracy of her judgment. The *Athenaeum* called her a "clever analyst of human nature," and the *Saturday Review* characterized her writing as subtle and introspective, saying her language had a "scholarly grace of style." [5]

Edith arrived in London in early summer carrying the address of James Bain, a bookseller with whom she would establish a long patronage. Visiting his shop at 14 King William Street, the Strand, she inquired about recent books and was handed her own volume, bound in dark olive ribbed cloth stamped with the same ornate design as the first Scribners printing. "This is what everybody in London is talking about just now," Mr. Bain said. His astonishment on learning her identity matched hers in learning that she was, so to speak, the talk of London town.[6]

Sometime later, a fashionable New York hostess invited Edith to a literary dinner. A friend warned her that the occasion would be "rather Bohemian." "Oh, what fun!" Edith exclaimed. "Who do you suppose they'll be?" The evening came, and the guests assembled in an ornate drawing room, "one of those from which 'The Decoration of Houses' had not cleared a single gewgaw," she later recalled. To her astonished amusement, the "Bohemians" turned out to be Edith herself and two longtime friends, society commentator Eliot Gregory and George Smalley, New York correspondent for the London *Times*. Seated "slightly below the salt" at the long table, the three exchanged witticisms while the heads of tiara-ed women and white-waistcoated millionaires "glittered between gold plate and orchids." The scene captured the contradictions of Edith's social and intellectual worlds—hers was one of the tiara-ed heads.[7]

The Greater Inclination announced her "vocation" and citizenship in "The Land of Letters." But her American life divided between the demands of society and the desires of her creativity. She saw herself as a failure in Boston society, where she was thought "too fashionable to be intelligent," and a failure in New York because "they were afraid I was too intelligent to be fashionable." Many years later, in the light of hard-won literary successes, she reexamined her development as a writer: Was it a good thing for an artist to grow up in a milieu in which the arts were "simply non-existent"? Was it a help or a hindrance to have "every aspiration ignored, or looked at askance"? Edith concluded that artists who in their early years must fight against derision and public ignorance find their way to real achievement. Her own "naturally slow" development had been retarded further by the general apathy about her, but having escaped "premature flattery" and "local celebrity" (being instead surrounded by "a thick fog of indifference, if not tacit disapproval"), she was all the more open to "kindred minds" when she met them. By summer 1899, Edith was eager for kindred minds and ready to abandon the long effort to adjust herself to the society into which she had been born.[8]

For some years, she had endured a barrage of conflicting advice, the more difficult to deal with because she had become habituated to "complying with the tastes of others." Egerton Winthrop had urged her to take a greater role in society, while Paul Bourget rebuked her for her "apathy in continuing a life of wearisome frivolity." At the "formative stage" of her career, she should be surrounded by people "who were thinking and creating," he said. When she convinced Winthrop of her intellectual needs, he urged Teddy to take her to London, where she could taste "old society" and meet "men of letters." Teddy agreed, but soon became restless. He preferred the sporting set to literary coteries, and when he did not succeed in the difficult task of gaining membership into London men's clubs, he had time on his hands. His boredom weighed on Edith, who observed that it was "depressing to live with the dissatisfied." She was not yet fully in tune with her own "greater inclination," but the short story volume was the first step in transforming the "insignificant *I* that I had always known" (as she described herself) into a woman of letters.

Writing was the catalyst for personal change in Edith Wharton, but she stood in wonder at the central mystery of *"how it is all done"*: "Exactly what happens at the 'fine point of the soul' where the creative act, like the mystic's union with the Unknowable, really seems to take place?" she asked. From youth until her middle years, Edith struggled to understand and master the enigmatic powers of her creativity. By age fifty, she had at last forged from the warring cultural prescriptions of woman and writer an independent and productive self.[9]

Travels and Trials

Seeing Teddy's discomfort in London, Edith took him to Paris, where she then gave in to fatigue. After resting for a few days, they traveled slowly to Ragatz, southeast of Zurich, where Minnie Bourget was taking a mineral bath cure. By July 11, the Whartons were settled at

L'Hermitage, a private chalet, and Edith's health and spirits improved in the high mountain air. While Minnie went to the baths and Teddy found his own interests, she took mountain walks with Bourget, who told her of his childhood in a provincial *petit bourgeois* family. They spoke of their respect for Stendhal (she favored *The Charterhouse of Parma* and *The Red and the Black*) and Balzac, the French writer who had the greatest influence on Edith's writing.

When the conversation turned to politics, a subject Edith usually avoided, they uncovered differences of opinion on the Dreyfus Affair. Alfred Dreyfus, the Jewish French army captain who in 1894 had been convicted of treason, court-martialed, stripped of his military rank, and imprisoned on Devil's Island in *"déportation perpétuelle,"* had appealed the sentence. On July 1, 1899, he entered France for a second court-martial trial, which opened in August and ended in another conviction on September 9, the day Edith and Teddy arrived in New York from Cherbourg. Outspokenly anti-Dreyfus, Bourget guarded his words in the presence of his Jewish wife, who (like Edith) believed Dreyfus innocent.

The second trial was not only the most important event of the summer, it was also the most celebrated legal case of the Belle Epoque and would play a defining role in forming the political consciousness of modern France. Hannah Arendt called the Dreyfus Affair a "dress rehearsal" for twentieth-century totalitarianism. Outside the courtroom, Dreyfus was tried by a French press dominated by some three hundred anti-Semitic newspapers. The affair catalyzed hatred against Jews, whom newspaper cartoonists portrayed with oversized noses and long, grasping fingers. In Faubourg salon society, where Bourget moved with ease, the affair divided royalists and Catholics, artists and intellectuals.

All the European newspapers and several American journals covered the trial, sending reporters to Rennes, the provincial northwestern town of sixty thousand people (including eleven Jewish families) chosen as the site of the second trial. Among the journalists was William Morton Fullerton, who would later become Edith Wharton's lover. Harvard-educated son of a Massachusetts cleric, he had worked in the Paris office of the London *Times* since 1891. He reported on the February 1898 conviction of Emile Zola for libel. In an open letter to President Félix Faure ("J'accuse"), printed in *L'Aurore* on January 13, 1898, Zola had accused the government of collusion with the military in making Dreyfus a scapegoat. His manifesto sparked anti-Semitic riots in the French provinces and Algeria. Fearing similar unrest during the sweltering summer of 1899, Rennes mobilized police squads to protect citizens and maintain order. No riots occurred. The local populace had taken to the seashore to escape the heat, and the curiosity seekers were outnumbered by government functionaries, military officers, journalists, and the police.[10]

The verdict in the long trial did not settle any of the complex issues the case raised. On a vote of five to two, the military tribunal court-martialed Dreyfus a second time and replaced the earlier decree of life imprisonment with a ten-year sentence. This was hardly the exoneration Dreyfus's family and supporters had hoped for. Fullerton, like many others, repudiated the decision: "For us to-night Rennes is the *ville maudite*," he wrote, "and we shall leave it in a few hours saying Anathema. Dreyfus alone is calm. He is beginning to comprehend the sublimity of his *rôle*." Even those who believed Dreyfus guilty (as did Paul Bourget) denounced the verdict, knowing that it would further divide French society. Fullerton, who had a taste for the dramatic and even bore a certain physical resemblance to Dreyfus, identified with his "*rôle*" as tragic outcast.[11]

The Bourgets returned briefly to France before the Dreyfus trial began on August 7. The Whartons traveled on to Splügen, a Swiss village perched on a ledge above the Rhine River at the entrance of the mountain pass into Italy. Edith would recount their stay at Splügen and the descent into the valley of the Lira in "An Alpine Posting-Inn," the opening essay of *Italian Backgrounds,* her first collection of travel writing. Her essays from this trip captured comic differences in national customs and attitudes, changes of scene, and the joys of traveling to out-of-the-way places.

Soon bored by fresh air, clear skies, and a village whose only entertainment was the arrival and departure of coaches filled with holiday-makers, Edith and Teddy decided to make the precipitous descent by diligence along the ice-covered Splügen Pass into Italy, land of "domes and spires," where they hoped to explore the "mysterious region" of the Bergamasque Alps. They crossed the Valtellina, a scenic region whose artistic legacy stretched back to prehistoric times, and joined the Bourgets. Hiring a private carriage and fancying themselves medieval pilgrims, the couples spent two nights at the monastery of St. Michael, where they dined each evening in its refectory, hung with portraits of cardinals and abbesses. In the morning, Teddy would ride ahead on his bicycle to secure rooms and order their evening meal, then circle back to meet the group for lunch. The third morning out, they crossed the Paseo dell'Aprica and descended into the Val Camonica, a smaller and more picturesque version of the Valtellina, its verdant splendor conjuring up for Edith the idyllic pastoral scenes of Giorgione.[12]

Having read about an interesting church in the hill village of Cerveno, Edith was again on the track of sacred art. After an arduous climb on foot when the rutted road grew too difficult for wheels, she discovered another group of remarkable terra cottas of Christ's Passion, whose figures of local types (dwarf, beggar, wagoner, and plowman) were rendered in frank realism. By day's end, the travelers had come to Lovere at the head of Lake Iseo, an old-fashioned resort town where Lady Mary Wortley Montagu had once had a summer villa. Although Edith's account gives the sense of late-summer languor and rich leisure, these modern pilgrims covered in a few days some one hundred miles of mountainous terrain on narrow switchback roads.

One August morning in a haze of golden heat, they sailed from Lovere to Iseo, at the southernmost tip of Lago d'Iseo. Edith recounted this spellbinding trip in the lyric "Midsummer Week's Dream," the second essay of *Italian Backgrounds*. The lake of "magic crystal" mirrored the *settecento* of Tiepolo and Goldoni, its shoreline villages the backdrop for scenes of eighteenth-century comedies enacted in the Bergamasque dialect, Harlequin sweeping by in his striped mantle and Pantaloon strutting in "black cloak and scarlet socks." The line between fact and fiction blurred before Edith's vision: "How much the eye receives and how much it contributes," she mused. Italy moved her deeply, and under its summer sun her creative spirit opened, flowerlike. *The Valley of Decision*, her "Italian opus," as she called it, had begun to take shape in her imagination.[13]

The two couples completed their trip by making a loop, traveling east to Brescia, where arcades and balconies provided shade from the heat, then turned west to Bergamo, Como, and finally to Lanzo d'Intervi. On the final day, "the most imperturbable member of the party" (probably Teddy) looked up from his guidebook to announce that they had never penetrated that mysterious and secret region of the Bergamasque or seen its Alps. Although agreeing to make another trip to this "promised land" another year, they never dared—"lest it should turn out to be less perfect." Edith would remember these weeks as among the happiest of her life, their enchantments surpassed only by the Aegean cruise of 1888.[14]

On returning to America in September 1899, she set to work on her first novel, a social history of eighteenth-century Italy. Soon Newport dampness drained her energies, however, and the "burst of lyric rapture" with which she had begun the project turned to discouragement. Feeling neglected by her publishers, she wrote an arch note to Charles Scribner's Sons. Would they explain why she had not yet received royalties on *The Greater Inclination* (now in its second edition), and why Mr. Codman had received his royalties on *The Decoration of Houses*, but she had not? The check for $441 had apparently been lost in the European mails, and W. C. Brownell sent another, enclosing with it a congratulatory note on the success of *The Greater Inclination*. She returned his favor by saying how pleased she was by the sales (three thousand copies) and remarking on the number of letters she had received from other publishers interested in her work.[15]

A Backward Glance portrays a less assured Edith. Opening the first book reviews with "trembling hands and a suffocated heart," she felt "humbled" by the critical praise but "bewildered" by reviewers' contradictory suggestions on how to improve her writing. She would emerge from this difficult period with confidence in her own literary judgment, but her fraught relationship with Scribners reflected her self-doubts and the stress of beginning a new project, the most ambitious she had yet attempted. Teddy and Walter believed she deserved better treatment from her publishers. Teddy wanted her to break with Scribners, while Walter professed amazement at her *"engouement"* (infatuation) with them.

Encouraging her to seek higher prices for her work, Walter advised her to play one publisher against another. When Scribners tried to cut the $175 fee on her magazine stories (a decision presumably necessitated by a Wall Street panic and business depression), he devised a counterattack: "Why not begin cheerfully by asking if it is customary that the publication of a Successful book lowers the value of future productions, and wind up by regretting that you can't write at 'scab' rates, as you belong to the Author's Union." She was, of course, not a union member, but the tone and logic of this stratagem would underwrite her dealings with all her publishers, present and future.[16]

Edith disparaged her writing in letters to Walter. Reading the work in draft, he countered her rueful remarks about a lack of talent and encouraged her to give the freest possible rein to her imagination. On business matters, he urged her to insist on being paid well, and promptly. Early in 1900, he reminded Edith, "Don't forget to strike for more each time." A few weeks later, he quoted a passage from the volume of Robert Louis Stevenson letters she had given him for Christmas. A Scribners author, Stevenson once had ordered some books from the firm that never arrived. He wrote Burlingame to say, "I conceive that 743 Broadway has fallen upon gentle and continuous slumber and is becoming an enchanted place among publishing houses!" Walter asked if Edith couldn't "work that quote on Mr. B some day."[17]

By October 22, 1899, Edith and Teddy were in Lenox, staying at Mrs. Wharton's "Pine Acre" cottage while she and Nannie were abroad. This was Edith's first extended visit to the Berkshires, and although she found the sprawling, dark-paneled, and heavily draped house a too-fine example of Victoriana, she fell in love with Lenox and its climate. Away from Newport's "sogginess," she quickly recovered her health, and Walter—who was spending a weekend in the country for his health (at Rhinecliff-on-Hudson, home of Edith's late aunt Elizabeth)—pleaded with her not to go back to Newport "except to pack up mss." He urged her to "keep on getting weller," encouraged her to finish her new novella, *The Touchstone*, and looked forward to being "introduced" to her Italian story. She wanted to read Casanova's memoirs for her research, and asked him to send her his copy. He did so, addressing the book, which included erotic illustrations, to Teddy in respect of her "pudeur." Meanwhile, she posted to him the opening pages of her novel. He found them "altogether delightful."[18]

Edith knew that every work of art contained "within itself the germ of its own particular form and dimensions," but once started on her Italian subject, she had no idea how to go on with it, and she asked for Walter's help. In the hands of a lesser talent, his advice might have produced disastrous results: "Don't worry about how you're going on. Just write down everything you feel like telling." Edith kept her eye on the "soul" of the novel, which should be, she later said, the writer's own soul. For the present, her soul—and that of her hero, Odo Vansecca—belonged to *settecento* Italy.[19]

Autumn in Lenox proved salutary, but she could not indefinitely postpone the return to Land's End. Teddy had put off a visit to Lenox by the Billy Whartons, whom everyone considered dull. "Dr. W. B." urged Edith to "chuck them" altogether: "Think what it means to have a relapse: your winter ruined." He wanted to see more of "The Valley," telling her that it was too soon for the "criticism" she had asked him to provide. *"Don't, don't go back,"* he pleaded. But to no avail. In late November, they set out for Newport, stopping in Groton, Massachusetts, to visit Billy and his family, who then promptly descended on Newport as soon as Edith and Teddy had returned. A few days later, Edith was beset by the inevitable flu and bronchitis with its accompanying fatigue, and she had run aground on *The Touchstone.* "I do wish you would take my advice just occasionally," Walter exclaimed. To console her, he sent a passage from George Eliot:

> 1869. Sept. 11. I do not feel very confident that I can make anything satisfactory of Middlemarch. . . . It is worth while to record my great depression of spirits that I may remember one more resurrection from the pit of melancholy.

Walter knew that Edith greatly admired *Middlemarch*. A reminder of another woman writer's self-doubt, the diary passage also offered inspiration and reassurance: Edith would find a way out of the current impasse. Many years later, long after Walter was dead, she confided to a friend that he had "understood always. He helped me more than anyone; in fact, he alone helped me believe in myself."[20]

By November, *The Greater Inclination* had gone into a fifth printing, and in announcing the new printing, the *New York Herald* extolled the book's merits. Minnie Jones, who had a good sense of the literary market, suggested to Edith a special edition to capture the holiday trade. Scribners liked the idea and produced a lovely white-and-gold-bound volume. December found Edith in an "all's-right-with-the world" mood despite "travail-pains" on *The Touchstone.* Walter, overworked and engaged in a prolonged legal fight involving inherited properties, was in a "low area" mentally and physically. "Please write and cheer me up. I need it badly." He visited Edith twice in New York, where she had room for overnight guests now that her little houses were "twinned," and he planned to return again in February. In addition to working on her novella, the "Italian opus," some travel essays and short stories, she was also writing a play entitled *The Tight-Rope*, a social comedy. While Walter stretched out on the chaise in her boudoir, she read the play aloud to him. No copy of the play exists, but its protagonists were the Perth and Malicent families, and Walter found them enormously amusing. ("What really interesting people one meets chez vous!" he wrote later.) Back in Washington for the new year, he was "thoroughly homesick for 884" and again begged her to write.[21]

These were their "great days," a period when Walter tried to see as much of Edith as possible. She depended on his emotional support and encouragement of her work; he relied on her affection, good humor, and hospitality. At her side, he felt cheered; away from her, he grew depressed. Their "orgies," as he called them, were not sexual, but intellectual—reading by the hour and talking constantly of literature. Walter and Teddy also enjoyed a lively friendship; they played pool for money (Teddy usually won), and joined forces to cheer Edith in her low moments and give aid and comfort when she was ill.

Walter was as attuned to Edith's periods of ill health as he was to her emerging importance on the literary scene. For some time, he had noted her pattern of overwork: she pushed herself not only beyond her physical strength but beyond exhaustion. Worried, he warned her against its consequences, but it was to become a lifelong habit. Endowed with extraordinary energy, she seemed to feel a moral responsibility to use it all up. Social activities and a restless "busyness" drained off some of this reserve, but she channeled her core energy into writing—an activity that encompassed more than the two or three hours each morning when she composed in bed. She rewrote extensively, editing her work by the time-honored method of scissors and paste; folding and cutting up pages, she created a layered manuscript whose seams hid earlier versions of her work. The cut-and-paste process consumed energy and saved paper, returning her to the childhood pleasures of writing on salvaged scraps of wrapping paper. The underside of this pleasure (like the hidden portions of her pasted text) was compulsion. Her childhood sense of being "driven to compose" gained strength as she grew older. Teddy, who in fifteen years of marriage had evinced little interest in her work, would soon show signs of being (in Edith's perception) "positively frightened by it. . . . he thought it was a kind of witchcraft." His fears grew as Edith's productivity increased.[22]

A CHANGE OF PLACE

Writing well and in several different genres in 1900, she drafted the first volume of *The Valley of Decision*, alternating long stretches of novel writing with work on short stories for her next volume, *Crucial Instances*—its title suggested by Burlingame. She had already tried her hand at a story composed entirely of dialogue ("Twilight of the God," in *The Greater Inclination*) and did so again in "Copy," a tale of a literary love affair between a woman novelist and a famous poet who later battle over the ownership of their love letters. These tales attempted to map the skeletal frame of the short story form, but they also revealed Edith's developing interest in drama. Having written an original play, *The Tight-Rope*, she now adapted *Manon Lescaut*, the Abbé Prévost novel, and tried to have it produced on the London stage. She would read both of her plays to a small audience of invited guests at the home of the George Goulds in Lenox the following summer. Attending theater in New York, London, and Paris, she assessed the quality of current productions, analyzed dramatic forms, and learned the technical aspects of staging. Neither of her plays was staged (she herself stopped the New York production of *Manon*), but the experiments in playwriting and adaptation led to her 1902 translation of Hermann Sudermann's *Es Lebe das Leben* (The Joy of Living).

The closing year of the nineteenth century was for Edith one of literary experiment and expanded cultural horizons. For Teddy, it marked the onset of mental illness, first evidenced in anxious restlessness and bursts of anger occasioned by money worries. Over the next decade, a variety of physicians struggled to diagnose his condition, identifying it as neurasthenia, melancholia, and senile dementia; today, we recognize his suffering as manic depression. For Walter, 1900 was a year of ill health and financial worries, eased only by his desire to be with Edith. He was not a man who employed the language of hearts and flowers or who sketched sexual fantasies in his letters. Thus, we take note when he compares a particularly golden, late-afternoon Boston sky to "the sun in your hair." He recorded a dream in which he took a train to Lenox, where Edith spent the summer (Teddy went to Newport), arriving "just in time for a good drive and a good long evening afterwards." Suffering from a bad headache one afternoon, he saw himself "stretched out on the sofa, là-bas." Edith was "reading Condorcet aloud, and would stop for a minute and come over and put both your hands on my forehead." He longed to see her, waited impatiently for her letters, and signed himself, "all yours, dear."[23]

In early spring, Edith was not in good health or high spirits. "Wretchedly unwell" at the end of March, she accepted Walter's invitation to visit Washington, announcing to Codman on April 5 that she was off for a week "to see if a change will help me." Suffering from digestive ailments (as was Walter, who lost ten pounds), she may have been too ill to travel to the capital. In another attempt to discover the cause of her flu and bronchial ailments, she consulted a new physician ("Dr. James"). Pleased at this news, but convinced that boredom was a "great part" of her "obscure and interesting case," Walter encouraged her to take a European trip.[24]

Perhaps she was bored, but fatigue and prepublication anxiety over *The Touchstone* also accounted for her ill health. She had experienced repeated setbacks and loss of confidence in writing this story, her first published novella; its serial run in March 1900 marked her first appearance in *Scribner's Magazine* in more than a year. *The Touchstone*'s psychological drama concerns publication of letters from a famous woman author to a younger lover; after her death, he sells them to finance his marriage, claiming that they were written not to him but to a "dead friend." Like "Copy," which ran in the June 1900 *Scribner's*, *The Touchstone* examines ownership rights to letters, the appeal of private correspondence between public figures, and the erotics of epistolarity. These two stories eerily forecast circumstances that would attend Edith's future love affair with Morton Fullerton. By then a famous author who feared her love letters might fall into the wrong hands, she repeatedly asked that Fullerton return them. (He did not.) After Walter Berry's death in 1927, she burned their forty-five-year correspondence, saving only his letters from the 1897–1902 period, when he served as her literary adviser.

When *The Touchstone* appeared in book form in April, Richard Le Gallienne, who was to have a distinguished career as poet and literary critic, heaped praise on it, as did other reviewers. He declared in the *Boston Evening Transcript* that the story's situation was its great distinction, and commended the quality of writing (as did virtually every other reviewer) and Edith's ability to render "almost a cruel enjoyment of the exquisite spiritual torture involved" in the drama. The *Atlantic Monthly* said the book was "more sustained" than her earlier work, and that although she had learned much from Henry James, "better things than he can inspire are . . . within the scope of her still widening possibilities"—a remark that must have pleased her. In England, where the book appeared as *A Gift from the Grave*, critics praised her literary style. The *Bookman* noted that her workmanship was "very far above the average of what comes to us from America."[25]

An unexpected letter of tribute came from Sara Norton, eldest daughter of Charles Eliot Norton, the recently retired Harvard professor of fine arts. "Sally" would become Edith's closest woman friend for the next several years. Although the Norton family moved in the same Boston circles as Teddy Wharton's family, Edith met Sally in New York, at the home of mutual friends. Unself-consciously charming, beautiful, and a gifted violinist, Sally had grown up in a world of intellectual and cultural values quite different from the society that made a claim to Edith's time and energy. When Charles Eliot Norton's wife died in childbirth with their sixth child in 1872, he raised the children aided by his sister, Grace. Brought up in a close-knit Cambridge family, Norton was a devoted father, so much so that he "cramped" his children's lives. His elder daughters, Sally and Elizabeth ("Lily"), never left home. In the late 1880s, Sally fell in love with the son of the late English poet Arthur Hugh Clough. Young Clough visited Cambridge and proposed marriage to her. His request threw Sally into emotional crisis: to marry him would mean living permanently in England, a choice her father had rejected after his wife's death. Breaking off her relationship with Clough, Sally remained at "Shady Hill," the Norton family home, and devoted herself to assisting her father. She was forty-four at his death in 1908, too old to marry and have children of her own; she devoted the rest of her life to editing his letters and manuscripts. A chilling version of Sally's story appears in Edith's 1901 tale "The Angel at the Grave."[26]

Like Edith, Sally had a gift for friendship. "You don't know how much pleasure your letter has given me," Edith wrote her on March 1, 1900. "I am so lacking in self-confidence and my work falls so far short of what I try for that I am almost childishly grateful for the least word of approval." She often disparaged herself in letters to friends, signs of her need for reassurance that her work had value. To Walter, she spoke of "fatuous, ineffectual yesterdays": *The Touchstone* was flat "like a plowed field"; her new story, "The Duchess at Prayer," revealed a *baissement* (lowering) in quality; *The Valley of Decision* was a "bowl of blue gruel." "I can't do it after all," she declared. Even praiseworthy reviews and strong sales of her books did not soothe her fears. *The Touchstone* sold five thousand copies in the first year, two thousand of them in England. This success gave a second "boom" to *The Greater Inclination*, which sold another fifteen hundred copies. Still, she remained unconvinced of her literary worth.[27]

In late spring, Edith and Teddy went to England, where she tried to launch a West End production of her play *Manon*, having enlisted the help of drama critic and translator of Ibsen William Archer and London *Times* correspondent George Smalley. The Whartons also traveled outside London, searching for an architectural model for the house they wanted to build near Lenox. A year earlier, Edith had told Codman that she wanted a "good house" in New York by 1900; if he could not join together 882 and 884, she would begin house-hunting in Manhattan. He joined the houses as best he could: the Whartons occupied 884, reserving 882 for servants and guests, but no interior door linked the two dwellings. By the time Codman finished his work on the houses, Edith had turned her attention to a country house. When she announced her English trip, he loaned her copies of *Country Life* and drew up a list of estates for her to visit. She and Teddy saw some half-dozen homes, among them Wilton (designed by Inigo Jones) and Holland House in Hampstead. After her English days, Edith found Paris "ugly" and took a "sightseeing rest" on her arrival there.[28]

The Paris International Exposition opened in June 1900 to record crowds. Edith and Teddy had planned to stay with Harry Jones in his Champs Elysées apartment, but discovered to their surprise that he had unexpectedly given it up. Unable to find a hotel room, they stayed with the Bourgets, newly resident at 20 rue Barbet-de-Jouy, around the corner from the rue de Varenne, where Edith would eventually reside. Minnie Bourget was translating into French "The Muse's Tragedy," a story from *The Greater Inclination*, and Edith assisted her. Written in 1898, this was the first of her three stories about literary love affairs. Faintly echoing Henry James's *The Aspern Papers*, it also forecast elements of *The Touchstone*. A young poet seeks out the famed "muse" of an acclaimed poet (now dead) and discovers that their relationship was not the romantic liaison the poet's love sonnets suggested. She was muse to his "intellectual life," nothing more; to keep alive the romantic pretense, however, she inserted ellipses in her published edition of his letters, making it appear that she had excised intimate passages. Trying to escape her role as mere "muse," she seduces the young poet as an "experiment." Their affair ends in tragedy when she comprehends the emotional losses of her earlier life. The tale appeared in the July 1900 *Revue Hebdomadaire* with an introductory note by Paul Bourget: it was Edith's first appearance in French.

The most difficult moment of Edith's Paris weeks was the visit to her bedridden mother, whom she had not seen since Lucretia moved to France some two years earlier. Having allied herself with Frederic in his divorce, Lucretia resented Edith's loyalty to Minnie and her refusal to recognize his second wife (and former lover), Elsie West. Harry had sided with Edith, and had taken the further step of legally adopting Frederic's daughter, Beatrix, to ensure that she inherit a portion of the Jones family fortune. When Lucretia learned of Harry's action, she broke with him. Against this background of divided family loyalties, Edith paid a duty visit to Lucretia. She reported to Walter that it went smoothly; he acknowledged that "it must have been a pull on your nerves, anyhow; and you aren't fit for that sort of thing, my dear." After Edith's visit, Lucretia made her last will and testament, a document that contained unhappy surprises both for Harry and for Edith. Several weeks later, Lucretia fell into a coma and never recovered.[29]

Her mission to Paris accomplished, Edith departed with the Bourgets and Teddy on a two-week tour of northern Italy to do research for *The Valley of Decision*. On their return to America, Edith and Teddy moved into The Poplars, a Lenox cottage owned by Leonard and Louisa Sands that would be their summer home for the next three years. Land's End (which Walter called "never never well land") was rented for the season. Located southeast of the village, The Poplars faced Laurel Lake Farm, the future site of Edith's house, The Mount. While Teddy took a yacht trip with a friend, she wrote the opening essay for *Italian Backgrounds*; in the afternoons, she rode her new white horse (a gift from Teddy) along back country roads. Happy in her new surroundings and buoyed by a sense of "*bien-être*," she wrote Codman, "The truth is, I am in love with the place—climate, scenery, life and all."[30]

WHILE THE LENOX climate boosted Edith's energy and put eight pounds on her thin frame, Walter's chronic health problems continued. His letters in spring and summer 1900 document ear infections, laryngitis, a hemorrhaged lung, weight loss, and a return of malaria. Continuous rain in the Adirondacks, where he had been sent to cure his lung, brought back the "old malaria," with fever and sweats. "I can find no simile to fit my raggedness," he wrote her in July. He passed his forty-first birthday in a depressed state and called himself "oldman."[31]

Returning to Washington from the Adirondacks, Walter paid a brief visit to Edith in Lenox and found her in excellent spirits as she awaited publication of a quartet of stories, three of which appeared in August: "The Duchess at Prayer" (*Scribner's*), "Rembrandt" (*Hearst's International*), and "Friends" (*Youth's Companion*). In October, after a delay of almost two years, *Lippincott's Magazine* in Philadelphia published "The Line of Least Resistance." Except for "Friends," a revised story written in 1894, these tales were recently composed and two would appear in *Crucial Instances* (1901), her next volume of short stories. Her self-confidence grew during the summer, and although she still depended on Walter's enthusiasm for her writing and his practical research help at the Library of Congress, she proved by steady work on *The Valley of Decision* over the next several months that she could conquer a vast subject outside her immediate experience. Charles Eliot Norton expressed interest in her topic and loaned her books from his extensive collections on Italian history and art. In the afternoons, she discovered the charms of the Lenox Library.

From August to early October, Edith worked for two to three hours every morning on *The Valley of Decision*, writing some forty thousand words—or about 150 pages of double-spaced typescript—"without a break." Finding her "tank empty," she turned to short stories, writing two in a month. When Burlingame told her that *Scribner's Magazine* could not take *The Valley* until 1903, she decided against serialization and notified Brownell of her wish to publish the story collection in February and the novel in June 1901. Lenox had been "a great success" for her, she remarked to Brownell, and she hoped New York would be "all the better."[32]

November 10 found Edith and Teddy at the Somerset Hotel in Boston, a blizzard "blowing great guns" around them. After a ten-day trip to Newport to close up Land's End (where they would never again live), they returned to 882–884 Park Avenue. Edith composed more stories for *Crucial Instances*, read proofs of the first half of *The Valley of Decision*, and developed an idea for a new stage play. The volume and intensity of this work fatigued her eyes, and by mid-December she was seeing "crystal zig-zags everywhere." She was again pushing herself to the point of exhaustion. On December 20, her secretary, Anna Bahlmann, who resided at 884, remarked in a letter to Brownell that "Mrs. Wharton is terribly driven this week." The play would come to nothing, the novel would be delayed a year, but the story volume appeared close to schedule—on April 27, 1901.[33]

CRUCIAL INSTANCES

Edith's literary pressures increased when she had to write two new stories to replace "The Line of Least Resistance," which was to have been the title story of her new volume. She withdrew the story because it had offended people in Lenox and Newport when it appeared in *Lippincott's Magazine* in October 1900. She quickly filled the gap with "The Moving Finger," a reversal of the Pygmalion story that turns a real woman into art, and "The Confessional," a tale of the Italian Risorgimento that she hurried to finish in the first weeks of 1901. Burlingame found "The Confessional" inappropriate for the volume and asked her to take it out. She first agreed, then stood her ground; the story appeared in the collection.[34]

Edith thought "The Line of Least Resistance" the best tale she had yet written and was proud enough of it to send a copy to Henry James. He declared it "a little *hard*, a little purely derisive," faults he attributed to her youth and cleverness. But his critical comments paled in comparison to the reaction of the Sloane-Vanderbilt families of Lenox and Newport. They considered the story indiscreet and insulting. Mrs. William Sloane, the former Emily Vanderbilt, generally was regarded as "the social queen of Lenox," reigning from her rambling villa, Elm Court. She recognized Edith's heroine, Mrs. Mindon, as her former sister-in-law Jessie Sloane, who had abandoned her husband, Henry, and her two daughters to marry Perry Belmont, scion of a family rumored to be partly Jewish. (Soon after the story appeared in *Lippincott's,* Walter wrote Edith to ask if anyone had "fitted the key" to its *donnée.*) Lenox society turned against Edith in spring 1901; to retrieve her place, she wrote Emily Sloane a letter of apology, and Teddy sent William Sloane a note. Amused by this circumstance, Ogden Codman added a clichéd moral: "People who live in glass houses ought not to throw stones." This remark suggests that Edith took her own marriage as a literary subject—Teddy, like Mr. Mindon in the story, turning a blind eye to her friendship with Walter Berry. Yet Codman seemed unaware of Walter's place in Edith's life, and general gossip about their "affair" would arise only some years later, when the Wharton marriage was breaking up.[35]

EARLY IN FEBRUARY 1901, the Whartons went to Lenox for several days, staying at Mrs. Curtis's lodging house. During their visit, they made an offer to buy Laurel Lake Farm. Exhausted from writing, Edith had been ordered by her doctor to rest. Codman reported to his mother that her ill health was due in part to the "failure to bring out her play."

For some months, Edith had worked with producer Charles Frohman and theatrical agent Elizabeth Marbury on a New York staging of *Manon*. She wanted the play produced, but feared the results would not be good: "I don't look forward to it with any enthusiasm," she wrote Sally Norton on February 28. When Shakespearean actress Julia Marlowe left the production, objecting to Manon's characterization, Elsie de Wolfe (Marbury's companion) was chosen to play the lead role. De Wolfe insisted that Edith rewrite the final drowning scene, which required the actress to jump into a tub of water. Edith refused, withdrew the script, and the production folded. Applauding her show of strength, Walter advised her to give up writing for the stage and the "monthlies" and "go hard" at *The Valley of Decision*, predicting it would have sales of forty thousand copies. This was excellent advice, and she took it.[36]

The publicity surrounding *Crucial Instances* in late April offset her disappointment in losing the play, but the short story collection was not the success she had hoped. It received fewer reviews than *The Greater Inclination*, and critics found it less good than its predecessor. Critical commentary focused on her writing method and style (her "delicate perception of forms and colors"), announcing themes that would become critical clichés: her indebtedness to Henry James, her weakness in depicting male characters, the restricted palette that upper-class New York offered. *Munsey's Magazine* classed her writing with that of other "rich women," calling it a "fad"; *Harper's Monthly*, where two of the stories had first been published, noted that she owed a great deal to James, but that "at her best, when her own poetical nature takes over, she writes wholly with her own authority." To Walter, however, it was "the best book of stories that is."[37]

By the time *Crucial Instances* appeared, Edith and Teddy had signed an agreement with Miss Georgiana Sargent—a painter and distant relation of John Singer Sargent—to buy Laurel Lake Farm for $40,600 (about $600,000 at today's rate). Edith wanted to begin construction in spring, a desire thwarted by disputes with Codman over the house plans. In the eight years since he had begun work on Land's End, Codman had become the darling of the moneyed set, his success spurred by his high-quality work and Edith's recommendations of him to her society friends. He had recently expanded his architectural practice beyond renovations and interior design to building from the "ground up" (thereby making "double the money"), and everyone assumed that he would build the Whartons' house. Busy with the really rich, he now had little time for Edith and Teddy, whom he thought would not "spend." He also found them difficult to work for: they "wear me to a shadow with their nonsense" and "fussing," he wrote his mother, whom he addressed as "Mère Cot."[38]

The threesome got off to a bad start. Edith and Teddy rejected Codman's first rough sketches for the house (probably because the design was too costly) and asked for revised plans. Teddy then suggested that he could purchase fittings (mantels, columns, cornices) direct from Codman's Paris supplier, thus saving the architect's 15 percent commission. Codman coolly responded that this would violate rules of the American Institute of Architects. Teddy flew into a rage, telling Codman he was not "easy to get on with." Codman reminded Teddy how unpopular he and Edith were in Lenox (a reference to the Emily Sloane contretemps), and Teddy "shut up right off." Thinking he had won, Codman assured his mother, "It will all come out right in the end." It did not.[39]

The tables turned when Edith engaged another architect—Francis L. V. Hoppin, whom she knew from New York and Newport. Codman maintained, at least to his mother, that *he* had walked out on the Whartons, admitting that even though he had not wanted to do the house, he "would have been better pleased if they had been *more upset*" by his leaving. "Their day of usefulness is over," he rationalized. "Poor Mrs. Pusscod must be replaced while she is still stunned." As a final turn of the screw, he recounted to his mother a story going round about the Tom Hastingses and the Teddy Whartons. They were couples, it was said, where the wife is a "wife in name only"—meaning, one supposes, that they did not maintain sexual relations. Codman was uncertain of the story's truth.[40]

He could not really afford an open break with Edith, and tried to patch things up. He blamed Teddy, and his friends Berkeley Updike and Eliot Gregory agreed that Teddy had become argumentative and difficult. He sent Edith "floral tributes" and friendly notes, which she answered by saying she set "great store" by their friendship:

> We are in such close sympathy in things architectural that it would have been a pleasure to me to work with you, but perhaps after all we know each other too well, and are disqualified by that very fact for professional collaboration. At any rate, having avoided that peril, I feel

that our escape ought to unite us more closely, and now that you need not be on your guard against me as a client perhaps I shall be all the more useful as a friend. I shall certainly try to be, for it has always been a great interest to me to follow your work and try to make people understand what it represents; and I *hope* you will not be too busy to be interested in *my* undertaking, and to come and talk over our plans some day when you have the time to spare. . . . Sincerely yr friend.

Walter called Codman's behavior "disgusting": "He ought to have made half a dozen plans, free, and begun over again, if necessary. You're dead right in chucking him," he wrote Edith. Some ten months later, Codman wrote his dear "Mère Cot" that he "had" the Wharton house. He was to do the interior.[41]

During these weeks, Edith was trying to write Book II of *The Valley*, sending Walter installments by express packets. In late April, she took a break from her literary labors to spend a long weekend in Boston with Teddy. They visited Isabella Stewart Gardner at her Italian Renaissance palace in the Fenway and paid calls on the Nortons at Shady Hill. Returning to Lenox, they learned that Mrs. Wharton, who had become ill in Europe earlier in the spring, was now very ill. Teddy arranged to sail for England on May 26, and Edith asked Sally to come stay with her in Lenox, where "the apple-blossoms are just showing themselves." She explained that Sally might find her "quiet and systematic kind of life" rather dull. First-time visitors always received this gentle forewarning that Edith's mornings were reserved for work and that she did not stay up late at night. Sally spent two days and adapted easily to Edith's routine.[42]

On June 1, Lucretia Jones died in Paris, having lain in a coma for nearly a year. Arriving in England to find his own mother improved, Teddy crossed the Channel to attend the funeral of his mother-in-law. "There is no room for anything but thankfulness at this sudden conclusion of it all," Edith wrote Sally on black-bordered notepaper. We know nothing of her real feelings on this occasion, but Edith entered into the traditional forms of mourning. Unable to find the proper clothes in Lenox, she made a hasty trip to New York to outfit herself. Her mother's death reopened a chapter in the Jones family troubles that had begun with Frederic's divorce some five years earlier. In late July, Edith went to Paris to confront her brothers about the terms of their mother's will. After cash bequests to her two sons, the estate (which included Rhinelander, Schermerhorn, and Jones properties) was divided equally among her three children. Frederic received outright $95,000 and additional real estate, including the family home on West Twenty-third Street; Harry, from whom Lucretia was estranged, received $50,000; Edith's $92,000 portion was held in a life trust.[43]

Until the late nineteenth century, laws in most states prevented women from inheriting legacies outright, a protection against gold-digging or spendthrift husbands. In 1901, Edith, a married woman approaching forty, felt betrayed by this old-fashioned practice, which prevented her from drawing on the capital in her lifetime and from passing it on to a survivor at her death. (The trust reverted to Frederic on Edith's death.) She threatened to break the will on the grounds that Frederic had exerted undue influence on his dying mother. Harry joined with her and together they forced Frederic to concede to their demands. In 1902, he resigned as trustee of Edith's estate (Teddy took his place), and legal papers were drawn up to dissolve the old trust and give Edith her fair share of the inheritance. One year after Lucretia's death, it appeared the problem had been solved. Edith's resentment toward her mother and Frederic continued all her life, however, and surfaced with renewed bitterness in 1931: while making a new will, her attorneys discovered that she had never fully recovered the money and property due her. This unhappy circumstance seems to have been caused not by malfeasance on Frederic's part, but rather by the incompetence of family lawyers and legal advisers.[44]

THE VALLEY

Lenox Life, the resort society paper of the cottagers, noted the comings and goings of the Wharton family in summer 1901. The first week of July marked the arrival of R. W. Curry of Newport and F. L. V. Hoppin and Beatrix Jones of New York—the engineer, architect, and landscape designer of "The Mount," which Edith named for the Long Island estate of her great-grandfather Stevens. Work began immediately after the Fourth of July holiday, in the middle of one of the hottest summers on record. Codman, observing from afar, kept his mother apprised of every event. Even before the real work had begun, Hoppin was having "an awful time with the house," he said, and hated traveling to Lenox from New York. Edith fussed over "every detail" and telegraphed Hoppin almost daily. He had already made three sets of plans for the house, which had been pared down "in every way," apparently because of financial constraints. "Poor Pussy" was still very unpopular.

> I always knew that she went out of her way to be rude and people don't seem to be willing to put up with it. Her story about the Sloanes finished her with all the Sloane Vanderbilt hangers on who are now hacking at her like a lot of yellow dogs.

In a *geste*, Codman declared that he had stood up for her, "as she was kind and helpful to me long ago, and as long as I am not working for her I have nothing against her."[45]

Lenox Life portrayed Edith and Teddy rather differently. The Whartons were "extremely cultivated people and well liked," and they would be missed when they sailed for Europe on July 31. The paper recalled the "little plays" (*The Tight-Rope* and *Manon*) written by Edith and performed at the George Gould home two years earlier and noted that she was going abroad to arrange English publication of her new novel. She sold *The Valley of Decision* to John Murray publishers, but her trip was marred by misfortune. They sailed from Boston on the *Commonwealth*. The day before landing in Liverpool, Edith fell violently ill with ptomaine poisoning and was carried off the ship on a stretcher. Although extremely weak and "unhinged" by the incident, she was eventually able to sightsee in London, taking in the Velázquez exhibition at the Royal Academy, enjoying the Turner landscapes in the National Gallery, and making a long-awaited trip to Oxford. Once in Paris, the dreary legal wrangles over her mother's estate were offset by visits to the Bourgets and browsing in antique shops. Edith and Teddy ended their stay on the Continent with a six-day visit to Belgium, where they toured Ghent, Antwerp, Bruges, and Brussels. The return home was even more dreadful than the first crossing. A "heavy sea" caused Edith's deck cabin to leak so profusely that on one day, she could not leave her bed and lay holding an umbrella over her head.[46]

While work proceeded on The Mount, she revised earlier portions of *The Valley* and read proofs (which were being set separately and simultaneously in the United States and England), and composed the final section of "Sub Umbra Liliorum," a travel essay about Parma for *Italian Backgrounds*. Working faster than ever, juggling a dozen different tasks, Edith found time to read Schopenhauer on the ascetic life.

On the night of November 26, Lenox was hit by a ninety-mile-an-hour gale that plunged the temperature to twelve degrees and heaped snow in the streets. Snowed under and "frozen out" of The Poplars, the Whartons packed up the next morning and Edith carried boxes of page proofs down slippery streets to Mrs. Wharton's house. She stole a few moments to record a "dream-poem" that had come to her as the night winds raged. The sonnet "Uses," dedicated to Sally, spoke of changing seasons and the rush of time, both of which weighed on Edith's mind. Sending their staff ahead to New York to prepare 882–884, Edith and Teddy accompanied Mrs. Wharton to Boston.

As Christmas approached, Edith accelerated her work, repeating the frantic activity that the previous year had induced headaches and eye problems. On December 22, she sent Brownell the penultimate chapter of *The Valley*. On Christmas Eve, Teddy, Edith, and Anna Bahlmann walked one block north to 53 East Seventy-ninth and joined Codman for dinner in the narrow house he had purchased several months earlier. On Christmas night, he dined with them. Their friendship had regained its former affection and camaraderie.[47]

Although delighted to be the author of a two-volume novel, Edith feared its price ($2) might "frighten away buyers for a new novelist, who has still to win her spurs." An "expensive novel" was, she said, "an impertinence." She greeted Brownell on the New Year with a furious letter of complaint about the book's design. Berkeley Updike, she rightly noted, had forgotton—or ignored—the page and type sizes she had selected the previous June. The two volumes, measuring five and one-half by three and one-half inches, lay easily in the palm of a hand; the dark red cloth binding was stamped in gold. But, to Edith, the "make-up" of the book seemed "as inappropriate for the style of the story as for its length." Pushing hard to finish the book, she asked, in vain, that its price be reduced to $1.75. Having composed the dedication, "To my friends Paul and Minnie Bourget, in remembrance of Italian days together," she sent Brownell the final chapter on January 7, with an enclosed note, "The end at last!"[48]

Between Walter Berry's arrival the following day and her fortieth birthday on the twenty-fourth, Edith fell ill with the flu. Her two closest women friends were also ill—Minnie Bourget worn out from months of serving as her husband's manuscript copyist, and Sally Norton, fatigued mentally and physically from household responsibilities caring for her aging father. Answering Sally's birthday letter, Edith empathized with her state: "Don't I know that feeling you describe, when one longs to go to a hospital and *have something cut out*, and come out minus an organ, but alive and active and like other people, instead of dragging on with this bloodless existence!! Only I fear you and I will never find a surgeon who will do us that service."[49]

These images of violent self-laceration betray Edith's sense that something akin to organic dysfunction prevented her from living fully. Worried about Teddy's health and weary of living with a dissatisfied husband, she desired intellectual companionship joined to sexual and emotional intimacy. These deeply submerged desires probably existed only at the level of fantasy and daydream, however. Edith's reigning conscious desire, one more powerful than her sexual needs, was for artistic recognition. Once she gained it with *The House of Mirth* in 1905, she never again resented her chronological age. Public acclaim of her work gave her the courage (and the opportunity) to act on her intellectual and emotional needs.

At forty, Edith was auburn-haired, straight-backed, and slim, an elegant rather than beautiful woman, whose facial expression in moments of repose was shadowed by an inner sadness. She spoke in a high, resonant voice, accenting her speech with rapid hand gestures, and had developed a social smile that countered the wary intelligence at play behind her hazel eyes. Her manner radiated a "calm tension," one observer remembered; her gaze was "straightforward, fearless, with the faint reminiscence of pain . . . that attracts and mystifies," her mouth a "challenge, intellectually severe, distinctly dangerous to the inefficient, to the untruthful, to the insincere." Dressed by high-fashion Paris couturiers, Edith wore textured silks and satins in muted browns that enhanced her dusky coloring and layered bodices with eighteenth-century Venetian lace from her mother's collection. She liked hats with feathers and veils, tucked her gloved hands into a mink muff, and carried an umbrella with a carved handle. She wore no makeup, used a floral scent from a London chemist, preferred her hankies small, square, and of the finest, purest Irish linen. She smoked gold-tipped English cigarettes in public but rarely drank wine and ate little.[50]

ON FEBRUARY 20, 1902, *The Valley of Decision* appeared in New York and London. Edith found herself explaining its *donnée* to several friends, including her editor at Scribners, William Crary Brownell, to whom she wrote on Valentine's Day:

> The Valley . . . is an attempt to picture Italy at the time of the break-
> ing up of the small principalities at the end of the 18th century, when
> all the old forms and traditions of court life were still preserved, but
> the immense intellectual and moral movement of the new regime was
> at work beneath the surface of things. . . . I have tried to reflect the
> traditional influences and customs of the day, together with the new
> ideas, in the mind of a cadet of one of the reigning houses, who is sud-
> denly called to succeed to the Dukedom of Pianura, and tries to apply
> the theories of the French encyclopaedists to his small principality.

Her background notes for the book show that she had steeped herself
in the history of Parma and Mantua (the "Pianura" of the novel), and
read memoirs of the period by Lady Mary Wortley Montagu and Mrs.
Pozzi, Casanova, Goldoni, Gozzi, and others. She explained to Sally
Norton that the turbulent phase of social history the novel traces
dwarfs the human histories it contains: "Fulvia and Oddo [sic] are just
little bits of looking-glass in which fragments of the great panorama
are reflected." Charles Eliot Norton, who praised the book, agreed that
its picture of Italy was more vivid than its characters, who were not
"convincingly alive." Eugene Lee-Hamilton (Vernon Lee's brother)
must have pleased Edith when he told her, "It requires a Stendhal or an
Edith Wharton to write a Charterhouse de Parma or a Valley of Decision." The Napoleonic era, with all its power and pageantry, served as a
"pivot" for both novels, but Stendhal's began where Edith's ended,
with the rise of Napoleon.[51]

Issues of freedom and tyranny drive both works, which take diamet-
rically opposed views on these issues. Victim of the tyrannical religious
feudalism of pre-Napoleonic Italy, the child Odo Vansecco, heir to the
throne of Pianura, comes to believe that the Catholic church has per-
verted man's essential humanity, which he believes is based in reason.
Enemies of reform murder Fulvia. When, after many years of exile and
suffering, Odo at last becomes the Duke of Pianura, he enacts reform
by freeing the subjects he has been crowned to rule over, thinking that
they desire freedom and know how to live with it. By this act, he becomes a victim of the very people he has freed. The novel shows
mankind driven by irrational, bestial, untamed forces that must be
suppressed. Authority, rather than freedom, is man's salvation.

A stark skepticism underwrites this richly colored historical pageant.
Although it would be unwise to press the parallels too far, two warring

sides of Edith Wharton appear in the novel's main characters. Like his creator, Odo is profoundly lonely, idealistic, filled with moral conviction and deep compassion. Fulvia Vivaldi, the woman "full of life," whom he desires, is the courageous and committed woman Edith longed to be (and was). Despite an opulent eighteenth-century setting painted with striking precision, revealing the secrets of the servant class and the vanities of aristocratic ladies, the novel offers a modern allegory of unrestrained forces kept in check by denial and repression. Readers found *The Valley of Decision* carefully wrought but lacking in passion. As Aline Gorren summed it up in the *Critic*, the book needed to be "a little more wrong to be a little more right." H. W. Boynton, writing for the *Atlantic Monthly*, observed that Edith Wharton's "art" was "a matter of greater moment to her than her audience"—a very perceptive comment. The London *Athenaeum* thought *The Valley of Decision* "rather congested and heavy and laboured in manner" but showing "considerable thought and careful observation." The *Catholic World* pronounced it "the subtlest assault ever invented in English literature against the Catholic Church. . . . The book is of so squalid a nature that no refined woman would be willing to associate her name even with the condemnation of it." What a compliment to Edith's success![52]

Scribners wanted her to write a sequel to her Italian opus; instead, she began a novel about contemporary New York, a work she had sketched out before starting *The Valley of Decision*. Although she abandoned it after writing some seventy pages, "Disintegration" pointed the way to *The House of Mirth*, the first of her New York society novels. She was already at work on what Henry James grandly called "the *American subject*" that he had "egged" her on to do when he read "The Line of Least Resistance" in 1900. Even then, his advice had come too late (she had already plotted out "Disintegration"), and although his letter about *The Valley* greatly pleased her, Edith found his "liking" the book "astonishing." He closed on the imperative "*Do New York!*"—an injunction that by August 1902 was superfluous.[53]

The Valley of Decision went into a second printing within three weeks of publication. When Sally sent her a glowing review of *The Valley* from the *Boston Evening Transcript*, Edith commented that "the American use of superlatives is so excusable when applied to one's self!" By early April, a "chorus of praise" from Maine to California spread "over the Valley" and department stores were unable to "keep up with the demand" for the book. On September 27, *Publisher's Weekly* announced that the novel was in its "25th 1000," and a one-volume edition of the book appeared the same week. By April 1903, Edith had earned almost $8,000 on the American edition, on a 15 percent royalty. Walter, who had anticipated large sales of the novel, thought the contract terms for advance royalties unfairly disadvantaged her: "It should be $2000 cash *and* royalties beginning with the first volume sold. By his royal advances [Charles Scribner] only loses interest on his money for a few months," he told her in autumn 1901. By spring 1902, she needed the money to defray rising construction costs on The Mount.

The house had become a source of great anxiety for Teddy, whose mental and physical health had noticeably deteriorated. He was so irritable and querulous with Edith that Walter "went for him strong," meaning, probably, that he spoke frankly to Teddy. Despite praise for *The Valley*, Edith was passing through an "arid time."[54]

In late January, Edith had a "sharp attack" of influenza that hit Teddy in early February and threatened pneumonia. On March 1, under doctor's orders to go south, he headed for George Vanderbilt's Biltmore estate in Asheville, North Carolina. Two days after his departure, Edith, alone in New York, experienced a "break-down" caused by a throat infection that produced nervous indigestion and confined her to bed for more than a week, forcing her to cancel a trip to Boston. Once recovered, she boarded a train for a ten-day visit to Washington in March. Teddy joined her, but still feeling unwell, he returned to North Carolina. Friends were beginning to talk about his restlessness and quick temper. Frank Hoppin, architect of The Mount, later recalled Teddy's coming to his office so enraged that he "foamed at the mouth." Desiring a private talk with him, Walter invited him to stop again in Washington on his return home from North Carolina—but Teddy passed by. Returning to New York "made over anew" by her time in Washington, Edith received a letter from Walter: "I had such a good dream of Summer, last night. You were sitting under a tree. Somewhere (it must have been in one of your boscos), and I was stretched out on the grass with my head in your lap, and you were reading aloud."[55]

Since January, Codman had worked on the interiors of The Mount's three main floors, placing door, window, and ceiling moldings, installing the Grinling Gibbons–style plasterwork of fruit, designing oak bookshelves for Edith's library, and fitting fireplace mantels. He wrote his mother that Edith and Teddy were "very dissatisfied" with Hoppin's work, adding, "Their only hope is that I may redeem it." By the end of March, Coddy had "domesticated" them, he said: they "eat out of my hand." Edith was still seeking new clients for him, and he was working up plans for a house she hoped to build on Park Avenue—an idea never realized. On an icy, gale-ridden weekend in mid-April, the countryside wearing its "grimmest look," she and Teddy accompanied him on a quick trip to Lenox to survey his work. Returning to New York in the afternoon, the Pittsfield Express train in which Edith was riding was struck by a switch engine and derailed, and she was thrown to the floor. She was not among the injured passengers, but the accident made newspaper headlines.[56]

Later that month, the Whartons made their long-delayed trip to Boston, visiting the Nortons in Cambridge, the Brooks Adamses in Quincy, and taking tea with Berkeley Updike. "I enjoyed it all," Edith wrote Sally, "as I always do my hurried incursions into Boston. It turns over my ideas." Once back in New York, she began treatments intended to reduce her vulnerability to sore throats and microbial infections, but the "throat-burning" (cauterizing) made her "achy and miserable." With her writing table stacked with requests for manuscripts, she resented such interruptions and remained unconvinced that the procedures would help her. Despite setbacks due to ill health, she published sixteen pieces in literary reviews in 1902, twice the number she had published in 1901. Three of her essays for *Italian Backgrounds* appeared in *Scribner's Magazine*, and Richard Watson Gilder, editor of *Century Magazine*, asked her to do a series on Italian villas and their gardens. Brownell urged her to prepare a volume of her poetry, and in spring, she wrote the title poem, "Artemis to Actaeon." Working in a half-dozen genres (poetry, short story, novella, novel, drama, and travel essays), she was making a reputation as a versatile and flexible writer.[57]

In spring 1902, she added a seventh genre to her repertoire, literary criticism: she reviewed Stephen Phillips's drama *Ulysses* and Leslie Stephen's biography of George Eliot for the *Bookman*. This book may have sparked Edith's interest in biography, especially the lives of women writers; from this moment on, she read voraciously in the genre. Edith's analysis of Eliot's life augured elements of her own future; she wanted to know how the provincial Mary Ann Evans, hampered by the "ethical pedantry" of the "narrowest evangelicalism," became "George Eliot." When Mary Ann Evans left the countryside for London, her "dormant" imagination flowered in the society of Herbert Spencer and George

Henry Lewes and other participants in the "speculative movement" in philosophy. Remarking on the impossibility of saying "what influences are likely to quicken the creative faculty," Edith argued that Eliot "flowered" when she found the milieu she needed—an observation that applies to Edith's own artistic development.

Her essay plumbs a central contradiction of Eliot's life: although her characters shrink from "any personal happiness acquired at the cost of the social organism," Eliot herself purchased happiness at "such cost" in her extramarital companionship with George Lewes, which many critics believed "thwarted" her development. Edith discovered in Eliot's "personal situation" an explanation for why Eliot's "mature" novels were "her worst as well as her greatest." Torn between passion and duty, Eliot (and her characters) transgress the laws of social convention while remaining faithful to inherited duty. They try to "reknit" the "ties which a moment of passion had so nearly severed." A major theme of Edith's writing, this reknitting process in future years became a primary theme of her life. Charles Scribner forecast the future when he called her "the George Eliot of her time."[58]

A HOUSE IN THE COUNTRY

When Edith and Teddy settled once again into the Sands villa in Lenox in late May 1902, Edith was reading Turgenev's *Un Bulgare*. She had borrowed it from Sally Norton, who wanted her to reconsider her opinion that Turgenev was a lesser writer than Tolstoy. His story only confirmed Edith's opinion that he was "unimaginative" and "colourless." Edith countered Sally's assumption that she wanted a novelist to be "intellectual": "I want him to be just what you say Turgeniev is to you—vivid, simple, dramatic, and the rest." She returned to work on her New York society novel, "Disintegration," which Walter urged her to do "off the reel."[59]

The Lenox climate once again had a "tonic effect": "I feel like a new edition, revised and corrected, in Berkeley's [Updike] best type," she wrote Sally in early June. The unpromising spring had burst forth in "cabbages and strawberries," "electric lights and plumbing" at The Mount. During the rainy weeks of this English summer, she worked on her novel "at a desultory pace," surveying the progress of her house and garden in the morning and riding horseback in the afternoon—excursions that left her "stupid with fresh air." She served on a committee chaired by Nannie Wharton that oversaw care of Lenox parks and streets and joined the Lenox Library Association. Teddy, still not in good health, went salmon fishing in Canada in late July, and Sally visited Edith in early August. "I miss you very much," Edith wrote after Sally returned to Ashfield, where the Norton family spent summers in a 1793 farmhouse called The Locusts.[60]

Edith joined Teddy at Newport, where they were guests of Winthrop and Daisy Chanler. They attended the finals of the American tennis championship at the Newport Casino, a scene so brilliant that it gave Edith the sense of being at a "Greek game." A "devout spectator" of tennis, Edith loved its rhythmic grace and the "setting of turf and sky," and regularly attended Tennis Week, one of the high points of the Newport summer season. The main event of the Whartons' visit, however, was the christening of Theodore Chanler, namesake and godson of President Theodore Roosevelt. Edith renewed her friendship with Roosevelt, whose courage and firm convictions she respected in the same degree that he admired her literary work. A week later, he spoke in Lenox on the Anti-Trust Act. Earlier that morning, his carriage was struck by a trolley car on the road between Dalton and Pittsfield; a Secret Service agent was killed and Roosevelt himself thrown onto the road. Bruised and bleeding, he said only a "few quiet words" to the assembled public at Lenox. Impressed by his dignity, Edith wrote Sally that he was not (as the Nortons thought him) a "bronco-buster."[61]

On September 20, Edith and Teddy began moving into their new (and unfinished) house. Many tensions surfaced in the weeks ahead, including money worries and complaints about the construction. The housewarming had been announced for Saturday, September 27, and in the preceding days the "Compleat Housekeeper" took the "upper hand" with Edith. She invited New York friends and Lenox summer society to her party, including William and Emily Vanderbilt Sloane, with whom the Whartons were now on polite terms. Despite fatigue, Edith delighted in her new home, the "delicious warm bloomy weather," and the sylvan country lanes purple with Michaelmas daisies.[62]

Berkshire Resort Topics did not feature an article on The Mount for two years, by which time the Whartons were finally settled and the gardens had begun to mature. Henry James's remark on seeing the estate in summer 1904 provides a snapshot of Edith's mansion: "A delicate French chateau mirrored in a Massachusetts pond." Built on the property's highest point and facing east over Laurel Lake, the three-and-a-half-story white stucco house was a classical blend of French, English, and Italian design. Its commanding east façade recalled Belton House (1684) in Lincolnshire, which Edith and Teddy may have visited on their summer 1900 English tour.

Then, as now, one approached the house along a winding drive designed by Beatrix Jones, bordered by sugar maples and wild woodland expanses of fern and periwinkle. A liveried footman escorted guests through a grottolike entryway to the second-floor reception rooms. These were arranged enfilade along a forty-four-foot vaulted gallery with arched windows designed by Ogden Codman. French windows in the dining room, drawing room, and library opened onto a canopied terrace below which extended to a walkway of linden trees flanked by formal gardens—the flower garden and reflecting pool to the north, a sunken Italian-style "secret garden" on the south. The reception rooms and the primary third-floor bedrooms looked eastward over the gardens, Laurel Lake, and the blue Tyringham Mountains.

House and gardens created a "harmonious symmetry" between public and private spaces that symbolized the central divisions of Edith's life and her need for order and balance. The architectural order of The Mount reveals a psychological principle that Edith some years later shared with Mary Berenson, who was suffering from suicidal depression: "Make one's centre of life inside oneself, not selfishly or excludingly but with a kind of unassailable serenity—to decorate one's inner house so richly that one is content there, glad to welcome anyone who wants to come and stay, but happy all the same in the hours when one is inevitably alone." As a metaphor of living, The Mount represents another of Edith's efforts to redesign the dark loneliness of her inner world: rising upward and outward to sun and air, the house commands the landscape that surrounds it while its inner spaces privilege quiet graciousness.

The oak-paneled library, where Edith entertained literary friends, encouraged reading and conversation. Appointed with low couches, Louis XVI–style chairs, and a *lit de repos*, it housed leather-bound volumes from George Frederic Jones's library, to which Edith had added an extensive collection of works on history, religion, moral philosophy, and architecture. At the two Regency-style writing tables, supplied with inkstands, engraved stationery, and postage stamps, guests could pen notes to their friends. Many visitors to The Mount over the next decade recorded its charms in letters to friends.

Above the library on the north wing was the master bedroom suite, which included Edith's boudoir, where she read, rested, wrote letters, and interviewed her household staff. Painted pale yellow and furnished in simple painted wood, her airy bedroom had views extending over the lake to the mountains, a scene she observed each morning as she sat writing in bed. Teddy's bedroom connected to hers through a dressing room that served as a private passageway. Separated from the row of bedrooms extending south along the third-floor passage, the master suite provided a retreat from guests and claims of the outer world.[63]

The design, construction, and decoration costs of The Mount were substantially less than any of the neighboring estates. The house cost $57,000 ($16,000 over the projected contract price), added to which were the architect's 10 percent fee and Codman's $3,500 interior decoration bill. The fourteen-stall white stucco stable capped by a Flemish-style spire, a replica of the Belton House stables, cost $20,000. Coachman William Parlett lived with his wife, son, and daughters in an apartment above the stables. A two-story gatehouse lodge, residence of the head gardener, Thomas Reynolds, and his family, cost $5,200. Total documented expenses (not counting landscaping and gardens) came to $87,000 ($1,500,000 at today's prices)—a tenth the price paid by Edith's nearest neighbor, George Westinghouse, when in 1893, he built Erskine Park, a nine-hundred-acre estate. In February 1902, Edith took out a $50,000 mortgage with the Berkshire Savings Bank in Lenox, co-signed by Teddy as "husband of said grantor." But creditors complained that the Whartons were slow in paying their bills.[64]

IN EARLY OCTOBER 1902, the Whartons summoned Codman to Lenox, complaining of "terrible mistakes" in the house construction. Just returned from a long European trip, Codman had not yet seen the finished house, but so much had to be "torn out and done over," Edith wrote Daisy Chanler, that she had reluctantly given up hope of inviting guests during the autumn. On stationery of the new four-hundred-room Aspinwall Hotel, Codman recounted the scene to his mother. The "terrible mistakes" were relatively minor and easily solved, although a dispute about hand-painted wall panels in her boudoir would result in a ten-year estrangement between Codman and the Whartons.

Codman's discerning eye focused not on his own work but on the failures of the basic house design. Reading beyond his gleeful snipes at Frank Hoppin's workmanship, one glimpses a truth about design failures in Edith's dream home. Its landscaping planned but not yet fully executed, the rooms inexpertly painted, the marble floors still unpolished, it looked to Codman *"forlorn* beyond *my* powers of description . . . bare and poverty stricken."* In the new setting, the Land's End furniture seemed an odds-and-ends collection, shoved into corners while gas fitters and laborers hastened to complete their work.[65]

His most devastating comments, however, concerned the circular forecourt on the west side of the house: an "utter failure, it looks like a clothes yard and is all out of proportion," he wrote his mother. Today, visitors can confirm the truth of Codman's claim. While other cottagers erred by expanding their mock villas and châteaux beyond human dimensions, Edith scaled down her country house to sustain the balance of structural elements. But in tightening the courtyard dimensions, she broke basic architectural rules. Codman sounded regretful, even a bit guilty about this mistake:

> I think they are somewhat hurt that I have not come up here oftener, as I could have helped them perhaps at times when they got in too deep, over their heads, and I am almost sorry I did not come, *as really it is a pity* to have it turn out so forlorn.

Although his primary target was Hoppin, a rival colleague and sometime friend, he felt Edith and Teddy had overreached themselves, as he explained to his mother: "The Whartons know just enough to be very *unhappy* but not enough to get anything done right, they have always supposed they knew all they knew and all I knew too. *Now they realize they don't."*[66]

THE JOY OF LIVING

Edith escaped The Mount's noisy clutter by traveling to New York for rehearsals of Hermann Sudermann's *Es Lebe das Leben,* which she had translated during late spring and summer at the request of Mrs. Patrick Campbell, who was making her American debut with her English theater company. Seeing her in Sudermann's *Magda* earlier that

year, Edith described Mrs. Campbell to Sally Norton as a "great rant-
ing gawk": "How I hate English and American acting! It's like an ele-
phant walking on the keyboard of a piano." But when they met in
person (probably at one of Minnie Jones's Sunday luncheons), they decided to collaborate on the most recent Sudermann play.

After a series of production delays, *The Joy of Living* opened at the
Garden Theater at Madison Square on Tuesday evening October 23
with Mrs. Campbell starring as Beata, the tragic heroine who commits
suicide to protect her former lover from political scandal. Directed by
Charles Frohman (with whom Edith had worked on *Manon*), it received
excellent reviews, despite subject matter that some reviewers found
morally questionable. One critic called it the "most notable play of the
year." The opening-night audience included Edith, Teddy, and Anna
Bahlmann (Edith's secretary), Minnie and Beatrix Jones, Eliot Gregory,
and most of New York high society.[67]

Mrs. Patrick Campbell's performance drew rave reviews, as did
Edith's translation: her name appeared prominently on the program,
and few critics failed to mention her excellent translation, which rendered Sudermann's German into "admirably simple" English, appropriate to the class of people it represented. Scribners' book version of the
play appeared in time for the opening and sold well for several years.
The Joy of Living ran the full New York season, touring theaters in the
five boroughs. In spring, Mrs. Campbell took it on a Midwest and
West Coast tour; by June 24, 1903, it was playing at the New Theatre
in London's St. Martin's Lane. Edith did not see the London production; she was in Italy, where she and Teddy had been since January.[68]

"Teddy is not well," Edith wrote Sally in early October 1902, "and I
am bothered about him and tired with the house." By mid-December,
things were very serious with him, and he was again at odds with Codman over bills for The Mount. The dispute, which began during the
summer and would rage intermittently over the next four years, resulted in Teddy's writing "strange letters." In November, he threatened to
put the matter of the bill for the boudoir panels into the hands of a
lawyer (Walter Berry). Codman confided his suspicions about Teddy's
mental and physical health in a long letter to Mère Cot that is virtually
a case history:

> Teddy Wharton seems to be losing his mind which makes it very hard
> for his wife. . . . Well he has been queer for a long time getting slowly
> worse I noticed it the day he came into my office two years ago

[1900]. . . . Part of the time he sat with his arms on the table and held his head in his hands. He looks very old and broken and has lost most of his hair on the top of his head.

He brought up a lot of strange accusations such as that I had written letters no gentleman would write to his wife, etc. I thought there must be no quarrel as no one wants to quarrel with a maniac so I merely remarked that the letters I had written would compare favourably with those I had received from him, after telling me that of course I was losing all my business because he had found me so hard to get on with he departed slamming the door.

I was rather prepared for this by what had gone before so was able to keep my cool [,] which was very important: I shall not do anything about it and expect that by end of next week she [Edith] will see that a cheque is sent me for my bill. . . . I should think she would send him to Waverly [McLean Hospital] then instead of going abroad as I hear they intend to do.

He has always been very strange about paying his bills, and the contractors have had great trouble in getting their money on the house. . . . As I know how Hoppin the other architect talks about the Whartons I feel I have said enough. . . . From something that happened the day I was at Lenox and from what Eliot Gregory and Berkeley Updike have said I am sure Mrs. Wharton is much troubled and worried about him.

I suppose she wants to put off shutting him up as long as she can, as he will probably never get any better. . . . [69]

Looking far older than his fifty-two years, Teddy experienced a series of physical problems, from headaches and facial neuralgia to gout and swollen, aching joints. Edith either did not suspect the mental sources of Teddy's suffering or so feared mental illness that she denied it entirely: her letters to friends describe her worry over his physical, rather than mental, condition.

After spending Christmas and New Year's Eve in New York, Edith and Teddy traveled to Boston on Thursday morning, January 1, 1903, to stay with Mrs. Wharton. That evening, Isabella Stewart Gardner presided over the gala opening of Fenway Court, a party to which several weeks earlier she had sent out 150 engraved invitations and arranged a special train carriage for New York guests. Edith eagerly awaited her invitation. When it had not arrived by December 30, she considered telephoning Mrs. Gardner and inviting herself, but then rejected the idea. Legend has it, however, that she attended the party. Sally Norton pasted the famous invitation for "nine o'clock punctually" in her Memory Book and told Bernard Berenson, who had helped Mrs. Gardner gather her magnificent art collection, that Fenway Court was "an expression of genius." Edith would not have agreed. The Italianate excess of its design and decor broke every rule of *The Decoration of Houses.*

The party of the decade, perhaps even of the century, took place on a frigid night. Gentlemen in evening clothes and ladies wrapped in fur and wearing tiaras waited in the cold to be led by Theobaldo Travi, the six-foot-five-inch major domo, up the curving staircase to greet the tiny woman dressed in black standing at attention on the circular balcony. For the event, Mrs. Gardner had draped herself in pearls, a huge ruby at her throat, and two diamonds—the twelve-carat Rajah and twenty-five-carat Light of India—winking in her dyed blond hair. Fifty Boston Symphony musicians, led by conductor William Gericke, gave a concert in the Music Room, after which a light dinner was served in the Dutch Room. No reliable account of the dinner menu exists, but it is said that Edith complained loudly (in French) that the cuisine was about what one would expect at a train station in the French provinces. This same legend records Isabella Gardner, as she bid farewell to Edith, remarking on how nice it was of her to come, but she needn't expect another invitation to eat in this railroad restaurant.[70]

ITALIAN VILLAS

In October 1902, Edith signed a contract with the Century Company for a book of essays on the relation of Italian villas to their gardens, all of them to be published serially in *Century Magazine.* Hoping to complete research for the book in spring 1903, she set herself the formidable task of touring some fifty villas in four months and arranging to have selected ones among them photographed. On January 3, two days after the Fenway Court fête, she and Teddy set out from Boston bound for Genoa.

Despite a "summer sea" along the Spanish coast, the voyage was a long "grey blank." The cold forced them to stop in San Remo, where they sat under palm trees for three weeks, Edith worrying about lost work time and Teddy profiting by the sun and warm air. Arriving in Genoa, Edith expeditiously completed her work, and they then traveled south by train along the coast to Rome—their first visit in eight years. During a month's stay, they drove out almost every day, seeing the Medici palace and Borghese gardens, in addition to villas hidden in the hills above the city. Edith's research opened her eyes to new splendors of the Italian eighteenth century, but it was time-consuming and exhausting, especially since the "acuteness" of her sensations tired her.[71]

Arriving in Florence on March 16, she discovered that in her eagerness to help, Vernon Lee had added a "prodigious" number of Tuscan villas to the original list. Edith quickened her pace, despite fatigue, continuing her investigations on a trip to the Brenta with the Bourgets, and on her travels in Lombardy and the Veneto. An exacting scholar who classified villas by architectural "school," region, and historical period, she verified her findings in old books on gardens and villas and consulted architectural drawings. Hers was to be a systematic, comprehensive study of a subject that heretofore had been treated in the "most amateurish fashion." The work was neither easy nor inexpensive, and hotel and transport costs had considerably increased her expenses. Richard Watson Gilder, editor of *Century Magazine,* agreed to her request for an extra $500 for eight essays; she earned $2,000 for them.[72]

Italian Villas and Their Gardens examines the origins and influence of Renaissance house and garden architecture by analyzing some eighty villas and gardens, many of them in ruins or virtually inaccessible even in Edith's time. Fifty-two sketches, photographs, and colored illustrations by Maxfield Parrish provide visual proof of the guiding thesis of the book: "The garden must be studied in relation to the house, and both in relation to the landscape." Dedicated to Vernon Lee, "who, better than any one else, has understood and interpreted the garden-magic of Italy," the book is a hymn of praise for Italian culture. In its first printings, it was also a sumptuous object, its cover embossed with a gold tablature, each drawing and photograph protected by engraved vellum. Reviews of the book were mixed. Commentators regretted the absence of house and garden plans (which Edith at one time hoped to include) and reserved praise for Maxfield Parrish's drawings at the expense of Edith Wharton's text, which some reviewers found too anecdotal and lacking in historical background. The *TLS* critic found her "almost too impartial in her appreciation."[73]

In June, tired and achy from her work, Edith went for the first time to Salsomaggiore, the mineral spa near Parma, where she took steam inhalations and massage treatments that relieved the sore throats and chest congestion she had suffered since childhood. "Salso," a kind of "Lourdes," would have a regular place on her summer calendar for many years to come. She described it to Brownell, who suffered from a similar nose-throat condition, as a "desperate-looking hole" situated on a "bare volcanic hill"—"as penitential a place as I ever came across outside of Dante's bolgia."[74]

Also taking the cure at Salso was Lady Sybil Cuffe, daughter of an Irish peer and bride of Bayard Cutting, a young friend of Edith's from New York. The Whartons had already spent time with the Cuttings in Florence, driving into the Fiesole hills with them to meet Vernon Lee at afternoon tea. Another day, Lady Sybil had gone antique shopping with Edith on the Via Maggio. She recalled how Edith's eyes, "bright and rapacious as a robin's, darted hither and thither" among the objects on display, then "pounced" on something she wanted. Bargaining with the dealer, her eyes darkened, their lids hooded and hawklike. In a voice heavy with regret, she pointed out flaws in the desired object. If the merchant did not meet her price, she swept out the door and repeated the performance at another shop.[75]

From the start, Edith had her guard up against Sybil, a petite blonde who spoke in a high voice accented by a slight lisp. Out of friendship for Bayard, she was pleasant to Sybil, but dismissed her as a lady of fashion. Two years earlier, when the Cuttings returned from their wedding trip to England, Edith had invited her to tea. Lady Sybil made her way in the winter snow to the narrow Park Avenue house with its high Dutch stoop, her excitement mixed with apprehension. "She was the person I most wished to meet in New York," Lady Sybil later recalled, but she found the house too studied in its perfection, its mistress "alarmingly neat in every detail." The game was lost entirely when Lady Sybil admitted that she had been occupied at balls and large parties in London and had not met any of the literati Edith inquired about.

When Ogden Codman appeared that afternoon, announcing that he had worked out "quite a good plan for the visitors' rooms" at 884, Lady Sybil took her leave, and he escorted her to the front door. Pulling on her overshoes, she heard Edith call out to him in a "warm kind almost humorous voice," the voice of someone Lady Sybil would have liked to know, asking if he thought a little house would allow a Chippendale clock on the hall table, or should it have only a card tray? Years later, after her husband died of tuberculosis, Lady Sybil married in succession two of Edith's friends, Geoffrey Scott and Percy Lubbock. Seeing Sybil as a manipulative sexual aggressor, Edith felt personally threatened and envisioned Sybil making off with every member of her "inner circle" of men friends. In these first years, Edith seemed to find Sybil silly but innocuous, someone she could not take seriously; later, she thought her insidious.[76]

DROUGHT AND DEPRESSION

The first sight of American streets, the first sound of American voices on returning home, reminded Edith of the vast gulf between the New World and the Old. She was "out of sympathy" with everything and heart-stricken at seeing The Mount. It was an "ugly burnt-up June" after nine weeks of drought, the grass parched with its "bald patches" showing, the flowers and vegetables dried and stunted. When a heavy rainstorm broke the drought, The Mount roof sprung a "big leak."

Edith withstood this stress, still feeling "wonderfully well" after her Salso cure, but for the next several months—between writing duties, civic activities, and hostessing—she ran a "hospital" at The Mount. Her first patient was Beatrix, who came to recuperate from an appendectomy. Edith consulted her about the gardens, left in ruin by a gardener who had spent the landscaping money on liquor. After firing the man, Teddy was haunted by the lost money. The Whartons should have been feeling "flush" following the sale of Land's End on June 13 to Eleanor Beeckman, wife of Robert Livingston Beeckman, future governor of Rhode Island. Edith made a $40,000 profit on the transaction, and Mrs. Beeckman took over the balance of the mortgage. Yet Teddy worried obsessively about finances and Edith spoke of fiscal constraints.[77]

By July 4, Beatrix was on her way to Europe with Minnie, Teddy had gone fishing, and Edith hosted Bay and Bessy Lodge, Daisy Chanler, and an exhausted and ill Walter Berry for a weekend party. On his return in early August, Teddy succumbed to nervous collapse: "Accumulated annoyances have taken a monstrous shape in his poor imagination," Edith wrote Sally. His brother, Billy, invited him to his seaside summer home in Nahant, while Edith remained in Lenox trying to finish literary work.[78]

Despite these troubles, Edith had a productive summer and autumn in 1903. *Sanctuary*, her second novella, began its run in the July *Scribner's*, and she read proof on it while composing another villa essay and two short stories. Brownell wanted her collection of Italian travel essays to appear in November, and she prepared a table of contents, although the book did not appear until 1905. They disagreed on a title for the book, finally settling on *Italian Backgrounds*, a title that illustrates its central thesis: "The most interesting Italy is the one in the background, behind the official guide-book Italy." By autumn, she had ten stories ready for a new volume, to be called *The Descent of Man* (a reference to Charles Darwin), all the stories under serial contracts at $500 each. In September, she began writing the novel that would make her career—*The House of Mirth*. Working from notes recorded some years earlier in her *donnée* book under the heading "A Moment's Ornament," she drafted the opening chapters and wrote steadily until December 2, when she and Teddy sailed for England. In spite of her husband's worsening health and the sudden illness in November of her mother-in-law, she wrote well and even took in stride public disinterest in *Sanctuary*. In this story of family corruption, a woman marries a man knowing that he dishonestly inherited his fortune and was indirectly responsible for the death of his late stepbrother's wife. She marries him in order to save his future children from the moral corruption of his actions, later preventing their son from committing a similarly dishonest act. The book received respectful reviews, although several critics found its premise unbelievable. Edith referred to it as "Sank."[79]

December found the Whartons in London, where they met Henry James, who had come up "to town" from his home in Rye. After lunching with Edith, he described her to Minnie Jones as "*really* conversable." It was the start of the most important literary friendship of her life. Twice before, she had been in Henry James's presence—first in 1887, at the Paris home of Edward Boit, a painter whom Teddy's family knew from Boston, and a second time in Venice at the palazzo of Ralph Curtis, another Boston painter friend of the Whartons. On the first occasion, she wore a Doucet gown, hoping to catch Mr. James's eye; the second time, she wore a new hat. Neither time did the great man pay her heed.

Their friendship began by letters and was facilitated by Minnie Jones, a longtime friend of Henry James's. The fastidious and bearded man Edith had first seen some fifteen years earlier had expanded to a "rolling and voluminous outline," his clean-shaven face revealing the "sculptural beauty" of a noble Roman head. At sixty-three, and in the last stage of his artistic apotheosis, he was in gradual retreat from the society life that had so occupied his middle age. Edith, an accomplished, well-traveled woman still enmeshed in society, was just making her entrance onto the international literary scene. The shy bride who had once hoped to win his favor in a Doucet dress was about to become his most famous literary invention—his Fire Bird, his whirling princess, his Angel of Devastation, his "dearest Edith." (She once described him to a friend as the "great master in the use of epithets.") He was her "Master" and her "dear H. J." About to purchase her first motorcar (a secondhand French Panhard of "moderate speed and capacious dimensions"), Edith would introduce Henry to the joys of automobile travel, their adventures recorded in published essays and private letters—her own contribution to the "Edith and Henry" myth.[80]

The first six weeks of their winter trip were so hectic that it was January 1904 before Edith found a moment to recount her experiences. She reported to Sally from the Riviera that Teddy had made an "extraordinary recovery" from his flu and depression: "He now looks back at his condition last summer as a bad dream, and enjoys the sense of bien être as he never did before his illness." His recovery released her pent-up anxiety of the previous six months, leaving her "limp as a rag" in December. She did not realize that his changed attitude was merely a turn from the depressive to the manic cycle of his disease. They toured the Riviera in their motorcar, Teddy at the wheel, and caught glimpses of the "radiant blue" Mediterranean beyond the hillside olive groves and fields of roses. Their spirits soared at these sights: "So many hours daily in the open air are incalculable," Edith concluded.[81]

The delights of motor travel turned to frustration, however, when they found themselves "storm-bound" at Cannes for ten days and then at Monte Carlo, places that did not appeal to Edith. Disconsolate, she sought in vain for interesting companions and new books to read. Passing their days reading newspapers, Edith and Teddy sympathized with Japan in the war with a "false and brutal" Russia, and rejoiced in having missed the most Arctic New England winter since the great storm of 1888. Trying to reach Genoa, they were forced back to Monte Carlo once again by bad weather, Edith by this time feverish with a cold and laryngitis. The stress and insecurity of their travel plans and the "Riviera Climate" caused her "old ailment" of headaches and nervous indigestion to reappear, a condition she blamed on the *désoeuvrement* of hotel life that prevented her from writing regularly and easily, as she did at home.[82]

Two weeks later, after a "glorious chevauchée" (gallop) across southern France from Cannes to Pau, she was rested and getting on well with "The Hermit and the Wild Woman," the title piece of her third short story collection. They drove south along the Spanish border before turning north to Périgueux and Limoges, Bourges, Blois, and on to Paris. Long days in the open air and "the rush of new impressions" had so stupefying an effect that Edith could hardly keep her eyes open in the evening. After several busy days in Paris, they crossed to England, driving up and down the countryside seeing friends, including Henry James. The high point of the English tour occurred on May 5, when they journeyed to Cambridge and saw the "Backs" of the Cam River bathed in a pale yellow sun, lime and beech trees in leaf, and the turf paths sown with daisies. "How much we miss in not having such accumulated beauties to feed on now and then at home!" she exclaimed to Sally.[83]

In London, Edith overcame her instinctive recoil from public gatherings and attended a Literary Fund banquet with 250 other "quill-drivers," a good number of whom praised her books. She felt good about her literary endeavors and was pleased to see copies of the American edition of her latest story collection, *The Descent of Man,* awaiting her at the Hyde Park Hotel. On the vivid red-cloth cover, stamped with an ornate gold design, the name "Edith Wharton" was "writ large enough to jump at the eyes." Dedicated to Edward L. Burlingame, "my first and kindest critic," the volume contained some excellent tales, including a chilling story of the supernatural ("The Lady's Maid's Bell") and a bitter comedy of modern marriage called "The Other Two," as well as two rather cynical stories about the writing trade ("The Descent of Man" and "Expiation"). Commenting that the tales were "exquisitely done," the *Bookman* summed up her strengths as "knowledge of the world, a sure psychology, and a well-bred cynicism." Although some reviewers found the maxims predictable ("Moral defeat is the sum total of every situation," wrote the *Independent*), the book received high praise, especially in England, although more than one reviewer detected "hints of Henry James."[84]

On her return to The Mount in June, Edith discovered in the accumulated mail reviews of *The Descent of Man* sent by Brownell. "I have never before been discouraged by criticism," she wrote him on June 25, "but the continued cry that I am an echo of Mr. James (whose books of the last ten years I can't read, much as I delight in the man), and the assumption that the people I write about are not 'real' because they are not navvies and char women, makes me feel rather hopeless. I write about what I see, what I happen to be nearest to, which is surely better than doing cowboys de chic." Reviewers had forged the link with Henry James in 1899, when *The Greater Inclination* appeared; trying to situate her within the Anglo-American literary scene, they heard "echoes" of James in her situations, sensibilities, and style. As most reviewers did not hold James's writing in high regard, the comparison of her work to his was not praiseworthy; she was said to reproduce his worst faults. (Literary history reversed these claims: James was the master, his work the model, by comparison to which Edith Wharton's writing was a pale shadow.) In 1902, the *Book-Buyer* asked her to review *The Wings of the Dove*, published by Scribners. She declined on the excuse of overwork, adding, "I have always made it a rule not to review novels" (a practice she maintained throughout her life). A week later, she penned a postscript to a letter to Brownell: "Don't ask me what I think of the Wings of the Dove."[85]

THE SEASON

Edith and Teddy had hoped to stay in England until the end of June, but the trip was cut short by the sudden announcement that all their Lenox servants—excluding, of course, Alfred White and Catherine Gross—refused to return for another year. This news upset Edith, who prided herself on fair treatment of her staff. The walkout may have been due to prospective rounds of houseguests (a feature of summer colony life), but it may also have resulted from village talk about the Whartons' unpaid bills. Francis Hoppin, for example, claimed they owed him $1,000, and Codman made no secret of his anger over the unpaid bill for the boudoir panels. White found replacement staff, and arriving home in June, Edith and Teddy prepared for the busy summer season that began on Independence Day. The house party included Daisy Chanler, Bay and Bessy Lodge, Egerton Winthrop, and Walter Berry—who spent several weeks at The Mount.[86]

Having sold the Panhard in England before returning to America, Teddy, on the morning of July 4, ordered a ten horsepower Pope-Hartford touring car "with removable tonneau and brass trimmings" from the Thomas S. Morse agency in Pittsfield. A medium-priced vehicle costing about $1,000, it was the first of three motors Teddy bought over three years, each more powerful than the last—and he purchased it despite his continuing anxieties about money. On July 6, he accompanied Mr. Morse to Hartford, Connecticut, and took delivery of the car. Three weeks later, "The Automobilists of Berkshire" columnist reported that the car was giving Mr. Wharton "the best satisfaction." Edith, Teddy, and Walter made their first long tour on August 10. Teddy hired as chauffeur Charles Cook, a lean and soft-spoken young man from nearby South Lee. The trip to eastern Massachusetts was the first of many road adventures with Cook that Edith described as their "epic *randonnées*." He proved not only an expert driver and mechanic, but became a lifelong friend as well.[87]

At a dinner in Manchester given by the Warder sisters (friends of Walter's from Washington, D.C.), Edith met thirty-three-year-old Gaillard Lapsley, an intimate of Henry James and a man whose talk engaged her. A Harvard graduate and tutor in medieval history at Trinity College, Cambridge, he would become a central figure in her emerging "inner circle." Edith impressed him as a "smartly dressed" woman wearing a pale blue and extremely décolleté dress; the only jarring element in her ensemble was a "shabby thumbstall" tied on her right hand, evidence of some unnamed injury. Her face was "worn and looked tired in repose," and her manner had a "metallic radiance" matched by a "like quality in her voice." Lapsley's recollection captures an image of a woman trying to rise above stress and fatigue. Headaches and vision problems that summer caused Edith to see printed text as wavy lines, and a few days after the Manchester dinner, she was rushed to a Boston oculist, who treated her eyes with belladonna, a muscle relaxant.[88]

In September 1904, family matters occupied Edith. Her godfather, Frederic Rhinelander, died suddenly while on holiday in Stockbridge, Massachusetts. Outfitting herself in the "black raiment" of mourning, she rescheduled dinners and houseguests. But a surprise cable from her brother Harry announcing his imminent arrival from Paris brought her back into the social whirl. This trip, his first return to America since leaving in 1896, gave her great pleasure. She proudly showed him the estate and escorted him on country drives. After several days at The

Mount, he was so taken with the Berkshires that he considered buying an adjoining property—a plan that came to nothing.[89]

Harry had no sooner departed than Henry James arrived at The Mount on October 15 for a stay of nearly two weeks. This was his first trip to America in twenty years, and he covered its length and breadth, from Massachusetts to Florida and California, during a ten-month tour in which he spoke to crowded lecture halls on "The Lesson of Balzac." He discovered at The Mount a household where "every comfort prevails." Urging his friend Howard Sturgis to join the group, he described Edith and Teddy as "kindness and hospitality incarnate." Sturgis, who was visiting his Boston relatives (Ogden Codman among them), accepted the invitation, and Walter Berry came up from Washington for his second stay of the season. On gentle Indian summer afternoons, Edith and Henry (not yet on a first-name basis) motored about the countryside in the Pope-Hartford. Swathed in protective veils, she sat straight-backed next to the goggled and touring-capped James, who sometimes catnapped as the "loud-puffing" motor took the curves of the Berkshire hills at what seemed breakneck speed. In the evenings, the group gathered in the library and James read poetry in his deep, sonorous voice—Matthew Arnold, Robert Browning, Baudelaire, and Leconte de Lisle. On warm nights, they sat on the east terrace, a shower of stars overhead, their laughter echoing across Laurel Lake.[90]

Did Edith and Henry discuss her work or his in their days and nights together? Writing from his brother's house in Cambridge in mid-November, he alluded to her "morning's work [which] will have been spreading its wings." After a period of "black despair," Edith now reported to Brownell that she was "fatuously pleased with 'The House of Mirth.'" She had written short stories and travel essays in the past two years but had been unable to complete a book-length work. Having abandoned "Distintegration" in autumn 1902, she had begun *The House of Mirth* in autumn 1903, then dropped it during her Europe trip. Now, after nearly a year's break, she had again taken it up. In the guest room next to Teddy's bedroom, its high window overlooking the lake, James struggled with the revisions and prefaces to the Scribners deluxe-bound "New York" edition of his works. He had sent Edith an advance copy of the two-volume *The Golden Bowl*, his latest novel, which she found hard to praise. It would have had "real greatness," she told Sally, "if only it had been written with the simplicity and straight forwardness of his early style, which was capable of mastering every shade of thought and emotion." She despaired of the "sterile word patterns" of his late style.[91]

A "glacial brilliant" cold settled over Lenox soon after James's departure, the air still and silent. Edith wrote *"very* hard" every morning. The serialized version of *The House of Mirth* was due to begin in the January *Scribner's*; correcting proof copy of the first chapters, she hurried to finish writing the final portions of the book. She interrupted her work in early December to close The Mount and return to 882–884 Park Avenue, where she and Teddy had not been for two years. The city was "execrable," Edith declared. Trying in vain to keep abreast of the "rising tide of notes, cards and such" that the winter social season occasioned, she longed for the country silence of Lenox.

Henry James was once again her guest, arriving in a snowstorm on January 2. He traveled by hansom cab the sixty blocks from Minnie Jones's town house on East Eleventh Street, near his childhood Washington Square neighborhood. This was the first of two visits he made to Edith in 1905. When he joined her at The Mount in late June, just before returning to England, they drove to Ashfield for a reunion with his old friend Charles Eliot Norton, making the eighty-mile round-trip journey in yet another of Teddy's new motors.[92]

ONCE THE WINTER snows melted in spring 1905, Teddy went to fish and golf at George Vanderbilt's Biltmore estate in Asheville, North Carolina. Edith planned to follow him, but her trip would be delayed until Christmas, when, under Ionian blue skies, she warmed herself in the sun and marveled at the "sheets of fruited ivy" hanging over terrace walls. The jasmine, honeysuckle, and laurel formed a green backdrop to a Christmas fête for 350 people who lived and worked on the estate. On her way to Biltmore in March 1905, however, Edith got no farther than Washington, where she visited her cousin, Mrs. Hamilton Webster. (The real purpose of her trip may have been to spend time with Walter.) She fell ill with flu and a recurrence of her throat and nose trouble, which turned to bronchial asthma. Teddy cut short his fishing vacation to accompany her to New York. Within days of returning to 882–884 Park Avenue, they had arranged for a quick trip to Italy so that Edith could take steam inhalations at Salsomaggiore.[93]

They sailed for Cherbourg on April 6. In Paris on that day, Frederic

Jones attended the funeral of his second wife, Elsie. A few days later, her body was interred in the family vault at Cannes. Edith was probably unaware of these events until she saw her brother Harry in Paris. Having refused to recognize Elsie Jones in life, she would not have attended the funeral or adopted formal mourning, even if Frederic had informed her of the situation. He fell heir to his wife's fortune and soon after her death lost all of it in bad investments, having already gone through more than $250,000 in Rhinelander Jones inheritances.

Literary rather than family matters headed Edith's agenda in late spring 1905, however. Before leaving New York, she met with Charles Scribner about a serial contract for her next novel, hoping to use the expressed interest of *Harper's* and *Century Magazine*, the two major competitors to *Scribner's Magazine*, to increase her literary earnings. Scribners had paid $7,500 for serial rights to *The House of Mirth* and 15 percent royalties on the book contract, with no advance against royalties. Amounting to some $75,000 today, this was a generous payment. Edith thought she could do better elsewhere, however, and her hint of a "probable future" at *Harper's* or *Century* made Charles Scribner nervous. She asked for an $8,000 advance on her new novel and a 20 percent royalty. These terms were based on the "incipient popularity of The House of Mirth," which had attracted a huge reading audience since beginning its run in the January *Scribner's Magazine*. Negotiations on the new book continued by letter over several weeks. In the end, Charles Scribner agreed to pay $10,000 in serial rights and increase Edith's royalty to 20 percent after sales of 10,000 copies. When *The Fruit of the Tree* began its serial run in January 1907, Edith Wharton's literary worth had far outdistanced the terms of her contract.[94]

Book Two

W

CHOICES

Chapter 4

W

AWAKENINGS

IN JULY 1904, AMIDST A BUSY SEASON AT THE MOUNT AND suffering eye problems from overwork, Edith wrote Edward Burlingame saying she would probably not complete *The House of Mirth* in time for the *Scribner's Magazine* deadline. This was disturbing news to an editor who had "counted heavily" on the work, reserving space for an eleven-month run. He decided to risk beginning the serial in January 1905, as planned, even though she had not finished the book. She would later say that writing *The House of Mirth* under pressure of editors' deadlines and printers' schedules taught her the "discipline of the daily task" and transformed her from a "drifting amateur into a professional" writer. This remark seems disingenuous: in the previous eight years, she had produced nine books, two of which (the novellas *Touchstone* and *Sanctuary*) appeared in *Scribner's Magazine*. But preparing a long work for the magazine was a far greater challenge. Serialization would be the crucible of Edith Wharton's art. Over a lifetime, it brought her vast sums of money, but its special requirements took a toll on her physical health and, some have said, on the quality of her fiction. It was a sign of things to come when an impatient readership ("fickle and featherheaded," in her opinion) lined up at newsstands across America in spring and summer 1905, eager to know more about Lily Bart's perilous adventures in high society.[1]

A daughter of New York society transformed by late-nineteenth-century industrial wealth, Lily Bart descended from prudent Anglo-Dutch settlers. Her ancestors were less wealthy than Edith Wharton's forebears, however; her father bankrupted himself while trying to further his wife's desire for a fashionable life. Mr. Bart died relatively young, and his penniless widow followed soon after. From her deathbed, Mrs. Bart urged her daughter to trade on her beauty. Emerging from this background of thwarted desires and early death, Lily Bart makes her way alone in a pleasure-seeking and self-interested environment. The novel charts her slow and seemingly inevitable descent from the ranks of the privileged, where she had hoped to make a good marriage, to a solitary life on the economic and social margins. She is the instrument of Edith Wharton's attack on a grasping, irresponsible, and morally corrupt upper class. At the close of the novel, Lily Bart is dead, her suicide (if, indeed, she died on purpose) having electrified a reading public that wanted Lawrence Selden to propose marriage to her, and thus save her from the horrors of penury and spinsterhood.

The somber twist of fate in the novel's final chapters guaranteed a bestseller. By October 28, two weeks after book publication, the first printing of forty thousand copies and a second printing of twenty thousand had sold out. A third edition of twenty thousand more copies was, in the parlance of the publishing trade, "almost exhausted." Edith recorded in her diary on October 28: "H. of M. bestselling book in New York." Three days later, she wrote Charles Scribner asking that the firm not give out her address: "I am so persecuted by letters since the appearance of this book." By year's end, 140,000 books had been printed, and in early 1906, the book climbed to the top of the bestseller list, surpassing Upton Sinclair's *Jungle* and its horrifying exposé of the Chicago meat-packing industry.[2]

Meanwhile, debate about the novel's meaning raged in the pages of newspapers and literary reviews. Readers and critics recognized the moral thrust of *The House of Mirth*, its title taken from Ecclesiastes: "The heart of the wise is in the house of mourning; but the heart of fools is in the house of mirth." They had three questions about its meaning. Was New York society as corrupt and corrupting as the novel portrayed it to be? If so, was a corrupt society a suitable subject for art? Need Lily Bart die for the novel to make its moral point? Edith had her own firmly fixed opinions on these issues, which she conveyed to Dr.

Morgan Dix, the man who had performed her marriage service twenty years earlier. He had written her to say, "This book places you at the head of the living novelists of our country or of the English-writing authors of our day. It is a terrible but just arraignment of the social misconduct which begins in folly and ends in moral and spiritual death." She responded that good fiction must treat the "relation of the eternal laws. . . . *No* novel worth anything can be anything but a novel `with a purpose,' and if anyone who cared for the moral issue did not see in my work that *I* care for it, I should have no one to blame but myself—or at least my inadequate means of rendering my effects." New wealth posed a dangerous threat to American society, she claimed, because it came "without inherited obligations, or any traditional sense of solidarity between the classes."[3]

The *New York Times* banner headline for Sunday, October 15, 1905, proclaimed, "New York Society Held Up to Scorn in Three New Books." (The other two were an anonymously written novel, *Our Best Society*, and a collection of nonfiction essays by David Graham Phillips entitled *The Reign of Gilt*.) By late November, a dispute focusing on the accuracy of Edith Wharton's portrait of high society burst forth in the *New York Times Saturday Review of Books* between two readers who identified themselves as "Lenox" and "Newport." "Newport" thought the book unjustly characterized the social scene. "Lenox" responded that "Newport" refused to recognize the truthful, if unflattering, portrait of society, and failed to see the book's "entire scheme and purposes." Most critics took the "Lenox" position, acknowledging Edith Wharton's profound knowledge of the social scene she examined, and praising the high quality of her writing.[4]

British reviewers protested less than Americans this grim picture of high society. One paper praised her courage in not shrinking from "the appalling facts of life" and another for registering "to the last degree of delicacy the jumble of crudity and over-civilization which she finds in New York to-day." Called both a realist and a satirist, she was praised for "searching into the causes of things." The *Spectator*, the prestigious English journal founded by Joseph Addison and Sir Richard Steele in the eighteenth century, lauded the skill with which she carried out the inevitable logic of the story. Her only error was a "too elaborate . . . ingenuity in contriving that every indiscretion, however venial, should ultimately recoil on her heroine with accumulated force." She would answer this charge thirty years later in *A Backward Glance*: "A frivolous society can acquire dramatic significance *only through what its frivolity destroys*. Its tragic implication lies in its power of debasing people and ideals."[5]

There was immediate interest in translating *The House of Mirth* into French, and Edith sought Paul Bourget's help. He recommended twenty-five-year-old Charles du Bos, "a very clever and agreeable" Frenchman. Long before it appeared in translation, the novel found an eager readership in the Faubourg St. Germain. At a tea given for her in April 1906 by the Bourgets, Edith was "amused" to discover that everyone was interested in the fate of *"cette pauvre Lily."* That spring trip to Paris was her first real taste of the intellectual and social pleasures available behind the shuttered gates of the old Faubourg, the setting of her future life. And it was the literary success of "poor" Lily Bart that underwrote Edith's richly cultured new life.[6]

She and Teddy had planned to spend the winter and spring of 1906 in Paris, residing in the Faubourg apartment of their friend George Vanderbilt, but the departure from New York was delayed first by their work for the New York Society for the Prevention of Cruelty to Animals and later by Edith's illness. Teddy was an officer of the SPCA, and Edith served on a five-member committee that created its new bylaws. In a rare act of public speaking, she addressed the membership, calling for a legislative investigation of the organization—her remarks quoted in the February 19, 1906, *New York Times*. Although Edith and Teddy believed that animals have a "natural right to a natural death," they recently had put down their fifteen-year-old dog, Miza, who was ill and suffering. At The Mount, Miza lies beneath a tree, her headstone one of four; the others commemorate Mimi (January 1902), Toto (November 18, 1904), and Jules (1907). Miza was survived by Mitou and Nicette, lapdogs who lived to great ages.

Edith's civic work and social commitments "paralyzed" her work on two literary projects. In November 1905, she had begun writing *The Fruit of the Tree*, and Burlingame had scheduled it for January 1907 serialization. She was also collaborating with popular New York playwright Clyde Fitch on a dramatic adaptation of *The House of Mirth*: he created the scenario, and she wrote the dialogue. Longing to escape the city, she managed to take one long weekend at The Mount, but returned to New York ill with flu and bronchitis. Her enforced "leisure" gave her the opportunity to read. She chose new works by European authors: a biography of St. Francis of Assisi, a history of the Roman

Catholic papacy, a translation into German of Aeschylus's *Oresteia* by scholar Wilamowitz-Moellendorff, and S. H. Butcher's *Aspects of Greek Genius*. The only American on her list was William Crary Brownell, who was writing a critical history of American literature. His recently published essay on James Fenimore Cooper, although a "tour de force," did not change Edith's negative opinion of Cooper's work. Praising his insights, she often did not share his enthusiasms (she thought Hawthorne overrated and he did not like Whitman), although she applauded his praise for Emerson.[7]

When Edith and Teddy finally left for Paris in mid-March, she went directly from her sickbed to the steamer and a stormy, difficult crossing. They stayed with Harry Jones, now installed in a town house on the place des Etats Unis on the Right Bank, and once Edith was fully recovered from the flu and the difficult voyage, she had a very social time in Paris, spending her evenings at the theater. (It was not very good, she admitted, especially compared to the Russian production of Henrik Ibsen's *Ghosts* she had seen in New York in January.) Bourget introduced her to new friends, the most important of whom were Rosa de Fitz-James, hostess of a famous Faubourg salon of writers and aristocrats, and the countess Anna de Noailles, a "little exotic bird," whose poetry moved Edith deeply. A six-week trip to England followed the Paris interval and included a motorcar "giro" with Henry James into Devonshire and Somersetshire. Bad weather cut short a trip that James described to his brother William as a "trying" experience, from which he "impatiently and prematurely and gleefully returned today"—May 4, 1906. Crossing the Channel to France, Edith and Teddy motored with Harry Jones for two weeks in the Clermont-Ferrand region and then made their first visit to George Sand's home, Nohant.[8]

Back in New York in mid-June, Edith began writing three "motor-flight" articles on France that appeared in the *Atlantic Monthly* between December 1906 and February 1907. She also corrected proofs on her novella *Madame de Treymes*, a story of tensions between the values of new America and old Faubourg society, which began its serial run in the August *Scribner's*. Readers responded enthusiastically to this story of thwarted love; its popularity, Edith remarked to Burlingame, was "breaking the "record" of her "short-story successes"—an event she credited to the "greater glory of Scribner's." Responding to a sales report showing that *The House of Mirth* had sold 127,709 copies, she expressed surprise that its February–August 1906 sales had not kept pace with autumn 1905 sales. To date, she had earned almost $34,000 in book royalties, added to the $10,000 Scribners paid her for serial rights and royalty advances. These earnings amounted to more than three times the money William Dean Howells, a venerated literary figure twenty-five years her senior, earned in a year.[9]

Hoping to surpass these sales figures with her next book, Edith dispatched to Burlingame the early chapters of her (as yet) "nameless novel." First conceived in 1904 as a play, she had called it "Shadow of a Doubt." That title seemed too theatrical for a novel, but she could not find an alternative. In late July, while spending a day in Tuxedo Park with the Winthrop Chanlers, a friend (probably Daisy) suggested "The Fruit of the Tree," a biblical reference.

The Fruit of the Tree is one of Edith Wharton's most ambitious literary works, a novel that explores the themes of industrial reform, the woman question, and the ethics of euthanasia through intersecting stories. Justine Brent, the tragic heroine, is a professional nurse who attends her childhood friend Bessy Westmore, a rich mill owner, when Bessy is left paralyzed after a fall from a horse. Her suffering relieved only by drugs, she begs Justine to release her; after debating the moral issues, Justine administers a lethal dose of morphine. Edith drew on the experiences of two women friends in Lenox to create Bessy's life-and-death struggle: Ethel Cram (former owner of Land's End in Newport) had been left comatose after a carriage accident in July 1905; Mrs. Hartmann Kuhn, who suffered from a painful illness (probably cancer), and eventually took her own life—a decision Edith supported. "If I had morphia in hand, as she has," Edith wrote Sally Norton in July 1908, "how quickly I'd cut the knot!"

After Bessy dies, Justine falls in love with her widowed husband, John Amherst, a man whose family background crosses social classes— his mother descending from an old family, his father a working man. Inheriting the cotton mill, he sets out with Justine to reform conditions for the workers. Their happiness crumbles when the "shadow of a doubt" about Bessy's death is revealed and Justine narrowly escapes being tried for murder.

Originally, this was to have been Justine's story. Edith wrote in her diary on Saturday, November 4, 1905: "Began *Justine Brent*." By November 25, she had written twenty thousand words. Work on the novel interrupted by her winter European travels, she began a new story, *Madame de Treymes*, wrote several motor-flight essays, and on returning to Lenox in spring, she began collaborating with Clyde Fitch on the stage adaptation of *The House of Mirth*. As summer turned to autumn in 1906 and she rushed to meet the January serial deadline for *Fruit of the Tree*, Edith described herself as an "anxious Parent," and she hovered over her text as if it were an ill child.[10]

In August, she and Clyde Fitch completed their script of *The House of Mirth*, and the play went into rehearsal. On September 14, they were in Detroit for the opening, Edith accompanied by Teddy and Walter Berry. An enthusiastic Opera House audience gave Fay Davis, a "simply perfect" Lily Bart, in Edith's opinion, fourteen curtain calls. Seeing that the last act needed revision, the playwrights rewrote it on the spot, and several nights later, Fitch reported that the play was going "splendidly." Its success was "assured," Edith thought. But the New York opening at the Savoy Theater on October 22 fell far short of success. The *New York Times* called it "doleful," and the *New York Herald* declared the play "not a success." Edith was disappointed, far more so than she let on to friends, and she was especially saddened on behalf of the actors.

She had refused to write a happy ending to accommodate the tastes of American theatergoers: Lily Bart must die. The play's failure in New York confirmed her doubt that a drama with a "sad ending" and "negative hero" could *"ever* get a hearing from an American audience"—literary realism, she believed, was not adaptable to the stage. Clyde Fitch supported this opinion, commenting that a "negative story" went against "the rules of the stage." They had agreed from the beginning, however, to try "an unusual experiment in playmaking," and with their producer, Charles Frohman, they were ready to "stand by the consequences"—which were predictable. As William Dean Howells once remarked to Edith about her play, the American public desires "a tragedy with a happy ending."[11]

A story recounted in the *Detroit Post* amusingly underwrote Howells's point. One afternoon in autumn 1905, just after *The House of Mirth* appeared in book form, Edith Wharton took a walk in Lenox. She met a friend whose face was "unaccountably sad" and who came up to her "full of virtuous indignation." "I have just finished *The House of Mirth*," the woman said. "It was bad enough that you had the heart to kill Lily. But here you are, shamelessly parading the streets in a red hat!"[12]

Edith had little time to brood over the failure of her play, as she was working at "white heat" to finish *The Fruit of the Tree*. She postponed social engagements and turned over all business and household responsibilities to Anna Bahlmann and Catherine Gross. When Burlingame read the completed novel in December, he felt the last chapters needed work and asked her to dramatize Justine Brent's emotions more fully. Edith's answer to his request shed light on her creative methods: "I am always afraid of my habit of *over-psychologizing*, and this has perhaps led me to the opposite extreme of not developing Justine's feelings enough after her marriage." While in Paris during the first months of 1907, she revised the last sections of the book, which began in *Scribner's Magazine* in January.[13]

EDITH BOARDED THE Hamburg-Amerika line ship bound for Le Havre on January 4 on the verge of collapse. Having once again pushed herself to the limit of her energy, she was "rest-curing" in the "demoralizing comfort" of a snug boudoir that at night converted into Teddy's bedroom. It was hung in vieux-rose silk and appointed with a Louis XVI writing desk on which sat a telephone (that never rang); a fat red azalea bloomed on a center table. The Whartons were traveling expansively—a half-dozen servants, two dogs, and a secondhand Panhard touring car. The cost of their suite for the eight-day voyage amounted to the cost of a Paris Faubourg apartment for the spring season—about $300, or $4,500 at today's rates. Millionaire industrialists reserved steamer accommodations at four to five times this cost, but Edith paid for her luxuries with hard-earned literary royalties. After several days of floating in luxury on an unseasonably warm sea, she exclaimed to Sally: "Rested at last!"[14]

Once in Paris, she filled her days with activities. By mid-February, she had corrected proof on the early chapters of *The Fruit of the Tree* and was making good progress on revisions of its final chapters. Two mornings a week she worked with a tutor to improve her idiomatic French. She continued her study of medieval French culture by reading Picaret's *Histoire des Philosophies Médiévales* and reread (in Italian) the "Paradiso" section of Dante's *Divine Comedy* in preparation for a series of lectures by a Sorbonne professor held at the Faubourg home of her American friend Matilda Gay. Edith filled her evenings with theater performances, feasting her eye on the elaborate scenery and sumptuous costumes while listening attentively to the quick repartee of stage

French. Shakespeare's *Julius Caesar*, performed in a mixed blank verse and prose translation, "fatigued and worried" her ear. Divested of its poetry, it seemed to her one of his least dramatically satisfactory plays. But *"any* Shakespeare on the stage is thrilling," she wrote Sally.[15]

The centerpiece of her gay *vie parisienne* was the 1750 town house at 58 rue de Varenne, sublet from George Vanderbilt. Built by a noble lord on land that had once been a game preserve, this *hôtel particulier* had the spaciousness and grace of a country estate. The Vanderbilt apartment occupied about two thousand square feet of the *piano nobile* level (one floor up from the street) and was furnished in the impeccable taste of an art connoisseur. Antique Chinese porcelains, bronzes, and period furniture were set against a background of original *boiseries*; overlaying the polished oak drawing room floor was the "Dear old Aubusson carpet" soon to be memorialized by James in letters to friends in England and America. Surrounded by the "stored beauty and tradition and amenity" of the aristocratic Faubourg St. Germain, Edith passed her forty-fifth birthday, "peacefully established" on the street that would become her future home.[16] By mid-February, she was bedridden with flu so severe that she had lost the hearing in one ear.

Sending off the proof copy of *The Fruit of the Tree*, she received by return mail two copies of her novella *Madame de Treymes*, scheduled to appear in New York on March 2. This story reveals the dark underside of old Faubourg life and satirizes the naïveté of Americans hoping to break through its class prejudices and papal customs. American Fanny Frisbee has been married for some years to the philandering Marquis de Malrive (whose name means "evil shore"), by whom she has a son. Once "dashing" and vibrant, Fanny has been "toned down" by her years among European aristocracy and forced to shape herself to their refined (and repressive) modes of living. Estranged from her husband, she has fallen in love with John Durham, a friend of her New York years whom she hopes to marry. Longing to return to "simple" American life, she fears the marquis (a Roman Catholic) will not agree to a divorce. A further concern is the fate of her son, heir to his father's title and fortune. Her future, the drama reveals, is mortgaged to her son's place in old French society.

The key figure of the story is the marquis's sister, Madame de Treymes, an adulterous woman involved with a playboy gambler who is ruining her financially. Although duped by her affections, Madame de Treymes has a wary and astute intelligence. When she was introduced to John Durham at a tea attended by his sister and mother, "her narrowed gaze like a knife [slit] open the unsuspicious personalities about her." An inscrutable woman, Madame de Treymes may either be duplicitous and self-serving like her brother, or, in her quiet sensibilities, a person of great worth. She shows her true colors by revealing to Durham the secret plan of the Malrive family. They will agree to the divorce, she confesses, but once Fanny has remarried, they will assert their rights to custody of her son in order to keep the boy within the fold of aristocratic religious, political, and class values. The story ends as Durham prepares to tell Fanny of the impossible choice that faces her—to choose between her lover and her son.

Generally speaking, the novella was well received, although critical opinion divided between those who praised its realism and those who thought it heartless—too analytic and discriminating. Mary Moss, who two years earlier had declared that Lily Bart could "only inspire interest and curiosity," pronounced *Madame de Treymes* "entirely above criticism" and lauded its "unimpeachable distinction of style." The *Nation* and the *North American Review* found *Madame de Treymes* realistic and believable, deftly sketched by "eliminations and reserves." The powerful institution of the French family "has never been better treated by a foreign pen," declared the *Spectator*. Reviewers detected Edith's debt to Henry James's 1876 novel *The American*, but the prestigious London *Athenaeum* thought her study the more subtle of these two works, as it revealed not only the self-enclosure of European life but exposed diseased and malign traditions that deny human freedom.

James himself thought the story "beautifully done . . . full of felicities and achieved values and pictures," but he warned Edith not to go too far with the "Franco-American" subject: "The real field of your extension is *here*"—that is, in New York. The Euro-American subject was, in his experience, as dangerous as it was seductive. The writer risked loss of literary identity and loss of readership. Ever more despairing of his own achievements, he associated his failures with his inability to live in America and the impossibility of fully embracing Europe. Edith classed him as one of the "wretched exotics"—Americans "produced in a European glass-house, the most déplacé and useless class on earth!" She counted herself among this group, too.[17]

She could no more turn away from the Franco-American subject in her writing (and in her life) than James could abandon his themes. As a glimpse of things to come in Edith Wharton's literary repertoire, *Madame de Treymes* is immensely revealing. Fanny de Malrive and John

Durham forecast Anna Leath and George Darrow, the thwarted lovers of *The Reef* (1912), who are themselves versions of Edith Wharton and her lover, Morton Fullerton. The Malrive family also prefigures the de Chelles in *The Custom of the Country* (1913), one of several works in which a child exemplifies the human cost of separation and divorce. Ellen Olenska in *The Age of Innocence* (1920), perhaps Edith's most brilliant portrait of expatriated womanhood, draws on elements of Madame de Treymes and Fanny de Malrive. Among these works, only *The Reef*, which James called Racinian in its unity and intensity, is as bitter as *Madame de Treymes* and as categorical in its denunciation of cultural traditions that Edith elsewhere praised, that nourished her creativity, and that ultimately pulled her out of her American roots. Casting a "long shaft of light . . . down the dark windings" of European codes and character, the story announced new and major themes of her writing.[18]

Edith had for some time been evaluating her relationship to Europe, weighing the moral and practical considerations of living permanently abroad. Although she sought the "mental refreshment" only Europe could give her (as she explained to Sally Norton), she thought expatriation would frustrate the impulse to civic duty, the "restless desire to better things about one": "If one lived in another country, [one would feel] the alien's inability to take part, help on, assert one's self for good. . . . The *social action* on the community would be impossible." Defining civic responsibility as a desire for social improvement, Edith's remarks were made in the context of her work in reforming the New York SPCA. She had no social improvement or political agenda and did not spend her time "doing good"; yet, her sense of responsible citizenship implicitly repudiated the narrow, self-serving attitudes of her parents and their friends. The ethical and moral considerations of expatriation formed a backdrop to Edith's fiction in the prewar years, judged in the same terms as issues of divorce, extramarital sexuality, and family loyalty.[19]

A SEASON FOR TRAVEL

Grown stout and slow-moving in his mid-sixties, James had been bracing himself "all appreciatively" for his first pilgrimage in many years to the "formidable Paris." The glittering city of light was challenge enough for him, but he most feared the pace of life *chez* Wharton, "the wild, the almost incoherent freedoms and restlessnesses of Wealth." On arrival, he succumbed to the influenza that had swept across Paris and plagued the Wharton household all winter. Teddy was still sick, and James, too, took to bed for a week. No sooner was he on his feet than Edith—eager to show him off—invited all the titled friends she could find to meet him. Many were "Fanny Frisbees," childhood friends who had married European nobility; most charming of all was Rosa de Fitz-James, a dark-eyed, rotund Viennese Jewess who charmed James. On March 20, Edith whisked him off on "india rubber wings" for a whirl-wind, three-week journey to Burgundy, Provence, the Basses-Pyrénées, and the Rhône Valley. Left breathless, nearly speechless, in its wake, he described the motor-flight to Howard Sturgis as "almost the time of my life."[20]

The trip's center of emotional gravity was a visit to George Sand's home in the Berry region southwest of Paris, where Edith and Teddy visited in May 1906. Receiving Edith's postcard from Nohant, James had fallen into a "disabled state." All "these (motorless) years," he wrote her, he had wanted to see the Sand shrine, remembering how in his youth he had heard Flaubert, Gautier, and Maupassant tell of their trips to Nohant by train and diligence. Should Edith decide to make a second visit, he would be a most willing passenger in her "Vehicle of Passion." Taking this hint, she arranged a second journey especially for him, an adventure recounted in the final four essays of *A Motor-Flight Through France*.[21]

"The motor-car has restored the romance of travel," she wrote, and certainly libidinal energy sped the travelers on their way on this occasion. It was the "blandest of late March mornings, all April in the air, and the Seine fringing itself with a mist of yellowish willows." The servants had been dispatched by train with the luggage. Teddy sat next to chauffeur Charles Cook in the front seat, James and Edith in the backseat, she with the *Guide Continental* in hand. The châteaux and cathedrals of Versailles, Rambouillet, Chartres, and Valençay cast "great loops of persuasion" on the road that led them into the Loire Valley.

Musing on the effects achieved by French frugality and compactness, Edith observed subtle variations in landscape and architecture, her novelist's eye assessing the physiognomy of French faces glimpsed in doorways as the motorcar swept through villages. By late afternoon, the sunset "burnished the great curves of the Loire" and gave a "plum-coloured bloom" to the slate-roofed houses of Blois. They arrived at day's end in Châteauroux, the northern gate of Sand country (and a profoundly disappointing town), having traveled almost 150 miles from Paris. At an average rate of fifteen miles an hour, and allowing time for a two-hour French lunch in Chartres, the day's drive had taken twelve hours. They would keep up this pace for three more weeks, motor travel with Edith requiring large measures of fortitude.[22]

After a night at the provincial Hôtel Sainte Catherine, they arrived at Nohant. James was lured by the scenes of "piggery" that its gray stones had witnessed during the early stormy years of Sand's rebellion against convention. In his private mythology, she was the "mighty and marvelous George," grotesque in her appetites and excesses of suffering and desire. It was the swashbuckling, booted, and cigar-smoking Sand of legend whom James adored, a tragicomic Circe presiding over the "greasiness and smelliness" of Nohant. Standing in the garden, his gaze following a line of shuttered windows, he searched in vain for signs of the "dark, disordered period" of her early life: "And in which of those rooms, I wonder, did George herself sleep?" he asked. Then, with a twinkling side glance at Edith, "Though in which, indeed, in which indeed, my dear, did she not?"[23]

For Edith, Nohant was the "image of aristocratic well-being," a "sober edifice conscious of its place in the social scale." She stood pondering the central mysteries of womanhood. How had the wild-hearted young Aurore Dupin become the timid and dutiful Mme Dudevant? By what force of courage and genius had she then transformed herself into George Sand, activist and *femme de lettres*, the woman Flaubert addressed as "Chère Maître," paying her double homage by linking the feminine form of the adjective ("*chère*") to the masculine noun? Nohant was a voyage of self-discovery for Edith, and she came armed with several volumes of Sand's autobiography, *Histoire de ma vie*, which served as her map to the inner landscape and secret suffering of Sand's life. Well-born and self-educated, the two women shared a passion for books and intellectual companionship, and for many years, they were lonely and dissatisfied. Following marriages to men with whom they had little in common, they tried to shape themselves to their husbands' desires and patterns of living. Married in 1822, Sand gave birth to her son, Maurice, nine months later; soon bored and restless, she sought distraction in travel and began to have affairs. In 1828, she gave birth to her daughter, Solange, probably the child of Stephane Ajasson de Grand-

sagne. Estranged from Dudevant (who had become drunken and abusive), she found her way into intellectual and literary circles in Paris,
where she lived half of the year; by 1832, she was publishing highly
successful novels under the name "G. Sand."[24]

Edith's slow transformation from dutiful daughter and timid young
matron into a woman of letters took place in a fashionable and bril-
liantly lit social setting, but her intellectual isolation was even greater
than Sand's. Nor was her intellectual awakening joined to social, sexual, and political rebellion, as was Sand's. Ten years after her marriage to
Teddy Wharton in 1885, Edith had published a few poems and short
stories, but had not yet attempted a novel. Twenty years after her marriage, she had emerged as an important, but rather solitary, figure on
the American literary scene, but had not yet found her way into European intellectual circles. She had been married almost twenty-five years
before she took a lover. Teddy had at first been amenable to her intellectual pursuits, even trying to keep up with them. He happily benefited by the earning powers of her pen, but as her writing became more
and more the center of her life, he felt alienated by it. As she moved
beyond New York and Newport to London and Paris, Teddy felt, as
one family friend put it, "dreadfully out of it."[25]

In 1912, Edith would give James the most recent volume of
Wladimir Karénine's *Life of George Sand* in which she had marked passages of interest to them both. "What a value it all gets from our
memory of that wondrous day when we explored the very scene where
they pigged so thrillingly together," he responded. Sand was to James's
last years what she had been to his youth—the "romancer" whose primary subject was love's passion. She was not, to his mind, a novelist of
the first rank. She was no Balzac attending to the manners and morals
of daily life, nor did she have the philosophic intellect of George Eliot,
whom James regarded as the only English novelist "to have powers of
thought commensurate with [Sand's] powers of imagination." He
stood awestruck before "George Sand" (a figure of his imagination),
and was always more interested in her life than her art. Edith, too, was
fascinated by Sand's life; she read and reread her *Histoire de ma vie* and
kept on her night table a volume of Flaubert's letters to Sand. Although she apparently did not own a single George Sand novel, her library shelves contained a complete set of Flaubert's works.

Soon after her return to Paris from this trip, Edith copied into her
Commonplace Book a statement by French social historian Georges Fa-

quet that seemed to confirm James's attitudes about Sand. Her intelligence, Faquet wrote, showed "a love of ideas without the capacity to fully understand them. She is a distinguished woman who would have had the instincts of a thinker without the force to be one." Beneath this comment Edith wrote, "applicable to any 'intellectual' woman." The meaning of her footnote to Faquet is not entirely self-evident. Was she saying that his complaint against Sand was one often used against "intellectual" women? Sand confided to Flaubert in an 1871 letter: "I'm a woman, I have feelings of affection, pity and anger. I'll never be a sage or scholar."[26]

IN HONOR OF their visit to Nohant, the travelers named the Wharton motor "George." It sped them southwest to the Pyrenees, transporting them from Angoulême to Bordeaux to Pau. Teddy fell ill with bronchitis, but James proved a hardy adventurer. "Never was there a more admirable travelling companion," Edith wrote Sally, "more ready to enjoy and unready to find fault—never bored, never disappointed, and never (*need* I say?) missing any of the little fine touches of sensation that enrich the moments of the really good traveller." James was fortunate to have such an excellent guide as Edith, whose motor-flight essays reveal her skill in capturing the scale and character of a place while also taking in every enlightening nuance—even of Lourdes, "a vast sea of vulgarism" set among sylvan meadows. The "cynical exploitation of superstition and fear" at the shrine of Bernadette, thronged with Holy Week pilgrims, disgusted Edith and exposed to her a grasping and misanthropic side of French character that she had not suspected.[27]

Easter Monday found the travelers in the busy market town of Montréjeau on the northeastern rim of the Pyrenees. Its "narrow streets packed with mild cream-coloured cattle" guided by "lively blue-smocked drivers," the town had a festive air. The Wharton entourage made its way to a large, galleried inn, where they were seated in the courtyard. In the "fragrance and sunshine" of an old walled garden "full of spring flowers and clipped yews," they enjoyed a "gay repast." After lunch, they climbed the steep mountain road to visit one last landmark of the Pyrenees, the Romanesque cathedral of Bertrand de Comminges (Pope Clement V) with its vast Gothic nave and choir.[28]

Edith's travels spurred her lifelong interest in medieval culture. In later years, she would read extensively—almost exclusively—in medieval art, history, and church architecture. But even in her mid-forties, she was something of an expert in the period, and *A Motor-Flight Through France* provides detailed analysis of architectural influences on ecclesiastical life and on the design of French towns and cities. She had an architect's eye for proportion and detail, an excellent visual memory, and an innate sense of the proper materials for construction. ("France has never wholly understood the use of brick," she declared.) She also commanded an extensive architectural vocabulary, speaking as fluently the language of transepts, sallies, and trefoils as she did the Latinate tongue of botany and horticulture. Every brick and cornerstone deserved to be called by its proper name.

Edith's childhood travels with her parents had impressed on her visual memory images of classic Italian architecture, which remained her models of excellence. She demanded that all parts of the construction—whether chapel or cathedral, hill village or great city—converge into a single effect blended into the landscape. She preferred buildings in the "scars and hues of old age" rather than restored by sandblasting. In decorative arts, she favored wood carving and statuary, especially wood aged to "the texture of old bronze." She loathed fakery (the "tout-and-tourist element") and could detect it at long-distance.[29]

Her special gift, as every page of *Motor-Flight* attests, was translating the visual into the verbal through word pictures. Standing in front of the cathedral at Rheims later that spring, she noted that the ideal experience of sculpture, painting, and architecture—arts that appeal first to the eye—demands that the viewer be able to reconstruct the individual elements, "conceive of them in a different relation, and visualise the total result of such modifications." This was a rare talent. Art historians Bernard Berenson and Kenneth Clark would later observe that she had no expertise or much interest in painting. Her preference for floral tableaux to adorn the walls of her houses would seem to confirm the accuracy of their observation; she believed that visual art must be architectural, matching and mirroring the lines, spaces, and textures of the building (as she proclaimed in *The Decoration of Houses*). Even an eye as discerning as Berenson's could not match Edith's mental facility for disassembling and reconstructing architectural edifices. Traveling with him in Germany in 1913, she discovered that the juxtaposition of landscape and edifice, the blend of nature and culture that she so loved, did not thrill him. His aesthetic sense was bounded by the walls of the museum or private collection, while hers opened onto the larger world.[30]

The landscape changed rapidly as "George" made her "comet-flight" across Provence, and Edith soon discovered a new theme in her litany of architectural wonders—Greek influence on Roman France. "It is as though, from that packed Provençal soil, some dust of Greece had passed into the Latin stem, clearing a little its thick sap." Attic lyricism faded and the Roman theme grew mighty when they turned northward up the Rhône Valley to Avignon, Montélimar, Valence, Lyons, and into Dijon, the seat of the dukes of Burgundy. If she thought of Rome—imperial and papal—she was also reminded at each turn of the road that the Rhône Valley represented *la France profonde*, a way of life deeply rooted in the soil and clinging to vestiges of feudalism and medieval class distinctions. For all their charm, these scenes could not erase Edith's awareness of the violent history of this land.

The Pyrenees had won James's heart ("*the* most sympathetic part of France"), but it was the small coastal village of Hyères on the road from Toulon to St. Tropez that captured Edith's. Each time she returned, she fell in love with it again. Hyères was their destination in early April, when they left behind the unfinished church of Saint Maximin and made their way across the "hermit-haunted" mountain range of the Sainte Baume into the pine woods of Costebelle. Here was another pagan scene, "beset by classic allusions, analogies of the golden age—so divinely does the green plain open to the sea, between mountain lines of such Attic purity." Descending the thyme-covered hillside, they came to Hyères, where historic and archaeological sensations "surrender to the spell of the landscape [that] tempts one to indefinite idling."[31]

The travelers were soon routed from this Eden by a strong mistral, the wind that slices down the Vaucluse from Avignon, the next stop on their itinerary. Under rain and heavy clouds that opened occasionally to provide sunset-filled views of Lyons and Valence, they wended their way north. The touring Panhard roared into Paris through the Porte de Choisy on the evening of April 12, twenty-three days and some one thousand miles after it had set out by the Porte de St. Cloud. Making their way toward the heart of the city, they felt the unaccustomed congestion of crowded streets and a certain lowering danger of converging masonry. This vague discomfort after weeks on the open road was relieved only by the sight of "lifted domes" and the symmetrical, elegant bridges of the Seine. What was "mean and huddled and confused" in other cities, Edith noted, cast a spell of beauty over Paris. They were hardly resettled in the rue de Varenne, where James would remain for a

month before traveling to Italy, when Gaillard Lapsley arrived and proposed a motor trip. The group (minus Teddy) set out again and re-
traced the homecoming route of the previous trip through the Morvan
Valley (Avallon, Vézelay, Auxerre), and reexperienced the art and history of Burgundy.[32]

IN PREPARATION FOR writing her motor-flight essays, Edith was reading French literature and history, including memoirs of the Revolution.
The subject had always fascinated her, but now she wanted to understand better "what turned the cannon on the castle." Ruined buildings
and monuments provided dramatic testimony for the necessity of the
Revolution while also recording its "senseless havoc." On the way north
from Aix, she had taken James to see the Château Grignan, where
Mme de Sévigné's son-in-law, the lieutenant governor of Provence, had
dispensed hospitality and "ruled with more than royal arrogance" from
a fortified château. Many years after his death, a revolutionary mob
who recalled the stories of his graft and extortion left it a blackened
ruin. Appalled at the fury directed at the château, Edith tried to imagine the inhuman life of serfs who had carried out the destruction, the
"swarthy livid animal," as La Bruyère had described him, "crouched
over the soil, which he digs and turns with invincible obstinacy, but
who, when he rises to his feet, *shows a human countenance.*"[33]

The Valley of Decision had already borne witness to Edith's curiosity
about revolutionary zeal. Mass violence, however legitimate its causes,
was to her the product of base instincts that once released could not
easily be contained. She believed in a system in which the rich and
privileged protected the poor and helpless, treating them with respect
and compassion. This code underwrote her own actions as a person of
wealth and privilege. Among forms of governance, she preferred an enlightened monarchy, not of the *noblesse oblige* variety, but one that took
seriously its responsibility to its subjects. Much as she loved France, she
never resolved what was for her a central contradiction in French character, the split between a desire for order and beauty—the cherished
equilibrium of daily life—and the overweening vanity and abuses that
bred reactionary violence and unbalanced this delicate structure. She
decried the wanton destruction of beauty. Visiting with Lapsley and
James the ruins of the thirteenth-century abbey of Port-Royal near
Chevreuse, west of Paris, she discovered a "touching poetic little valley
with the merest relics . . . of the monastery and church." Its clerics sus-

pected of Jansenist leanings, it was destroyed by decree of Louis XIV, the last act he signed into law. The "cold fury which had passed a law decreeing the ruin of Port Royal," Edith commented, "was ten times more odious when one was face to face with its work."[34]

Yet another form of violence occupied her thoughts during these weeks—the internal, hidden violence of self-denial that undermines creativity. Mme de Sévigné (once protectoress of the Port-Royal Abbey) created in her Paris salon an order of cultured brilliance unsurpassed in French history. She left it behind during the last years of her life to enter a melancholy self-exile at her son-in-law's Château Grignan, some four hundred miles from Paris. She wanted to be near her daughter, whom she adored and without whom she could not live. Thus, she cut herself off from an intellectual world that had nourished her spirit. Pondering the reasons for her exile, Edith concluded that Mme de Sévigné was "a victim of maternal passion." George Sand also in her later years gave up literary Paris to be near her son and grandchildren. Edith was touched by the emblems of maternal love she had seen at Nohant—the costumes Sand had made for her son's marionette theater, the tombstone of her daughter, Solange, who died at age twenty-six. The epitaph on her tomb—"four tragic words, *La mère de Jeanne"*—defined Solange as mother (and only mother) and commemorated the birth and death of her first baby and only daughter, an infant who was cared for by Sand, and who died in childhood. In Edith's account, the ruins of the Château Grignan and the tombstones of mothers and children in the graveyard at Nohant suggest a sinister link between maternal passion and death.[35]

In light of her remarks on Mme de Sévigné and George Sand, two literary women dedicated to the maternal, one puzzles anew over Edith Wharton's childlessness. In the last years of her life, she told two of her close women friends that not having had children was a "great grief" to her. Her remark seems to reverse the popular belief that she did not like children (and therefore did not want to have any), but it tells us nothing about the causes of her childlessness. The generally accepted explanation for the absence of children in the Wharton household is that Edith and Teddy did not maintain sexual relations. If that were true (as gossips hinted), then her regret at not having children was joined to another sorrow—the absence of a fulfilling sexual life. Yet, in her childbearing years, she apparently never spoke of her desire to have children. She lived "on" herself, intellectually and emotionally.[36]

Returning from her motor-flight through French history in spring

1907, Edith seemed to feel the need of taking her life into her own hands and shaping it to her needs and desires. Many passages in her Commonplace Book during this period speak to issues of fate, choice, rebirth, and regret, but a stanza from Matthew Arnold's "Resignation" captures her sense of urgency:

> *They, believe me, who await*
> *No gifts from chance, have conquered fate.*
> *They, winning room to see and hear,*
> *And to men's business not too near,*
> *Through clouds of individual strife*
> *Draw homeward to the general life.*

Wanting to conquer her own fate, she turned her steps toward the "general life."[37]

A few weeks after returning from the Pyrenees, she was given another view of French history, this time from the viewpoint of its ecclesiastical heritage. Her insights suggest that she was engaged in an intense internal debate about Christianity as a moral and political force. During the Whitsuntide weekend, ten days before they were due to leave for America, Edith and Teddy took a "little flight" northeast of Paris into Picardy. They stopped the first night at Rheims, at an inn facing the great Gothic cathedral, and the next morning viewed the medieval fortress of Coucy (which Edith contrasted to the feudal secular architecture of Carcassonne), and saw the cathedral and Hôtel de Ville of Noyon. They then motored across the valley of the Somme and Aisne rivers, where the worst fighting of World War I would take place and where the occluded light of the lowlands reminded her of the Dutch landscapes of her ancestors.

After a stop at St. Quentin to view the portraits of the eighteenth-century *pastelliste* Quentin de Latour, they drove southeast to Laon, its plain crowned by the seven towers of the cathedral. A "wonderful place," she wrote in *A Motor-Flight*, comparing it to an Umbrian hill town. Teddy loved the open niches inside the church that housed huge stone statues of oxen modeled with a "bold realism" and commemorating the beasts who dragged the stone for the cathedral up the "cruel hill" of Laon. Like the angels of St. Père de Vézelay, seen on their trip with James, the oxen represented a visionary passion that had aroused the extraordinary religious activity of the Late Middle Ages. Experiencing doubts about her own religious beliefs, and having essentially cast aside all but the language of faith (the King James version of the Bible and the Book of Common Prayer), Edith was especially sensitive to the "moral and material cost at which Christianity reared its monuments." The underside of the fervored Middle Ages was human and animal drudgery, a "vast sum of dull, unrewarded, unintelligible toil." She hoped, but was not at all certain of its truth, that the more stable fibers of European character had grown up from this toil. After all, the monument toiler and the face of La Bruyère's rebellious serf, poised for revolution, displayed the same countenance.[38]

BEFORE DEBARKING from Le Havre for the return trip to New York, Edith wrote several letters to the American journalist Morton Fullerton, whom she had met recently in Paris. He had offered to help her arrange serialization of the French translation of *The House of Mirth*. Learning that the newspaper *Le Temps* wanted to publish her book but would require large cuts in it, she asked him whether the *Revue de Paris*, which earlier in the spring had published his travel series on the Rhône Valley, might print it without cuts. Arrangements with the *Revue de Paris* were not finalized until autumn, by which time Morton Fullerton (who had taken "endless trouble" on her behalf) was her houseguest and they were beginning a slow, secret courtship. Her last note to him before she boarded the *Adriatic* reminded him that she was "findable at 'The Mount, Lenox, Mass' from now till Christmas."[39]

They had met for the first time in January 1907 in the red damask drawing room of Rosa de Fitz-James's town house, one street away from Edith on the rue de Grenelle. A dapper, dark-haired man with intense blue eyes and a thick mustache, Fullerton turned up at Rosa's with his playwright friend Paul Hervieu, an acquaintance of Edith's and a "regular" at the salon. Edith quickly discovered that she and "Mr. Fullerton" shared literary and intellectual interests and a set of American friends that included Henry James and the Nortons. (Charles Eliot Norton had been Fullerton's mentor at Harvard.) A year later, she described her feelings on first meeting him in a phrase from Sophocles that she had discovered in an essay by Ralph Waldo Emerson: "The moment my eyes fell on him I was content." Her recorded impressions from spring 1907 do not support this retrospective reading of their early encounters. A frequent guest at her tea table during James's Paris sojourn, he left her perplexed. She confessed to Sally: "Your friend Fullerton . . . is very intelligent, but slightly mysterious, I think." Their lovers' progress was fraught with intrigue resulting from his covert sexual escapades; she did not fathom certain aspects of his character and never suspected others.[40]

Edith never realized the extent of Fullerton's heterosexual pursuits, and she knew nothing of his homosexual affairs, including his erotic interest in Henry James, which dated to the late 1880s, Fullerton's years in London. Then in his mid-twenties, he moved on the fringes of the Oscar Wilde circle and had affairs with the sculptor Ronald Sutherland, known as Lord Gower, and with Percy Anderson. He also had an impassioned liaison with Margaret Brooke, estranged wife of James Brooke (the rajah of Sarawak), whom she had left in India. James introduced Fullerton to this flamboyant, rich woman with literary interests, and he played "facilitator-voyeur" to their affair, arranging lunches and dinners *à trois*. James's interest in these meetings was fueled by his erotic interest in Fullerton, who teased and tantalized him. When the *Times* transferred Fullerton to its Paris office in 1891, James wrote fulsome letters to his "dearest boy" and "cher enfant," employing the traditional rhetoric of the absent and longing lover. Fullerton answered his messages with silence. James visited him in Paris on several occasions, his interest peaking in the late 1890s; the affair was never consummated.[41]

REVERSALS

During her five months in France, Edith had motored for thirty-one days, the hardy "George" covering a distance of two thousand miles without suffering so much as a punctured tire. She had enjoyed it all, the more so because her enthusiasm for epic motor adventures was matched by Teddy's pleasure in every aspect of road travel. His spirits seemed to soar at the prospect of motor-flights, and despite recurrences of flu during the trip with Henry James, Teddy proved a resilient and good-humored companion. In retrospect, these months were a charmed period for both of them. Their last glimpse of France was a two-day excursion in Normandy occasioned by the steamer's delayed departure. After spending a "delightful evening" at an inn in Bayeux, a

gray stone structure complete with a walled garden of "pleached ar-
bours and lilies and roses behind box-borders," Edith and Teddy cast a
quick glance the next morning at the medieval Bayeux tapestry in the
local museum and flew down the road to Cherbourg.

"We are returning to a country where the atmosphere is thin enough
to permit my over-crowded sensations to 'settle,'" she had written
Charles Eliot Norton in mid-May. The Normandy "downs with broom
in flower" contrasted sharply with the stark, drought-ridden Berkshire
landscape that greeted her return to The Mount: "Oh, how the landscape and the life *lack juice!*" she exclaimed to Sally. Nothing on her
horizon boded well, certainly not the announcement by Harvard president Charles Eliot that the university would institute a course in business studies (a sign of future directions in higher education) or his
declaration that the urban skyscraper portended America's future. "It is
bad enough to break with all that adorns life, as one does on leaving
Europe—but if, in compensation, one could find here that which . . .
'lifts the souls of the citizens rather than the roofs of the houses'; then I
think one might be consoled for the absent church-towns and domes
and pinnacles. But sky-scrapers don't symbolize a lifting of the soul,
and President Eliot's manifesto proves it." In this arid atmosphere,
Edith worked on a novel about America's worship of money and power—*The Custom of the Country*.[42]

She took long motor-flights, including a trip up Mount Greylock,
the highest promontory in Massachusetts, and spent her evenings
stargazing from the east terrace. Seeing Capella, a "handsome new luminary in the East," she made it her lucky star. Edith's inner eye gazed
steadily at France as she completed four more motor-flight essays for
the *Atlantic Monthly* and continued a program of reading begun early in
the year: Georges Faquet's *Socialisme en 1907* and *Anticléricalisme* (books
she wanted to discuss with Fullerton) and Gustave Le Bon's *Evolution de
la Matière*—nothing since Darwin's *Origin of Species* had so "thrilled and
impressed" her, she wrote Sally.[43]

To these tomes, she added works in astronomy, philosophy, and literature—the Chinese mystics, Immanuel Kant, George Meredith's "Lu-
cifer in Starlight" and "Modern Love" (among other of his poems),
John Milton's *Paradise Lost*, Aristotle's *Poetics*, Emerson's "Threnody,"
and Matthew Arnold's "Resignation." But French novelist and poet
Anna de Noailles merited the most space in her Commonplace Book,
where she copied lyrics and epigrams from *Les Eblouissements* ("Flower-

ings")—meditations on womanhood, love, death, loss, and regret that eerily projected the tenor of lived experiences just ahead for Edith. The 420-page *Eblouissements* appeared in April 1907 to immense acclaim, Marcel Proust sounding the first note of fanfare in the literary supplement of *Le Figaro*: Mme de Noailles's book, he said, ranked with Charles Baudelaire's *Fleurs du mal.*[44]

Edith met the comtesse de Noailles in spring 1906, when Bourget brought her to tea. Twenty-nine years old, she had already made her name with two volumes of poems and three novels, of which *Domination* (1905), a *roman à clef* of her love affair with the writer and journalist Maurice Barrès, excited controversy in Paris intellectual circles. Endowed with quick intelligence and sensitivity to nature, the comtesse had (like Edith) survived a grave childhood illness that left her permanently weakened and vulnerable to flu and pneumonia. As an adult, she had a tendency to migraine headaches (misdiagnosed as neurasthenia) and was often ordered by her doctors to take bed rest. An outspoken social activist, she did not toe the Catholic-royalist line in politics (she and her husband, Mathieu, were outspokenly Dreyfusard), and her intellectual eclecticism drew her to writers as diverse as Taine, Huysmans, Loti, Michelet, Anatole France, Gide, and Nietzsche. Friedrich Nietzsche had a greater influence on her than any other thinker, and she may have awakened Edith's interest in him—in 1907 and 1908, Edith read all his works, as part of her reading program in philosophy.[45]

During the summer of 1907, she made extensive notes for an essay in French that, as she explained to Brownell in November, would demonstrate Mme de Noailles's "utterly un-French" resemblance to Walt Whitman and their poetic treatments of the natural world. Never before had she been moved by "the poems of *any* lady in *any* language," Edith told him: the originality of her work "grows as *she* grows, which is the great thing about her." No enthusiast of Walt Whitman, Brownell did appreciate Anna de Noailles, and he praised Edith's idiomatic French, encouraging her to publish the essay. She did not publish it, and perhaps never completed it. The loss is regrettable for several reasons. It would have provided a rare opportunity to hear Edith Wharton's reactions to a contemporary woman writer whom she respected (quite apart from what she might have said about Whitman's writing), and it might have opened the way to real friendship between the two women.

Autumn 1907 was an unexpectedly stressful period for Edith, which may explain why she abandoned the essay. After an intense advertising campaign that predicted *The Fruit of the Tree* would be a greater success than *The House of Mirth*, the new novel appeared on October 19, its first edition of fifty thousand copies having sold out in advance. Thirty thousand more copies sold within the first week after publication, and all signs portended a bestseller. Scribners banked on such a success to recoup the $10,000 they had paid for serial rights, while Edith needed money to finance an ambitious remodeling project at The Mount. Hopes were running high for *The Fruit of the Tree* when she sent Burlingame the first chapter of a new novel, *The Custom of the Country*, which she described as a comedy of manners "of the Gelegenheits Ge-dict order" (a novel of the current moment). She had begun it in Paris the previous spring and planned to have it ready for serialization by January 1909. But plans went awry, her work on the book interrupted many times, and *The Custom of the Country* did not appear until 1913.[46]

She initially lost interest in her comedy of manners when *The Fruit of the Tree* did not fulfill its early sales promise, despite good reviews in the literary supplements. Sales dropped after a financial panic, brought on by overproduction in the industrial sector, hit Wall Street. J. P. Morgan, aided by President Teddy Roosevelt, intervened to stem the tide of fear and restore order to the markets, but Edith's book never regained its initial momentum. Serial publication, ironically, had also contributed to slackening sales. The book engendered such controversy during the months of its *Scribner's* run that everyone knew the central event of its plot (Justine's "mercy killing" of her childhood friend Bessy West-more), and no surprise ending recaptured reader interest, as had been the case with *The House of Mirth*. Sales of *The Fruit of the Tree* were less than half those of *The House of Mirth*, and the difference in financial re-turn to publisher and author was enormous. The American edition of *The House of Mirth* earned Edith almost $29,000 in 1906 on a 15 per-cent royalty. She negotiated a 20 percent royalty on *The Fruit of the Tree*, earning $2,500 on it in 1907 and $14,500 in 1908. In 1906, her total literary income was $42,790.06, but she earned only one-third of that amount in 1907.[47]

Edith's disappointment about the book extended beyond the loss of expected sales. In widening the focus of her social criticism, she invited the charge that she was not expert in the subjects her novel addressed. Industrialists disputed the authenticity of the factory scenes; physicians and lawyers doubted the accuracy of the story's medical and legal issues. She had tried to establish the verisimilitude of the mill scenes, she explained to Burlingame, and to learn the required technical terminology. At her request, Massachusetts senator Crane secured permission for her to tour a cotton mill in Adams, probably the Berkshire Cotton Manufacturing Company, which produced fine cotton and gingham and employed fifteen hundred workers. But the superintendent, a Mr. Plunkett, "rather snubbed" her. He seemed unaware of who she was or why she was making her inquiries. She did not feel welcome at the mill, and the "stunning noise" of the workroom machines—an occupational condition described in detail in her book—made it difficult to hear the superintendent's comments.[48]

Lawyers complained that in administering the lethal dose of morphine to Bessy Westmore, Justine Brent was without question a murderess, and in real life would not have been allowed to escape the consequences. Furthermore, Edith did not have her facts straight regarding the legalities of Bessy Westmore's will. The *Medical Journal* claimed Justine was not believable as a trained nurse: "It is incredible that any tumult of sentiment should sweep a trained nurse of Justine's character and discernment from the anchorage of the discipline and traditions of her order and cause her to commit murder in order to shorten suffering." Edith corrected some factual errors while reading proofs on the book, but the wealth of complaints made her feel that in taking up this large subject, she may have ventured too far beyond the limits of her expertise. Reviewers overlooked (or were unaware of) factual errors in the book and focused instead on her treatment of the "controversial" and "daring" theme of euthanasia. The *Dial* praised Edith's "accomplished artistry" and strong sense of "ethical responsibility." The *Bookman* was less generous: acknowledging her "fine and exceptional gift," the reviewer noted that the novel lacked unity and coherence and was marked by "structural deficiencies."

This was the second season in a row that she faced artistic defeat; at this same moment in 1906, the stage version of *The House of Mirth* was closing after its brief run. The failure of the stage play and the disappointing reception of her new novel bruised her self-confidence, but these responses to her work also fostered her growing pessimism about her American readership.[49]

IN THE THIRD WEEK of October, while *The Fruit of the Tree* still held promise of success, Morton Fullerton arrived at The Mount from Bryn Mawr College, where he had given a lecture on Henry James. His brief stay in Lenox opened an unbridgeable gulf with all that had gone before in Edith's life. A week after his departure, she reopened an old leather-bound notebook and began to write what has come to be known as the Love Diary.

THE LIFE APART. (L'AME CLOSE.)
The Mount. Oct. 29th 1907.

If you had not enclosed that sprig of wych-hazel in your note I should not have opened this long-abandoned book; for the note in itself might have meant nothing—would have meant nothing to me—beyond the inference that you had a more "personal" accent than week-end visitors usually put into their leave-takings. But you sent the wych-hazel—and sent it without a word—thus telling me (as I choose to think!) that you knew what was in my mind when I found it blooming on that wet bank in the woods, where we sat together and smoked a cigarette while the chains were put on the wheels of the motor.

And so it happens that, finding myself—after so long!—with some one to talk to, I take up this empty volume, in which, long ago, I made one or two spasmodic attempts to keep a diary. For I had no one but myself to talk to, and it is absurd to write down what one says to one's self; but now I shall have the illusion that I am talking to you, and that—as when I picked the wych-hazel—something of what I say will somehow reach you. . . . [EW's ellipses.]

Your evening here the other day was marked by curious symbols; for the day before you arrived we had our first autumn snow-storm (we have October snow in these hills); and on the bank where you and I sat we found the first sprig of the "old woman's flower"—the flower that blooms in the autumn!

In response to his letter enclosing the witch hazel, Edith sent an eccentric hand-drawn illustration whose message was wholly at odds with her feelings. Its reference was a trip they made on the last day of his visit, Tuesday, October 22. Edith and her friend Eliot Gregory were on their way to visit William Sheffield Cowles and his wife, Anna Roosevelt (Teddy Roosevelt's sister), in Farmington, Connecticut. After a "dazzling run across blue mountains, through arches and long vistas of gold and amber," they dropped Fullerton at the Westfield train station, and he made his way to Cambridge, where he was to lecture at Harvard. He did not know the Cowleses and never saw their house, Oldgate, but on its stationery, Edith sketched for him a smiling image of herself wearing a three-quarter-length coat and long skirt, skating between two top-hatted bears. She entitled the scene "Little Edith & her Teddy Pair," sent "From Wharton, Compliments of One of the Pair." The obvious other of the "pair" was Teddy, who had not joined the motor party that day, but instead had visited his sick mother in Lenox. The clue to the third bear's identity is perhaps found in Anna Cowles's nickname for her broad-shouldered husband, "Bear-o," a term of endearment that Fullerton could not have known.[50]

The enigmatic card suggests a deep division between Edith's inner feelings, confessed in the pages of her secret journal, and her outward demeanor. Despite wealth, social standing, and literary accomplishments, she harbored insecurities about her looks, her desirability, and her age. (She was nearly four years older than Fullerton.) The son of a retired Congregational minister in Brockton, Massachusetts, Fullerton came from a genteel but poor family. After leaving America in the late 1880s, he transformed himself from a small-town boy to a dandyish cosmopolitan. His long residence in Europe and his wide experiences (including his bisexual liaisons) allowed him to move easily among all types of people. But as ensuing events revealed, he was confounded by Edith's behavior. She was by turns gracious, imperious, expectant, and paralyzed by shyness. He would soon complain to her that he had no idea how she really felt about him.

After the first long entry, she wrote nothing in the Love Diary until November 27: "Your letter from Paris . . . ," her ellipses a metonym of the hours and days of waiting during the intervening five weeks since receiving his first letter. One week after she dropped him at the Westfield train station, she advanced her departure date to Europe, and gave friends the most mundane of excuses for her rapid departure—heating problems in the servants' wing of The Mount— blaming her architect for delays in producing the plans for the necessary alterations. "Don't put your visit off too late," she urged Sally, "for we have decided to sail on Dec. 5th, so we shall have to leave here on the 1st." She eventually abandoned her plans to add more guest rooms to The Mount and install a steam furnace for the servants' wing. Poor sales of *The Fruit of the Tree* meant that she lacked the necessary money to pay for the construction, but she also had a new set of personal priorities.[51]

By mid-December, after a brief trip in Normandy with Harry Jones, Edith and Teddy were back in Paris, and *The House of Mirth* in its "French dress" (*Chez les heureux du monde*) had begun its run in the *Revue de Paris*. It was having "a wild, fantastic, unprecedented success, the likes of which the 'Revue' has not had in years," she wrote Charles Scribner, "and in consequence I am seeing amusing people." Among the most amusing was Fullerton, who accompanied her to lectures at the Sorbonne and joined the group of American and French friends gathered at her tea table. On Christmas night, coming home from dinner at a Left Bank restaurant, she spotted the star she had first seen above Laurel Lake in the summer. "I saw hanging above Notre Dame a blue star which surely, surely was Capella!" she wrote Sally.[52]

WINTER LIGHT

Nineteen hundred eight, a Leap Year, dawned snowy and frozen. Edith did not immediately take the initiative in love, but she inscribed on the frontispiece of her daily diary the couplet from the sixteenth-century French poet Pierre Ronsard that she had already taken as the title of her secret Love Diary.

> *Une tristesse dans l'âme close*
> *Me nourrit, et non autre chose.*
> *(A sadness in my shut-in soul*
> *Nourishes me, and no other thing.)*

She had recently discovered in lines from Giuseppe Tigri, a nineteenth-century Pistoian poet, another vision of the shut-in soul. It served as the only diary entry for January 1, 1908.

> *I have been to hell, and I have come back.*
> *Mercy! How many people were there.*
> *There was a well-lighted room,*
> *And therein was my Hope.*

The speaker in the poem visits his lover, Hope, who is imprisoned in Hell. She asks for a kiss, and when he has complied, she says, "Do not hope to leave this place."[53]

Some weeks later, after a visit with Fullerton to the village of Herblay, northwest of Paris, Edith wrote a poem, *Ame Close*, using Tigri's image of the illuminated chamber:

> *My soul is like a house that*
> *Dwellers nigh can see no light in.*
> *"Ah, poor house," they say,*
> *"Long since its owners died or*
> *Went their way." Thick ivy*
> *Loops the rusted door-latch tie.*
> *The chimney rises cold against the sky*
> *And flowers turned to weed down the*
> *Bare path's decay . . .*
> *Yet one stray passer, at the shut of day,*
> *Sees a light trembling in a casement high.*
> *Even so, my soul would set a light for you,*
> *A light invisible to all beside,*
> *As though a lover's ghost should yearn and glide*
> *From pane to pane, to let the flame shine through.*
> *Yet enter not, lest, as it flits ahead*
> *You see the hand that carries it is dead.*

Employing her familiar metaphor of the human being as house, this macabre poem articulates a new version of the old fear that life would pass her by, that her soul would remain imprisoned in the "dark and silence" of its loneliness. In the Love Diary, she recounted an event at the Herblay church: "A veiled figure stole up and looked at me a moment. Was its name happiness? I dared not lift the veil. . . ." Haunted by unconscious fears and joys, Edith was unable to lift the veil of her own feelings, except on the pages of her private diaries.[54]

The trip to Herblay took place on February 15, the first of ten motor trips to villages surrounding Paris that she and Fullerton took in spring 1908. Earlier in the winter, wanting to spend an evening with him alone, she had invited him to accompany her to see a group of Sicilian players perform Gabriele D'Annunzio's *La Figlia di Iorio*. She chose the play with care and penned a discreet invitation: "As my husband objects to the language of the play [i.e., the Sicilian dialect in which it was performed], I am obliged to throw myself on the charity of my friends." Fullerton replied that he did not care for D'Annunzio.

This play was different, she countered, "simple and dramatic." A tragedy about forbidden love—a father's desire for his son's lover—and the patricidal violence it breeds, the drama had caused a scandal when first performed in 1904.[55]

On Monday, January 13, Fullerton dined with the Whartons and then accompanied Edith to the Théâtre de Marigny just off the Champs Elysées. *Unvergessliche Stunden*, "unforgettable hours," she noted in her diary. Seated in the darkened *baignoire*, the velvet side curtains hiding them from the gaze of others, the setting portended intimate communion, and the powerful sexuality of the drama stirred Edith's emotions. When in the play, Iorio's daughter is unable to send her lover away once he has kissed her, Fullerton leaned over to her and said laughingly, "That's something you don't know anything about." Perceiving that Edith had no experience of passion, his remark was an aggressive strike against her protective social armor. We do not know her response, but however she answered him, it did not bring them into immediate intimacy.

She had a quite different romantic vision from Fullerton's. She believed in "doubles," twin souls who mirror one another; recognizing the other's desires, they are fated to lose their individuality in the abyss of the other's love. This is the message of the Tigri canto and Edith's Herblay poem—the lover is an echo of the self. Real-life lovers, however, speak their needs and desires. Fullerton wanted her to express her feelings and demonstrate her affection for him. Was she toying with him, "amusing" herself? he would soon ask. She answered him in a letter, explaining that theirs was a "fugitive" relation, which inhibited her. Fullerton thrived on mystery and intrigue, but Edith preferred to approach things straightforwardly. She disliked the deceit required by illicit love. The Love Diary also reveals that her heart had fed on loneliness so long that her desire had turned morbid. When she could at last speak her feelings, "unpack her trunk," as she called it, he could not bear her sadness—loving him "sadly," as he described it.[56]

Seeking occasions to see him, Edith entertained at a frantic rate and invited him to lunch, dinner, and tea. She even gave him carte blanche to invite himself anytime—a liberty he never took. Between January 1 and February 29, she saw him twenty-four times; on eighteen of these occasions, he was a guest in her home. As she had always enjoyed the friendship of bachelors (Walter Berry, Egerton Winthrop, Ogden Codman, Eliot Gregory, Berkeley Updike), Fullerton's constant presence did not appear unusual. When Edith was not entertaining at home, she could be found at the theater, often accompanied by Rosa de Fitz-James, Matilda Gay, or another of her women friends. She saw seventeen plays that season, among them Bourget's smash hit *Un Divorce,* dramatized from his 1904 novel of the same title. Although unenthusiastic about his work, Edith loyally attended both an afternoon general rehearsal and an evening performance, noting in her diary that it was "beautifully played" by Georges Brandes. Preferring classical drama, she attended in January a magnificent production of Euripides' *Andromache,* and in March went with Matilda Gay to see Mme Silvain in Sophocles' *Electra: "finer* than ever."[57]

In late February, she joined the Bourgets at a gala general rehearsal of Henri Bataille's *La Femme nue,* starring Berthe Mady and Sacha Guitry. During the performance, Fullerton quietly slipped into the loge to pay her a surprise visit. It was a moment of anguished joy (*"Ach, Gott, Gott"*), and several days later she re-created the scene in her journal:

> March 3
>
> The other night at the theatre, when you came into the box—that little, dim baignoire (no. 13, I shall always remember!) I felt for the first time that indescribable current of communication flowing between myself and someone else—felt it, I mean, uninterruptedly, securely, so that it penetrated every sense and every thought . . . and said to myself: "This must be what happy women feel." . . . (The theatre was the Renaissance.)[58]

She brought to her fantasy of silent communion between lovers all the familiar props of romantic love. Numbers and dates had special meaning and words had special resonance ("renaissance"). Fullerton now appeared as M.F. in her daily diary, her comments on their hours together phrased in elliptical German, the language of Goethe and Heine, whose works she was rereading.

All this time Teddy stayed near the fire, ill with gout, slipping slowly into depression and invalidism, steadfastly refusing his doctor's advice to get away from the Paris cold. Irritable and uncommunicative, he rarely left the apartment and interested himself in little else but his symptoms. Finally persuaded to visit Ralph and Lise Curtis at their villa Beaulieu near Cannes, he departed by train on Wednesday, February 12. The following Saturday, Edith and Morton took their trip to

Edith at age six, photographed in England in autumn 1868, when her brother Harry entered Trinity Hall, Cambridge University. (The Lilly Library, Indiana University, Bloomington, Indiana)

Edith in Switzerland 1870, following her battle against deadly typhoid fever. Usually beribboned and frilled, she appears here with uncurled hair and badly cut bangs: "I was much the least good-looking of the family, [and] the consciousness of my physical shortcomings was heightened by the beauty of the persons about me," she recalled. (Beinecke Library, Yale University)

Irish nanny Hannah Doyle ("Doyley"), whose "rich all-permeating presence" enclosed Edith's childhood in a "warm cocoon." (Beinecke Library, Yale University)

Henry Edward Jones ("Harry," age six, c. 1856), whom Edith called the "dearest of brothers to all my youth." In 1913, his gold-digging mistress effected an estrangement with Edith that resulted in Harry's disinheriting both his sister and his niece, Beatrix. (Portrait by John Whitten Ehninger, Edith Wharton Restoration, Lenox, Massachusetts)

Frederic Rhinelander Jones (age ten, c. 1856). Seventeen years old at Edith's birth, he entered Columbia College when she was eight months old. Sexually promiscuous and profligate, he cheated her out of a portion of her mother's inheritance, and his scandalous liaison with a New York socialite forced him to live in Europe under a pseudonym. (Portrait by John Whitten Ehninger, Edith Wharton Restoration, Lenox, Massachusetts)

George Frederic Jones (age twenty-four, c. 1845), Edith's father, courted Lucretia Stevens Rhinelander by sailing up Long Island Sound in a catboat at dawn, having contrived a mast from an oar, rigged with a bed quilt. (Portrait by John Whitten Ehninger, Edith Wharton Restoration, Lenox, Massachusetts)

Henry Brougham, First Baron of Brougham and Vaux, rumored to be Edith's father. Their similar gestures and appearance (red hair, the shape of nose and hands), restless behavior, and extraordinary intellectual gifts led to speculation that Edith was born of a secret affair between Lord Brougham and Lucretia Jones in Cannes, France, during spring 1861. (Portrait by Sir Thomas Lawrence, 1825, National Portrait Gallery, London)

George Frederic Jones in 1880, age fifty-nine, two years before his death from a paralytic stroke. Prematurely aged by ill health, he appeared to Edith a "lonely" man, "haunted by something always unexpressed and unattained." (Beinecke Library, Yale University)

Lucretia Jones in her early fifties with Edith and Harry Jones (New York, c. 1877). Ultra-fashionable Lucretia dressed in velvet, satin, and furs. (Beinecke Library, Yale University)

Edith at twenty-one, on her reentry into New York society in January 1883 after her father's death. She wore an extremely décolleté dress of black satin, velvet, and appliquéd lace. Pearls and diamond jewelry are from Cartier, gifts of her mother. (The Lilly Library, Indiana University, Bloomington, Indiana)

Edward ("Teddy") Robbins Wharton, future husband of Edith Jones, on his graduation from Harvard University in 1873, ranking in the lower third of his class; his best subject was natural history. (Pusey Library, Harvard University Archives)

Walter Van Rensselaer Berry, age twenty-four in 1883, when Edith met him in Bar Harbor, Maine. She turned his early romantic gestures toward an intimate friendship; at his death in 1927, she called him "the love of all my life." (Beinecke Library, Yale University)

Edith photographed in Paris, spring 1886, one year after her marriage. While in Paris, she sat for a portrait by Teddy's Boston friend Julian Story; although she used the portrait for publicity purposes (*The Greater Inclination* and *The Touchstone*), she thought it a "failure" and was never again painted. (Columbia County Historical Society, Kinderhook, New York)

Pencraig Cottage, Edith and Teddy Wharton's first home (1885–1893). In this "little house," owned by Lucretia Jones and located across the street from her estate "Pencraig" in Newport, Rhode Island, Edith first tested her interior decorating ideas. (The Lilly Library, Indiana University, Bloomington, Indiana)

Ogden Codman, Jr., the "clever Boston architect" who worked on three of her homes—Pencraig Cottage and Land's End in Newport, and The Mount in Lenox, Massachusetts—and with whom she wrote *The Decoration of Houses* (1897). In gossipy letters to his mother, he provided startling views of Edith and Teddy Wharton's marital and social life. (Courtesy of the Society for the Preservation of New England Antiquities)

Edith at age twenty-eight, photographed in Newport in 1890, five years after her marriage. Thin, hollow-eyed, her skin heavily freckled and lined from sun exposure, she suffered from recurrent ill health—bronchitis and flu—caused by Newport's damp weather. (Beinecke Library, Yale University)

Teddy Wharton with dogs Jules, Miza, and Mimi (c. 1898). Age forty-eight in this picture, his eyes already pouched and red-rimmed, Teddy would soon show signs of the inherited manic depression that destroyed his marriage and his life. (Beinecke Library, Yale University)

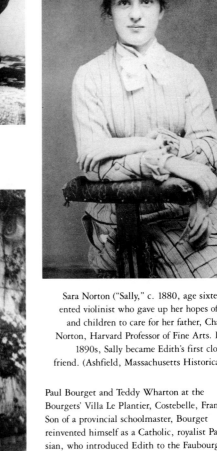

Sara Norton ("Sally," c. 1880, age sixteen), a talented violinist who gave up her hopes of marriage and children to care for her father, Charles Eliot Norton, Harvard Professor of Fine Arts. In the late 1890s, Sally became Edith's first close woman friend. (Ashfield, Massachusetts Historical Society)

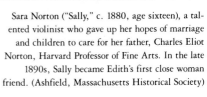

Paul Bourget and Teddy Wharton at the Bourgets' Villa Le Plantier, Costebelle, France. Son of a provincial schoolmaster, Bourget reinvented himself as a Catholic, royalist Parisian, who introduced Edith to the Faubourg St. Germain in 1906. Edith preferred Bourget's "talk" to his writings, and her greatest affection was for his Jewish wife, Minnie David. (The Lilly Library, Indiana University, Bloomington, Indiana)

The Mount, Lenox, Massachusetts
(c. 1905), view of the east terrace from
lime walk. Edith's bedroom, where she
wrote each morning, is behind the two
upper-right-hand-corner windows.
(Beinecke Library, Yale University)

Vista toward Laurel Lake from
east terrace, looking toward the
Tyringham mountains. Henry
James described The Mount as a
"delicate French chateau mir-
rored in a Massachusetts pond."
(Beinecke Library, Yale
University)

Edith seated at her desk in The Mount library.
This publicity photo for *The House of Mirth* (1905)
shows her triple Tiffany engagement ring, two
diamond bands and one of rubies. Teddy purchased one diamond hoop; Lucretia Jones gave her
daughter the two other rings. (Gessford Studio,
New York City)

Herblay: *Wir waren zusammen*—"We were together." After a three-month silence, she again took up her pen and addressed herself to Fullerton in the Love Diary: "All these months I thought after all I had been mistaken; and my poor 'âme close' barred its shutters and bolted its doors again, and the dust gathered and the cobwebs thickened in the empty rooms, where for a moment I had heard an echo. . . . Then we went to Herblay." Their mission was to find the home of Hortense Allart, French writer and mistress of Chateaubriand, Sainte-Beuve, and Henry Bulwer-Lytton, and friend of George Sand's. Calling Allart a "George Sand without hypocrisy" (a strange remark, given Sand's openness about her intimate life), Edith had discovered this second muse to her passional life in Leon Seché's biography of Allart, just published by Mercure de France. It was the talk of Paris.[59]

Two nights after the Herblay trip, Edith and Morton were seated near the fire in the library at 58 rue de Varenne. He was reading aloud an article on George Meredith by André Chevrillon, editor of the *Revue de Paris*. Wearing a tea gown that Morton particularly liked, Edith sat knitting. The moment was "exquisite." She had "the illusion . . . of a life in which such evenings might be a dear accepted habit." She tracked his mind as it "discriminated, classified, with that flashing, illuminating sense of differences and relations that so exquisitely distinguishes your thought." At that moment, "the hour became her husband." Then he broke the spell: "You said things that distressed me." What he said constituted a breach in "mental companionship," as she wrote to him in the Love Diary. Some days later, after evaluating the situation, she confessed: "I'm so afraid that the treasures I long to unpack for you, that have come to me in magic ships from enchanted islands, are only, to you, the old familiar red calico and beads of the clever trader, who has had dealings in every latitude, and knows just what to carry in the hold to please the simple native." (She quite accurately guessed what his reactions might be to her avowals.) Beyond her fears, or allied to them, was a "scruple" that kept her from speaking her feelings freely.[60]

Teddy returned from the Riviera little improved by his stay on the south coast, and by March 21, he was on a boat to America and would soon begin a cure at Hot Springs, Arkansas. The rhetoric of Edith's passion for Fullerton escalated: "Nothing else lives in me but *you*—I have no conscious existence outside the thought of you, the feeling of you." She, who just a few weeks earlier had experienced such difficulty speaking her emotions, now wrote him that his mere presence in a room sent a "ripple of flame" through her: "If, wherever you touch me, a heart beats under your touch, and if, when you hold me, and I don't speak, it's because all the words in me seem to have become throbbing pulses, and all my thoughts are a great gold blur." Despite her sexually charged language, Edith was not yet his lover. He was now in the uncomfortable (and unusual) position of waiting for a sign that she desired greater physical intimacy. He waited all spring.[61]

"I am a little humbled," Edith wrote in her journal on April 25, "a little ashamed, to find how poor a thing I am, how the personality I had moulded into such strong, firm lines has crumbled into a pinch of ashes in this flame!" She was "*anéantie*" by the flame—annihilated. Searching for herself in the ashes of passion, she exclaimed, "Oh my free, proud, secure soul, where are you? *What were you*, to escape me like this?" Choosing poems for *Artemis to Actaeon*, her Scribners collection, she thought it "curious" that some of her old verses expressed more than she had known or understood at the time: "They go straight to you," she wrote in the journal, "like homing birds released long ago by a hand that knew not whence they came!"

Literature had become the vehicle of her lovemaking. The sacred text was Dante's *Divine Comedy*—as it had been for Edith and Walter. (He had even made a failed effort to learn Italian, hoping to increase his enjoyment.) She addressed Morton in lyrics, love letters, and the Love Diary, and awoke each morning to find a note from him, mailed in the midnight hours as he left the *Times* offices:

A note comes almost every morning now. It is brought in on my breakfast-tray with the other letters, and there is the delicious moment of postponement, when one leaves it unopened while one pours the tea, just in order to "savourer" longer the joy that is coming! . . . And then comes the opening of the letter, the slipping of the little silver knife under the flap (which one would never tear!), the first glance to see how many pages there are, the second to see how it ends, and then the return to the beginning, the breathless first reading, the slow lingering again over each phrase and each word, the taking possession, the absorbing of them one by one, and finally the choosing of the one that will be carried in one's thoughts all day, making an exquisite accompaniment to the dull prose of life.

In this ritual enactment of sexual intercourse, Edith took the man's part, opening the letter and possessing its words as though they were the gift of a woman's body.

But the immediate obstacle to acting on her fantasies of sexual seduction was logistics: how to arrange trysts in absolute secrecy? Her ingenuity had been stretched to the limit during the early weeks of 1908 as she contrived assignations in art galleries and museums, places where they could be alone and out of earshot of her household staff. She even sent Fullerton instructions about how to present himself to the footman when he dropped in for tea, and she became upset if he did not follow her directions to the letter—fearing that she would be caught in lies. Very soon, the circumventions of intrigue began to wear on both of them. To have arranged afternoon trysts in her bedroom suite was beyond imagining. Her letters and notes to Fullerton in spring 1908 reveal that her prime concern was to protect her reputation with her household staff while at the same time being with him as often as possible. (Paulina Trant, the heroine of her 1912 story "The Long Run," faced similar problems and also refused to compromise herself.)

If chauffeur Charles Cook suspected the true nature of Edith's Saturday drives in the country, he never gave expression to his thoughts; Fullerton felt uncomfortable, however, and asked that they take the train. Edith was more concerned about butler Alfred White, who for many years had served as Teddy's valet. She may have had less concern about her housekeeper, Catherine Gross, who had come into service with Edith in 1884 to escape her own sexual past. As a teenager, Gross was seduced by a man who abandoned her. She gave birth to a son, whom she put in foster care, keeping in touch with him by letter. She gave him a good education and set him up as a farmer in Algiers. After he married, she visited him in Algiers and realized that he was ashamed of her—not because of the circumstances of his birth, but because she was a servant. She returned to Edith saying that she would never see him again.[62]

In mid-April, when the lease was up on the rue de Varenne apartment, Edith gave her staff a month's vacation and moved into her brother Harry's town house. He was in America on business, and except for her lady's maid, she was served by Harry's staff. Soon, she sensed they were watching her and Fullerton, and her worries about gossip increased.

HENRY JAMES SPENT three weeks in Paris during April and May, and Edith's last days with Fullerton before her departure for America were spent in his company. James arrived with a particular interest in secret love affairs, Edith having written him of Hortense Allart and the house at Herblay. He asked to see the "shrine of the *inouïe* Hortense." On May 1, in radiant spring sunshine, they drove to Herblay. Fullerton accompanied them the following day to Beauvais, where they lunched in the courtyard of the Hôtel d'Angleterre to the sounds of canaries singing, dogs barking, and children's thin-voiced shouts. After coffee and cigarettes, they walked through little back streets to the Church of St. Etienne to see its famous Jesse-tree window, and then turned northward to the Cathedral of St. Peter, with its "soaring, wheeling choir." While James walked in the ambulatory, Edith and Fullerton sat on the cathedral steps, enjoying a rare moment of privacy.[63]

The next day, Edith decided to consummate her love for Fullerton: "*I will go with him once before we separate,*" she promised herself. Her idea was to go to "a little inn in the country in the depths of a green wood," where she would be "held fast" in his arms:

> How strange to feel one's self all at once "*Jenseits von Gut und Böse*" [Beyond Good and Evil, title of Friedrich Nietzsche's most famous work] .
> . . . It would hurt no one—it would give me my first, last, draught of life. . . . Why not? I have always laughed at the "*mala prohibita*"—the "bugbears to frighten children." The anti-social act is the only one that is harmful "per se." And, as you told me the other day—*and as I needed no telling*—what I have given already is far, far more. . . ."

The decision to enter fully into a love affair with Fullerton radically altered Edith's view of the world. She was "a new creature opening dazzled eyes on a new world! C'est l'aube."

But it was already too late: the return to America was only three weeks distant. She tried to find a suitable locale and fix a date for the tryst, but Fullerton suddenly found himself too busy to leave Paris. She had predicted that something like this would occur, the result of her delays and scruples: "Why didn't I speak my heart out at once?"[64]

As the days dwindled down and the moment of separation was at hand, her mood shifted again. Overcome with gratitude and self-satisfaction for the events of the spring, she poured her emotions onto the diary pages: "O Life, Life, how I give thanks to you for this! How right I was to trust you, to know that my day would come, and to be too proud, and too confident of my fate, to take for a moment any lesser gift." But she consigned her great experience to the past ("the day has *been*"), and her thankfulness was directly proportional to all she felt had been denied her. "One should be happy in one's youth to be happy freely, carelessly, extravagantly! How I hoard and tremble over each incident and sign! I am like a hungry beggar who crumbles up the crust he has found in order to make it last longer!"[65]

On her last day in Paris, Edith gave Fullerton the Love Diary to read. He returned it to her at the station, having made some notes on a page that she later tore out. In giving him the diary, a record of her most intimate self, Edith unwittingly reversed the power balance of their relationship. From their first meeting, she had set the terms of their friendship; for most of the spring, she kept him guessing about his place in her affections. But the diary, a record of her vulnerability, confirmed that from the weekend at The Mount, she had been his.

As the train pulled out of the station en route to Le Havre on May 23, she smiled and waved ("to smile at that moment!"), but by midafternoon, when the *Provence* slipped its moorings and headed out toward sea, she declared in her diary: "It is over, my Heart, all over! . . . *Et on n'en meurt, hélas!*"—Alas, she did not die of it. A rhetoric of despair replaced the exultant voice of a few days earlier. Lurking doubts, which Fullerton's presence had pushed away, now crowded her consciousness. As darkness and silence began to descend around her, she nursed her grief, fears, and love for him in long letters. In the first week after her departure, he wrote three letters. Then, after a disconcerting lapse, two others followed; finally, and inexplicably, there was no word at all. Withdrawing into silence (a technique he used with all his women lovers), he left her confused and desperate.[66]

THE SEASONS OF HER DISCONTENT

Edith's despondency on leaving Fullerton owed less to the prospect of long absence from him (he expected to be in America within a few weeks) than her remorse at having lost the chance to have a real love affair. Such an opportunity as they had had might never come again.

Her diary entries and letters brimmed with sorrow and regret, but she portrayed a quite different set of feelings in a short story, "The Choice," written on the boat. Teddy and Edith are recognizable as Cobham Stilling, a pompous, affable bore, and his wife, Isabel, who loves another man but is held to her marriage by duty and consideration for her son. Isabel's lover, Wrayford, urges her to save herself. "I'm not the saint you suppose," she responds. "Day by day, hour by hour, I wish him dead." Fate intervenes after a dinner party on a stormy summer evening. The lovers meet at the boathouse, where Wrayford tells Isabel that her husband—trustee of her estate—has speculated with her moneys and lost heavily on the stock market. (This situation forecast one that Edith herself would soon face.) Hearing the approach of Stilling, drunk on after-dinner brandy, Wrayford opens the sliding floor and Stilling falls into the deep water beneath the boathouse. Inexplicably, Wrayford then attempts a rescue effort. Isabel tries to save her lover, but in the darkness saves her husband instead. Wrayford dies, and "the choice" has been made. The tale's violence dramatizes the intensity of Edith's feelings about her marriage—powerlessness, rage, guilt, futility. If either Teddy or Morton read the story, no record of their responses exists.

Teddy met her at the New York pier, and they traveled by afternoon train to Lenox. She took up Robert H. Lock's *Heredity and Variation*, a scientific study of evolution she had begun reading on the boat. Finding an interesting passage, she held the book out to Teddy and said, "Read that." After a pause, he replied, "Does that sort of thing really amuse you?" "I heard the key turn in my prison-lock," she confided to the Love Diary. "Oh, Gods of derision! . . . And you've given me over twenty years of it! *Je n'en peux plus*! [I can't take it anymore.]" She soon turned anger at her "fate" against herself. Among the letters stacked on her desk at The Mount was Fullerton's note of the previous October, in which he had enclosed the sprig of witch hazel. Her country house was now a prison. She wrote in her diary, "*Ici, j'étouffe*"—I am suffocating here.[67]

Edith entered a period of emotional paralysis that brought on headaches, insomnia, and agitated depression. She fell ill with a six-week bout of hay fever. Writing Fullerton of her despair, she said: "I have stood it all these years, and hardly felt it, because I had created a world of my own, in which I lived without heeding what went on outside. But since I have known what it was to have some one enter into that world, and live there with me, the mortal solitude I come back to has become terrible." She confessed to having once taken strength from the line from Matthew Arnold's poem "Resignation": "They, believe me, who await no gifts from chance, have conquered fate." But no more. "Wear the mask," he advised.[68]

"I steep myself in books, I stupefy myself with long walks," she wrote him. She could not avoid for long the formidable editorial work awaiting her. She revised "The Choice," which appeared in the November issue of *Century Magazine*. She proofread translations of several previously published short stories scheduled in French reviews and edited *A Motor-Flight Through France* and *The Hermit and the Wild Woman*, a volume of seven stories. Only two of the tales in it were new, "The Verdict" and "The Pretext," both written during her weeks in Paris. "The Verdict" is an acidly etched portrait of a society painter of little talent who weds a rich widow and now lives lavishly on the Riviera. In real life, the couple were Ralph Curtis (Henry James once commented that Curtis made "a profession of merely knowing everybody and doing nothing") and his wife, Lise, who had inherited money from her former husband. When the story appeared, Mrs. Curtis took umbrage, just as Mrs. Sloane had seven years earlier over "The Line of Least Resistance." Lise Curtis undoubtedly suspected that Teddy's February visit to her Riviera home had occasioned the story. Teddy was a good raconteur with a quick eye for social foibles, and Edith often drew on his impressions. At that very moment she was using his verbal sketches of the clientele of the Hot Springs spa where he had spent the spring for *The Custom of the Country*.[69]

The second new story, "The Pretext," tells of young Guy Dawnish, an Englishman who woos an older American matron. The woman later learns that his interest in her had been a pretext to mask his attentions to a younger woman. This story presumably reversed the terms of a real incident (recounted to Edith by Henry James) in which the son of an English lord studying at Harvard fell in love with a professor's wife and broke off his engagement to the daughter of Pre-Raphaelite painter Holman Hunt. Ogden Codman, amused by her satire of pretensions in Cambridge, Massachusetts (where the story caused a good deal of "talk"), thought it a clever trick. "As usual," he commented to his mother, "Mrs. Wharton has just changed a few names, and altered peoples [sic] character a bit."[70]

To outward appearances, Edith worked well in early summer 1908, balancing writing, editorial, and translation projects. She continued to "grind steadily" every morning at *The Custom of the Country*, and in late July sent its first six chapters, about one-eighth of the book, to Burlingame, who scheduled it for January publication in the magazine. It was "distinctly and aggressively in the earlier field" (i.e., *The House of Mirth*), he told Charles Scribner, and would "do much to revive interest" in her work. The comic and briskly energetic tone of her correspondence with the men of Scribners in June and July so markedly contrasts with letters she wrote Fullerton during this period that the letters appear not to have been written by the same person. Yet, as the summer wore on, life became more difficult, and she finally stopped writing. Her last piece of fiction was a story in French, requested by Francis Charmes, editor of *La Revue des deux mondes*. "Les Metteurs en scène" ("The Stage Managers") tells of an American woman who arranges marriages between Faubourg nobility and American ladies.[71]

The story was written as a lark, but Henry James, when he read it in the October number of the *Revue*, received it with mock seriousness. He called it "an altogether astonishing feat" and congratulated Edith on having "picked up every old worn-out literary phrase that's been lying about the streets of Paris for the last twenty years, and manag[ing] to pack them all into those few pages." To a mutual friend, he pronounced it a "very credible episode in her career. *But she must never do it again*." (She did not.)[72]

Edith laughed at James's remarks and even repeated them as a joke on herself. This incident reveals how freely James offered his opinions on her work and with what frequency he prescribed the boundaries of her literary terrain. In a 1902 letter, he had "admonish[ed]" her toward "the *American subject*." At the same moment, he described her talent to her sister-in-law, Minnie Jones, as a "diabolical little cleverness," saying that he wanted to "get hold of the little lady and pump the pure essence of my wisdom and experience into her. She *must* be tethered in native pastures, even if it reduce her to a back-yard in New York," admitting that he wanted to "write" her work "over in my own way." The ferocity of James's rhetoric betrays his fear of Edith (as woman and as artist) and no small measure of hostility toward her. By 1908, she had long since leaped the fence of her New York "back-yard," and although she would never leave behind the "American subject," she followed her creative instincts wherever they led her. Because Henry James's friendship mattered to her, she answered his literary ultimata and cutting remarks with grace and wit. One imagines that lesser beings, had they spoken to her in such terms, would have received a quite different response.[73]

The glittering surface of "The Stage Managers" was wholly at odds with Edith's private depression and malaise of summer 1908. She wrote it shortly after Walter Berry made his annual visit to Lenox, and his accounts of wealthy ladies at the Paris Ritz (the "Nouveau Luxe" in the tale) may have provided her pretext. Bay Lodge, the young poet whom she had met a decade earlier in Washington, recalled the flashes of wit between Edith and Walter that summer, dramatizing the scene for his mother, Mrs. Henry Cabot Lodge:

> I have lunched twice with Mrs. Wharton and Walter whose keen little minds crackle and sparkle together unremittingly as of old, reminding one, for sheer continuity of sharp explosive wit, of some endless string of [small] prompt fire-crackers. They—especially she—are astonishing; the quick dry continual flash, coming briefly and brilliantly in unexpected right places, like the complicated lights of some restless electrical advertisement, leaving one, after all, admiring but rather unable, on one's own account, to hold the pace.

Thrust-and-parry was Edith's favorite social game. It relieved intellectual tensions and gave rise to sidesplitting laughter, but revealed little of her private self. Aware of her worries about Teddy (in Canada on his annual fishing trip), Walter knew nothing about Fullerton, whom he had not yet met. Walter still played the role of Edith's friend and adviser, but the subliminal eroticism that sparked their relationship some years earlier had faded. He now flirted with much younger women, society types whom Edith could not abide.[74]

When Edith's motor arrived from France, where it had undergone repairs following a June road accident, she traveled with Walter to Boston—her first excursion since returning from France three months earlier. (Her immobility and consequent isolation in this period undoubtedly had contributed to her ill health and unhappiness.) Eager to see Sally Norton, who had spent the summer at Shady Hill nursing her dying father, Edith paid her last visit to Charles Eliot Norton, her longtime friend and mentor. He would die on October 19, aged eighty-one; two weeks before his death, Sally wrote Edith of her intense suffering and regret. The letter recalled to Edith her own sense of self-loss, and the responsibility she bore for her own condition. "I should like to get up on the house-top and cry to all who come after us: 'Take your own life, every one of you!'" She begged Sally not to "ever regret having cried out your pain to me, or how shall *I* feel over my self-abandonment?" The opening stanza of Arthur C. Benson's poem "Self," recorded in her Commonplace Book, pictures Edith's condition:

> *This is my chiefest torment, that behind*
> *This brave and subtle spirit, this swift brain,*
> *There sits and shivers, in a cell of pain,*
> *A central atom, melancholy, blind,*
> *Which is myself. . . .*

With Fullerton at her side in the spring, the weight of her sadness had momentarily lifted. Now facing his inexplicable silence, she inhabited the "gross darkness, tangible, abhorred" that Benson wrote about.[75]

When news came of Charles Eliot Norton's death, Edith loaned Sally a tailored suit and black mourning veil (probably the outfit she wore for her uncle Fred Rhinelander in 1904) and suggested that she make a "complete break from present conditions" by coming to Europe. But Sally remained in Cambridge while Edith—unable to bear her own pain any longer—left for Europe. On October 20, one year after Fullerton had first appeared at The Mount, one year after the disappointing publication of *The Fruit of the Tree*, she withdrew *The Custom of the Country* from *Scribner's Magazine* and announced her immediate departure. "I have suffered so much from insomnia for the last two months that my work has been paralyzed by it."[76]

She had had no word from Paris since late June. "What was I to him?" she repeatedly asked herself. Worried that Morton might be ill, she cabled him. Receiving no response, she wrote on August 26: "Dear, won't you tell me soon the meaning of this silence?" He had awakened her from a "long lethargy, a dull acquiescence in conventional restrictions, a needless self-effacement," she wrote, and had she been "younger and prettier," things might have been different. She had loved him—and did love him—but she would not write again, "unless the strange spell is broken." Her last word was one of "tenderness for the friend I love—for the lover I worshipped. Goodbye dear."[77]

This letter, which was as much a memoriam of their brief time together as a plea for reassurance that nothing had changed between them, brought no answer. She had already memorialized herself for him in one of her best love poems (which he may not yet have seen), composed on the boat returning home in May:

> *When I am gone, recall my hair,*
> *Not for the light it used to hold,*
> *But that your touch, enmeshèd there,*
> *Has turned it to a younger gold.*
>
> *Recall my hands, that were not soft*
> *Or white or fine beyond expressing,*
> *Till they had slept so long and oft,*
> *So warm and close in your possessing.*
>
> *Recall my eyes, that used to lie*
> *Blind pools with summer's wreckage strewn.*
> *You cleared the drift, but in their sky*
> *You hung no image but your own.*
>
> *Recall my mouth, that knew not how*
> *A kiss is cradled and takes wing.*
> *Yet fluttered like a nest-hung bough*
> *When you touched it like the Spring.*

In this unpublished poem, one hears echoes of Shakespeare and John Donne (whom she was rereading), but its greatest debt is to William Butler Yeats. In spring, she had copied into her Commonplace Book his poem in tribute to Maude Gonne, "When you are old and grey and full of sleep," which recalls the afterlife of love in old age. Edith's poem reverses this perspective; her speaker springs to life at the lover's touch, her youth and beauty restored. The closing pun on "Spring"—more Donne than Yeats—retroactively charges the poem with erotic energy and establishes a wholly new perspective on the preceding lines. Edith used poetry to focus her intense emotional responses, and in the months ahead—unable to concentrate on novel-writing—she wrote verses. Before leaving for England on October 28, she began a remarkable eight-part sonnet sequence in honor of Fullerton entitled "The Mortal Lease." The centerpiece of *Artemis to Actaeon*, it would prove to be her finest poem.[78]

In late September, she wrote Henry James two distressing letters. These missives no longer exist, but we can infer from his response that she told him of her ill health, her worries about Teddy, and her concerns about Fullerton's mysterious silence. James had had no news from his young friend in three months, "and there are *kinds* of news I can't ask for." He hinted darkly, however, that "a great trouble, an infinite worry or a situation of the last anxiety or uncertainty are conceivable—though I don't see that such things, I admit, can explain *all*."

This reply was disingenuous. James had known for nearly a year that a woman in Paris had been trying for some time to get money out of Fullerton, but it was not for him to reveal the situation to Edith. How much she revealed of her relations with Fullerton, or how much James had deduced from his Paris trip, we do not know. Both Edith and Fullerton had reasons for not revealing themselves fully to James, and they had been especially discreet in his presence. Edith certainly would not have confessed everything in a letter. "Don't conclude," James cautioned: "sit tight." Before receiving this advice, she had already sent James a one-sentence announcement of her imminent arrival in England. The servants closed The Mount, Teddy checked into the Knickerbocker Club in New York for a stay of several weeks, and Edith sailed on the *Provence*, the ship that had brought her back from France five months earlier.[79]

She was accompanied by Walter, on his way to Cairo for a three-year appointment on the International Tribunal. His twenty-five years of law practice in Washington were at an end, although he would formally leave the firm only after he returned from Cairo. Some unpleasantness apparently occurred on the boat when Walter's behavior offended Edith—he seems to have flirted too openly with another woman. Landing at Le Havre, they detoured to Paris for a two-night stay at the Hôtel Dominici before taking the boat-train to Southampton. The Paris visit allowed Edith to see Fullerton, whom Walter met for the first time. Walter seemed more irritated than jealous at the delay; he was eager to get to London and spend a few days with a certain "Lady G"—Elsie Goelet. How much he ever knew or suspected of Edith's relationship with Morton Fullerton remains lost to history, but the two men later established a comradely friendship.[80]

The Paris detour raised more questions for Edith than it answered. She apparently did not ascertain the cause of Morton's long silence. Six weeks later, she wrote him from Lady St. Helier's London town house, addressing him as "Dear Mr. Fullerton" and requesting that he return to her "a few notes and letters of no value to your archives, but which happen to fill a deplorable lacuna in those of their writer." Twice before, she had asked that he return her letters, but now she wanted them sent registered mail (to Harry Jones's address on the place des Etats Unis) to ensure that they come "straight into my own hands." He did not return her letters, but sent a reassuring message: "The letters survive, and everything survives."[81]

ENGLISH SCENES

Edith had not been to England in more than two years, and when she and Walter pulled up at the Berkeley Hotel on Sunday, November 8, something like a royal welcome awaited her. Old friends gathered round, new acquaintances invited her into their drawing rooms, and for the next six weeks, she was caught up in the most exuberant, crowded social season she was ever to know in London. Her "inner circle" gathered around—Henry James, Howard Sturgis, and Gaillard Lapsley on hand to accompany her to lunch and tea, theater and art galleries. Even before arriving to the late-summer warmth and golden sunshine in the British Isles, her mood and health had begun to improve. She slept and ate better. "The change and movement carry me along, help to form an *outer surface*," she wrote Sally, "but the mortal desolation is there, will always be there." By "mortal desolation" she presumably meant the core of loneliness in her inner being.[82]

James later reported to Walter, whom they had seen off at the Southampton pier, that Edith was having the "Time of her Life" in a "wild, extravagant, desperate, detached fashion." He worried about her interest in English "society" and decried her "too rich and abysmal" life. Still, he matched her pace during these crowded weeks and even arranged a literary surprise for her. En route to Windsor to visit Sturgis, they stopped at Box Hill so that James could pay a visit to his old friend George Meredith. Edith wanted to wait in the motor, but at his insistence, she followed "somewhat sulkily" up the garden path.[83]

In a low sitting room sat Meredith—eighty years old, immobilized by illness, and completely deaf—"statuesquely throned in a Bath chair." She was face-to-face with one of her greatest literary heroes, author of "treasured" poetry and the invaluable *Harry Richmond* and *The*

Egoist, which she counted among her eight most favorite novels. In an agony of embarrassment, she waited while James tried to make Meredith understand who she was: "The room rang and rang again with my unintelligible name." But then the old man recognized that the figure standing before him was Edith Wharton. He lifted the book that lay at his elbow: "My dear child . . . I've read every word you've written, and I've always wanted to see you! I'm flying through France in your motor at this moment." This was a moment James had desired for Edith, but unable to make herself heard, she drew back to a corner and watched as their profiles leaned toward one another, Meredith's classically distinguished, James's heavy and Roman: "It was a fine impression."[84]

Although she claimed that her most cherished hours were spent with Dear Henry at Rye and Dear Howard at Windsor, Edith spent the bulk of her time on the London and country house social circuit. Doubtless, she wanted to be recognized by English high society, needing to taste its delights, rise to its occasions, and measure herself in its regard. The London social season added a third image to the hinged reflections thrown back to her by New York and Paris. Lady St. Helier, with whom Edith stayed for a few days, dedicated her life to providing a surfeit of kingly pleasures to aristocrats. She entertained nearly every night of the week; her spirits never flagged, her welcoming smile never drooped. Guests at her dinners sometimes numbered fifty, tiara-ed women in wasp-waist gowns and waistcoated men with monocles sitting at table for upwards of four hours while phalanxes of butlers served as many as ten courses. An endurance test, it required entertaining companions. Mary St. Helier had a fondness for literary and artistic figures, and Edith was always well placed at her table. She met Sir George Trevelyan, whose history of the American Revolution she held in high regard, discussed German literature with Lord Haldane and Lord Goschen, and (at a dinner for the princess of Schleswig-Holstein) carried on a one-sided conversation with Thomas Hardy, whom she found "as remote and uncommunicative as our most unsocial American men of letters." On another evening, she sat between Philip Burne-Jones and John Galsworthy.[85]

At the Mayfair town house of Lady Essex (Adele Grant from Boston), she was greeted by Edmund Gosse, H. G. Wells ("most stirring and responsive of talkers"), and the "matchless" Max Beerbohm. She also renewed her friendship with drama critic William Archer, who eight years earlier had tried to help her mount her play *Manon* on the

London stage. At a dinner given by the marchioness of Ripon, whom Edith had met at the Salsomaggiore spa and a woman known in the annals of Edwardiana for her love affairs, she found herself matching wits with an engaging man in his mid-thirties with an eager, "radio-active" intelligence. Taken by his conversation, she seems not to have noticed his sapphire-eyed good looks or even to have caught his name. He was Harry Cust, editor of the *Pall Mall Gazette*, who was a favorite of society hostesses and reputed to have fathered many a blue-eyed baby in peerage nurseries. They discussed one of Edith's favorite subjects, famous kisses in literature. She chose the kiss on the stairs in James's *Spoils of Poynton*. He quoted Shakespeare's Troilus:

> *Injurious Time now with a robber's haste*
> *Crams his rich thievery up, he knows not how;*
> *As many farewells as be stars in heaven . . .*
> *He fumbles up into a loose adieu,*
> *And scants us with a single famished kiss*
> *Distasted with the salt of broken tears.*[86]

Shakespeare's image of robber Time cramming his rich thievery fit the Edwardian age admirably well. It grew fat on excesses of food and wine, pleasure and promiscuity, as the clock ticked away to August 1914.

To Edith's great surprise, women writers sat at aristocratic tables: Lady Millicent St. Claire Erskine, the duchess of Sutherland (a novelist and friend of James's), and Lady Winifred Burghclere, who wrote on English history. More surprising, they did not hide their literary activities from the eyes of society, nor were their families embarrassed that wife and mother was also an author. Edith observed that poet and essayist Alice Meynell (who had reviewed several of her novels) was treated by her husband as a reigning sovereign; in conversation, he made constant reference to his wife's profound sayings. "I, who had been accustomed at home to dissemble my literary pursuits (as though, to borrow Dr. Johnson's phrase about portrait painting, they were 'indelicate in a female'), was astonished at the prestige surrounding Mrs. Meynell in her own family; and at the Humphry Wards' I found the same affectionate deference toward the household celebrity." Poet Alice Meynell and novelist Mrs. Ward took great interest in Edith's work and introduced her to people of similar interests, as did Mrs. Austin, wife of poet laureate Alfred Austin, and Lady Mary Elcho (later Lady Weymss), mistress of Stanway, a Renaissance house in the Cotswolds, where in December a weekend party was given in Edith's honor.[87]

Among the guests at Stanway were two men who would join Edith's enlarging "inner circle." The first was Robert Norton, the slim, handsome "Norts," whom she had met in 1905. After one year at Cambridge University, he first served as private secretary to the Conservative prime minister, Lord Robert Salisbury, and then went into business in the "City." At age forty, he was now about to retire to travel and paint. Edith introduced Norton to John Hugh Smith, a Cambridge-educated banker in his late twenties whom literary critic Percy Lubbock had brought along to dinner at Qu'acre, Howard Sturgis's home in Windsor, a few weeks earlier. On a foggy weekend in late November, she and Hugh Smith had met again at Cliveden, the three-hundred-acre Thames Valley estate of William Waldorf Astor and his wife, Nancy Langhorne. By then, John Hugh Smith was a little in love with Edith, and she was prepared to declare him "the most brilliant young man I have met in England." Years later, he recalled their first encounters in autumn 1908 and saw in his mind's eye a well-dressed woman of "exuberant vitality," her figure youthful, her face lined, her talk entertaining and stimulating. "You often spoke to me of Edith's books with admiration and of Edith herself with bewilderment," he told Lubbock, but "the more I saw of her, the more there was to learn and to enjoy—it seemed endless." James congratulated him on making friends with Edith Wharton: "You may find her difficult, but you will never find her stupid, and you will never find her mean"—an evaluation composed entirely of negative terms.[88]

When Edith's triumphant six weeks in England ended, she escorted Howard Sturgis and his nephew William Haynes-Smith (known as the "Babe," although he was nearly forty) on a motor-flight to Provence. She referred to this excursion as an "elopement." She collected them in her motor on Saturday, December 19, and whisked them to Lamb House, where they spent two nights. James, wanting to hear the full story of John Hugh Smith's lovesick condition, urged a "motor run" during her visit so that his nephew Aleck, who was also staying at Rye, would not overhear the gossip. On the twenty-first, Edith and her group took the ferry from Folkestone to Boulogne, and James collapsed, so he said, in an exhausted heap.[89]

By the twenty-third, the entourage had arrived in Dijon and pro-

ceeded as far south as Avignon before turning back (having encountered a fierce blizzard) toward Paris, where they dined at the Café de
Paris on New Year's Eve. Edith needed her "frame of steel," as James
had once called it, to face her return to Paris, where the situation with
Fullerton remained clouded and where Teddy would soon arrive for the
winter season. Several months later, James described her autumn 1908
idyll in England to Gaillard Lapsley, employing the metaphors of rapacious vampirism that he reserved just for her. There had been "general
eagle-pounces and eagle-flights of her deranging and desolating, rav-
aging, burning and destroying energy. . . . The Angel of Devastation
was the mildest name we knew her by." Earthbound James, gazing
skyward, envisioned Edith as a swooping, diving bird of prey. He
feared for his life, and also hers.[90]

THE WOMAN QUESTION

Sometime in the first week of January 1909, Edith and Fullerton spoke
privately of his "hell of a summer." Finding a moment for such a conversation must have been difficult, as she was busy escorting Howard
and the "Babe" to the theater and entertaining them at teas. The story
came to her piecemeal over several months, and one must consult Henry James's letters to her and her notes and *petits bleus* to Fullerton to
glean the general outline of the narrative: a Parisian named Mme Mirecourt had in her possession some old and compromising letters of
Fullerton's; during summer 1908, she had again threatened to make
them public (perhaps by sending them to his superior at the *Times*) if he
did not pay her money that she claimed he owed her. This was a severely truncated version of the story he had told James in November
1907, when he wrote in despair over the woman, who had been threatening him for several years. A worried James had little to give but
sympathy.[91]

When Edith told James in January that she and Fullerton had at last
talked, he declared himself "immensely relieved and fortified." Knowing what he did of the participants in these events, which dated from
the 1890s, he would hardly have thought that Fullerton would make a
clean breast of his past—the homosexual affairs with Lord Ronald
Gower and Percy Anderson, the disastrous affair with Margaret

Brooke, an emotionally unstable woman, who (in a foretaste of Mme Mirecourt) became domineering and demanding when Fullerton broke off their relationship.

Leaving behind a messy and entangled sexual past in London, Fullerton immediately involved himself in complicated liaisons on his arrival in Paris in 1891. He took up with Blanche Roosevelt Tucker, a writer and singer much older than himself, and also courted the young and very beautiful Anna Gould (later the wife of Boni de Castellane), whom he apparently almost married. In 1903, at age thirty-eight, he married a Frenchwoman, Victoria Camille Chabert, fourteen years younger than himself and the mother of a three-year-old girl, Mireille. (She was not Fullerton's child.) The unexpected marriage took his family in America by surprise. Deeply hurt, they pretended to friends that they had known of his plans for some time. Almost immediately after he married, the *Times* sent him to Madrid on an extended journalism assignment, and it was apparently in this period that Mme Mirecourt discovered the incriminating documents. He returned to Paris in January 1904, already separated from Camille, who was fed up with his affairs and had refused him his "marital rights." A Paris court granted him a divorce. Soon after, Mme Mirecourt made her first attempt to get money from him. In letters home, he told his parents of the difficult situation he faced and the kind of information contained in letters now in Mme Mirecourt's hands.[92]

We do not know how much Fullerton told Edith of his circumstances, but he probably revealed no more than absolutely necessary to explain his long silence during the summer. Although he remained friendly with his former wife, Camille Chabert, until his death, Edith seems never to have known that Fullerton was once married. Henry James, who cultivated discretion as a screen to hide his own latent desire for Fullerton, knew of the marriage but remained unaware of other aspects of his young friend's private life. He thought Morton suffered too much from unsteady nerves with Mme Mirecourt, and when he learned they resided in the same building, he urged him to move out immediately. Fullerton was, James said, "*hypnotized* by nearness and converse" with this "dangerous blackmailer." But in January 1909, Fullerton was still a resident at 40 bis rue Fabert, a street of eighteenth-century *hôtels* forming the western border of the esplanade des Invalides—less than a half-mile from the rue de Varenne.

Little about Morton Fullerton's relationship with the domineering Mme Mirecourt is self-evident. They apparently had been (and perhaps still were) lovers; the claim that he owed her money may have had some basis. She was not, as has been alleged, his landlady or concierge at the rue Fabert address, nor did she own the building. A firsthand account, given by a man who had known her for thirty years, described her as a self-possessed woman of "*estime*." Fullerton had once told his parents that he felt "profound sympathy and compassion" for her, and he apparently used a similar phrase in speaking of her to Edith.[93]

Such remarks only confirmed Edith's worst fear: there was another woman in Morton's life. But in telling her of Mme Mirecourt, who was apparently not the youthful beauty Edith might have imagined, he let her believe there was only *one* other woman in his life. In fact, there were several others, including his cousin Katharine Fullerton, who was deeply in love with him. Fourteen years younger than Morton, she was a lecturer in English literature at Bryn Mawr College, and in 1908–1909 she took a sabbatical leave in France. She had arranged his October 1907 lecture at Bryn Mawr, and during that visit—just days before Morton was Edith's guest at The Mount—he asked Katharine to marry him. When Morton's parents learned of these plans, they were distressed. Mrs. Fullerton accused Katharine of having "impertinently made love" to Morton, and Katharine felt "flayed alive" by this reaction.[94]

The domestic drama occasioned by news of the prospective marriage had roots in confused familial relations between Morton and Katharine. She was born Catherine Elizabeth Fullerton on February 6, 1879, in Brockton, the daughter of Bradford Fullerton's younger half brother, Charles, a bank cashier. Her mother, Elizabeth Prince Fullerton, died a month later, on March 4, of septicemia, aged twenty-eight. Bradford and his wife, Julia, the parents of two adolescent sons (William Morton and Robert), took baby Catherine into their home. Charles left Massachusetts, having apparently cheated his stepbrother out of a family inheritance. Catherine (whose name was later spelled "Katharine") grew up knowing the circumstances of her birth, thought of Bradford and Julia Fullerton as her parents and addressed them as "Father" and "Mother," although they never formally adopted her. From her earliest years, she gave Morton a special place in her heart. He encouraged her intellectual and literary interests, and she called him "the unforgettable miracle of my childhood." In 1891, when she was twelve, Katharine attended a convent school in Paris, and during this period, the bonds with Morton strengthened.[95]

An emotionally fragile girl, she was intensely romantic, impulsive, and strong-willed. She developed fantasies of Morton, spilling out her dreams and desires in long letters to him. Among the letters to him from her student days at Radcliffe College is one of angry warning. Should he ever have a daughter, he must not create dependencies in her and then abandon her: "Of course you couldn't help leaving me—and with the most constant care I never should be worth much anyway—but I should like you to realize that I am not the dupe of events." A more intense sorrow came with the news of his marriage to Camille Chabert. The failure of Morton's brief marriage, which hurt his parents, renewed Katharine's fantasy of marriage to him.[96]

She was convinced that he loved her only because of their "strange story," but in their hours at Bryn Mawr, he said "sacred words" that won her to him: "Without marriage there is no life for you nor for me." Although they were not sister and brother, and even though they never had sexual relations with each other, the emotional dynamics of their affair were incestuous. Indeed, the incest taboo fueled their desires for one another. Katharine spoke of "quivering from head to foot with love for you."[97]

No date had been set, but by early January 1908, Mrs. Fullerton had done an about-face in her resistance to the marriage and was already planning the wedding breakfast. As the weeks wore on, Morton fell silent and Katharine began to doubt his love. Were they to marry or not? If so, when? She became suicidally depressed: "I am terribly afraid of you," she wrote him, "but you are irresistible to me. . . . You have said nothing to me about destroying my letters. I want from you *at once please* the explicit assurance that you have destroyed them all."[98]

Receiving no answers to her questions and no assurance that he had destroyed the letters, Katharine made plans to come to Europe. She requested sabbatical leave from M. Carey Thomas, president of Bryn Mawr College, and after spring graduation ceremonies, she sailed to England. Following several weeks in London, where she visited Henry James, she arrived in Paris. Morton squired her around the city, introducing her to his friends. Dolly Wilde (niece of Oscar Wilde), a friend of Fullerton's and quite probably his sometime lover, warned him that he was playing with fire: "As you have told me," she wrote in misspelled French, "your little sister loves you. Don't break her heart if you are incapable of attaching yourself to her." Petite, brown-eyed Katharine, whose wavy, dark hair hung loose on her shoulders, making her look far younger than her twenty-nine years, dreamt of a wedding at the American Pro-Cathedral on the avenue George V—the most elegant and fashionable of the churches that served the expatriate community. Edith apparently met Katharine during her two-day visit to Paris with Walter in October 1908. But by the time she returned to 58 rue de Varenne at the end of December, Katharine had taken a room at the convent of Tours in the Loire, at work on her first novel.[99]

EDITH HOPED TO put her relations with Fullerton on a new footing, but in the first weeks of the new year, they were preoccupied with domestic problems. Trying to retrieve his letters from Mme Mirecourt, Fullerton was also dealing with problems at the *Times*. Edith was simultaneously house-hunting and searching for a cook to replace the alcoholic, unreliable "empoisonneuse" (figuratively, a "poisoner") she had just fired. Determined to take a long-term lease on a Paris property, she set up a business meeting with her brother Harry to discuss her trust funds on January 19, the day after Teddy's arrival from New York. Teddy arrived after a "frightful crossing" in no condition to make any decisions. John Hugh Smith, whose planned visit she had put off, arrived on January 21, expecting to play golf with Teddy (whom he had not yet met) and discovered him bedridden with gout, grippe, and severe headaches. Edith escorted John Hugh to art galleries and museums and a round of theatergoing, but Teddy's illness forced her to forgo the small dinner parties she usually arranged for visitors. Instead, she asked a few people to Sunday luncheons, Fullerton among them. John Hugh's visit occasioned many good talks—"quick 'wirelesses'" of feelings and intuitions—and soon he became one of her closest confidants.[100]

Returning to London after a brief trip south, he sent Edith an "admirable" silver cigarette case that cheered her. She flaunted and flashed it in front of envious friends ("female especially"), and felt "enormously adorned and enhanced by it." Her gift to him was the volume of Flaubert's letters to George Sand, and she encouraged him to read Sand's responses. A second gift was Benjamin Constant's *Adolphe*, the story of a seducer pursued by his victim. She enjoyed their mild flirtation, and if these works fed John Hugh's romantic fantasies, Edith—writing him in the marital "we"—felt trapped in her marriage and buffeted by vicissitudes. Life was so "jerky and incoherent," she wrote, that she could not make quick progress on *Tales of Men and Ghosts*, the volume of short stories she was planning.[101]

As she established herself in the Faubourg intellectual community, Teddy was pushed farther to the margins of her life. Unable to speak French, lacking business and legal expertise in international property matters, he could not play the managerial, advisory, and investment roles for her in Paris that he did in America. Edith needed Walter, expert in all these matters, but he was facing formidable challenges in adapting to the rigors of life in Egypt, suffering stomach pains and intestinal viruses that produced the old malarial symptoms. Meanwhile, Teddy's physical and psychological distress increased alarmingly, and he sank into almost total self-absorption. "He's the worst 'patient' I've ever seen," Edith wrote Sally, who was due to arrive soon in Paris for a visit intended to help her get over the death of her father. A few days later, Edith cabled Sally, advising that she go first to England. The doctors wanted Teddy to go south, and Edith accompanied him on a ten-day trip to the Riviera. When Sally did at last arrive in Paris, Edith sent her to a hotel.[102]

By late February 1909, Teddy was so ill that they could not entertain overnight guests in the apartment. He saw a Paris specialist, who recommended a two-month series of massage and electricity treatments for his gout and facial neuralgia. By the third week in April, the lease was up on the Vanderbilt apartment and Teddy was on a boat back to New York. Edith moved to the Hôtel de Crillon on the place de la Concorde, not far from Fullerton's office on the rue de la Chaussée d'Antin.

To friends back home, she played down the seriousness of Teddy's illness. Writing to Robert Grant, who had sent her his latest novel (*The Chippendales*, a study of Boston life), she remarked on recent changes in herself, telling him how much she had enjoyed the "whole glittering procession" in England:

Then I came here, and picked up the threads again, finding as usual plenty to pick! It is curious that when I was younger, and busy with my own slow development, I could subsist on *myself* indefinitely with only a vague unformulated need of companionship "de l'esprit"; whereas now I find myself greatly stimulated by it, and consequently more and more dependent on having it for at least a few months of each year. Hence my great enjoyment of London and Paris.[103]

Grant envisioned her moving beyond the New York–Lenox–Boston–

Newport axis. From foggy, chilly London, John Hugh imagined her as an unclouded luminary, tracing serene curves through the seventh heaven. To Henry James, she was an eagle in flight. In fact, she was feeling "shabby," "dim," and in need of sympathy. She kept a tight rein on her emotions at home, trying not to betray her anxieties to the servants; but in social situations, her pent-up anger and distress at her marriage and frustrations with Fullerton were expressed in barbed *répliques*.[104]

One such moment occurred at a Sunday luncheon at the home of society painter Jacques-Emile Blanche, whom she had commissioned the previous spring to paint Henry James (a portrait she probably paid for). Blanche knew everyone who was anyone, and on this occasion, his guest was his friend, the Irish novelist George Moore, the literary lion of expatriate London hostess Emerald Cunard, rumored to be his mistress. Famously conceited and rude, he showed himself on this day so "repulsive a bounder" that Edith decided to "annihilate him." She succeeded admirably, she told John Hugh: "There were no recognizable fragments to gather up." Moore had made the fatal mistake of commenting that the women of his *Confessions of a Young Man* (1888, but revised and expanded in several later editions) had been "rather flattered" to be mentioned in his book. "I should think *you* would have been flattered at their even having heard of your book," she retorted. "Having tasted blood, I proceeded to wade in it." To what depths she waded, we do not know.[105]

In all these weeks, James had had only "the faintest and most roundabout" echoes of Edith, and from the end of January to mid-April, she had no word from him. Like Teddy, he worried about his failing health; fearing heart trouble and struggling with his writing, he worked himself into nervous depression. James was at a low moment, and things were soon to get worse. The primary causes of his distress were economic and professional. In 1908, he had earned only $1,000 (to Edith's nearly $14,000, a year of poor earnings for her). It was the least profitable year of his career, and because of his winter illness, he had lost valuable time in preparing the "New York" edition of his novels that Charles Scribner's Sons was publishing. He and his publishers hoped that the edition would revive American interest in his writing. It proved a financial and critical disaster, and James's despair over it resulted in physical illnesses and depression that dominated his last years.[106]

Adding to his current woes, two American magazines had rejected his short story "The Velvet Glove," a *conte à clef* based on an evening drive through Paris with Edith to St. Cloud in spring 1907. When it was at last published, in the March 1909 *English Review*, she sent him a letter of praise (a letter that no longer exists), for which he was deeply grateful: "As I seem to be living on into evil days, your exquisite hand of reassurance and comfort scatters celestial balm—and makes me de nouveau believe a little in myself, which is what I infinitely need and yearn for . . . so that in short, dearest Edith, you are a direct agent of the Most High for keeping alive *in the me* the vital spark. You've blown upon it so charmingly to-day that it's quite a brave little flame."[107]

In the next years, James depended on her friendship and was solicitous of her as she tried to cope with Teddy's illness. In early May, a few weeks before she was due to visit England, he wrote frankly of her situation to Gaillard Lapsley:

> I fear she has had a baddish, anxious overloaded winter in Paris. Teddy is worryingly, nervously, a bit ominously ill—on the best "advice" even that he may be cerebrally compromised. This is the first "cross" I really imagine that she has had to bear, and I seem to make out that it comes terribly hard. He is gone back to America for the time, but they have *let* the Mount this summer (for a million or two!) and are to drift or "hoard" or whatever, according to his condition.

What James actually knew of Teddy's condition and what he meant by "cerebrally compromised" we can only guess. But rumors were beginning to circulate: in autumn 1908, while Edith was in England, Teddy had reportedly been seen in New York and Boston with young actresses from the musical stage.[108]

Chapter 5

ESTRANGEMENTS

DESPITE EDITH'S DOMESTIC WOES AND CARES OF THE heart, spring 1909 was an exceptionally energetic period of her writing career in which she produced not only her best poetry but also some of her most memorable short stories. She again set aside *The Custom of the Country*, this time to write ten new short stories for *Tales of Men and Ghosts*, a volume under contract to Scribners. She completed her long sonnet sequence, "The Mortal Lease," and revised sections of "Ogrin the Hermit," a 170-line poem on a theme from the myth of Tristan and Iseult, which appeared in the December 1909 *Atlantic Monthly*. "The Mortal Lease" and "Life" (a poem begun in May 1908) provide hinged-mirror responses to Fullerton, while "Ogrin the Hermit" allegorizes a moral struggle on the question of extramarital love.

"Life" echoes the hymn of thanksgiving recorded in the May 16, 1908, Love Diary entry: "Oh Life, Life, how I give thanks to you for this!" In tone, rhythm, and sensuality, and in the pure energy of its joyfulness, "Life" is unlike any other Edith Wharton poem. Set in a springtime wood, the poem's speaker is a reed growing among the rushes of the Lethe-bank, a shoal of forgetfulness. Life—a feminine Pan—makes the reed the instrument of her music:

> *Nay, lift me to thy lips, Life, and once more*
> *Pour the wild music through me—*

Playing tunes on the reed, Life travels the world from woodland and seashore to cities, from the depths of Hell to Mount Olympus and on into interstellar space.

The immediate source for this work is Herbert Trench's poem "Apollo and the Seaman," which Edith copied into her Commonplace Book early in the year. It explores the nature of selfhood, comparing it to a ship awash on the tides of Life, guided by unseen forces. Apollo, god of music and prophecy, speaks to the seaman whom he has invented as his human "other": "Ah, fragment of my soul." Edith's poem rejoices in the "demi-urgic powers" that surge beneath human hopes and fears (Nietzsche's influence is evident); Trench's poem strikes a more somber note, reminding the sea-tossed sailor that self-determination is a delusion:

> *Deem'st those old faceless images,*
> *"Truth," "Justice," "Liberty,"*
> *Heralding symbols thou employ'st?*
> *They are employing thee!*

Throughout 1909, Edith struggled with the faceless images of "truth," "justice," and "liberty." She also felt the strong undertow of old forces of convention and duty that had shaped her and that she could not completely disown.

"The Mortal Lease" mirrors "Life" by casting human experience within a time-space continuum that forms a double perspective, at once cosmic and personal. Collectively, the sonnets compose a meditation on love; individually, they trace the stages of love's progress and forecast reversals of love's promise. Read literally, and biographically, the poems reconstruct her hesitation in meeting her lover's desire (and her own) to enter into physical intimacy with him. She reexamines her initial confusion and inability to act and acknowledges her sexual vulnerability. A second perspective, which focuses the universal and eternal through the human spirit, recounts a chronological narrative that moves across the vast sweep of history, from the world's creation to a faraway future seen from a distant planet. "The Mortal Lease" constituted Edith Wharton's most challenging poetic endeavor, and undoubtedly her clearest success. The eight sonnets form linked dialogues: first, between the speaker and lover, and then between the speaker and Time, personified as "the Moment." The speaker is pulled between the desire to live in the moment *and* her very human longing for eternity. In an elaborate metaphysical conceit, the poet imagines the world as the circle of the lovers' kisses—a kind of eternity in the present. "The Moment" arrives bearing a "sacramental cup," but flees when the woman hides her face before its wonder. A ghostly vision (recalling the veiled figure at Herblay) whispers "with lips derisive": "Now thou shalt not know." The woman has lost her chance, as Edith feared she had lost hers.

The next sonnet harks back to the agonized weeks of self-scrutiny early in 1908:

> *Shall I not know? I, that could always catch*
> *The sunrise in one beam along the wall,*
> *The nests of June in April's mating call,*
> *And ruinous autumn in the wind's first snatch*
> *At summer's green impenetrable thatch—*
> *That always knew far off the secret fall*
> *Of a god's feet across the city's brawl,*
> *The touch of silent fingers on my latch?*

Edith did not make a religion of her love for Fullerton nor did she return to her youthful religious orthodoxy. Rather, she sought ways to reconcile the sexual and the sacred, to undo oppositions and to see how the sacred—whether Attic or Christian—folds mortality into immortality.

"The Mortal Lease" is contemplative, taking a retrospective look at human nature. In the early stages of its composition, Edith assumed that her relationship with Fullerton had already ended. She regretted her *manque de volonté*, the diseased will that prohibited her from enacting—physically, sexually—her love for him. Time was her enemy. When she left Paris in May 1908, she did not believe that the occasion for erotic intimacy would again present itself. But it did. When "the Moment" came, she acted without guilt.

An unpublished sequel to this poem, entitled "Colophon to The Mortal Lease," re-creates a scene of sexual love that builds to the moment of climax, in which spirit and flesh seem to be one. As the moment falls away into silence, the woman looks into her lover's eyes to realize that he has not glimpsed that other scene—eternity irradiated in the Moment—as she has. Unable to bear looking at his eyes, she asks him to close them. Edith's own copy of this undated poem apparently no longer exists; but in March 1912, Fullerton made a copy for himself, adding a postscript that provided his own "colophon" to the poem and an epitaph to his love affair with Edith Wharton: "I saw not what she saw, and that's the tragedy of it."

Edith included "The Mortal Lease" and "Life" in her poetry collection *Artemis to Actaeon*, published in April 1909. Although response was generally praiseworthy, most critics thought her poetry did not reach the level of her prose and found the poems more intellectual than emotional. William Morton Payne, writing for the *Dial*, concluded that her poetry was "too sicklied o'er with the pale cast of thought, its artifice is too evident, its song (as far as it sings at all) does not well straight up from the heart." The *Independent* reviewer said the poems were "too precious and curious"—indeed, too "unnatural."

"Ogrin the Hermit," the third poem she had begun writing in 1908, had as creative impetus Joseph Bédier's retelling of *The Romance of Tristan and Iseult*, first published in 1900. Edith used only one scene from the story, in which Ogrin, a religious hermit, protects Iseult after Tristan has helped her escape the leper colony where her legal husband, old King Mark, had consigned her when he discovered that she loved his nephew Tristan. Elements of this legendary threat to an old man's proprietary interests and the quasi-incestuous rivalry between young and old were themes of D'Annunzio's *La Figlia di Iorio*, which she and Morton had seen in January 1908, and the legend of Lancelot and Queen Guenevere. (She copied William Morris's "Defence of Guenevere" into her Commonplace Book.) The *Divine Comedy*, a favorite work of both Edith and Morton, also echoes in "Ogrin," where pity (in Dante's sense of "worthy of compassion") is the instrument of spiritual awakening.

Ogrin recalls how he abhorred the young couple's sin of illicit love but pitied their "great extremity." He tried to teach Iseult holiness, only to realize that she was a child of "ancient lore," born in an antediluvian Paradise where evil did not exist: her "heart lives in heathen innocence/With earth's innocuous creatures." She represents a pre-Christian view of love and compels the hermit's attention not by justifying her actions, but by opening new perspectives on the relation of love and life to mortality and sin. In renewing the human spirit, acts of love (including sexuality) are sacred and repeat the initial gesture with which God created the world out of love.

Underwriting the poem is Edith's belief—expressed in letters to friends, diary entries, and commentaries on her reading of Nietzsche—that traditional Christian dogma had so narrowed the definition of the spiritual and so brutally denied the body's natural impulses that it embraced death rather than life. The lover's kiss becomes—quite literally in Bédier's reading of the Tristan and Iseult legend—the kiss of death.

She dedicated the poem to Fullerton ("Per Te, Sempre per Te"), claiming not only that it was written for him but *by him* as well. She presented it to him on a spring 1909 evening when things were very bad with Teddy and asked him to read it aloud to her. Fullerton had known in spring 1908 that she was working on the poem; one of its most memorable conceits, "Close as lips lean/lean the thoughts between," became a refrain of her letters to him. She copied these lines and Ogrin's meditation on the quality of Tristan and Iseult's love into the Commonplace Book:

> *Such music of the heart as lovers hear,*
> *When close as lips lean, lean the thoughts between—*
> *When the cold world, no more a lonely orb*
> *Circling the unimagined track of Time,*
> *I like a beating heart between their hands,*
> *A numb bird that they warm, feel its wings—*
> *Such music once I heard.*

The morning after Fullerton read her poem aloud, Edith wrote to him: "I am so happy at what you told me about 'Ogrin.'"

> You'd understand why, if you knew how often and often I've said to myself (like the Jongleur de N. Dame): "Oh, if once I could *make* something for him that people—indifferent strangers—might talk about and find good; and if he might hear them praising it, while he sat silent and said to himself: 'good people, it's not *hers*, it's mine!'" Et voilà—cela m'est arrivé, et je suis heureuse. [And it came to me, and I am happy.]

In the tale, the juggler of Notre Dame is caught performing his acrobatic feats before the statue of the Virgin Mary. He explains to the priest that he has no other gift to bring her but the gift of his "art." Edith's gift carries a pointed message to Fullerton: like Iseult in Bédier's reading of the legend, she will remain, out of pity and loyalty, with her husband. (His mental illness, not her affair with Fullerton, would later force her to reverse this decision.) She asked him not to think her "sentimental or 'petite fille'—still less, a woman who tries to make herself more interesting":

> It's just this—the situation *is* changed, and I, who like to *walk up to things*, recognize it, and am ready to accept it—only it must be nettement [clear]! I recognize, also, perfect freedom in loving and in un-loving; but only on condition that it is associated with equal sincerity.
>
> Since things are as they are now, I look on you as free to carry your soucis cardiaques [concerns of the heart] where you please; *but* on condition that you and I become again, in our talk and our gestes, the good comrades we were two years ago. If I thought that you could continue to talk to me and to *be* with me as you were this afternoon, while you had, at the same time, even transiently, a fleur d'épiderme [heart throb], the same attitude to anyone else, I should think you had failed in the loyalty due to a love like mine, as freely and unconditionally given as mine has been.

She asks that they "go back gaily and goodhumouredly" to their former state. "That is the form my fierté [pride] takes!" She would repeat her request for friendship rather than the pretense of "Love" a dozen times over the next three years, and only by her continued persistence did Fullerton finally acquiesce.[1]

The changed "situation" to which she referred in her letter was Fullerton's entanglement with Mme Mirecourt, to whom (he said) he was bound by loyalty and compassion—just as she was bound to Teddy. Edith and Morton had seen little of each other in spring 1909, and when they were together, she was, by her own admission, often "stupid, disappointing, altogether impossible," and "inarticulate." She was beset with fears that he was making a pretense of loving her or that her letters to him might fall into the wrong hands—Mme Mirecourt's, for example. These fears were hardly irrational given what she now knew of his situation, but they added to the strain on her overworked nervous system. On one late-February morning she became frightened: "I was *paralyzed* by not getting your note till 11, knowing it must have been written, and having the conviction that it must have got into the wrong hands, yet being unable to find out. . . ." Asking him to drop the pose that theirs was anything other than friendship ("Don't, above all, feel obliged to try to make *me* think what isn't!"), she then reversed herself: "So, if you come and dine, let it be with the old friend of last year, who knits and reads—qui t'aime, qui t'aime, mais qui sait qu'elle ne sait pas te le dire, et qui se taira désormais [the one who loves you, who loves you, but who knows that she doesn't know how to tell you and who will henceforth keep silent]."[2]

Sometime earlier, Edith had responded to a poem that Katharine Fullerton had sent her. The dramatic monologue "Gemma to Beatrice" was occasioned by a comment Morton made to his cousin in a letter of late 1907: he apparently called her his "Beatrice," a reference to the virginal Beatrice Portinari, who inspired Dante Alighieri and served as a symbol of eternal love in his *Divine Comedy*. Katharine angrily rejected this role for herself. She did not want to "triumph in some fantastic Heaven": "You shall have me yet—flesh and blood, on this Earth," she wrote him. Her poem gives voice to Gemma, Dante's wife and the mother of his children, who at the end of her life prays to "Madonna Beatrice," the Queen of Heaven:

> *I have shed many tears, Madonna, for your sake:*
> *Now I am wise, and would not change with you,*
> *Who have known love but as the angels know it,*
> *In Heaven, where none gives or takes to wife.*
> *I have loved Dante, whom you did not love;*
> *I wedded Dante, whom you did not wed:*
> *I hold no woman is so blest as I—*
> *No other woman born will have had this.*

The price of Gemma's earthly love was long years in Purgatory: "I have had earth, Madonna. Heaven is yours."

A tour de force, the poem gives clear evidence that thirty-year-old Katharine Fullerton, who would become a respected novelist, essayist, and literary critic, had a great poetic gift. Edith praised its terse, vigorous expression and advised that she send it to Richard Gilder at *Century*. But Edith also mentioned the poem to Edward Burlingame, who accepted it for the June 1910 *Scribner's*. Wanting to know Katharine better, Edith invited her to make an overnight visit from Tours and stay at the rue de Varenne—this despite Teddy's illness. She suggested that they might persuade "Mr. Fullerton" to join them for an evening performance by Isadora Duncan, whom Edith regarded as the greatest of contemporary dancers. The overnight visit never took place, probably because Katharine was not eager to see Morton, having fled Paris several months earlier expressly to escape him. Katharine knew there was another woman in his life, and someone other than Mme Mirecourt, whom she probably had known about since 1904, when Morton told his parents the story of her blackmail attempts. But she had no idea—and would never learn—that the "other woman" of 1909 was Edith Wharton. Nor would Edith ever learn that Morton and Katharine were engaged to be married during this period. Indeed, it was not until some years later that she learned Morton and Katharine were cousins, not siblings. Fullerton, a master of deception, spoke to each woman about the other, all the while hiding his real relations with them.[3]

Critics have suggested that Fullerton may have shared Katharine's letters to him with Edith, letting her glimpse the "strange story" that crisscrossed the boundaries of brother-sister-lover, and that Edith then put the letters to literary uses (in her 1910 story "The Letters," for example). Not only is there no evidence to support this claim, but it also seems entirely out of character, both for Fullerton and for Edith. Leading multiple lives, he kept multiple secrets. When Edith suspected his duplicity (with Mme Mirecourt, for example), he tried to dissemble. The best evidence that Edith knew nothing of his desirous relations with Katharine is her sustained admiration for the younger woman. If she had read Katharine's letters to Morton from the 1908–1909 period, she would have formed quite a different view of her—and of Fullerton.[4]

PASSAGES

On June 1, Edith left the Hôtel de Crillon for London. Cook was at the wheel of her Panhard, a bonneted Gross sat by his side; Fullerton and Edith shared the backseat. Their moment was almost at hand: they were soon to spend a "long secret night" together. The setting was not the green wood she had dreamed of, but instead a grimy railroad hotel, and before it took place, they had one more night alone, in separate rooms at Folkestone (and seasick from the Channel crossing).

Fullerton was in transit to America, his first visit home since the fateful weekend in November 1907 when he had announced his engagement to Katharine. Relieved as he may have been to escape Paris, where Mme Mirecourt had made yet another attempt to get money out of him, he knew there were troubles ahead—his father, now in his early seventies, was ill; the family was suffering financial hardships; and his brother Rob was suffering an embarrassing personal crisis. An insurance agent, unhappily married and the father of two young children, he had apparently contracted syphilis and was taking a two-year mercury cure for ulcers on his mouth and genitals. Julia Ball Fullerton, whose relationship with her sons combined coquetry, maternal suffering, and wheedling dependence, had taken Morton into her confidence about this situation and made him swear to keep these events secret from Katharine, who was still in France. Rob's wife, a much disliked daughter-in-law who suffered incapacitating depressions rather like Teddy Wharton's, feared that she, too, would become infected. (She did not.) Edith knew nothing of this situation.[5]

Fullerton had taken a suite in the Charing Cross Hotel, two bedrooms and a salon (Apartment 92), where he and Edith spent the night. The station hotel was in his price range, its location convenient—he was leaving by train in the morning for Southampton—and distant from the Mayfair area where Edith usually stayed. Gross and Cook were probably also lodged in the hotel, but as we know from Edith's poem commemorating the occasion, Gross did not wait on her mistress that evening. Henry James roused himself from his own troubles to come to town, and he dined with Edith and Morton. Where they dined and what they discussed are lost to history, as are James's conclusions (if any) about his friends' relationship. He had not seen Fullerton since they parted in Paris in May 1908 and had heard virtually nothing from him in the intervening year. He knew only by hints and rumors of Edith's present domestic problems. The following morning, a dark and rainy one, Fullerton said good-bye to Edith, who—in his memory of some forty years later—was propped up in bed writing. In parting, he sent her roses.

She may or may not have been composing "Terminus," the fifty-two-line poem that recalls (and imaginatively recasts) the events of the previous night, a work she presented to Fullerton five weeks later. The poem astonishes as much by its existence as its frankness. It employs powerful sexual images—the long windings of passion, the pressure of ecstatic bodies—and the singsong rhythms of its dactylic hexameter (borrowed from Longfellow) repeat the "shaking and shrieking of

trains, the night-long shudder of traffic." The scene is both extraordinary and commonplace, the night of lovemaking set in a red-lamped
room of an impersonal hotel with soot-sodden chintz and grimy brass-
es. Except that the woman in the rutted and worn bed is the poetic re-
creation of Edith Wharton—who on no other occasion tolerated
dust-eddied hotel rooms—the acts that take place under the black rain
of midnight are predictable.

"Terminus" describes not the exceptional or noteworthy, but the routine and prosaic. The "faces innumerous" reflected in the mirror and
the dust-stained, fagged bodies that lay on the low, wide bed belong to
"travelling automata," workers of the world who are indifferent and
weary, hurried and aimless. Ordinary souls, the "human unceasing current" of their daily lives, had long sparked Edith's curiosity. She felt
joined at last to the human throng: "Thus, like us they have lain and
felt, breast to breast in the dark." The experience alleviated somewhat
her sometimes bitter jealousy of other women—plain, dull, poor
women—who accepted as a matter of course their right to sexual pleasure.

The lyric, celebratory note takes an ominous turn, however, as the
male lover is carried into the "wide flair of cities," while the woman
fares forth in the morning to "waste land and stretches of low-skied
marsh" (a scene not unlike Rye, where Edith was headed), a dying
landscape in which the wrecks of houses metamorphose on a pale winter evening into gravestones, and ghosts stand at train carriage doors.
The woman finds herself among the living dead, a scene Edith had
plotted in numerous stories of the supernatural. Two women appear in
the poem, the speaker ("I") and a silent, ordinary woman who leaves
the room to follow the "fixed rail of habit by the hand of implacable
fate." The second woman is a shadow of Edith Wharton, who must return to her marriage. The closing lines of the poem draw mirror images
of the two women as they lean to kiss the sleeping man—a lover im-
aged only as a pair of "sleeping lips," the kiss reflected as "shadow-
mouths" in the mirror. The scene is vampirish, and the poem ends on
the word "oblivion," the desired, deadly unconsciousness that Edith's
heroines Lily Bart and Bessy Westmore had sought and found:

> *Thus may another have thought; thus, as I turned,*
> *may have turned*
> *To the sleeping lips at her side, to drink, as I drank there, oblivion.*

As its title suggests, "Terminus" does not signal life and light. Set in shadows and "gloom," it is steeped in darkness (a word repeated four times in ten lines), and sunrise never comes. The woman's night of passion leads not to regeneration but to the old path of duty. The poem is depressing, even frightening, its terminus a "no exit" from death-in-life. Fullerton noted that it owed something to Goethe's *Roman Elegies*, a series of poems that celebrated his sexual liberation with an enigmatic woman named Faustina, who embodied the spirit of Rome. The *Roman Elegies* are not elegiac in the usual sense, however. They are filled with light and energy, and portray myth, history, and daily life against the dignified splendor of the classical past. Edith's poem, by contrast, summons up industrial-age London, the scream of trains carrying away "the nameless, the many." No line of "Terminus" has the energy of Goethe's rapture. The undated note in which Edith enclosed the poem to Fullerton comes closer to Goethean joy than anything in the poem itself: "I beg you dear, send back the poem soon. *Je suis si heureuse* [I am so happy]—it breaks over me like a great sweet tide." This lyrical evocation of female eroticism, conceived as a rhythmic, repeated, orgasmic wave, reveals a sensual and romantic Edith Wharton rarely seen.[6]

A few hours after Fullerton departed, she set out in "Hortense" (her motor named in honor of Hortense Allart) for a dark, wet, and cold weekend at Windsor with Howard Sturgis. The following day, Edith made a special trip to Rye to collect Henry James. Resident at Qu'acre for ten days, she made almost daily trips to London for luncheons and sightseeing, and in so doing gave Howard the impression that she was bored by his company. The Babe wore on her nerves, as he did on everyone except Howard, who, it was rumored in the family, provided him a home in return for sexual favors. Edith would have liked to attend Cup Day at Ascot, where she had never been, but turned down the Babe's invitation to accompany her. She wanted to discuss Racine with John Hugh and to hear his comments on *Artemis to Actaeon*, but all this had to await their reunion on June 14, when she visited Lady St. Helier in London and another round of banquets and theater parties.[7]

Between social engagements, Edith had important editorial business to attend to. In mid-May, she had received a letter from Frederick Macmillan that gave her the idea for a possible solution to Fullerton's financial woes with Mme Mirecourt. Macmillan asked her to write a book on Paris, explaining that the firm had contracted the project with someone else, who was now unable to complete it. She politely refused his request, saying she had neither the ability nor the inclination to do the work: a book on Paris, "in addition to special qualifications in the author, requires an intimate and varied acquaintance with the most complex of cities, in all its aspects, historical, architectural and socio-logical." She recommended Morton Fullerton, who combined "an un-usual number of these qualities," she said. She proceeded to laud his past accomplishments, and asked Macmillan to speak with Henry James, who would "confirm what I say as to his ability to do the kind of book you want."

By the time Edith arrived in England in June, Macmillan had al-ready written Fullerton, who—to Edith's dismay—had not answered the letter. She urged him to do so, thus setting the stage for part two of the scheme, for which she sought James's complicity: an "advance" of £100 (about $2,500 at today's rates) against book royalties. The mon-ey went from Edith's Barclay account to James to Macmillan to Fuller-ton. Macmillan believed the money came from James; Fullerton was supposed to believe that the money came from Macmillan. Only Edith Wharton and Henry James were to know the real source, but the only person who remained completely in the dark was Macmillan. Fullerton never wrote the book, despite encouraging, chiding, and finally angry words from both Henry and Edith, and he seems to have learned the identity of his benefactress. He did pay off Mme Mirecourt and move to a different apartment, as Edith and Henry urged him to do, but these measures by no means extricated him from her.[8]

With no sick husband to attend to and no enigmatic lover to worry her, Edith made the most of her English idyll. The primary compass points of her travels were Qu'acre, Lamb House, and Lady St. Helier's Portland Place mansion in London. But she motored to Cliveden (the Waldorf Astors) in the Thames Valley, to Stocks (the Humphry Wards) in the Epping Forest, and southward to Stanway (Lord and Lady Elcho) in Gloucestershire. Her tour included Oxford to see Percy Lubbock, a librarian at the Bodleian, and Cambridge, where Gaillard Lapsley was a tutor in history. His Majesty's telephone and postal service were abuzz with changes in plans and switches of venue. "Hortense" crisscrossed the island with breathless speed as Edith's friends and hosts looked on agog. What a way to organize one's life! Henry groaned.

Amused, Howard Sturgis composed a mock scientific narrative, "Studies in Bird-Life," in which Edith appears as the "Editten Steelpen-nata" and as the *l'oiseau de feu*, a reference to Stravinsky's *Firebird* ballet, which had already been performed in Moscow and would take Paris by storm in spring 1910. Slender and delicate, this intelligent, exquisite little creature is endowed with "unexampled strength and ferocity." It nests in "the most unlikely places, and is seldom long in one place as it is a true bird of passage." Henry James appears as the Ryebird, *Laureatus poeticus,* and Howard himself as a near-extinct Quacker goose, "graceless, greedy, lazy" and with no sex instinct. Edith read the comic send-up on returning to Lamb House with Henry after a four-day motor tour of Sussex in July. He reported to Howard that "the Fire-Bird was convulsed by and infinitely charmed with [it], but not, I make bold to say, to her faintest amendment or amelioration." Between themselves the two men fussed and fumed over Edith's changes of mind and fell prostrate (metaphorically speaking) before her immense energy. She was having a good time, and it was not over yet.[9]

While visiting the poet laureate Alfred Austin and his wife on the Dover coast, her last stop before returning to Paris, Edith was summoned by telegram to Lamb House. Henry wanted another little motor trip, she reported to John Hugh, "and with my usual docility I countermanded Paris plans" (which included final arrangements for leasing an apartment) "and turned Hortense's prow westward." She descended from her room on the evening of July 12 to discover Fullerton standing before the hearth, deep in conversation with Henry. "Your back was turned to the door, and you didn't *feel me come in*, but went on talking." His presence at Lamb House seems to have been a surprise to her. Perhaps it was for this reason that Henry James had suddenly called her back. The next morning, they all set out in the motor, Charles Cook at the wheel, for a three-day run across Essex. To their delight, they experienced a rare respite of sunny weather in a summer of cold rain.

During this trip, Fullerton and Edith resumed sexual relations. Her poem "The Room" probably dates from this period; it re-creates a scene in which the poet's lover comes to his beloved late at night. They lie beneath a window, the "singing stars" looking on as the "summer night turned to grey" dawn. As he opens the door to leave, he gives her a last glance:

> O, all my world in the world,
> Heart in my breast, O room!
> That held a million spheres enfurled
> And are straiter now than a tomb.

The emotional level of the eighteen-line poem is overwrought, its rhetoric sometimes bathetic. In an apostrophe to the "room," the poet exclaims, "How your curtained silence calls/His name, his name, his name!" The room/tomb conceit in the final lines reworks Edith's familiar metaphor of rooms as prison cells.

The rhetoric of these lines matches in banality and intensity the language of other women who desired Fullerton; suspended between despair and ecstasy, longing for his presence, they beg for his attentions and describe the emptiness of their worlds after his departure. Fullerton's bisexuality undoubtedly contributed to his erotic powers. Playing the male role as sexual partner, he also knew from the "other" side what a woman felt and wanted. A bisexual Don Juan, he took double pleasure in every encounter: in some sense, he was both seducer and seduced.

HENRY JAMES KEPT Howard Sturgis apprised of their pilgrims' progress through Essex by frequent telegrams, but neither these announcements nor James's letters of this period give clues to how much he knew—or did not know—about Edith and Morton's affair. Howard was less discreet than James and more frankly curious. In answer to her facetious letter to the "*Spectator*" (her response to Howard's "Studies in Bird-Life"), he asked, "Pray what has become of the *immediate* necessity for your presence in Paris, to secure the house or apartment or 'whatever?'" Advising her to "Run your race. Fly your flight. Live your romances. Drain the cup of pleasure of the dregs," he added, "polite greetings to Mr. Fullerton."

Edith and Morton said good-bye to Henry at Canterbury and, having sent Charles Cook and Catherine Gross ahead to Paris with the motor, they "dashed across the Channel" to spend a night in Boulogne before returning to the city. Back at the Hôtel de Crillon, "high up in the sky, overlooking the whole of Paris," Edith confessed, "Oh, my dearest, our week has spoiled me for brief interrupted minutes—I, who said I would never complain!"[10]

Almost from the moment of his return, Fullerton was preoccupied with Mme Mirecourt, who again was causing trouble. Edith was involved in domestic concerns as she arranged the lease on a large second-floor apartment at 53 rue de Varenne, a building with a southern exposure onto the Cité de Varenne and the Doudeauville gardens. She was moving to the more desirable side of the street, as the houses on the north had no gardens; but the drawing rooms, library, and her bedroom at number 53 overlooked the cobblestone street, which was noisy, as her future neighbor Ogden Codman observed. Her new residence had a separate guest suite (with its own latchkey), which she offered to John Hugh for his proposed winter visit. Teddy's bedroom would give him greater privacy than he had had in the Vanderbilt apartment at number 58; he could come and go without crossing through the drawing room, and he would no longer need to keep his boots in the library, Edith quipped. She had already begun shopping for seasonal bargains and prowling for furniture when news came from Lenox that Mrs. Wharton, now nearly ninety, was seriously ill, and Teddy was forced to delay his August 1 sailing date. Anna Bahlmann arrived on July 30 and assisted Edith in organizing repair work and painting on the apartment. Harry Jones lent advice and support on Edith's legal and financial matters.[11]

Summer news of Teddy had at first been relatively cheerful. He had gone fishing in Canada in "great spirits" following a series of serum treatments for gum disease. Teddy had a strong physique, as did his mother, who—according to Edith—was endowed with "boundless" powers of resistance. But the end came for Nancy Spring Wharton on August 17. She died at Pine Acre and was buried nearby in the cemetery of the Church on the Hill. Teddy later erected a memorial to her in the churchyard, a drinking fountain on a marble slab. Edith used her small legacy ($1,000) to buy books for the Lenox Library.

Francis P. Kinnicutt, Teddy's New York doctor, himself a cottager at Lenox, had visited The Mount early in the summer. Teddy seemed to him then "very natural" and "keenly interested in all he showed us," especially in plans for an addition to the service wing of the house and further development of the working farm at The Mount. But Dr. Kinnicutt noted that following the second set of serum treatments, Teddy had entered a phase of excitability and was now "in a distinctly exalted state." He had purchased a new car during the summer and was enjoying country drives; several friends who had seen him racing about were worried about him.

Edith, focusing her energies on decorating and furnishing their new home in Paris, was not cheered by these reports, especially since Dr. Kinnicutt urged her to encourage Teddy's interest in their Lenox home: "At present it is the one place in the world he is most fond of." He was convinced that mental disturbance was the root of Teddy's physical problems, and he noted (not for the first time) the cyclical pattern of

Teddy's emotional responses, which moved from exalted energy to lethargy and despair:

> From the reports which I have mentioned, from my knowledge of his past [a reference to Teddy's prolonged illness from summer 1902 until winter 1904], and from my experience in similar cases, I am not free from anxiety about him. My fear is that on his return to Paris, in an environment which does not appeal to him apart from the helpfulness of your presence, there may be another swing back of the pendulum.

Underneath this diplomatic, even guarded, résumé of Teddy's illness lay the unstated suggestion that Teddy's health would continue to improve if the Whartons were to resume their life together at The Mount rather than removing him to a European environment that did not appeal to him. "Local irritations and suffering directly affect the deeper evil," Kinnicutt had told Edith earlier in the summer, referring to Teddy's gout pains and facial neuralgia. Geographic locale was also a "local irritation." "Remove them and by just so much you retard the progress and manifestation of the other"—the "deeper evil" of mental illness. This diagnosis handed Edith an impossible choice: return to America and face illness and unhappiness herself, or remain in Paris with an ill and irritable husband.[12]

She searched for some compromise solution and undoubtedly discussed these matters with Walter Berry, who arrived from Egypt on August 15 for a much-needed holiday from his duties as judge on the International Tribunal. Fatigued and despairing of the torrid Cairo heat, he was experiencing stomach pain and other ailments. Edith had looked forward with pleasure to his visit (their nine-month separation was the longest in almost fifteen years), but his Paris stop was a mere way station on his way to England. James proposed that she accompany Walter to Folkestone and spend a few days, à trois, at Lamb House. James also had a "little vision" of Walter, "straining the leash to rush to the arms of Lady G," in whom he still had a romantic interest. The visit to England was not to be: Walter instead sailed to the United States, where his aged mother lay ill. She died later in the autumn, and he spent the next four years trying to settle her estate and claim his right to his inheritance. Throughout the autumn, Edith's concern about Teddy was matched by her worry about Walter's health and Morton's difficulties. In letters to Henry James, she spoke of Walter in terms of

Morton Fullerton—both men caught, in her opinion, by vengeful and tenacious Fates. James saw Teddy passing through a *mauvais moment*.[13]

On the heels of Walter's departure came the news that Bay Lodge had died suddenly on August 21 at age thirty-six after suffering a heart attack brought on by food poisoning. He and his wife, Bessy, were staying with their three young children at the summer home of Sturgis Bigelow (also a friend of Edith's) on Tuckernuck Island off Nantucket. Bay's death was a major loss to Edith, who had loved him as a younger brother. His death cut another of her links with America, especially with The Mount, where he and Bessy had often visited.

Senator Henry Cabot Lodge asked Edith to write a remembrance of his son, which *Scribner's Magazine* published in February 1910. In her memorial, she spoke of the qualities of friendship she valued and that Bay had represented. Recalling their first meeting in 1898 at the Gordon Hotel in Washington, D.C., Edith said that he was a man who kept no reserves but gave himself wholly, showing all sides of his nature—a sense of beauty, his kindness and laughter, his hatred of meanness: "For he, who had so many gifts, had above all, the gift of life; and that is the best, since it gives all the others their savour." Writing the memoir was a taxing effort because, although she loved Bay Lodge, she had never been wholly enthusiastic about his writing. She used the occasion to set out her own aesthetic and artistic principles. She contested Théophile Gautier's notion that artists should "sacrifice much to produce little," arguing that it was dangerous for an artist to "draw all his effects from his inner experience." It was easier, she wrote, to characterize one's neighbor than to draw "one's self as seen by one's neighbor"—this remark is an important hint on her own methods of characterization.[14]

Soon after Bay Lodge's death, she discovered a new friend, who appeared from an unexpected quarter. In September, she ran into Elizabeth Cameron, companion and Paris hostess to historian Henry Adams (now in his early seventies), who asked her to pay Mr. Adams a visit. Edith agreed, and went along to Elizabeth's house on the avenue du Bois de Boulogne, a few doors away from the residence where Lucretia Jones had died eight years earlier. As Edith and Elizabeth entered the drawing room, Bernard Berenson was just leaving. He did not recognize Edith, whom he had met in 1903 and had instantly disliked. "She did not look the least like the woman we met six or seven years ago," he reported to his wife, Mary. Other observers noted that Edith seemed aged and appeared to be under great stress. Francesca d'Aulby, a friend of Katharine Fullerton's and probably one of Morton's lovers in this period, commented that Mrs. Wharton looked "worn out and nervous." Katharine passed this remark to Fullerton, obviously unaware that he was frequently in the company of both women. For some time, Henry Adams had wanted to bring Berenson and Edith Wharton together, but after Berenson's first encounter with her in 1903, he had issued an ultimatum that he would attend no social function at which she was present. Ignoring this old declaration (or perhaps unaware of it), Adams invited them to dine with him at Voisin, one of the city's best restaurants. Located at the corner of the rue Cambon and the rue St. Honoré, only a few steps away from the Ritz Hotel, where Berenson was staying, the restaurant was near Morton Fullerton's office. Edith arranged that he, a former classmate of Berenson's from Harvard, should join the happy "combination." Indeed, the date of the dinner, September 30, was set to accommodate Fullerton's schedule at the *Times*. Although more grave and mature, Morton looked to Berenson much as he had twenty-three years earlier, when they shared a short stint on the *Harvard Monthly*.[15]

It was a lively party of six, including Elizabeth Cameron and her beautiful twenty-three-year-old daughter, Martha. Adams had arranged for a private upstairs room, its windows open onto the fading sunset. Diminutive, dapper, and looking a little like his friend Paul Bourget, Berenson engaged in lively conversation with a woman seated next to him whose face was shadowed by a black lace veil. He later claimed to have recognized her as Edith Wharton only when the restaurant lights came on. This version of their second meeting has become legend, although it strains credulity that the sharp-eyed art critic who could establish the provenance of a Renaissance portrait from a few selected details could have been twice blinded to Edith's identity.

The dinner marked the beginning of a long friendship in which each was to count the other as among the closest friends of a lifetime. Three years younger than Edith, Berenson viewed her as an affectionate older sister; she confided and trusted in him to a degree exceeded only by her reliance on Walter Berry. Their letters to each other over nearly thirty years range across art, archaeology, history, literature, and religion, Edith and "B.B.," as he was known to his friends, revealing to each other their most cultured and intellectually curious sides. They also wrote openly of their fears and joys, longings and sufferings, disclosing to one another hidden aspects of themselves.

Still, theirs was an unlikely pairing. Adviser to Joseph and Louis Duveen, the insatiable and successful London gallery owners, Berenson spent his time brokering art purchases for nouveau riche Americans—the very people Edith satirized in her novels and stories. She forgave him these associations and overlooked as well his lack of aristocratic pedigree. She marveled at the story of his family's emigration from a Lithuanian *shtetl* to a North Boston working-class community and his rise to a brilliant career at Harvard (supported by a scholarship) and his fame as the world's foremost expert on Renaissance art. She also came to love his wife, Mary, a Quaker, feminist, political activist, and partner in his business enterprise. Most surprising, given Edith's background, she turned a blind eye to his Jewishness.

They loved jokes and good stories and were inveterate travelers; when they met, Berenson was considering the purchase of his first motorcar and would soon begin his long years of motor adventures. They were also, in summer 1909, involved in passionate, secret love affairs. Both the Wharton marriage of twenty-four years and the Berenson marriage of nine years were in crisis. All four spouses were having affairs, and Teddy Wharton and Mary Berenson showed symptoms of crippling mental problems. Berenson's inamorata was Belle da Costa Greene, a sensuous woman of exotic beauty and mysterious origins whom he had met a year earlier in New York. Twenty years younger than Berenson, she was the guiding genius behind J. P. Morgan's rare book and manuscript collection. Mary Berenson was in love with Geoffrey Scott, a man many years younger than she. A protégé of Berenson's, he would become a noted cultural historian. On the summer evening of the Voisin's dinner, Scott was at I Tatti, the Berensons' eighteenth-century *pavillon* in the olive groves above Florence, helping Mary design extensive gardens for the estate. Teddy Wharton was in Boston, keeping the company of a much younger woman, while Edith and Morton Fullerton in Paris were making a pretense of casual friendship. As Berenson had written in his notebook many years earlier, "Marriage is a sacrament tempered by adultery."[16]

The evening at Voisin was a tonic for both Berenson and Edith, and they saw a great deal of each other before he departed for I Tatti two weeks later. She opened her eyes anew to medieval and Renaissance painting, and he introduced her to Oriental art, which was enjoying a certain vogue. She soon reported that, thanks to him, she was walking through galleries "in a Paradise of Chinese pictures." Before he left Paris, she sought his advice on an artifact she owned, a "little Asia minor toy," a terra-cotta piece with figures—something she probably had brought back from her 1888 trip to the Aegean. Was the female figure Europa, as she thought? (Berenson's answer to the question is not known.) He was buying art for himself, and returned to Italy with an eighth-century Javanese stone Buddha purchased from Bing, the Paris dealer specializing in Chinese antiquities. Mary Berenson thought it "creeping with tactile values" but otherwise frightful.[17]

After suffering a mild case of flu in early October that pulled her down "out of all proportion to its severity," Edith left Paris to spend a few days at Offranville (near Dieppe), where the portrait painter Jacques-Emile Blanche and his wife had a Louis XIV Normandy manor house. She knew little of the "immense richness and variety of appeal" of this area of France, and during her stay, she made daily motor trips into the countryside, Blanche at her side. They talked as they drove, and he realized that she was unhappy. Teddy's recent illness, his six-month absence in America, and her evident weariness signaled distress in her domestic life. Soon after, a rumor that she was separating from Teddy appeared in a Paris newspaper. Distressed by this indiscretion, Rosa de Fitz-James appealed to Fullerton to intervene in the journalistic community and put an end to the rumors. Edith spent nearly two months tracing the source of the false story, a trail that led back to Blanche and their conversations during her visit. Knowing he was a gossip, she should have been on her guard, and the incident made her even more protective of her private life.[18]

Driving back from her weekend in Normandy, she spent Saturday night, October 23, at an inn called Le Fayel-Oise in the river valley north of Paris near Chantilly. The route had taken her that afternoon through Creil, where she caught a glimpse of the "old crooked church" of St. Medard that she and Fullerton had visited on their final motor trip in spring 1908. Addressing him in a letter as "My Dearest Love," she recalled that day almost a year and a half earlier when she had had as yet no personal life: "since then you have given me all imaginable joy." She confessed, and not for the first time, her "besetting fear"— that the love that had "set my whole being free may gradually, imperceptibly, have become a kind of irksome bondage to you." Accepting the fact that their lives could not "run parallel much longer" (Teddy was due to arrive in Paris), she announced herself ready to make the transition, when the time came, "to be again the good comrade you once found me." Afraid that her love might blind her to the inevitability of that moment, that she might try to hold him longer than he wanted, she proposed that he give her a signal: "One day simply call me 'mon ami' instead of 'mon amie,'" a grammatical gender shift from feminine to masculine in French that cannot be heard in the spoken word. She was asking, in sum, that he treat her as he would a male friend. Five weeks later, she asked that he return her letters, reminding him that she had asked several times for these "fragments of correspondence," but that he had not acquiesced to her wishes. "In one sense, as I told you, I am indifferent to the fate of this literature. In another sense, my love of order makes me resent the way in which inanimate things survive their uses!" But it was more than this. Her fear that they would fall into Mme Mirecourt's hands and then find their way into a newspaper was heightened by the incident of Jacques-Emile Blanche's gossip.[19]

By October 1909, Edith was casting a remorseful backward glance on their love affair, especially its sexual aspects, and it may have been in these weeks that she wrote "Colophon to The Mortal Lease." Certainly, it would have been difficult for her to continue the intimacies of the summer once she was back in Paris, surrounded again by her servants and her secretary in the suite at the Crillon. Although one cannot date the end of the affair with absolute certainty, references in Edith's later letters suggest that its sexual component was framed by her summer sojourn in England—"some divine hours," as she would later refer to them. If so, their trysts included one night of lovemaking at the Charing Cross Hotel in London in June 1909, another at a hotel in Boulogne on the return trip in August, and several more nights during the week of their motor-flight with Henry James. Edith seems to have taken enough from these few experiences—and their love letters, afternoon drives in the country, stolen kisses, and handholding—to ease her anger and anxiety at having been denied something she assumed other women took for granted.

Although her poetic accounts of their lovemaking should never be read as factual accounts, they nonetheless suggest that she was at ease with sexual intimacy, that she reached orgasm, and that even in the first sexual encounters, there were no embarrassments or awkwardnesses. In "Terminus," presumably a poetic rendering of their initial seduction, the lovers watch each other in the mirror, smiling as the man helps the woman to loosen her dress. One wonders how a woman who apparently had spent twenty-five years in a sexless marriage could find the savoir faire to carry through such an encounter without a false step, or how her years of sexual repression were suddenly and painlessly transformed into sexual bliss. That the moment had been so long delayed undoubtedly fueled Edith's desire, and she had no intention of letting the opportunity slip through her fingers—as she had in spring 1908. Still, these scenes of passion raise real questions about her supposed naïveté and sexual repression.

Fullerton's few comments on the subject credit Edith with courage and perspicacity in her desire for sexual fulfillment. When he learned in 1950 that Elisina Tyler, executor of Edith Wharton's estate, planned to write a memoir of her friend (a book she never wrote), he urged her to "seize the event, however delicate the problem, to destroy the myth of your heroine's frigidity." In love, he said, Edith had "the courage of George Sand." She was "fearless, reckless even." As "proof" of his claim, he sent Mrs. Tyler a copy of "Terminus" and told her of the circumstances that had led to its composition. Fullerton perhaps wanted to believe that Edith was "reckless," yet her letters to him show how carefully she judged the risks, weighing and measuring the price she would pay. She did not risk her reputation, her literary work, or her marriage. Indeed, from autumn 1909 until spring 1913, her concern about Teddy's well-being took precedence over everything else in her life and threatened to eclipse her writing.

When Teddy returned from Boston in early November with his sister, Edith was eager to get out of Paris on an extended "motor-dash" and hoped that he would be in the mood for one, too. He arrived looking well—"*much* too well," she noted. He rambled on, often incoherently, about his investment successes; his buoyancy of spirit did not ring true to Edith. Very soon, the pendulum swung back, as Dr. Kinnicutt had predicted, and his mood changed from one of excited optimism to depression. "The breakdown has come exactly *as* and *when* Dr. Kinnicutt said it would," she wrote Sally. Nannie Wharton, who was now staying at the Crillon, insisted that her brother was perfectly well. Edith faced her sister-in-law's "incredible blindness and stupidity, and determination not to recognise *any* nervous disorder."[20]

Nannie played a crucial role in the family crisis that unfolded in November and December 1909. The eldest of the three Wharton children, she had not married or established an independent life outside the parental home, except to take on church and community work. Affable, even charming (so Henry James found her), she was also willful, childish, unpredictable, and stubborn—traits that had recently come to dominate Teddy's personality. With her mother dead, Nannie—now in her mid-sixties—had no fixed future, and she interposed herself at every juncture of Teddy's life. The *folie à deux* that some thought characterized Edith and Teddy's relations for the past year now transferred itself to brother and sister.

When Edith proposed a motor trip, Teddy demurred, "indisposed to move." He lounged in the Crillon suite while Edith and Anna Bahlmann (now also serving as Nannie's companion) organized the renovations to the rue de Varenne apartment. Days passed in a kind of limbo. "I can make no plans, but only live again from hand to mouth, as before," she wrote Sally. Sturgis Bigelow, who had come to Paris for a health cure, took Teddy off her hands, motoring around the city and in the countryside with him. Finally, Nannie announced that she wanted to visit Pau in the Basse-Pyrénées. After wrangles and reconsiderations, it was at last decided that Teddy would take his sister to Pau in the motor. Edith departed in a different direction, taking Anna on a trip to Munich, which they both "hugely" enjoyed. It was Edith's first trip to Germany in many years, and it renewed the love of German culture that Anna, as her governess, had first instilled in her some forty years earlier. They stayed at the Vier Jahreszeiten (the best hotel in Munich) and spent their days "excursioning." Although the Pinakothek Museum was closed for repairs and Edith caught a cold in the Glyptothek (which "drips with sepulchral damp"), they visited the Schauspielhaus and saw two performances of Schiller's *Intrigue and Love*. From Munich, they traveled to Würzburg to view the Tiepolos at the Prince Bishop's Palace, and then made their way to Bruchsal, Karlsruhe, and back to Paris. It was a very "rococo" trip; Edith's love of Goethe and her general interest in eighteenth-century culture made it so.

Teddy returned to Paris alone and in worse shape than when he had left. Nannie wrote from Pau, where she stayed for the winter, to say that the trip south had been splendid. "Parting with him yesterday was awfully hard." Perhaps this statement appeared to Edith as sisterly devotion, but it portended something quite different. On the trip, Teddy had told his sister a little about his summer's financial dealings. On his return to Paris, he unburdened himself to Edith, telling her a story so lurid and grotesque that she was left in stunned silence. She wrote to Morton:

Cher ami—Things are serious here, and I cannot be free tomorrow. . . .
Teddy arrived just after you left, and I saw at once that his condition
had grown *much worse*. This morning comes a letter from my cousin
[Herman Edgar], throwing light on the causes of this *crise*. He has put
my affairs into rather serious (temporary) confusion, and is of course
brooding over this, and trying to work it out in his poor confused
head. I am so sorry for him! His state is piteous, and I feel—oh,
irony—that if I had been less "delicate," less desirous of letting him
feel that he was completely trusted, things might have not turned out
so. *Mais quelle folie*! [But what madness!] As if the disease would not
have found another outlet.

Edith immediately sought advice from her brother Harry, Herman
Edgar, and Walter Berry, who had returned to Paris and would soon replace Teddy as the second trustee of her estate. Giving Henry James a
curtailed account of events, she then wrote to Nannie inquiring what,
if anything, she knew of the story.

Nannie admitted that the second round of serum treatments in the
summer had seemed to excite Teddy unduly and that she and their
brother, Billy, had been very worried about him in the autumn. She
knew that Teddy had been speculating on the stock market, "but I had
no idea that it was with your Trust Funds." As to the "other matter,"
Teddy's purchase of a property on Mountfort Street in Boston and the
young mistress he established there, Nannie had suspected that something was wrong but had learned the full truth only in a letter from
Teddy written after he had confessed to Edith.

Edith took immediate steps to correct the damage Teddy had done
to her finances. He was to pay her back with money from the inheritance from his mother, and he set out for Boston to settle the matter.
Unwell and desperate for Edith's forgiveness, he was pitiable. She did
not yet know the full story of what had happened the previous summer, or even how much money Teddy had taken from her accounts.
The larger picture would emerge slowly in January and February 1910.
In New York, Dr. Kinnicutt set out to learn everything he could about
the summer's events so as to prescribe suitable treatment.[21]

It was with relief rather than sadness, then, that Edith faced Christmas alone in the hotel. Morton often came for tea. When she moved
out of the Crillon, she sent him a sheaf of poems in memory of these
times. He had paid a visit to Suite 403 on New Year's Eve afternoon
and later, as she awaited the new year, she wrote to him:

My Dearest and Ever Dearest,

Are you happy when you sit and talk to me like that? If you are, nothing else matters—at least not this last day of December, just a little more than a year after the day on which you wrote me: "The letters survive, and everything survives."

During that year you have given me some divine hours, and I want to remember them alone tonight.

It's true that I'm not "strong" when you are near me, but when I leave here next week the change will come of itself, naturally, and I shall get gradually used to seeing you less—I suppose!

All the ghosts of the old kisses come back, Darling, and live again in the one I send you tonight.

Morton Fullerton probably had never received a love letter as beautiful as this one. Even Katharine's passionate lyricism could not match the beauty of Edith's calm reflection. Her tone betrayed no lingering sorrow or anger, and despite her present difficulties, the letter revealed no desperation. The "ghosts of the old kisses," however, were a reminder that one side of their relationship had been consigned to the past.

THRESHOLD OF CHANGE

On January 3, 1910, Edith moved into 53 rue de Varenne, her Paris address for the next nine years. Later that month, a flood inundated the city, turning the Faubourg St. Germain into a little Venice. Rowboats carried passengers down streets that had become canals, and pedestrians used hastily built wooden bridges to cross over the lake that now covered the rue du Bac. The rue de Varenne was spared the worst of the flood's ravages, but on her excursions in the neighborhood, Edith observed volunteer relief activities for those left homeless by the storm. Until the isolation and inconvenience of it all began to wear on her nerves, she thought the drama "magnificent." Her apartment, freshly painted and wallpapered, stood virtually empty as rain sheeted its tall windows. Edith was awaiting the arrival of her furniture from New York: she had sold her twin houses to help finance the Paris leasehold. Anna Bahlmann had returned to New York to supervise the shipping of the contents of 882–884 Park Avenue to France. Teddy remained in Boston with his sister.[22]

After the revelations of the previous December, Edith was in a state of "exasperated sensitiveness." She lay awake crying at night, "the despair of the future" with Teddy before her. Her forty-eighth birthday passed "soberly and sadly," but in spite of anxiety and vaguely ill health, she was "writing hard" to complete the four remaining stories for *Tales of Men and Ghosts*. The usual Paris diversions held no charm for her, not even Edmond Rostand's *Chantecler*, a verse play based on the beast fable, which was the talk of the winter season. The role of the aggrandizing cock had been written especially for the rotund French comedian Constant Coquelin (whose name meant "little cock"). Thirty years earlier, during a period when New York society had attempted to reproduce French "salon" evenings, he had performed in Caroline Astor's drawing room. Coquelin died unexpectedly before *Chantecler* went into production and was replaced in what might have been his greatest role by Lucien Guitry, whose performance drew rave reviews. Audiences loved the play, but when Edith saw it in late February, she thought it "drivelling" and "hideous," and made no concessions to Rostand, whom she knew slightly. "It was like some awful night-mare in the unimaginative realism of the costumes and scenery," she told Sally. Edith and Fullerton walked out after the first act.

King Edward VII saw the production and paid for it with his life. Theater heating had been kept at a low level because the actors were enveloped in feathers, but at the news of the king's arrival, the manager turned the theater into something like a steam bath. Flushed, the king presumably caught a chill as he waited for his motor after the performance. His head cold turned to bronchitis and less than a month later, on May 6, he died. The Edwardian era was technically at an end. A spark would flicker into flame during the gala season of 1911 and the crowning of George V, only to be extinguished forever in the muddy trenches of the Great War. There were already signs on the European horizon that the old order would soon end (class conflict, the rise of socialism, colonial unrest, militarism), but Edith—like many others—was too preoccupied with her own life to notice.[23]

Uneasy about Teddy, she kept in close contact by letter and cable with Billy Wharton, who was looking after his brother, and with Dr. Kinnicutt, who reported to her about Teddy's behavior during the previous summer and autumn. The delusional aspects of his disease, combined with shame and regret, had led him to make an exaggerated confession in December. Kinnicutt found no evidence that he had rented out rooms in the

Boston house to chorus girls, as had been rumored. Teddy appeared to have lived quietly with a woman some thirty years his junior (he was sixty in April 1910) in an apartment on Mountfort Street that he had purchased for about $17,000—a scene of extramarital domesticity that almost exactly reproduced Fred Jones's New York arrangements in the early 1890s and the life that Harry Jones was now setting up for himself in Paris.

Dr. Kinnicutt and his partner agreed that Teddy belonged in a sanatorium, a suggestion rejected outright by Billy and Nannie Wharton, and by Teddy himself. They no doubt feared that once admitted to McLean Hospital or a similar institution, he would never return to active life, but die in hospital. The greater fear was that he would commit suicide, as his father had done. As talk about appropriate treatment and the outlook for his future swirled around him, as gossips in New York and Boston chattered about his follies, Teddy insisted that he wanted nothing more than to return to Edith. Dr. Kinnicutt recommended that a physician travel with him, but restated to Edith his conviction that the Paris environment contributed to Teddy's depression. Using both his authority as a medical doctor and his position as a personal friend to the Whartons, he urged her to return with Teddy to The Mount the following summer. The rural environment would soothe his state of mind and her presence (Kinnicutt implied) would hush the gossip. In a quandary, she first proposed to send Alfred White to accompany Teddy to Paris, then decided to give up the lease on the apartment into which she had moved only the month before and sail by herself to New York. In the end, she sent White.[24]

Just how bad things were for her in these weeks can be gleaned from a letter she wrote in April to her friend Robert Grant, a friend of Teddy's since childhood and the judge who had probated Mrs. Wharton's will the previous October. Edith had been through a "dreadful year," and she was now caught in a "deadly inertia":

> Teddy has always been extremely self-willed, and has done, all his life, exactly what he chose; and it is hopeless to try to direct him now, unless all those about him unite in trying to carry out what the Drs suggest. I can only watch passively, shelter Teddy as much as I can from worry, and from the curiosity and comments which are inevitable when a man in his condition attempts to live in the world, and be prepared for the fact that any day he may yield to some impulse like those which wrought such havoc in his life last summer.

The situation "coloured" her whole existence: Teddy was never "out of" her mind or "*off* her mind." Unable to work well, she also found it impossible to read anything except Goethe and Schopenhauer, "the two authors with whom I always take refuge when everything else becomes meaningless." This last remark was intended to explain why she had not been able to finish Robert Grant's latest novel, *The Chippendales*, a story of a South Boston boardinghouse. But it was not only worry that distracted her. She was unable to relate the story's characters to "anything in my experience, or attach them to any social order known to me." Aware that the novel was receiving "serious" attention by critics, she admitted that her own difficulties with it were probably due to her limited range of social types.[25]

More surprising than her frank remarks about Teddy to Grant, whom she had known for many years, was the tone of her April 9 letter to William Crary Brownell, her editor at Scribners, a man to whom she rarely made mention of personal matters. Stating her anxiety about Henry James, who was suffering from a suicidal neurasthenia almost as grave as Teddy's manic depression, she remarked that her husband was "no better," and there seemed "nothing to do" about it. She was seeing things "à la manière noire, shading to grisaille." When Teddy arrived in Paris, he was "very depressed and listless," as she knew he would be. Awaiting his reappearance, Edith sensed the shadows closing around her, just as she had in summer 1908 at The Mount. Before entering again into "les ténèbres" of her life with Teddy, she wanted to talk with Fullerton.[26]

Some weeks earlier, she had sent him a few verses from the previous autumn. Yet again, she proposed that they shift the terms of their relationship. "I want to love you in any way that gives you peace, and not more bother," she wrote him. He was too preoccupied with work and his move from the rue Fabert to the Hôtel Vouillement on the Right Bank, too weighed down with his own worries (paramount among them his unhappiness at the *Times*), to give due consideration to her request. He got the flu, and sent her a note: "I am too ill to see you."

Thinking him seriously ill, she sent a note to his hotel early one morning. He was not there. "You know what I must think," she wrote him—that he was with someone else, perhaps his "Equitable friend," the mercurial Mme Mirecourt. Although he no longer lived under the same roof as this woman, she evidently still had claims on him. Angry, hurt, and again baffled by the inconsistencies of his behavior, Edith did not want to be "the woman who has to be lied to." "What you wish, apparently, is to take of my life the inmost and uttermost that a woman—a woman like me—can give, for an hour, now and then, when it suits you; and when the hour is over, to leave me out of your mind and out of your life as a man leaves the companion who has accorded him a transient distraction [i.e., a prostitute]. I think I am worth more than that, or worth, perhaps I had better say, something quite different." The "inmost and uttermost" that a woman like Edith could give was not sex in the afternoon (as her reference to "something quite different" makes clear) but rather her heart and soul—her love, in short. She wanted him to stop courting her, talking love and making promises he could not keep: "I know that a relation like ours has its inevitable stages, and that *that* stage is past." But each time they agreed to put their relationship on the footing of friendship, he either abandoned her altogether ("You could let nine days pass—living at my very door—without concerning yourself to know if I were well or ill, happy or unhappy, here or away") or pressed his attentions by telephone calls, *petits bleus*, and little notes, as he would do when she made a brief mid-March trip to see Henry James.[27]

She had decided to settle Teddy into a rest cure at Neuilly (a plan he agreed to), and then get away to England for a fortnight. This program was countermanded by Nannie Wharton, who was back in Paris. Caught again between her husband and her sister-in-law, Edith departed for Folkestone, leaving Teddy in his sister's care. Arriving at the Berkeley Hotel on Wednesday, March 17, she found a note from Harry James (Henry's nephew) saying that his uncle was ill and would not be able to see her until the next day, when she found him lying motionless on a sofa in his room at Garland's Hotel, his eyes dark with despair. He "cried out" to her his fear and loneliness, and his craving for a "cessation of consciousness." He was poised, she wrote Fullerton, above the "abysses" of his own fictions. He seemed to her like John Pellerin, the character in "The Legend" (one of her *Men and Ghosts* tales) who disappeared from the world when his ideas were disregarded by the public. She understood that James's despair sprang from a sense of failure and lost hope caused by the public indifference and critical silence that had greeted the Scribners "New York" edition of his works. Hungering for companionship, he was unable to bear the presence of other people, and Edith sensed that even as he begged her to stay with him, he really wanted her "out of the door."

The next day, however, he was well enough to join her for an hour at the Repertory Theatre matinee, where he had offered her his box. He then went down to Rye, and she motored to Windsor to spend the remainder of the weekend with Howard Sturgis. In the week that followed, she accompanied Robert Norton to a performance of *Othello* starring Ernesto Grasso, the Italian actor-manager who had organized the Sicilian theater company appearances two years earlier in Paris. She made the rounds of museums and galleries, was escorted by the Babe to see Lady Constance Stewart Richardson "caper amateurishly through a country-house imitation" of Isadora Duncan. It was a week of distractions to ward off worries about James and Teddy.

She took steps to keep Henry company until his brother William arrived from America. William James, far more seriously ill than his brother, was en route from America to a rest cure in Germany for his bad heart. Edith's plan was to bring Teddy to Folkestone so that she could shuttle back and forth to Rye, caring for him and Henry. Teddy's Paris physician, Dr. Magun, approved the scheme, and Teddy arrived at Folkestone on March 25, accompanied by Alfred White. Edith joined them, taking rooms at the Metropole Hotel. "What queer uses destiny makes of me!" she wrote Fullerton, "so different from those I fancied I was made for." On Easter Sunday, the Whartons motored to Rye in the hope of seeing Henry James, but were told that he could have no visitors. His physician, Dr. William Osler, who years earlier had served as first consultant to Dr. Weir Mitchell at the Orthopaedic Hospital in Philadelphia, had now imposed a strict *"rest cure"* on his patient—open windows, massage, feeding, "packing" (enemas), all under the supervision of a specialist nurse. The cure was a complete failure. Henry later wrote Fullerton that he had threatened Osler and the nurse that if they "touched" him again with massages and "water-cure 'packing,'" he would throw himself out the window. They called an immediate halt to the cure.[28]

Edith's plan to assist Henry had failed, but after she returned to Paris, she sent her motor to England with a hired chauffeur to drive the Jameses around the countryside. William and his wife, Alice, enjoyed the trips, but the touring, which in better times gave Henry great pleasure, now made him restless and fretful. After four days, he apologetically sent the motor back across the Channel. In May, Edith met William James for the first time when he called on her at the rue de Varenne to bring news of Henry and to thank her for giving his brother her motor and chauffeur during his bad depression.[29]

While Edith was in England, Fullerton wrote her loving letters near-ly every day, and she responded in kind. Driving out from Charing Cross station on her arrival, she had strained to see the window of Apartment 92, in which they had spent their "Terminus" night: "I can't tell you, Dear, 'what heart was mine,'" she wrote him. A few days later, she concluded a long letter about her efforts to cheer Henry James by saying, "Tu es venu hier soir, mon aimé. Nous étions au Ter-minus. [You came last night, my love. We were at the Terminus.]" Yet, when she returned to Paris, he ignored her. She was "sad and bewil-dered beyond words": "Write me no more such letters as you sent me in England," she said. Referring to his "enigmatic change" the previous December, she declared that her life had been better before she knew him. By late May, however, she had reassessed her feelings. "I said once that my life was better before I knew you. That is not so, for it is good to have lived once *in the round*, for ever so short a time. But my life *is* harder now because of those few months last summer, when I had my one glimpse of what a good camaraderie might be—the kind of thing that some women have at least for a few years!" His courting her by letter, then turning the tables on her when she returned to Paris, had aroused her anger at him and her old jealousy of "other women."[30]

Later in the spring, she sent Fullerton a sonnet in which a woman offers herself body and soul to her lover. The ceremony of Christian Communion serves as metaphor for sexual passion in a poetic conceit that is at once metaphysical and mystical:

> She said to me: "Nay, take my body and eat,
> And give it beauty, breaking it for bread.
> Or else, your hunger sated, drain instead
> The chalice of my soul, wherein, to meet
> Your longed-for lips, the bitter and the sweet
> Of passion's mystic vintage have been shed,
> And through the clear cold crystals of the head
> Tremble the ardours of the central heat."
> She said: "Your thirst appeased, rest you yet
> A quiet moment in the thought of me . . .
> Then pass upon your way, and quite forget;
> Or dimly—as one inland feels the sea—
> Recall that once a summer hour long set
> Hung over you the murmur of leaf and bee . . ."

This verse commemorates their wondrous summer of 1909, rekindling its ardors even as it consigns them to memory. Although they were no longer lovers, each of them toyed with the memories of their experiences together, and neither let the other forget that they shared a past. Inviting him to a tea in honor of former president Theodore Roosevelt, she asked why her sonnet had "met with silence."[31]

SINCE LEAVING THE presidency in 1909, Roosevelt had been making a much-publicized tour of Africa, where he was hunting big game. His illustrated articles—which pictured the bounty of elephants, wild buffalo, and other game killed on the trip—appeared throughout 1910 in *Scribner's Magazine*, alongside Edith's stories from *Tales of Men and Ghosts*. Angered that his handpicked successor, President William Howard Taft, had failed to carry out his policies, Roosevelt returned home to proclaim the "New Nationalism," keynote of the Progressive party on which he would run for election in 1912. En route to New York, he stopped in Paris to speak at the Sorbonne. Entitled "Citizenship in a Republic," his talk praised manliness and courage in the effort to achieve a better society and decried intellectual cynicism and the rise of socialism. The speech, which was widely reported in the press, inflamed Socialists and trade union members and caused riots in Paris a week later, on May Day—by which time Roosevelt had left the city.

Before arriving in Paris, he sent word through the American ambassador that he wanted to see Edith Wharton. She gave a tea for him at the rue de Varenne on April 25, and in preparation for it consulted Fullerton about the guest list, which included diplomats, academicians, and members of the aristocracy. "No women," she remarked to Fullerton: "il redoute les 'mondanités' autant que vous! [He dreads "society occasions" as much as you.]" She meant by this remark that the party was arranged to provide Roosevelt an opportunity for serious talk among men. Her decision not to include women reveals not only her dislike of the presumed worldliness of her own sex (a prejudice she believed Fullerton held, too), but it also placed her in a solitary and special position as the only woman present.[32]

Guests were selected for yet another reason. She wanted to frame Fullerton to his best advantage, surrounded by powerful diplomats, intellectuals, and littérateurs. For some time, he had desired to leave the *Times*, where he worked long hours for low wages with apparently no hope of advancement. The moment was at hand, as the newspaper was undergoing a change of ownership and management. She wanted him to "see the man" Roosevelt because she realized the advantages that acquaintance with the former president could give him.

Her plan got off to a good start. Fullerton managed to get in ten minutes' conversation with Roosevelt at the tea, and he passed along to Edith a lengthy response he had written to the Sorbonne speech (later published in *Scribner's* as "Roosevelt and France"), and asked her to hand it to the president. Roosevelt had been "greatly struck" by his brief conversation with Morton and asked Edith to invite him to the American Embassy reception the next evening. She forwarded the invitation, but Fullerton did not appear. Not knowing what to make of his absence, she wrote him the following day to express "regret at having been importunate in trying to help you." Her words were charged with anger and shame, and Fullerton himself regretted his cowardice: he was afraid that the "embassy crush" would have "fumbled" his ideas and "undone the impression" he had made at the tea party—an explanation that made no sense to Edith.

Fullerton may have judged correctly that a large embassy party was not an appropriate moment for a tête-à-tête with the guest of honor. But he misread the realities of Edith's current domestic situation, despite her constant references to the difficulties of her home life. "Your vision of our ménage as flitting from one fête to another, fills me with amazement," Edith wrote him. Teddy had made a brief appearance at the tea party, she explained, only out of regard for Roosevelt. He was not well enough to go out; indeed, things were growing "rapidly and terribly worse."[33]

In early May, she took Teddy to Lausanne to see a Dr. Vittoz, an eminent neurologist, who told them that Teddy suffered from neurasthenia, which was not the doctor's medical specialty. "Oh, the Molière play that I could write on specialists!" she wrote Berenson, who had invited her for a visit to I Tatti. She had hoped to travel south to Rome while Teddy "cured" at Lausanne. Instead, they searched for a sanatorium, "the day he dreads so much," she wrote Fullerton. Teddy chose a clinic in Kreuzlingen, Switzerland. After a return to Paris to gather his things, he traveled to Switzerland by train, escorted by White, who took advantage of the sunshine and good air to improve his own health. Within days of his arrival, Teddy began to complain: the place was too isolated, there was no golf and no one to talk with. He wanted to come home. White didn't know "what to think" about the situation. His letter to Edith was followed by one from Dr. Binswanger, director of the clinic, informing her that massage and water therapy and Teddy's daily work in the garden had already improved his appetite and sleep patterns, and that he had gained weight.

Teddy was convinced to stay. His absence provided Edith two months of relative freedom, during which she took up again her *Tales of Men and Ghosts*: "My work is, must be, my only refuge, my only raison d'être," she wrote Fullerton. She took time for the pleasures unavailable to her during the weeks of caring for Teddy—seeing friends, lunching and dining out, going to the opera, and entertaining houseguests. On July 3, accompanied by Fullerton, Berenson, and Walter Berry (who had just returned from Cairo), she saw Serge Diaghilev's production of Stravinsky's *L'Oiseau de feu*, with its sumptuous costumes and set designs. Minnie and Beatrix, on their summer travels, spent several weeks in a neighboring apartment at number 53. As Minnie often brought the mail up from the loge, Edith asked Fullerton not to use stationery and envelopes from his new residence, the Hôtel Vouillement, when writing to her.[34]

On one of his trips to Paris that summer, Berenson stayed at the rue de Varenne. "I like Mrs. Wharton better and better," he wrote his wife, Mary. He later wrote Edith from London to say that she had been "like a fairy godmother to me at a moment when I particularly needed just that kind of treatment." His troubles included overwork and unhappiness with the business side of his art activities, but his chief problems were worry about his marriage and depression at his stalled love affair with Belle da Costa Greene in New York. Just as Edith did not reveal to him the special nature of her friendship with Fullerton, he did not tell her of his affair. Berenson was emotionally vulnerable. "She *may* mean something to me," he would write his wife in the autumn about Edith, "for she really seems just now to care for me." By then, however, he was also aware that Edith's primary affection was for Walter Berry: "I envy them both such a friendship," he wrote Mary.

Walter had resigned his judgeship on the International Tribunal in Cairo effective June 26. A week later, he was back in "God's Country," but still suffering from the stomach illness that had afflicted him during his two years in Egypt. He had found the food and heat intolerable and denounced as lamentable the "uplift and education" program put in place by the British protectorate. "This is a dreadful country to be anything but a nigger in—or a digger," he had written Berenson the previous April, an assessment underwritten by race and class prejudices, but also a deep resentment of British imperialism. Walter was now hunting for a job and a place to live, and in the autumn, he moved into Edith's adjoining guest apartment, where he lived for the next six months while searching for a permanent residence. A rumor circulated that they were living together as a couple. The story was patently untrue, although Walter was urging Edith to break with Teddy—not out of his own self-interest but because he thought Teddy was destroying her life. [35]

"Do you feel no *resentment* when you think of what your life is to be?" Fullerton had asked her in the spring. Yes, she felt the most bitter resentment: "I had to 'hold myself' yesterday to keep from putting my head down beside you, and crying my soul out. . . . Think of having had the chance of complete liberation—and when that went, the prospect, at least, of *a life of my own*, in which I could write and think; and now *this*!" In early July, when Teddy threatened a second time to leave the sanatorium, Dr. Isch Wall, a Paris physician and friend to the Whartons, wrote him a frank letter urging that he travel for "several months" after the Kreuzlingen cure in order to spare his wife. She was weak, tired, and in need of a "grand repose physique et moral [a physical and mental rest]." To protect her, Dr. Wall ordered that she be "isolated from her family," by which he meant Teddy. Dr. Binswanger, who had developed a fondness for Teddy, agreed that he should not return home immediately. [36]

Where could Teddy travel? Edith encouraged him to follow the desire he had expressed the previous year—to see California. She offered him a new "open" motor (a cabriolet), saying that her "sage economies" had made her "flush." More likely, the profits from the sale of her New York houses had occasioned her financial health. On the eve of leaving the sanatorium, he cabled to say that a motor trip was "impossible" for him now. He was going instead to Thun, another Swiss spa town. Again, she dispatched Alfred White to Switzerland.

White returned to Paris with a forlorn and visibly aged Teddy who was apparently little better than when he had gone away in May. Disturbed by her description of Teddy's illness, her Boston friend Sturgis Bigelow (a medical doctor) advised her not to be alone with him, as his tensions could become "explosive." He urged that she put him "under restraint." In his professional opinion, it was "very like criminal neglect" that Billy Wharton had not taken such action a year earlier, and Nannie's "dogged and indiscriminate opposition" to all advice, including the best medical opinions in Europe, could no longer be tolerated. For too long, he told Edith, she had tried to "adapt" herself to Nannie's attitude. She accepted his advice about Nannie, who was unreasonable and irresponsible in ways similar to Teddy's (she seemed to suffer a milder form of his disease), but Edith could not bear to put Teddy under restraint. Neither could she live with him. As soon as he was safely back in Paris under White's watchful eye, she traveled to England with Walter, who was sailing to America for a few weeks. She spent a weekend with James and Sturgis at Qu'acre.[37]

While Teddy was in Switzerland, Henry James, deep in the throes of his own depression, had been at the German spa Bad Nauheim with William and Alice. He spent the afternoons trying to restore his physical and mental health by taking long walks in the surrounding forests, and he returned to England somewhat improved. His brother was decidedly weakened, however. Now the William Jameses, with Henry in tow, were leaving for America. Henry could not face another winter at Lamb House, and King Edward VII's death on May 6 had canceled plans for the opening of his play *The Outcry*. With the country in official mourning, there would be no London "season." They sailed from Liverpool on August 12; two weeks later, William James died at his summer home in New Hampshire. Henry was paralyzed with grief and confessed to Edith that "my relation to him and affection for him, and the different aspect his extinction has given for me to my life, are all unutterable matters." She received the news of William James's death while traveling with Teddy in the hills of the Côte d'Or, where she was trying to recover from a severe attack of hay fever. "It's a sorry picture, your being driven to such restless repose," Henry wrote, but the clear air did her good, and she was amused by her stay in a former Carthusian monastery that had been turned into a charming (but badly run) hotel.[38]

Three weeks later, she was in New York with Teddy, who was to leave with Johnson Morton, a writer, editor, and professional social worker among Boston's poor, who had agreed (for a fee) to escort Teddy on a six-month round-the-world voyage. The Whartons took a suite on the upper floors of the Belmont Hotel on Park Avenue at Forty-first Street. Twenty-two stories of luxury, the tallest structure in midtown, it had been built by August Belmont in 1906. They might have been in Paris, as everything from tapestries to paintings, furniture, and antiques had been imported from France. In these marbled surroundings, they waited ten days while Dr. Kinnicutt recovered from influenza. He was to give Teddy a thorough physical checkup and approve the trip.

Edith was again suffering from hay fever. The late-summer heat was extreme, and the waiting wore badly on her nerves—and no doubt on Teddy's as well. The "appalling city," she wrote Berenson, who was at that moment arriving in Paris, "plunged" her into "dumb despair." She described for him the Dantesque scene below her "high-perched apartment." The city was "a Mercator's projection of hell—with the river of pitch, and the iron bridges, and the 'elevated' marking off the bolgie, and Blackwell's Island opposite for the City of Dis!" Even Dr. Kinnicutt's approval of Teddy's expedition did little to relieve her unhappiness, nor did his reassurance that her own symptoms—of "senile decay, if not of mortal disease"—were due to nervous strain. They would disappear with their "cause."[39]

While Edith was awaiting Kinnicutt's assessment of Teddy, Johnson Morton was lingering in Paris before sailing to New York to meet up with the Whartons. At the Ritz one evening, Ogden Codman encountered him at a table with the Berensons, and learned that Teddy's illness was being described as senile dementia. Codman was "immensely interested" in all that Johnson Morton had to say, but thought it in "unutterably bad taste" to discuss Teddy's condition publicly, especially as he was now working for Edith, who hired him (in Codman's phrase) as an "inexpensive keeper" for Teddy. Codman, who had recently received from Teddy full payment plus six and a half years' interest on the disputed decoration bill for The Mount, now realized that his earlier troubles with the Whartons were due to Teddy's illness. He was still estranged from Edith, but was being urged by several mutual friends—Egerton Winthrop, Eliot Gregory, and Berkeley Updike—to make up their old quarrel. Winthrop, a reliable witness to the Wharton marriage, explained to Codman that Edith had not realized how sick Teddy was and that she had believed his interpretation of the misunderstandings with Codman over The Mount. Codman at first rejected this idea. Edith was a woman "lacking in womanly feeling," he told his mother. "She really is as much to blame as [Teddy] is, for she knew what a liar he was." Meanwhile, in New York, the society journal *Town Topics* was keeping an eye on Edith Wharton and would soon hint that Teddy's trip was arranged so that she and Walter Berry could see more of each other.[40]

In the days leading up to Teddy's departure on October 16, Edith assembled her friends to lend moral support. Henry James responded immediately to the "silver steam-whistle of the Devastating Angel," and admitted to Sturgis a certain eagerness to leave the "dismal associations" of Chocorua, New Hampshire, where he was staying with his sister-in-law, Alice. Edith had heard gossip that Alice James was giving Henry a "faith-cure" to help ease his lingering depression (a true story), and Edith was happy to get him away from her even for a short time. Morton Fullerton came to New York from Brockton, where he had been visiting his parents, and Walter Berry came up from Washington. The foursome gathered for a gala dinner at the Hotel Belmont's Rotunda restaurant on the eve of Edith's departure for France on the *Prinzcessin Cecile*. Once at sea, her hay fever cleared up, but she was by no means well, and on her return to Paris, she "went to bits . . . in nerves and digestion." Berenson, who had stayed on in Paris at her request, thought she looked terrible. James told Sturgis that she had been in "rags" in New York.[41]

On the day of Edith's departure for France, Fullerton, James, and Berry had a last lunch at the Rotunda before going their separate ways. Walter headed to Washington, where he was closing up his former law practice. While in the capital, he spoke with the editor of the *Washington Herald*, who expressed interest in Fullerton's writing on French topics. Edith had enlisted his help in securing commissions and making State Department connections for Fullerton, a service Walter was happy to do, since Fullerton recently had put him in touch with a man who would become his future law partner in Paris.

About this time, Fullerton asked for a leave of absence from the *Times* to write a book and had been told that he would be fired and refused his last month's salary if the newspaper could not immediately find a replacement for him. At this news, Henry James cried outrage. How could "those vulgar and odious people" treat him in this manner after twenty years of an "admirable career"? But Edith saw Fullerton's current predicament as a great opportunity. She had been urging him for some time to remake his life by exerting "interior discipline" rather than submitting any longer to "routine obedience" imposed from the outside. "A man of your age, and your ability and your 'record,' who says: 'I am afraid to strike out for myself' . . . *really means*: 'I am afraid to give up many small pleasant things which now compensate me for the sacrifice of the distant hope.'" He now had no choice but to "strike out" for himself, but he also had no assurance that he could succeed.[42]

FABLES OF DARKNESS

While Edith was en route to France, her new book of short stories, *Tales of Men and Ghosts*, was published in New York and London to mixed reviews. Between March 1909 and September 1910, individual stories from the collection appeared in *Scribner's* and *Century*. One reviewer detected a "cramping of influence" in the tales and noted that they were of "strangely unequal merit." While the American Library Association judged them too subtle, inconclusive, and "deficient in action" to please the average reader, the *Nation* thought their ingenuity too "patent." *Bookman* and *Athenaeum* praised Edith Wharton for her understanding of human nature. Despite its title, the collection explores the human psyche rather than purely social situations or the worlds of ghosts and goblins. It traces a symptomatology of fear, desire, obsession, and repression that today's readers, familiar with psychoanalytic theories of human behavior, find less troubling than did Edith Wharton's contemporaries. She was aware of Freud's theories of sexuality and the emerging field of psychoanalysis. Her studies of the human psyche dramatize a truth that Freud might have recognized (the eerie, the uncanny, the violent, the inexplicable) but to a different end: she meant to send shivers down the spines of her readers.

By 1910, it should have been obvious to Edith Wharton's readers and reviewers that she presented two faces to the public. A satirist of people and institutions, ideas and art forms, she decried the absence of culture and lack of moral standards, and ridiculed the notions of progressivism and get-rich-quickism of modern industrial life. Her critical regard of society broadened as she grew older, so that her satires of contemporary experience (*The Custom of the Country*, for example) required the large canvas of the novel, where she painted in wide brush strokes and bright colors. She used the smaller canvases of short stories and novellas to probe the psychological and parapsychological worlds, casting a handful of characters into a mold whose finely wrought shape revealed an inner truth. These two forms of her writing required quite separate skills, and it was for this reason that there came a moment in every long project when she turned back to short story writing or a novella. She needed to shift both the scale and the subject, an exercise that served as a resting place and also a spur to her creativity.

The *Tales of Men and Ghosts* were composed during a two-year period of stressful change in her life when she was unable to find the energy and peace of mind to continue her work on *The Custom of the Country*. The stories in this volume throw into relief the shadows of her troubled inner world, worries about her marriage, her work, even her sanity, while also drawing acute psychological portraits of those closest to her: Henry James's sorrow over his failure to gain wide readership ("The Legend") and her own concerns about literary fame ("The Bolted Door," "Full Circle"); Fullerton's lapses into silence ("The Letters"); mysteries of paternity and creative expression ("His Father's Son"); Teddy's mental and physical degradation ("The Eyes"); the egotism of connoisseurship and art collecting ("The Daunt Diana," where we catch glimpses of Egerton Winthrop, Ogden Codman, and Bernard Berenson); public stewardship and civic responsibility ("The Blond Beast," whose title is taken from Nietzsche). She recognized the failure of at least two of the stories, agreeing with Fullerton that "The Legend" required a larger background and should have been a novel; she admitted to John Hugh Smith that although the subject of "The Blond Beast" was a good one, she had failed to fulfill the story's promise.

The first of the ten stories, "The Bolted Door" (which some reviewers thought the best in the volume), was written during her sojourn in England in autumn 1908. She credited John Hugh Smith with the idea for it: a man proclaims himself a murderer but no one believes his story. After he is committed to a rest home for the mentally disturbed, a journalist discovers the truth of his claims. The murderer's psychological situation—he feels himself a "prisoner of consciousness," alone, alienated, living behind a locked door—was true to Edith's experience during that dreadful summer. The victim, an aged uncle bloated with self-absorption and resembling the hothouse melons he raises, is a grotesque version of Teddy, whose joints and big toes were swollen with gout, his face now a mask of pain and his eyelids heavy and pouchy. When Percy Lubbock read the story in the March 1909 *Scribner's Magazine*, he dismissed it as a "rotten little melodramatic anecdote." The story may seem to create an atmosphere of excess emotion in response to insufficient motive, but it also shows that surface irrationalism and overstatement—the man's claim to be a murderer—can hide a psychological truth that has its own logic.[43]

The most enduring story of *Men and Ghosts* is a macabre tale in which a man is twice haunted by a pair of disembodied eyes that sear his soul. They appear when dilettante Andrew Culwin denies his own desires. On the first occasion, he becomes engaged to his cousin, who is "wholesome as fresh water" but fails to excite his passion, and then abandons her by fleeing to Europe. Two years later, he praises a failed work by his literary protégé Gilbert Noyes, and the eyes come to haunt him until he is at last forced to tell Noyes the truth. All the elements of Edith Wharton's world are to be found in this vision of egotism and self-deception overlaid by a cultured refinement that replaces human warmth and engagement with the world. A spectator on life, Culwin inhabits an arid, enclosed, effete, and latently homosexual environment. At the end of his tale, told before a flickering fire in his library, Culwin's own eyes—reflected in a mirror—have become the very image of the evil, hateful eyes that had long ago frightened him.

Critics have identified in Culwin elements of Walter Berry and Morton Fullerton, with touches of Howard Sturgis and Egerton Winthrop brushed in. Yet, the red-rimmed and feverish eyes, the gouty hands, shrunken figure, and "congested face" also belonged to Teddy Wharton, who by spring 1910 (when the tale was written) had aged well beyond his years. The most striking feature of photographs from this period are his eyes, which have an otherworldly gaze, staring out of the death mask of his face. Henry James's eyes had also taken on a haunted look; they were the eyes of a man who had "looked on the Medusa," Edith told Fullerton; he stared out of a "stony stricken face" with "tragic eyes" that elicited her compassion. Teddy, whom she pitied, had now become the agent of her imprisonment, and she found it ever more difficult to look on him with sympathy, or even to look at him. *"J'en ai assez, et à quel point,"* she wrote Fullerton in June: "I've had enough of it, and to what point!"[44]

Remembered as a supreme artist of the ghost story genre, Edith Wharton counted among her mentors Robert Louis Stevenson, Sheridan Le Fanu, Fitz James O'Brien, Marion Crawford (Daisy Chanler's half brother, who wrote only one ghost tale), Walter de la Mare, and Henry James. Her criterion for a good ghost story was that its *effect* should be "thermometrical": "If it sends a cold shiver down one's spine, it has done its job and done it well." She understood that there was no fixed rule for inducing this response, that what made one reader cringe left another (often herself) "peacefully tepid." She believed, too, that the teller of supernatural tales should be "well frightened in the telling." She had hoped for such effects in two stories written in late 1909. The first of these, "Afterward," stirred reader interest when it appeared in *Century Magazine* in January 1910. The story takes place in a haunted English manor house, recently purchased by an American couple, in which the ghost is known only by its aftereffects—in this case, the inexplicable disappearance of the new owner. The second story, "Triumph of the Night," was written during the Paris flood but not published until 1914. It is a tale of inheritances, fiscal misdealings, mysterious death, haunting eyes, and bloodstained hands.

Neither story compares with "The Eyes" (or with "The Lady's Maid's Bell," her first published ghost story, written in 1902), because neither provides the "continuity and silence" that allow ghosts to enter the world of the living—the quiet that the author creates through tone. Every ghostly appearance is a *re*-appearance. In a preface to a collection of her previously printed short stories that appeared a few weeks after her death in 1937, Edith observed that the faculty required for enjoying ghost stories had "almost atrophied" in contemporary life, that her readers no longer met her "halfway among the primeval shadows." She held the cinema and "wireless" responsible for the loss of the "ghost instinct": ghosts need "silent hours," an all too rare occurrence in "a roaring and discontinuous universe." One might also observe that in a world in which science was rapidly solving the mysteries of the cosmos and psychoanalysis was explaining the operations of human emotions, there was little place left for the ghostly.[45]

A friend once asked Edith whether, given her attraction to ghosts, she was interested in spiritualism. She responded that she had no desire to talk with the dead. The question continued to nag at her, however, until Berenson provided an explanation. "What appeals to your imagination in ghost stories is something immediate, atavistic, and far deeper than your reason; while the interest in spiritualism and mediums is a reasoned intellectual curiosity, and one need not necessarily lead to the other."[46]

WHEN *Tales of Men and Ghosts* was completed in June 1910, she turned to work on her best-known tale, *Ethan Frome*, which she first described to friends as a long short story and then as a "young novel." Taking up this story of lonely lives in half-deserted New England villages, Edith returned to a sketch she had begun some three years earlier, written in French as an exercise for her Paris tutor. She abandoned the story when her language lessons ended and picked it up again after Teddy left for Switzerland in summer 1910. Interrupted by the New York trip and her illness, she did not turn to it again until January 1911, when she withdrew completely from society and wrote steadily over a six-week period. Each evening, she read aloud what she had written that day to Walter Berry, who was still resident in her guest suite at number 53. This novella was destined to become a standard item on middle-school reading lists, and it met with a rare compliment from Henry James, who praised it without reservation: "A beautiful art and tone and truth—a beautiful artful *kept-downness*, and yet effective accumulation."[47]

Ten years of summer residence in western Massachusetts had given Edith a sense of the spiritual and economic poverty of its local people. But the chilling spirit of the story, its dark loneliness and emotional paralysis, belonged to the interior world of her fears, a lonely landscape that she projected onto the winter beauty of the Berkshires. In spring 1907, when she first conceived this tale of a fated extramarital liaison, she had as yet no real hope that such an event would ever occur in her own life. By winter 1911, her hours of sexual passion had come and gone. Disillusioned with her lover, her husband in the throes of mental illness, Edith felt as tied to Teddy as Ethan Frome was to his bedridden wife, Zeena.

Set in the fictional village of Starkfield, the drama involves a poor farmer, his wife, and her niece, Mattie Silver, who comes to keep house when Mrs. Frome is invalided. Wedded for many years in mutual misery and dependency, Ethan has retreated behind a mask of silent avoidance, and his wife speaks only to complain. Mattie's entrance into this frozen world awakens Ethan's slumbering desire. Sensing the change, Zeena insists that they cannot afford to keep Mattie, and orders her sent away. Ethan dreams of escaping with the girl, but in the end, he cannot summon the courage or energy to do so. Driving her to the train station, he agrees to her impulsive desire to take a sled run down School House Hill. In what may have been a failed suicide attempt, the ride ends in an accident that cripples Mattie. Zeena rises from her sickbed to care for her niece, who turns bitter as she ages. Ethan retreats deeper into silence. This little tale—a "volumelet" less than a hundred pages in print—bitterly condemns the human weakness and inertia that chain people in what Edith once called "sterile pain."

Emotionally and materially, *Ethan Frome* is a frigid moonscape. While the imaginary Starkfield has no intellectual equivalent to Lenox life, it is not without communal activities—sleigh rides, church socials, and dances, like the one from which a flushed and smiling Mattie emerges when we first see her. The isolation of the Frome household that destroys its inhabitants and renders Mattie a younger version of Zeena is self-enforced by separation from the human community and a turning inward on themselves. One might imagine that in writing the tale, Edith's own mood matched the tone of the story. Yet, her letters reveal the fun she had with it: "It amuses me to do that decor"—Starkfield and Shadd's Falls—"in the rue de Varenne," she wrote Berenson. She re-created in the sledding scene a real incident that had occurred on March 11, 1904. On a Friday afternoon, four girls from the Lenox Academy and a young man ran a "double ripper" bobsled down the slope south from the Egleson Patterson monument at the center of Lenox onto the Old Stockbridge Road. The sled attained a speed of fifty miles an hour before it hit a gaslight pole, throwing the passengers onto the ice.[48]

One young woman died and two others were badly injured in the accident, among them Kate Spencer, who like Mattie Silver was badly scarred. A 1904 graduate of the academy, she later worked at the Lenox Library, where she met Edith Wharton. The library setting is fictionalized in *Summer,* the twin tale to *Ethan Frome.* The heroine of *Summer*, which Edith wrote in Paris during the war and published in 1917, is a young woman who works as the village librarian. Any similarity between Kate Spencer, daughter of a prestigious Lenox family, and the fictional character Charity Royall stops at the library door, however. Edith referred to *Summer* as "Hot Ethan" because it reversed the thematic and structural principles of her winter story. It takes place in a verdant Berkshire summer painted in vibrant colors, as the scent of thyme and wild honeysuckle blows across the blue New England hills. Stellar cold has been transformed into summer's heat, lovelessness ignites in sexual passion, passivity is converted into assertive energy.[49]

Ethan Frome was published serially from August to October 1911 in *Scribner's Magazine*; the firm paid $2,500 for the serial rights and also gave Edith a $2,000 advance against book royalties. It appeared in book form simultaneously in New York and London (where it was published by Macmillan), and, in February 1912, in the *Revue des deux mondes* in an unsigned translation entitled *Sous la neige*, revised by Edith and Charles du Bos. Her friends agreed that the novella was a remarkable piece of work, New York reviewers offered qualified praise, and she was pleased with it herself. The reviewers, she wrote Fullerton, "don't know *why* it's good, but they are right: it *is*." The *New York Times Book Review* called it a cruel, haunting story, saying that Edith Wharton was a dramatist who passed for a novelist. *Outlook* praised its unity of structure and style, but hoped that in her next book, she would bring her "great talent" to focus on "normal people and situations." The American *Bookman* could not forgive the "utter remorselessness" of the tale, and the *Nation* thought Ethan "hag-ridden" by fate: "the wonder is that the spectacle of so much pain can be made to yield to so much beauty." In England, the *Saturday Review* complained that the story lacked "motive," while the *Bookman* found it an "intensely human story, working out to its final conclusion with all the inevitability of a great Greek tragedy."[50]

With congratulatory letters from friends in New York and Boston "pouring in," Edith assumed that *Ethan Frome* was having the financial success of *The House of Mirth*. Initial sales in America, however, were disappointing (forty-two hundred copies sold in the first six weeks), and there was no mention of a second edition, even though Charles Scribner had agreed to her request of an additional advance of $1,000. She complained of printing errors and the absence of advertising. In her November 27 letter, she reminded Mr. Scribner that because Mr. Burlingame had been unable to "make room" for *The Custom of the Country* in the magazine, she had set the novel aside in lieu of something she wanted to finish first. That "something" was *The Reef*, which Charles Scribner had known of since summer 1910, when Burlingame warned him that the *Century*, which had published two stories from *Tales of Men and Ghosts* ("Afterward" and "The Letters"), was making a "dead set" at her—that is, trying to win her away from *Scribner's Magazine*. When Edith announced that she wanted to write a short novel before completing *The Custom of the Country*, Burlingame, afraid that she was looking for an excuse to leave the firm, offered to make space in the magazine for *The Reef* at whatever date she completed it. It was a "good strategy," Charles Scribner said, but her novel was not "really wanted."

Burlingame's ploy did not work. Edith did not want just page space in *Scribner's Magazine*: she wanted a substantial payment for serial rights. She had made her case to Charles Scribner five years earlier when she negotiated with him a $10,000 contract for serial rights on *The Fruit of the Tree*. He had agreed to that exceptional contract because he expected (as did Edith) that the novel would match sales of *The*

House of Mirth. It did not, and Edith was not in a good position to insist on an even higher contract price for her new book. Without a word to her editors at Scribners, she sold *The Reef* in May 1912 for $15,000 to D. Appleton and Company, an old firm, founded in Boston and later transferred to New York, that had published Hamlin Garland, Stephen Crane, and Joseph Conrad.

Fullerton, who had become Appleton's representative in Europe in 1911, helped negotiate the contract. When it was all settled, she wrote Charles Scribner of her decision. He was so shocked by her announcement that it took him a month to reply to her letter. "Mr. Scribner is mortally hurt by my infidelity," Edith told Fullerton in June 1912.[51]

WHILE TEDDY TRAVELED in Southeast Asia and India in spring 1911, Edith finished writing *Ethan Frome*. She attended some theater and ballet performances, seeing Isadora Duncan dance in January and taking in a May appearance of the Ballet Russe in a lavish production of Stravinsky's *Petrushka*. She thought Hofmannsthal's *Oedipus* "very fine" and Bourget's dramatization of his own novel, *Le Tribun*, "really good." She convinced Fullerton, who was busy meeting orders for articles that were "pouring in," to translate it into English. He was "so much happier since he has been a free man," she told Berenson. She socialized primarily with the men of "*la bande*." They were the "Bs"—Berry, Blanche, Bourget, du Bos, Léon Bélugou (an engineer with mining interests in Indochina), and Berenson, when he was in town. There would be no gathering of the Anglo-American "inner circle" until December at Qu'acre, but three of its members (Henry James, Gaillard Lapsley, and John Hugh Smith) gathered at The Mount in July. Plunged into the "deep dark hole" of depression, James spent nearly two months with Minnie Jones in New York City during the spring, unable to live alone in Cambridge. Desperate to leave the United States ("terrible country"), he was even more afraid to return to Lamb House, where his troubles had begun. His mental suffering had increased to such a degree that he even submitted for a time to Freudian analysis with Dr. James Jackson Putnam, a neurologist who had once been a devotee of the Weir Mitchell cure.[52]

While Minnie tried to cheer up James, Edith began an effort to secure the Nobel Prize in literature for him. She had two motivations: to give him the international recognition he deserved and to relieve him of financial worries. As she explained to Edmund Gosse, whom she asked to lead the Nobel Prize effort in England, and to William Dean Howells, who sought American support for his nomination, James needed the relief from "material anxiety" that the prize could provide. Working tirelessly at this project with "unexpectedly encouraging" results, especially in America, she was taken completely by surprise later in the year when the Nobel Foundation announced that the prize had gone to Belgian writer Maurice Maeterlinck. The prize had been awarded before the Nobel Institute committee in England had even voted on its list of candidates and before James's name had been brought to the Swedish committee. Determined not to go down to defeat, she wrote Gosse that they would "hatch a fresh plot" when she visited England in December. But her efforts to put James in competition for the award did not succeed.[53]

On an afternoon in early March, she returned from an excursion to Versailles with Fullerton to find a letter from Johnson Morton announcing his arrival with Teddy in Marseilles on April 4. Her six-month interval of peace and independence was at an end. Teddy arrived looking physically fit, but she knew from Harvard professor Barrett Wendell, who had seen him in India, that Teddy still suffered periods of irritability and agitation. Teddy's stay in Paris was brief, but his fleeting presence in the household created unbearable havoc. Ill with hay fever, Edith could not tolerate his constant talk about money and the daily scenes of anger and humiliation. After his departure for London, where he outfitted himself with a new Savile Row wardrobe, she succumbed to the flu. "I am feeling considerably bluer than this paper," she wrote Berenson.

To cheer her up, Fullerton brought the news that, after a long labor, Katharine had given birth to a baby boy, Christopher, on April 9—ten months to the day after her marriage to Gordon Hall Gerould, a Princeton University professor of folklore and medieval studies. They had been married on June 9, 1910, at the Fullerton family home on Newberry Street in Brockton. The Reverend Bradford Fullerton officiated at the ceremony, and Robert Fullerton gave Katharine away. Morton was not present. Katharine was not in love with Gerould when she married him, but she accepted his proposal in "utter despair" at Morton's inability to commit himself to her. "I do not think any human being has the right to hurt another like this," she had written him in January 1910. "I would not treat a slave so." Meanwhile, Gerould—

who knew enough about Morton Fullerton to believe that he had an unhealthy influence over Katharine—pressed his case with her. After making her decision, she cabled Morton in Paris: "Courage dearest love, Katharine." She asked for his blessing on her union—"the last balm you can give to the heart you have so subtly tortured all these years." He gave it.[54]

Edith was impressed with what Fullerton told her of Gordon Gerould, who helped with household duties so that Katharine had time for her literary work. "What a good fellow your brother-in-law must be!" Edith exclaimed. "Think of having a husband who thought one ought to have a chance to write! C'est invraisemblable. [It's improbable.] The only interest my works ever excited was purely mercantile." This bitter comment about Teddy had a solid core of truth to it. Some years earlier, he had confided to Walter Berry that when they could not afford the new "piggery" needed for the farm operation at The Mount, Edith had solved the problem by publishing some poetry. He had come to rely on her ability to raise needed cash by selling her literary work. His role had been to oversee her investments, and as soon as he returned to America from his trip with Johnson Morton, he mounted a campaign to resume control of her financial affairs: "I want to feel still that I know about them [investments] and can be of some use to her," he told Herman Edgar. In the past, Teddy had shown a certain flair for investments; Walter, who had lost heavily in mining, metals, and commodities, respected Teddy's ability to choose stocks wisely. But after his losses with her trust money in 1909, Edith would not consent to Teddy's having any control over her money, "whether income or capital," and Walter agreed.[55]

By mid-May 1911, she was at Salsomaggiore, where she had not been in five years. After a complete medical examination, her doctors reported that the "dry congestion" she was experiencing was not caused by external, environmental irritation (as she had thought), but rather by a "disturbance of the circulation" that indicated high blood pressure. This appraisal was the first notice of the circulatory problems that, along with successive heart attacks, would eventually kill her. The doctors asked her to extend her stay at Salso for special medical treatments, and to return again for a second series in the autumn.

Lonely, she closed her shutters against the full moon "soaring above the hills at night," and read into the wee hours, having armed herself with enough reading material to last her for months. Her book box held Victor Hugo's posthumously published autobiography, *Post-scriptum de ma vie*, Ernest Renan's *Averroès*, Flaubert's *Novembre*, George Henry Lewes's *History of Philosophy from Thales to Comte*, Sir Joshua Reynolds's *Discourses on Art*, Dostoevsky's *Idiot*, Melville's *Moby Dick*, Ludwig Woltmann's *Die Germanen in Frankreich*, and Léon Bazalgette's translation of Whitman's *Leaves of Grass*. But her favorite text, the one she portioned out to "prolong the feast as long as I can," was Richard Wagner's autobiography, *Mein Leben*, the agonizing story of his personal and creative life, and of his political exile from Germany. What would she do when she had finished it? she asked Fullerton. "Je suis triste à mourir [I am sad enough to die]," she said, adding that she wished she had known him when she was twenty-five. "We might have had some good days together."

In the afternoons at Salso, she walked the dusty roads near the hotel in an effort to lose weight (over several years, she had gained some fifteen pounds and now weighed 140); in the evenings, she read. But in the mornings, she was at work on *The Custom of the Country*, revising portions she had not looked at since summer 1908, and introducing a new character, Indiana Frusk, whose unlikely name reviewers considered outrageous. She "interests me very much," Edith wrote Fullerton, "but when, at this rate, will the poor book be done?" She soon put it aside to work on *The Reef*, the contract for which she had just signed.

Edith had hoped that Berenson might pay her a visit at Salso, but he was too busy with visitors to leave I Tatti. Eager to get away from the place that resembled the "backyards of Jersey City, as seen from the train," she took a day trip to Parma in a rented motor and "scuttled" in and out of cold churches. Enjoying the Duomo and its baptistery, which she had not seen in many years, she was amused by the Correggio cupids on the ceiling of the Camera di San Paolo, but the trip did not ease her bored restlessness. She wanted conversation and companionship. "You are the only light spot in the sky just now," she wrote Fullerton. "Please keep on shining, and shedding your beneficent ray on your affectionate EW."[56]

Chapter 6

W

DEPARTURES

EDITH ACQUIESCED TO DR. KINNICUTT'S SUGGESTION
that she spend summer 1911 at The Mount. Teddy was in
Canada fishing with his brother, Billy, when she arrived for
her first visit in three years. The July heat was intense and her emotions were a confused tangle. To calm herself, she took a long tour of
The Mount grounds with her gardener, Thomas Reynolds. "Decidedly
I'm a better landscape gardener than novelist," she wrote Fullerton,
"and this place, every line of which is my own work, far surpasses the
House of Mirth." Strolling on the terrace that evening, she communed
with Vega, Arcturus, and Altair and pondered her future, one as "impenetrable" as the moonless sky.[1]

The next day, she set to work preparing the house for the arrival of
Henry James, Gaillard Lapsley, and John Hugh Smith. James was the
first to arrive, apparently in good mental health but suffering from
heat so intense that it would, according to Edith, have "inspired Dante
to draw an additional *bolgia*." He sat for hours in front of a small electric fan sucking oranges, a "mere prostrate, panting, liquefying mass,"
he wrote Howard Sturgis, "waiting to be removed" from America. In
the mornings, Edith worked on *The Custom of the Country*; in the afternoons, she motored in her new fifty-horsepower Mercedes; and in the
evenings, the group gathered on the terrace to talk and stargaze and

listen to James's rambling anecdotes about remote members of his family. At work on the first volume of his autobiography, *A Small Boy and Others*, he had many stories to tell. He was, as Edith recalled to John Hugh several weeks later, "completely and lavishly himself; and that *greatness* in him is just the all-enclosing fact."[2]

Despite the heat, those days with her three comrades were the only pleasant ones of Edith's summer. The party began to break up when John Hugh departed on the twelfth. (Edith provided him with a letter of introduction to Theodore Roosevelt, who was at Sagamore Hill, his country place in Oyster Bay, New York; two weeks later, Edith and Teddy were Roosevelt's guests.) Lapsley left on the thirteenth, and Teddy turned up later that same day. He immediately resumed his litany of recriminations against Edith: she was mean and vindictive and responsible for his unhappiness. He again demanded the right to control certain aspects of her finances. James was horror-struck by what he saw and heard, and he departed for Boston the following morning worried about Edith. Responding to a sad letter from her several days later, he spoke frankly of her "actual, dreadful history." She must rid herself of the "absolutely unworkable burden and complication of the Mount"; now that "scenes of violence" had recurred (by which he meant shouting and verbal abuse), she must save her life by establishing a "separate existence." He spoke to Minnie Jones of Teddy's "childishness of mind," and portrayed him to Howard Sturgis as "perfectly sane and in the stoutest, toughest physical health, but utterly quarrelsome, abusive, perpetual-scene-making and impossible. He simply and absolutely . . . will do her to death, and then where should we be?" Edith wrote Minnie that the weeks after James left Lenox were "about as bad as they could be."[3]

Teddy's primary anger at Edith arose from his forced abdication in December 1909 of fiscal control over her estate. Worn down by his protests, she proposed an alternative arrangement: if he resigned as trustee of her inheritance, he could manage The Mount (as he wished to do), and she would deposit money for that purpose in a special account. He agreed to her offer, and she sat down to write his brother, Billy, about the agreement. When she asked Teddy to read her letter and approve it, he again became enraged and claimed she was inflicting a "cruel and unnecessary humiliation" on him. He had never consented to resign the trusteeship, he said, and if he was turned out of the trust, he would take no responsibility for The Mount's upkeep. He demanded a final break with her. (Many years later, Edith remarked to a friend that Teddy had "no cruelty and no unkindness in him. Yet," she said, "he was cruel through weakness.")[4]

The next day, Sunday, July 23, Edith detailed these events in a second letter to Billy. In closing, she thanked him and his wife, Susan, for their understanding. Billy wrote back that he and Susan believed the source of Teddy's unhappiness was the estrangement in his marriage. Now it was Edith's turn to deny charges she felt were unfair. She had not changed her behavior toward Teddy, she said, and there was no reason for estrangement except that caused by Teddy's "disregard of all courtesy and self-control in his behaviour to me." Only ten days earlier, however, *Town Topics* had speculated on Edith's relationship with Walter Berry, the second such item they had printed in a year.[5]

On Monday, July 24, Teddy reversed himself and consented to resign from the trust; Edith agreed they should live apart. She outlined these arrangements in a letter hand-delivered to him in his bedroom at The Mount by a servant. She then departed for Newport to spend several days with Egerton Winthrop; Walter, who had just arrived from France, accompanied her. The Whartons' marital drama had several more acts to run. Billy intervened, asking her to "give another trial" to living with Teddy. By July 29, she was back at The Mount and Teddy was on his best behavior. Earlier that summer, they had received a purchase offer for the estate, and now received a second offer, "a *very* large" one. The question of selling or keeping the property again lay on the table. "I have had a terrible two years," she wrote Sara Norton, confiding that she thought it would be better for Teddy to have a small house at the seashore where he could swim and sail. She admitted to Berenson that The Mount, in which she had invested so much of her creative spirit, was the only thing that could "reconcile" her to America. She loved its "stillness, the greenness, the exuberance of my flowers, the perfume of my hemlock woods, and above all the moonlight nights on my big terrace."[6]

Returning from Newport to Lenox alone, Edith called on Fullerton's parents in their little Brockton house. She wanted to give him "eyewitness" news of his family, but it seems more likely that her curiosity spurred the visit. (Fullerton, due to land in New York in four weeks' time, would soon see his parents in person.) Her Mercedes turned into Newberry Street just at teatime, and the Reverend and Mrs. Bradford

Fullerton welcomed her graciously. They were charming, she wrote Morton, and stronger-looking than he had led her to believe: "You are *so* like them both, with such differences!" Surely her visit must have disconcerted him, as it gave her a view of his family's economic circumstances. The Fullertons were poor, and Edith knew that they sometimes asked Morton for financial help. On this occasion, however, she did not remind him that money that might have gone to help his parents instead went to Mme Mirecourt.[7]

Edith's long, hot American summer ended when Teddy headed west to French Lick, Indiana, to undergo physical therapy at a spa, and she sailed to Europe for her second cure of the season at Salso. Halfway across the ocean, she received the news that Teddy had sold The Mount and was forwarding papers that required her signature. Earlier in the summer, she had left him to decide "as he thought best" about the house sale, and on September 2, she signed a document giving him legal authority to rent or sell The Mount. But she also made him promise that he would not sell the property before she reached Paris. Angered by his willfulness, she protested his action to friends. For Edith, selling The Mount was fraught with conflicting emotions; recognizing that she could no longer bear its financial and managerial burdens and could not live there with Teddy, she still put off making a final decision. A few weeks later, she signed the sale agreement, an act that effectively put the seal on her life in America. The sale would not be finalized until the following summer. In the interim, she tried to put the matter out of her mind.[8]

After a few days at the Crillon in Paris, she went to Salso, where Walter joined her. They traveled for several weeks in northern Italy, cheering themselves in the bone-chilling cold and rainy autumn weather by composing postcard jingles for James, whom they had invited along but who had chosen to settle down to work on his autobiography: "Climbing hills and fording torrents/Here we are at last in Florence. . . . " On October 15, they wound their way up from the city into the Settignano hills, arriving at the gate of the Villa I Tatti, where Bernard and Mary Berenson awaited them. It was their first visit to I Tatti, and many more would follow. During the past seven years, the Berensons had renovated and enlarged the original two-story pavilion on the estate, designed a series of libraries for Berenson's art books, and created gardens that capitalized on the landscape's natural beauty. Mary supervised the architects and engineers and teams of local workers, while her husband raised the funds to pay for the increasingly expensive venture. Together, they created a work of art on a human scale—welcoming, intimate, and charming. But the effort on the house, with its accumulated tensions and anger, had torn the fabric of their marriage and left both of them deeply scarred.[9]

For most of 1911, the Berensons lived in a kind of marital truce, dire rumors circulating about the state of their union. Edith may never have learned the full story of their marriage and probably never suspected at what cost Mary had joined her life to Bernard's. Educated at Smith College and the Harvard Annex, Mary made an unhappy early marriage to an Irish jurist nine years her senior with whom she had little in common. They moved to London, where he practiced law. In late 1891, she left him to pursue her career as a professional art expert in Italy. He refused her a divorce and denied her access to her two daughters. Given time and freedom, Mary had once told her mother, "I can become one of the most important people in my own profession, as well as one of the most interesting women to cultured people." But when she left England for Italy, her mother accused her of abandoning her children. By 1892, she and Berenson were lovers; indeed, she was pregnant with his child. As he was "deadset against having children," she had an abortion, an act that haunted her, although she admitted to being torn between being a "person" and being a "mother." After her husband died, she married Berenson and they lived at I Tatti. They were a comical-looking couple, as she was far larger than he, and he soon complained about her appearance. "Whenever he looks at me," she confided to her diary, "I am fat, or red, or hairy, or slouchy or untidy."[10]

While he wanted "perfection of physical surroundings" and an income adequate to support this style of life, she resisted "fashionableness in any form," admitting that her "bad dressing and lack of French" cut her off from *mondaine* joys. She loved his "stimulating mind" and "amusing talk," but was alienated by "scenes" in which he shouted and shook his fists, made faces and mimicked her in a high voice, beat his head against the wall and screamed that he hated her and her children and that she had "utterly ruined" his life. By 1906, his "rages" had intensified frighteningly; by 1910, in the heat of his affair with Belle da Costa Greene, Mary threatened to leave him. But she could not live without him, nor he without her.[11]

While Edith and Walter motored with Berenson in the countryside on October afternoons in 1911, Mary remained at I Tatti to oversee the planting of some three hundred ilexes that would create a wooded area on the slopes beneath the house. Although preoccupied with household concerns, she spent time with Edith and revised her unfavorable impression from their first meeting in 1903. Walter's presence eased Mary's anxiety that Edith might have eyes for B.B. From Paris several weeks later, Edith wrote Berenson to say that getting to know Mary was "one of the pleasantest things that has happened to me in a long time, and I want to go on with the process, please tell her!"[12]

While Edith was enjoying the pleasures of I Tatti, Teddy was spreading rumors about her: she had "insisted" on selling The Mount, he said, and thereby "deprived him in his old age of a home and of his one hope of getting well." More discouraging news of Teddy greeted her return to Paris on November 7. Dr. George A. Kahlo, medical director at the French Lick spa, was convinced that Teddy suffered from psychosis and held little hope for his recovery. Dr. Kinnicutt concurred. He acknowledged Edith's "untiring and unavailing efforts" to help her husband recover, but thought she must place him in a sanatorium. She should secure Teddy's consent for such a step—an impossibility, as Kinnicutt must have realized.

He congratulated her on *Ethan Frome* ("a classic that will be read and re-read") and wondered how she had found time and energy "in the pressing anxieties of the past two years" to write such a book. Her "present makeshift existence," as she explained to Fullerton, was "utterly destructive to any sustained imaginative work." But the call to write was "irresistible," the very ground of "the last struggle for an individual existence." The question of Teddy's immediate future was tabled when he suddenly decided to go to Bermuda instead of returning to Paris.[13]

Family matters pursued her from yet another direction in these weeks. Returning to France from her Italian trip, Edith learned that her brother Frederic, age sixty-six, had suffered a paralytic stroke and had been taken to the American Hospital in Neuilly. Although she and Harry had maintained only minimal relations with their brother since Lucretia's death, they now joined forces to help him, visiting him regularly and paying his medical expenses. Edith wired New York, thinking Beatrix might want to see him (she did not), and as the days wore on, it became clear that while he could not recover, he was not in immediate danger of death. Back in Paris, she kept up a hectic social schedule. When a friend of Henry James's observed her dining one evening at the Ritz "en nombreuse compagnie," he thought her "looking awfully handsome and stunningly dressed."[14]

The climax of Edith's current troubles came with a bad case of conjunctivitis, which prevented her from writing, and the death of her "world-worn" little dog, Mitou. She fled Paris for London in early December, where James—happy that his novel *The Outcry* was finding commercial success—squired her to lunches and dinners. They spent a country weekend at Hill Hall, the home of Charles and Mary Hunter in the Epping Forest, where James was a frequent guest. Edith described the experience to Fullerton as "like walking a ploughed field against the wind," adding, "How Henry can stand it I can't think!" But she exploited her society connections to arrange a production of Paul Bourget's *Le Tribun*, which Fullerton was translating into English. (The play was not produced.) On her return to London, she indulged James's desire to see *Kismet*, a dramatization of the novel by his old friend Constance Fletcher. Visiting galleries and museums, she called on John Singer Sargent at his studio in Tite Street to commission a charcoal drawing of Henry James, and on Friday, December 15, she and Henry motored together to Qu'acre for a long and lively weekend with the "inner circle." Logan Pearsall Smith (Mary Berenson's brother) joined the group, and when the party broke up, Robert Norton—en route to the Riviera on a painting expedition—accompanied Edith to Paris. They spent Christmas together at the rue de Varenne.

On December 20, in an apparent reversal of her decision to separate permanently from Teddy, Edith dispatched White to bring him back to Paris. While awaiting their arrival, she attended a series of Beethoven concerts with Daisy Chanler and continued work on her new novel, *The Reef*, a story based in part on her affair with Fullerton.[15]

THE LONG RUN

The health problems Edith had suffered for some eight months continued into January 1912 with disturbing new symptoms. In addition to conjunctivitis in her "bad eye" (the left one), she had begun to have "horrid sudden attacks" of vertigo that left her "utterly demoralized." The doctors diagnosed an inner ear problem related to the anemia she also suffered and prescribed blood builders and rest. The condition eventually disappeared, but it was undoubtedly related to the elevated blood pressure levels that her Salso doctors had discovered a year earlier. Her Paris doctors were not entirely certain what brought on the dizzy spells, but James, who had suffered from them during the 1890s, thought their source lay in her personal problems and her inability, as yet, to see a way out of these difficulties. "You'll find, of a sudden, the right thing to do *or* not to do—and then they will drop like a wounded bird."[16]

By summer, James would envision her as a rapacious bird of prey— eagle and Devastatrix, an elemental figure who "rode the whirlwind" and "played with the storm." For the present, though, his wounded- bird image was all too appropriate. Alone and feeling "very poorly," Edith passed her fiftieth birthday at home on the rue de Varenne, as she had done for the previous six years. She took to her bed as a rest from "talking, translating, 'attending to things.'" She read Keats, "the greatest joy I know." The "sober anniversary," she joked to Sally, made her feel that "getting old" was only "an illusion of youth." Yet, she had no illusions of youth. "The thing is not to watch one's self shrink," she wrote Berenson.[17]

Edith was in no sense "shrinking," but overwork and anxiety were taking their toll. Writing of these years in *A Backward Glance*, she described the "core" of her writing, work that was "growing and spreading," and "absorbing more and more of . . . [her] imagination." The challenge was to shape her daily existence so that her creativity could prosper and her health flourish. In 1912, she had just passed the mid-point of a literary career that would span sixty years, from the publication of *Verses* (1878) to the posthumous publication in 1938 of *The Buccaneers*. By 1912, eighteen of the forty-seven books that would comprise her life's work were in print, thirteen of them having appeared in the decade since *The Valley of Decision*. From 1905, the year she began keeping an account book of her literary income, she had earned some $125,000 in book royalties and serial contracts (almost $2,000,000 pretax dollars today). An Edith Wharton short story cost $1,000 (the price established in 1909 for the stories in *Tales of Men and Ghosts*); her poems sold for $200 each. The $15,000 advance Appleton paid for *The Reef* established a baseline for her future book contracts.[18]

WHEN TEDDY RETURNED to Paris in mid-February, Edith was at work on *The Reef* despite her continuing episodes of vertigo. Rather than heading south to warmer weather, as she had hoped he would, Teddy settled down in the apartment. Walter Berry, who had moved some nine months earlier to his own apartment, a short walk away at 12 rue St. Guillaume, temporarily reinstated himself in the guest quarters of number 53 to serve as a "shock-absorber." He could provide little but moral support for Edith, however. Teddy's restlessness, as he reported to James (who then relayed the news to Howard Sturgis), was intolerable: "He can't 'endure' . . . and from the same cause, he can't be endured, or scarcely." In the grip of the bipolar cycles of his disease, Teddy drew energy from others to renew himself, exhausting everyone around him: "With these renewals he may go on and on," James remarked.[19]

In a pathetic effort to fit into Edith's life, Teddy decided to learn French. During the morning hours usually reserved for her writing, Edith tutored him. After a particularly difficult morning, she wrote Fullerton:

> "Learning French" has become an obsession (*why?* that is so strange!), and we have been having a "lesson," and he has been crying, and saying over and over again: "My mind is going, and the Drs don't see it." It seems to me that he is failing *very* fast mentally. It is too terrible! In some far off moment of respite from work, could you, would you, see [Dr.] Janet for me, and get at the bottom of it all? My brother [Harry] is not the kind of man who can get much information in such cases, and perhaps Janet doesn't realize that I can be told everything—and *must* be, since there's no one far or near to help me. You can tell him that I'm strong.
>
> Oh, when I think of *ten years of it*! My dearest, dearest, I won't trouble you with it.

Tears and recriminations had been the pattern of Teddy's behavior for more than two years. Making himself completely dependent on Edith, he refused to leave the apartment without her, and she spent time taking him "round" the city. Meanwhile, *The Reef*, "at its mid-crisis," wailed for her "every morning like an infant for the bottle." After a month of constant tending to Teddy, she felt "the dead weight of it." "I can naturally make no plans," she wrote Berenson.[20]

She did make plans, however: she proposed a yacht trip along the southeastern coast of France. An excursion of this kind would put Teddy in the fresh air and sunshine he loved, she thought. But the plan threw him into such agitated indecision that she abandoned it and instead escaped herself on a "quick trip" to Spain during the Easter holidays with Rosa de Fitz-James and her young friend, Jean du Breuil de St. Germain. Teddy remained in Paris in the care of White and his sister Nannie, presumably making plans for his return to America during the summer. From Madrid on Easter weekend, Edith wrote Fullerton that Teddy had as yet made no plans to return to America: "I can't tell you how I dread to go back [to Paris]. I shall put it off as long as possible."[21]

The trip to Spain was the first of eight junkets Edith made in 1912, and her final stop en route to Paris was Nohant. She had last been there with James, and, in remembrance of spring 1907, she sent him a picture postcard of "dear old George" and volume three of Wladimir Karénine's biography of Sand. The desire to see George Sand's house again was perhaps never more powerful—or painful—than on this visit, her third in six years. As Edith scanned the façade of the old house, she must have felt the imminent loss of The Mount and the cold shadow of Teddy's illness that was splitting her life apart. How to live—and write—under such conditions?[22]

She made little progress on *The Reef* until the final days of the trip, when she dropped Rosa de Fitz-James at Biarritz and then turned eastward toward Provence. Once back in Paris, she saw Teddy off to New York, six days after their twenty-seventh wedding anniversary. He never again entered the foyer of 53 rue de Varenne; they never again lived as man and wife.

DURING THE WEEKS Edith had toured Spain and southwestern France, world attention focused on several unrelated but disturbing sets of events. England was in the grip of violent social upheaval. One million coal miners had walked off the job in a strike that caused severe coal shortages and threw the country into darkness and cold. Militant suffragettes planted bombs, set letter boxes afire, poured acid on golf greens, horsewhipped visiting politicians, and hammered down shop windows. "The impossible wears on us," James wrote from London on March 13. The atmosphere was "unspeakably dismal and depressing," he said, "to which the window-smashing women add a darker shade." Tensions between social classes and sexes, and between labor and management, erupted into violence as the old aristocratic and colonial order began to crumble.[23]

The loss of the *Titanic* on its maiden voyage seemed yet another sign that some kind of apocalyptic change was at hand. Many viewed the disaster as a warning from God that the excesses of rich industrialists and financiers would be punished. When the luxury liner sank in the early hours of April 15, Edith was asleep in her suite at the Madrid Hotel Ritz; the following morning, she departed for Zaragoza unaware of the tragedy. Although she knew people who died that night, the tragedy did not take on human form until July, when she visited Cliveden, the Waldorf Astor estate in England, and met the nineteen-year-old widow of John Jacob Astor IV. On the night of the accident, forty-eight-year-old Astor, perhaps the richest of the men who went down on the *Titanic*, reportedly put on his tuxedo, escorted his bride to a lifeboat, and then returned to the gentlemen's lounge, where he played cards until the ship sank at 2:20 A.M. He was said to have faced death with great calm.

The last hours of those fifteen hundred people, awaiting death in the bitter cold of the moonlit sea as the band played on, became the stuff of myth. Viewed in the light of August 1914, the *Titanic* seemed to have forecast the end of economic expansionism, of American optimism and opportunism that divided the superrich on board the floating Ritz from the lower and middle classes. Sometime later, it was revealed that the tragedy was occasioned by intense competition between the two steamship companies that controlled passenger service in the North Atlantic—White Star Lines, owners of the *Titanic*, and Cunard, whose liner *Carpathia* came to the aid of the doomed ship that night, saving the pregnant Mrs. Astor and some seven hundred others. Financed by J. P. Morgan, the *Titanic* was the last word in opulence, but it failed to meet even minimal safety standards. Thomas Hardy's poem on the occasion, "The Convergence of the Twain," suggests that while shipbuilders were "fashioning/This creature of cleavining wing," the "Immanent Will" of God had "prepared a sinister mate/For her—so gaily great—/A Shape of Ice, for the time far and dissociate." The convergence of cosmic forces and industrial capitalism had spelled tragedy.[24]

At Cliveden in July, there was talk of the dockworkers' strike, whose consequences were being debated in the House of Commons. Waldorf Astor had been elected to Parliament from Plymouth in 1910. Nine years later, his wife, Nancy Langhorne, born of a Virginia tobacco auctioneer, would become the first woman to be seated in the House of Commons. She won the seat her husband vacated when he became Viscount Astor and ascended to the House of Lords. In summer 1912, Nancy Astor was thirty-three years old and the mother of a new baby, her third son. Troubled by health problems for several years, she was undergoing rest cures that kept her isolated for days and left her "numb in body and mind"; after two failed surgeries, she would convert to Christian Science. Meeting her for the first time, James found her "full of possibilities and fine material—though but a reclaimed barbarian, with all her bounty, spontaneity and charm, too." (Commentators usually cut short James's remark, and thus reduce her to a "reclaimed barbarian.") Watching James and Nancy Astor together, Edith thought him "captivated" by her.[25]

Edith apparently enjoyed Nancy Astor. The two women had certain personality traits in common: quick wit and sharp tongues, energy and determination, compassion for those less fortunate, and a dark, sometimes brooding side rarely seen by others. A social activist and feminist, Mrs. Astor worked with the poor in London's East End and in Plymouth. She would be a tireless worker during the war, when some twenty-four thousand wounded soldiers passed through the Canadian Red Cross Hospital set up on the grounds at Cliveden. Edith would not, however, have had much sympathy for Nancy Astor's enthusiastic commitment to the mix of science and religion in Mary Baker Eddy's philosophy, or for her outspoken support of women's suffrage. When, more than a decade later, the editor of an American magazine asked Edith to write an essay on the question "Women: Have They Got What They Want?," she said she was too busy with literary work to write the essay but that she had always been "entirely out of sympathy with woman-suffrage." Now that American women had the right to vote, she hoped "sincerely" that they would "find they have *not* got what they want." In the context of Edith's other remarks on women in American society, this statement suggests that she thought the vote irrelevant to achieving equality for women. She apparently never exercised her right to vote after the woman suffrage amendment was ratified in 1920.[26]

IN MID-MAY 1912, after Teddy returned to the United States, Edith began a five-month series of travels that took her south to Rome and north to London. The first stop was Salso, where, in the company of

Anna Bahlmann and Catherine Gross, she submitted to her third cure in twelve months. The results were salutary. Within days, her mental attitude underwent a remarkable change: the weather was "perfect"; she was "blissfully steeped in ink and iodine" and making good progress on the novel. "Do come and join the dance," she wrote Berenson; "fiction in the morning and friction in the pomeriggio." He could not leave I Tatti and its stream of visitors, but Walter appeared (as arranged), and together they set out on their second Italian trip in seven months. They headed south on a journey cut short by illnesses and travel mishaps.[27]

By the end of her Salso stay, Edith had completed almost two-thirds of *The Reef*. She sent a copy of the manuscript to Fullerton, saying that she could "see the end," but could not "go on alone" without his help. Her first attempt at a love story, *The Reef* is the most autobiographical of her novels and the only work of fiction in which she depended so completely on the advice of another person. This was especially true in June and early July 1912, when she was constructing the crucial "recognition" scene between Anna Leath (the "Edith" figure) and her unfaithful lover, George Darrow ("Morton"). Anna and Darrow are descendants of Old New York, who in their youth had fallen in love, then drifted apart to go separate ways—Darrow into a diplomatic career, Anna to become the wife of Fraser Leath, a dilettante of the Egerton Winthrop type. When they meet again in their forties, Anna is the widowed mother of two children and living in France at her château, Givré (which means "frosted"); Darrow lives in London. They fall in love and plan a life together, but the road is blocked by Anna's ambivalence, which appears to derive from a deep-seated sense of inadequacy. Her upbringing, which mirrors Edith's own background, has stifled her spontaneity, and her sexuality has never been awakened. She lives behind a social mask, elusive and inaccessible.[28]

The book opens with Anna's telegram to Darrow as he is about to leave for France to meet her: "Unexpected obstacle. Please don't come till thirtieth." This is the second time she has put him off, and in his bewilderment at what he takes to be her rejection of him, he falls in with a young woman he meets on the boat train, Sophie Viner, who is on her way to Paris to become an actress. They spend a weekend together at the Hotel Terminus near the Gare du Nord (once a trysting place of Fred Jones and Mrs. West). Some four months later, when Anna again invites Darrow to Givré, he arrives to discover that Sophie is governess to Anna's nine-year-old daughter, Effie (a self-portrait of Edith at the same age) and also engaged to Anna's stepson, Owen. In a series of scenes staged almost as theater, all the interdependent relations come into the light—Sophie's love for Darrow and the secret of their days together in Paris; Owen's jealousy of Darrow and his suspicion that Sophie has had an affair with him; Anna's shattered happiness when she learns that Sophie and Darrow had once been lovers. There is not just one "recognition scene" but several, and they come enfilade, as doors opening onto a line of drawing rooms in which the mirrors of each salon provide a new perspective on the drama.

Wound tight, *The Reef* relentlessly searches for the truth of the relationships it portrays. Its central drama is contained within a double viewpoint. Seen from the perspective of Darrow, Anna is the woman who keeps him at arm's length, refuses to tell him what she feels for him or take him into her confidence; she toys with him, mocks him, and succeeds in humiliating him. Seeing Anna from the inside, the reader discovers a sensitive woman capable of great depths of feeling; proud, articulate, but afraid of her own desires. Edith shines a powerful searchlight on Fullerton's weaknesses, of course, but also on her own, and she does not turn her eyes away from what she sees. She confronts her proprietary and controlling nature, her desire to own her lover: "He's mine—he's mine! He's no one else's," Anna thinks as Darrow leaves Givré for the last time. Seated next to Fullerton at the theater one afternoon in May 1908, Edith had gazed at his profile and the curve of his hair across his forehead. Recalling the moment in her diary, she wrote, "Every drop of blood in my body whispers: 'Mine—mine—mine!'"[29]

Chapter 27 of *The Reef*, in which the truth of their relationship comes out, is the shortest in the book. Edith thought it "unconventional" because its subject is Sophie and Owen, not Anna and Darrow. She wanted Fullerton's advice on the narrative method of the scene. His letter on the subject no longer exists, but he was evidently worried about how much of the story Walter had read. Edith's answer was categorical: "No—Walter Berry has never read a line of The Reef, and does not even know its donnée. He takes not the slightest interest in my literature." How can one explain this flat denial of Walter Berry's longtime interest in her work? In *A Backward Glance*, she would credit him with having encouraged and patiently guided her writing; as recently as winter 1911, he had listened to her read aloud the draft of *Ethan*

Frome. Edith reassured Fullerton that she had not revealed their own little secret; there would be no recognition scene exposing the hidden attachments of their triangle. To neutralize his suspicions and assuage his evident jealousy, she blatantly flattered him: it was because he was "kind enough" to read her work and because he did it in a "way so intelligent, and so stimulating to the poor scribe, that she appeals to you for aid."[30]

Edith's responses to Fullerton's writing, however, were less than encouraging. In this same letter, she spared nothing in her comments on his Paris book, the one for which he had received a royalty advance of £100 (from Edith via Macmillan) almost a year ago: "Cher ami, If you would burn all your notes you'd do a better book! don't think me brutal; but your preparations are *unconsciously* prolonging themselves as a pretext for not doing the book." More advice of this sort followed several months later, when he sent her a portion of his book on international politics. She offered excellent advice on the manuscript, but the tone of utter frankness she adopted would have discouraged any but the most competent and self-assured of writers: "Mow down every old cliché, uproot all the dragging circumlocutions, compress, diversify, clarify, vivify." Her own writing sped along that summer at a pace matching that of the mighty Mercedes as it flew across Italy and France. Meanwhile, a discouraged Fullerton was writing in "the language of fatigue." Edith had known for many months that he would not finish the Paris book, and she had said as much to James, who also recognized the truth: "I groan for the verisimilitude of it when you tell me that Morton the book-maker *défaillit* [failed]. There it deplorably is—that he isn't,—won't be, probably *can't* be—a book-maker."[31]

EDITH SPENT THE last days of June 1912 at the Grand Hôtel de Vevey in Switzerland recovering from her Italian *giro.* She and Walter had intended to travel in the Abruzzi, the mountainous rural region of southeast Italy, but a combination of hot weather and a flare-up of Walter's enteritis forced them to abandon that plan and also its alternative, a trip to Sicily. They found themselves instead one night "hanging over dizzy precipices" in the Apennines in an effort to find the monastery of La Verna, a site in Tuscany overlooking steep chalk cliffs where in 1224, St. Francis reputedly received the stigmata. The road was barely a mule path, and as they inched forward in the darkness, Charles Cook guiding the motor with "wonderful coolness and skill," peasants appeared from the shadows and placed stones behind the wheels to prevent its slipping backward. At last, they arrived at the gates of La Verna and raised the sleeping monks, who served them a supper of olive oil soup, anchovies, and cheese (no diet for a man with enteritis). The next morning, Cook steered the motor while twenty men eased it down a three-quarter-mile descent on ropes, peasants taking their luggage down on a cart.

As he watched this slow process, Walter began to feel the pain of an inflamed tooth. Strapping the luggage atop the Mercedes, they sped to Florence, where a dentist concluded that it would take ten days for Walter's tooth to heal. They set out again, this time for Milan and the night train to Paris, where Walter's own dentist awaited him. En route, their motor was hit broadside by a "crazy coachman." The accident smashed the windshield and injured Catherine Gross, who was thrown into a roadside stream and nearly drowned. Quickly patching up the motor, they proceeded to Milan, Edith holding open her umbrella to keep the night wind blowing through the broken windshield off Gross's wet head and away from Walter's painful tooth. Walter made the train with three minutes to spare, after which Edith booked rooms at the Hotel Cavour for two days of rest. Notifying her servants of her return to Paris, she went on to Vevey, Switzerland, where she passed the time working on *The Reef* while 53 rue de Varenne was being cleaned.[32]

She did not want to return to Paris, but for the moment, there was no alternative. Gross needed time to heal from her injuries. "I feel chilly and grown old," Edith confided to Berenson. He was in Paris on business, and she invited him to lunch, where she unburdened herself of her marital problems and recounted the story of Fullerton's blackmail intrigue. He sympathized with her situation, as did Mary when she learned of it, professing shock and dismay at Fullerton's troubles. Although her work on the novel went well ("I'm just bobbing along on it like a drowned dog!"), she could not bear another minute of Paris. She wired James to announce the "Coming of Edith" in England, and he assured her of the "fondest accueil." Privately, he wanted nothing more than to work on his autobiography. By the eve of her arrival, he was verging on panic and dated a letter to Sturgis, "Reign of Terror ce vingt juillet 1912." Her proposed plan of travel and social engagements—in which he was included—filled him with dread, but he lacked the energy and ingenuity to counter it. The "whirr and wind" of her "great pinions," he said, were "already cold" on his "foredoomed brow": the Ryebird was to be caught "struggling in her talons" and carried off from the Lamb House barnyard.[33]

She arrived on July 21 and stayed in England two days short of three weeks. In that time, the "Bird o'-freedom" did indeed spread her wings, making not one but two visits to each point on her compass. After spending two nights with Howard Sturgis, Edith and James went to Cliveden, a stately home the size of a hotel. Liveried footmen in yellow breeches ushered them to rooms with views of the lawns and gardens, but with no running water or private bath. They returned to Qu'acre the following day, using it as a base for a trip to Ascot, where they visited James's old friend, Margaret Brooke, the ranee of Sarawak. Now a corpulent, bewigged, rouged, and wildly eccentric old woman, she had been some twenty years earlier Fullerton's passion. (Edith knew nothing of their affair.) The object of this trip was not Brooke but her guest, Vernon Lee, whom James had known since the mid-1880s. He found her "monstrous clever," but had avoided her since 1892, when she publicly criticized his theatrical adaptation of *The American* and caricatured him in her story *Vanitas*. "She's a tiger-cat," Henry had told his brother, William. On this occasion, however, Lee and James had "a good deal of talk."[34]

On the last weekend of July, Henry and Edith returned to Cliveden. While strolling through the gardens, he suffered an attack of angina. On the following day, Cook motored him to Lamb House, stopping en route for luncheon at Qu'acre, while Edith stayed on with the Astors, awaiting the return of her motor. After another stay in London, she drove to Rye to spend a last night with James. They were joined by Claude Phillips, curator of the Wallace Collection in London, who came for tea. On Saturday, August 10, Edith and Phillips attended the Beauty Queen of England pageant at the Victoria Pier Pavilion in Folkestone. A capacity crowd watched eighteen contestants compete for a first prize of a 26-guinea piano. (Edith joked to Fullerton that she and Phillips had tied for first prize.) It was a lark, but one amusing enough that she returned in future years.

By teatime on Sunday the eleventh, she was in Normandy, visiting Jacques-Emile Blanche and his wife at Offranville, and the following day fell sick with a nose-and-throat infection that delayed her return to Paris. Such was the price of her "whirligig" life, as James called it. She left James "reduced to pulp, consumed utterly." But he had to admit that her "admirable talk" with Claude Phillips had held him "spell-bound." "She never was more wound up and going, or more ready, it would appear, for new worlds to conquer." From her sickbed on Monday, she wrote Fullerton that the final six chapters of *The Reef* would "*positively*" go to Appleton within the week, and asked him to forewarn them.[35]

After a brief rest at number 53, where she entertained Minnie Jones, Edith set off to visit Paul and Minnie Bourget. They were on their annual cure, "sunk to their chins" in "drug-dreariness," she said, in a "sinister little mouldy villa" at Pougues-les-Eaux, near Bourges. It was all too dreary for Edith, who immersed herself in work, putting the finishing touches on *The Reef* before moving on to her next destination, the summer home in the Lyonnais of the French ambassador to the United States, Jules Jusserand and his wife. She then traveled for three weeks in the Massif du Cantal with a longtime friend, Marion Richards, sister of Elise Jusserand. They stopped overnight at the château of Prosper de Barante, a Paris friend of Edith's whose grandfather had been a convive of Mme de Staël and Mme de Récamier, and stayed up late reading aloud letters written by members of this group. By September 20, after a quick run through the Pyrenees, Edith was again in Paris, where she awaited the arrival of Teddy, who had spent his summer in America, having his teeth extracted.[36]

ON JUNE 21, the day of Edith and Walter's Spoleto to La Verna adventure, The Mount and its 126-acre domain legally passed into the hands of Albert R. Shattuck of Greenwich, Connecticut. According to the deed of sale, he paid one dollar and "other valuable considerations"—a sum that came to $180,000, for which he received the house and virtually all its contents, the outlying buildings, and farm implements. In the twenty years since rich industrialists first put up sprawling summer cottages around Lenox, the town had not fulfilled its dream of becoming a society capital on a par with Newport. Property values were in decline, and the Whartons were fortunate not to have taken a loss on The Mount. Taking into account the cost of the land, design and construction expenses for the house, gardens, and driveway, architects' fees, Ogden Codman's commissions, and real estate fees, Edith and Teddy made a profit of about $15,000. In Teddy's words, it was a "magnificent" sale, but the emotional losses out-weighed the profits for Edith. Two months later, she wrote Lapsley, who was in Rhode Island visiting his family: "Write me soon, dear Gaillard. But don't tell me anything about the Mount, for there's a great ache there still."[37]

Early in July, she had proposed to Teddy that they sublet the Paris apartment and take a house in New York for the winter. They could then search for a small country place nearby. She wanted to "settle down quietly" somewhere that satisfied him and where she could write steadily and avoid the "ever-recurring uncertainties of the present situation." Her letter occasioned a frantic cable from him ("entirely disapprove plan"), followed by a twenty-page letter of reproach for having worried him with "such an absurd suggestion." On the face of it, her suggestion was absurd. It was little more than a year since she sold her twin New York houses, and only a matter of days since the sale of The Mount had been finalized. The distress of her marriage had sent her searching frantically for people and places to ease her restlessness. James, in an apt phrase, called her a "female Ulysses." Despite the pain of losing The Mount, she told Sally that the "most earnest self-searching will *not* discover in me the least regret for having left America."[38]

Edith returned to Paris alone, and a few weeks later motored to Avignon, where she met the Berensons. They traveled together as far as Portofino, east of Genoa, when she suddenly collapsed from fatigue, unable to keep up with the twelve-hour travel days. She described herself to Mary as an "over-wound watch." A few days of rest and long walks on the high ridges above the coastal town restored her strength. She watched sunsets and star-risings, and worked on *The Custom of the Country* "at a Lazenby pace." She had returned to her long-neglected novel in late August; it was scheduled to begin its serial run in the January *Scribner's Magazine*, and she was not close to finishing it. After a stay at I Tatti, followed by a brief visit to La Spezia, she returned to Paris, where for the next five months, she devoted herself to writing.[39]

The Reef appeared on November 15, 1912, to unfavorable reviews and poor sales. The *Nation* found its story "paltry" and its theme "impossible of dramatic solution." The *New York Times Book Review* thought it a "conspicuous failure," except for the character Sophie Viner. The *New York Sun* called it "sordid," and wished that Mrs. Wharton would "look on brighter and nobler aspects of life." Among American critics, only M. P. Willcocks of the *Bookman* called it a fine book, "a revelation in spiritual tragedy of the subtlest" kind. In London, the *Saturday Review* decried the "abnormal circumstances" of its characters, saying that "Mrs. Wharton could do much better work than this, for she has style and understanding."[40]

Sending a copy of it to Berenson, Edith described her book as a "poor miserable lifeless lump." She asked that he put it in the guest room, "or lend it to somebody to read in the train and let it get lost"—"*please* don't read it!" This moment of self-denigration was the result of having put so much of herself into the novel, and of struggling to keep in motion the reversals and counterreversals of its oscillating plot. In closing, she said to B.B., "Remember it's not *me*, though I thought it was when I was writing it—and that *next time* I'm going to do something worthwhile!"[41]

A copy of *The Reef* also went to Henry James, who wrote her from his sickbed of pain. Although suffering from shingles, he had no doubt about the novel's quality—it was, simply, "quite the finest thing you have done." Whereas echoes of "the good George Eliot" often sounded in Edith's writing, *The Reef*, James proposed, was rather more like an "ancient" Greek text from which Eliot might have captured some "weaker reflection" in her own writing. Edith had created a drama rather than a narrative, he said, a Racinian tragedy of the proportions of his *Iphigénie en Aulide* and *Bérénice*. Charles du Bos, who had read the book in page proofs in October, assessed the novel in exactly the same terms. By its "small number of protagonists, the passionate poignancy enhanced by the rigorous restraint of expression, no novel came closer to the quality of a tragedy of Racine."[42]

Amid this flurry of compliments, James had only one question: Why was this story of non-French people "localised" in France, he asked? The real "drawback," he said, was not any fault of the novel but the problem of her life—of "not having the homeliness and the inevitability and the happy limitation and the affluent poverty, of a Country of your Own." His words reflected as much on his own state of expatriation as hers. In the midst of her current troubles, "big black balls of worry and weariness," as she expressed it to Berenson, praise of her work—even flattery from Henry James—could not convince her of her literary worth. "If only my work were better," she wrote John Hugh Smith, "it would be all I need! But my kind of half-talent isn't much use as an escape—at least more than temporarily." She was in a "stagnant back-water of indifference," she said, and asked him to come pull her "out into mid-current." The language of her request anticipated James's rhetoric: "Clearly you have only to pull," he wrote, referring to her literary abilities, "and everything will come."[43]

During these weeks, disturbing reports of Teddy's activities in London and Monte Carlo reached Edith in Paris. The first ill omens came from her butler, Alfred White, who was traveling with him. She asked her brother Harry, in London on business, to see Teddy and report on his condition. The news was not good. From New York, Dr. Kinnicutt wrote to warn her against trying to live with him again. James began to receive wildly megalomaniacal letters from Teddy. He threatened to descend on Lamb House at any moment, but then did not appear. When he arrived in Paris in early December, Teddy gave his wife a "wide berth," but contacted several of her friends, among them Matilda and Walter Gay. They described their encounter with him to Henry James, who passed the news to Minnie Jones. Teddy had bragged of his powerful American motor (purchased with money from the sale of The Mount), which he claimed he drove at one hundred miles an hour. He detailed his exploits with variety-theater ladies and boasted of the money he spent on them. On arriving at La Bréau, the Gays' château south of Paris, he promptly pulled up his trousers to reveal his "gold garters," wide circles of gold that held up his stockings.

More disturbing was his appearance. The Gays reported that his faced showed "strong marks of 'la débauche,' vinous and other," James reported, barely able to control his syntax, "and of that terribly and distressfully insane character of his eyes," caused by his "great physical pain." Unaware that his facial expression revealed either debauchery or physical pain, Teddy instead worried that his recent teeth extractions, a process he described in detail to the Gays, had "unfavourably affected" the form of his face.[44]

Although Walter Berry was away from Paris in December, making a last—and finally successful—trip to America to gain his inheritance, Edith was surrounded by supportive friends. Mary Berenson, on her way to London to spend Christmas with her family, stayed several days at the rue de Varenne. She and Edith had grown close to one another on the Avignon trip and were eager to see each other again. "That beautiful smile of hers," Edith wrote Berenson on December 23, "really gave me two days of Florentine weather." The next day, Gaillard Lapsley and Percy Lubbock arrived to spend the holidays. In the last hours of the year, she reread *Gil-Blas de Santillane*, Alain-René Lesage's eighteenth-century picaresque novel, which Fullerton had translated into English in 1911. Edith had at last succeeded in putting her relationship with Morton on the footing of friendship and professional collaboration. But he still had the power to disconcert her; any gesture from him that hinted of *l'amour* rather than *l'amitié* weakened her resolve to maintain a friendship rather than a love affair. "Last night I cleared up all my old papers and letters, against the coming break-up," she wrote him, "and found at last, thank heaven, the 50 missing pages of 'The Custom of the Country.'—Je vais m'y remettre de suite. —I found many other things too! All my life of the last four years." The "coming break-up" was her divorce from Teddy.[45]

BEGINNING AGAIN

The first days of 1913 found Edith reclined on her bed, dictating answers to Christmas cards and sending belated New Year's greetings. The winter was unusually mild, and in mid-month she went to Versailles to get away from the Paris hubbub and take country walks along roads "lined with broom in full bloom." The tranquillity she sought eluded her, however, because the new president of the Republic, Raymond Poincaré, was to be installed at the Palace of Versailles on January 17. Thronged with crowds, the town had a festive air, and by the luck of her friendship with Bourget, Edith witnessed the great event. A member of the Académie Française with an official invitation, he "smuggled" Edith into the Salle de Congrès at just the moment when the proclamation of the new president echoed through the hall—"really an *émotionnant* moment, for feeling ran high and everybody had the sense that history was being made," she wrote Mary Berenson. Certainly, this was a political turning point for France. Unrest among the Balkan states had heightened war fears, and Germany's industrial and technological advances worried her neighboring nations. In electing Poincaré, the populace had voted for a militarized France, thus bringing war—which they ostensibly hoped to avoid—one step closer.[46]

Edith returned from Versailles intending to go to England for a few days to see James. Instead, she greeted her cousin Herman Edgar, who had come from New York to help her with financial matters. Herman was in Paris when she learned that her brother Harry was angry with her—a "perfectly horrible and tragic" estrangement, she wrote Gaillard Lapsley. Now almost sixty-three years old, Harry had been since her childhood a loyal friend. The split between brother and sister came about (as it had with Fred Jones) over a woman. She was Anna Julia Caroline Marie Vanherle Tekla, a countess (so she claimed), who had been living for some time with Harry as his wife; they would be legally married in 1920, two years before his death. Herman Edgar admitted that he had seen signs of Harry's "smouldering 'rancune,'" but had been helpless to do anything about it.

Harry's bad feelings seem to have arisen about the time of Fred's stroke in 1911 and may have surfaced in the discussions of family wills and inheritances. When Fred remarried after Minnie divorced him in 1896, he made his second wife beneficiary of his estate. To assure that Beatrix would not be disinherited, Harry then legally adopted her, and named her and Edith as sole beneficiaries of his own estate. When Countess Tekla came into his life, she set out to alter this arrangement by alienating Harry from his sister and niece so that she herself could inherit his wealth. As Edith told the story to Gaillard Lapsley, the countess took a "violent dislike" to Edith because Edith had not asked to make her acquaintance. "How could I," she asked, "when [Harry] never even spoke to me of her?" However the break came about, and whatever its real causes, the blow could not have fallen at a worse moment for Edith, especially since Harry sided with Teddy in the divorce, saying that Edith had mistreated her husband.[47]

News was reaching Edith that Teddy's recent exploits in New York and Boston were being talked about. She wanted to avoid publicity, but she agreed with Mary Berenson—who had heard the stories in London—that "it's as well they should be known." Friends and family urged her to act quickly, and Herman was on hand to set the stage for her divorce, which was pleaded in a Paris court to avoid publicity in New York. "I hope something may soon be decently, silently and soberly arranged," she wrote Mary in early February. Among those offering information and advice was Daisy Chanler's husband, Winthrop, a longtime friend of Teddy's. "I think the Bostonians are persuaded that his mind has gone," he wrote her, "that he is going as his father did, and that nothing he says is worth anything." He described the previous four years of her life in the very terms she herself used—as *nerve waste* and a health waste." The present situation of waiting for Teddy to appear in Paris so that he could be served with papers for a divorce action made her desperate.[48]

While Herman Edgar was in Monte Carlo collecting evidence for the adultery charges that would form the grounds for Edith's divorce, she mounted a secret campaign among American friends of Henry James to present him with a special gift on April 15, his seventieth birthday. A similar effort, organized by writer Edmund Gosse and playwright James Barrie, was already under way in London. In early March, she sent a circular letter to some forty people, asking for monetary contributions toward a gift of $5,000 that James could use however he pleased. Co-signed by William Dean Howells, the letter mentioned James's three years of ill health and the "consequent postponement of all his work," and specified that the gift would provide a "practical form" of "sympathy and admiration" for him. Within ten days, Edith had collected $1,000 for the "Henry fund," half of which was her own donation to which was added $100 from Isabella Stewart Gardner, and a few other contributions.[49]

Teddy arrived in Paris before Easter and was immediately served with a court citation; twenty-four hours later, Edith's divorce was settled. She was "pinching" herself at the prospect that the nightmare would soon be over. Already hounded by reporters who had gotten wind of Teddy's exploits, she planned to be far away on the day the decree was "pronounced." Friends in England wanted her to come in that direction (Henry was ill again, and Howard Sturgis was undergoing surgery), but she longed to see spring in Italy and even dreamed of a trip to Egypt. In the end, she and Walter went to Sicily.

On March 28, they set out for La Spezia and I Tatti as first stops on their way south. The previous day, Henry James had received word that Edith was raising money on his behalf. He cabled his nephew William in Cambridge, Massachusetts, declaring his "horror" of the idea. Edith had not yet reached the Italian border when she received a cable from Sturgis Bigelow in Boston relaying James's protest. "You may imagine my feelings, and those of the other friends," she wrote Sally some weeks later.[50]

Howells had "betrayed" their confidence to Mrs. William James, she said; only later did she learn that the culprit was George Abbot James (no relation of Henry's), one of those who had received her circular letter. "A more reckless and indiscreet undertaking, with no ghost of a preliminary leave asked, no hint of a sounding taken, I cannot possibly conceive—and am still rubbing my eyes for incredulity," James wrote to William. "My trip has been completely poisoned by Henry's letter," Edith told Gaillard Lapsley, who then intervened with James on her behalf. "There was nothing on earth I valued as much as his affection. I can never get over this."[51]

She immediately returned the money that had so far been collected by the American committee, but the plans of the English group went forward. In London, on his birthday, he was presented with a "golden bowl" and the John Singer Sargent portrait he had sat for during the winter, a painting that now hangs in the National Portrait Gallery in London. In gratitude for the gifts, he sent a printed letter to each subscriber acknowledging his "boundless pleasure," appending to it the list of contributors. He added two names from the defunct American committee—Walter Berry and Edith Wharton.

This gesture did not ease Edith's pain. She felt that James had wronged his American friends, and—having refused their gift—he should have refused as well the English tribute: "He put himself doubly in the wrong," she wrote Fullerton, adding that James's Boston friends—Barrett Wendell, Sturgis Bigelow, and others—were "as indignant and disgusted as I am." Edith could not have withstood an open break with James, given her emotional fragility in these weeks. She directed her anger instead at the James family, especially young Henry James, who had written her to say that his family had considered it their "duty" to warn James because she had tried twice before to "relieve" their uncle of financial worries and had "been stopped." He referred, presumably, to two occasions in 1910 and 1911 when Edith had directly offered James financial aid, which he refused.[52]

James never learned of her one successful effort to provide him monetary assistance, however. She used the plan they had conceived four years earlier to aid Fullerton; she proposed to Scribners that they offer James an advance against royalties for his novel-in-progress, *The Ivory Tower.* In January 1913, a contract was drawn up in which Edith agreed to pay Scribners $8,000, a sum dispensed to James in two installments. Charles Scribner, who went along with the scheme only to please Edith, felt squeamish about the whole enterprise. "I feel rather mean and caddish," he wrote her, "and must continue so to the end of my days. Please never give me away." She kept the secret, but Henry James never completed the book.[53]

Teddy was proclaiming his new freedom to all who would listen, saying that it was "damned bad form of Puss to divorce him," but that he was "damned well rid of her." He was also writing letters to friends accusing Edith of "improper relations with Walter Berry and several others," tales that were repeated in *Town Topics* and European newspapers. Ogden Codman dismissed the accusations, saying that he never thought Edith had much "temperament" (meaning romantic passion) and that Walter Berry was so "anaemic" that he did not think she would have found him "much use in a naughty way." While Teddy and his most recent girlfriend were seen dining in expensive Paris restaurants with Harry Jones and the countess Tekla, Edith was receiving letters from friends who expressed their sympathy for her situation and support for her decision to divorce her husband. Berkeley Updike expressed his wish to be with her now, so that they "could talk and be silent and understand, as old friends can." Lapsley forwarded a letter from Professor Barrett Wendell, who, having seen Teddy in India two years earlier, regretted that Teddy had not been admitted to "formal guardianship," an opinion also expressed by Robert Grant, Berkeley Updike, and others. Wendell could not "imagine more admirable and simple devotion" than Edith had shown. It was a "great comfort," she wrote Lapsley, that Wendell saw the situation so clearly, "for I do sometimes feel a great soreness and indignation at the way in which the Whartons have treated me."[54]

These expressions of compassion did not dispel the anger she felt toward Teddy's family. Billy Wharton had slandered her by portraying Teddy as a "homeless martyr," she wrote Minnie, a victim of his wife's "frivolous tastes for an effete society"; the impression he created was, to Edith's mind, a "deliberate parti pris to relieve his family of any responsibility." Her own friends, she said, knew from personal experience how impossible Teddy had become. "Tant pis pour les autres [Too bad for the others]," she concluded. Back in New York, her cousins Herman Edgar and Tom Newbold were trying to settle her affairs. Tom was particularly pleased that there had been no newspaper notoriety. She should now think only of her future, he said: "Your life and work are far too important to be interfered with by these horrid annoyances." He urged her to choose the name she wanted to be known by. She took "Edith Newbold Wharton" as her legal name and "Mrs. Wharton" as her form of address. To gain the legal right to keep the Wharton name, she brought a legal case, arguing that it was her professional name, her nom de plume.[55]

When her divorce was granted by the Tribunal de Grande Instance in Paris on April 16, she was in Palermo under an "Ionian" sun. By law, French court records were unavailable to the public, so reporters had no means of access to the supporting documents in the case. They sought out Fullerton, who claimed to know nothing about Mrs. Wharton's divorce. In a letter to him, Edith explained that the decree was obtained on grounds of Teddy's adultery, dating back to 1908 and documented in Boston, London, and France. He should feel free to give friends this explanation: "It's a tiresome moment to traverse," she wrote, "but no more."[56]

Motoring south on "great adventurous flights over unknown roads," Edith watched her worries fade in "sun and air and sweetness." She was drinking up "all the wonders of the world" from Rome to Naples and Sicily, where she had not been since 1888. While she and Walter crisscrossed Sicily, the motor fairly leaping from one mountain view to the next, she dreamed of a summer cruise around the island, with ascents to Mount Etna and Mount Eryx—a dream that would not become reality for another thirteen years. From Palermo, they motored to Agrigento, site of Greek and Etruscan ruins, then to Taormina, perched high above the sea, a spot Edith considered to be among the most beautiful in the world. After a boat crossing to Rome, they continued by motor to Naples, Amalfi, Ravello, Paestum—all places new to her. Friends in America and Europe received breathless, almost delirious letters from her. "It has been one long radiance from shore to shore," she wrote Berenson. That afternoon, April 28, she and Walter had stretched out among the palmetto bushes on the crest of the Soluntum above Rome. Five days later, scurrying up the west coast of Italy because Walter's stomach problems had recurred, she had time to cast only a "fugitive glance" at Cunae. But she was returning with her "mental and visual trunks *so* full that the left-outs are not bothering me." After a few days at I Tatti, Walter departed alone; Edith returned to Paris with Geoffrey Scott, the thirty-year-old Englishman who was an architect of I Tatti and the man Mary Berenson loved. Their last stop was the Cathedral of Sens in Burgundy, which they viewed during a "tremendous black thunderstorm, with the lightning illuminating the smoldering reds and blues." Back in "Paris mud," literal and metaphoric, Edith was again in a "submerged" state of daily life— "notes, telephones, compatriots, clothes, and all sorts of futilities."[57]

EDITH RETURNED TO Paris and into the public eye just in time to witness the event that many believe gave birth to modern art. Stravinsky's *Le Sacre du printemps* played for four performances at the recently opened and starkly modern Théâtre des Champs Elysées. She attended, but perhaps not opening night on May 29, when the *beau monde*, dressed in tails and tiaras, hissed and jeered Nijinsky's choreography, the dancers moving awkwardly to the unconventional rhythms of

Stravinsky's score, their feet turned inward. The brutal primitivism of the sacrifice itself was pronounced obscene, more shocking even than Nijinsky's interpretation of *L'Après-midi d'un faune* in spring 1912 (which Edith missed because of her Salso trip).

A Russian enthusiast if not a committed avant-gardiste, she proclaimed *Le Sacre du printemps* "extraordinary (in the good sense)," which says nothing of what she really thought of it, but she was given to one-word pronouncements: Diaghilev's production of Mussorgsky's *Khovantchina*, she told Berenson, was "magnificent." She was seeing a good deal of Jean Cocteau, whom she had first met at Jacques-Emile Blanche's home in 1910. He had a studio a few doors away from her apartment, in the former Hôtel Biron, which had been converted into artists' studios. (Isadora Duncan was there, too.) Everyone was talking about the *Sacre du printemps*, especially "adorable" Cocteau, as she referred to him, who claimed to have seen Diaghilev in the Bois de Boulogne after the opening-night performance reciting Pushkin, tears streaming down his face.[58]

Berenson would soon arrive in Paris, and he wanted to see everything that was new. Edith bought him a ticket for Maurice Ravel's ballet *Daphnis and Chloë*, which was opening at the opera and would be remembered as his great masterpiece. She did not accompany him to the performance, however, saying that she knew nothing about the ballet. Not to have heard Ravel's haunting impressionist music after listening to the clamorous Stravinsky seems an imponderable contradiction. Ravel was, of course, present at opening night of *Le Sacre du printemps*. A quiet, even shy man who did not draw attention to himself, he was so angered by the hissing of the *haut monde* seated in the boxes that he reportedly became "truculent as a fighting cock."[59]

According to received opinion, Edith Wharton cared little for the modern in any of its artistic forms, but we know all too little about how she formed her judgments of modern art and music; in many cases, we do not know what those judgments were. In the years leading up to the Diaghilev takeover of Paris opera, ballet, and symphony, she had grown bored with the predictable menu of the season. Never a devotee of symphony concerts, she attended the opera occasionally rather than habitually; she disliked traditional ballet but had developed a passion for Isadora Duncan, whose Nietzschean and Dionysian fantasies excited her. She appreciated certain kinds of modern painting. Walter Berry collected modern art and owned a few pieces that she cared for, but, in general, her preferences concurred with Berenson's

Italian Renaissance tastes, and she had little to say about Picasso, Matisse, and their contemporaries.

In literature, she had a strongly antiexperimental bias, especially against stream-of-consciousness narrative. (She made an exception for Proust.) She deplored artistic self-consciousness and the "cult of the self" in the manner of Joyce and Lawrence. She had wider tastes in poetry than in narrative fiction—from Homer, the Nordic *Eddas*, the metaphysicals, to Whitman, Matthew Arnold, and Cocteau. She preferred classical theater to domestic drama of the Paul Bourget type, and after the war, she said flatly that she hated the theater. She knew the works of D'Annunzio and Hauptmann, had sampled Strindberg and Bataille, but said nothing of Wedekind and Brieux. She saw Minnie Maddern Fiske in New York as Nora in Ibsen's *Doll's House,* and later saw *Ghosts,* but she had nothing to say about these or other of his tragedies, although Ibsen was the primary influence on Sudermann, whose work she much admired and whose *Es Lebe das Leben* she had translated. Among American playwrights, she thought only Eugene O'Neill had stature. Some of her artistic likes and dislikes—her preference for the Victorians, for example—seemed to derive from her upbringing and early reading, while other choices, such as Anna de Noailles's poetry, were clearly her own. Gaillard Lapsley claimed that she had no interest in aesthetic theories, an opinion that may be open to question, given her knowledge of John Ruskin, Walter Pater, and Matthew Arnold. She was far more interested in the aesthetics of the visual (architecture and landscape) than in literary theory. Once her opinions on art movements and individual works were formed, she did not seem to care whether others agreed with them. Describing Edith's flow of "talk" as "*scherzo . . .* verging on *pizzicato,*" Charles du Bos remarked that she "too swiftly shelved" topics of conversation rather than immersing herself in discussions of cultural events and trends. She read journals, reviews, and newspapers, and although she cast a wary eye on "fads," she did not reject the modern just because it was new.[60]

Edith passed six weeks in the rue de Varenne in summer 1913, during which time she tried to finish *The Custom of the Country.* By the end of June, she had revised galleys on the first ten chapters, but had not yet finished writing the final portion of the book. In these weeks, she was also searching the Paris area for a country house, set in a "little green place," to take on a long lease. When the search proved fruitless, she decided to look in England, establishing herself at the Cavendish Hotel in Jermyn Street (a "squalid little" place). James came up to town to meet her, their first face-to-face encounter since the birthday-gift incident.

Their mutual impressions at this moment reveal a widening distance in their personal energies and interests. Five weeks after her visit, James pictured himself to Sturgis as David to Edith's Goliath. She had been "our colossal Edith," and he had "wrestled with" her "social presence." She was now "lay[ing] waste to North Germany and the surrounding parts—her *tenth* big rush about, of the last eight or ten months, as one figures it up," he wrote. "She now moves, for me, on another and sublimer plane altogether, and I somehow feel her look down on mine, where I sit doubled up, with *inevitable* alienation." Before leaving England, she had made a purchase offer on Coopersale, a house near Mary Hunter's Hill Hall in the Epping Forest. The sale was "hanging fire," and James quaked at the "magnitude" of her adventures and the risks involved in such responsibility. The property needed extensive work, which must be done "without Teddy's former practical aid," James remarked, aid that had been "very great in their constructive days."[61]

Edith returned to Paris to put the finishing touches on *Custom* before meeting Berenson in Luxembourg for their trip to northern Germany. Undine Spragg, the central figure of her novel, had for some time been "making the press ring" in her monthly appearances in *Scribner's Magazine*, but with the final episodes soon to appear on newsstands, Edith had two chapters yet to write. She had written *The Reef* in a record six months, the book composed almost entirely while she was on her road travels. *The Custom of the Country*, in contrast, had spread over five years, its composition interrupted by a love affair, extensive travel, changes of residence, illnesses, and a disintegrating marriage. Between February 1912 and August 1913, she had composed about half of *The Custom of the Country* (some two hundred pages) and all of *The Reef*. No wonder, then, that she was fatigued almost to illness as she faced its final chapters.[62]

In some sense, her difficulties with *The Custom of the Country* had always turned on the question of energy. A story of ambition and moral corruption, it portrays a new breed of American—reckless, selfish, adventurist real estate speculators and stock market deal-makers—whose life goal is acquiring wealth. They had crashed the gates of the Old New York citadel, marrying their daughters to the scions of the patriarchy. In their conservatism, disengagement from social issues, and customary lethargy, the old aristocrats had created the grounds for their own destruction. A "satire on certain demoralizing tendencies in our modern society" (as the *New York Times Book Review* put it), the novel's irony cut several ways at once. Its success depended on fast-paced action fueled by the devouring energy and restless desire of its protagonists. To create this atmosphere, Edith had to summon her deepest energies. The conditions of her life in the past five years had, on many occasions, prevented her from doing this.[63]

Undine Spragg, whose first name means "water sprite," is the most self-centered and outrageous of Edith Wharton's heroines—and a favorite of Edith's, who listed *The Custom of the Country* among the top five of her best-liked books. The British journal *Nation*, however, saw Undine, daughter of a "new rich" entrepreneur of the American Midwest, as a "mere monster of vulgarity." Desiring social status, beautiful clothes, luxurious surroundings, and the distractions of wealthy society, Undine is on a quest that takes her from Apex, Illinois, to New York City to Paris and back again. Trading on her youth and vitality, she accumulates husbands and houses, beginning with Ralph Marvell, scion of an old New York family, by whom she has a son. She next conquers the Faubourg St. Germain, marrying Raymond de Chelles, a French count, but returns to Apex at the novel's close as wife of Elmer Moffatt, a hometown boy turned successful real estate speculator, the man to whom she had been married before her round-robin career began.[64]

Having survived three marriages and a rough-and-tumble voyage in the waters of international society, she has not yet satisfied her desires at the novel's close, but she has outdistanced her ability to name her longings. "She had everything she wanted, but she still felt, at times, that there were other things she might want if she knew about them." A version of Theodore Dreiser's Sister Carrie, Undine is restless, stylish, and doomed. Bound by no rites and customs of tradition, she has been an "easy prey to the powers of folly," to vulgarity, just as Ralph Marvell had feared. During the first decade of the new century, Edith Wharton had strained against the limitations of those rites and customs, inherited from her Anglo-Dutch ancestors. By 1913, horrified at what America had become, she had decided to keep what was best in its traditions and dispense with the rest.

The Custom of the Country appeared in a first edition of thirty thousand, half of this number having sold before the book appeared on October 18, 1913. Scribners paid $6,000 for serial rights and a royalty advance of $7,500. Although Edith described it as having a "languid debut," the novel was widely reviewed and (despite the *Nation*) received high praise in Great Britain. The *Athenaeum* called it a courageous and sympathetic study, "no mere entertaining story," while the *Saturday Review* thought it should be read as a parable of modern life. Among general praise from American reviewers (the *Bookman* praised its unity, penetration, and incision), the *Boston Evening Transcript* thought the book "decidedly beneath" Edith Wharton, that she wrote to startle and slander rather than describe accurately, "to hyperbolize rather than convince." The American Library Association *Booklist* commented, "It is devoutly hoped that the title is a libel." Henry James, in an article on fiction for the *Times Literary Supplement*, commented that only by its "satiric light" could the story's elements "be focused together." He said little to Edith directly about the novel, except to note that her choice of American names, especially Elmer Moffatt, was "inspired."[65]

Although rewriting and proofreading remained to be done, Edith had closed the book on *The Custom of the Country* in the first days of August. Due to meet Berenson for a motor trip in northern Germany, she wrote asking that they spend some time in a "green woody *walky* place" before attacking the "big towns," where he wanted to visit museums. She needed to "recover" her nerves. Knowing his impatience, she reminded him that everything his "all-beneficent Mary" did for him she had to do for herself, from paying bills to firing a "heartless chef" who had abused one of her kitchen boys. While waiting for her to arrive, Berenson began to fear that she was trying to slip out of her agreement to travel with him or merely playing for time, in case Walter—who was away on a cure—grew bored and called her to his side. "She would chuck me to join him," he wrote Mary. Jealous of Walter and irritated at her delays, he overlooked important information that Edith was giving him about her travel priorities and the limits of her strength.[66]

She arrived in Luxembourg on August 7, accompanied by Catherine Gross and they headed northeast into Germany toward Copenhagen, as they had originally planned. Before the first day was out, Edith collapsed from exhaustion. She offered to send Berenson on in her motor in Charles Cook's care, but he refused, "partly, I suspect, because it bores him to travel alone," she wrote Fullerton, who was in America on a lecture tour. Berenson summoned his diminishing reserve of patience and stayed by her. Convinced that her troubles were mental rather than physical, he quietly procured the addresses of the best "alienists" (psychotherapists) in Cologne. After a few days' rest, she was ready to travel, and they turned east to Dresden and Berlin, stopping at "green places" along the way.[67]

Letters from the traveling twosome filled the I Tatti letter box. Edith's long epistle to Mary of August 14 takes the view of an indulgent but observant governess toward a headstrong and self-important adolescent. Berenson had insisted on taking over map-reading duties, and by the end of the preceding day, he had directed the motor west into a "particularly showy sunset," all the time claiming they were heading due east. They passed the night at Fulva, only a few miles from Frankfurt, where they had set out from early that same morning. Edith wrote Mary:

> In addition to this negative progress, he has learned several useful things that appear to have been omitted from his earlier education, such as going through galleries with a quick firm step instead of gaping and dawdling; letting Nicette [Edith's dog] sit on his lap when she feels like it; getting out of the motor to ask the way of an intelligent-looking person on the corner, instead of calling out to the village idiot or a deaf octogenarian from one's seat; and abstaining from shallow generalizations such as: "You'll find it's always safe in Germany to follow the telegraph poles," or: "On mountain roads there are never any cross-roads one need bother about," with geological remarks about his companion's "not understanding the conformation of the country."[68]

The comic flair with which Edith sketches this portrait suggests that she knew very well how it would be received by Mary, who had her own stories to tell of motor adventures with Bernard. And he had his own stories to tell about Edith.

After Dresden, whose beauty outweighed the bad food, incompetent service, and "cheeky" people, they traveled to Berlin, a "model modern Town," where they settled in for ten days. Berenson guided Edith around the galleries, but she grew restless at his commentaries on painting, finding them "much too purely technical." He reminded her, she wrote John Hugh Smith, of a hero in a story she had conceived but never written—a man who committed suicide because his "continuous chemical research" had led him to "see people and things only as aggregated atoms." Berenson also was finding museum-going difficult, with Edith casting only cursory glances at paintings, showing impatience with his lengthy explanations. "Art is a sealed book to her," he wrote Mary; she "sees only the subject, and in the subject only what appeals to her literary sense." On September 2, they parted amicably but with some relief. (They never traveled together again.) Berenson went to France and Edith motored to Baden-Baden, where Gross visited her family. Edith had last visited Baden-Baden in 1887, and now found it very "second Empire" and rather amusing. But she was at a "low ebb," she wrote John Hugh, with "no heart for anything," and unable even to read: "One goes through some things—at least I have—that turn everything bitter." She encouraged him to "have all the good days you can."[69]

If her recent experiences had turned everything "bitter," they had also enlarged her understanding of life. "I'm inclined to think that people who haven't lived much emotionally take their physical woes a good deal harder," she wrote Sally Norton, "because comfort has replaced so many other things to them." She was thinking of Charles du Bos and Howard Sturgis, both of whom had had recent surgeries and were "nervous and worried" about themselves. Henry James, who earlier in the year had seemed so beset by a "thousand little incidental nervousnesses" that kept him "from easy communion with the people he likes and wants to see," was now better than she had seen him in five years. But he kept a close watch on himself, avoiding both physical and emotional stress. She seemed to sense, perhaps for the first time, that she had surrounded herself with people who had not lived broadly and deeply. The men of the inner circle in England and *la bande* in Paris lived, for the most part, behind the protective high walls of self-involvement, risking neither passion nor commitment.

Apart from Henry James, none of these men had the breadth of character and generosity that defined Edith Wharton. Seeing the emotional limitations of her men friends, she may also have perceived that by encircling herself with those who dared not plumb the depths of life, she had set limits on her own experience. Moreover, she had reached the stage in life when her world would inevitably narrow and bind her more closely to those few she really loved. "I live, really, with and *on* very few people," she confessed to William Crary Brownell that autumn. It was the "very breath of my life," she told him, "to communicate with the few people who make me feel my shortcomings." She was speaking of her intellectual limitations, but her remark radiates in a wide arc.[70]

By September 21, just ten days after her return from Germany, she was once again lunching at Lamb House, this time with Bessy Lodge, whom she had brought with her for the second round of negotiations

on Coopersale, the house she hoped to buy. "Edith is really more wonderful than ever," James wrote Minnie. She was at work on a new novel, "Literature," and had, in his words, "lost her harassed look." Three
weeks later, she was back in England for her third visit in as many
months, trying again to arrange the house purchase. This time, she
spent ten days at the Ritz Hotel in London and made trips to Qu'acre
and Rye. James formed another vision of her. "Edith's image has in a
manner become terrific and troublesome to me," he wrote Minnie, "a
figure of entirely unmitigated *agitation*; out of which considered 'literary art' is by way of coming—all in so confounding and upsetting a
fashion. How I wouldn't *be* her—for all her possessions!" Edith's image
swung like a giant clock pendulum before James's eyes. At one extreme, she was awesome, "colossal," "wonderful," and wholly remarkable; at the other, she was a source of fear and intimidation and an
object of irritation and pity. Always larger than life, she was never in
his view merely human.[71]

Two American friends of long acquaintance with Edith saw her in
Paris during this period and gave disturbing reports. Moncure Robinson, a Bostonian who was especially kind to her during the months before the divorce, described her as "old and sad and forlorn—and
lonely." A friend from Lenox, Clem March, said she so impressed him
with her discontent that she made him feel discontented with his own
environment. ("Just as she used to make me feel," Codman remarked
when he heard the story.) These two friends were trying to effect a *rap-
prochement* between Edith and Codman, who now lived at number 60
rue de Varenne, next door to the George Vanderbilt apartment. The
original cause of their estrangement (a disputed bill) had long been settled, but Codman had been angered anew in autumn 1904, when
Edith and Teddy did not respond to the announcement of his forthcoming marriage to Leila Griswold Webb, widow of a wealthy New
York physician and a longtime friend of Teddy Wharton's family. Leila
died suddenly in January 1910 of complications following a hysterecto-
my, and in his grief, Codman was further embittered with Edith because she did not send a note of condolence. Edith had no "heart," he
said. (This comment echoes Edith's parents, who told her that she had
"less heart" than her brothers.)[72]

Part of Edith's worry in autumn 1913 may have been about Walter.
Gossips had it that Mrs. Robert Goelet was divorcing her drunken and
stingy husband to marry Walter Berry, who had made four trips to
America in the past year to see her. (Another rumor had it that Elsie

Goelet would marry Henry Clews, a wealthy New Yorker. In the end, she remained with her husband.) Edith's anxiety about Walter's roving eye became apparent to her New York acquaintances later in the year when she returned to America for her niece Beatrix's wedding.

Beatrix Jones, now forty-one years old, was to marry Max Farrand, a professor of American political economy, on December 17. They met when she was commissioned to design gardens for the residential colleges at Yale University. Invited to dinner at the president's home one spring evening, she was seated next to Max Farrand, a last-minute addition to the party owing to another guest's unexpected absence. He and Beatrix fell into conversation, and love. Their friends were taken completely by surprise, everyone having assumed that Max was a confirmed bachelor and that Beatrix's professional commitments precluded marriage and motherhood. A tall woman with striking good looks that combined her mother's dark coloring and her father's high forehead, Beatrix could be chillingly formal in the Old New York way. She also had a dry wit and an unexpected flirtatious and captivating side. She loved the outdoors, was expert at hunting and fishing (Max enjoyed salmon fishing), and preferred the country to the city.[73]

Beatrix had lived her entire life with her mother. They divided their time between the Reef Point estate in Bar Harbor that Minnie and Frederic had built in 1880 and 21 East Eleventh Street, where Beatrix opened her first office as a landscape architect in 1895, converting the attic into a large workroom. She was devoted to her mother, in comparison to whose youthful gaiety and slim, petite figure she felt old and "elephantine." The only cloud on her horizon was how Minnie would adjust to the changed circumstances. She asked Henry James, "What will become of Mummy?" Sensing Beatrix's worry about her mother's future, James wrote Minnie to say that he knew full well that she was "incapable" of setting the condition that her daughter "should not be a married lady." In this way, he underscored his belief in Trix's right to an independent life. He believed, correctly, that Minnie saw Trix's marriage as a gain rather than a loss, an "*extension* of sympathy and confidence." But mother and daughter had been bound together for so many years that any change that might distance them from one another was painful.[74]

At a prenuptial dinner given by Minnie on Sunday, December 7, Codman sat next to Beatrix, whom he had known for many years both as his professional colleague and friend. She confided to him that members of the Jones family were so completely divided against each other that she considered Edith her only close relative, and she was very pleased her aunt was coming for the wedding. She hardly knew the extended family of Rhinelander and Newbold cousins; within her generation, Beatrix was an isolated figure. The prolific Jones family had shrunk, since neither Edith nor Harry had had children. "The Jones[es] are rather down on their luck just now," Codman told his mother. "Fred Jones['s] divorce and second marriage, the worst of all his losing all his 'harlots earnings' inherited from his second wife. Then Harry Jones['s] unedifying condition with another ancient harlot, and Puss and Ted's divorce . . . have made them rather forlorn." It was to be a small wedding, but the meager representation from the Jones side was reduced further when Minnie was confined to bed after an operation on her ear and Edith fell ill with a "violent grippe and bronchitis" and collapsed on December 10 while boarding the steamer *Olympic* for New York. Walter departed without her, and she returned to Paris.[75]

Forced to wait a week for another steamer, she missed the wedding. Celebratory luncheons and dinners with friends had been postponed. When they did take place, Walter enjoyed himself, but Edith, who had collapsed again en route to New York, had little strength for them. It was her first winter in the city in eight years, and her two weeks there were "cracking and bursting with obligations." From the Ritz Carlton on New Year's Eve, she wrote to Daisy Chanler, who had had a difficult year because of her husband's illnesses: "I hope 1914 will make up. I don't feel as if anything could obliterate 1913 for *me*." She felt "battered" by the "winds and waves" of the old year.

Edith's letter of good wishes to Beatrix, written during her return trip to France, disclosed an unspoken sadness at all that she had not had in her own marriage. Chief among her regrets was the absence of children:

> Blessedness gives such a bloom even to chairs and tables—and how the sunlight strikes on a bowl of flowers, when one looks at it through a haze of happiness! Fasten with all your might on the inestimable treasure of your liking for each other and your understanding of each other—build your life on its serene foundations, and let everything you do and think be a part of it. And if you have a boy or girl, to prolong the joy, so much the better. Be sure it's worthwhile. *And times come when one would give anything in the world for a reason like that for living on.*[76]

In the aftermath of her divorce, with all its cumulative losses, Edith was clearly searching for a reason to live. On the eve of her fifty-first birthday, she might now have had children and grandchildren to ease her loneliness and take away the bitter taste of the final years of her marriage. For her, marriage was the primary relationship between adults, a relation built on mutual "liking" and "understanding," and children prolonged its joys. Her apparent regret over not having had children opens a set of questions that shadow her life. Had she, during her childbearing years, wanted to have a baby? Had she and Teddy tried to have children? Her letters and diaries give no clues to help us answer these questions. Beatrix's evident happiness seems to have unleashed old longings in Edith.

GOOD-BYE TO ALL THAT

The return trip to France gave Edith a week of "blue sea and sunshine" in which to assess her "mad fortnight" in New York. Her experiences reinforced the general impression she had gathered in autumn 1912, when she had seen New York as Dante's Inferno. The city's life was "hurried and purposeless"; she was a mere "jeton" in a game of "nightmare chess without rules or issue." Feeling her own individuality "shrivelling a little every day," she was aware of the city's new self-consciousness, how it stepped back from itself to "measure and generalize." This posturing self-regard brought no advantages, in her opinion. Behind its glittering, "vertiginous" surface and beneath "all the new ardours and the new attitudes," nothing much had really changed: New York was still "ugly, patchy, scrappy."[77]

She had intended to stay until January 19, but she fled the "queer rootless life" on the seventh, taking a very reluctant Walter Berry with her. He was quite enjoying his time in the city—too much so for Edith's comfort. This was Mary Berenson's impression when she arrived in New York from Boston. "Edith was *indiablée*," she wrote Geoffrey Scott. "She spoiled several evenings especially arranged for her by evidently hating everything and has left some bitter enemies behind." She "could not control herself" because (Mary speculated) she was "nervous with jealousy" over Berry's absences. Mary criticized Edith's "unseemly and misplaced archness and coquetry" and recalled that there had been a good deal of support for Teddy Wharton during their divorce case. Edith was, she said, spoiled and immature and apparently so accustomed to criticism that she was "quite indifferent" to it.[78]

Behind the image of a restless and endeviled Edith was a woman facing a New York mired in gossip of her divorce, tales of Teddy's wild doings, and speculation about her relationship with Walter and his feelings for Elsie Goelet. She may have recalled in some back corner of her mind the night in January 1883 when she had appeared at the Patriarchs Ball to face the disapproving glares of New York matrons after the Harry Stevens debacle. The Edith Jones of thirty years ago shook in fright as she entered Delmonico's on the arm of Willie Buckler. In the intervening years, she had created a defensive social pose: arched brows, squared jaw, and voice pitched to slice the air. Under stress, she could become the sneering and snobbish Edith Wharton of legend.

Social encounters were for her devouring experiences, a civilized form of emotional cannibalism. "People are so friendly and hospitable here to the prodigal," she wrote Daisy, "that a fortnight is not enough to exhaust their ardour!" She felt duty-bound to see all her friends and relations: "I *can't* be 'apache'—I'm too old to begin." In French argot, "apache" means "thug" or "villain," but Edith uses it to mean "uncivilized." Leaving behind an impression of her own incivility, she found the "maelstrom" of New York a "soul-destroying experience." Back in Paris, under the shade of her "village clocher," she worked steadily on her new work, "Literature," spent "long book-evenings" reading Theodore Roosevelt's autobiography and Proust's *Du Côté de Chez Swann*. When she ventured out, it was to hear performances of Bach's *Well-tempered Clavier* and the Beethoven quartets. Her interests were changing, music taking the place of theater, and her need for new friendships was waning. "I'm less and less disposed to make new acquisitions, to throw out feelers," she wrote Sally. "So I've crawled into myself as into a kind of Esquimau hut," an image appropriate to the bitterly cold late-January weather.[79]

The furnace at number 53 could not meet the demands put on it, and in February, a series of chimney fires left the apartment without heat for four days. Edith fell ill with flu (her third case in three months), and Anna, suffering from rheumatism and neuralgia, also showed signs of deafness and made "scenes" when she could not understand what was said to her. "By scenes, of course, I mean sadness, and notes left on table-corners," Edith explained to Minnie, who herself was almost stone-deaf. Anna had become a chronically discontented person, "always complaining" and "unhappy wherever she is." Fred Jones, whom Edith had visited several times in the first months after his stroke in 1911, was now unable to leave his bed and reported to be failing mentally. Henry James was undergoing teeth extractions in hopes of improving his health; Howard Sturgis was suffering mysterious stomach ailments that would later prove to be cancer. Near and far, Edith's friends were drawing into themselves and leading what she called "little lives." Bourget refused to travel beyond his known territories, increasingly "'maniaque' about drugs, diseases and diets." Charles du Bos, following an appendectomy, had now "rooted" himself and his wife in a little flat where he gave little teas and offered "little pontifications."[80]

Walter, by contrast, was approaching Ceylon on a "Passage to India" that had begun on February 14 from Marseilles and would end on May 18. "I am delighted at his decision," Edith wrote Berenson, "for I don't think he has been well lately, and nothing seems to do him as much good as swallowing sea-air in long unbroken draughts." She was determined to resist the "tropism" she saw about her as she planned an excursion to Algeria and Tunisia with Lapsley and Lubbock. It was to be a five-week adventure, Percy's portion of it underwritten by Edith, since he was between jobs. She would cap the trip with a long visit to I Tatti. "I've made up my mind, for the next few years, to eat the world leaf by leaf," she informed Berenson, "and I have projets de voyage to unfold that will, I hope, make you follow me as if I were the Pied Piper."[81]

Edith and her friends sailed from Marseilles to Algiers on March 29 on the S.S. *Timgad*. If one believed in ill omens, the name of the ship foreshadowed a terrifying adventure in which Edith awakened during the night in a remote inn at Timgad, on the African campagna, to discover a man in her room. After a brief struggle with her assailant, she fled into the corridor where her screams awakened the others. She was neither hurt nor robbed, but the event was "indescribably sinister," the dark side of the exoticism of the desert whose daylight so captivated her. She had once again sailed beyond the rim of Europe, and her responses to people, customs, and costumes were much the same as in 1888, when, under the shade of her white parasol, she had stepped from the gangplank of the *Vanadis* onto Malta. Accompanied by Anna Bahlmann, Lubbock, Cook (at the wheel of the Mercedes), and her new maid, Elise Duvinck, Edith left the "narrow thread of civilization along the coast" at Algiers (a city full of "native types"—"all effeminacy, obesity, obscenity or black savageness") to venture inland for what she called their "spicy days in the desert," a reference to the sandalwood, jasmine, attar of roses, and other essences sold in the oasis bazaars. Gross, no longer able to undertake the rigors of this kind of travel, had stayed home. Lapsley, ill with dysentery, had returned to Cambridge.[82]

They traveled in southern Tunisia as far as the "motor road" would take them—to the borders of Tripoli. They saw Carthage, "so august and so shadowy," and spent ten days in Tunis, then sailed to Palermo and on to Naples. For Edith, it was a voyage into the Arabian Nights, a feast for all the senses, but particularly for the eye. Coming back to Naples on May 1, she complained to Berenson of the necessity to "*look away* from people in the streets, instead of gloating on them as we've been doing for this last month." Europeans were "ugly monkeys in comic clothes," she wrote Fullerton. "*How* I understand Lady Hester Stanhope!" Yet, Lady Stanhope, who had put down roots in North Africa and lived among its peoples, might have viewed Edith Wharton as a wealthy, self-interested tourist ogling natives.

Edith captured the shifting scenes of this landscape in verbal snap-shots rich in color and sound. She told of "stumbling over snake-charmers" and storytellers, watching beautiful youths carry huge trays of "snowy cream-cheeses veiled in gold and violet gauze, others selling rosettes of orange-blossoms and pink rose-buds." The white heat, green oases, and "desert magic" aroused her senses. Taking undisguised interest in the erotic habits of the Eastern world, she bartered in a Tunisian bazaar for an aphrodisiac elixir made of sandalwood and sycamore, a gift for Gaillard Lapsley (the most staunchly formal of all her men friends); in Sfax, she bargained with a "'coloured' prostitute" for an ambergris necklace, whose scent was supposedly irresistible. The "East" filled her with "incurable nostalgia." After such "peace and loveliness, and such a quieting of the Western fever," she wrote Sally, "I don't know how to take up life again."[83]

The return to "civilization" was difficult for her. While en route to I Tatti, she learned that Teddy, now in Paris with his sister, had suffered a bad breakdown. The mania of the last two years had finally reversed itself, and he was paralyzed by depression. The attack was "critical," she wrote Mary. "I send you word because I naturally feel rather sad, and you will excuse me, I know, if I don't 'play up' at dinner, and perhaps excuse myself afterward." Her emotional ties to Teddy were by no means broken ("It is dreadful to me not to be able to do anything for him," she wrote Fullerton), nor had her rage at the Wharton family's blindness to his condition diminished: "Nothing will enlighten them, because they don't want to be enlightened."[84]

Fullerton had sadnesses and worries of his own. His father was dying slowly of myocarditis. Too poor to afford a nurse, Mrs. Fullerton cared for him around the clock. It was unconscionable, Edith wrote, that the money he should be giving his parents was instead "going to a woman who got it from you only because you were afraid she would blackmail you."

> I know you think there were other reasons—there were, no doubt, reasons for giving her some compensation, but none whatever for binding yourself for life to pension her, when you had no settled means of support. Every penny you can spare belongs to your mother after your father's death, and you ought to make some sort of fight, now [that] you are not afraid of a scandal at the Times, to free yourself from being bled any longer.

The Reverend Bradford Fullerton lived on until October, and Morton arrived in America for his lecture tour just in time to attend his father's funeral. There is no evidence, however, that he sent money to his family.[85]

Fullerton renewed his old seductive games with Edith. She invited him to dinner one evening before her departure for North Africa, and their conversation took a disturbing turn.

> You said things then that touched me, you voluntarily appealed to old memories, and then you left me—for many days—to conclude that you had used them as a mere conversational convenience.
>
> Perhaps you didn't—but in that case it's *I* who don't "understand," and who feel the uselessness of trying—since the real things don't need so much annotation, but say themselves simply and indelibly.
>
> I have been sad, thinking of all this, and have felt the inability to talk of indifferent things with you just now.

Her letters to Fullerton in this period adopted a new tone, giving free expression to her feelings, desires, and needs, but without the pleading and posturing that sometimes marked the early years of their affair. Recognizing her vulnerability to his seductive maneuvers, she refused to play the game and instead insisted on her rights within their friendship.[86]

As Edith's dependence on Morton waned, her reliance on Walter grew, as did her trust in him, now that the crisis over Elsie Goelet had passed. Mary and Bernard Berenson were quite right in assuming only one man figured in Edith Wharton's life—Walter Berry. In July 1914, at the very moment she was supposed to have moved into Stocks, the thousand-acre Buckinghamshire estate of the Humphry Wards that she had rented for the summer, she instead went to Spain with Walter, "like another George Sand and another Chopin," James remarked to Howard Sturgis.

Walter had travel in his blood, and he was ready for more. His India trip had been such a success that he planned to do "All-the-Way-Round" in 1915. In retrospect, their motor trip to Spain served as an almost-too-perfect metaphor for the end of the Belle Epoque. In their own way, they were capturing the last ray of afternoon sun on the Edwardian garden party in one of the most beautiful summers in memory. That the season was so lovely and the sights so unforgettable lent a special poignancy to all that was to follow. Had war not come, Edith might have divided her time between the rue de Varenne and an English country house with extensive gardens. In between her novel writing and Berry's practice of law, they might have toured the far reaches of the world, drinking in fresh air and sunshine.[87]

Their July trip took them to the French Pyrenees, then south along the Bay of Biscay, inland to Burgos and Pamplona and, three weeks later, back to Paris. It was a journey of contrasts between ancient and modern. They went to a cinema at Bilbao, where they saw a travelogue entitled *How to Visit a City at a Gallop,* in which panting travelers marched across the screen. From the tone of Edith's account to Berenson, this was the first "movie" she ever saw. (It was not her last.) On another day, they entered the prehistoric world. They motored the short distance from Santander to Santillana along the coast road and then walked across "grassy heights and hay fields" to spend an afternoon viewing the recently discovered cave paintings at Altamira. Walter kept repeating, "I can't believe it—I can't believe it!" In the magic of the cave, they stood outside time.[88]

Time was tracking them, however. "The international news . . . is pretty black," Edith wrote Berenson from Burgos on Sunday, July 26. The newspaper she read was two days old, and completely outdated. Russia had begun premobilization, ready to strike if Austrian troops crossed the Serbian frontier. Earlier that summer, on an afternoon at the end of June, Edith had gone to tea at Jacques-Emile Blanche's studio at Auteuil. Groups of people had already gathered in the garden where blue forget-me-nots bordered the walk, and quiet talk drifted on the summer air. It had been an "exceptionally gay season," she recalled, "full of new literary and artistic emotions," but that afternoon was darkened by a "cloud-shadow" that swept over the tea tables. "Haven't you heard? The Archduke Ferdinand assassinated . . . at Serajevo . . . where *is* Serajevo [sic]? His wife was with him. What was her name? Both shot dead." The date then was June 28, and although the assassination of the archduke Ferdinand in the capital city of Bosnia was not the first in the long chain of events that led to world war, it was the incident that ignited the tinderbox. That few people could have located Sarajevo on a map or had any idea why the Austrian archduke had traveled there made the war that followed all the more tragic.[89]

Walter and Edith hastened back to Paris by way of Poitiers at the end of July; in the square under their hotel windows, they heard crowds singing the *Marseillaise* all night long. The next day, they stopped for an hour in the cathedral at Chartres and drew spiritual strength from its "tranquillizing power." They reached Paris that evening, July 29. For the next seventy-two hours, France's fate hung in the balance as diplomats frantically negotiated, telegraph wires carrying urgent messages between Vienna, St. Petersburg, Belgrade, London, Paris, and Berlin. Austria and Russia ordered general mobilization; Germany and France would follow suit three days later.[90]

In Paris on July 29, Jean Jaurès, editor of the Socialist newspaper *L'Humanité*, pleaded for reason and continued negotiation. He painted war as Apocalypse: "millions and millions of men . . . destroying each other." As war fever had grown during the summer, Jaurès was attacked in the press and parliament as a German sympathizer. That evening, as he sat at a café near the offices of *L'Humanité*, he was murdered by Raoul Villain (so aptly named), a follower of the anti-Semitic group Action Française. The young Villain carried a high-caliber revolver in one hand and two pages of Maurice Maeterlinck's symbolist poem *The Blue Bird* in the other. Helmuth von Moltke, the man who would implement the Schlieffen plan, the German military strategy for fighting a two-front war with France and Russia, also loved Maeterlinck's writing and was at work on a German translation of his *Pelléas et Mélisande*. His other passion was Goethe, whose *Faust* he carried in his pocket.[91]

Count von Moltke was as much artist as military man. The coming war revealed the tensions between culture and technology and the ways avant-garde art (Expressionism and Futurism) joined the two. For Germany, the war was an effort fueled in large part by Nietzschean egotism and energy. Although Germany believed it was forced to go to war, its artists and students, academics and intellectuals, were seized by "war fever." For England, the war was primarily a defensive action to conserve order and tradition. France was caught between these two positions: enamored of technology and energized by the new arts, it also fought to save its own cultural history and political sovereignty. In Edith's memory of the tea party in Auteuil, the "new literary and artistic emotions" that were in the air were joined to the incongruous but troubling news of the archduke's murder, news that in June 1914 had caused a momentary "shiver" in an otherwise golden summer.

The "dust of ideas" that floated on the summer's air exploded into gunfire when German armies marched through Belgium and France. Edith, who read Heine, Schiller, Kant, and Nietzsche, and whose favorite text was Goethe's *Faust*, joined the English and French in seeing the new Germans as barbarians, the destroyers of civilization. "The 'atrocities' one hears of *are true*," she wrote Sally Norton on September 2, the day the French government moved to Bordeaux in flight from an expected German siege of the city. "It should be known that it is to America's interest to help stem this hideous flood of savagery by opinion if it may not be by action." A novelized memoir of one family's response to the German advance was *Les Cloches de St. Amarain*. Privately printed after the war and written under a pseudonym, it told of Jacques-Emile Blanche's flight from Normandy. He and his family took refuge in an improvised *pension* in a convent on the Rhône River. The story of their life among other "fugitive froussards [chicken hearts]" entertained Edith. She sent a copy of the book to John Hugh Smith as a Christmas present in 1927, commenting that it was a "soul-baring" and "amazing glimpse into the arcana of French bourgeois life."[92]

The war energized, and ultimately consolidated, Edith's most conservative tendencies. In her humanitarian activism, she saved lives and gave hope to the war's victims. Raising money for her charities, she became a propagandist, skillfully employing an anti-Boche rhetoric whose "truth" she apparently believed: Allied soldiers were heroes; German soldiers were savages. When America entered the war in 1917, she developed a belated and (from a contemporary perspective) somewhat embarrassing patriotism. Once the war was over, she wanted to forget its darkness. She had paid heavily in the deaths of friends and in the loss of her health. There were other, unspoken losses: she never traveled in Germany again; she rarely spoke of German literature and art, and certainly not of its radical avant-garde. Turning aside from the outrage and hyperbole of the "new" art, she was in some sense turning her back on the new Germany.

Book Three

W

REWARDS

Chapter 7

W

CHARITY

FOR THE FRENCH, THE GREAT WAR WAS HERALDED BY three murders: of Gaston Calmette, the archduke Ferdinand, and Jean Jaurès. The first to be killed, Calmette was editor of *Le Figaro* and an outspoken supporter of President Poincaré's anti-German policies, who fought battles in 1912 and 1913 against the "new art." His prime target was Vaslav Nijinsky, whose interpretation of the faun in Debussy's *L'Après-midi d'un faune* he called—in a front-page editorial in his newspaper—filthy, bestial, crude, and indecent. Nijinsky's interpretation was purposely provocative, intended to challenge ruling dance conventions and the canons of taste. Dressed in a leotard stretched tight as a second skin, he made orgiastic love on stage to a scarf belonging to the wood nymph with whom he had fallen in love. It was a hypnotic, masturbatory scene. When sculptor Auguste Rodin tried to defend Nijinsky's interpretation, Calmette publicly denounced Rodin as an "immoral dilettante." In spring 1914, Calmette's editorial pugilism backfired when he threatened the former prime minister, Joseph Caillaux.

A wealthy banker, Caillaux was minister of finance and head of the anticlerical and antimilitary Radical party. He opposed Poincaré's militarism and supported détente with Germany; his politics, many claimed, were based on self-interest. Powerful and unscrupulous, as war drew closer, he came under ever more virulent attacks in the Chamber of Deputies and in the press. Compromising letters between Caillaux and his former mistress, Henriette (now his wife), fell into Calmette's hands. The newspaper editor threatened to publish them and thus force Caillaux's resignation from the cabinet. Mme Caillaux took action. She went to the *Figaro* offices one morning, waited while Calmette finished a meeting with writer Paul Bourget, then entered the office and discharged her revolver at Calmette. Hearing the shots, Bourget rushed back in and found Mme Caillaux looking, in Edith's account to Minnie, "perfectly calm and expressionless." Calmette died that evening.

Caillaux resigned his post, and his antimilitarist voice was silenced; after the war, he was jailed for his efforts to gain a settlement with Germany. His wife went on trial in July, a month of oppressive heat and humidity in France. The trial was front-page news in the Parisian papers, the public eager to read courtroom testimony that revealed government, financial, legal, and press scandals. On August 1, however, Mme Caillaux was relegated to page two: the front page was devoted to the international crisis.[1]

Edith was to have left for England on August 1 to take up residence at Stocks, the house she had rented from the Humphry Wards. Alfred White, who had overseen preparations for her arrival there, returned to Paris to accompany her on the Channel crossing. The French government ordered general mobilization that afternoon, and all civilian travel was banned. The "plunge of civilization into this abyss of blood and darkness," as Henry James called it, had begun. Dining that evening in the rue Royale (no doubt at Larue, a fashionable place with music), Edith and Walter watched as streams of conscripts passed in the street, their luggage pushed on handcarts, the restaurant band playing the *Marseillaise* and the Russian national anthem. In following days, Edith and Walter (like other foreigners) had to obtain identity papers. People who wanted to leave France stood in long lines at Cook's travel agency; even longer lines formed at police stations, where boat-train tickets were stamped with French visas. Shops and banks closed, and Red Cross flags announcing "Ouvroir" (workroom) and "Hôpital" appeared on town house façades. Inside the fashionable *hôtels*, women gathered to make bandages and bed sheets. Streets fell silent, empty of traffic; Parisians walked in the "blue-grey softness" of afternoons and under a ripe moon in the evening. Within a fortnight, some seven thousand French trains carried 3 million men to the front lines.[2]

Henry James, looking across the Channel from Rye, imagined Edith helpless, desperate, and motorless due to the transport confiscations. In reality, she was "cheerful and calm," finding it all "thrillingly interesting." Running short of cash after two nights at the Hôtel de Crillon, she reopened her rue de Varenne apartment, which had been closed for the season. Soon, she was preoccupied with charity work. At the request of the comtesse d'Haussonville, president of a French Red Cross affiliate, Edith raised almost $2,000 and found available space for a workroom to employ neighborhood seamstresses left without work when wealthy Faubourg women formed sewing circles to make clothing for the troops. Edith paid them 20 cents a day in return for six hours' work and provided a hot midday meal. The *ouvroir* was the first of "Mrs. Wharton's Charities," the most diverse privately funded charity in France during the war, second in size only to the American Hospital at Neuilly. By the third week in August, she reported to Berenson that the *ouvroir* had already excited a "good deal of interest."[3]

Having sent White back to England on August 4, Edith worried about how he was managing to meet household expenses in her absence. She wanted to settle her affairs there, hand Stocks back to the Humphry Wards, and return to Paris to oversee her workroom. Borrowing money from Walter, she crossed from Calais, arriving on Thursday, August 27, at Folkestone, where Henry James met her. They had not seen each other in a year; despite his recent digestive attack, she found him in better health than expected. After dinner at Lamb House and a night at the George Hotel in Rye, she traveled to Stocks. In the days ahead, she tried in vain to secure a return visa to France, appealing both to the French and American ambassadors. Rumors of an impending "decisive battle" halted travel in northern France.[4]

In the weeks since hostilities had begun, 1 million German soldiers (a quarter of Germany's trained military forces) had waged war on Belgium, opening a corridor for the army's sweep toward Paris. The German advance into France, which cut a swath seventy-five miles wide, had begun even before Edith crossed the Channel. The success of the Schlieffen plan seemed inevitable when, on August 24, beleaguered French troops were ordered to "fight in retreat." The following day, the Germans began to sack the medieval Belgian city of Louvain, committing atrocities against the population and destroying property, including the university library, which housed irreplaceable manuscripts and books. Some weeks later, on a tour through Belgium and Germany, Walter Berry brought back what he believed to be all that remained of the Louvain library, a tiny iron dragon found in the charred rubble by some children.[5]

The assault against neutral Belgium and the outrages against its people fueled international hatred of the "Boche beasts." Edith was no less horrified than Henry James by this "infamous violation." Like him, she was deeply ashamed that America hid behind a pledge of neutrality. While James believed Britain was demonstrating moral courage in fighting against the "butchery and atrocity" in Belgium, Edith's loyalties were with France. Seeing British men of the upper classes "playing cricket and philandering with girls" disgusted her. "I find the egoistic apathy here very trying," she wrote Robert Grant. The German bombardment of the Rheims cathedral on September 17 and 18 was a defining moment. It was, James wrote to Edith at Stocks, "the most unspeakable and immeasurable terror and infamy—and what is appalling and heartbreaking is that it's *forever and ever*!"[6]

The first authoritative report of the cathedral's destruction appeared in the September 22 *New York Tribune*, written by veteran American war correspondent Richard Harding Davis, who had begun his career as a military reporter in the Spanish-American War. He and several colleagues rented a chauffeured limousine and drove to Rheims from Paris, passing checkpoints by flashing an official-looking (but bogus) pass. Although the cathedral was under bombardment, a young priest gave Davis a tour. Red and blue glass from the stained-glass windows crunched under Davis's feet as he walked, and tangled window sashes and fragments of statuary littered the stone floor. Used as an aid station, the church gave shelter to injured and dying German soldiers, who lay on blood-soaked straw, unable to escape the falling masonry caused by shelling from their own artillery. The noise of the explosions was deafening. Touring the town a year later, Edith described the cathedral as "glowing and dying before us like a sunset." The west front of the building had been covered in scaffolding, which caught fire from the shells, melting ivory and glass, and reducing the stone to a glaze of "umber and burnt sienna"—a new, but terrible beauty.[7]

Destruction of the Louvain library and damage to the Rheims cathedral were cultural losses every bit as terrible to Edith Wharton and Henry James as the devastating human toll of the war. Unlike Howard Sturgis, who was so overcome with depression about the war that he became physically ill, they were drawn into active participation in the war effort. In James's case, this aid took two forms—opening his

Watchbell Street studio in London to Belgian refugees, and agreeing to accept the chairmanship of the American Volunteer Motor-Ambulance Corps.[8]

Edith spent two uneasy weeks at Stocks worrying about her *ouvroir*. Under other conditions, she would have relished the summer loveliness of the gardens and countryside, but without a motor or a telephone, she felt isolated. She also felt a "little aggrieved" that the Wards had never mentioned the absence of a telephone, for they had driven a hard bargain on the rental price, even charging her for garden vegetables. Eager to do purposeful work, she restlessly waited out the Battle of the Marne, perhaps the most important battle of the war.[9]

With the Germans bearing down toward Paris, General Joffre ordered the French army on September 5 to "die where you stand rather than give way." In a matter of hours, Joseph Gallieni, military governor of Paris, rushed six thousand men to the front in Paris taxicabs—the "taxis of the Marne"—and the following morning the battle began. During the next six days, British and French forces not only held their positions (thus preventing the dreaded "siege of Paris"), but also retook Châlons and Rheims and drove the German army back across the Marne as far as the Aisne River. The fiercest fighting raged in the area northeast of Paris where Edith and Teddy had toured during Whitsuntide weekend 1908, a trip she described in loving detail in *A Motor-Flight Through France*. The Battle of the Marne cost each side a half-million casualties. During autumn 1914, the opposing armies built hundreds of miles of trenches, between which lay a barbed-wire no-man's-land. A war of stagnation and stalemate had begun.[10]

Unable to tolerate the quiet of the English countryside, Edith moved into the Humphry Wards' town house on Grosvenor Place, where James visited for four days in mid-September. News came from Paris that the "philanthropic lady" who served as treasurer of her *ouvroir* had fled the city ahead of the German advance, taking with her $2,000 meant to support the workroom. The fifty women employees were again out of work, and Edith was desperate to return to Paris. Her crossing from Folkestone on September 24 took twenty-two hours—three times longer than normal. By September 27, however, she had traced the appropriated money and found new quarters for the workroom at 23 bis rue de l'Université. She hired Renée and Gabrielle Landormy, nieces of Paris music critic Jean Landormy, to run it.[11]

When it opened, the *ouvroir* made clothing for donation to hospitals and other charities, including the Red Cross, and Edith collected money to underwrite the expenses. When hope of victory by Christmas disappeared, she decided to make the workroom self-supporting by selling for a modest 5 percent profit the dresses, blouses, and specialty items (low-necked shirts for American artists in Montparnasse) created by the skilled designers and *lingères* whom she employed. She succeeded beyond her expectations, in part because the French fashion industry had collapsed; she added a knitting room to produce sweaters, socks, and mittens. In the sewing rooms, displaced Belgian lace-makers made lingerie, christening gowns, veils, and other delicate articles that were sold to American society women. One year after it opened, the *ouvroir* employed a permanent staff of ten women and provided temporary work to another fifty. In that time, they had produced 15,200 garments, sales of which brought a profit of $5,000. Edith claimed that hers was the first "paying" workroom in Paris, a source of great pride to her.[12]

By September 1914, the war had already reaped a grim harvest. In Paris, German prisoners marched in rank under the silent stares of city residents, and wave upon wave of refugees poured in from the war zones. They slept on street benches and in railway stations and wandered aimlessly, searching for food and shelter. Edith joined in creating the "Foyer Franco-Belge," a clearinghouse for refugees run by Charles du Bos, translator of *The House of Mirth*, and writer André Gide. To feed, clothe, house, and provide medical care for the displaced, Edith and some friends founded the "American Hostels for Refugees," which began its work with about $250 cash, three donated houses, and some furniture. Within a fortnight, two of these houses had been converted into institutional residences for a hundred refugees and the third house operated as a restaurant that fed 550 people a day. A free clinic and medical dispensary opened, and soon a clothing depot. Each step in easing the suffering of the war's victims led to expansion of the hostels' operation. Founding a day nursery and a workroom where fifty women made garments for the clothing depot, the organization also created several schools offering courses in sewing and lace-making, and language training in English and French. The hostels established an employment agency and financial assistance office.[13]

From the outset, Edith's approach to helping those in need contrasted sharply with the philosophy of other charities. The hostels offered basic support services, but their larger aims were to give people confidence, hope, and the practical help to become independent. Guided by Edith's conservative social and economic philosophy, the operation was run on strict business principles. She had no experience in business or philanthropy when the American Hostels opened, yet she presided over an international organization whose administrative and finance structures resembled a modern-day corporation and whose physical operations spread out across the city and into the countryside. In its first months, the organization survived from week to week on ad hoc donations and on money diverted from the *ouvroir*, but Edith soon realized that she must systematize the solicitation of funds.

The Battle of Ypres in mid-October marked a turning point for the American Hostels. Called the "children's massacre," it killed or displaced thousands of infants and young children. The regular armies on both sides had already been decimated in the Battle of the Marne, and the Germans were now forced to use huge numbers of reserves to try to break the Allied line. British soldiers, unable to pronounce the name of the Belgian town Ypres, called it "Wipers," a suitable eponym because they were virtually wiped out there, losing four-fifths of their 250,000-man fighting force in a three-week battle that left ten thousand people homeless. They made a "miserable procession," Edith wrote, a gathering of cripples and crying children, the old and infirm conveyed by carts. "Where are these unhappy people going?" she asked in her fund-raising circular. To Paris. Between November 1 and 20, the hostels provided ten thousand meals, found clothing and obtained lodging for innumerable refugees—all on 12,000 francs (about $1,500). Edith mounted a "Belgian appeal" in American newspapers, becoming a "brazen beggar" to the New York–Newport society worlds she satirized in her books and stories. Between September 1914 and December 1915, she raised $82,000. Adjusted for inflation, this sum amounts today to over $1,000,000. Her fund-raising activities during the next four years were on a scale that in our time only corporations could undertake.[14]

In order to assure continuing American support for the American Hostels and its fourteen dependent organizations, Edith asked Minnie Jones to organize a network of fund-raising committees in New York, Boston, Baltimore, and Washington. "We *must* get money from America," she wrote her in November; "$3000 a month (perhaps only for 3 or 4 months) would enable us to lodge, clothe and feed 300 desolate creatures but for whom Paris would now be German, and all humane humanity in peril." She urged Minnie to "give it all the push you can."

Her rhetoric was "rather sensational," she admitted, but the need was "desperate." Working twelve-hour days, Edith set aside literary activities to write letters appealing for funds. "I'm not used to philanthropy," she wrote Berenson in fatigued handwriting. The "fluffy fuzzy" people, she said, had all left Paris; those who remained assisted in war relief.[15]

During these first busy weeks, Edith worked without support staff of any kind, not even a secretary. She had sent Anna Bahlmann (a German citizen) to New York to protect her against anti-German sentiment in Paris and possible deportation to her native land. In mid-November, Edith asked Minnie to send Anna back to Europe: "I need a typist 'every hour,'" she said, quoting an old hymn. More than a typist, she required someone with managerial skills to supervise the daily activities of the charities. It took her five months to find such a person. Elisina Tyler, a woman Edith had met socially but did not know well, volunteered her services and those of her husband. Thirty-nine years old, Elisina was born of aristocratic Italian background, a woman of quick intelligence and slender, fragile beauty. Royall Tyler, a direct descendant of the eighteenth-century American playwright Royall Tyler, had graduated several years earlier from Harvard in art history, with a specialty in Spanish art and culture. Recently married, the couple moved to Paris from London, where they edited sixteenth-century diplomatic papers concerning relations between England and Spain. Edith took them both "on," as she put it, and made Elisina Tyler vice president of two of her charities.[16]

Edith later claimed that she and Elisina "hooked" with each other immediately, but Elisina, although a woman not easily daunted, remembered being at first rather frightened of Mme Wharton. Their war work joined them in mutual admiration and friendship, however, and Edith soon learned Elisina's story. Born in Florence, Elisina Palamadessi di Castelvecchio was convent-educated and trilingual in Italian, French, and English. At a young age, she married Grant Richards, the London publisher of George Bernard Shaw and James Joyce, and had three children by him. In 1909, Royall Tyler, then twenty-five years old, visited Richards in London to discuss a publishing project. He fell in love with the beautiful Mrs. Richards, his senior by nine years, and like a fairy tale prince soon carried her away with him.[17]

Their story repeated certain elements of the Bernard Berenson and Mary Costelloe affair. When Elisina and Royall came to Paris in 1914, she left her older children in England, where they were enrolled in

public schools. In 1910, she had given birth to a child by Royall, a little boy named William Royall Tyler, who would soon find a place in
Edith Wharton's heart. Although Elisina was "Mme Tyler" to everyone
she met, she and Royall did not marry until their son was nearly five
years old. When New York society women later tried to portray Elisina
as a woman no better than she should be, Edith came staunchly to her
defense. Her "'past' is what mine is, and yours," she wrote Minnie.
"She was very unhappily married to Grant Richards, and got a divorce
and married Royall." Rather than taking offense at Elisina's story (as
Beatrix Farrand would do), Edith was charmed by its romance and admired her young friend's courage in starting a new life.[18]

Elisina brought energy, stamina, and dedication to her war work;
like Edith, she negotiated Franco-American culture with ease. The
"Chief" and her commandant viewed situations from comparable perspectives, mastered large and complex problems without overlooking
crucial details, and foresaw the implications of each decision. Strong-
minded, determined, and independent, they collaborated for seven
years (well beyond the official end of the war) with only occasional
strains between them. Their harmony was remarkable, not only because the stalemated war produced difficult working conditions, but
also because they were both considered "difficult" women. Edith reputedly did not like other women, and men found Elisina self-willed, even
aggressive. Berenson was taken with "Peter," as Royall Tyler was
known to his friends, finding him a cultivated, urbane, engaging, and
lovable human being. But he could hardly tolerate Elisina, and certainly did not find her "lovable." Her "terrifically efficient and commanding manner" and "sing-song" voice sometimes put people off. But as
Edith explained to Daisy Chanler some years later, "When we get past
that funny little 1875 mincing manner there is much to be enjoyed
and appreciated." The men in Edith's "inner circle," however, thought
Elisina overbearing. When invited to the rue de Varenne for Thanksgiving dinner in 1913, Berenson asked whether she would be present.
He was told that the Tylers were "indivisible, alas!"[19]

By Christmas 1914, the French government had returned from Bordeaux, where it had retreated at news of the German advance; Walter
Berry was back from Berlin; and Percy Lubbock occupied Edith's bachelor quarters. Paris was filling up and looking "very usual," she wrote
Minnie, but the "solitary months" had made her withdrawn, and she
found "dinner talk" an effort. In the little free time available to her,

Edith read European history to understand better background events of the war. Describing herself as a "beginner," she praised a book by Charles Downer Hazen, a professor of history at Smith College in Northampton, Massachusetts. She found his massive study, *Europe Since 1815*, "clear and architectural, and well mapped and bibliographed. . . . I have really got a picture of things out of it," she wrote Mary Berenson.

Edith also listened closely as Walter gave his impressions of Germany: prices were no higher as the result of war, troops were moving westward rather than east to the Russian front (as had been reported), the prisoner of war camps were "fairly decent." The war that Germany felt had been forced on it by Great Britain was, he said, "universally popular." Rather than isolated facts and opinion, Edith wanted an "illuminating incident" of the kind she used in her public appeals for charity money. She thought Walter's imagination "less sensitive than it used to be." Henry James, by contrast, was disconcerted by Walter's "detachment," his "judicial and impartial ease." James admitted to being "fanatical" in his anger, no less so in winter than he had been in September when he visited Edith in London. Berry's "charming mirth" in the face of "this plunge of civilization" troubled him. "How much I wish," he wrote Edith, "he were not so anxious to amuse himself at our expense." (By February 1915, Walter would complain to Berenson, "It's appalling here. I am more and more fed-up with the obsession of refugees and relief.")[20]

Edith felt a deep sense of historical displacement in these weeks, as though she were "living again in the year 1000, with the last trump imminent." She referred to people who tried to carry on their lives in the old way as "left-overs." They were like "dead flies shaken down out of a summer hotel window curtain," she wrote Lapsley. "We shall never lodge in *that* summer hotel again!" As the "overwhelming horrors" mounted, she tried to recall the silence and emptiness of Paris in early August, before its streets were filled with the hungry and homeless. "It is really impossible to write of other things," she wrote Sally, speaking of the refugee crisis, "and I know you feel this, and are in the same state of mind, so I make no excuse."[21]

In December 1914, the French army stood 2,500,000 strong (many of them untrained volunteers) and defended 543 miles of trenches. The British, who had raised 1,000,000 men since August, held thirty-one miles of line and the Belgians patrolled eighteen miles. The total distance of Allied defenses extended from the English Channel to the bor-

der of Switzerland, roughly the distance from New York City to Toledo, Ohio. On Christmas Day, with the waterlogged trenches frozen
over, soldiers from opposing camps crawled out into no-man's-land,
where they exchanged gifts, trading Princess Mary's boxes of tobacco
and cigarettes for beer and cheese. They sang songs and read prayers; a
German barber set up shop and gave haircuts and shaves to British re-
cruits. In Paris, Edith celebrated the day by giving a party for eight
hundred refugees—most of them Belgians—in the Hostels restaurant
on the rue Taitbout. Cardinal Mercier, the Catholic primate of Belgium, declared that "God will save Belgium." "Which of us," he asked
in a letter to parish priests, "would have the courage to tear out this
last page of our national history? Which of us does not exult in the
brightness of the glory of this shattered nation?"[22]

THE HOME FRONT

Across the English Channel, James tried to "form some sort of approxi-
mate image" of Edith's life, concluding, grandly, that she was a "great
generalissima." She referred to her war work as "philanthropy" and repeated as a *bon mot* Percy Lubbock's quip that he could forgive her for
her industry because she "so visibly" hated what she was doing. The remark perhaps says more about Percy, who spent his evenings seated by
her fire knitting garments for refugees, than it does about Edith. Her
letters from this period reveal a deep commitment to her charity work
and pride in its success. The war had thrust her into social activism, a
role for which she had no training and (she thought) no talent. Although women of her class had participated historically in such activities, in her own family, the word "social" was rarely, if ever, joined to
"service," and she acknowledged her own "innate distaste for anything
like 'social service.'" Yet she cleverly joined philanthropy to propagan-
dism, using all her social, diplomatic, and political connections to further the war relief effort. She must have taken special pleasure in
putting the wealth of nouveau riche industrialists to good use.[23]

Shortly after the new year, Edith dined at the Ritz with Lady Essex
(her friend Adele Grant from New York) and Nancy Astor, who had established a war hospital at Cliveden. Only four other tables in the vast
restaurant were occupied. "I never saw anything so spectral," she wrote

Mary Berenson. Dinner over, the three women huddled together on a couch to keep warm as a "ghost of a waiter in a long apron shuffled up and down the endless empty vista of the hall, obviously revisiting the scene of his earthly activities." Two weeks later, she gave B.B. another little sketch of the Ritz. "Walter tries to pretend, by means of one professional beauty, a restaurant table, and a new cigarette case, that he is Seeing Life in the good old Ritzian style, but all the rest of us have given up the pretense, and surrendered to the dim and dowdy." Edith did not bemoan the loss of Parisian elegance and style. Instead, she felt the war's "motionless horror" and the oppression of always having to do what one *must* do. "The ouvroir and the oeuvres help to keep one from hanging over the abyss of the war," she wrote Berenson, "but not, alas, from breathing the chill of one's private abyss." As the months wore on with no end to the conflict in sight, she often spoke of her loneliness and fatigue. Walter kept to his usual schedule, playing tennis three mornings a week in the closed courts of the Bois de Boulogne. When he was not trying to resurrect the "old Ritzian style," he spent evenings at home reading. He was not always patient with the increasing demands made on Edith's time and strength; until he too undertook charity work, he seemed puzzled by her unflagging devotion. She often asked for his help, however, and he never turned her down. "All the Belgians in Paris are feeding out of Edith's hand," he wrote Berenson in early February 1915. "She's half a wreck but keeps on quand même."[24]

The war cast several of Edith's Faubourg friends in a new and less kindly light. The abbé Mugnier, head of the parish of Ste. Clotilde, had always amused her; she now found him "pleasant" but "a little inadequate." Portrait painter Jacques-Emile Blanche was "lucid but depressing." Léon Bélugou, an engineer, was still a "dear," but preoccupied with a belated grand passion for a "silly and unsatisfactory" twenty-five-year-old who did not suit him. Young Charles du Bos, director of the "Foyer Franco-Belge," had only a few months earlier taken to his sickbed; resurrected by his call to war work, he was, in Edith's first assessment, "wonderful and admirable." But he soon proved too disorganized and undisciplined to meet her exacting standards for charity workers. Writer Paul Bourget displayed the lovable and irritating contradictions of character that had first drawn her to him: "whimsical, fanatical and foolish, and at the same time dear and sensible and *solid* just when one least expects it!" (He did not, however, do much to aid the war effort.) She gained new respect for her English friend Robert Norton, now working for the British Admiralty, who had forecast the

current situation: "a long long struggle, with the all-too-great probability of a stale-mate at the end." Agreeing with Norton's assessment,
Edith could no longer discuss the war with those who "serve up the old
optimistic sugar plums of last August."[25]

During that first year, she found it impossible to write fiction, describing herself to Charles Scribner as "pen-tied." "I had a really big
novel in me . . . a year ago," she told Berenson in February 1915, "but
things have killed it—one thing after another." The novel was *Literature*, a *Kunstlerroman* that was to have begun its serial run in *Scribner's
Magazine* in 1915. Her 1914 literary earnings amounted to about $900
(a drop of $11,000 from 1913), on which she paid the United States
government an 11 percent income tax. Her account book shows only
two entries, £73.2.1 from Macmillan for the English edition of *The
Custom of the Country* and a Scribners general royalty of 900 francs
($150). Berenson sent large contributions to her *oeuvres*, which now had
taken in eight hundred refugees ("for life apparently"). Ogden Codman
won his way back into her heart by sending "massive checks" to her
charities. She contributed her own dwindling funds to the refugee effort, but by April 1915, she was "blood poor." She had begun writing
articles on the war for *Scribner's Magazine*, earning $500 each. Now
that Elisina Tyler helped administer the expanding charity operation,
Edith devoted herself to the conjoined activities of writing and raising
money.[26]

Early in 1915, she completed "The Look of Paris" for *Scribner's Magazine*, an essay that described the changes in the city's aspect from "sunlit
silent" August, with its "smiling fatalism," to the wartime darkness of
February fog that obscured faces and heightened the sound of footsteps
echoing on a neighborhood street. "It's not much good," she wrote Minnie Jones. "I'm too close to Paris to see its features clearly." Yet the essay
announced the signature style of Edith's war writing, combining the
evocative qualities of travelogue with moral instruction: she discovered
the "moral health" of France in the calm courage of Paris citizens. In
October 1914, she described Paris to Charles Scribner as "magnificent in
its coolness, serenity and seriousness." Its citizens had resolved that the
"great sacrifice" would not be in vain, she said. "I hope America is beginning to understand this, and that there is no more talk there of 'hon-
ourable peace.'" Deeply ashamed and angered that President Woodrow
Wilson persisted in his neutrality policy, she confessed to Minnie, "I'm
not very proud just now of being an American."[27]

On January 12, Edith motored to Chartres, casting a quick glance at the cathedral "in a glow of winter sun," before visiting Isch Wall's nearby hospital for war wounded. This was her first trip out of Paris since her return from Stocks in September. In early February, Germany declared the English Channel a war zone; travel to England was allowed only in special circumstances. Italy had not yet entered the war, and Edith, oppressed by the "awful loneliness of the world," dreamed of a trip to I Tatti: "How I wish I were just scurrying down to the salottino before dinner, with the prospect of a long warm evening by the library fire." Instead, she went to the war zone, at the request of representatives from the French Red Cross, who asked her to report on needs of military hospitals at the front.[28]

Two weeks earlier, Walter had accompanied Nancy Astor to the Marne battlefields and Rheims. He now went with Edith to Verdun, joined by Mildred Bliss, wife of Robert Woods Bliss, secretary to the American Legation in Paris, and writer Victor Bérard. Loading the motor with bandages, medicine, clothes, boxes of fresh eggs, and bags of oranges, they set off, Charles Cook at the wheel of Edith's Mercedes. This was the first of four trips to the front in 1915: twice in two weeks Edith visited Verdun; in May, she toured Lorraine and the Vosges; in June, she went to western Belgium, where Ypres and Poperinghe were again the scenes of dreadful fighting. In August, she toured the Alsace front, an "eager grotesque figure" in tight skirts astride a mule, she recalled in *A Backward Glance*, a woman laden with cigarettes for the legendary *Chasseurs Alpins* that held the mountain positions. She recalled the scarred land, the faces of the men in the trenches, her emotion at arriving at the posts, the astonishment of the officers and men who greeted her, the summer picnics on improvised tables, the good-byes and the messages she carried to wives and mothers. Collectively, these expeditions gave her a view of the entire western front.[29]

Her reports from the front give the impression that she was the first civilian woman allowed into the battle areas, but, strictly speaking, that was not true. Women relief workers could travel to the front under official military permit, and although their presence was anomalous, they were in no real danger. Edith sold her war articles to *Scribner's Magazine* on the premise that she had privileged access and portrayed herself as a singular figure. Journalist Henri de Jouvenel (husband of Colette Willy), the officer who checked her papers at Verdun, exclaimed in amazement that she had succeeded in getting to the front: no other woman had yet come to Verdun, he said.[30]

Certainly, Edith Wharton was the first American woman writer to provide an account of events at the front lines. Her articles for *Scribner's Magazine*, gathered into a book entitled *Fighting France: From Dunkerque to Belfort*, appeared in November 1915 to excellent reviews. The *New York Times Book Review* described her writing style as "carved ivory," and the *Bookman* praised the ways her "seeing eye" captured scenes of daily life. Edith used the essays to raise the consciousness (of Americans especially) to the grim brutalities of the war. Despite the tales told by refugees who appeared at the Foyer Franco-Belge and who were themselves the visible emblems of the war's ravages, she was unprepared for the devastation she witnessed, especially the disease—typhoid and tuberculosis—that were the by-products of trench warfare. At Châlons, she and Walter visited a hospital with nine hundred typhoid patients—"No bath, no bedpans—one thermometer for 30 men," Walter reported to Berenson. "We have just sent them a whole freight-car, full up." Edith was taxed to find new words to describe the repeated scenes of horror. Clermont-en-Argonne was "utterly ravaged," another Pompeii; Verdun was "dead and desolate" and Gerbevillier "incredibly destroyed"; a "death-silence" hung over Ypres, whose very name was synonymous with torture and death. Churches had been turned into hospitals; chapels were observation posts; cripples were gathered into "depots" for transport to the rear of the lines; bandaged creatures huddled in doorways. The heavy boom of guns echoed in the distance by day; after nightfall, skyrocketing flares and German Very lights lit up no-man's-land.[31]

Edith played the double roles of relief worker and foreign war correspondent, a woman who stood out amid soldiers in battle dress, nuns in their habits, and nurses in their uniforms. Among the photographs of fortified trenches, graveyards, and devastated towns that accompany her essays, she included one of herself—it is the only image of a woman in the book. She stands in front of a boundary fence; two French officers in a wooden enclosure behind her have their backs to the camera. Dressed in an ankle-length fitted suit, behatted and booted, her gloved hands resting on an elegant umbrella, she looks directly into the camera. Nothing in the picture betrays the horror taking place some hundred yards beyond the fencing. Caught on a bitter-cold night at Châlons and unable to find rooms in which to sleep, Edith and Walter were aided by a French friend who occasionally visited her at the rue de Varenne. When, in the "pitch blackness of the deserted street," he gave her the password ("Jéna"), she could not believe that "*any* of it was true, or happening to *me*." Such otherworldly scenes played on her imagination. Hiding from the eyes of an invisible enemy gave her "an even acuter sense of being in the very gates of Hell."[32]

EDITH BEGAN TO lose friends to the war. The first was Jean du Breuil de St. Germain, the man who had traveled with her and Rosa de Fitz-James to Spain in spring of 1913. He had fallen in love with the widowed Bessy Lodge, and they hoped to marry. But as he was Catholic, the Lodge family opposed the match and threatened to take away her children if she married Jean du Breuil, a situation that ironically mirrored Fanny de Malrive's in *Madame de Treymes*. Bessy left France for London in August 1914 and never saw her lover again. She settled in Washington, D.C., under the observant eyes of the Lodges, and her father-in-law began grooming her eldest son, Henry Cabot, for a political and diplomatic career. Observing from afar as Bessy raised her three children alone and scrimped to meet expenses, Edith grew to detest the Lodges, who had proclaimed such love for their son, Bay, but who provided little for his children. When news came of Jean du Breuil's death, she asked Daisy Chanler, then living in Washington, to be especially kind to Bessy: "Too much bitter sorrow is shut up in her lonely heart"—a comment Edith might have applied to herself.[33]

In June, Robert d'Humières died at the front. Friend of Marcel Proust and translator of Rudyard Kipling and Thomas Hardy, he had completed only a third of his French translation of *The Custom of the Country*. Edith had known him since her early days in Paris, and felt his loss deeply. Her former footman Henri, who had become Berenson's valet, returned to France and worked in her charities while waiting to be called up. He died on September 30, 1915, soon after he went on active duty in the Dardanelles. "All my servants are crying their eyes out," she wrote Berenson, and she, too, mourned Henri's "eager spirit." In summer, Anna Bahlmann discovered she had cancer. Isch Wall operated on her in July, but the surgery provided only temporary relief. "I've been to too many funerals," Edith told Berenson, adding that she could not bear weddings either.[34]

In April 1915, when the Germans began a second wave of bombardments in western Belgium, and now were also spraying deadly nerve gas on its fields and villages, the Belgian government asked if

Edith Wharton's War Charities could provide housing for two hundred children on forty-eight hours' notice. Soon, they asked if the charities could take one hundred nuns, a colony of old women, and six hundred children who had been found in the trenches and in cellars of abandoned towns, or "picking up their food in the streets like dogs." Edith and Elisina formed the "Children of Flanders Rescue Committee" to meet their diverse needs. Under its auspices, they rented several residences near Paris and, later, two houses in Arromanches on the Normandy coast for those suffering from anemia or tuberculosis. Eventually, the Children of Flanders occupied six houses, all directed by the Flemish Sisters of Charity. A teaching order, the nuns set up schools for the refugees in their care. Two lace-making schools were established, giving girls the opportunity to learn a trade and participate in the lace-industry revival. Boys at another colony learned agriculture and gardening. By January 1917, the Children of Flanders charity cared for nearly a thousand people, including infants and infirm people in their eighties.

In a memoir of this work written almost twenty years after the war, Elisina Tyler remembered the circumstances that brought the first group of two hundred girls to safety in 1915. At four o'clock in the morning on April 23, the superior of the "Grands Hospices" at Poperinghe opened her window to discover the convent garden filled with "immobile shadows." British soldiers had leapt the wall and waited in silence until the clock sounded for morning prayers. Standing guard while the girls were hastily dressed in their Sunday clothes, the soldiers escorted them to an emergency train bound for Paris. Elisina first saw the girls lined up along the station *quai* at the Gare du Nord. Dressed in black, each clutching her umbrella, they looked like "little widows." Elisina, "the Lady in Charge," solved the problem of transporting them to Sèvres by asking the director of the Paris municipal police to lend her the tour buses the Cook's agency had put at his disposition when war was declared. The procession to Sèvres included four buses filled with refugees and eight coal carts loaded with beds, matresses, cooking utensils, and furniture.[35]

Edith considered the "Children of Flanders" her "prettiest and showiest" charity, and she spent the next three years raising money to keep it functioning. To sustain the "American Hostels for Refugees" and "Children of Flanders" through winter 1915–1916, she edited *The Book of the Homeless*, a collection of original poetry, prose, musical scores, drawings, and paintings by some sixty writers and artists from Belgium, France, Italy, Great Britain, and the United States. The list of contributors is a roll call of the era's most important artists. It includes those whose work dominated the late-nineteenth century—Thomas Hardy, John Galsworthy, Henry James, Joseph Conrad, William Dean Howells, Claude Monet, Pierre-Auguste Renoir, John Singer Sargent, and Jacques-Emile Blanche, who contributed his portrait of Igor Stravinsky—as well as moderns—Jean Cocteau, William Butler Yeats, Edmond Rostand, Rupert Brooke, Anna de Noailles, Paul Claudel, Maurice Maeterlinck, Auguste Rodin, and Léon Bakst. Edith lost respect for those who declined her invitation—illustrator Maxfield Parrish, whom she asked to design the book cover, and writers Pierre Loti and Rudyard Kipling, who later lost a son in battle.

Edith oversaw every aspect of the bookmaking process, from enlisting its contributors to translating the French and Italian contributions: "I could have cried for weariness . . . but the overwhelming needs of the hour doubled every one's [sic] strength." Published by Scribners in New York and Macmillan in London on January 22, 1916, the 155-page volume was printed by Berkeley Updike's Merrymount Press in a regular edition that sold for $5 and two deluxe editions that sold at $25 and $50 respectively. It was undoubtedly the most prestigious of the memorial books produced during the war and received excellent press coverage and reviews. The *New York Times Book Review* observed that its famous contributors "have given their best." Advance notices of the book described Edith Wharton's charities and appealed for more funds; book reviewers supplied the addresses to which contributions should be sent and included Edith's detailed instructions for labeling gifts of clothing and money.[36]

Minnie Jones organized an auction of the original art and manuscripts from the volume at the American Art Galleries at 6 West Twenty-third Street in Manhattan, a few doors from Edith Wharton's birthplace. To spark interest in the sale, she arranged a benefit reading of poems and essays from the book by French actress Yvonne Garrick on January 23, an event attended by socially prominent New York matrons. Two days later, at three o'clock in the afternoon, auctioneer Thomas E. Kirby opened the sale. The group was small but bidding was brisk, and in a very short time, sales had reached almost $7,000. General Joffre's letter of tribute to the American relief effort, written on August 18 from his field headquarters as commander in chief of the

French armies, sold for more money ($575) than any other item. It was purchased by Charles Scribner's Sons, which contributed another $400 to the cause by purchasing a Claude Monet landscape pastel. Charles Scribner purchased for himself a pen-and-ink drawing by Charles Dana Gibson, "The Girl He Left Behind" ($100), and a manuscript poem by Edmond Rostand. The typescript of Henry James's poem "The Long Wards," drawn from his experience of visiting wounded soldiers in London, brought in $500 and Edith's contribution, "The Tryst" (a piece of "doggerel," she said), sold for $350. Printing and production costs for the volume were high ($7,500), and when these were deducted, sales of twenty-five hundred copies earned about $1,500. Taken together, book sales and auction proceeds netted Edith's charities some $9,500, enough to get them through the winter.[37]

Publication of *The Book of the Homeless* brought tremendous publicity to Edith's war efforts. Even Teddy Wharton, whose mental capacities were failing as his manic-depression worsened, came briefly into the spotlight in a totally inaccurate international news service item about the team efforts of husbands and wives. The squib beneath a photograph of Teddy Wharton read:

> Over in France an American and his wife, among other American husbands and wives, are doing splendid things in the hospitals. The wife is one of our best-known American women and it is her many years of life alternately in France and America that compelled her, two years ago, to go to France to do all in her power to alleviate the misery of the wounded in France's glorious army. Save for the briefest of returns, she has been constantly on duty there. She is Edith Wharton, author, among other books, of "The House of Mirth"—and this is her guide, counselor and husband, Edward Wharton.

In September 1915, struggling to finish her work on *The Book of the Homeless*, Edith was overcome with fatigue. Gathering together the manuscript material, she set off for a three-week trip in Normandy and Brittany. On the eve of departure, she received a letter from Theodora Bosanquet, Henry James's secretary, telling her that he had collapsed from what seemed to be a gastric crisis. A week later, he dictated a cheery note saying that he was better and wanted her to come for a visit. By early October, she had finished all but her preface for the book. When her request for an emergency visa to cross the English Channel was approved, she traveled to London on a "Scotland Yard" permit to see James. Finding him depressed and withdrawn, she paid only a brief visit before going to Howard Sturgis's at Windsor, where several of the "inner circle" gathered. She did not see James again and never received another letter from him. Ensuing communications were with Miss Bosanquet, who reported that after several weeks of improvement, his condition worsened.[38]

Ashamed at America's refusal to join the Allied war effort, horrified at the sinking of the *Lusitania* in April, and saddened by the injuries to his valet, Burgess Noakes, who was wounded in action in late spring, Henry James decided to renounce his American citizenship. On July 26, 1915, he swore allegiance to the British crown. He did not discuss his decision with Edith before the event, nor did he tell her of it afterward, although he wrote to her on the day it happened. When she learned of his action, she at first thought him misled. By April 1916, she had revised her opinion. "It is indeed hard for some of us to 'accept America as it seems to be today,'" she wrote Barrett Wendell: "His change of citizenship was the revolt of a sensitive conscience bred in the old ideals, and outraged by the divergence between act and utterance which has come to be a matter of course for the new American."

In a memorial essay on James, Wendell declared that his "last months were tragic." In October 1915, Edith observed that "the sadness of every one about him is beginning to tell on him." She found England far sadder than France, despite its gala theater season and crowded restaurants and cafés. The "German horror," she wrote Sally Norton, "is becoming an ever blacker nightmare."[39]

Returning from England, Edith devoted herself to charity work. She procured coal and groceries for the hostels at wholesale prices, "remodelled" the organization's committee structure and general management, planned an advertising campaign for *The Book of the Homeless*, and arranged for Anna Bahlmann, whose health problems and secretarial inefficiencies complicated daily life, to spend the winter with relatives in the United States. Anna's tasks were reassigned to an English woman, Leanora ("Dolly") Herbert, and Elisina and Lizzie Cameron shared administrative duties.[40]

The hostels had grown enormously in the year since they were founded. Three lodging houses, two restaurants, a clinic and dispensary, a day nursery, and a clothing depot operated under their auspices. Since October 1914, they had provided shelter, food, and medical care for more than ten thousand refugees and twelve thousand sick persons and found employment for forty-two hundred people. Their workrooms employed one hundred women, whose children were cared for in the nursery; a free clinic opened two days a week for medical consultations. In addition to serving nearly 150,000 meals and distributing fifty-eight thousand garments, the hostels maintained a grocery depot and coal distribution center. The total expenses to date were something over $100,000—nearly all of it raised by Edith and Minnie—and monthly operating expenses were about $5,000. In spring 1916, the hostels were scheduled to open a model lodgings program to provide inexpensive housing for refugee families who, arriving in Paris destitute and dazed, starved and ill, were often preyed upon by dishonest boardinghouse owners and hoteliers. The American committees could not raise enough money to support all this work, and Edith had organized a monthly subscription program by which donors—she first among them—made regular contributions to the hostels' budget. Minnie, who had been working as a volunteer, now earned a $500 salary, paid quarterly out of Edith's trust money. That "Edith Wharton's War Charities" were transformed into quasi-permanent organizations with payrolls and fixed budgets confirmed the reality of a stalemated war.

By November 20, Edith was again leaving Paris, this time for an informal rest cure on the Riviera. She motored down with Léon Bélugou and André Gide, who since 1914 had worked with the Foyer Franco-Belge and whom Edith had recently appointed to the general committee for the Hostels. (She addressed him formally as "M. Gide," however.) They were joined by Robert Norton, who was on a brief leave from his work at the British Admiralty in London. Edith settled into a sunny hotel near the Bourgets at Costebelle. "It is heavenly here," she wrote Lizzie Cameron, "and I marvel at the thought that I used to be *bored* on the Riviera!"[41]

The respite was brief. She received a telegram from Miss Bosanquet on December 4 that James had suffered a stroke at his Chelsea lodgings two days earlier. "There is nothing to do now," Edith wrote Minnie, "but to wish that 'all that mighty heart were lying still.'" Winston Churchill intervened with Prime Minister Asquith to secure the Order of Merit for James, the highest honor England could bestow on a civilian. On New Year's Day, Henry James was included in the 1916 list of honors, and the insignia of the Order was brought to his bedside. "Yes—all my 'blue distances' will be shut out forever when he goes," she wrote Gaillard Lapsley. "His friendship has been the pride and honour of my life. Plus ne m'est rien after such a gift as that—except the memory of it." He died on February 28. Two days later, Edith wrote Lapsley: "Let us keep together all the closer now, we few who had him at his best." The desire to "keep together all the closer" became a refrain in letters to the men of her inner circle until the war was over.[42]

Edith returned to Paris in mid-December 1915, her Riviera trip "shattered" by the news of James's stroke, to face the major task of moving her *ouvroir* into larger quarters in a building on the boulevard St. Germain. She searched for a new secretary, Dolly Herbert having proved unsatisfactory. In early January, she wrote Minnie, "I am on the brink of a complete break-down." Visiting Edith some six months earlier, Mary Berenson had described her situation to Bernard: "She must have some intelligent person to help her. . . . In short, a sympathetic and clever secretary." Percy Lubbock, who was then staying with Edith, was almost useless, Mary said, since he was partially deaf and also unable to speak French. She asked Bernard to come to Paris and save Edith from a breakdown. If he could not come, would he send Geoffrey Scott? Scott arrived in early January, moved into the guest quarters that Lubbock had vacated, and for the next four months served both as friend and aide-de-camp. They spent long evenings discussing books and art, telling stories and laughing. His presence helped her through the sad winter of deadly fighting, increased charity responsibilities, and another series of personal losses.[43]

THE BATTLE OF VERDUN, which lasted twenty-two months, from February 21, 1916, until December 15, 1917, was the most formidable contest of the war. It began with heavy German bombardment that drove thousands of people from their homes; within days, those refugees were in Paris seeking food and shelter. In March 1915, Edith and Walter had toured this region, which she described as a "mud-and-cinder-coloured landscape, with the steel-cold Meuse winding between beaten poplars." The view was of "Winter War to the fullest. . . . I shall never forget the 15 mile run from Verdun to that particular ambulance [post], across a snow-covered rolling country sweeping up to the white sky, with no one in sight but now and then a cavalry patrol with a blown cloak struggling along against the wind." By 1916, the poplar groves that might have sheltered the French artillery had been obliterated by the German bombardment. The battlefield was a cratered, trenched, barbed-wire, and frozen slough of mud.[44]

With some thirty-three hundred refugees in permanent care, twenty-eight hundred of them from invaded provinces and bombarded towns in France, the hostels were now asked to take women, children, and old people who had hidden in snowy ravines under an "icy blizzard" without food or shelter, the roar of the big guns overhead. In her general report to the hostels' committees, Edith turned her novelist's eye on the horror and pathos of those who appeared at the grocery depot at the end of February 1916. One little boy had lost his ability to speak. He clung to his mother and stared "with vacant eyes." A woman, "Mme Marguerite M.," had spent fourteen months in a straw kennel in a German prison with some five thousand civilian prisoners. During that time, she received the news that her husband, a soldier, had died in a military prison camp. She watched her seven-year-old daughter die before her eyes. She heard the screams of her sister, lodged in an adjoining kennel, as she was raped by German officers in front of her two children. The sister died; her children were taken away and never seen again. "Mme Marguerite M." fell ill with grief and, thinking her insane, the guards released her. Discovered in a Paris railway station by a policeman, she was sent to one of the hostels' rest homes. "She had been there for several weeks when I first saw her," Edith wrote, "but even then I could not wonder that her gaolers thought her mad. Today, she is quiet and has recovered her self-control; but she remains an irreparable wreck, a wasted life. . . . I could tell of many others like her."[45]

Behind the committee reports with their tallies of money raised and meals served were the faces and stories of the people the hostels cared for and those who worked to save them. The war revealed itself to Edith, as it no doubt did to her co-workers, in individual cases, those who separated themselves from the masses either by the extremity of their need or the strength of their resistance against impossible odds. She had a gift for seeing a problem clearly and conceiving its solution. She started from a specific case (the little boy who could not speak, for example) and imagined all that it would take to answer his needs. The complex and interlocking organizations she established began with simple questions: What must this child have to survive?

Edith Wharton was not a Lady Bountiful who appeared occasionally to hand out clothing or preside at Christmas fêtes, though many of her social class practiced such *noblesse oblige*, even as they sent large donations to her charities. She made daily visits to the placement offices and the hostels themselves, and biweekly visits to the residences, schools, and lace-making enterprises. She saw the women and children, heard their cries and smelled their misery. Determined to give hope to those who had lost everything, she set the tone and example for those who worked with her, hiding her own sorrows and discouragement behind a smiling face. Her New York friend Eunice Maynard spoke of Edith's tenderness and sympathy: "Every face—adults and children alike—lit with pleasure when she entered the wards." Edith's correspondence with nurses and teachers reveals her regard for them; her letters to children (and theirs to her) are spontaneous and full of affection.[46]

A casual snapshot from this period, taken by a soldier on a Paris street, shows Edith standing behind an ambulance convoy she was seeing off to the front. She is handsomely dressed in a gray wool walking suit, fur pelts wrapped around her shoulders. The strong, square lines of her face frame a radiant, open smile. This is not her fixed "social smile" that sometimes betrayed boredom or suppressed anxiety. This expression reveals secret happiness—the joy of full engagement in life. The photograph appeared on the cover of *Heroes of France*, bulletin of the French Heroes Lafayette Memorial Fund in New York, which ran a story on her charities. She chose the photograph, but remarked to the editor of the issue, "I make such hideous photographs that there is no use trying for anything else."[47]

In spring 1916, Edith suggested to Elisina that they begin a rotation to "spell" each other every six or eight weeks, giving the other an opportunity for rest. While the rue de Varenne apartment was being repainted, Edith went to Costebelle for several weeks, her second trip to the Riviera in four months. She wanted to work on a new novel, *Summer*, a companion piece to *Ethan Frome* that, as she later told Charles Scribner, she had "wanted to do for years." She was also putting together a collection of short stories, *Xingu*, to be published by Scribners in October. All but one tale, "Coming Home" (a war story), was written before the war.[48]

Edith was far from Paris when it was publicly announced that on March 28, 1916, she had been made Chevalier of the French Legion of Honor, a recognition of her war work made all the more precious because it was the last award given to a civilian and foreigner until after the war. She had not attended the ceremony at which President Poincaré decorated the recipients, and her absence encouraged the myth that she wore her accolades lightly: "She does good works without seeming to notice it," wrote *Le Temps*. Perhaps she wished to create such an effect, but it was not true to her everyday experience; indeed, increasing charity responsibilities were beginning to take a toll on her health.

News of the award brought an outpouring of congratulatory letters and telegrams from friends near and far. Her old friend Egerton Winthrop cabled from New York: "Congratulations with all my heart." A week later, a little note arrived from him enclosing $250 for her work. By the time she received his check, he had been dead for several days. A friend from the earliest days of her marriage, Winthrop had served as her mentor, traveling companion, and confidant. She had not had time to recover from the news of his death when word came that Anna Bahlmann had died in Kansas City. Edith had been a child of ten when she crossed through the back gate joining the Jones property to the Rutherfurd estate in Newport to take lessons with her new governess. Their last days together in the rue de Varenne were difficult ones, as Anna tried to be useful but instead complicated the situation. Edith was now full of regrets—"Poor little unquiet bewildered and tender soul!"—and wished that Anna had remained in Paris so that she could have "been with her to the end." She asked Beatrix Farrand to design a "very simple" headstone for the grave. Friends raised money for a bed in Anna Bahlmann's name in Edith's newest charity, the Maisons Américaines de Convalescence, a charity for tubercular patients.[49]

These new losses renewed Edith's sense of loneliness; she felt increasingly cut off from her past. The "mourning on all sides" as the war's death toll mounted intensified her distress. "I can't shake off the thought of all I've lost," she wrote Berenson. Henry James had been to her "an atmosphere, a sort of mountain-height"; Egerton Winthrop, whom everyone mistook as merely conventional, was to her "dear and good and wise." Together, they comprised "the best I have known in human nature." In the shadow of these deaths was America—the most persistent and painful of all her losses. In June, she wrote Sally Norton, "I'm glad your father didn't live to see what America has become." In August, having retreated to Fontainebleau to work on *Summer*, a love story evoking the beauty of New England and the Berkshire Hills, summers at The Mount and Fourth of July celebrations, she wrote Minnie, "I want to go home for a while." She meant "go home to

America," but in every important way, America was no longer her home.[50]

During spring and summer 1916, Edith balanced charity work with literary endeavors. *Summer*, she told Berenson, was "taking every bit of grey matter that isn't used for greasing the philanthropic machinery." She had drafted nearly half the novel when news reached her at Fontainebleau that Elisina's fifteen-year-old son by her first marriage—Gerard Grant Richards—had been smothered by sand in a tragic beach accident. Still suffering from a recent attack of flu, Edith rushed back to Paris to take over for Elisina, who went to England for her son's funeral. Edith faced terrible pressures during the next six weeks as she supervised day-to-day charity work while also writing her novel. She had first offered the book to *Scribner's Magazine*, but because her 1893 novella *Bunner Sisters* was scheduled to appear there in the autumn, the magazine had no space for *Summer*. With Morton Fullerton's help, she sold the novel to D. Appleton and Company, which paid a $7,000 advance against royalties and sold the serial rights to *Cosmopolitan* for another $7,000.[51]

In need of "lucre," Edith signed the contract with *Cosmopolitan* magazine, despite her "loathing" of its owner, William Randolph Hearst. She decided to withdraw her novel after reading a Hearst editorial on behalf of Sir Roger Casement, who was executed on August 3, 1916, for obtaining arms from Germany to assist the Irish in their war against England. In a rather confused and emotional letter to Fullerton, Edith explained that she had forgotten Hearst was a "pro-Boche propagandist." (Prior to the outbreak of war, his newspapers had adopted an editorial policy of conciliation with Germany.) His "mourning page" for Casement, however, put her "in rather a bad posture to be begging day after day for the Allies, and at the same time helping to 'boom' a filthy Boche-Irish publisher by giving him [the] book." She asked Fullerton to use a "little diplomacy-delay on account of illness" to get her out of the contract.

He reluctantly intervened with Joseph Sears, vice president of Appleton, who withdrew her novel, managing to save the $7,000 serial rights money. He sold *Summer* to *McClure's* magazine for the same price. *Cosmopolitan* agreed to relinquish the story if Edith would give them something else later; after the war, they published several essays from *French Ways and Their Meaning*. She did not lose money on the arrangement, but she did lose time: *McClure's* required that her novel be completed by year's end.[52]

Several weeks later, on the evening of November 9, Catherine Gross discovered Edith unconscious on the drawing room floor. She had fainted from fatigue. This incident disturbed Edith enough that she took a day's rest and canceled a dinner with Berenson, who was in Paris. But there was no escaping her charity work or the deadline for her novel. By month's end, she had sent the last chapters of *Summer* to *McClure's*, where it was to begin serial publication in February 1917. "I don't know how on earth the thing got itself written in the scramble and scuffle of my present life: but it *did*, and I think you'll like it," she wrote Gaillard Lapsley. "Anyhow the setting will amuse you."[53]

In February 1938, six months after Edith Wharton's death, Elisina Tyler wrote to Robert Grant, the Boston novelist and retired probate judge, about Edith's jealousy of *Ethan Frome*'s "high fame." Edith preferred *Summer*, Elisina explained, and wrote the novel because she had once seen a newspaper account of a crime committed by "Charity Royall," a black girl descended from a slave formerly owned by the southern branch of the Royall family. Her "fine" name captured Edith's imagination. The central meanings of *Summer* arise from the name given its heroine by Lawyer Royall, the most prominent citizen of North Dormer, who "brought [her] down from the Mountain" as an orphan and made her his ward. He named her "Charity" to mark his "disinterestedness" and "to keep alive in her a becoming sense of dependence."[54]

During a remarkably beautiful New England summer, Charity falls in love with Lucius Harney, a handsome city architect who visits North Dormer. Their passionate lovemaking takes place in an abandoned house outside of town. Charity becomes pregnant, but keeps her condition secret both from Lucius (who is engaged to a woman of his own social class) and from Lawyer Royall, who in his jealousy of the two young people has suspected everything about their relationship. As the cold winds of winter begin to blow, Charity fears the "derision" of the village matrons if they learn of her pregnancy; she returns to the Mountain and to the mother who abandoned her. Mr. Miles, the minister, gives her a ride up the Mountain, and they arrive to find her mother dead on a filthy straw pallet in a hovel. (Edith took this scene from an account given to her by the Anglican pastor in Lenox, who had officiated at such a service.) After a night on the Mountain, Charity makes her way slowly back to North Dormer, overtaken en route by Lawyer Royall, who brings her home. In a second act of charity, but also out of his own loneliness, he marries her and agrees to accept her child as his own.[55]

To Edith, Lawyer Royall was the most important character in the book: "Old man Royall . . . *he's* the book," she wrote Berenson. He is certainly the most complex and mysterious of its figures, a man who is first Charity's guardian and then her husband. The book resolves its sexual puzzle in a union that is psychologically, if not in fact, incestuous. But neither Edith nor her reviewers seemed to notice it. Relieved perhaps that the story did not end in frozen tragedy, as *Ethan Frome* had, one reviewer saw Charity's marriage to her guardian as a "foothold of safety and of real, if wintery [sic], sunshine." Except for the *Bookman*, which said the novel displayed all the virtue of Edith Wharton's style and none of its weakness, American critics did not like the book. They thought it was artificial, unconvincing, and had struck a false note. The *New Republic* accused Edith Wharton of "going slumming among souls."[56]

In England, however, critics gave it high praise. Percy Lubbock, in an anonymous review for the *Times Literary Supplement*, said it matched and surpassed *Ethan Frome*: "Anyone who cares about the way in which a pen is handled should take this book and read, and read again, such pages as those which record the excursion to the country town for the Fourth of July celebration, or the girl's visit to the insinuating lady-doctor [an abortionist], or the wild night-piece of the funeral on the mountain." T. S. Eliot, writing for *The Egoist*, called Edith Wharton a "satirist's satirist," saying that in *Summer* she had dealt a "death-blow" to the New England novel of "stunted firs and . . . granite boulders." Constructing a "deliberate and consistent realism," she "refrain[ed] from the slightest touch of irony by suppressing all evidence of European culture"—the European culture that she (and Eliot) so admired. These remarks were high praise from an acclaimed young poet who would become a major figure in the modernist literary revolution already under way in London, Paris, and New York. In Pittsfield, Massachusetts, the setting for the novel's Fourth of July celebration (an event Edith and Lapsley had attended some years earlier), response to the novel was less praiseworthy. The library refused to purchase the book, judging it unfit for their readers. This news, which came to Edith from a local contributor to her charities, amused her.[57]

Her friends liked *Summer*, and she was more than usually pleased by Berenson's reactions. "It's such a wonderful sensation to find, when one comes out from behind the 'haute lisse' frame of the story-teller, that one's picture lives to other eyes as well as to one's own!" Joseph Conrad wrote a charming letter of appreciation: he noted Charity's "bewildered hurtfulness and her innate generosity"; "old Royall" was "immense"; everything in the book presented itself "*en beauté*," he said, the beauty of nature. For English readers, the lush rural setting recalled Thomas Hardy, the untutored Charity a silhouette of *Tess of the d'Urbervilles*. The churlish reviewer for the *Boston Evening Transcript* called *Summer* a New England *Adam Bede*.

The sale of *Summer* to D. Appleton and Company complicated Edith's relations with Scribners at a moment when her publishers had done everything possible to make *The Book of the Homeless* a critical and financial success for her charities. When Charles Scribner wrote in summer 1916 to say that they could not find room in the magazine for Edith's new novel, he offered to act as her agent in placing it as a serial. When he later inquired about book publication of *Summer*, knowing she had sold the serial rights to *McClure's*, Edith replied that she had accepted a "long standing offer of Messrs Appleton" combining serial and book publication "on terms so advantageous" that she could not reject the opportunity.[58]

A few weeks after its publication, Edith had occasion to write William Crary Brownell, who had sent her his new book, *Standards*, inscribing it to a "lovely writer." Admiring his courage in writing a book on cultural standards in the "New America," she told him that every word in it was "precious" to her. "It is the very voice of all my years of literary loneliness!" The primary source of her "literary loneliness" in America was her affinity with Continental and British traditions, a preference Brownell shared. In passing, she apologized for having forgotten to send him a copy of *Summer*, a novel that indicts American provincialism while invoking rural beauty: "what I really forgot was, that it was not published by Scribner!" In the months since Charles Scribner had written to apologize for letting it "get away," she had apparently convinced herself that he had rejected it: "I don't know why Mr. Scribner didn't want 'Summer.'" The idea that Scribners had rejected her work became fixed in her mind, and she repeated it in future correspondence with Brownell.[59]

THE LONG CONFLICT that brought America into the war began on the night of June 30, 1916. The Battle of the Somme opened with French howitzers shelling German positions near Bapaume and Péronne. The sound of the guns could be heard in Paris, eighty miles south. Forcing the Germans to respond to a massive attack while they were still trying to advance on Verdun, the Allied command hoped to divide the western front and break the stalemate, and perhaps even secure a rapid victory. Between July 1 and July 14, the French took 12,200 German prisoners of war. Walter Berry reported to Bernard Berenson that Paris was "cheerful" and everyone was "feeling good about the war outlook." These hopes died slowly and painfully over the next five months as casualties rose to unheard-of rates. By December 1, the Germans lost 700,000 men defending the Somme, a total of almost four million casualties since the war began. The British lost 450,000 men in the Somme campaign and the French 225,000.[60]

Among the victims were men suffering from tuberculosis, which spread rapidly in the filth and damp of trench life and reached epidemic proportions with the onset of September rains. Civilians living in unsanitary conditions also succumbed to the disease. Edith participated in a Franco-American effort to create rest homes for soldiers who needed more treatment than the limited care provided by the government, and to find facilities for pregnant women and mothers of small children at risk of infection from their diseased husbands. By rule of the French War Office, soldiers "invalided home" received pensions only if they had been wounded in battle. Men invalided because of tuberculosis—some 100,000 by September 1916—received no military pension or other form of financial assistance, or any further medical care. Because there was no free hospital for tubercular patients in France, these men went home, where they infected their wives and children. The civilian community so feared the malady that French law forbade the word "*tuberculose*" to appear on death certificates. People referred to it in whispered euphemisms, and physicians called the disease by one of its major symptoms, "chronic bronchitis."

The "French Tuberculous War-Victims" organization, whose offices were a few doors away from Edith at number 61 rue de Varenne, had as its honorary presidents William G. Sharp, the American ambassador to France (a close friend of Walter Berry's), and Léon Bourgeois, a cabinet minister and president of a permanent commission studying tuberculosis in France. An honorary medical committee of four physicians and researchers oversaw the charity's facilities. In summer 1916, Edith established her third charity, the "Maisons Américaines de Convalescence," which provided rest homes for tuberculosis patients. (The vague name given to this charity was purposefully chosen to avoid resistance from local authorities who feared the spread of tuberculosis in their own communities.) Seven homes opened in 1916 and 1917—two at Groslay; two at Arromanches on the Normandy coast for children suffering from tuberculosis of the bone; one in the Château de Tuyolle at Taverny, and another on the rue du Dr. Blanche in Paris. The charity also set up a halfway house providing a six-week program of reeducation for patients released from the rest homes. By June 1917, the American Hostels, Children of Flanders, Maisons Américaines de Convalescence, and Tuberculous War-Victims managed twenty-one houses in Paris and outlying regions.[61]

The Château de Groslay establishment was uniquely prepared to serve mothers and children. By November 1916, the nurses and administrators had been hired and the laboratory and kitchen were equipped. Edith and Elisina had rented two adjoining properties, which they named "Belle Alliance" and "Bon Acceuil"; separated by a garden wall, they overlooked the sun-filled fields and kitchen gardens surrounding the village. The tubercular mothers and pregnant women lived in one house (a "sanatorium"), while their children (who were not ill) lived in the other. This second house served as an experimental "preventorium." From the sunny garden, the mothers could hear their children's voices from over the wall, sounds that gave them hope and renewed their will to live.

The fight against tuberculosis added enormously to Edith's charitable work. When the French Ministry of War inspection team praised the model program of the Groslay sanatorium-preventorium, the government asked her to expand the network of rest homes. She founded new committees in New York to raise money especially for the sanatoria. During this same period, her *ouvroir*, which had become a profitable enterprise, was "overwhelmed" with orders from hospitals at the front lines. Troops needed every kind of clothing as winter settled over the western front, and the enormous casualty rates from the Verdun and Somme campaigns had depleted medical supplies. The scale of operations was such that she could no longer use her own motor to deliver supplies to the hostels and convalescent homes, or to the front lines. For over a year, she had borrowed cars and small delivery vans to run these errands. At last, the government agreed to give her charities the same privileges accorded the American Ambulance Corps. "Edith Wharton's War Charities" were "militarized." In January 1917, she purchased a fleet of trucks for deliveries to the front lines.[62]

SEASONS OF CHANGE

For many, the early weeks of 1917 were the darkest of the war. The lofty ideals and high sentiment of the first years died with the hopes for the Somme campaign and its enormous toll of human life. British poet David Jones described it as the last action of the Old World; all that followed was "the Break." The war had become an end in itself, and no language had words to describe its horrors or the sense of utter futility. Autumn floods were followed by a winter so brutally cold that hand grenades froze in their casings. Wilfred Owen's poem "Exposure" pictured shriveled skin and eyes of ice. The Russian army starved because supply routes were blocked with snow.[63]

In Paris, ice blocks on the Seine prevented tankers from delivering fuel. Coal rationing and electricity cuts forced Edith to close the larger rooms in her apartment; she lived and worked in the dining room. Playing down these woes, she conceived a variant of President Wilson's motto "Too proud to fight": "Too cold to sleep." Huddled in bed for warmth, she read most of the night, her choice of books severely limited, as she had sealed her "Grand Saloon," which housed the bulk of her library. Thus she rediscovered the Icelandic *Edda* and thirteenth-century German *Minnelieder*, epic poems she had first read as an adolescent in Dr. Washburn's library in New York. She rediscovered Horace Traubel's account of his conversations with Walt Whitman in Camden, Edgar Lee Masters's *Spoon River Anthology*, and Ernest Renan's *La Vie de Jésus* (which led her to reread portions of the New Testament). She tried, not for the first time, to get into the "swim" of the Goethe-Schiller correspondence, but concluded that "this book is not for me." Goethe lost his authentic voice in these letters: he "Schillered." "People talk more for themselves, apparently," she wrote Berenson, "and write more for their correspondents," an observation that does not accurately describe Edith's epistolary style. She wanted to discuss her reading with Berenson, in person: "Sometimes my heart gets so tight from that sort of loneliness."[64]

After two or three hours of fitful sleep, she awoke to face a day of mounting difficulties in providing the hostels and rest homes with food and fuel. How to transport wood and deliver flannel nightgowns to the women at the Maisons de Convalescence without petrol for the delivery trucks? "The situation of some of our refugee families is too terrible for words," she wrote Minnie in early February. When President Woodrow

Wilson appeared before a joint session of Congress on April 2 to rec-
ommend that America enter the war, she declared, "It's made me
young again to be an 'Ally' at last!" She immediately began her search
for a country house. Her desire to leave Paris and live permanently in
the countryside was joined to a firm belief that the American army
would break the stalemate and end the war.[65]

Soon after turning fifty-five on January 24, Edith fell ill with flu that
resulted in pneumonia and anemia and damaged her heart. Her team of
stalwart co-workers were also feeling the effects of two years of nonstop
charity work. After the death of her eldest son, Elisina had plunged
more deeply into administrative duties to escape her grief; she now
verged on psychological and physical breakdown. Minnie, age sixty-
seven, and on her third American lecture tour in less than a year, raised
money in "fat hauls." She appeared to be indefatigable, organizing "Red
Cross Day" events, managing the accounts for the American contributions to Edith's charities, and serving as Edith's proofreader and literary
representative in New York. But nerves were strained.[66]

In March, when Elisina went to the Riviera for several weeks of rest,
Edith apprised her by letter and telegram of crises at Groslay. These
missives reveal the day-to-day work of the charity organization in all its
mind-numbing particulars, especially the problems of personnel management. In Elisina's absence, Edith inspected the rest homes outside
Paris, often accompanied by Royall Tyler, treasurer of the hostels. They
discovered a poisonous cloud of enmity hanging over Groslay. Workers
in the two houses told tales about each other; an alcoholic manager
abused his workers and stole coal; standards of cleanliness were inadequate and morale was low. "It is hard for me to judge just what is
best," Edith wrote Elisina, "as I have not been au courant of your
house-keeping decisions." She then probed the sagacity and questioned
the logic of those decisions. Elisina answered every letter (and every
charge), and by the end of March, she was sicker than when she left
Paris.[67]

Unlike Goethe, who in his letters to Schiller adopted the tone and
perspective of his correspondent, Edith seemed unaware of the effect
her brisk manner and quick eye for every detail might have on her
reader. Part of her tonal blindness was due to her sense of inadequacy.
When new, and more devastating, problems arose in late summer, she
admitted to Elisina that she was of "little practical use in 'running' the
work" because until now, her participation had consisted primarily in

raising money for the organization. Their habit of "spelling" one another for rest breaks began to have negative effects for both of them. Elisina, overseeing the *ouvroir* in Edith's absence, raised questions about the quality of fabrics chosen and craftsmanship of the clothes it produced, and cast doubt on the managerial capabilities of Renée Landormy. "I feel the results of my own incompetence," Edith responded. "I never knew how to choose the material of my own clothes, much less anyone else's!" Her statement is disingenuous, given the care she paid to her own dress, but she was on the defensive—as Elisina had been in the spring. Acknowledging her own inexperience in such matters, she concluded, "All you say confirms my conviction that I had better close the ouvroir." (She did not close it.)[68]

In early April 1917, Edith and Walter made their final trip to the front, spending two and a half days touring the Somme. They witnessed the effects of the German "strategic retreat," enemy troops evacuating and devastating three hundred towns and villages in a thousand-mile-square area. A "Land of Death," as she described it to Berenson, its horrors were "unimaginable." By April 6, the refugees from Bapaume, Péronne, Chaulnes, and Noyon were pouring into Paris, the largest influx since the first days of the war. They required ever more resources. Edith's newfound pride at America's announced entry into the war turned to despair when she realized that a massive fund-raising campaign in May and June 1917 by the American Red Cross diverted funds that otherwise would have come to her charities. The newly formed Rockefeller Commission on Tuberculosis competed with her Maisons de Convalescence for American money and support staff. Despite her sense that the leaders of these organizations understood little about French life and customs or foresaw the challenges ahead of them, she hoped to turn her charities over to them. Yet, the hostels and convalescent homes were linked in ways that made it impossible for the Red Cross and the Rockefeller Commission to take over their work immediately.[69]

The future of Edith Wharton's War Charities hung fire for another year while the major charity organizations jockeyed for position and competed for money. Meanwhile, refugees streamed into Paris, tuberculosis was on the rise, and each day's mail brought some two dozen or so letters that Edith answered personally. Her days were so crowded that she used inspection tours of her facilities in Burgundy and Normandy in June as vacations, her doctor having ordered her to rest, and during the summer divided her time between Paris and Fontainebleau. While resting at Fontainebleau in late July, she received a letter from Elisina warning her that she was surrounded by people who disliked and resented her. This news came as no surprise. Edith admitted to having known for some time that Mildred Bliss was "doing her utmost" to undermine her position with the Rockefeller Commission. Daughter of an Ohio congressman and educated in Paris, Mildred was married to Robert Woods Bliss, counselor to the American Embassy in Paris. Since the beginning of the war, when she helped Edith organize concerts by unemployed Paris musicians (revenue from which went to the hostels), Mildred had devoted herself to refugee work. An elegantly slim woman in her late thirties, she had immense energy, wide contacts in the diplomatic community, and an ability to organize others. Edith appointed her to the executive committee of the Maisons de Convalescence, and soon after, rumors began circulating that the two women did not "get on"—rumors Edith initially tried to discount.[70]

By late summer 1917, an incredible and completely unfounded story circulated in Paris. According to the tale, Edith opposed the policies of the French government, and her charities were said to be politically motivated and controlled by unnamed "party organisations." The rumor took hold to the extent that the Rockefeller Commission, headed by Livingston Farrand (Max Farrand's brother), was advised not to "get mixed up" with her work. Although Edith firmly believed that Mildred was behind this plot (an unlikely event), she never forgave Livingston Farrand for trying to "ruin" her charities. Elisina knew the rumor, and she also knew that Mildred criticized Edith. Mildred's primary complaint—that Edith was capricious and given to reversals of mood and opinion—echoed the frustrations of others who had worked closely with her. Frank Hoppin and Ogden Codman, the two architects of The Mount, described her in similar terms. Another American friend remarked that she was "more changeable than the New York climate," and a Paris acquaintance once said that Edith required too much *hommage*. There was a growing consensus (undoubtedly spurred by the rivalries among charity organizations) that in the limelight of her fund-raising and charity successes, Edith had become too *grande dame*.

Yet, Edith's chief concern was her charities, prime among them the hostels. As she explained to Elisina, they represented "so many months of harmonious collaboration with you, and I am so proud of what your energy and your intelligence have made of them, that I want above everything else to see them survive." While rumors swirled around her, and as she waited to learn the future of her charities, Edith joined Walter, the newly elected president of the American Chamber of Commerce in Paris, and a group of French officials on a tour of Morocco. This was her first trip outside of France since visiting the ailing James in London two years earlier, and she was eager to escape the war's misery. Before leaving, she interested Scribners in a series of travel essays for the magazine (later collected into the volume *In Morocco*), an effort to fill her empty charity coffers.[71]

Since 1912, when he put down an uprising and helped establish a French protectorate in Morocco, General Hubert Lyautey modernized the country while also preserving Arab customs and Islamic religious traditions. The fruits of this experiment in Moroccan arts and industry were displayed at Rabat's annual fair in October 1917. Edith secured a promise from General Lyautey that she could see "everything," and under escort of government officials and French military, driving in chauffeured cars over roads built by German prisoners of war, she gained access to places usually forbidden to Westerners and to women. There was the "Sacrifice of the Sheep," a religious ceremony attended by the sultan in state with all his feudal chiefs; a visit to the sultan's harem, where he reclined surrounded by "lovely ballet russe concubines, in clothes such as [Léon] Bakst never dreamed of"; tours of wealthy estates in the hills above Fez, Edith astride a pink-saddled mule; attendance at a violent dance of ritual self-mutilation at the holy place Moulay Idriss; sightseeing in the El Kaironan mosque during prayer hour, where—accompanied by the French government architect overseeing repairs to the building—she and Walter could "linger and gaze" as much as they wanted. The gates of high castellated enclosures and palaces in Marrakech, Meknes, and Fez swung open at their arrival as though someone had spoken the magic words "Open Sesame." It was a "fairy tale every minute," as they walked in flowered courtyards where blue-and-white-tiled fountains merrily splashed and the scent of jasmine hung in the air—a turbaned caïd bowing them forward with each step. Edith came again under the mystery of the "East," just as she had in Tunisia and Algeria in 1914.[72]

By October 17, she was in Biarritz, having missed her train to Paris. Feverish with flu, she glimpsed the "land of fairy-tale" through "an endless perspective of railway tunnels and dreary wagon-lits vigils." The trip had been more than worth it, she told Minnie, but it was the most difficult traveling she had ever done, despite the luxe amenities provided by General Lyautey. Although she hoped to transcribe her Moroccan impressions on returning to Paris, war work interrupted her plans and the four essays did not begin their run in *Scribner's Magazine* until July 1919. The book appeared a year later, reviewed as a travel narrative whose freshness had not been dimmed by the delays and intrusions on its writing. Most commentators remarked on her gift of "vivid description," her personal observations and her attention to Moroccan atmosphere, and were fascinated by her depictions of places and ceremonies usually inaccessible to foreigners. The *Saturday Review* noted that her "nervous style never fails to convey the effect at which she aims."[73]

Several critics, however, commented on her many references to General Lyautey's work. She dedicated the book to him and his wife, whom she had first known as Faubourg neighbors. Two English reviewers offered opposed opinions on Edith's description of French colonialism. The *Spectator* noted that Lyautey deserved her tributes, as he was a proconsul who could rival "some of our best colonial governors." Irita Van Doren, writing for the *Nation*, noted that Edith's fulsome praise of the French administration sprang from her acceptance of the "general theory of imperialism." As a guest of the French government, she could have done no less than laud General Lyautey's administration, but Edith also believed strongly in what he was doing. This, in her view, was how colonialism should work: "natives" were to be educated in European ways but without destroying their own customs. She had been hypnotized by the beauty and exoticism of the culture, its "rounded orientalism." She did indeed see "everything" she had asked to see; but in some sense, she saw just what General Lyautey wanted her to see.[74]

Returning to Paris, Edith launched an $8,000 fund-raising campaign to maintain the Groslay and Arromanches convalescent homes throughout the winter. Elisina, meanwhile, responded to a request from the French Ministry of the Interior that the Maisons Américaines de Convalescence establish and administer, at government expense, three houses on the Groslay model for tubercular women and children from the Evian region. Tensions with the Red Cross had eased in early autumn, but news came that the Refugees War Relief Fund, which had supported Edith's work for nearly a year, had been shut down. Apart from the subsidy provided by the Belgian government for the Children of Flanders, Edith's charities once more depended on assistance from the Red Cross, and tensions again rose. The weeks since her return from Morocco had been "one long infernal drudge," she wrote Lapsley. She had caught a fever in North Africa that persisted; by November, she was near collapse. She worked only one or two hours a day, and her Paris physician, Isch Wall, wanted her to take a three-month leave from the charities. But she could leave Paris only after the Christmas holidays and the seasonal parties for residents of the rest homes and the hostels.[75]

On Christmas Day, as heavy snow blanketed the city, Edith served up an Anglo-American dinner of turkey and plum pudding to the Tyler family, her young cousins Le Roy and Freddy King, Rosa de Fitz-James, and Berenson, who was now working as an intelligence officer for the American Embassy, reporting to Royall Tyler. Berenson enjoyed the work, but was quickly disillusioned by the "sordid" network of agreements that bound the Allied forces and at times doubted whether any fundamental differences existed between the warring camps. He probably did not have the temerity to share these opinions with Edith, who was entering a patriotic phase.

Allied forces had endured a disastrous year. The Bolshevik revolution resulted in Russia's withdrawal from the war, giving Germany an enormous advantage. ("Russian treachery," Edith called it.) The British, having lost many thousand men in the Somme campaign in 1916, were nearly decimated in trying to hold the Vimy Ridge near Arras. From April to November, the French sacrificed men regaining the Chemin des Dames, a beautiful shaded road constructed by Louis XV along the northern heights of the Aisne River near Laon. Conditions were so terrible that French troops mutinied. The July–December British offensive along the Passchendaele Ridge near Ypres cost 300,000 lives, many men drowned in the mud of autumn rains. In late October, the German army drove the Italians out of Austria, and by year's end occupied four thousand square miles of Italy. That they had not succeeded in taking Venice, inflicting on it damage equivalent to that of Louvain and Rheims in 1914, was the only cheer in a year of horrors.[76]

AT THE NEW year, 1918, Edith went south for two months, her doctor having once again ordered her to rest. She had hoped to work on her Morocco essays but was so exhausted that she could do little but enjoy the warm weather. Mid-February found her resting on a pine-treed slope above the Mediterranean near Marseilles trying to get over the shock of Geoffrey Scott's announcement that he was planning to marry Lady Sybil Cutting. ("I have been *practising liking* it for 24 hours now," she wrote Berenson, "and am obliged to own that the results are not promising.") At this moment, Mary Berenson was just arriving in Paris, emotionally shattered by Scott's news.

A handsome and talented man of thirty-five, Geoffrey Scott had published in 1914 a mammoth cultural study, *The Architecture of Humanism*, which Edith, in her review for the *Times Literary Supplement*, had called "brilliant and discriminating." For some time, he had been looking for a wife, but his choice of spouse made Mary and Edith despair. The beautiful Lady Sybil Cutting, now in her late thirties, had lived for several years with her daughter Iris at the Villa Medici in the Settignano hills, near I Tatti. In 1914, she and Berenson had entered into a "rather romantic friendship" (only recently ended) that Mary initially encouraged, in the hope that her husband would be pried away from Belle da Costa Greene. She soon thought Lady Sybil no less "vulgar" than Belle Greene.[77]

Berenson was not entirely sympathetic to Mary's sufferings when she arrived at their apartment on the avenue du Trocadéro. Jealous of her feelings for Scott, he described his former protégé to her as "an aspiring little brother of the rich and well placed" and added further to her heartache by confessing that all he wanted to remember of Mary was her eyes at the moment of sexual climax with him—and also the look of Belle da Costa Greene at such a moment, and of Baroness Gabrielle La Caze, his latest Paris lover. (Berenson was also pursuing at this moment the "profoundly unattainable" Natalie Clifford Barney, a poet and salon hostess, perhaps the most famous lesbian in Paris; he pursued her until 1922.) Despite the quality of French farce in these tales of love requited and unrequited, their effect on Mary was disastrous. Unable to live either in Paris, where her husband was seeing Mme La Caze, or at I Tatti, where Geoffrey and Sybil were nearby, she went to England for the next year and a half. While there, she had a serious emotional breakdown and tried to commit suicide; she also underwent a series of painful surgeries for cystitis and urinary tract disorders.[78]

Edith looked on from afar, horror-struck at Mary's condition. Berenson shared her letters and medical documents with Edith, perhaps hoping that her experience with Teddy could shed some light on the situation. These materials depressed Edith, who believed that Mary must exert her will against this "hard and weary illness": "*Count your mercies,*" she wrote her, "gather up the fragments." Worried that Mary's condition would destroy Berenson, Edith several times urged him to leave her. She also urged Mary to put her faith in self-discipline, "the weighed and measured science acquired painfully, drop by drop, grain by grain, in the laboratory of continuous effort."[79]

But it may not have been possible for Mary to overcome her illness by sheer willpower. The emotional history of her family mirrored the constellation of mental illnesses among the Whartons. Her father, Robert Smith, had experienced manic-depressive spells, as did his brother Horace, and by the 1930s, Logan Pearsall Smith—Mary's brother—endured crippling episodes of the disease far worse than his father's. Mary's daughter, Karin, a psychoanalyst who suffered depression throughout her life, would kill herself at age sixty-four. When she returned from her eighteen-month separation from her husband, Mary charted a new course. She continued to serve as Berenson's business manager, but distanced herself from other professional obligations and from the social demands of the household. As the years went on, she turned many of these duties over to Elisabetta Mariano ("Nicky"), whom she hired as the I Tatti librarian. Nicky became Berenson's lover and devoted companion, and her mediating presence calmed family tensions.[80]

Elizabeth Cameron, a good friend of the Berensons and a co-worker in Edith's charities, also suffered a severe psychological breakdown in 1918. Within the space of a few months, she lost Henry Adams, her companion of nearly forty years, and her estranged husband, Senator James Donald Cameron of Pennsylvania. At their deaths, both men were in their eighties. The most terrible blow, however, was the death of Lizzie's beloved daughter Martha, wife of British diplomat Ronald Lindsay. She died after a long illness, and Lizzie gave up her war work in Paris to go into seclusion at Stepleton, her country house in Dorset, on whose grounds Martha was buried. In her grief, she sometimes threw herself on Martha's gravesite. Worried that Lizzie might commit suicide, her niece Elizabeth Hoyt left her new position as general administrator of the American Red Cross in Paris to care for her. Shocked that Lizzie would let Elizabeth risk her job in this way, Edith wrote her bluntly, "You are putting her in a very cruel dilemma." Elizabeth Hoyt (who later married Ronald Lindsay) recalled how kind Edith was to her in these difficult

Edith at age forty-five, dressed in silks and fur in 1907, when she met American journalist William Morton Fullerton in Paris. Taking the lead in their relationship, she invited him to The Mount and fell in love with him on a motor drive in the Berkshire countryside. (The Lilly Library, Indiana University, Bloomington, Indiana)

William Morton Fullerton in Paris (c. 1908), at age forty-three. A blue-eyed, bisexual charmer, he had once moved on the fringes of the Oscar Wilde circle. He carried on simultaneous, secret affairs while involved with Edith and was subjected to "blackmail" threats by a mysterious Parisienne, Madame Mirecourt. (Beinecke Library, Yale University)

Katharine Fullerton, Morton's first cousin, age twenty-two, at a May Day 1901 school celebration at Bryn Mawr College, where she taught English literature. Fourteen years younger than Morton, she was orphaned at birth and raised as his sister. Morton asked Katharine to marry him in October 1907, a few days before he visited Edith at The Mount. (Bryn Mawr College Archives)

Henry James, age sixty-nine. Edith commissioned this charcoal drawing by John Singer Sargent in 1912. Displeased with the artist's rendering, she then offered the drawing to James as a gift. (Beinecke Library, Yale University)

Edith's niece, landscape architect Beatrix Jones, sometime after her marriage. Daughter of Frederic and Mary Cadwalader Jones, she was married at age forty-two in 1913 to Max Farrand, a Yale professor. Beatrix loved and admired her aunt Edith, who served her as "an example and a light to follow." (Louisa Farrand Wood Collection)

American Hostels day nursery at Arromanches (Normandy), France, one of Edith's war charities for children suffering from tuberculosis of the bone. (Beinecke Library, Yale University)

"Belle Alliance," one of two *Maisons Américaines de Convalescence* for tubercular mothers and their children at Groslay, northwest of Paris. Part of "Edith Wharton's Charities," the two houses included a sanatorium and a preventorium.

A smiling, energetic Edith in 1916 seeing an ambulance convoy off to the front. Taken by an Allied soldier, the photo appeared on the cover of *Heroes of France*, the bulletin of the French Heroes Lafayette Memorial Fund in New York, on 18 November 1918. "I make such hideous photographs," Edith wrote the journal's editor, "that there is no use trying for anything else." (Jacques Fosse Collection)

Edith and Walter Berry with two members of the French military at Nieuport in western Belgium. Her four 1915 trips to the front included Lorraine, the Vosges, Alsace, and Verdun, which she described in *Scribner's Magazine* articles later collected in *Fighting France: From Dunquerque to Belfort*. (Beinecke Library, Yale University)

Elisina Tyler, photographed in Geneva, Switzerland, in the late 1920s, served during the war as Vice President of the American Hostels for Refugees and the Children of Flanders Rescue Committee, two of "Edith Wharton's Charities." (The Lilly Library, Indiana University, Bloomington, Indiana)

Pavillon Colombe in St. Brice-sous-Forêt, northwest of Paris. The eighteenth-century dwelling was built on a walled six-acre estate in the heart of the village as a pleasure house for a young actress of the Comédie-Italienne who took "Colombe" (dove) as her stage name. (Jacques Fosse Collection)

Pencil sketch of Minnie Jones signed by Edith, "Minnie reading," dated July 1920. Edith's sketchbook contains many drawings of her gardens. (The Lilly Library, Indiana University, Bloomington, Indiana)

Catherine Gross, who served as Edith's companion and housekeeper from 10 October 1884 until her death in spring 1933. Photographed in the Pavillon Colombe gardens, she shared Edith's love of Pekingese dogs. (Beinecke Library, Yale University)

The last formal photograph of Edith Wharton (1921), made into a cameo for *The Glimpses of the Moon* book jacket and also used as frontispiece to her autobiography, *A Backward Glance* (1934). Seed pearls twined in her hair, furs draped around her shoulders, the portrait deliberately evoked a lost past. (The Lilly Library, Indiana University, Bloomington, Indiana)

Edith at Yale University commencement exercises, 20 June 1923, when she received an honorary Doctor of Letters degree, the first woman to be so honored at Yale. (Yale University Library Archives)

Walter Berry, age sixty-six, in 1925, two years before his death in Paris from a stroke. (The Lilly Library, Indiana University, Bloomington, Indiana)

Ste. Claire le Château, Hyères, France, looking toward the terrace and the "Tour Jeanne," a remnant of the fortified château. Robert Norton described

the setting as "pure Albrecht Dürer background." (The Lilly Library, Indiana University, Bloomington, Indiana)

Edith in the early 1920s, seated on east terrace of Ste. Claire le Château, surrounded by her twenty-eight terraced gardens. (The Lilly Library, Indiana University, Bloomington, Indiana)

Edith in the early 1930s at Ste. Claire with three members of her "inner circle" of men (l. to r., John Hugh Smith, Robert Norton, Gaillard Lapsley) and Mme Homberg. (Beinecke Library, Yale University)

Bernard Berenson, Edith's "Dearest B.B.," with whom she shared a friendship of nearly thirty years. "Hearing you read your own prose, and even reading it without you, is one of the few pleasures I still look forward to," he wrote her on 20 May 1931. (Beinecke Library, Yale University)

The last photograph of Edith, in doorway of Pavillon Colombe in late July 1937, taken days before her death. "I'm used to invalidism now," she wrote Berenson, "and find it full of oases and hidden springs." (The Lilly Library, Indiana University, Bloomington, Indiana)

weeks, writing her almost every day during her two-month stay at Stepleton. "There can have been no one more reserved," she later wrote, "and yet more actively desirous of frank and outspoken understanding."[81]

Edith held up to Lizzie the example of Minnie Jones, who in spite of terrible financial crises was "younger, braver, more gallant and altogether admirable" than ever. Lizzie was behaving "like a mad-woman," Edith wrote Minnie; "sometimes I feel like saying simply 'like a woman.'" To Berenson, she decried Lizzie's "barbarous ostentation of grief" and observed that both Mary and Lizzie had "a real sorrow, a great deal of undiscipline, and the absence of certain experiences that make women really grow up." Calling Mary a "spoilt-child," she told Berenson he was being "vampired" by her, and urged that she be put in the hands of a "good neurologist," who would, Edith was sure, advise that he immediately separate from her. About this time, Minnie sent news of Teddy's worsening condition. Comparing Mary to Teddy, Edith pondered whether Berenson would be able to "stand it" for twelve years, as she had.[82]

Edith did not specify the "certain experiences" that make women grow up, but she believed that American society kept women childishly dependent. In *French Ways and Their Meaning*, she unfavorably compared American women, who were still in the "kindergarten," with French women, who by culture and training grew to responsible maturity. Her judgments of friends' suffering, and the swiftness with which she labeled others as lacking in self-discipline, seemed to betray a certain disregard of their feelings. On a visit to Lenox, Minnie Jones learned that Teddy was very weak and rarely left his bed. Nannie Wharton still maintained there was "nothing whatever wrong with his mind," although townspeople observed that he was "nasty" and abusive to her. For Edith, pity overrode empathy: Teddy's story was "horribly sad," and Mary Berenson was a "poor, poor dear." The war's destruction had perhaps caused Edith to lose perspective on human suffering. Soon, she spoke of herself as the "Incassable," the unbreakable one.[83]

In June, Lizzie Cameron had written her a sympathy letter on the death of Edith's brother Frederic. He died on June 7 at the Villa Victor Hugo, his home on the rue de Bassano, in Paris. Edith received no notice of the funeral from her own family, nor was it announced in the Paris papers. She went through "the hollow gestures of conventional mourning," wearing black and using black-bordered notepaper for her letters to American friends. The real sadness was being "cut off" from her brother Harry. She was also concerned about the financial consequences of Frederic's death on Minnie and Beatrix; they compensated for her own "wretched family," she wrote Lizzie. "The real thing nowadays concerns the real people, and not the poor phantoms who have voluntarily ceased to live so long ago."[84]

Less than two months after she wrote this letter, on a sunny August day at Fontainebleau, she received the wholly unexpected news that thirty-one-year-old Ronald Simmons, former secretary to the Tuberculous War-Victims Committee and now a captain with American Intelligence in Marseilles, had died of pneumonia, one of the first victims of the Spanish influenza that swept Europe and America in 1918–1919 and killed even more people than the war. "This breaks me down to the depths," she wrote Berenson. "I really loved him dearly—and he had a great sort of younger brotherly affection for me." Idealizing him, she told Elisina that he helped make up to her all that her two older brothers had not been. She was "paralyzed"; her heart was "murdered." In letters to friends, she described Simmons as a "pathetic figure" whose "jolly fatness" had awakened her affection and pity; shy, extremely modest, he was in her view a "frustrated, unappreciated, *undiscovered* being."[85]

Edith's men friends thought she had been a little bit in love with Simmons. But her immediate recognition of his inner self—"all the fine things shyly vibrating in his heart and mind"—suggests that she saw something of her childhood self in him. Psychically speaking, they were twinned. Everyone who knew him was heartbroken, she wrote Minnie, "and I perhaps most of all because I am lonelier than all the others." She, who had been so rich in friendships, she told Berenson, was now "so poor."

Six weeks later, Edith had another shock. Her youngest cousin, the "golden-haired" Newbold Rhinelander, who was serving with the Army Air Corps, had been shot down behind enemy lines. It would not be known for nearly three months that he had died instantly when his plane crashed. Trying to determine his fate, she used every diplomatic and military connection at her means. Meanwhile, his parents, Tom and Kit Rhinelander, held out hope—a hope that dimmed as the weeks went on. When his body was at last recovered, Edith arranged a funeral for him in the village of Murville, France, where he had fallen, and presided as next of kin in the absence of his parents.[86]

The lessons 1918 held for Edith concerned parents and children—a mother watching her daughter's slow death; a father searching for his missing son; a woman nearing sixty who had never had a child but who, in her grief for her young cousin and for the pathetic Simmons, came to know something of the special sorrow reserved for those who are asked to bury their children. She thought of Simmons's mother in Rhode Island, who learned of her son's death in the newspaper, and of "Bo" Rhinelander, whose father had "specially entrusted him to me." She no doubt thought of Elisina's loss two years earlier, and of Elisina's strength in bearing her sorrow without show of grief.[87]

Through her charity work, Edith observed many sides of parent-child relations. Some parents made enormous sacrifices to save their children, and others abandoned their responsibilities. The plight of four young brothers from the northern region of France came to her attention in 1917. The Herrewynn children, aged three to eight, had been abandoned by their mother during the German retreat from the Somme. Their father, a soldier who had been gassed in combat, was a man of "weak character," she determined, "quite unequal to bringing up four children." Starving and clinging to one another in fear when they arrived in Paris, they represented for Edith the suffering of all children victimized by war.

Because the hostels grouped children according to sex and age, the two older Herrewynn boys were sent to a home near Paris, and the two younger ones—who were at risk for tuberculosis—went to one in the Auvergne. This separation from his older brothers so disturbed the youngest child, George, that the nuns feared for his life. Edith determined that the boys must live close to one another, and she managed—despite many difficulties—to place them at two Lafayette Heroes Fund establishments in the Haute Loire, where they remained until the end of the war, when they again faced displacement and separation. From the moment she learned of their situation, she paid for their housing, food, and medical expenses, wrote to them regularly, and took an avid interest in their education. On October 27, 1921, she and Mr. Herrewynn signed a formal agreement at the Chamber of Commerce in Paris entrusting to Edith responsibilities for the boys' upkeep and education.[88]

IN JULY 1918, Edith Wharton and Elisina Tyler were awarded the Médaille Reine Elisabeth by the Belgian government for their refugee work. When Edith first learned about the award, she asked Boccon-Gibod (legal counsel to the hostels) to refuse it, saying that France had "long ago recompensed" her for her work. She referred to the huge gold medal as the Belgian "dole," and was irked by this tardy recognition of organizations established in direct response to the invasion of Belgium almost four years earlier. Elisina also received in 1918 the French Medal of Honor for "devotion," but in sharing the Belgian award, they were the "Great Twin Sisters." "It bores us both very much," Edith wrote Minnie. The Belgian government had been "consistently rude and indifferent" to their work; she would have preferred "common courtesy" to a medal, and in 1919, King Albert of Belgium did her the "courtesy" of naming her Chevalier of the Order of Leopold, the equivalent of the French Legion of Honor. Edith urged Minnie to announce the news for advertising and fund-raising purposes.

The Prix de Vertu, awarded by the Académie Française for virtuous achievements, better pleased Edith and Elisina. Raymond Poincaré, president of France, wrote a moving memoir of their work, which he read at the ceremony on November 25, 1920. He quoted Edith's own words: "When the eloquent expression of a sentiment does not translate itself into action, it falls to the level of rhetoric."[89]

The most difficult crises facing the charities occurred at the war's end. In early August 1918, Homer Folks, director of the American Red Cross in Paris, wrote Elisina about plans to place the hostels under the umbrella organization of the Red Cross, which wanted to showcase the hostels as advertisement for the quality of Red Cross work. The hostels' governing executive committee and Elisina and all of her co-workers— the very people whose constant attention to the hostels had ensured their superiority among charity organizations—would be dismissed. When the news came, Elisina and Edith were both away from Paris, and a good deal of confusion and misunderstanding ensued. Edith immediately opposed the takeover, writing a letter to Folks that Elisina felt was "ill-timed and unfortunately worded," and also appeared to "diminish" Elisina's authority. Edith thought Elisina's letter to Folks (a letter never sent) appeared to "virtually accept" the takeover. Telephone calls and tedious explanations followed. Edith rehearsed with Elisina the entire history of the hostels and—her feelings hurt—announced that "after this conflict is over, I will withdraw altogether from the Hostels to avoid such malentendus hereafter." This was a difficult moment for the charity, but the women's friendship was also at risk.

Walter Berry resolved the administrative crisis. The Lafayette Heroes Fund, a New York–based charity of which he was the newly elected president, offered to take over the financial support of the hostels, providing an $8,000 monthly budget for operations but leaving the charity's management to Elisina and her committee. The hostels escaped the Red Cross ("that slimy gang," in Edith's words), and the misunderstanding between the "twin sisters" was apparently resolved without lingering resentments. But Edith's proprietary interests in Royall Tyler may have added to tensions in their personal relationship.[90]

Elisina had been resting in the country for most of July while her husband continued his work at the American Legation in Paris. Edith saw a great deal of him. They dined with friends at her apartment or at Left Bank restaurants such as Lapérouse. He brought news of American advances in the Vosges (whispering the latest bulletins in Edith's ear as he slipped into his place at the dinner table), spent evenings in conversation with her, and was a comforting presence when Big Bertha's shells came too close—as they did on several occasions. Coming into the rue de Varenne one afternoon, Edith watched a shell drop down with a "dull thud" in front of her former residence, number 58.

Her accounts to Elisina of evenings with Royall were peppered with flirtatious references. Elisina was a constant topic of their conversations, but as reported by Edith, the talk about her was vaguely derogatory. In one letter to Elisina, she mentioned her "stupid little crise cardiaque" (which happened in July), then moved on to a brief discussion of charity matters, and finally to her decision to take a rest cure. "How shall I tear myself from Royall on Sat? *He's* given me another kind of cardiac crisis—but that one has been chronic since I first laid eyes on him.— My only consolation is that I know he's been giving up a lot of nice parties to keep me company in the evening—and now he'll be a free man again!" This message would not have comforted a wife on a rest cure in the country, while her young, handsome, and charming husband lived a bachelor life in Paris. Yet Edith, the writer so adept at catching the nuances of human interchange, appeared tone deaf to the possible readings of her text.[91]

Edith's heart attack at the end of July followed several months of hard writing. At age fifty-six, she had suffered three heart attacks in fifteen months (the first two occurred in May 1917 and May 1918), the last one serious enough to prevent her from taking an allergy treatment in the Auvergne that Isch Wall had offered to supervise personally. After each attack, Dr. Wall had ordered her to rest, but he now treated her with digitalis to regulate her heartbeat. She was at work on two projects, a war novel (*The Marne*) and the series of essays entitled *French Ways and Their Meaning*, the first five of which appeared in *Hearst's International Cosmopolitan* magazine between October 1918 and June 1919 under the title "The French We Are Learning to Know." These essays fulfilled her agreement with the magazine to replace *Summer*, which she had withdrawn three years earlier and published in *McClure's*.[92]

Appleton gave her a $4,000 advance against royalties on *The Marne* and sold the serial rights to the *Saturday Evening Post* for $2,000. Dedicated to Ronald Simmons, this story tells of an artistic American boy caught in Paris with his mother during the first Battle of the Marne in 1914. He returns to America to finish his schooling, haunted by the memories of what he saw in those days and thinking of his young tutor, who has since been killed in the battle. In 1918, at age eighteen, he returns to France as a Red Cross ambulance driver and joins in the second Battle of the Marne. He is wounded on July 18, 1918, during the street fighting in Château-Thierry, a decisive battle that turned the Germans back. Patriotic (propagandistic, even), the story captures the high-flying sentiments of that summer, when the armies of Pershing and Foch checked the last German offensive and brought an end to the war.

The Marne appeared on December 13, 1918, to rave reviews. Initial sales were so strong that it appeared to be a bestseller. The *New York Times* remarked that the "reader's first sensation on closing the volume is one of sheer wonder at its richness." She had never written a "broader, keener criticism than this." The *Times Literary Supplement* said the story was "carved like a gem . . . [that] glows with an inner light," a remark foreshadowing Frederic Cooper's statement in *Publisher's Weekly* that it was a "clear-cut, pure-water, almost flawless gem of war fiction." Several reviewers commented that France itself was the central figure of the story ("not France the pitied, but . . . France the adored," as the *Nation* put it). Edith Wharton gave "significance" to the activities of American youth in time of war, according to the *Boston Evening Transcript*. This early enthusiasm for the book did not hold up. In spring 1919, sales dropped off, and by the time John Dos Passos, Ernest Hemingway, E.E. Cummings, and others had written their war books, literary historians dismissed *The Marne* (and her later *A Son at the Front*) as dated and maudlin.[93]

AFTER JULY 18, 1918, Allied forces were continually victorious everywhere on the western front. Fighting stopped on November 11, the armistice signed at daybreak in Maréchal Foch's railway car at Rethondes, six miles east of Compiègne. Edith, like thousands of others in cities and villages throughout France, learned the news when the ringing of church bells replaced the roar of the big guns. She and members of her household went to the balcony overlooking the rue de Varenne and listened to the bells of Ste. Clotilde. Echoed and repeated by bells from other parts of the city, they rang in a "crash of triumph." The war was over. Within weeks, the fighting machine was disassembled, soldiers demobilized, and trenches abandoned. Normal life could begin again.[94]

But what was "normal life" in the wake of this catastrophe? Nine months passed before the last "Children of Flanders" returned to their native land; three years passed before the Maisons de Convalescence were turned over to the Department of Public Hygiene of the Seine-et-Oise region. In the interim, Edith, Elisina, Minnie, and their co-workers mounted new (and more difficult) fund-raising campaigns to sustain operations. The Conference of Paris to draw up peace terms with Germany opened on January 18, 1919, an antagonistic, futile, and ultimately bitter affair. The Germans, whose newly elected democratic government collapsed in the face of the treaty's demands, thought the terms too severe (as indeed they proved to be); the Allies thought the terms too lenient. Berenson, an official observer at the conference, became disillusioned and embittered. Eight million men—an entire generation from Germany, Belgium, France, and Great Britain—lay in graves that would soon bear military crosses. Another six million were missing, eighteen million more were wounded. Russia, which had sustained greater losses than any other country in the three years she participated in the war, had fallen to communism. Economically and politically, the war left Italy in a state of crisis, her government paralyzed.

By the time the Treaty of Versailles was signed on June 28, 1919 (the fifth anniversary of Austrian Archduke Ferdinand's assassination), all parties to the agreement were disenchanted. The United States refused either to ratify the treaty or to support its primary contribution to peace, the League of Nations, the brainchild of President Woodrow Wilson. The treaty officially ending a conflict that was to have ended all wars instead laid the groundwork for another war.

During the final months of conflict, Edith reconsidered questions of national habits and culture, the war having revealed the French in a new light. If her long residence in France had once seemed a matter of chance, *French Ways and Their Meaning* (most of it written in 1917) revealed her commitment to its cultural and political values. Intended to instruct American military men about French mores, the book was chosen by the United States Navy Department for ships' libraries. Opening with a quick—and highly derogatory—sketch of the German people, it then compares and contrasts French traditions to those of a "pioneer people" in the United States. The essays isolate four defining qualities of the French: taste, reverence, continuity, and intellectual honesty. Her book is a shorter, simpler version of two works on France by friends—William Crary Brownell's *French Traits* (1889) and Barrett Wendell's 1907 *The France of Today*, written after his year as visiting lecturer at the Sorbonne in 1904–1905. Edith's opinions parallel those expressed by Brownell and Wendell, especially on the nature of French women, relations between the sexes, and child-raising practices.[95]

She devoted a chapter of her book to "The New Frenchwoman," the woman of the war years, who faced peril with *sangfroid* and who, whatever social class she was born to, had benefited from France's "highly civilised" culture. French women "rule life," make an art of it, and have a purposeful role to play in their society, Edith commented. American women, by contrast, are concerned with trifles, their interests narrow, their manners, taste, ideals, and judgment unformed. She concludes that "only in a civilisation where the power of each sex is balanced by that of the other" is it possible for women and men to grow up—that is, to mature.[96]

Whatever truths about French, German, and American societies emerge in these essays (and there are many), their insights reflect most clearly Edith Wharton's personal values. The key element is intellectual honesty, synonymous with "wisdom" in her vocabulary. Its component elements are fearless self-regard, maturity achieved through courage, the ability to see and accept things as they are, the will to learn, a commitment to self-discipline and principled conviction, and loyalty to established values, however attractive the latest fad might be.

French Ways and Their Meaning received mixed reviews. Virtually every commentator took exception to at least one of her claims. The *Nation* disagreed with her opinion of the intellectual capacities of women and disputed her claim that "intelligent women will never talk together when they can talk to men or even listen to them." This journal also regretted her silence on the growing spirit of internationalism among French workers. This new spirit of international brotherhood fostered by the Bolshevik revolution was not one that Edith Wharton would celebrate. Indeed, she came to fear it. The *New Republic* asked, "Can it be possible that America will survive this apologist and France this defender?" Edith posed a parallel question to Barrett Wendell: "How much longer are we going to think it necessary to be 'American' before (or in contradistinction to) being cultivated, being enlightened, being humane, and having the same intellectual discipline as other civilized countries? It is really too easy a disguise for our shortcomings to dress them up as a form of patriotism!"

ON BASTILLE DAY, 1919, Edith watched from a sixth-floor apartment in the Champs Elysées as the "Great Procession" of the victory parade, a "poet's Vision of Victory," passed below her. She was deeply moved by what she saw—the "perfectly ordered" and solemn majesty of flags, tanks, soldiers marching in rhythm—and could barely express her feelings: "All the while . . . our hearts were choking and bursting with the too-muchness of what it all meant."[97]

Chapter 8

W

PROFITS

O N December 28, 1918, ill with flu brought on
by inadequate heating in her rue de Varenne apartment,
Edith left Paris by motor for the village of Hyères on the
south coast, where she would spend the next four months. She was accompanied by her lady's maid and Robert Norton (ill with pneumonia
and pleurisy), who had recently been released from his wartime work
at the British Admiralty. After a delay in Lyons when chauffeur
Charles Cook suffered an attack of appendicitis, they arrived at the
Hôtel du Parc. The "frowsty" pension-style hotel was decidedly below
her usual standards, but she was traveling inexpensively in deference
to Norton's small income.

Edith had hardly settled in when news came of Theodore Roosevelt's death on January 6 of pneumonia. In poor health for several
years, his last months were spent grieving over the wartime loss of his
youngest son. The news of Roosevelt's death struck a deep chord in
Edith, who mourned "the lost friend and . . . the great leader gone
when he was most needed," as she wrote to his sister Corinne. She
wrote a memorial poem, "With the Tide," which appeared in the
March 29 *Saturday Evening Post*. It drew on an ancient legend described
in Sir James Fraser's *The Golden Bough*: friends gather at the shore at
twilight to escort the dead by boat to the blessed isles. The Mediter-

ranean view from the sunlit hotel terrace no doubt inspired Edith's vision. The golden isles of the Porquerolles in the blue distance beyond Hyères were always to her the islands of the "blessed."[1]

Her daily routine during these weeks varied little. Each morning she worked for two hours on her *Morocco* essays, scheduled to begin in the July *Scribner's Magazine*, while Norton sketched or painted on the hillside. Toward noon, she took a brisk walk, then joined him for a picnic in the pine forests above the Mediterranean. After lunch, they took "dithy rambles" in sun-drenched fields of wildflowers along the sea before returning to the hotel for tea and a light dinner. She quickly recovered her energy and soon was "bustling up and down mountains like an English old maid." The mails to Paris hummed with directives to her charity workers, lists of errands for her household staff, and orders for her shoemaker and couturière.

The couture industry was making a slow but colorful return to life now that cloth dyes were no longer needed for camouflage and fabrics requisitioned for military uses. Choosing designs from newspaper and magazine ads, she asked her tailor and dressmaker to copy them in the fabrics and colors she selected. Gone were the somber gray, blue, and black wools of the war years, when women avoided ostentatious dress. Gone, too, the cinched waists, tufted bosoms, and hourglass shapes of the Belle Epoque. Postwar fashion featured softly draped short skirts (hemlines had risen six inches since 1914) and loose waistlines—a boon to Edith, who, despite illness and food shortages, had gained weight during the war years. No longer endowed with a slim neck and pencil-thin waist, she bought two of the new combination corsets (one in white and one in pink, both with lace trim) and sent her six-strand pearl "dog collar" to be enlarged. Counting and numbering the pearls according to size, she provided precise instructions for restringing the necklace. She also placed an order with Monguignon, her Paris shoemaker, for three pairs of handmade oxfords—two in yellow leather, one in black—and a pair of pearl-encrusted satin mules. Pearls were her favorite jewel, and she twined them in her hair, had them sewn onto wide velvet neck ribbons, embroidered on dresses and tea gowns, and affixed to shoe buckles and combs.[2]

The rue de Varenne apartment, once the symbol of her cultured and elegant French life, now represented the last link to an urban existence she had grown to detest. She hoped to sublet it from February to August, and Gross and White had stayed behind in Paris to supervise preparations for a possible future tenant. The asking price was 60,000 francs for the six-month period (about $6,000), a not unreasonable rate for the size and elegance of the furnished dwelling. Coal shortages made the apartment impractical (and uncomfortable), and no renter appeared. She did not wait to rid herself of number 53 before setting up a new life in the country, where she would write, garden, and entertain friends. Renovation work had already begun on a property she had purchased northwest of Paris, and before leaving Hyères, she would enter into negotiations on a Mediterranean property.[3]

During an afternoon ramble on the heights above the village, she discovered the ruined ramparts and tower of a fourteenth-century château. Built into its crumbling walls was a low, two-storied structure that had once been the convent of the "Clarisses," the order of Sainte Claire. With its "pure Albrecht Durer background," as Norton described it, this group of buildings overlooking the rocky, steep hillside and clustered red-roofed houses below it would become Edith's winter home. Accessible only on foot, its gardens an overgrown wilderness and the two-story pavilion empty for almost a half century, the setting stirred her imagination. Paul and Minnie Bourget, who lived nearby at Costebelle, shook their heads in dismay as she described her plans for gardens, an orchard, an enlarged and modernized house with guest rooms, a stone terrace from which to gaze across the hills and to watch the night sky. By January 1920, Alfred White took up residence in the village to oversee the renovations. The pavilion was gutted, roofs rebuilt, drains installed, a road made through the pine trees, garages and staff residences constructed, and soil imported for twenty-eight terraced gardens that Edith would design. Total costs for the project, which took several years to complete and included acquisition of additional land, came to over 1,000,000 francs, about $60,000. (The dollar had quadrupled in value, from 6 francs during the war to 26 francs in 1925.)[4]

As Edith and Norton stood gazing at the crumbling tower of the château above Hyères, a similar reconstruction process was taking place in the small village of St. Brice-sous-Forêt at the edge of the Montmorency Forest. On a visit to the Groslay convalescent homes early in 1918, Elisina Tyler had stopped in St. Brice to inquire whether the walled estate in the heart of the town was for sale. Like many properties north of Paris, this one had been abandoned during the final advance of the German armies. Tall oaks and elms towered above a deteriorating eighteenth-century pavilion and six acres of tangled, weedy undergrowth. Elisina saw possibilities in the ruin and returned the following day with Edith, who fell in love with the little house. Because properties near the war zone were vastly devalued, Edith was able to buy the domain for 90,000 francs (about $10,000), less than she had paid for her first Park Avenue row house in 1891. It took nearly a year to finalize the purchase and complete restorations; in the meantime, the property had become a symbol of Edith's conviction that the war would end in Allied victory.[5]

St. Brice-sous-Forêt, a village dating from before the Middle Ages, had long served aristocrats from Paris as a country hideaway. The property on which Edith's pavilion stood was originally a dependency of the Château de St. Brice, built at the end of the seventeenth century. The house itself had a rather risqué history that charmed her. It was built as a *folie*, or pleasure house, for actress Marie-Thérèse Colombe. She and her younger sister, Marie-Madeleine, daughters of a wandering Venetian musician named Rombocoli-Riggieri took "Colombe" (dove) as their stage name when, as young adolescents, they joined the Comédie-Italienne in Paris in 1766. The "Pavillon Colombe," as it was called, was the shady retreat to which they brought their lovers for secret assignations. Edith loved the story, believing that it brought her good luck.

In the nineteenth century, aristocratic Parisians came to St. Brice for their health, and at the beginning of the twentieth century, it became a refuge for writers. Edmond Rostand, whose 1910 *Chantecler* had so appalled Edith, was her neighbor in St. Brice, and his sister, Jeanne de Margarie, became a close friend. The town was also the unlikely center of Surrealist thought. From 1920 to 1923, poet Paul Eluard and his wife, Gala, lived near Edith at 3 rue Chaussée, where the movement's leaders—André Breton, Louis Aragon, Robert Desnos, Philippe Soupault, René Crevel, and Max Ernst—met to write, paint, and debate the tenets of one of the most influential artistic movements of the century. Edith was either unaware of (or preferred to ignore) the presence of Eluard and his band of artistic rebels, yet her name and his are coupled today as cultural icons of the village.[6]

In spring 1919, as she came back to life in the Riviera sunshine, all her hopes for a quiet life of writing and gardening were centered on St. Brice. She conceived of a classically ordered space sealed off from the horn-tooting, bustling postwar world. Working from architect's plans on which each room of the house was measured and numbered, she plotted furniture arrangements, made lists of accessories to purchase, and chose wallpaper and slipcovers from samples sent by the Paris firm of Allioli. Her architect, Charles Knight, drew up plans to convert the old stable adjacent to the pavilion into a summer house to provide extra space for guests, and she sketched garden designs to fit the new scheme. By midspring, major structural work on the property was well under way. No record of renovation costs exists, but at Edith's death in 1937, the property was valued at 1,000,000 francs.

On her return to Paris from Hyères in May, she drove out to St. Brice several times a week to supervise the last stages of work. The exterior was covered with scaffolding, and rough boards charted a path from street to house, whose interior was littered with paint pails, ladders, and assorted impedimenta of the reconstruction process. The house was not yet habitable when, on an afternoon in late July, two horse-drawn flatbed wagons from a moving firm owned by Widow Noiret pulled into the rue de Varenne. Four men loaded the carts with furniture, books, linens, and kitchen equipment, and the entourage made its way slowly along the *quai*, north across the river and out of the city by the Porte St. Denis. Edith gave a housewarming party on August 7, but she did not herself move to the country until later in the month, and even then, plasterers and paperhangers were still at work on the upstairs rooms. She left behind in Paris about half of her furniture and a variety of other items, including some of her mother's things and memorabilia from The Mount, which were stored in warehouses or with friends. All this would go to Hyères when the time came.[7]

As THE DREAM of a Mediterranean residence took shape in Edith's mind early in 1919, she wondered how to pay for it. The visit in February by Rutger Bleecker Jewett, an experienced and energetic senior editor at Appleton, was fortuitous. "He knows all about your manuscripts," Joseph Sears, vice president of Appleton, assured her. Jewett had negotiated the sale of serial rights on *Summer*, *The Marne*, and *French Ways and Their Meaning*, and when ill health forced Sears to retire in summer 1919, he was promoted to Sears's position. For the next sixteen years, Jewett devoted himself to advancing Edith Wharton's career, nominating her work for literary prizes and securing for her the largest royalty advances and serial rights contracts then known in American publishing. They met in person for the first time on February 16, 1919, and on no more than a half-dozen occasions thereafter, but their professional collaboration was strengthened by a friendship based on shared literary tastes and political beliefs, and a network of New York friends, including Minnie Jones and Beatrix Farrand. A bachelor a few years younger than Edith, Jewett was descended from an Anglo-Dutch family, and his courtesy and kindness represented the best of that old world. He shared her love of gardening and her appreciation of the rugged beauty of upstate New York and New England. He quickly gained her respect, and in the years ahead, there were only rare moments of tension between them.[8]

"Writing is my business as well as my passion," Edith wrote Minnie early that spring, noting that she had sacrificed business opportunities and writing pleasures to continue her "endless" war work. Indeed, her literary earnings had dropped to an all-time low during the war years, and her trust income was now reduced by a depression in the New York real estate and rental markets. (She confided to Beatrix in autumn 1920 that her combined literary and trust income had dropped in the previous three years from $45,000 to about $18,000, out of which she was paying both French and American taxes.) Minnie's financial situation had become so desperate that she closed her Manhattan house and moved in with Beatrix and Max in New Haven. Edith had hoped that *The Marne*, which had had such a "glorious debut," would sell so well that she could finance Minnie's return to 21 East Eleventh Street. These hopes were dashed when she received her April 1919 royalty report. In four months, the book sold eighty-two hundred copies, earning back about half of the $4,000 advance.[9]

Resistance among readers to war stories occasioned the low sales: "It was almost grotesque to see the aversion which the American public had for purely war literature" after the Armistice, Sears commented. Edith was aware of this reaction. She had sold two pieces of war fiction to American magazines but could interest no one in her proposed essay "How Victory Came to Paris." The war figured so vividly in her mind that she could not turn away from it. In summer 1918, she outlined a novel entitled *A Son at the Front*, a psychological study of an artist father and his son set in wartime France. With four chapters of the book in hand, Sears had been trying to sell the serial rights to this novel since October, without luck. He wanted $15,000 for the contract, but discovered that editors who would pay such a price for something by Edith Wharton did not want a war story. *A Son at the Front* was not a war novel, she maintained, but a study of French-American life in Paris in 1915–1916, "somewhat on the scale of the social studies of The House of Mirth." She changed its title to "Paris" and "Their Son," but still no one wanted it.[10]

Publishers wanted another *House of Mirth*, a modern-day novel of manners that would capture a wide American readership. Edith had signed an $18,000 serial rights contract with the *Pictorial Review* in 1916 for just such a book ("The Glimpses of the Moon"). Having missed several publishing deadlines due to ill health and her war work, she had set aside the project. She now tried to substitute *A Son at the Front* for the story she was pledged to write for the *Pictorial Review*. At first, the magazine's editor, Arthur Vance, agreed to the exchange, and after completing the *Morocco* essays, she devoted herself to *A Son at the Front*, working "like a nigger" at it through the late spring and summer. But when Vance read the later chapters, he changed his mind, telling Jewett that the book did not "possess the suspense and carrying-on quality which the magazine editor always hopes to find in a serial story." He proposed delaying it for one year in the hope that public resistance to war stories would lessen. This piece of bad news was quickly followed by another. Appleton had agreed to pay a $15,000 royalty advance for her next novel. If that novel was *A Son at the Front*, they would have to withdraw the advance. Like other publishers, they hedged their bets against war fiction.[11]

The wartime setting of *A Son at the Front* intensifies the novel's primary themes—art, self-sacrifice, and parental responsibility. The story idea derived, probably, from Pierre-Auguste Renoir's charcoal sketch of his son, wounded at the front, his contribution to *The Book of the Homeless* and considered the most moving image in the collection. Edith dedicated the book to Ronald Simmons, who for her was both war hero and artist. (A painter, he studied at Yale and the Ecole des Beaux-Arts in Paris.) Even though young George Campton, a "son at the front," gives his life for the Allied cause, the story belongs to his father, John Campton, a portrait painter whose artistic struggle has been long and painful. Guilty about the son born of a "stupid ill-fated marriage" that ended in divorce, he repeatedly paints George, and his art portfolio is silent testimony to George's place in his art. The novel ends as Campton begins to sculpt his dead son into art.

A Son at the Front ran in *Scribner's Magazine* from December 1922 until September 1923, when it was published in a first book edition of sixty thousand copies. By this time, the novel seemed to be—in the words of the *Bookman*—"a belated essay in propaganda." The book received a few generous reviews. The *Spectator* called it "deeply affecting," its characters and scenes vividly presented with a "certainty of touch that few living novelists can command"; the *Times Literary Supplement* concluded that although a war novel seemed "dull" and "unnecessary," the day would come when it would have "permanent value among the minor documents of the war"; the *New York Times Book Review* praised its absence of sentiment. But most critics found it not only bad, but egregiously so; no other novel by Edith Wharton was so severely criticized or roundly dismissed.[12]

A Son at the Front had lost the prescience and poignancy of 1919. But in August 1919, with bills from architects, engineers, painters, and tradesmen pouring in, Edith could not afford to lose the $33,000 in literary contracts that the novel represented to her, a sum that at today's rates is almost half a million dollars. Although she objected to delaying publication of the novel, she wisely decided not to fight against it. Instead, she offered *The Age of Innocence*, a novel of Old New York set in the 1870s, to the *Pictorial Review* on the same terms they were to have paid for *Son* ($18,000) and insisted that Appleton pay a $15,000 royalty advance for it. Enclosing the first two chapters of *The Age of Innocence* with her letter of proposal, she agreed to have the novel ready for serialization in spring 1920. In a separate packet, she sent the nearly completed *Son*, asking Jewett to put it in the Appleton safe until further notice.

On September 19, little more than two weeks after she put forth her offer, Jewett wrote to say that he and Vance had agreed to her terms. Their payment and publication schedule, however, required that she submit the first half of the novel in December and the second half a month later, on January 1, 1920, when it was due to begin its serial run. This timetable was clearly impossible, and she asked for an extension of two months for the completed book. They acquiesced; she had won.[13]

THE AGE OF INNOCENCE

In 1918, Edith had begun a journal entitled "Subjects and Notes," in which she recorded story ideas. She outlined there three plots for *The Age of Innocence* and gave brief descriptions of its central characters—a young man from a "very good 'Old New York'" family (Newland

Archer); his fiancée, a charming girl of the same social set (May Welland); and her cousin, Ellen Mingott, a woman in her late twenties, unhappily married to the Polish count Olenski, who returns from Europe to the "simpler life" and "purer atmosphere" of New York. Newland falls in love with Ellen, whom he has known since childhood, and the novel recounts their secret courtship in scenes drawn from Edith's memories of Old New York. The themes and characters of the novel recall two of her earlier works, the 1907 novella *Madame de Treymes*, with its clash of Old Faubourg and Old New York, and her 1912 story, "The Long Run," in which lovers renounce their desires and conform to society's dictates.[14]

The Age of Innocence re-creates a world bound by form and convention. For its large cast of characters, Edith drew freely on her family and friends, mixing and matching their qualities. The most easily recognizable of these are her "old aunt," Mary Mason Jones, re-created as Ellen's grandmother, the aged, obese, and opinionated Mrs. Mingott; and nouveau riche Mrs. Paran Stevens (mother of Edith's fiancé Harry Stevens), satirized in the bewigged and blowsy Mrs. Lemuel Struthers, widow of a shoe polish magnate who had once used her image in his advertising. Edith drew from memory Mary Mason Jones's Upper Fifth Avenue mansion, built in the 1850s, when fashionable New York still lived below Thirtieth Street. After the ancient widow Jones died in 1891, Marietta Stevens bought the Marble Row house, getting her revenge against the family that had snubbed her years earlier.

In the novel, Mrs. Struthers shocks Old New York by giving musical evenings on the Sabbath (just as Mrs. Stevens had done in real life), and Ellen shocks Archer by attending the champagne-and-lobster suppers on the arm of Julius Beaufort—a married man and a Jew. Edith based Beaufort on financier August Belmont (rumored to be Jewish), who kept a mistress in an apartment on Madison Avenue and provided her with a canary-yellow carriage that shocked proper ladies like Lucretia Jones. Aspects of Lucretia appear in three characters: Mrs. Welland, whose smiling placidity masks the strain of coping with her husband's ill health; Mrs. Archer, who mouths Lucretia's opinions about Old New York society; and Louisa van der Luyden, a straitlaced and socially unapproachable matron who is given Lucretia's sobriquet ("Louisa"). Edith even includes a veiled reference to her own amorous past. When Archer visits Paris many years later, he discovers Mme Olenska living in a square west of the place des Invalides. Fullerton had lived there during his years with Mme Mirecourt, while Edith resided on the other side of the *place*, on the rue de Varenne.

Soon after the book began its serial run, Jewett noted that "Society (spelled with a capital `S') is trying to fit familiar New York names to your characters." Edith denied that she had taken her subjects direct from real life, but there are many clear echoes of people and events. Minnie Jones did much of the research for the book in the Yale library, where she consulted a copy of *Society as I Have Found It*, the privately printed memoir of Ward McAllister, self-appointed arbiter of Old New York society. He appears in the novel as Sillerton Jackson, who studies his fellow citizens with "the patience of a naturalist," and as Lawrence Lefferts, who, like McAllister, is a captious philanderer with a curving mustache. "Little did I think I'd ever consult him!" Minnie wrote Edith; "such bosh I never tackled."[15]

Edith "plunged" into writing the novel in late summer 1919, and by November 7, she had sent Jewett its first fifteen chapters (about one-third of the book), promising to send another ten thousand words by the next steamer. She finished the novel toward the end of March 1920, revising its last chapters in Hyères. Despite arduous research and documentation, Edith completed this prizewinning bestseller in little more than seven months, almost as quickly as she had written *The Reef* in 1912. She would never again agree to such a demanding publication timetable. Revising the serialized version for book publication, she regretted that the magazine schedule prevented her from "work[ing] incessantly" on her text, as she usually did. She had had no time to "brood over" it, and a printers' strike made the production program tighter than usual. Some obvious errors, including anachronisms, were not initially caught. Most glaringly, she used the Book of Common Prayer liturgy for the burial of the dead at Newland and May's marriage service. This mistake caused her a sleepless night, but she admitted to a friend that in quoting poetry, prose, or prayer services, she often put down the phrase whose rhythm and cadence fit her sentence. An embarrassed Rutger Jewett remarked to her, "I am not cynical enough to insinuate that perhaps for Archer you selected the correct service after all."[16]

Edith's journal entries for *The Age of Innocence* and letters to Jewett and Minnie outline her creative process and writing methods. Of the three synopses she wrote in her "Subjects and Notes" book, Jewett saw only the final sketch, which closely approximates the published novel.

When he asked for "additional descriptive points," she refused to give them, saying that in her compositional method, "the minor incidents always grow out of the theme as I write."[17]

Such a moment occurred early in the book. Edith wanted to advance the story of Newland's growing interest in the Countess Olenska through a series of Old New York society events. To balance the opening scene, in which the Swedish soprano Christine Nilsson sings *Faust* at the Academy of Music on Fourteenth Street, she needed an evening at the theater. Minnie searched the back files of the *New York Tribune* and sent Edith a list of plays performed in the mid-1870s. Dion Boucicault's *The Shaughraun* had run at Wallack's Theater from November 1874 until April 1875. (Edith, age thirteen, had seen it with her parents.) Minnie recalled the "great love scene" in which the hero—after a sad good-bye to his beloved—turned to see her leaning against the mantelpiece and gazing into the dying fire. Quietly stealing up to her, he lifted one of the ends of the black ribbon around her neck, kissed it, and departed unnoticed. Since most "love-making had been more downright, face to face, this scored," Minnie noted.

As Minnie was describing that long-ago evening at the theater in a letter, Edith was composing the opening of chapter 13: "It was a crowded night at Wallack's Theater." She found it "positively uncanny" that Minnie should have recalled the "black velvet ribbon scene" at the very moment she herself was writing it. She had placed Newland at Wallack's Theater in spring 1875 "for the sake of that particular scene."[18]

"You bring back that time as if it were last week," Minnie remarked on reading the early chapters. But she wondered whether readers would recognize Aunt Mary Mason and August Belmont in their fictional portraits. Walter Berry, more cynically, said it was a good book, "but of course you and I are the only people who will ever read it." They were the last who remembered New York and Newport in those days, he claimed, "and nobody else will be interested." Recalling his discouraging words in her autobiography, Edith admitted to having agreed with him secretly. When the novel was published in late October 1920, they were both proven wrong. The compelling story, set against a perfectly realized background, made it an immediate success. Appleton mounted an aggressive advertising campaign that proclaimed *The Age of Innocence* "the literary treat of the year"; press notices on the book jacket described Edith Wharton as America's "foremost," "greatest," and "leading" novelist.[19]

In the first year, *The Age of Innocence* sold 115,000 copies in America, Canada, and Great Britain; two years after publication, she had earned $50,000 on it, a figure that included a $9,000 Warner Brothers movie contract for a seven-reel silent version of the novel. When Edith learned that Jewett had tried to get $20,000 for the "fillum" rights, she thought it a "preposterous price," but she soon realized that Hollywood could be an important source of income for her. This was the second novel she sold to the movies. In 1918, Metro studios produced *The House of Mirth*, and in her lifetime, five of her works were adapted for film, including a second version of *The Age of Innocence*, produced in 1934 by RKO and starring Irene Dunne, John Boles, and Julie Haydon. She did not see any of these films, nor had she anything to do with their production.[20]

The Age of Innocence had just begun its serial run in the *Pictorial Review* when Arthur Vance asked to be released from his agreement to publish *A Son at the Front*. Edith let him withdraw from the contract, but she set favorable terms for her next novel, *The Glimpses of the Moon*—a delivery date of May 1922 (two years in the future) and a strict schedule of advance payments on the $18,000 serial rights contract. "I fear my terms on the Pictorial may have seemed to you rather grasping," she admitted to Jewett, reminding him that she had written two novels in little more than a year and had as yet been paid for only one. Scribners, eager to have her on their list again, bought the serial rights to *A Son at the Front* for $15,000 and paid her another $15,000 in advance book royalties. It was the last Edith Wharton novel they published.[21]

Vance soon wrote Jewett that *The Age of Innocence* was posing difficulties for his readership. The *Pictorial*, he explained, was a popular magazine, and its subscribers were more "at home" with Kathleen Norris and Booth Tarkington (middle-brow writers). In her next novel, would Mrs. Wharton please divide the story into four parts, each section leading to a climax or "interesting situation that will leave the reader in suspense and eager to get the next issue of the magazine"? He wanted the story to have more than "literary interest"; this could be accomplished, he said, in a "dignified, artistic way." A rather shamefaced Jewett relayed Vance's request to Edith, reminding her that only the Hearst periodicals could match the "topnotch" money the *Pictorial* offered her. Having already protested against cuts that Vance wanted to make in *The Age of Innocence* to save space for illustrations and advertisements for detergents and home cleaning products ("I cannot consent to have my work treated as prose by the yard"), she deliberately ignored his plea for story divisions that would leave the "reader in suspense."[22]

Meanwhile, Appleton's advertising campaign succeeded. The *New York Times* featured a special review by Yale professor William Lyon Phelps. Formerly an outspoken detractor of her work, he now compared Edith Wharton favorably to Joseph Conrad and Henry James and spoke of the "glory" she brought her native country. Henry Seidel Canby struck a similar theme in the *New York Evening Post*, but compared Edith to Jane Austen and Guy de Maupassant, who had studied the "articulate" rather than broad-ranging manifestations of human nature. In the *Nation*, Carl Van Doren noted that she portrayed the rituals of Old New York "as familiarly as if she loved them and as lucidly as if she hated them." At the *Athenaeum*, Katherine Mansfield asked, "Does Mrs. Wharton expect us to grow warm in a gallery where the temperature is so sparklingly cool?" The central characters were, in her opinion, "infinitely dignified," but she wanted their feeling to be "greater than the cause that excites it."[23]

The *Boston Evening Transcript*, which usually praised Edith Wharton's work, turned against this novel. Its "unintelligent and prejudiced" attack on society had hurt its sales in the "quaint village" of Boston, the reviewer said. Appleton decided to "declare war," and inserted ads protesting the review in all the Boston papers, including the *Transcript*. "You can depend upon us," Jewett wrote Edith, "to protect your interests, advertise and feature your books to the very best of our ability." He capped his comforting words with an invitation to submit a "novelette," for which he had a prospective buyer. Six days later, he wrote to say he wanted to enter *The Age of Innocence* in competition for the Pulitzer Prize, and had already sent the entry forms to Minnie Jones.[24]

Edith acted immediately on Jewett's suggestion for a "novelette." She returned to the detailed genealogies of the Mingott and Manson families she had prepared for *The Age of Innocence* with the idea of writing two novellas collectively entitled "Among the Mingotts." She set the first of these, *The Old Maid*, in New York of the 1850s. Built on themes of secrecy, jealousy, and mutual dependency in one of New York's ruling families, the story is one of Edith Wharton's most memorable. Unmarried Charlotte Lovell, a niece of old Mrs. Manson Mingott, had years earlier given birth to a daughter, the product of her secret affair with an impecunious suitor. Her married cousin Delia agrees to raise little Tina, and Charlotte plays the demeaning role of

Tina's old maid aunt. She confides to Delia the identity of the child's father, a man who had once been Delia's lover as well, but whom she rejected in favor of her conventional and socially acceptable husband. The final scene of the tale occurs on the eve of Tina's wedding, when the two women argue about their maternal rights over the bride-to-be, and which of them will give her "mother's counsel" as she faces marriage—an oblique reference to Edith's conversation with Lucretia before her own wedding.

She completed the story early in 1921 in Hyères and read it aloud to Lapsley and Norton as they sat before an olive-wood fire in the evenings. Incorporating their suggestions for revision (and those of the Berensons, who read the story in draft), she sent it to Jewett. The *Ladies' Home Journal* (his prospective buyer) found its subject too "vigorous" and unpleasant. It was rejected, Edith wrote Mary, because of its "immorality." Good fortune with *The Age of Innocence* changed the fate of *The Old Maid*.[25]

The "most satisfactory thing about 'The Age of Innocence,'" Edith wrote Berenson in February 1921, was that it enabled her to "build walls and plant orange-orchards." The extensive renovations and additions to the Hyères property—which she named "Sainte Claire le Château"—would not be completed for some time, but the house was habitable, and under her watchful eye, gardeners were laying out terraces and walkways. The move from Paris had taken place in December, a complicated, costly, and sometimes comic endeavor. A gale had damaged the pavilion roof, causing water leaks that ruined wallpaper, but even this event could not diminish Edith's joy in her new surroundings. The views stretched away to the golden islands of the Porquerolles, and the sky was cerulean blue. In the evening on her terrace, as the scent of an olive-wood fire drifted from the chimney, she watched the "wheeling of the great winter constellations." Walter Berry, meanwhile, was moving into number 53. When her effort to find a tenant ended in failure, he agreed to take over her lease (which had two years to run), and by January 1921, he was shivering in the drafty apartment as he shelved his ten-thousand-volume library of rare books and manuscripts. He admitted to Berenson that "53 hasn't the charm of 14" (his old address on rue St. Guillaume), but he intended to stay in it "till I go out feet first"—which he would do six years later.[26]

Edith was back at the Pavillon Colombe when news came that *The Age of Innocence* had won the Pulitzer Prize for literature, the award to

be officially bestowed at the Columbia University commencement ceremonies in mid-June. Given annually, the prize had been endowed by
the late Joseph Pulitzer, New York journalist, owner of the *World* newspaper (where Edith published her first poem, "Only a Child," in 1879),
and founder of the Columbia University School of Journalism. She was
the first woman to receive the Pulitzer Prize for fiction (first given in
1918), but not the first choice of the committee.[27]

Chaired by Hamlin Garland, the jury included two journalists-
turned-academicians, Robert Morss Lovett (who had a brief tenure as
editor of the *New Republic*, and one of Edith Wharton's severest critics)
and Stuart Pratt Sherman, who would become editor of the *New York
Herald Tribune* book section. The committee had midwestern associations: Garland was born in Wisconsin; Sherman was a former faculty
member at the University of Illinois; and Lovett, a Bostonian, taught
for more than thirty years at the University of Chicago. They represented the westward directions and middle-class sympathies in American fiction over the past fifty years. Lovett and Sherman acknowledged
voting for Sinclair Lewis's *Main Street*, which Lovett considered a living
commentary on the American scene. *The Age of Innocence* was, in his
words, "dead." In 1920, Garland noted in his diary the passing of Old
New York and the "tall, grey eyed, straight-nosed aristocrats of other
years." One of the last representatives of that era and its most important chronicler, Edith Wharton also represented a dying literary
breed—writers born into the New York and Boston upper classes.

Hamlin Garland transmitted the votes to university authorities, and
he may have registered his own sense (as recorded in his diary) that
Lewis's novel was "depressing . . . and vengeful," an attack on small midwestern towns. When the prize was announced, everyone was taken by
surprise. Sherman was so angered that he threatened not to serve on future juries. Lovett openly criticized the decision in a letter to the *New Republic*. He believed that the Columbia Advisory Board had overruled a
unanimous jury recommendation, but he later learned from the secretary
of the Advisory Board, F. D. Fackenthal, that the board was not at fault.[28]

Who (if anyone) on the jury voted for *The Age of Innocence* and how
the award came to be given to Edith Wharton remain a mystery, but
Sinclair Lewis considered himself "robbed" of a prize that he had already
failed to get in 1920 for his novel *Free Air*. He directed his anger at Columbia University rather than Edith Wharton (to whom he sent a letter
of congratulations), but he brooded on the wrong done to him for five

years, planning the letter he would write should he ever be offered the Pulitzer Prize. By the time he won it in 1926 for *Arrowsmith*, he and Edith were friends; indeed, he had dedicated *Babbitt* to her, and she was greatly pleased by his gesture. She held Lewis's work in high regard ("He really *is* an artist," she told John Hugh Smith), although she advised him to use slang "more sparingly" in dialogue.

Lewis's refusal of the Pulitzer was a media event, extracts from his carefully composed letter appearing in all the major American papers. He sent back the $1,000 honorarium, which Edith had spent on her Ste. Claire gardens. He convinced her (and a few others) that literary prizes were a bad thing and that she should be suspicious as well of literary organizations, such as the Authors' League—which she refused to join, considering it a "union."[29]

She knew nothing about the Pulitzer Prize when she won it, and later expressed dismay that it was awarded for "uplifting American morals." (According to Joseph Pulitzer's will, the prize was for the novel judged to "best present the wholesome atmosphere of American life and the highest standard of American manners and manhood.") Her "disgust was added to despair," she wrote Lewis, when she learned that *Main Street* had presumably been rejected because it had offended "prominent persons" in the Midwest. She joked, not a little disparagingly, that the Pulitzer was the "Virtue Prize." She did not attend the award ceremony, but the publicity surrounding the event spurred the editor of *Red Book* to accept *The Old Maid*, which sold for a remarkable $7,500 (minus the Appleton agent's fees)—"a price beyond my dreams, if not of Avarice," Edith wrote Mary Berenson.[30]

IN SPRING AND summer 1921, Edith worked on *The Glimpses of the Moon,* completing this short novel in mid-September, nine months ahead of her own contractual deadline. On September 17, she wrote Berenson, "For the first time in three years I've stopped working, and working against time." The next day, she departed for a two-week trip to England—her second visit there since the war's end. Henceforth, a fortnight in England, during which time her staff took a paid vacation, was a regular event on her summer calendar. She visited friends, beginning with Robert Norton, now the resident custodian of Lamb House, where the "sense of the Master" still lingered among "gayety, life, activity." At Trinity College, Cambridge, where Lapsley tutored in medieval history, she passed an evening with A. E. Housman, professor of Latin, whose poetry she admired. John Hugh Smith accompanied her on a country weekend to Hill Hall, the home of her friend Mary Hunter. Queen's Acre at Windsor, once a regular stopping point on her compass, existed only in memory. After Howard Sturgis's death in 1920, the house fell into other hands. At the end of the war, feeling the weight of her losses (especially the absence of Henry James), she had told Lapsley that she might never return to England. But it drew her back, and the remaining members of the "inner circle" (Lapsley, Norton, and John Hugh) were all the more precious to her.[31]

On her return to France, she answered Jewett's request for a novella to pair with *The Old Maid* for book publication. Before the year was out, she had begun *New Year's Day*, a tale of New York in the 1870s and one that drew on her own memories and on Minnie's research for *The Age of Innocence*. She finished it in mid-February 1922, and by April, Jewett had sold it to *Red Book* for $6,000. These prices took her breath away, especially since in real income, her literary earnings were enhanced by a strong dollar. During the war, the French franc had held relatively steady at six and seven to the dollar; by early 1922, the franc was fifteen to the dollar and losing ground. The war had devastated the French economy, making it impossible for France to meet the schedule of war debt repayments to the United States, a matter that caused riots in Paris and attacks against American tourists. The French currency was in free fall, and by 1925, it would drop to twenty-six to the dollar. In May 1922, she wrote Jewett to ask for a larger advance royalty on *The Glimpses of the Moon* than they had agreed to ($15,000). She wished to "profit by the exchange": "I know that I can get practically any advance royalty I like from other publishers," she added.[32]

A writer who lived by the pen and knew her literary worth, Edith capitalized on the current business climate. Jewett did not take exception to her request. His salesmen in the field—from New England to the Mississippi Basin to the Pacific Coast—reported excellent advance sales of *Glimpses*, and he agreed to an additional advance on royalties. He also sent her a descriptive list of six American magazines that paid "top-notch" prices. The *Ladies' Home Journal* could never print "anything that deals too frankly with the sex problem." The *Saturday Evening Post* could tolerate "more frankness," but did not have as much freedom in this matter as did *Red Book* and *Pictorial Review*. The *Woman's Home Companion* was "not afraid of sex when handled in a serious way, especially if some moral lesson is included," but the *Delineator* (where Edith would begin to publish in 1928) was almost as "restricted in choice of stories" as the *Ladies' Home Journal*. Karl Harriman, editor of *Red Book*, accepted *New Year's Day,* although he found it a "trifle strong for home circulation." He hoped that her next work would be "less strong in theme." "If the story is too frank," Jewett wrote, "it means letters of protest and loss of subscribers."

Jewett's role as middle man between an author whose themes focused ever more directly on controversial moral issues and editors of magazines who were (in his words) "victims of the bromidic taste and the moral tremors of our dear reading public" was not an easy one. He couched his warnings to Edith about the moral and intellectual climate of postwar America in diplomatic terms: "Perhaps it is difficult for you to sense the limitations which bind the magazine editor." The taboo topic was sex.[33]

Middle-class America, Edith Wharton's primary reading public in the 1920s, denounced extramarital sexuality in the same tone as does the narrator's mother in *New Year's Day*: "She was *bad* . . . always. They used to meet at the Fifth Avenue Hotel." In this opening sentence, Edith captured the "hiss" of Lucretia Jones's "uncharitable words" when she spoke of George Alfred Jones; she also invoked the ghost of Mrs. Paran Stevens, whose husband had once owned the Fifth Avenue Hotel. A New Year's Day fire at the hotel sends its occupants—many of them ladies who wear full décolletage and short sleeves in midafternoon—running into the streets. Gathered at Grandmamma's house on West Twenty-third Street (which faces the elegant white marble hotel), the Parrett family watches in horror as Mrs. Lizzie Hazeldean, a respectable society matron, flees the burning structure with Henry Prest, a wealthy bachelor who in looks and demeanor resembles a young Walter Berry. At this sight, the dead silence among the men in the family drawing room is broken by the gasps and "Ohs!" of the women.

Mrs. Hazeldean must be banished from society. But her loss of place in the Old New York world is not the primary subject of the tale, which focuses instead on how she came to marry Charles Hazeldean— who dies from a lingering heart ailment the very night of the hotel fire—and why she became involved with Henry Prest. Like Lily Bart, she had been left in her youth to fend for herself, after her father—a popular rector of a fashionable church—had been forced to leave town when rumors circulated that he was on too easy terms with some of his lady parishioners. His wife, "crushed" by the blow, later died. (The Reverend and Mrs. Arcadius Winter are comic versions of the scholarly and very proper Reverend E. A. Washburn of Calvary Church and his wife.) When Lizzie returns to New York penniless, taken in by an aunt jealous of her looks and youth, she marries Charles Hazeldean, a bookish, distinguished man considered a prize catch.

Six years after their marriage, he falls ill and is forced to give up his law practice. Lizzie's reasons for the affair with Prest are neither sentimental nor sexual. They are economic: she invests the money Prest gives her. He is aghast to learn the real reasons for their liaison, his pride wounded by her confession that she acted out of love for her husband. She refuses to marry Prest after her husband's death. Living alone, and ignoring the comments of society ladies, she gathers around her interesting and intellectual young men who remind her of her youthful dead husband. By the story's end, some fifteen years after the Fifth Avenue Hotel fire, Lizzie Hazeldean has established in Old New York a life that distantly mirrors the one Ellen Olenska in *The Age of Innocence* created on the Paris Left Bank.

New Year's Day recapitulated familiar themes of Edith Wharton's writing and interweaved versions of her family and friends. She herself appears as the young male narrator (a boy of twelve on the New Year's Day of the fire), and her voice condemns both "modern" attitudes toward women and old society prejudices: "Among the young women now growing up about me I find none with enough imagination to picture the helpless incapacity of the pretty girl of the 'seventies, the girl without money or vocation, seemingly put into the world only to please, and unlearned in any way of maintaining herself there by her own efforts." Of the friends who appear in cameo in the story, Bay Lodge is the book-loving Charles Hazeldean, who dies before he can reach middle age, and Lizzie Hazeldean has aspects of Bessy Lodge's strength, beauty, and fidelity. Just as Edith was beginning to write *New Year's Day*, she and Walter visited Bessy in Brittany in August 1921, where she was on holiday with her children. She described Bessy to Berenson as a "marsupial seraph—marsupial because [she is] so primitively made, and always carrying her children in her pouch." In Edith's story, Lizzie Hazeldean carries her husband—even after his death—in this same primitive, protective way.[34]

NEW WORLDS AND OLD SECRETS

The Glimpses of the Moon, the "House of Mirth" type of story Edith had begun in 1919 but put away to write *The Old Maid*, takes a thoroughly modern attitude toward marriage. As she explained to Berenson, it was a love story about "a young couple who believe themselves to be completely *affranchis* [emancipated] and up-to-date, but are continually tripped up by obsolete sensibilities and discarded ideals." It was a "difficult subject," she admitted, "which of course seemed the easiest in the world when I began it." Susy Branch and Nick Lansing, children of socially prominent New York families, are penniless. He has literary interests; she earns her keep as a companion to rich women. They marry for love, but agree that should either get a "better chance" (someone rich), each is free to leave without regret. Meanwhile, they live on the margins of high society and on the largesse of wealthy friends.[35]

Generally dismissed by critics today, *The Glimpses of the Moon* was widely reviewed when it appeared on July 21, 1922, wrapped in a book jacket that promoted it as a "novel of society to-day." The inside front flap of the dark-blue jacket displayed a cameo portrait of Edith Wharton, made in Paris in 1921. The last formal portrait she would have made, it reveals a woman considerably aged since the war years. Sad-eyed, even somber, she is dressed in décolletage and the fur-draped formality of the 1870s, seed pearls woven through her hair. Beneath it, an advertising encomium proclaimed *The Glimpses of the Moon* as the "finest flowering" of Edith Wharton's literary talent—"the perfectly wrought story, the notable gift for characterizations, the ability to depict a situation and wring from it every atom of truth." Notice of the Pulitzer Prize and a list of praiseworthy comments about *The Age of Innocence* completed the promotion.[36]

No critic dared to dismiss out of hand the novel that followed *The Age of Innocence*, although reviewers both in New York and London expressed reservations. Katharine Fullerton Gerould, in a thoughtful and highly praiseworthy essay in the *New York Times Book Review*, praised the "reality" (realism) of the Nick-Susy love story and the architectonics of its plot, the absence of sentimentality, and Edith Wharton's "masculine" sense of humor. (Edith told Jewett that she "deserved" a "good word" from Katharine for having brought her to the attention of Scribners in 1910.) Other reviews were more circumspect. Henry Seidel Canby thought the book neither as amusing, picturesque, nor important as *The Age of Innocence*, but he found its theme "sharper and simpler," its moral problems well conceived, beautifully balanced, and skillfully developed. Carl Van Doren praised her for handling a theme that other novelists might have used to illustrate the maxim that love reforms morals. Wilson Follett, writing for the *Atlantic Monthly*, said the book was either a "promise of new powers or the collapse of old ones"; he preferred to take *Glimpses* as promissory of Edith Wharton's maturing genius.[37]

There was a collective voice of dissent against these opinions, however; younger writers and literary critics in New York and London called the book lifeless. Acknowledging that it was written with "supreme accomplishment," Rebecca West called it a "dead thing" (a comment that echoed the Pulitzer Prize jury). She pointed to two adverse circumstances that had restricted Edith Wharton's literary development: she was born in America at a time when artistic "novelty" was unfashionable (an astute observation), and she was content to write books in the Jamesian mode that did not extend "humanity's knowledge of itself." West shared with most other writers of her generation the assumption that Edith Wharton's failings stemmed from her mimicry of Henry James—who, in the postwar years, symbolized for young moderns all that they hoped to overthrow.

Gilbert Seldes entitled his review for the *Dial* "The Altar of the Dead": Susy and Nick were pale ghosts of Lily Bart and Lawrence Selden. "In her failure to suggest the richness of life, and in the refusal to render the passion of love, Mrs. Wharton has left her work empty." He felt cheated by the "watered wine of her plot." Ruth Hale in *Bookman* called *Glimpses* a "gaudy thing with no sincerity whatever"; it was a "puppet show." J. Middleton Murry, writing for *Nation and Athenaeum*, was kinder than some others of his generation: the book was interesting but not worth rereading—"the standard that really good books must meet." The *Times Literary Supplement* remarked that it was "slight" and the major characters "algebraical symbols."[38]

From his office on West Thirty-second Street in Manhattan, Jewett observed dryly, "The Young intellectuals . . . like young terriers worrying a muff, have lashed themselves into a rage over your novel." Critics had always taken Edith Wharton to task for concerning herself with frivolous, shallow society types who seemed unworthy of her interest or the skill with which she delineated them, but the debate now focused on what H. W. Boynton called "negative realism"—subjects and situations drawn from a modern society so artificial, alien, and empty that it was difficult, if not impossible, to invest the story with the necessary emotional and moral force to give it meaning. Virtually every postwar writer faced this problem. As Edith read reviews of her book, she was also reading recent fiction from England, America, and France to settle this question for herself.[39]

Because it captured the 1920s spirit, the story of Nick and Susy was a runaway bestseller, selling sixty thousand copies within three weeks of publication. The film rights sold for $15,000 to Paramount in late August 1922, and Jewett sold *The Age of Innocence* to Warner Brothers. Edith was considering a sequel to *The Age* that would take up the story of young Dallas Archer and his wife, Fanny Beaufort. Some in the publishing industry were already recommending that she do a sequel to *The Glimpses of the Moon*, and for several weeks in summer 1922, *McCall's* magazine and the *Pictorial Review* were in a bidding war for her next novel. *McCall's* outbid Arthur Vance at the *Pictorial*, but he matched their offer ($27,000 after agent's fees) so that she would not lose money. The battle over, he remarked wearily to Jewett, "I do wish Mrs. Wharton would regard herself as one of the Pictorial Review family."[40]

Appleton mounted a strenuous advertising campaign for *The Glimpses of the Moon*. Five weeks after its publication, they placed a notice entitled "Silence is Approval" in *Publisher's Weekly*. A dramatic block chart compared advance sales and reorders on *Glimpses* and *The Age of Innocence*. The later novel was shown to have outsold the earlier book three to one during the first month of publication. Jewett enclosed the *Publisher's Weekly* ad in a letter to Edith and reported that Appleton had flooded Los Angeles and Hollywood newspapers with advertisements to create a demand for film rights to her works. She penned a note in the margin: "Left matter entirely in Mr. Jewett's hands." Two years after they had begun working together, she had great confidence in his judgment, and seemed pleased rather than embarrassed by Appleton's aggressive advertising methods. She would soon complain, however, that Appleton's London house did not energetically promote her books.[41]

In mid-September, Jewett reported that Somerset Maugham might dramatize *Glimpses*. Edith was skeptical, and indeed the project was never taken up. In April 1923, however, a seven-reel silent film version opened in major American cities to enthusiastic reviews. It starred Bebe Daniels as Susy Lansing, David Powell as Nick, and Nita Naldi and Maurice Costello as Mrs. and Mrs. Vanderlyn, a millionaire couple in a troubled marriage. F. Scott Fitzgerald—promising young chronicler of the Jazz Age—earned $500 by writing the film's dialogue, but his script apparently was not used; the screenplay is credited to Lloyd Shelton and Edfrid Bingham. In 1922, Edith earned nearly $60,000 in royalties, serial and film rights for *Glimpses*, to which she added another $10,000 from sales of some short stories and the novella *False Dawn*, the third of the Old New York stories, which *Ladies' Home Journal* had purchased for $5,500.[42]

In September 1922, shortly after she signed over serial rights to the *Pictorial Review* for her next novel, Vance began to push for delivery of a finished manuscript by autumn 1923. Vance was "deluded," she wrote Jewett, if he thought she could—or would—produce a new novel within a year. She was only now beginning to consider the subject of her new work, which would be *The Mother's Recompense*, and insisted on an autumn 1924 delivery date. Meanwhile, she had completed half of *False Dawn*, a story of the 1840s about a young art connoisseur on the Grand Tour. *A Son at the Front* was due to begin in the December *Scribner's Magazine* and would appear in book form in September 1923. Jewett wanted to issue her three novellas (there would eventually be a fourth) as a set. She asked that Appleton schedule the publication so as not to compete against Scribners. Having finally found a publisher for *A Son at the Front*, which she sold for almost as much money as the *Pictorial* had originally agreed to pay for it, she was in a mood to be generous. "I am in the happy position of an author who has received only consideration and kindness from her successive publishers," she wrote Jewett, "and I am most anxious to make the same return to you both."[43]

BY 1922, EDITH had established a predictable routine in her rural life, dividing her time between the Pavillon Colombe (June–November) and Ste. Claire (December–May). After a two-year search for a pied-à-terre in Paris ended in failure, she made the Hôtel de Crillon her temporary residence during the two weeks each November required for her staff to close up the St. Brice house and move to Hyères. She packed those two weeks with business appointments, social engagements, and shopping. In the spring, while her staff prepared the Pavillon Colombe for her arrival, she traveled in Spain or Italy (taking in

Salso or I Tatti, or both), arriving at St. Brice in time to see her rose garden come into bloom. Her "little" houses provided settings for a life that was ever more focused on literary activities.

To her permanent household staff of seven, she added seasonal staff—kitchen helpers, footmen, and gardeners. By the 1920s, those servants who had been with her longest were ready either for retirement or promotion. In autumn 1921, Charles Cook, her chauffeur for twenty years, had a slight stroke. The doctors warned that he must never again drive professionally. This was a blow to a man in his midforties and a "tragedy" to Edith, who was deeply saddened by his illness. He took a long paid holiday and in 1922, Edith gave him the old Hotchkiss motor she had purchased secondhand during the war and pensioned him off. Returning to western Massachusetts, he wrote several times a year, keeping her apprised of events in Berkshire County. An Englishman named Franklin (outfitted in Savile Row livery) replaced Cook. He kept Edith's four motorcars in good running condition—a new Panhard, a new Morgan, and, soon, a Torpedo Delage and a Peugeot. Catherine Gross was, at seventy-two, still a central figure in the household, although she had retired from service and no longer traveled with Edith. She had promoted Alfred White, age fifty-five, to "general agent" for her estates, and a Frenchman named Favre replaced him as butler.

Central to Edith's literary and business enterprises was Jeanne Duprat, a young Parisian who since 1917 had typed her manuscripts and handled her correspondence. Several days a week, she took a train through the working-class suburbs northwest of Paris to the village of Sarcelles, the station nearest St. Brice-sous-Forêt, where Edith's chauffeured motorcar waited to bring her to the Pavillon Colombe. After a day of typing, filing, telephoning, sorting mail, and paying bills, Mlle Duprat returned to Paris with a thick folder of blue, unlined stationery sheets on which Edith drafted her fiction. She transcribed this work at home on her Remington typewriter, sometimes typing as many as a half-dozen revisions of a novel.

During Edith's winter months at Hyères, all this work was done by mail. Mlle Duprat did not admit to disliking the Riviera climate and Ste. Claire le Château (although Edith sensed her feelings); instead, she used her mother's ill health as an excuse to remain in Paris. Only after prolonged negotiations did Edith succeed in convincing Mlle Duprat (by then a married woman) to spend a few weeks each winter in

Hyères. For several years, however, Edith endured the considerable in-convenience of having her secretary at long distance for half the year. Why she tolerated this situation, we do not know. Certainly, Mlle Duprat worked hard, was extraordinarily reliable, dealt efficiently with the complications of postwar French life, and relieved Edith of many routine tasks. Beyond the polite, but cool, tone in which Edith spoke of her in letters to friends, few clues exist to her real feelings about her secretary. Although Mlle Duprat was with her for twenty years, she never entered the charmed circle of affection that Edith reserved for Gross, Elise, White, and Charles Cook.[44]

Behind her energy, productivity, and manifest happiness at having established a life that suited her tastes and temperament, Edith felt a deep sense of loss in the postwar years. Country living had a salutary effect on her own health, but the roll call of her dead continued to sound. In 1919, Isch Wall, her Paris physician, died of anemia, and Renée Landormy, the young woman who had managed Edith's *ouvroir*, died of heart failure. In January 1920, Howard Sturgis died of cancer. Gone, too, were Eliot Gregory and Robert Minturn, Edith Fairchild and Margaret Rutherfurd White—all of them friends from the New York–Boston–Newport days. Early in 1921, she lost Barrett Wendell, whose literary and cultural studies she admired. ("The last of the tradi-tion we care for," she told Berenson, who had been his student at Har-vard.) Six months later, she suffered a loss from a different quarter: Numa Herrewynn, one of the four children of a refugee family she pro-vided for, fell ill with typhoid. He battled the illness for six months, and died in June, a few days before his eleventh birthday, at the hospice St. Michel in Poperinghe, Belgium, where he had lived with his older brother Albert since the war. Recalling her own childhood battle with typhoid, Edith kept in close contact with the mother superior about his condition. Distressed at the news of his death, she intended to go to Poperinghe herself. When that proved impossible, she arranged to bring the Herrewynn family together in northern France for his funer-al. She paid for Numa's burial and purchased a headstone for his grave. In October 1921, three months after Numa's death, she took legal re-sponsibility for the education of his three remaining brothers.[45]

The year 1921 brought more deaths. Nannie Wharton died, leaving her part of the family estate to the grown children of her brother, the late William Wharton. Teddy had been for some time in the care of a nurse; Edith wrote him a condolence letter on his sister's death, but received no answer. Rosa de Fitz-James, her neighbor in the Faubourg, was diagnosed with cancer and died, after terrible suffering, in 1923. Edith wrote Minnie Jones about her early days in Paris: "I hardly went anywhere but her house," and "her kindness from the first was unvarying." In summer 1922, Sally Norton died of cancer at her home in Cambridge. Three weeks later, news came that Edith's brother Harry had died on August 14. He was the last connection to her parental family; she confided to Berenson her "sadness at the years of lost affection and companionship, and all the reawakened memories of youth."[46]

Her sharpened interest in family relations and human sexuality, the "strong" themes of illegitimacy, extramarital liaisons, and incest that editors of family magazines wanted her to tone down, were linked to events rumored to be part of her own history. Harry's death left her with the bitter mystery of his anger and also with a set of unanswered questions about sibling and parental relations in their family—questions that became *données* for her fiction. She had first written of illegitimacy and infidelity in 1894 ("That Good May Come"), and these themes continued to appear with regularity. But from *Summer* (1917) until the mid-1920s, they recurred with marked intensity.

Sometime after her divorce, perhaps in the interval between Frederic Jones's death in June 1918 and Harry's death in August 1922, Edith learned of the rumor about her paternity—that she was the child of her mother's affair with the Englishman who had tutored Frederic and Harry in the late 1850s. Matilda Gay, Edith's childhood friend and later her Faubourg neighbor, told Elisina Tyler of the rumor in summer of 1937, as Edith was dying. It was not *what* Edith had learned that so surprised her, but rather *how* she came to know it, Matilda said. She may have heard the story by accident from any of the sons and daughters of New York families who joined the charity effort in Paris during the war, or the tale may have circulated along with other gossip about her during the months in 1918 when competition among the Paris charity organizations was particularly fierce. Possibly, she heard the rumor during a visit to her brother Harry on a Sunday in autumn 1920. Susy Gray, an old friend, arranged the meeting, and it ended disastrously.[47]

Returning to Paris from that trip, Edith wrote Fullerton, "My day yesterday at Compiègne can only be described by saying that I *drank mud*, and came back heart-sick with the hopelessness of doing anything for my poor poor brother." The general circumstances of this visit were confirmed in a 1962 letter from Edith's cousin Frederic Rhinelander

King to writer Louis Auchincloss. She had told King of a "painful visit" to Harry when he was very ill and living in a "squalid bourgeois apartment" with the mistress he had by then married, a woman whose "parsimony" (in King's words) "deprived him of proper comfort [in order] to store up a cache of Louis d'or."[48]

Edith deplored the circumstances in which Harry lived in his last years. Apart from a chance encounter in Paris, when he gave the impression of being "enslaved and silenced," the visit to Compiègne was her only face-to-face meeting with him in the years of their estrangement. She knew that he had changed his will to favor the countess Tekla and her daughter, his "niece" to whom he gave financial support. (This young woman had been born out of wedlock, but Edith was uncertain whether Harry himself was her father.) In changing his will, he disinherited Edith and his niece, Beatrix Farrand. Among the bitterness Edith swallowed that day may have been the accusation that she was not George Frederic Jones's daughter and therefore not entitled to Harry's portion of his legacy. The news, if it indeed came on that fateful Sunday, was probably delivered by the countess Tekla rather than Harry, who withdrew into silence and illness.[49]

For reasons probably associated with legal matters, Harry Jones's funeral took place two months after he died. In the interim, his widow sailed to New York to meet with Herman Edgar, the Jones cousin who served as family accountant and trustee. At these meetings, she spoke against Edith and Minnie, co-owners with Harry of several Manhattan properties. When she returned to Paris, an elaborate funeral was held on October 13 in the American Pro-Cathedral on the avenue George V. Edith attended the "ghastly performance," accompanied by Walter Berry and Susy Gray. The coffin, covered with a "pall of wired carnations," stood in front of the altar, and the church was full of people Edith did not recognize. She sat in the front pew, opposite the woman she called the "Bereaved One," but refused Dean Frederick Beekman's invitation to join a small reception in the sacristy following the service. The widow left the church sobbing, and Edith—flanked by Walter and Susy—departed down the long central aisle, making certain the few Americans among the mourners saw that she was present. "Then *that* book closed for me," she wrote Trix.

The book, of course, was not closed. Edith was now the sole survivor of George Frederic and Lucretia Jones, yet everything that Harry had kept of their parents—family portraits, mementos, the silver service, and his portion of the inheritance—was left to the countess Tekla. When she died in 1928, the countess was buried in the family mausoleum in Cannes. Lucretia Jones, who in life had turned in disgust at the idea of divorce, lay in death beside her sons' second wives, women of questionable repute. Only by legal maneuverings did Edith finally retrieve a few souvenirs and the Jones family portraits from Tekla Jones's estate.[50]

The rumor that Edith was the daughter of her brothers' tutor was not the only one circulating about her paternity. The tale of Lord Brougham also made the rounds: Marian Bell recounted it to Ogden Codman, who repeated it in a 1926 letter to his brother. Only the tutor story reached Edith's ears, however, and her childhood friend Daisy Chanler was convinced that she believed it. They had once driven through an English village together, she said, and Edith commented, "My father was born here." Daisy told her daughter, Hester Pickman, that in her periods of anti-Americanism after the war, Edith declared herself pleased that her father was English. Beatrix Farrand in her old age confirmed that Edith had known the story but had "realized the entire unlikelihood of a happening of this sort." Given the family's efforts to hide the scandal of Frederic's infidelities, however, Beatrix had every reason for wishing to dismiss the rumor of her aunt's parentage. The fictional portraits Edith painted of her family in the early 1920s— stories she described to Minnie Jones as "left-over reminiscences picked up from Mamma, grandmamma, and Egerton [Winthrop]"—cast a questioning glance over the supposedly harmonious relations of the Jones family.[51]

False Dawn, a novella Edith began writing in the weeks between Harry's death and his burial, satirizes connoisseurship and society attitudes toward art. Berenson's ideas hover on the edges, but the story satirizes Lucretia Jones's taste for Italian landscape paintings and "morality" pictures. The opening scene is a page from George Frederic's courtship of Lucretia. At the dawn of their relationship, when love was young, Lewis Raycie rigs his bed quilt to the mast of his boat and sails up Long Island Sound on a summer morning for a secret meeting with his love, Beatrice Kent, a poor and not very pretty orphan of distant cousins. (Lucretia was not an orphan, but as a young woman, she was poor and not very pretty.) The silvery dawn promises much that the events of their lives later deny, but through all their travails, the couple remain faithful to one another.

In contrast, *The Spark*, a novella set in the 1860s (when Lucretia was supposed to have been playing the unfaithful wife), paints a malicious portrait of the card-playing, sexually promiscuous Leila Delane, mother of two teenage sons and a little girl, who takes holidays from her maternal duties to pursue younger men—polo players and Italian counts—at Newport. While society gossips, her husband turns a blind eye to her tawdry and pathetic intrigues. The satire of Lucretia as unfaithful spouse is too broad to be successful, but the anger and derision that fuel the characterization of Leila/Lucretia are palpable.

When the four stories appeared in a boxed set under the collective title *Old New York*, reviewers were divided between those who extolled the technical perfection of these tales and those who dismissed them as "unreal" and lacking historical authenticity. Calling Edith Wharton the John Singer Sargent of American fiction, Edmund Wilson hinted that, as with the great portrait painter, success had made her self-satisfied: "As time goes on [she] seems to become more and more willing to deal facilely with her subjects." John Jay Chapman (brother-in-law of Daisy Chanler) wrote in the *Atlantic Monthly* that Edith's characters were "staged rather than studied," the historical coloring "inaccurately splashed in." Other critics, however, saw beneath the stylized surface of the stories to a disturbing underside. Edwin Edgett of the *Boston Evening Transcript* called them "hole-in-the-corner stories"; the author's words "eat like acid into the souls of her personages." L. P. Hartley said her art had an "affinity with blackmail" (effective only when it threatens, but "refrains from damaging disclosures"). No one, he said, conveyed more admirably than Edith Wharton the "intimate discomfort of a false and tainted relationship."[52]

In spring 1921, while Edith was at work on these tales, her niece, Beatrix, underwent minor uterine surgery, a procedure that frightened her and that, according to Minnie, turned her "odd." Edith responded to this remark with her most acute, and certainly her most disconcerting, observation on family resemblances among the Joneses: "I've always felt in [Beatrix], since she was a girl, a mysterious impenetrability, a locked room full of bats and darkness—as I did in Mamma, whom Fred so much resembled." Beatrix Farrand's "mysterious impenetrability" displayed itself in her later life in a firm jaw and intractable nature. But her forbidding Old New York demeanor masked adolescent insecurities: a perfectionist, she repeatedly described herself in letters to Edith as "stupid," "silly," and "idiotic," and often worried that by some oversight she had offended her aunt. Despite the sometimes childlike tone of Beatrix's letters, Edith remarked to Minnie that she seemed "many years older than you and I are."[53]

AT SOME UNSPECIFIED time in the postwar years, Edith wrote a plot summary of a story for a volume called "Powers of Darkness." The volume never materialized and the story, entitled "Beatrice Palmato," was never written. The plot summary and a dramatized scene of father-daughter incest (labeled "unpublishable fragment") were among the papers included in Edith Wharton's literary estate. Historical and literary reference for the fragment is Beatrice Cenci, the sixteenth-century Roman woman sexually abused by her father, whose story Percy Bysshe Shelley told in one of Edith's favorite dramas, *The Cenci*. The family background includes the suicide of an older daughter and the mother's madness and death. After the death of his wife, the father—a handsome, rich Levantine-Portuguese banker in London—takes special interest in his daughter, Beatrice, but his sexual relations with her do not begin until after she is married and the mother of two young children. She takes a trip with him to Paris and returns "brilliant, febrile and restless." The story fragment reveals what happens when she visits him in London.[54]

The seduction scene powerfully dramatizes female sexuality, infusing it with an exoticism more Oriental than European. Palmato's London apartment combines elements of a Parisian *maison close* with a North African brothel. The surroundings in which Beatrice throws off the "dull misery of her marriage" are sensual—a "deep divan," a "lustrous black bear-skin rug," velvet cushions strewn on the floor, the heat of the fire and the pink of low lamps. A Levantine (Edith's word for "Jewish" in her fiction), Palmato both attracts and repels by his exotic otherness. He achieves power over his daughter by guiding her to the pleasures of her own body. Beatrice vibrates, writhes, swoons, and swells under the touch of his hands and tongue. He brings her to orgasm, calling her his "little girl." When Beatrice Palmato returns to the country from London and watches her husband kiss their daughter, she sees the "incest vision." Screaming, "Don't kiss my child," she unwittingly gives him the clue to "many mysterious things" in their married life. She then runs to her bedroom and shoots herself.[55]

Much has been written about this fragment in the twenty years since it was first made public. Its Orientalism looks back to Edith's 1914 trip to Tunisia and Algeria, when she took a frank interest in the eroticism of Eastern cultures, and of her 1917 trip to Morocco, when she observed lethargic concubines awaiting the sultan and saw fear in the eyes of young girls who were sold into prostitution. The cultivated and charming Palmato bears a certain resemblance to Morton Fullerton, but the name "Palmato" has led some critics to connect the story with an early scene in Edith's memoir, *A Backward Glance*, in which she and her father walk up Fifth Avenue in the winter, her hand enclosed in the "large safe hollow" (the "palm") of his "bare hand." They suggest that "Beatrice Palmato" reveals Edith's repressed erotic longings for her father ("and now his warm palms were holding each breast as in a cup"). Some critics claim that Edith was, in fact, the victim of father-daughter incest; others assert that her affair with Fullerton unleashed her sexuality. Although the "unpublishable fragment" opens itself to endless interpretation, its passionate eroticism seems to undercut the likelihood that it was composed by an incest survivor. Nor is there verifying evidence from Edith's personal life to support the claim that she was sexually abused, either by her father or her brothers. It is difficult to imagine, however, that Edith could have scripted the scene of Beatrice's seduction without having on some occasion experienced her own body in similar ways, and Fullerton's comments suggest that she did in summer 1909.[56]

WOMAN OF LETTERS

Early in 1923, Edith received the news that Yale University wanted to offer her an honorary doctor of letters. It was "the one sort of honour I have ever imagined that could please me," she wrote Berenson, "because I have so loved Letters all my days." In future years, Columbia and Rutgers universities would also offer her honorary doctorates, but ill health prevented her from traveling to the United States to accept them. Severe flu almost prevented her from accepting the Yale award, but a two-week cure in mid-May proved successful. While she took inhalations at Salso, Walter (from his law office in Paris) booked passage for her on the *Mauretania* for June 9.

Edith landed in New York on June 15 during a scorching heat wave.

Minnie Jones and the Farrands met her at the boat and accompanied her to the St. Regis Hotel, where they dined privately in her suite. In the next days, she and Minnie visited friends on Long Island, stopping first at the home of Olivia Cutting. Her granddaughter Iris (twenty-one-year-old daughter of Lady Sybil Cutting) recalled Edith as "elegant, formidable, as hard and dry as porcelain," but a woman immensely interested in the gossip and goings-on of New York. At the end of a social evening, as Edith climbed the stairs to her second-floor bedroom, Iris caught a glimpse of another woman behind the social mask: "As she looked down on her old friends, the face softened, even the erectness of her spine relaxed a little. She was no longer the trim, hard European hostess, but a nice old American lady. Edith had come home." Certainly, Edith was eager to see as many friends as possible and to take the measure of her old American world, which she had not seen since late 1913, when she came for Beatrix's wedding.[57]

She described the graduation ceremony of June 20 as a "mediaeval pageant." Edith donned cap and gown and marched in slow procession with university dignitaries and other honoraries across New Haven Green and into Woolsey Hall. Of fifteen honorary degree recipients, only two were women—Edith and Mary Emma Woolley, president of Mount Holyoke College, who on this day became the first woman to receive an honorary doctor of law degree—her second honorary degree from Yale. Edith was the first woman to receive an honorary doctor of letters from Yale. Presenting Edith for her degree, Professor William Lyon Phelps, who had so often reviewed her books in the *New York Times*, hailed her as a writer who held a "universally recognized place in the front rank of the world's living novelists." She "elevated the level of American literature," he proclaimed. "We are proud that she is an American, and especially proud to enroll her name among the daughters of Yale." These last words were inscribed on the citation of merit accompanying her degree.[58]

Although the heat was unrelenting, Edith enjoyed the solemn ceremony, which was so "impressive and beautiful that it would have been worth crossing the Atlantic to see [it] merely as a spectator," she wrote James Barbour, a Paris friend and a Yale alumnus. In the days remaining, she saw more friends, met with her estate trustees, and consulted with editors at Scribners and Appleton. On June 26, she boarded the *Berengaria* for the journey to France, never again to set foot on American soil.[59]

While meeting with Charles Scribner in his office at 597 Fifth Avenue, she is said to have first encountered twenty-six-year-old F. Scott Fitzgerald. He burst into the office unannounced and, in one version of the legend, threw himself at her feet in homage; in another version, he tried to throw himself out the window. The stories cannot be corroborated, but if true, one can imagine Edith's startled, stiffened reaction. Talented and ambitious, Fitzgerald was a rising star in 1923, and saw himself in the tradition of Edith Wharton, as chronicler of an American leisure class that, in his opinion, had "no consciousness that leisure is a privilege, not a right, and that privilege always implies a responsibility." A midwesterner who sometimes felt an outsider among wealthy easterners, Fitzgerald was both jealous of and attracted to their world. He had already established a self-destructive life-style, spending money more quickly than he earned it. By 1923, his short story fee was $1,000; Edith Wharton, after thirty-five years of magazine publishing, earned the same amount. His yearly literary income in this period, including film writing, was about $25,000—half of hers. Their work appeared in some of the same magazines, and they both struggled against restrictive editorial policies of magazines marketed to a middle-class readership. The Hearst group, for example, had refused to serialize Fitzgerald's *The Great Gatsby* because its subject was too "strong" for their female readers.[60]

In spring 1924, Fitzgerald lived for several weeks at the Hôtel du Parc in Hyères, where Edith had spent the first months of 1919. He was at work on *The Great Gatsby*. The French franc had slipped to 19.92 against the dollar, less than a third of its value of five years earlier, and he was one of several American writers who took up a nomadic existence on the Riviera, moving from hotel to hotel and enjoying the nightlife. A year later, when *The Great Gatsby* appeared from Scribners, Fitzgerald sent Edith a copy—and ones to T. S. Eliot, Gertrude Stein, and Willa Cather, receiving enthusiastic responses from them all. His book, with its "friendly" dedication, awaited her return from a trip to the Pyrenees with Robert Norton. His gesture "touched" her because she thought his generation found her "the literary equivalent of tufted furniture and gas chandeliers." (When in 1921 Sinclair Lewis congratulated Edith on *The Age of Innocence* and the Pulitzer Prize, she responded to his "generous and so unexpected" comments by saying that she had long since resigned herself to thinking that "les jeunes" thought of her as the "Mrs. Humphry Ward of the Western Hemisphere.")

Praising *The Great Gatsby*, she noted Fitzgerald's strength of characterization (Wolfsheim was the *"perfect* jew") and praised the scene in the Buchanan flat where the "dazed puppy" watched the "seedy orgy." In a complaint that echoed his editor, Maxwell Perkins, and Charles Scribner, she remarked that he should have dramatized Gatsby's early career rather than summarizing it. Recognizing *Gatsby* as an important book, and in a "spirit of sincere deprecation," she sent him *The Mother's Recompense*, describing it in the parlance of nineteenth-century industrialism as the "last [latest] product of my manufactory."[61]

She also invited him to the Pavillon Colombe for tea at four on Sunday afternoon, July 5, 1925. A disaster, the afternoon of "steady rain" became a literary legend. She was at her most grande dameish and he was either inebriated or terrified, or both. He told a story about a couple (the Fitzgeralds) who spent several nights in a Paris brothel, thinking it was a hotel. Edith missed (or feigned to miss) its point. Her diary reads: "To tea, Teddy Chanler and Scott Fitzgerald, the novelist (horrible)." Gaillard Lapsley maintained that Fitzgerald was drunk. Teddy Chanler (Daisy's son), another member of the party, said that Fitzgerald was unnerved by Edith's "unyielding formality and stiffness." Edith thought he was "ill," and claimed never before to have met "anyone in that condition."

Fitzgerald did not respond to Edith's gift of *The Mother's Recompense*, but in a letter to Maxwell Perkins in December, he commented on a group of novels by American writers: "I thought the books by [Sinclair] Lewis, [Carl] Van Vechten, Edith Wharton, Floyd Dell, Tom Boyd, and Sherwood Anderson were just *lousy!*"[62]

Nineteen twenty-five was an extraordinarily good year for American fiction, which saw publication of Sinclair Lewis's *Arrowsmith* (the novel, which Fitzgerald called "lousy," was chosen for the Pulitzer Prize), John Dos Passos's *Manhattan Transfer*, Hemingway's short story volume *In Our Time*, Sherwood Anderson's *Dark Laughter*, Willa Cather's *The Professor's House*, Ellen Glasgow's *Barren Ground*, and Margaret Kennedy's *The Constant Nymph* (which Edith read and recommended to friends). Added to these were *The Great Gatsby* and *The Mother's Recompense*, which were widely reviewed and often compared to one another. They competed for top spot on the bestseller list: Edith Wharton's novel was number one in April and May, but Scott Fitzgerald's book soon took that place—and kept it for a while.

In a *Dial* review of *Gatsby*, Gilbert Seldes noted that Fitzgerald had

learned from Henry James through Edith Wharton how to structure
his novel in scenes. Louis Bromfield, whose first novel, *The Green Bay
Tree* (1924), Edith had praised to her friends, remarked in his *New York
Evening Post* review that the only novel of the year that "approached"
the "technical skill" of F. Scott Fitzgerald's book was Edith Wharton's
new novel. Her interest in the "sociological and social aspects of American life" matched that of Fitzgerald. He praised her as un-Victorian, a
view echoed in the *New York Herald Tribune* by Stuart Pratt Sherman,
who took Robert Morss Lovett to task for characterizing Edith Wharton as bound by culture, class, and morality. In a book-length critical
study of her work published in 1925, Lovett claimed that she was out
of touch with the modern vision, her voice "whisper[ing] the last enchantments of the Victorian age."[63]

Edith did not know what to make of these critical responses to her
work. Answering Daisy Chanler's letter of appreciation for her novel,
she remarked that one commentator thought her new novel raised her
to the "same height as Galsworthy," while another (Bromfield) said she
was "now equal to Scott Fitzgerald": "As my work reaches its close, I
feel so sure that it is either nothing, or far more than they know. . . .
And I wonder, a little desolately, which?" This final decade of her literary career was marked by mixed signals about the value of her writing.
Still a bestselling author and the recipient of prizes and academic honors (more were to come), Edith Wharton was her generation's most important American writer. Yet, as critics revised upward the quality of
her prewar writing, the more they demanded of her —and the less they
agreed on what directions her work should now take.[64]

Reviewers had no idea what to make of *The Mother's Recompense*, a
psychological study that turns on relations between parents and children—a theme heralded by *A Son at the Front* that would carry through
her next three novels. The "strong" theme of sexual desire between
generations invokes the subject of incest (as in *The Reef* and *Summer*).
Kate Clephane, an unhappily married woman of New York society,
long ago abandoned her husband and baby daughter and spent twenty
aimless years on the Riviera. After the death of her husband and mother-in-law, she is invited to New York by her daughter and welcomed
back into old society, as Ellen Olenska is in *The Age of Innocence*. She
then learns that her daughter is about to marry Chris Fenno, a young
man with whom Kate had an affair during the war and for whom she
still has longings. Fenno, a journalist, is a likeness of Fullerton. He

awakened Kate's sexuality in her middle years, and thus put her in his power: "His ways of being cruel were innumerable." The pain of their relationship mirrors Edith's during the period of her intense involvement with Fullerton.

Without giving her daughter reasons for her resistance to the marriage, Kate tries (unsuccessfully) to stop it. As Edith explained to John Hugh Smith, when Kate sees Fenno holding her daughter in his arms, it is an "incest-vision" that justifies Kate's anguish and determines the dénouement of the story. She flees New York on the wedding day, keeping her secret and Fenno's. The incest theme remains a backdrop to the contradictory tensions that arise in Kate.[65]

In the London *Saturday Review*, Gerald Bullett described *The Mother's Recompense* as a "well-staged drama in which the expected always happens." Comparing it to Virginia Woolf's new novel, *Mrs. Dalloway*, he called Woolf a "brilliant experimentalist," while Edith Wharton was "content to practice good craftsmanship without enlarging" the scope of the novel as a genre. Edith agreed that it was an "old-fashioned novel." She was not trying to follow the new methods ("as May Sinclair so pantingly and anxiously does"), she wrote John Hugh: "My heroine belongs to the day when scruples existed."[66]

Later in summer 1925, Virginia Woolf's essay "American Fiction" appeared in the *Saturday Review of Literature*, a new journal published in New York. Woolf declared that English readers were not interested in Americans who wrote in the European tradition, but wanted to hear from those who were developing American storytelling forms and writing in a new idiom rather than aping the English. Although she gave "qualified praise" to Edith Wharton and the late Henry James, in her opinion, they were not Americans: "They do not give us anything we have not got already." She then discussed the work of Sherwood Anderson, Sinclair Lewis, Ring Lardner, Willa Cather, and Fanny Hurst. Reading the article, Edith let out a cry of despair—angry and frustrated, she felt dismissed.[67]

EDITH HAD NOT been dismissed; indeed, this was her Age of Acclaim. In January 1925, she received the gold medal for "distinguished service to . . . letters in the creation of an original work" from the National Institute of Arts and Letters, the parent organization of the American Academy of Arts and Letters—both groups comprised entirely of men.

The first woman to receive the gold medal (in literature and drama, William Dean Howells and Eugene O'Neill had preceded her), Edith was nominated by Brand Whitlock, a writer of social reform novels whom she had met during the war, when he served as minister to Belgium. She initially rejected the gold medal, but was convinced to accept it when Robert Bridges, editor of *Scribner's Magazine*, assured her that the National Institute of Arts and Letters was a "respectable institution" and that both he and William Crary Brownell were members. Elected to the National Institute of Arts and Letters in 1926, Edith was nominated for the Nobel Prize in 1927. Robert Woods Bliss, then American ambassador to Sweden, helped organize the Nobel Prize effort. She did not win it, nor did she ever believe she had a chance of winning the prize. French philosopher Henri Bergson, whom Edith knew personally and had read avidly in her early days in Paris, won the Nobel Prize in 1927. Art historian Kenneth Clark, whom Edith met for the first time in spring 1927, later declared in his autobiography that *The Custom of the Country* cost her the prize. The Swedish committee, he said, found it too cynical. In the 1930s, apparently hoping that she would be renominated for the prize, she made a point of arranging translations of her works into Swedish.[68]

In 1929, she received the American Academy of Arts and Letters Gold Medal for "special distinction in literature." Only one other woman had received this award, Mrs. John King Van Rensselaer, a novelist and the author of *The Social Ladder* (1923), a book that interested survivors of Old New York society. (On seeing a notice of its publication, Rutger Jewett made a little note to himself to ask Edith about writing her memoirs.) On November 30, 1930, Edith entered the American Academy, only the second woman in its ranks. (The other was Julia Ward Howe, inducted in extreme old age.) Ellen Glasgow followed Edith into the Academy in 1938, Edith's death having created a vacancy.

In a commemorative tribute to Edith Wharton published after her death by the American Academy of Arts and Letters, novelist Robert Grant explained that although much of the best American fiction of the previous thirty years had been written by women, the Academy was "managed by men." Her nomination had sprung from "enthusiastic recognition of her genius as a novelist and as a consummate artist in the use of pure English." In his memorial, Grant quoted from Arthur Hobson Quinn's evaluation of Edith Wharton in *American Fiction*

(1936). Quinn described her as the "supreme artist in modern American fiction," a writer who, though "belonging to no movement or group, [but] following her own standards," remained "essentially American in her choice of material and in her artistic point of view." Quinn had put his finger on the reasons critics found it difficult to place Edith Wharton in a single literary tradition: she belonged to no movement or group; she followed her own standards and her own artistic viewpoint.[69]

EXPANSIVE YEARS

For some time, Jewett had kept Edith apprised of changes in class structure and social organization in America. He seemed to be encouraging her toward new themes in her writing. "We are still suffering from growing pains," he wrote; "nothing is settled; there is an upward and onward [movement] which expresses itself in fantastic form and mad developments." He admitted that men still had an edge over women in entering business, politics, and the professions, but the changing nature of opportunities for women interested him as a subject of fiction: "Novels . . . are being lived (if not written) year by year in this country." He sketched scenes from his own experiences—a dinner party among the Old New York rich, at which he sat next to a woman engaged to young Abraham Hewitt, son of the steel manufacturer. She had no intention of wasting her time on "dinners and balls" but was instead taking a graduate degree in psychology from the University of Wisconsin![70]

Edith was oppposed to educating women for the professions. At Ogden Codman's request, she endowed a $500 scholarship for a student at the Paris division of the newly organized New York School of Design (later the Parsons School): she specified that the recipient be a male. When asked to contribute to a fund for travel scholarships for women, she sought Minnie's advice about whether it was "worthwhile." She was "not much interested in travelling scholarships for women," she wrote, "or in fact in scholarship, tout court!—they'd much better stay at home and mind the baby." She was even less interested in helping "female Yids, and young ladies who address a stranger as 'Chère Madame' and sign 'meilleurs sentiments'" (modes of address that suggest familiarity). In these nasty remarks, she appears to have forgotten her own longings for the education her brothers took for granted; she also disregarded the challenges her niece Beatrix had faced in becoming a recognized landscape designer. (No evidence exists to show that Edith contributed to this scholarship fund.)

The reference to "female Yids," perhaps her most derogatory recorded statement on women and Jews, reveals her growing anti-Semitism in the postwar years. Like many of her class, she resented the "new" Europe and America, in which immigration had created ethnic diversity. She believed the misapprehension touted by banker John Hugh Smith (with whom she swapped anti-Semitic jokes) that Jews controlled the international monetary system, mining it for their own profit. The more important element, however, was her return to Christianity and her attraction to Roman Catholicism. In her last days, she spoke to Elisina Tyler of her moral and religious beliefs: "I hate the Jews, and I don't like the thought that they have given us our Faith. When I was a child the story of the crucifixion used to harrow me so." She perhaps did not see how her pattern of beliefs tracked those of Paul Bourget, with whom she had disagreed on the Dreyfus case many years before: his anti-Semitism was directly related to his Catholic and royalist loyalties.[71]

As the years passed, Edith more firmly believed that erasing differences between sexes and social classes, the intermingling of customs, and the overthrow of traditions could bear no rich cultural fruit. She marcel-waved and tinted her hair, wore cloche hats, straight-waisted dresses with midcalf hemlines (nothing "flapperish"), and admitted that when she peered through her tortoiseshell lorgnette at the world of her youth, it appeared shrunken, as though seen from the wrong end of a telescope. Rather than bridging the distance between Edith and her native land, however, Jewett's observations on the new America seemed to widen the gulf.[72]

If she set aside his ideas for novel subjects, Edith did respond to Jewett's request for a commentary on fiction writing (a volume she sold to Scribners). In November 1923, she wrote Robert Bridges at *Scribner's Magazine*, to apologize for her long delay in delivering the first portion of the manuscript. She had been absorbed in reading novels and stories by the "rising generation in England and America," and the article she had just completed on Marcel Proust was an effort to "clear" her thoughts on the subject. She had read everything from *A la recherche du temps perdu* to *Babbitt* to *Ulysses*, describing the latter to Berenson as "a turgid welter of pornography (the rudest school-boy kind), and unformed and unimportant drivel."

The Writing of Fiction began its serial run in *Scribner's* in late 1924. It appeared in book form in October 1925, bound in a yellow-gray cover. She dedicated it to Gaillard Lapsley, the man who would become her literary executor, and chose as the headnote to the volume her favorite line of poetry, taken from the seventeenth-century metaphysical poet Thomas Traherne: "Order the beauty even of beauty is." This statement, the guiding principle of her own artistic aesthetic, provides a key to her critique of modern writing. The reviewer for the *Times Literary Supplement* astutely observed that the instruction she offered in her book was essentially "negative," a series of warnings about the dire consequences to follow if writers abandoned order and beauty for literary experiment. Her own talent, he said, gave weight to her words. She envisioned younger writers laying siege to fundamental principles of composition and to the novel as a genre. Their "distrust of technique and the fear of being unoriginal" would lead, she claimed, to "pure anarchy in fiction." They had not read widely or deeply enough, in her opinion, and their writing betrayed a narrowing intellectual scope and intrusive authorial methods. Some years later, she wrote a friend to say, "Palates accustomed to William Falkner [*sic*] no longer care for delicate fare."[73]

Edith's audience for *The Writing of Fiction* was not so much critics and students of literature as practicing writers. Its literary reference points are the nineteenth-century English and French writers who influenced Edith Wharton's writing and whose works filled her library shelves: Balzac, Flaubert, Jane Austen, George Eliot, Thackeray, Dickens, Meredith, Tolstoy, Conrad, and James. (She considered James's fiction in the European tradition.) Except in the essay on Proust, which many reviewers singled out for praise, she did not discuss recent writing. Although she greatly admired Proust, he did not escape her criticism, discreet and carefully worded though it was. His beautiful storytelling forms delicately disguised the absence of a defining moral sensibility, and this hole at the center of a work of fiction amounted, for her, to a tragic flaw.

Edith Wharton was not a prude, as some of her detractors may have assumed, nor did she turn her eyes away from unpleasantness, as her comments about Joyce's *Ulysses* might suggest. She did not shrink from the erotic range of Proust's *Sodome et Gomorrhe* (which Walter Berry called "terrific . . . nothing like it outside of Krafft-Ebing"), nor did she believe that good literature must avoid the "immoral." On the contrary, she championed the rights of authors to treat openly all the taboo bourgeois subjects—sexuality, adultery, divorce, illegitimacy. Aesthetics and ethics, however, were indivisible. At the core of her argument with Modernism was a belief she had stated to the Reverend Morgan Dix twenty years earlier, in response to his letter of praise for *The House of Mirth*: "No novel worth anything can be anything but a novel 'with a purpose,' and if anyone who cared for the moral issue did not see in my work that *I* care for it, I should have no one to blame but myself—or at least my inadequate means of rendering my effects."[74]

BY 1925, EDITH had made up all the financial losses of the war years. She was rich by virtue of her pen, and with the French franc at twenty-six to the dollar, her riches went a long way. Her wealth allowed her to fulfill a long-held dream—to retrace her 1888 voyage in the Aegean. Literary projects, publishing deadlines, and the schedules of friends whom she had invited to accompany her forced delays, but in late summer 1925, en route to England for a three-week holiday, she inspected a yacht moored at Rouen. By the time she and Walter departed for Spain in September, a "miracle month," when they traveled to the "most unknown parts" of the country in search of early church architecture, she had dispatched Robert Norton to look at available yachts in the Southampton harbor. In November, John Hugh Smith interviewed Captain MacLean of the *S. Y. Osprey* in London, and she made her choice. Charter and fuel costs for the 360-ton steam yacht for ten weeks was £4,000 ($200,000 today), of which Edith paid a little more than half, her four guests contributing the balance.

The party included Robert Norton, Daisy Chanler, Logan Pearsall Smith, and Harry Lawrence, an Englishman who was director of the Medici Society in London. That she did not know well one of her traveling companions (Pearsall Smith) and another not at all (Harry Lawrence) suggests that few of the friends she really enjoyed had the leisure and money to embark on such an adventure. The little group proved congenial, however, and Edith took special pleasure in Daisy Chanler's company, their friendship now spanning nearly sixty years.[75]

Equipping herself with map books from Larousse and the *Times* of London atlas, she plotted a course from Hyères through the Straits of

Messina and the Corinth Canal to Crete, and Cyprus (with a stop at Alexandria, Egypt), the Aegean Sea and its tiny islands, then returning by way of Sicily and the eastern Italian coast. Rereading her diary of the 1888 trip, she was dismayed to see how little it revealed of the wonders of the ancient world. The trip had been the "crowning wonder of my life, and yet how ignorant I was," she told Berenson. The diary provided a detailed itinerary and record of travel times and weather, however, and served as a general scheme for the second trip. As they steamed from port to port, she compared changes in landscape and habitat. Where she had last seen "depths of Turkish squalour and *laissez-faire*" at Rhodes (recorded in some detail in the 1888 diary), she now discovered a city "magically restored to its ancient beauty."[76]

Edith took pleasure planning the trip, charting the course, ordering suitable clothing and provisions, and stocking the ship's library. The voyagers, she told Berenson, were to have read the "big works" on the ancient world prior to boarding the yacht. She gathered a collection of thirty-four books in English and French, most of them from her own library. There were cultural guides to the ancient world, works on sacred and secular art, classical dictionaries, Gilbert Murray's *Ancient Greek Literature* and *Four Stages of Greek Religion*, *The Oxford Book of English Verse*, and the collected poems of Keats, Shelley, and Browning. She included a guidebook to the stars, one to flowers, and a book on "camping in Crete." The traveling library contained only one piece of light reading, E. C. Bentley's classic detective novel *Trent's Last Case*. The major works of literature were Homer's *Iliad* and *Odyssey* in the Butcher and Lang translations, from which Robert Norton read in the evenings. She confessed to Gaillard Lapsley that some nights, they dipped into *Gentlemen Prefer Blondes* (not listed in the ship's library), the Anita Loos novel that the "literary committee of Ste. Claire" had earlier in the year declared "the greatest novel since *Manon Lescaut*."[77]

Provisions lists from Hyères, Marseilles, and the British Levant Shipstores Company reveal that the group ate plentifully of both fresh and preserved foods. In addition to 168 bottles of rosé wine, they drank two dozen bottles of *vin mousseux*, twenty-five bottles (and five half bottles) of Veuve Clicquot champagne, and were supplied with brandy and liquors, as well as herb teas, cigarettes, cigars, and kerosene lamps. Edith left nothing to chance; every need or desire was anticipated, from international newspapers to mosquito netting for campouts (ordered from Harrods' colonial supplies cataloges and never used).

On the "serene and sunny" morning of March 31, 1926, Edith and her little group boarded the *S. Y. Osprey* at Les Sablettes, the old port a few miles to the west of Hyères. It was from here that Saint Louis, king of France, had sailed forth on his last Crusade. To honor the occasion, the staff of Ste. Claire arranged themselves along the dock to wave good-bye as the *Osprey* slipped its anchor.[78]

Edith had told Jewett that the Aegean cruise was the "most reckless extravagance" she had ever undertaken. She intended to pay for it, she said, by writing a set of travel essays, some short stories, and a novel set in the Greek isles. She first proposed these projects to Scribners in 1924 and mentioned them to Jewett on the eve of her departure, when she sent him the opening chapters of her new novel, *Twilight Sleep*. He was "keenly interested" in her impressions. She soon dropped the idea of the travel essays (they needed photographs, and she had none of the kind needed for publication), and the trip yielded only one story, a tale based on her visit on muleback to the twelfth-century castle on Cyprus, set on a rocky peak two thousand feet above the sea and surrounded by precipices. The Crusaders called it "Dieu d'Amour," named for the god Eros, and she took this as the title of her story, which she started writing the day after their climb. This was a rare moment of industry, since she had purposely set aside her literary work and put off all business matters until her return home.

Hoping to sell the serial rights of her proposed novel, Jewett pressed her for a synopsis. In *A Backward Glance*, Edith calls this never-written story "The Sapphire Way," a title that suggests something of her "unbroken bliss" during these weeks. By December 1926, she had written three or four chapters of the book, which was set in colonial New York but recounted a trip its hero made to Hyères and Toulon. She put it aside, telling Jewett that it was a story she wished to write "at leisure, without any definite time," and never took it up again.[79]

The only book publication to result from the cruise was a slim volume entitled *Twelve Poems* printed by the Medici Society of London. It appeared in December 1926 in an elegant gold-stamped cloth edition of 130 numbered copies. Casting an appraising eye over it, Edith remarked to Jewett that its "make-up" was "a credit to the Medici Society." It was perhaps the only volume of her work whose physical properties—weight, size, quality of paper and print—thoroughly pleased her.[80]

Edith's other book-length publication of 1926 was a volume of short stories, *Here and Beyond*. It was her first collection in ten years and one that most reviewers found undistinguished, although it included three stories of the supernatural that would rank among her most enduring: "The Seed of the Faith" (set in North Africa), "Bewitched," and "Miss Mary Pask." "Why does she fail now where she has succeeded so notably before?" asked Garreta Busey in her *New York Herald Tribune* review. "Has she relaxed her efforts toward technical perfection or has she underestimated the importance of the muse—inspiration in the sense of that sudden and unaccountable quickening of his capacities which enables a writer to see all the artistic possibilities of his subject?" Later generations of critics would conclude that Edith Wharton was writing too quickly in these years, directing her work at a popular readership that had no standards of taste; she had lost touch with her American roots, some said, and was out of touch with modern life.[81]

An element of truth inheres in these assessments, and yet they explain neither her extraordinary productivity in the 1920s nor the varied quality of her work. *The House of Mirth*, *Ethan Frome*, and *The Age of Innocence*, which are today considered among her best works, received mixed reviews when they first appeared. Critical opinion of them was later revised upward, often by reviewers who had first raised doubts about their quality. Reviewing *Here and Beyond* for the *New Republic*, Dorothy Bacon Woolsey said it was unjust always to hold Edith Wharton to the excellence of *Ethan Frome* and *The Fruit of the Tree* (a novel almost forgotten by the 1920s). If this new book had "come to hand under an unknown name," she said, "it would be received with praise if not general enthusiasm."[82]

Since the war, Edith had devoted herself to long fiction, producing a novel a year since 1917—except for 1919, when *French Ways and Their Meaning* appeared. The quantity and range of her work had long since made Jewett "bow low" before her energy. Calling her a "wonder," he avowed that her "fertility and ingenuity" filled him with envy. In New York, two people tried to keep up with Edith Wharton's literary enterprise. Minnie Jones, her cinema and theater representative since 1919, dealt with requests from producers and agents interested in putting various of her stories and novels on the stage and screen. Jewett, meanwhile, lined up serial contracts for her work.

Edith was more than ever in need of serial rights money to maintain her style of living, yet she admitted that her "working powers" were not as "reliable as they once were." In July 1926, she had asked for a two-month extension to finish *Twilight Sleep*, her new novel. While she worked on its final chapters, Jewett sought buyers for her future work. She had already informally agreed to give her Aegean novel (which was never completed) to the *Pictorial*, and Vance had offered $35,000 for it. She had two more novels in mind, both on "modern" subjects, and he set about to secure contracts from Vance and from Loren Palmer, the new editor in chief of the *Delineator*, a magazine owned by the Butterick sewing pattern company. Jewett arranged a bidding war between them.[83]

When negotiations were finally settled, the *Delineator* had agreed to pay $42,000 for a work entitled *The Children*. She sent Jewett a summary and opening chapter of the book in February 1927, and one month later added four more chapters. Vance, who could not exceed an offer of $35,000, had lost out in the bidding and now needed to be appeased. "Have you another full length story in mind which you could finish for Vance before you write the Delineator novel?" Jewett asked. She had written several chapters of her Aegean novel, but now set it aside to work on one called "The Keys of Heaven."[84]

The sale of serial rights for this novel (which was never written, but for which Edith prepared two separate plot outlines) was the most difficult Jewett ever undertook. Not only was an immense amount of money involved, but he had to establish a publishing schedule suitable both for Edith and for the two magazine editors. Her primary concern was money. On January 1, 1927, she bought "Clairfont," an acreage across the road from the Pavillon Colombe to be used as a kitchen garden, paying 475,000 French francs for it—about $20,000. At the close of 1926 (and at Walter's urging), she had purchased Ste. Claire le Château and all its surrounding acreage (about twenty acres), including a property called "Pierre Lisse" that she wanted for Alfred White, who had recently remarried. The value of Edith's total investment in Ste. Claire was 1,120,000 francs—about $45,000 at the current exchange rate. When it was settled, she owned everything on her mountaintop, "all round to the sea." She borrowed money to pay for it, however, and as she wrote Jewett, her "'bourgeois' mind [was] oppressed by the thought of so large a loan." These expenditures, added to her United States tax bill for 1926 ($28,500), made it imperative that she earn as much as possible from her writing. She therefore insisted that Vance match the $42,000 serial contract offer from the *Delineator*.[85]

She had spent liberally in 1926, not only on travel ($15,000 for her portion of the Aegean voyage), but on gardens, house decoration, motors (a new Peugeot and a Torpedo Delage at a cost of 130,000 francs), additions to her Spode dinner set, and the replating of her entire silver service. In February 1927, she ordered a specially designed diamond-and-emerald necklace from Cartier's. The emeralds were her own, as were some of the diamonds. By July, Cartier's had made fourteen separate sketches for the necklace, and she had rejected them all as too expensive. Finally, she decided to postpone buying the necklace, and instead had the jewelers reset her pearl necklace.

Meanwhile, negotiations on her serial rights contracts were entering a new, and far more complicated, phase. Arthur Vance of the *Pictorial* had agreed to pay $40,000 for *The Children*, which Loren Palmer of the *Delineator* had relinquished on the agreement that his magazine would publish "The Keys of Heaven," a story based on an 1847 Paris murder that Edith reset in a "Young Ladies' Academy" in "Sloebridge," Massachusetts (a play on "Stockbridge"). He had offered $42,000 for that novel, and $50,000 for the one that would follow it. Vance "begged to remain in contention" for this one (the third in the lineup), and the editor of the *Ladies' Home Journal* wrote to say he was interested in her fourth novel down the line! In a feat of stamina, diplomacy, and skillful wheeling and dealing, Jewett completed these arrangements in June 1927. He wrote Edith a charming letter of confirmation:

> Do you remember the dance card of your youth, ornamented with a silken tassel and sometimes brave with a miniature pencil? I recall those innocent monstrosities with glee and remember how we boys fought wildly in our effort to fill up our cards with dance after dance with the same girl because she was the belle of the ball. I feel somehow as though I were chaperoning you under such hectic circumstances, as I check up the different offers for serials which are now coming in.

Edith fulfilled the three *Pictorial* and *Delineator* contracts, which collectively amounted to $132,000, although she substituted new subjects for two of the books. At today's rates, these contracts came to $1,500,000, added to which were the advances against royalties paid her by Appleton—a grand total of almost $2 million.[86]

Chapter 9

W

LOSSES

RETURNING FROM THE AEGEAN, EDITH MOVED HER household to a rainy, cold St. Brice, where she took up her work on *Twilight Sleep*, due to begin its run in the *Pictorial Review* in February 1927. Minnie Jones came for a long visit, and Ogden Codman, arriving at the Pavillon Colombe for a June tea party in honor of visiting American friends, described Minnie as looking like "Time in the Primer" and remarked that Edith seemed worn and "broken." Edith described the friends from New York and Boston who visited her in summer as "green isles in that sea of misery" that was modern America. During their Aegean voyage, Daisy had tried to soften Edith's attitudes about America, but to no avail. The "green isles" were too few and far between and did not "encircle one dancingly, like some islands we know," Edith remarked.[1]

In September, she and Walter went to northern Italy, where they planned to retrace the 1899 trip she took with Teddy and the Bourgets. The trip began well. They found the old walled city of Bergamo charming and picturesque, but as they descended into the Po Valley, "nauseating heat and dust" assaulted them. They went to Venice (no doubt Walter's choice), where, after seeing the Veroneses at the Accademia, they found themselves for five days amid the "human wreckage" of the Lido season. Songwriter Cole Porter had rented the Rezzonico

Palace, where he re-created a Venetian festival, complete with rope dancing. Edith disliked attempts to resurrect lost folklore, and she watched the spectacle of writhing bodies with growing horror. Meanwhile, the princess San Faustino, seated next to her, became misty-eyed with emotion: "It was really magnificent," she gushed. "He revived all the ancient glories of Venice." Walter probably enjoyed the evening. Still elegantly slim, he was a striking figure who caught the eye of much younger women. He observed the Paris Jazz Age scene through his friendship with a young cousin, Harry Grew Crosby, and his wife, Caresse, the former Mary Phelps of Boston, a niece of J. P. Morgan. They founded the Black Sun Press, publishing hand-printed, gold-leafed editions of their own poetry and work by other avant-gardists. Their legendary dusk-to-dawn parties, where sex, drugs, and drink prevailed, expressed the frenzied dark side of Left Bank living. Edith could not tolerate such excesses; nor could Walter, now in his late sixties, have withstood the rigors of such nightlife. Fleeing the "shallow abyss" of the Lido, they motored to the relative cool and calm of the Dolomites and then drove west through the lower Tyrol to Lake Garda and back to Bergamo.[2]

The trip did not match Edith's hopes for it. Forced to change plans several times, she could not recapture the sense of leisure and adventure that characterized the 1899 tour. Instead, she was pulled into an artificial world of meaningless diversions. This world was the backdrop of her new novel. *Twilight Sleep* (whose title refers to anesthetizing women in childbirth) satirizes New York nouveau riche bent on getting through life without suffering—at any cost. Pauline Manford, a twice-married mother with two grown children, is an energetic, optimistic, and socially ambitious woman in her fifties. To escape boredom, she fills her life with trivial pursuits, devoting time to social activities hardly worth her energy; her goal is to stay busy and cheerful and avoid pain and scandal. In the end, she is nearly consumed by her undirected energies—a tragicomic vision of what Edith Wharton might have become in middle age had she not disciplined her talents and directed her energy.

Twilight Sleep is not ranked today among Edith's best work, but it received some laudatory reviews when it appeared in May 1927. English critics were enthusiastic, but American reviewers less generous. Pauline Manford seemed to them a "too perfect specimen of a type" rather than an actual person; no scene in the book seemed "inevitable, or in any way heroic or arresting." The *New York Herald Tribune* (a newspaper read by the Paris expatriate community) remarked that Edith had not examined the "nature of human institutions," as great satirists do. Percy Hutchinson, in the *New York Times Book Review*, disagreed. Edith Wharton had never told a tale with "equal refinement of method," he said. The tragedy's flat tone matched its emotion, a sense of being lulled into disaster.[3]

Edith believed not only that this theme was timely, but also that society would pay heavily for its continued evasion and emotional bankruptcy. She no doubt realized that *Twilight Sleep* fell short of its grand theme, but its subject continued to trouble her, and in her next novel, *The Children*, she dramatized how children pay for the sins of the parents. The scene at the Lido still fresh in her mind, she went back to work on *Twilight Sleep* on her return from Italy and kept at it through the late autumn. The weather was cold and damp as her household staff prepared for the winter move to Hyères.

The season's last official function was a surprise champagne celebration on November 1 for Catherine Gross. Edith arranged for her to receive a Medal of Honor from the French government for her "devoted services" during the war. (She assisted at Edith's charities.) The award was a source of great pride to Gross, who in 1870, as a young woman of twenty, had become a French citizen when Germany invaded France. Edith gave Gross a fur coat, which she first wore during the two weeks she spent in Paris before departing for Ste. Claire with Edith.[4]

Postwar Paris with its crowds and noise had become hateful to Edith, and her yearly stay at the Hôtel de Crillon was a "severe discipline" that she survived, she told Lapsley, only by living on the "rooftop and thanking heaven I'm not at the Ritz"—the hotel that catered to noisy and reckless Jazz Age sophisticates. She was in Paris on November 13, when Jules Beaurain, Walter Berry's valet, telephoned to say that Walter was ill. Arriving at 53 rue de Varenne, she found him in acute pain from what appeared to be an attack of appendicitis. She summoned Dr. de Martel, a prominent Paris surgeon who was away in Brussels on business. He took the overnight train, and the following morning performed the operation.

Walter disliked being ill and detested being fussed over. Made nervous by the French nurse, a "chocolate box beauty of 18," he shocked Edith by exclaiming, "Oh, for God's sake get me one who's old and ugly." She found a good English nurse (perhaps neither old nor ugly), and by December 21, he was well enough to take the *train bleu* to Ste. Claire, where he joined the annual Christmas fête. Returning to Paris on New Year's Day, he resumed his usual activities—business, charity, and legal affairs, and society gatherings. Early in the new year, Dr. de Martel gave him permission to resume his triweekly games of tennis. He played a set on January 11, and the next morning suffered a stroke.[5]

Edith received the news of his illness too late to catch the night train from Toulon, and static on the telephone line made it difficult to hear clearly the doctor's words. She understood that Walter's situation was "pretty bad." At noon the following day, she went to Paris. "I hope with all my soul," she wrote John Hugh Smith, that "it will be short and fatal. Anything else for him won't bear thinking of." Ten days later, however, she reported to him that she lunched with Walter almost every day and that they had taken two short motor drives. As he began to recover his physical health, he fell into depression. "He is like a great powerful bird caught in a net," Edith wrote Minnie.[6]

A full recovery required six months of complete rest, and Walter's doctors wanted him to go south for the sunshine. He initially refused to return to Ste. Claire, not wanting Edith "hovering over him." He eventually did go to Hyères (joining a household where everyone was ill, even the Pekingese dogs), but not before he flared up angrily at her. He had asked Edith not to alert his sister, Nathalie Alden, of Washington, D.C. When she suddenly appeared in Paris, telling Walter that Edith's many cables had frightened her into making the transatlantic voyage, he was furious. He sent Edith the only unkind letter she ever received from him, a stinging reproach written "in his poor halting hand." Nineteen twenty-seven had begun like a "Comet Year," she told Minnie. "I only hope there is better in store bye and bye." Her sixty-fifth birthday passed virtually unnoticed.[7]

By early March, Walter was making "very slow progress." He had been visited by a brain specialist from Marseilles, who predicted that if he led a quiet life for several months, he would recover completely. On Mary Berenson's advice, he arranged to see a renowned physician in Berne, Switzerland, and from there wrote a letter to his "dearest Edith": "I'm missing Ste. Claire dreadfully—though what it must have been for you dear, I can't think: tied down to a stuttering paralytic." Walter was not a "stuttering paralytic," but his self-description casts a bright light on his inner suffering and broken pride at being ill and at having Edith see him in such a condition. Late in April, she wrote Lap-sley that his sadness had been "so profound, and so penetrating" that she was "benumbed by it, in spite of his constant effort to hide it." His mind was as quick and flashing as ever, but his "bodily fatigue hangs on him like lead."[8]

During the summer, he moved very slowly toward recovery, under-going rest cures in Switzerland and Germany. (Gossip had it that he was taking monkey-gland treatments.) Edith went to Salsomaggiore for two weeks, following up her cure with a ten-day motor trip in France. Returning to Paris, she found Walter tired out by his spa "ex-periments." In September, some ten thousand American Legion war veterans arrived to celebrate the tenth anniversary of America's en-trance into World War I. Berry, something of an elder statesman in France, was called on to make a few appearances. Even before he was appointed president of the Chamber of Commerce in 1917, he lobbied harder, and to greater purpose, than any of his compatriots in Paris to bring the United States into the war. Made a commander of the French Legion of Honor in 1918, he was arguably the most influential Ameri-can in the city (except for the United States ambassador) and certainly the most revered. Marcel Proust, who had become a close friend of Berry's during the war, dedicated his collection *Pastiches et mélanges* (1919) to him: "To Mr. Walter Berry, lawyer and man of letters who, from the first day of the war, confronting an indecisive America, ar-gued France's cause with an incomparable energy and talent, and won. His friend, Marcel Proust."

When Edith and Walter dined together on September 23 and at-tended a rehearsal of a friend's play, she thought it a good sign that he was getting out into society again. A few days later, he felt a recurrence of abdominal pain. He dismissed Edith's doctor, who had tended him during his stroke in January, and called in a surgeon, who saw him sev-eral times and visited him the day before his fatal attack on October 2—a day Edith described as "anxious" and "endless."[9]

Paralyzed and unable to speak, he lay for seven days, seeing no one. The doctors concurred that, as they could do nothing for him, it was best to accede to his wish to be alone. Edith suspected that he feared they would try to prolong his life by modern technology (an ethical problem she had examined twenty years earlier in *The Fruit of the Tree*). She waited at the Crillon for a sign that he wanted to see her. It came on October 9: she entered the bedroom at 53 that had once been hers and promised him that she would not agree to any procedure to extend his life. Over the next three days, she sat with him for a half hour each morning and afternoon. Holding him in her arms, she repeated the names of friends and recalled their old times together. On October 11, she noted that he was "failing fast." As she rose to leave, he held her, kissed her, and called her "dear." The following morning, Jules telephoned to say that she should come quickly. She arrived at the rue de Varenne too late. He died at 8:05, aged sixty-eight.[10]

At first relieved that Walter's suffering had ceased, Edith was soon desolate at the prospect of the "great desert" of loneliness that lay ahead of her. Of all the letters she wrote to friends about her last hours with Walter, the most revealing was her October 15 letter to John Hugh Smith. In those final days, she said, "all the old flame and glory came back, in the cold shadow of death and parting. . . . I am proud of having kept such a perfect friendship after the great days were over, and always to have felt that, through all the coming and going of things in his eager ambitious life, I was there, in the place he put me in so many years ago, the place of perfect understanding." She said he liked to be with her because she was not given to "humbug." Indeed, intellectual honesty, the opposite of "humbug," was at the core of their mutual respect.

Walter's dry wit, which Edith so loved, was evident even in the instructions he left for the disposal of his body. He ordered that his funeral take place at the Church of the Holy Trinity (the Pro-Cathedral), that his body be cremated following the services, and that his "so-called 'ashes' be chucked-out anywhere." These instructions accompanied his last will and testament, made in Paris on June 19, 1927.[11]

His funeral, one of the most resplendent Paris ever witnessed, was planned in the salon of 53 rue de Varenne by Harry Crosby, the marquise de Polignac (the former Nina Crosby, a favorite young cousin of Walter's), and Edith Wharton—"ghastly hours," she noted in her diary. It was virtually a state event, attended by cabinet members, diplomats, titled aristocrats, war veterans and military heroes, including General John J. Pershing. On Monday morning, October 17, a silver-inlaid, plumed hearse drawn by four black horses led the cortège from the rue de Varenne to the Pro-Cathedral, many mourners following on foot. (Edith arrived at the church from the Pavillon Colombe in her chauffeured car.) A newspaper account described the scene: "Slowly, with stately dignity, the funeral procession wound its way through the streets of the Left Bank, across the Seine and up the Avenue des Champs Elysées to the church in the Avenue George V. The entrance to the church was heavily draped in black." Rector Frederick W. Beekman officiated at a service in which some eight hundred mourners, "shaken with grief," Edith recalled, crowded into the nave. Heavily veiled, she sat with the cousins who represented the family, Berry's sister Nathalie too ill to make the voyage.[12]

Following the service, Walter's body was transported to Père Lachaise Cemetery in northeast Paris for cremation. Fortified by brandy, Harry Crosby (residuary legatee of the estate) and the marquis de Polignac fulfilled their duty of witnessing the cremation. According to Caresse Crosby's account, they then made their way to the Pavillon Colombe, where Edith had planned a requiem mass. A black sedan followed their motor, and no sooner were they inside the salon where the service was to take place than there was a loud pounding on the front door. Two gendarmes spoke in harsh argot to Edith, demanding to know what she intended to do with the casket of Walter Berry's ashes. According to this story, she apparently had intended to bury the casket at the bottom of her garden, but they reminded her that according to French law, human remains had to be interred in consecrated ground. She must find a proper burial place or risk punitive action. Harry dealt with the gendarmes; Edith was, Caresse noted, close to tears.[13]

Edith's diary entry for Monday, October 17, reveals nothing of this wild tale: "The funeral. In the p.m. the Marquis de Polignac and H. Crosby brought the ashes here." Photographs show the altar, adorned with a *pietà* Edith had brought back from her trip to Sicily with Walter in 1913, that held the velvet-covered box of ashes. Spread before the altar on an Oriental carpet was the large wreath that had rested on Walter's funeral bier. For twelve days, Edith kept vigil over this *chapelle ardente* while Harry Crosby searched for a burial plot for his cousin.

On October 29, in a service attended only by Edith and the family (Nathalie Alden having arrived from Washington), Walter Berry's remains were buried on the outermost *allée* of the Protestant Cimetière des Gonards at Versailles, at the edge of the forest. In her diary, Edith wrote, "The stone closed over all my life."[14]

Edith faced Walter's death, the greatest loss of her life, with stoicism. She kept to her daily routine and did not give in to ostentatious displays of grief. Elisina Tyler, reading of his death in the newspaper, took the train to Paris from her house in Burgundy. Robert Norton, on his way to Tunisia, escorted Edith to the funeral. The Berensons arrived in early November. While her staff closed up the Pavillon Colombe, Edith moved back to the Hôtel de Crillon. The weather was warm and summery, and the city had a gay air about it—a "mockery" to her feelings. On a particularly beautiful afternoon, she went with Nathalie Alden to 53 rue de Varenne, where she burned in the fireplace grate the letters Walter had kept from her over the forty-five years of their friendship: "Every time I think of that apartment, and what I have lived through there of joy and sorrow," she wrote Lapsley, "my soul recoils from the idea of ever crossing its threshold again."[15]

The wrangling over bequests began in earnest, and she was called in to "advise and arbitrate and pacify." Harry Crosby proved to be "inexperienced and unmanageable," in her opinion; she called him a "half-crazy cad." From his point of view, Edith's "Grab Act" caused rancor and resentment. Walter had left her some paintings that she particularly liked (including a Cézanne, *Jas du Bouffon*) and also his library, one of the most beautiful in France, according to *Le Figaro*. A dispute arose when Harry claimed that the library belonged to him as residuary legatee of Walter's estate. To avoid public argument, Edith gave him a "great many" of Walter's books, but she insisted that the collection be cataloged (a process that took several months), during which time she designed a new room at Ste. Claire to accommodate her enlarged holdings. In May 1928, the police seal on number 53 was lifted, and she was at last allowed to retrieve the furniture, paintings, and silver she had left behind in 1920 for Walter's use. No sooner had Crosby transported his portion of Walter's books to his rue de Lille apartment than he felt oppressed by them. He gave away illuminated manuscripts to people he met on the street and left valuable first editions in bookstalls along the Paris *quais*, penciling in ridiculously low prices on the frontispiece.

A macabre footnote to the story of Harry Crosby came in late 1929, when he killed his Boston society mistress in a friend's art studio on the ninth floor of the Hotel des Artistes on Manhattan's Upper West Side. Meanwhile, Crosby's wife, mother, and poet Hart Crane awaited him at the Caviar restaurant, where he was to join them for dinner. The killings may have been part of a suicide pact, but the autopsy showed that Crosby shot himself several hours after his mistress died. Edith afterward referred to him as the "murderer."[16]

Walter's death had left her in a "passion of loneliness." "For the first time in my life," she wrote Berenson, "I feel totally rudderless. I had foreseen this, and thought I had arranged my life in such a way that the old props would hold; but the awful situation in which I found myself, and then the strange desolating communication of those last days, have knocked everything to splinters except my ever-deeper affection for the friends who were Walter's too—and you most and first."

Edith apparently never realized that several men of her inner circle disliked Walter. The most devastating sketch of him is the one Percy Lubbock provides in his *Portrait of Edith Wharton*: Walter Berry was a "gracious mould of a man," he wrote, a "shell, a simulacrum with nothing inside." Where a heart and soul should have been, there was a "deep vault of egotism within, spacious and cool, sealed against the variable currents of sympathy and humanity." In Lubbock's view, Berry lowered the temperature of life around him, "deaden[ed] its charm and cheapen[ed] its value." John Hugh Smith, whom Edith thought to have had greater sympathy for her loss than any other of her friends, dismissed him in a sentence: "Of course, there was Walter Berry." Lapsley thought him a "ferocious snob," noting (with some pleasure) that he was a blue blood only on his mother's side, the Van Rennselaers. His father, Nathaniel Berry, had brought neither an old family name nor money to the marriage. Lapsley's main complaint about Berry—one shared by others—was the powerful hold he seemed to have over Edith's thoughts and actions, encouraging her class consciousness and convincing her to accept late-nineteenth-century rationalist materialism. If it was true that she adhered to this dogma, Walter Berry's death marked her turning away from it. In the last decade of her life, she grew more deeply spiritual, moving (as Lapsley noted) toward the Roman Catholic church. Indeed, the requiem mass she planned for Walter, officiated by the abbé Mugnier, was a sign of the future directions of her spirituality.[17]

Berenson, always jealous of the pride of place Berry held in Edith's life, was said to have described him in the terms Lubbock used—selfish, clever, and cold. Yet, he and Mary were grieved "beyond measure" over his death, and it was their friendship, more than any other, Edith said, that sustained her in the first weeks after his death. It is safe to say that she knew nothing of Berenson's real feelings toward Walter (if, indeed, he had turned against him). She described Berenson to Nathalie Alden in 1931, when there was talk of a biography of Berry, as "one of Walter's dearest and most intimate friends, and no one is more qualified to advise you on the subject."

Protective of Walter's memory, Edith put a stop to a proposed biography of him by French critic Gaston Riou, whom she and Walter little respected. She headed off a supposed biographical project by a young student at the Sorbonne, Leon Edel, who was at the time completing a thesis on Henry James. She recommended to Nathalie that Morton Fullerton undertake a biography, offering to make available to him her letters from Walter; she even volunteered to help him write the book. Fullerton, of course, did not take up the project. One can envision a scene in which Edith assisted her former lover in writing the biography of the man she considered her "beloved." Had Berry ever suspected her affair with Fullerton? Had she confided to Morton the intimate details, if any, of her relationship with Walter? From all available evidence, the answer to both questions is no: the two men occupied separate quarters of her heart.[18]

Before leaving Paris in November, Edith wrote a memorial poem for Walter. To the readers of the January 1928 issue of *Scribner's Magazine*, "Garden Valedictory" may have yielded no clues to the identity of the "you" it addressed.

> *I will not say that you are dead, but only*
> *Scattered like seed upon the autumn breeze,*
> *Renewing life where all seemed locked and lonely,*
> *Stored in shut buds and inarticulate trees,*
> *So that this earth, this meaningless earth, may yet*
> *Regain some sense for me, because a word*
> *You spoke in passing trembles in the jet*
> *Of the frail fountain in my garden-close,*
> *Because you stopped one day before this rose,*
> *Or I can hear you in the migrant bird*
> *Throating goodbye along the lime-tree aisle*
> *And feel your hand in mine, and breathe awhile.*

"I know that I shall be back in a few weeks at my usual business," Edith wrote Berenson shortly after Walter's death. At work on *The Children* even before leaving Paris in November, she finished the book in Hyères in mid-January 1928. Three weeks later, she received a cable from Billy Wharton's widow saying that Teddy had died in New York City on February 7—two months short of his seventy-eighth birthday. He was buried at the Church on the Hill in Lenox next to his mother and sister. "It is a happy release," Edith wrote Gaillard, "for the real Teddy went years ago, and these survivals of the body are ghastly beyond expression." In four months, almost to the day, she had lost her dearest love and the husband to whom she still felt spiritually bound by the marital ties that were never, in her mind, quite dissolved.[19]

Since Nannie Wharton's death in 1921, Teddy had been in the care of a devoted nurse, to whom he left $14,000 and other gifts amounting to $65,000. William Wharton's children (Teddy's closest living relatives) contested the will, but the court found in favor of his nurse, Pearl Leota Barrett. His last years, as Edith knew from friends, had been slow agony. He spent his days wrapped in a shawl and seated in a chair in his bedroom. The gregarious young man who had once been "sunshine in the house" had become a silent recluse.

From Ste. Claire, Edith wrote to Judge Robert Grant: "You will go back to the far-off past of our youths together, as I do tonight, and will remember many things that I am remembering. . . . Teddy was the kindest of companions till that dreadful blighting illness came upon him, and you knew how much I appreciated his good qualities, and for how many years I struggled to carry on some sort of life with him. Your help and understanding . . . were a greater comfort to me than you can know in those dark ten years of my life, and I want to thank you for them now." Edith had by now buried all but three of the family members and close friends who went back to those early years—Minnie, Beatrix, and Gross. She would live to bury two of these women. As the shadows gathered, she was more determined than ever to live fully and intensely: "At my age, and with a will-to-live (and to work) as strong as mine," she wrote Mary Berenson, who was again passing through a period of depression, "one comes soon, I find, to accept sorrows and renunciations, and to *build* with them, instead of letting them tear me down. I had the best that life can give, and for all my grown-up life, enclosing the best, an unswerving untiring friendship, the wisest and kindest that woman ever had—and in the end, I could not have wished Walter to live another hour; and the last hours, for all the agony, were sweet. So I go on—."[20]

LOYALTIES

The Children, a story about offspring born of "careless couplings" who become victims of their parents' "careless divorces," began its serial run in the *Pictorial Review* in April 1928. The seven Wheater children range in age from an infant to fifteen-year-old Judith, who assumes responsibility for them, and is determined to make them a family. On a boat from Algiers to Europe, they meet Martin Boyne, an unmarried engineer in his early forties and a friend of Judith's parents. Drawn into this makeshift family, he finds himself serving as their unofficial guardian. His initial compassion toward Judith, a girl of an age to "be his daughter," turns to love (a version of Lawyer Royall and Charity in *Summer*) that alienates his fiancée, Rose Sellars, a woman his own age. In the synopsis Edith sent to Jewett in February 1927, the novel ended with the marriage of Martin Boyne and Judith, who then legally adopts her siblings. In the published novel, Boyne loses both Rose and Judith, who misunderstands his proposal of marriage to her as a proposal to *adopt* her along with her siblings. She returns to her mother, who has reformed her irresponsible life, and Boyne boards a ship for South America, planning to fill his empty life with work.

Edith dedicated the book to her "Patient Listeners at Ste. Claire," a group that included Norton, Lapsley, Geoffrey Scott, and Mary and Bernard Berenson, who followed the story as she read sections aloud to them during the winter of 1927–1928. They objected, as with one voice, to the story's tragic close. Mary even wept over it. Edith was primarily interested in the psychological situation represented by her characters, and had once described her writing to Jewett as constructed from "shades of character rather than dramatic situations." Thus, she was pleased with the novel's effect on her friends. It was "reserved to the end of my long literary career," she wrote Mary in March 1928, "to taste the Sweets of Success. No one before has ever cursed me for the ending of any of my books as my little group of Patient Listeners have over 'The Children.'" On the eve of book publication in August, Edith wrote Mary again: "I shall always feel I owe its success to the way you all listened and laughed while I was doing it. I wish I could reconstitute the group, to lend an ear to what I am now doing." By this time, she was well into the work she hoped to make her masterpiece, *Hudson River Bracketed*.[21]

The Children was a huge commercial success, earning over $95,000 from the serial rights contract, Book-of-the-Month Club sales of more than fifty thousand copies, and a $25,000 contract from Paramount Pictures for the film rights. (The sound movie, starring Fredric March, was entitled *The Marriage Playground*.) Reviewers, however, found *The Children* uninspired, artificial, and slick, its plot verging on the preposterous. The *Times Literary Supplement* regretted that such a good novelist as Edith Wharton could find no better theme than the "vagaries and immoralities of ultra-rich Americans"; the *Independent* thought the book "scarcely credible." Declaring it a minor effort, Clifton Fadiman noted that Wharton "still glitters, winds, surprises."

Edith thought the reviews "uncomprehending drivel (laudatory or other)." Her longtime friend Royal Cortissoz, art critic for the *New York Times*, wrote her a "life-giving" letter about the book, in answer to which she described her weary indignation and discouragement at its reception by the press. The reviews deeply depressed her, and she imagined the novel selling wildly (as it was) to people who had no idea what they were buying. No reviewer, apparently, had seen the "vision" she had tried to convey. She had failed, she concluded. Literary historians agreed: *The Children* was unworthy of her and clear proof of the decline of her literary powers. Out of print for decades, it has only recently stirred critical interest, perhaps because the circumstances in which the Wheater children find themselves are not seen today—as they were in 1928—as a vulgar "caricature" of modern society.[22]

Immediately after completing *The Children* in January 1928, Edith returned to her work on *Hudson River Bracketed*, the first chapters of which were due at the *Delineator* on June 1. A story of a young man's search for social and artistic freedom, this novel returned her to the subject of "Literature," the book she had promised to Scribners in 1915. Before war work forced her to abandon it, she had blocked out its plot and written some seventy pages. The opening scene was taken directly from her own childhood memories of sitting with her friend Emelyn Washburn in the rector's pew at Calvary Episcopal Church, listening with rapt attention as Dr. Washburn read "O my son Absalom" from the Old Testament. In the fictional scene, Edith is Dicky Thaxter, son of a preacher, who hears in his father's voice a "rain of celestial syllables pouring down on him from heights higher than the swallow's nest and the summer sky." Glancing up at the church ceiling, he sees the place in the "steep brown roof" where it "jig-sawed into a Hudson River carpenter's version of Perpendicular Gothic." *Hudson River Bracketed* takes its title from this ugly and almost forgotten nineteenth-century style of building. Loren Palmer of the *Delineator* thought the title "unfortunate" because it required explanation, but the outmoded architectural style serves Edith's young artist as a pathway for his growth and a metaphor for gentility denied him by his upbringing.[23]

Vance Weston is nineteen years old when the story opens, a child of the raw and "crude" America. He flees his native Midwest town of "Advance" when he discovers his dissolute grandfather having sexual relations with Floss Delaney, Vance's first love. The sight of them slipping into the hidden grove where he used to make love to her brings on a life-threatening fever. To recover his health, he goes East to visit relations in New York's Hudson Valley. There, in the library of The Willows, a rambling Hudson River mansion owned by a distant cousin, he discovers the world of imagination, mystery, and fantasy—he finds "literature." Weston is less easily identifiable as a fictional counterpart of Edith Wharton than was Dicky Thaxter in "Literature," but the grandfather's rampant sexuality seems to burlesque the seduction of Lucretia Jones by an aged Lord Brougham—yet, no evidence suggests that Edith knew this story about her birth.

As she worked at her new novel, whose scope would require a second volume, Jewett was busy negotiating a sale of the serial rights to her "reminiscences," the book that would become *A Backward Glance.* She wanted to publish it in a literary review like *Scribner's Magazine,* but Jewett thought it a mistake to bury her memoir in journals with limited circulation. It was especially "bad business," he said, to give it to Scribners, where she would be forced to publish both the serial and book versions. The serial market had "changed radically" since the days when *Scribner's* and *Century* had "stood aloof in splendid literary isolation," he explained. They were no more "literary" now than the popular magazines that could pay top prices. Edith reluctantly agreed with him about Scribners: "There is nothing left of the old tradition, and I see no advantages in associating my name with the kind of literature they publish nowadays." There were two offers for the memoirs, but he accepted the *Ladies' Home Journal* bid of $25,000 over one from the *Saturday Evening Post* because serialization in the widely read *Post* would mean lower book sales.[24]

Meanwhile, plans were under way to stage two of Edith Wharton's works. In January 1921, Elizabeth Marbury, vice president of the American Play Company and longtime acquaintance of Edith's, had proposed mounting a theatrical adaptation of *The Age of Innocence.* An agreement was drawn up and signed with the American playwright Zoë Akins and British actress Doris Keane, who was to play Ellen Olenska, but the project was abandoned when complications arose with Miss Keane's repertory schedule. In spring 1927, Zoë Akins, by this time one of the most sought-after playwrights in New York, pro-

posed a dramatic version of *The Old Maid*. Minnie and Jewett handled
the negotiations and secured a royalty agreement in which Edith received half of all proceeds. Production was delayed for several years by
financial problems arising from the economic depression that followed
the 1929 stock market crash, but when it finally opened, the play was
the most talked about production of the 1935 Broadway season, won
Zoë Akins the Pulitzer Prize for drama, and earned Edith about $200 a
week.

A dramatic version of *The Age of Innocence*, scripted by novelist Margaret Ayer Barnes and starring Katharine Cornell, opened in November 1928. Although Edith was not involved in the production, she
followed its progress through Minnie and her friend Edward Sheldon, a
young New York playwright whose promising career had ended when
he was paralyzed and blinded by a virulent form of rheumatoid arthri-
tis. Concerned that the staging might be too modern, Edith worried
that details of dress and gesture would not reflect accurately the New
York of the 1870s or give the flavor and atmosphere of that long-lost
period. As it turned out, she needn't have worried.[25]

The play opened at the Empire Theater in Manhattan on November
27 after a two-week trial run in Albany. Jewett saw it in early December and remarked that advance ticket sales were so "brisk" he had been
unable to get a good seat. "Miss Cornell plays the Countess Olenska
with charm and sympathetic understanding," he wrote. He noted, as
did virtually every reviewer, that the play was literary rather than dramatic; "but as the story is unfolded the audience is carried along on a
stream of interest and expectation." One critic thought Katharine Cornell overly "accentuated" her part, another complained that the love
scenes with Newland Archer (Roland Peters) were too prolonged and
not convincing, but everyone predicted a brilliant career for young
Franchot Tone, who played Newland Archer's son.

The Age of Innocence ran to packed houses for the full New York season; a year later, in autumn 1929, it toured cities from Baltimore to
Chicago. This was a sweet success for Edith, a counterbalance to the
"sad disaster" of *The House of Mirth* in 1906, which in retrospect she
thought had been caused by a "vulgar" interpretation by the director
rather than any fault of the play itself. She sent Katharine Cornell a
bound copy of *The Age of Innocence* for Christmas and thanked her for
her beautiful performance. Edith was discovering how profitable the
theater could be. Her portion of box office receipts averaged $600 a

week in January 1929; by the end of the New York run, she had earned a total of $15,000.[26]

Financially, 1928 was a "banner year." Edith would never have another as good. In July, Jewett sent her an accounting of earnings to date—$25,373.99 on back sales and book advances, plus an estimated $48,000 for the balance of the year. He asked her to decide how she wanted to divide the payments to avoid a surcharge on her United States income tax. She deferred until the following year all payments except for the $7,500 first installment on the Book-of-the-Month Club advance sales of *The Children*. On January 9, 1929, a check from Appleton for $57,122.59 was paid into her New York Bankers Trust Company account. Jewett asked whether she would consider turning back some of her earnings to make up negative balances on her earlier novels as a way of reducing her tax bill. He had failed, despite repeated efforts, to sell *The Reef* (1912) to reprint houses and film producers. It had an account deficit of $7,000. She did not take up his offer.

Edith spent lavishly from her record earnings in 1928. The major expense was a new "wing" at Ste. Claire—"an event as great to me as Versailles to Louis XIV!" she told Mary Berenson. The enlargement provided four more guest rooms and a library lined in natural-colored walnut that could house her portion of Walter's library with room to spare for volumes on art and archaeology that she purchased to complete his collection. With her own library of three thousand books, her holdings comprised six thousand volumes, with another thousand or so at St. Brice. The new room at Ste. Claire, she told Mary, was a "lizard-hole" compared with even the smallest library at I Tatti, but it was nonetheless a source of tremendous pleasure and pride for her.[27]

Even to members of her intimate circle, Edith appeared to have hardly missed a step after Walter's death. Keeping a watchful eye on her, they were relieved to see her take up with enthusiasm her old loves—literary work, gardening, and travel. In the daytime, she was all efficiency: she bought a plot in the Cimetière des Gonards as near as possible to Walter's, ordered a gravestone for his plot, and paid 150 francs a year for cleaning and upkeep of his tomb, which she visited in September 1928, her first visit since his burial. At night, as her diary reveals, she nursed her grief and loneliness. On the first anniversary of his death, she thanked the Berensons for having answered her "cry of despair" the previous autumn. "Those few weeks surrounded by the warmth of your affection put me on my feet again, and gave me back my interest in my work, which I have never lost—Bless you for it!"

In spring 1928, she made a new French will. A complicated affair, it required that she reconstitute the wartime committee of the Maisons de Convalescence so that she could bequeath her St. Brice and Hyères properties for the construction of tuberculosis sanatoria under the status of a *utilité publique* of the French government. (The plan to use the proceeds from the sale of Ste. Claire to build two sanatoria on the grounds of St. Brice was abandoned shortly before her death, because her properties were encumbered by back taxes.) She gave 40,000 francs toward endowing the "Walter Berry Room" at the Fondation Foch, a charity with which he had been associated that built a hospital for poor English-speaking expatriates in France. In the coming years, she organized a joint charity sale each winter for the Fondation Foch and the Maisons de Convalescence, the single event in the year at which she made a public appearance.[28]

Edith was acutely aware of the different ways her friends and family members faced old age and death. Minnie Bourget had for some time been in a slow retreat into morbidity that Edith blamed on Paul Bourget. He had shut her away from life: "It is all his fault," she told her friend Madeleine St.-René Taillandier. Suffering from senile dementia, Minnie (age sixty-two) became so ill in June 1928 that Bourget had to place her in a sanatorium, where she spent the last five years of her life. He rented a little house nearby and visited her regularly, but he soon became a recluse. "It makes me shudder," Edith wrote Berenson, "to think how those two played at being ill till the Furies could stand it no longer." Minnie Jones, by comparison, thought that in the previous two winters, she had been "too much shut up" and in her "shell," so at age seventy-eight, she planned to reconquer New York society. On her arrival in France for a summer visit, she ordered new dinner dresses for the winter season. "I envy that Berserk fire!" Edith wrote Lapsley. (Jewett later reported on a dinner at which Minnie was present, beautifully dressed and livelier than people half her age.) At seventy, Daisy Chanler was riding to hounds at the hunt club; "Your tempo is going to get ahead of you again, I see!" Edith joked to her.

Almost two decades earlier, when Edith was fifty years old, she had discussed with Mary Berenson the experience of "Growing Old." She remarked that growing older was the "most interesting thing that [had] ever happened to her" ("I wish I could say the same," Mary commented)

and confessed to having "wasted her youth trying to be beautiful." Now
that she had "given up all hope" of being beautiful, Edith felt "freer." This
emphasis on living fully and freely, of cultivating spiritual rather than
physical beauty, grew stronger as Edith entered the last stage of her life.

In May, Edith and Daisy made a three-week motor tour in central
and northwest Spain. This was known territory to Edith, but she gave
a breathless account of the trip to the Berensons: "How full of good
things the world still is!" When Berenson asked her to name the perfect traveling companion she would bring on their Syria and Palestine
sojourn, planned for spring 1929, she answered, "Alas, he lies at Versailles, under his cold stone."[29]

A string of three deaths came in summer. She lost Tom Newbold, a
favorite cousin who had provided legal counsel and practical aid after
her divorce, and William Crary Brownell, her editor at Scribners since
1889. She described Brownell to Charles Scribner as "one of the friends
of all my life, and seldom as I saw him his friendship was a constant
presence to me." Scribner asked her to write a memorial article on
Brownell, which appeared in the November 1928 magazine. A third
death occurred while Edith was on her annual fortnight in England,
when M. Friderich, the husband of her secretary, Jeanne Duprat, died
of pneumonia. The couple had been married less than a year. Edith
gave the young widow an extra month's paid vacation, and in September, Mme Friderich was back in Paris, at work.

Edith's visit to England was a pale shadow of the Edwardian summers she had once known, yet she saw a great number of people,
among them Mary Hunter, "down on her luck" financially because of
the drop in coal prices, and Mrs. Alfred Austin, widow of the poet laureate. She visited Robert Norton at Lamb House, where she met young
Evelyn Waugh. (She would later praise his novel *Vile Bodies*.) Eric
Maclagan, an art historian whom she had recently met through Kenneth Clark, arrived to join her and Norton for a day-trip to Sandwich
and Canterbury. The high point of her stay was a visit to the Devonshire and the Cornwall coast, a "tiny giro" she had long dreamed of.
She wanted to see Tintagel headland, where King Arthur's castle lay
wrapped in a veil of fog. It was as "wild and lonely and haunting as its
name," she wrote Mary Berenson. Although she was hard at work on
Hudson River Bracketed, writing it even as she traveled, the rocky coast-
land so captured her imagination that she reserved the name "Tintagel"
for the young duke and duchess of her final novel, *The Buccaneers*, and

later drew on her memories of this trip in her descriptions of the countryside surrounding their estate.[30]

John Hugh Smith came to the Pavillon Colombe in August, and one
afternoon, they visited the armistice memorial near Compiègne,
the centerpiece of which was Maréchal Foch's railroad car in which the
cease-fire was signed on November 11, 1918. "I was moved to the mar-
row," Edith wrote Lapsley, "as it was the first time I had been in that
part of the world since 1917." Apart from a few day-trips to Beauvais
Cathedral and Laon, she spent the last weeks of summer at work on her
novel. In September, she learned that—without consulting anyone—
Oscar Graeve, literary editor of the *Delineator*, had begun serializing
Hudson River Bracketed. Edith was forced to double her writing pace. By
Christmas, she had completed twenty-three chapters, almost half the
novel. The story exceeded the length appropriate for serialization, but
the theme of a young artist's development so engaged her that she
could not curtail the story. "I must have full swing!" she had written
Jewett in July. He encouraged her to take the space she needed, repeat-
edly voicing his enthusiasm for the book: "I love this story and have an
Oliver Twist appetite for more."[31]

Her two weeks at the Crillon in November left her "shattered with
fatigue," and she fell ill with an "undeveloped grippe." Once out of the
"slime and darkness" of Paris and into the sunshine at Hyères, she began to feel better. The new year held the promise of a trip to Syria and
Palestine with the Berensons and a voyage to New York to accept an
honorary doctor of letters from Columbia University. She planned to
see *The Age of Innocence*, which was "booming." As it turned out, the
most serious illness of her adult life canceled all her spring plans. In
January, an intense cold front swept across France and dropped temperatures at Hyères into the teens. Edith and her guests shivered inside
the walls of Ste. Claire while the terrace gardens shriveled and turned
black. The bitter cold lasted six weeks, during which time Edith struggled to recover from her third bout of flu in as many months. By the
first week in March, she was dangerously ill, having suffered a "violent"
heart attack, followed by a throat infection, high fever, and vomiting
that brought on "fievrous angina." Her illness was later diagnosed as
infectious flu accompanied by heart failure (she did not have a stroke,
as has often been assumed), but her symptoms resembled diphtheria.
Her local physician treated her with an appropriate medication, to
which he added digitalis to help regulate her heart.[32]

She was first cared for by Robert Norton and the comtesse de Béhague, a friend who had contributed generously to her war charities and who lived nearby at Villa Polynésie. But when the illness dragged on, they summoned Elisina, who, when she arrived, took over the household management. The weather was still wintry in mid-April, but Edith sat up for a couple of hours in the salon. On warm days, bundled in blankets, she lay on a chaise on the terrace, the ruins of her gardens in full view. By month's end, she could climb the stairs once a day and was allowed to take short rides in the motor, but in early May, she suffered a serious relapse. She weighed 130 pounds, fifteen pounds less than normal.

Fatigue, flu, the frigid weather, and the destruction of her garden all contributed to the onset of this illness, but the primary cause was overwork. In January, Graeve sent a plea to Jewett on behalf of the illustrator, who needed more chapters to create the sketches to accompany the text. Edith was then working at top speed, writing far more quickly than she ever had before. She felt "hunted."

Angered at the magazine editor's mercenary ways, Edith also felt ashamed: "The sense of failing to keep an obligation . . . made me so nervous that the work has gone much more slowly than it would have otherwise," she wrote Jewett. By the end of March, after the first terrible stage of her illness, she sent six more chapters. Jewett wrote to say that the pressure of publishing deadlines had developed into a "mental and moral hazard" for her, and urged her to "forget the magazine editors." In early April, Minnie sought Elisina's advice on whether Edith would be able to complete the installments or whether the magazine must halt publication.[33]

Despite the seriousness of her illness and her periodic relapses, Edith managed to keep pace with the magazine schedule. Oscar Graeve, worried that she might not be able to complete the novel and concerned about its growing length, asked her to find an ending for the serialized version. His assistant, Eleanor Carroll, disagreed with this suggestion, and wrote to Jewett in July: "My feeling is that, with so much that is already unsatisfactory, a special ending to lop it off short would be indeed the last straw." Jewett passed her letter on to Edith: "When I consider what the Delineator is," she wrote him, "and what the poorest of my work is in comparison, I confess that I feel indignant at such a tone, and I will never again willingly give a line of mine to the Delineator." She hoped to finish the novel by November, she said, adding, "I have been so harassed by the Delineator that the more I am asked when I shall finish the longer the delay is likely to be."[34]

By the end of July, Edith seemed to have recovered her health, and she took the boat-train to England for her annual holiday. In London, she spent an afternoon at the National Gallery with Geoffrey Scott, finding him in excellent health and spirits. He was sailing in a few days to New York to continue work on his edition of recently discovered James Boswell papers, now housed on Long Island. After his estrangement and divorce from Sybil Cutting, he passed through a long period of depression capped by an unhappy affair with Vita Sackville-West. Lady Sybil, in the interim, had become an outspoken supporter of Mussolini's Fascist government. (Berenson, her former lover, could scarcely abide her.) Edith's antipathy to her had strengthened when she heard reports of Sybil's mistreatment of Geoffrey and her determined pursuit of Percy Lubbock, to whom she was now married. To Edith, she was a vampire and vulture, a destroyer of human lives. Edith's affection for Lubbock was waning now that he was in Sybil's grasp, but she had an abiding love for Scott, and high hopes for his future. She rejoiced that he was "happy, ambitious, hard at work, full of courage and enthusiasm."

Thus, Edith was completely unprepared for news of his death, which came on August 15, while she was visiting Lamb House. He had died the day before in a New York City hotel of pneumonia. Pitched into grief and guilt, Edith had regrets. "How I wish I'd wired to the steamer!" she cried out, remembering Scott's hasty leave-taking a few days earlier. "I hope Percy [Lubbock] will be ashamed now of having cut him the other day in London. It wounded him so bitterly," she said. "Why do our friends die one after the other?" she and Gaillard had recently asked one another. Her "uncommonly rich" month in England was colored by Scott's death, which left her dazed and heartbroken. To Mary Berenson, she spoke openly of her anger at Sybil and Percy: "Sybil's crocodile tears revolt me, and I don't feel in the least sorry for Percy, who knew exactly what she was when he married her." To Minnie Jones, she wrote, "I championed Sybil for years against the whole Cutting family, but her behavior to Geoffrey finished that for good. Edith locked the door of her heart against Sybil and resisted Percy's efforts to win back her friendship.[35]

DESPITE HER REMARK to Jewett that she would take her time finishing *Hudson River Bracketed*, Edith worked on the book during her English sojourn and kept up the pace once she returned to France. In October, she traveled to Hyères to hire a new gardener and undertake restoration of the Ste. Claire gardens. On October 22, back at her desk at the Pavillon Colombe, she finished the novel. Already over five hundred pages long, the story of Vance Weston would not be complete until publication of its sequel, *The Gods Arrive*, in 1932. She thought it her best book, and listed it among her personal favorites, but she was convinced the public would disagree.

November 8, 1929, marked the official publication date of *Hudson River Bracketed*—one week after Wall Street's Black Friday. The final chapters, which she had rushed to New York on a fast steamer, arrived days before the book was due to appear. Jewett, who underwent surgery in October, read the last chapters on leaving the hospital. "Here's hoping," he wrote her, that "the great American reading public will respond to the passion and beauty which lift *Hudson River Bracketed* miles above the standard of the average novel."[36]

Although advance orders of twenty-six thousand copies seemed to augur strong sales, his hope was only partially fulfilled. The stock market crash immediately affected the publishing industry, although Edith's worst fears—that "nobody will buy a book" until Wall Street recovers—were not realized. It was not her best novel, and certainly not the masterpiece she had hoped it would be. Considering the formidable obstacles she faced during the months of its composition, however, the book is a remarkable achievement. Of the six novels and four novellas by her that Jewett had seen through production over the previous nine years, this one was his favorite. It was at her own "highest standard," he said. But when she received her copy in December, she was greatly disappointed. The misprints angered her, and she thought the texture of the blue binding "very ugly." Meanwhile, the serial version continued to run in the *Delineator* until February 1930—the extended run owing to the book's length.[37]

The *Nation* declared *Hudson River Bracketed* a failure, the *New Statesman* called her characters "marionettes," and Gilbert Seldes in the *New Republic* thought the novel lacked freshness and vitality. Other reviewers, however, found much to praise. Percy Hutchinson saw "human sympathy" rather than irony in the story, and Mary Ross in the *New York Herald Tribune* declared it the "most generous" book that Edith Wharton had yet written. *Century Magazine* said the novel commended virtues that the machine age sorely needed: dignity and poise, steadfast honesty, and penetrating intelligence and sympathy. The reviewer praised Edith Wharton's courage in remaining loyal to her own inner vision of wisdom and beauty. L. P. Hartley, in the *Saturday Review*, compared its sweeping European perspective of America to a painter's canvas, and the *Times Literary Supplement* called *Hudson River Bracketed* a fine "reflection of modern American life and its contradictions in the mirror of a mind nourished on tradition." The novel took a "worthy place" in Edith Wharton's work, the reviewer said. This was high praise, but the reviewer's reference to her as "Miss Edith Wharton" offended her: "I feel the discourtesy very much," she wrote Berenson. She also hated being called "Mrs. Edith Wharton" (which to her Old New York sensibilities proclaimed her a divorcée); but she raged at those who thought her an old maid. Berenson asked his brother-in-law, Logan Pearsall Smith, to ask the *TLS* editor to use her preferred mode of address ("Mrs. Wharton"). Smith intervened, but the mistake recurred in the future as though it were a "fatality."[38]

THE DRAMATIC *"tournée"* of *The Age of Innocence* continued to put coins into Edith Wharton's coffers, making Christmas 1929 at Ste. Claire particularly gay. Norton, Lapsley, Hugh Smith, Berenson, and Nicky Mariano were on hand, and Daisy Chanler arrived by steamer in Cannes at the beginning of February in advance of another trip to Spain with Edith. The only cloud on the horizon was the lackluster response to Edith's fund-raising efforts for beds in her tuberculosis sanatoria. Her richest friends—the princesse de Poix and the comtesse de Béhague, who had made substantial contributions to her charities during the war—unblushingly persisted in not giving money to further their peacetime work. Edith made up these deficiencies out of her own funds and endowed a new bed from the honorarium of Louis Gillet's "admirable" translation of *The Children* (*Leurs Enfants*). The *Revue des deux mondes*, which had been publishing Edith's work since 1907, had paid 15,000 francs (about $600) for it, which she divided with Gillet, an art historian and critic whom she had known for several years.

Gillet was a regular contributor to the *Deux mondes*, a highly respected, conservative (some thought reactionary) Catholic journal that since 1916 had been under the direction of his father-in-law, René Doumic, secretary to the Académie Française and a wealthy aristocrat, whom Edith had known since before the war. This was the third novel by Edith Wharton that Gillet translated. In 1916, he and his wife, Dominique Gillet, translated *Summer*, and in 1927, he published *The Mother's Recompense* in the *Deux mondes* under the title *Le Bilan* (The Balance Sheet)—a title she did not like, thinking it rang too much of the "Rue Barbet," that is, of Paul Bourget. She had never highly regarded Bourget's writing and did not read his late work, which overlaid his adult Catholicism on the somber Protestantism of his youth.[39]

Louis Gillet by the mid-1920s was a rising star in artistic and intellectual circles in Paris and the curator of the Abbaye de Chaalis Museum, near Senlis. A bearded, rather severe-looking man, he was the most intensely intellectual of her younger French friends, and he approached the new art movements with scholarly seriousness. Among the writers he knew personally, he held two in the highest regard— Edith Wharton and James Joyce. She no doubt would have been astounded at this coupling had she known of it, especially since Gillet initially disliked Joyce's work. In the August 1925 *Revue des deux mondes*, he wrote a long and quite critical essay on *Ulysses* (which Edith undoubtedly read and applauded). But he reversed his opinion. Six years later, he was in Sylvia Beach's rue de l'Odéon bookshop for a reading by Edith Sitwell. He introduced himself to Joyce and apologized for the article. As his friendship with Edith Wharton ripened into real affection in the 1930s, he drew near to Joyce as well.

Edith's letters to Gillet make no mention of Joyce, the modern writer whose work she disliked more strongly than any other—although she spared no kind words for D. H. Lawrence, William Faulkner, T. S. Eliot, or Virginia Woolf. She had left Paris for the countryside by the time Joyce arrived in 1920, but they shared the same ophthalmologist, the famous Swiss physician Dr. Louis Borsch. There was never the possibility of an encounter in his waiting room, however. Edith patronized his rue de la Paix office, while Joyce met him at his clinic for indigent patients on the rue du Cherche-Midi. (Joyce's choice of venue was one of convenience rather than financial necessity—he lived on the Left Bank.)[40]

Trusting Gillet's opinion on literary matters, and unaware that he had changed his mind about Joyce's *Ulysses*, Edith shared her opinions on modern writing and often asked him about avant-garde French writers—for example, her Riviera neighbor Paul Valéry, one of the most important experimenters in poetry in the early years of this century. "I don't like Valéry's writing," she said. "When you have a free moment, please tell me how he impresses you." Gillet's answer, unfortunately, has not survived. This question, and others she put to him, marks a rare moment in her literary correspondence. Her letters were not a stage for intellectual debate, nor did she often fully explore a topic in "letter talk," as Sand and Flaubert did, for example. Rather, she suggested topics for future discussion—the talk itself to take place in person. Because she saw Gillet infrequently (despite the proximity of their villages), letters were their primary means of communication.

He did not know Edith well when he wrote her in 1924 a long letter of appreciation of *Un fils au front*, the translation of *A Son at the Front*. She turned to him in summer 1925 for advice on finding a good translator for *The Mother's Recompense*, and when he himself volunteered for the job, she sent a charming letter in response to his offer: "I am honored and elated, but I don't dare believe it!" A year later, as he began work on the book, she was still amazed that he would give up his own literary work to devote himself to hers. Of the French translations of her writing, his received the greatest praise. When *Le Bilan*, an unsigned translation, was read aloud to Edith's old, blind friend Gustave Schlumberger, he exclaimed, "How marvelously Mme Wharton writes French!"[41]

Edith actively participated in translating her work into French, and even Louis Gillet did not escape her blue-penciled revisions. From 1907, when she worked with twenty-five-year-old Charles du Bos on the translation of *The House of Mirth*, she knew that her literary reputation in France depended not only on the quality of her writing, but also on the rendering of its style in French. Du Bos later recalled that Edith "enjoyed to the utmost all the problems involved in translation, [and] took the greatest interest in the process." Du Bos did not enjoy the process and did not translate any other of her books, although he helped her revise translations of *Ethan Frome* (*Sous la Neige*) and *Summer* (*L'Eté*). She had first approached André Gide to do *Summer*, since he had expressed interest in translating some of her work and she admired his writing style. When he refused, she was *"désolée,"* primarily because she wanted the book done in "very sober and very simple" language.[42]

For a brief moment in early 1915, after the death at the front of Comte Robert d'Humières, who was translating *The Custom of the Country*, there was talk of Marcel Proust completing the translation. Gide apparently mentioned the subject to him. Deep in his own work and fighting ill health, Proust did not take up the suggestion, and no French translation of *Custom* appeared. In 1929, when Edith was asked to translate *Le Temps retrouvé*, the last volume of Proust's *À la recherche du temps perdu*, after the death of the English translator, C. K. Scott

Moncrieff, she turned it down. Flattered, and perhaps amused, she told Berenson that she might have accepted the project had she been "40 or 50 years younger!" Her real reason was the same as Proust's fourteen years earlier: she wanted to do her own work.[43]

As the French audience for her writings grew, Edith felt no compunction in firing translators. In 1921, she rejected a translation of *The Age of Innocence* just as it was about to appear in the *Revue des deux mondes*—thereby forcing the magazine to fill its pages with another work. She wrote to Madeleine St.-René Taillandier, sister of André Chevrillon (former editor of the *Revue de Paris*), to ask if she knew anyone who could rework the material into acceptable French. Mme Taillandier accepted the assignment, aided by her daughter Mariane, who had translated John Galsworthy's *The Man of Property*. The result was *Au Temps de l'innocence*, which was a great success in France.

THE GODS ARRIVE

On New Year's Day, 1930, Edith wrote Elisina Tyler from Ste. Claire thanking her for her kind words about *Hudson River Bracketed*. "I would rather hear it of this than of any other [book] I have written," she said, recalling that its theme of the artist's development was one that Walter (to whom she dedicated the book) had often urged her to write. She was relieved to see 1929 pass into history, a year that had begun with her near-fatal illness and ended with the New York stock market crash. Celebrating its end, she picnicked beneath the walls of the ruined Salliès-Ville Castle near Toulon with Norton, Lapsley, and Berenson, after which they took a "long mountain walk" through pine forests and olive groves. Rejoicing at having fully recovered her health, she again expressed her gratitude to Elisina for having assisted her the previous spring: "I can never forget what you did."[44]

Edith had originally planned to rest awhile before attacking the sequel to *Hudson River Bracketed*, but a few days into the new year, she announced to Jewett that it would be called *The Gods Arrive*, taken from a poem by Ralph Waldo Emerson: "When half gods go / The gods arrive." She began writing it on January 25, the day after her sixty-eighth birthday. *Hudson River* covered two years of Vance Weston's life, a period in which he published one novel, began work on another, and entered New York literary circles. The book ended with the death of his first wife, the untutored and socially graceless Laura Lou. In financial straits because of her illness and guilt-ridden by her death, he thought of returning to his family in the Midwest. But Halo Tarrant, wife of his editor, seeks him out, and he changes his plans. In *The Gods Arrive*, they run away together to Europe, she becomes pregnant, is abandoned, and (in an all-too-hopeful ending) they are later reconciled. The major theme is Vance's development as an artist, the tug-and-pull of tension between the "lived" life and the writing life. Endowing Vance with her own ambitions and insights and inner loneliness, Edith tried to imagine through him how it feels to be an aspiring author in the competitively mercantile climate of the modern literary world. Vance learns that he must attend to the business, editorial, and publicity aspects of his writing career (as Edith herself continued to do), while also listening to the inner voices of his creative self.[45]

When Edith returned from her trip to Spain with Daisy Chanler in April, Rutger Jewett paid her a visit at Ste. Claire; it was their sixth meeting in eleven years. She wanted better distribution of her books in Great Britain and a more aggressive effort to sell the translation rights. She had by this time hired a literary agent, Curtis Brown, whom she had met seven years earlier in London, and she delegated him to sell the Swedish rights to *Hudson River Bracketed*. Confusion arose when she discovered that Appleton's London agent, Mr. Blaber, had also sold these rights. She protested Blaber's "very casual way of doing business." When Jewett arrived in Hyères, her dispute with Appleton had reached crisis level. He was able, for a time, to smooth things over.

Only when she received her November 1930 royalty statement from Appleton did Edith realize how her illness and the stock market crash had affected her literary income: it amounted to little more than $5,000, some $90,000 less than in 1929. "Yes, times are hard," Jewett wrote her, "but you must not feel poor. Your work was never more in demand." She saw no immediate opportunity for making money, even though she had completed forty thousand words of *The Gods Arrive*. Fearing that Oscar Graeve might begin publishing the novel as soon as he had its opening chapters, as he had done with *Hudson River Bracketed*, she forbade Jewett to show him the manuscript until twenty of the proposed thirty-three chapters were completed. Thus, she did not receive the first payment on her $50,000 serial contract with the *Delineator* until June 1931. In the intervening months, she lived on the declining interest money from her trust fund and rents from a lagging New York real estate market. When Munroe's Bank in Paris failed (she lost 10,000 francs, a minimal amount in better times), she resolved to do "some hard work" in the next year.[46]

Edith's sole publications for 1930 were one magazine story and *Certain People*, her eighth volume of short fiction, which appeared on November 1, 1930. Its six stories, which were written before her serious illness, had all appeared previously in magazines, one of them ("The Refugees") as far back as 1919. The *New York Times Book Review* declared it a "fine collection," and in London, the *Times Literary Supplement* said it was a "happy reminder of her vitality and contemporaneousness." Some critics thought the collection uneven and questioned whether the stories had "universal appeal," but everyone agreed that "After Holbein" was a triumph of short story writing. It tells of a senile New York hostess (probably based on Caroline Schermerhorn Astor, a cousin of George Frederic Jones's) who carries on imaginary conversations with long-dead guests. Edith dedicated the book to New York playwright Edward Sheldon, an avid reader of murder mysteries and supernatural tales. Both genres are represented in the collection: "Atrophy" is a disturbing story about aging; "Mr. Jones," whose title figure recalls aspects of the reclusive miser Joshua Jones (from whom Edith inherited a sizable fortune), tells of a murder in a haunted house; "A Bottle of Perrier," set in North Africa, recounts the aftereffects of a mysterious disappearance. She wrote this story in less than a week, North Africa still a powerful imaginative force some thirteen years after she last visited there. Berenson mistakenly thought she had composed the tale in a single day, and he grumbled at the facility with which she turned out stories. But he praised *Certain People*, questioning only her use of ghost lore in "Mr. Jones." "Didn't you know," she wrote him, that "a ghost could strangle? It's the reason why I'm so afraid of them."[47]

Three violent events in Edith's domestic life in summer 1930 rivaled scenes from her fiction. Her "fool of a cook" Roger, a man in his mid-thirties who had begun his career as a chef's helper in her kitchen some eighteen years earlier, died on July 1 of injuries he received in a motorcycle accident, leaving behind a wife and young son. After a similar accident a year earlier, Edith had warned him that he must be more careful, since he was now a man with responsibilities. (His response was to buy a larger, faster bike.) The same day Roger died, Romano, a footman of Italian origin in the Ste. Claire household, was shot to death by his wife, a woman thought to be the town prostitute. Edith quickly found a replacement for Roger, hiring a man who was "old," and did not "motor-cycle." Three weeks after he was engaged, with the guest rooms at the Pavillon Colombe full, he was found lying on the kitchen floor covered in blood. The local doctor determined that he had suffered a hemorrhage from an abscessed liver and would not survive. Transported by ambulance to a hospital in St. Denis, he died in late August. This string of events upset and saddened Edith: "Gloom in household. Every one distressed," she noted in her diary. The accidents were costly as well; she paid all the medical bills and also provided for Roger's young wife and child. Having hired a third cook (whom she later fired), she set off on a ten-day trip to Anjou and Poitou in western France with John Hugh Smith, where they visited ruined castles and attended services in out-of-the-way churches.[48]

Edith had taken time away from *The Gods Arrive* and work on her memoirs in late autumn 1929 to write a long ghost story, "The Pomegranate Seed," generally considered one of her two best tales. (The other is "All Souls," the last story she ever wrote.) The plot turns on the mysterious appearance of letters that arrive soon after Kenneth Ashby remarries. His second wife, who had known the first Mrs. Ashby before her death, begins to feel haunted. The background myth is the abduction of Persephone, daughter of the fertility goddess Demeter, into the underworld by Pluto. When Edith read the story aloud to the Ste. Claire Christmas group (Norton, Lapsley, Hugh Smith, Berenson, and Nicky Mariano), everyone guessed that the letters came from Ashby's dead wife. When Loring Schuler, editor of the *Ladies' Home Journal*, asked Edith to clarify the nature of these letters (how could a ghost write letters?), and to explain the story's ending, Edith caught another glimpse of her American readership, with its limited imagination and lack of classical learning.

Although Edith revised the story, Schuler refused it. Jewett sold "The Pomegranate Seed" to the *Saturday Evening Post*, and when it appeared in April 1931, letters poured into the offices of the *Post* from people who offered other examples of psychic phenomena. Thinking there might be a market for such stories, Edith proposed that Appleton publish a volume of her early supernatural tales. Jewett thought it an excellent idea, but suggested that early publication of such a book might interfere with the excellent sales of *Certain People*, which had earned $4,000 by January 1, 1931. The proposed collection, *Ghosts*, did not appear until after her death, when it was published not by Appleton but by Scribners.[49]

Jewett sold "The Pomegranate Seed" and a second story, "Diagnosis," for $3,000 each. These were the highest prices Edith had yet received for short fiction, and they were all the more remarkable given the depressed magazine market. But she did not succeed in getting a good price for a novella-length story, "Her Son," another of her tales of illegitimacy and social shame. Written in spring 1931, the story rings changes on *The Old Maid*, *A Son at the Front*, and *The Mother's Recompense*. It was based on a true story of a couple who gave up their first son because he was born out of wedlock; they marry and have a second son, who is killed in the Great War. After the death of her husband, the wife searches for the child she abandoned. "*What* a subject!" Edith wrote in her *donnée* book in June 1925. In her story, the mother, a respectable woman of social standing, finds her abandoned son. He is a talented painter suffering from a fatal case of tuberculosis. After his death, the couple who raised him to manhood try to coerce her to sell his paintings in order to pay her "debt" to them. The real truth about "her son" (a truth she never learns) is that he was weak and self-serving, had once been the lover of his adoptive mother, and was not, in reality, her son.

Not only did the subject of this tale fly in the face of middle-class American morality, but the story was too long for most magazines. By autumn 1931, when Edith tried to place it, the bottom had dropped out of the magazine market. She sold it for a mere $750 to *Scribner's Magazine*, agreeing to this low sum only because they submitted the story for a $5,000 prize they felt certain she would win. She did not win.[50]

As EDITH GREW older, she found it increasingly difficult to see "new people," by which she meant those outside her usual group of friends. Yet, in late 1930, she did form bonds with several younger people. Aldous Huxley, grandson of naturalist Thomas H. Huxley and nephew of Mrs. Humphry Ward, joined her Riviera circle. Huxley and his wife, Maria, took a house at Sanary, about twenty minutes away, and Edith found them "delightful" and "pleasant" neighbors. They introduced her to another couple who wintered in the South of France, English writer Cyril Connolly and his American wife, Jean. In his mid-twenties, Connolly was already making a name for himself as literary critic in the *New Statesman*. Among her younger friends, Edith's special favorites were art historian Kenneth Clark and his wife, Jane. In 1931, when they visited Ste. Claire for the first time, Clark, not yet twenty-eight years old, had just been appointed keeper of the Department of Fine Art at the Ashmolean Museum at Oxford. Soon, he would become director of the National Gallery in London.[51]

When Edith first met Kenneth Clark in 1927, he was assisting Berenson in his research at I Tatti. She was unaware that both Mary and Bernard had already begun to dislike him. From the first, Mary thought her husband's sponsorship of Clark was a "mistake"; she later described him as a "queer mixture of arrogance and sensitive humility." When he married in January 1927, she thought his bride a "complication," as did Berenson, who preferred his protégés unencumbered by family responsibilities. By the time Jane gave birth to their first child in spring 1929, Berenson's hope of making Kenneth Clark his heir apparent had faded.

The marriage proved to be less than either Kenneth or Jane had hoped. When their twins were born in autumn 1932, they were already experiencing serious marital strain. They asked Edith to be godmother to their son Colin (Nicky Mariano sponsored daughter Colette Clark), a responsibility she accepted with great pleasure and a certain high seriousness. On his christening, she gave him the silver mug that Lucretia had furnished for her own baptism more than seventy years earlier, and on her death, she bequeathed to Colin Clark (then age five) the greater part of her library. Edith was apparently oblivious—as the Berensons were not—to the Clarks' marital difficulties. Jane, suffering from serious allergies and prone to rapid weight loss, alternated between periods of flourishing health and desperate illness. Worried about her, Edith wrote endearing and supportive letters, but she did not suspect that depression and alcohol and cocaine addiction lay behind the ups and downs of Jane's health. While Kenneth Clark charted a meteoric rise in the art history world, his wife struggled to be the perfect companion and hostess, and cope with raising three children. She felt herself a failure at every turn.[52]

The Clarks were part of a wave of visitors who occupied guest rooms at Ste. Claire and St. Brice in spring and summer 1931—Alfred de St. André, Logan Pearsall Smith, Bessy Lodge, Lily Norton, Mary Berenson, and many others. There was no "closed season," Edith explained to Minnie, and virtually no weekday without guests for lunch or tea. Despite another serious battle with flu, she made steady progress on *The Gods Arrive*. The novel writing was slow going, she told Berenson, consoling herself with the knowledge that she had not been able to write much faster than at her current pace when she was young: "I suppose it's my natural tempo." Fatigue and illness showed themselves in her handwriting, however, which degenerated into an almost unreadable scrawl. Her doctors began a treatment to correct a glandular deficiency, which they now thought was the cause of her nose and throat irritations and the constant battles with flu that had already done serious damage to her heart.[53]

She was also busy with charitable activities, raising money for more sanatoria beds and attending countless meetings with officials of the public hygiene office regarding the sanatorium at La Tuyolle. If the Maisons de Convalescence added to her daily stress, another charity project left over from the war gave her great joy in summer 1931. For more than a decade, she had sponsored an auction each autumn for the abbé Compteur, a young priest who ministered to those living in the "zone rouge" encircling Paris. The "red zone," the northern ring of working-class suburbs, had suffered impoverishment during the war and a continuing low standard of living in the years since. Their inhabitants were thought to be vulnerable to Socialist-Communist thought, which the Catholic church tried to counter by offering various kinds of aid and activities. The abbé had prayed for a church of his own, and at last—with Edith's help—his prayer had been answered. In an elaborate ceremony in August 1931, the Chamoine of Garges de Gonnesse (a friend of Edith's) christened a bronze bell for the church, paid for by funds raised by members of this poverty-stricken parish. The bell was named "Edith-Matilda," in honor of Edith Wharton and Matilda Gay. Brioche and *vin mousseux* were served to the entire parish following the ceremony. Ogden Codman was so moved by the event and by the abbé's devotion to his people that he gave $4,500 (about 110,000 francs) to complete the cement belfry. By mid-October, the "campanile" was nearly completed.[54]

In Europe, Edith Wharton was seen more and more frequently inside Catholic churches. Three of her closest women friends were Catholic—Daisy Chanler and Matilda Gay (both of whom converted in young adulthood), and Elisina Tyler. Her lady's maid, Elise Devinck, was a devout Catholic, and Catherine Gross would soon begin instruction to convert to Catholicism. In her private moments, Edith read Roman church history, and on All Souls' Eve, 1930, had read the Roman *"Office des Morts"* and thought of her "Beloved" Walter. Each August 15, she opened the Pavillon Colombe to the local convent to celebrate the Virgin Mary's Assumption, when girls from the school, dressed all in white with flowers twined in their hair, paraded through the gardens. She made pledges to the Catholic parish of both St. Brice and Hyères and regularly entertained the local curé.

In America, meanwhile, magazine editors coped with the ever-more risqué subjects of her fiction. *The Gods Arrive* was turned down by the *Saturday Evening Post, Liberty,* and *Collier's.* Thus, she was forced to return to the *Delineator,* where she had sworn never to publish again after they prematurely began serializing *Hudson River Bracketed* in 1928. The *Delineator* described itself as one of the most "liberal-minded of the women's magazines," but its editor was nonetheless "startled" at the situation dramatized in *The Gods Arrive* in which Vance and Halo live together unmarried. Only Edith Wharton's prestige as a writer enabled the magazine to publish such a story; "We will, of course, get protests," Oscar Graeve told Jewett. "What fools these mortals be!" Jewett exclaimed, referring (he said) not to the magazine editors but to their "dear subscribers." Edith's novel was, in his opinion, "as moral as a church sermon," as moral even as *The Scarlet Letter,* which in its day was "undoubtedly considered alluringly wicked."[55]

When the first advance payment from the *Delineator* arrived in late June 1931, Edith again felt flush. To rest from her labors, she took her usual fortnight in England in July, spending three "lightning" days in London and environs during which she saw some half-dozen writers, critics, and journalists, including the Kenneth Clarks in Richmond, Sacheverell Sitwell, Harold Nicolson, Desmond MacCarthy and his son-in-law David Cecil, H. G. Wells, and Sir James Barrie.

Returning to St. Brice after a tour on the Cotswolds country house and garden circuit, Edith encountered weather so cold she was forced to run the central heating at the Pavillon Colombe, and by early September, she was ill with flu. Two weeks later, still not well, she fainted in the train. As a stream of visitors and houseguests continued unabated, she tried to recover her health and keep apace with her literary work, writing so furiously at *The Gods Arrive* that she became "work-blind." Although due to begin serialization in February, the novel was still far from finished, yet she had already proposed to Jewett a title and subject for the novel that would follow it. In *The Buccaneers,* she planned to picture again the "Age of Innocence" period in American life, telling the story of how wealthy nouveaux riches married their daughters to English lords. Jewett enthusiastically embraced the idea, commenting that the very landmarks of mid-nineteenth-century America were disappearing from sight. Looking out from his office on West Thirty-second Street, he could see on the skyline the new Empire State Building. "Does it seem possible," he wrote Edith, "that this structure towers to heaven on the site of those two red brick houses which we knew in our youth as the homes of 'old John Jacob' and William Astor," the son and grandson of the family founder.[56]

The Gods Arrive was still unfinished when Edith left for I Tatti at the end of October, but she needed a real holiday. Mary Berenson was ill again with cystitis and facing another surgery to correct the condition, and Edith, seeing that Nicky Mariano was nearly sick from exhaustion and worry over Mary, took Nicky on a trip to Rome. Except for an afternoon on the hills above Rome in 1925 with Walter, Edith had not visited the city in seventeen years.

For Nicky, who felt "real devotion" to Edith but also found her formidable, the trip revealed unexpected and apparently contradictory aspects of her. Edith booked rooms at the Albergo Palazzo, one of Rome's best hotels, but for their daily excursions, she hired the "oldest and dirtiest and most ramshackle" of taxicabs, one driven by a man whose black coat had turned green with age. Nicky rebelled at the indignity of this conveyance and suggested they hire a car more in keeping with Edith's "station in life." She refused, saying that she had chosen the man because she thought he would be good to her little dog Linky, her ancient and beloved Pekingese, while they toured early Christian churches. In an eye blink, Edith had taken in "details of expression, subtle nuances of mood" in the man that Nicky had missed. It was true: the cabdriver with tattered coat was very tender with the dog.[57]

Nicky caught another insightful glimpse into Edith at a pontifical mass sung by Benedictine fathers to celebrate the consecration of the churches of St. Peter and St. Paul. They went to the Basilica of S. Paolo fuori le Mure, situated in a poor parish, for a ceremony that was dignified in a "severely classical" manner. Deeply moved, Nicky also knew that Edith—who she had feared would be bored and restless—sat very still, carried away "into another sphere" by the service. Later that day, they went to St. Peter's to observe the display of the holy reliques at vespers. This was Edith's favorite service, one to which Walter Berry, Robert Norton, John Hugh Smith, and Daisy Chanler had at various times accompanied her. By week's end, and at Edith's request, they had attended services at some half-dozen churches, among them obscure and outlying ones.

Nicky and a few other of Edith's close friends believed that she came close to converting to the Roman church before her death. Her diary reveals that in the last decade of her life, she frequently attended Catholic services. But when Nicky expressed this opinion to a member of Edith's inner circle (probably Lapsley), she was greeted with surprised skepticism. He admitted that Edith was "sensitive to the beauty of ritual," but doubted that there was anything more to it than this. "Anyway," he quipped, "if Edith should be converted to Catholicism, my heart would go out to her confessor!" This remark derives from Lapsley's conviction that her "inexpungeable and self-sufficing pride kept her an intellectual rationalist." At her core, he believed, was a "tough and unreduced *ego* that would have made submission impossible for her." He assumed that mysticism, which she had explored in several early works (the 1901 poem "Margaret of Cortona," for example) was closed to her as well. She was "in the main," he said, "a just, reasonable, compassionate and generous woman, but she was not consistently nor constantly that."[58]

Kenneth Clark offered another perspective. The division of her world between those who were inside her charmed circle (the "elect") and those who were not, derived, in Clark's opinion, from a conflict between her Protestant and Catholic attitudes. When he remarked to Edith that he had never known anyone who so thoroughly understood both viewpoints, she answered that she had always wanted to write a novel that would dramatize the conflict between the two impulses. On a drive back from Beauvais Cathedral one afternoon, she outlined the story to him in great detail. The expansive side of her nature—her kindness to servants and dependents, her generosity to the two villages in which she lived, and her interest in human nature—derived from the "Catholic side" of her character, he thought. "But I would not press the analogy too far," he told Percy Lubbock.

After Rome, Edith returned to I Tatti to spend two weeks, working on *The Gods Arrive* in the mornings and taking "enchanting excursions" into the countryside in the afternoons. By Christmas, Mary was convalescing at I Tatti, and Berenson joined Norton and Lapsley at Hyères for a less than happy Yuletide season, despite plentiful sunshine and beautiful flowers. Berenson, "in a perpetual state of nerves," fretted over Mary's health and waited impatiently for the arrival of Nicky, who had spent the holidays with her family. Catherine Gross, her mind fading in this, the forty-seventh Christmas she had spent with Edith, walked in the terraced gardens with her nurse, a nun of the local convent. While her guests basked in sunshine, Edith pushed to finish *The Gods Arrive.*[59]

In January 1932, Gross celebrated her eightieth birthday and Edith passed her seventieth. Minnie, aged eighty-two, saw to it that her letter of condolence for the "woes and privations of old age" arrived on the eve of the "great day," but Edith repudiated its sentiments. "The farther I have penetrated into this ill-famed Valley the more full of interest, and beauty too, have I found it. It is full of its own quiet radiance, and in that light I discover many enchanting details which the midday dazzle obscured. As long as I love books and flowers and travel—and my friends—and good food, as much as I do now, I want no allowances made for me!"

Edith sent the last chapters of *The Gods Arrive* to Berenson, who was reading it in draft, and received in response a telegram saying that Mary was dying. Beside himself with worry, he poured out his misery to Edith in almost daily letters. The crisis of Mary's illness was worsened for him by the "Economic Black Death," as he called the Great Depression. By 1932, Berenson's income had been cut virtually to nothing. He had lost his £10,000 retainer from Joseph Duveen, his stock portfolio was all but wiped out, and he now feared losing I Tatti. All this weighed on him as Mary slipped toward death. Kneeling at her bedside in late January, he called out, "Don't desert me, Mary." The sound of his voice, she said, pulled her back toward life.[60]

After several spells of irregular heartbeat brought on by fatigue and hurry in spring 1932, Edith decided not to make the trip to New York to accept the honorary doctorate that Columbia University was once again offering her. "I am so sickened at the thought of what America has become," she wrote Minnie, "that I want to stop [up] my ears and close my eyes when it is mentioned! I can't be thankful enough that I am ending my days among civilized people." Except for Minnie, the Max Farrands, and Edward Sheldon, she said, there was no one in America she wanted to see or felt stimulated by. She was appalled as much by the collapse in social values as by the country's puritanism, and followed the accounts of the Lindbergh baby kidnapping with growing horror, noting in her diary on May 15, "I am haunted by murder of Lindbergh baby—What a sad Whitsunday."[61]

In late spring, she received the news that the mortgage on 737 Broadway was at risk of foreclosure. Edith, Minnie, and Beatrix needed to raise $153,000 to pay it off and thereby protect two other trust properties—Minnie's home, 21 East Eleventh Street, and Edith's birthplace, 14 West Twenty-third Street, both of which held second mortgages. Minnie once again faced losing her home, and Beatrix and Edith, aided by attorneys in Paris and New York, worked to forestall such an eventuality. Meanwhile, Minnie was writing her reminiscences, entitled "Lantern Slides," hoping they would bring in some money. She did not live to complete the book, but in 1937, two years after her death, Berkeley Updike agreed to print a private edition.[62]

In an effort to "forget what the world is like now," Edith turned to work on her own memoirs, but as she wrote about her early years, she longed to be writing a novel. "I can never keep up my interest in my own past history for more than an hour or two a week, whereas I am always longing to tell about the life of the imaginary people who populate my dreams," she wrote Sheldon. She recommended Aldous Huxley's Brave New World to him and any number of other friends. "I suffer from a complete inability to read novels about a future state of society," she wrote Sheldon, "but in this case, although it pretends to be a prophecy of the future it is really a cruelly true picture of the present." The rise of the modern, mechanized totalitarian state, whether in the form of Soviet communism or German and Italian fascism, was appalling to Edith, and she thought Huxley's novel had captured something of its terror. Her daily worries were spurred by efforts to care for people whose needs were overlooked by the modern republican state, and she was saddened when even the most stalwart supporters of her charities were forced to reduce their contributions. Meanwhile, her personal charities ("lame ducks," as she called them) required increasing assistance. Everything depended on her continued ability to write quickly and to second-guess accurately the American literary market.[63]

The Gods Arrive was published in book form in September 1932. As Edith explained to Robert Grant, writing it had proved more difficult than expected. A sequel to Hudson River Bracketed, it had to stand as a self-contained novel and also refer briefly to events described in the

novel published three years earlier. In solving these structural problems, she had rewritten portions of the story as many as five times, and
the book version differed in certain respects from the magazine version.
In an interview with Eleanor Carroll, associate editor of the *Delineator*,
Edith was quoted as saying that her ambition was to portray the "half-
gods that are worshipped by all people—but especially by the creative
artist—the mistakes, the sufferings, the glimpses of glory, that go into
the painful perfecting of the human spirit." This goal was perhaps the
greatest challenge she had undertaken as a writer, and by her own esti-
mation, she had not succeeded in reaching it. Among her friends, Bessy
Lodge and Royall Tyler wrote to say how much they liked the book,
but readers who knew nothing of the workings of the "creative mind"
were puzzled.[64]

In general, reviewers praised what May Lamberton Becker in the
Saturday Review of Literature called Edith Wharton's attempt to fathom
the novelist's processes of creation and chart the cultural evolution of a
writer. Some readers complained that the book lacked unity and that
sketchy secondary characters merely provided a background for Halo
Tarrant and Vance Weston. To William Lyon Phelps, however, Edith
Wharton was a patrician in art, a writer without a "trace of the common or vulgar in her mind." She was a pure artist, writer and nothing
else. Isabel Paterson remarked that in satirizing the modernists, the
novel conceded "not the fraction of an inch in either theory or practice
to their literary claims."[65]

Jewett reported on September 29, 1932, some ten days after publication of *The Gods Arrive*, that the book had started off well with reviews that were, "in the main," good. But it did not sell many copies.
By summer 1934, it had earned little more than $8,000 in royalties.
(*Hudson River Bracketed* had earned over $18,000 by this time.) An
American middle-class readership was perhaps bored by her detailed
analysis of the literary process, while the Left Bank experimenters the
story satirizes took themselves for the gods who had arrived. When
Edith received her copy of the book, whose gold-stamped flower and
leaf design on dark-blue cloth pleased her, she was already working
hard on her reminiscences and had sent Jewett the first installment of
the memoir. The search for an appropriate title had been a long and
frustrating one, but a phrase from Walt Whitman—"a backward
glance o'er travell'd roads"—came to her on the morning of July 20,
1933. Unable to put aside fiction, she planned two new volumes of

short stories and had already written the first chapter of *The Bucca-neers*.[66]

"IF THERE IS any money left in the world by April 18, let's blow in a little, and take one more look!" Edith suggested to Daisy early in 1933. They planned a trip to Rome, and to save on expenses, Daisy would share Edith's maid, Elise. The trip was canceled when Elise collapsed from what at first appeared to be a nervous breakdown. She had been suffering spells of inexplicable fatigue for almost two years, and when her condition suddenly changed for the worse, she assumed she had only a short time to live. Edith believed the trouble was some "temporary physiological disturbance" and declared that Elise was behaving childishly. "The servant class can never grasp anything like that," she wrote Daisy; "if they could (as dear Egerton used to tell me) they wouldn't be servants, but Presidents and Prime Ministers!" But Elise's premonition was correct. She had anemia. Attended by two doctors and two nurses, she lingered for several weeks and finally died during the night of May 29. Many of her friends and Edith's attended the funeral service at the village church in Hyères. Within days of her burial, Edith was involved in a legal battle to protect the inheritance rights of Elise's niece. At the same time, she was arranging for Gross, now in the later stages of senile dementia, to enter into the care of the sisters of the L'Espérance Convent in Hyères.[67]

It was not a year since Gross had converted from the Lutheran faith to Roman Catholicism. She had certainly been guided toward this decision by the example of Elise's strong faith and that of the abbé Compteur, the parish priest of the "zone rouge" who received her into the church. In late September, Edith's old servant fell into a coma, and on October 3, Alfred White telegraphed from Hyères to say that she had died. Catherine Gross was buried next to Elise Devinck in the village churchyard, and Edith erected twin monuments for the two women who were closer to her than any others, except her childhood nurse, Doyley.

Without these friends of many years, Edith's life was "emptier than ever." In their forty-eight years together, Gross had never fallen below her own high standard of "perfect honesty, loyalty, and fidelity," Edith explained in a letter to Berenson. Shortly after Gross's death, Edith took a three-week trip to Holland with her new lady's maid, Marie. It was an effort to "fill up some of the numerous lacunae in my world map before the curtain falls," she told Berenson. She had "madly rich" days—Amsterdam was "all jade and agate and topaze, and the Hague all the marbled reds and greens." But when darkness fell early in the afternoon, she felt closed in by loneliness.[68]

BUCCANEERING

In 1933, a year of financial reversals, deaths, and household upheavals, Edith completed *A Backward Glance* and successfully battled an effort by the *Ladies' Home Journal* to reduce by $5,000 its contract price of $25,000. Loring Schuler had purchased the rights in 1928, when the book trade was booming. In the wake of the economic depression, he could not fulfill the original contract, he said, nor could he use all 450 manuscript pages she had submitted. Parts of the book were "decidedly dull," he wrote Jewett, and he suggested judicious cutting of almost half—about fifty thousand words—and reducing the fee by one-fifth. Sending Edith a copy of Schuler's letter, Jewett explained that the *Journal*, like other magazines, had experienced a drop in advertising and was rumored to be losing money.[69]

Edith replied that she was not at all surprised that Mr. Schuler found her memoir too long and parts of it "dull." He was at liberty to cut anything he wanted, she said—except the price. She would neither take back the manuscript nor accept a lower fee for it. Those who had read the manuscript (including Desmond MacCarthy, editor of the *Saturday Review*) were enthusiastic about it, she said, and letters were pouring in from readers praising "Confessions of a Novelist," a section of the autobiography recently published in the *Atlantic Monthly*. While Jewett pressed the case with Schuler, Edith stood her ground and threatened to sue the magazine. No doubt they were "hard up," but so was she, "and I imagine that they have larger funds to draw upon than I have." Schuler eventually agreed to pay the full price.[70]

In March 1933, while Edith was struggling to complete her memoirs, her ninth volume of stories, *Human Nature*, appeared to mixed reviews. (The weakest story in the volume, "Diagnosis," which Jewett had sold to the *Ladies' Home Journal* in 1930 for $3,000, was rejected by fourteen British magazines before Edith withdrew it from circulation.) She dedicated the book to Bernard Berenson, an enthusiastic reader of her short fiction. The four stories and a novella ("Her Son") repeat the familiar themes of her later period—emotional betrayal, parental abandonment of children, and the quality of artistic talent. Several reviewers noted that the stories had the virtues of a "commanding maturity," and Graham Greene—a writer of the new generation—found her attitude "cool, aloof, a little withering," betraying the influence of her "master," James. The long shadow of Henry James again fell across Edith Wharton's literary career as reviewers repeated the familiar refrain that her greatest strengths and weaknesses reflected James's influence. In according him a central place in her memoirs, the only chapter devoted to a single person, Edith made it seem that James, if not her "master," was still the most important literary person in her life.[71]

A Backward Glance—cut up into segments by the "untutored tooth of some office underling," as she later complained to Berenson—would begin its serial run in October and appeared in book form in late April 1934. Edith hated the serialized version so much that she advised her friends to wait for the book. And the book was worth waiting for. Bound in a diagonal-ribbed deep-blue cloth, its cover had a gold facsimile of Edith Wharton's signature and pale-yellow woven endpapers. It included precious portraits of her father, her grandparents, and great-grandparents (retrieved from Harry Jones's Versailles apartment after the death of his widow in 1928), a casual photograph of Henry James, and pictures of Pencraig, The Mount, and Edith's two French homes. Searching through photographs and memorabilia for the book early in 1934, she destroyed many old pictures, letters, and literary documents, and chose not to include in the memoir photographs of her mother, her two brothers, Teddy Wharton, or of Land's End. The sad-eyed portrait made of her in 1921 faced the poignant dedication:

> *To the Friends*
> *Who Every Year on All Souls' Night*
> *Come and Sit with Me*
> *By the Fire*

By 1934, Edith's dead friends outnumbered her living ones. The more their numbers grew, the more she felt their absence in her daily life. In an early draft of the book, she wrote, "I have reached the age when the only night of the year when my little house is really crowded is on All Souls' Eve when I sit alone and *they* come who have been the joy and solace of my life, the friends who, when I think of them, live again, whose voices I hear, whose eyes I look into, whose hearts melt into mine."[72] Aware of having escaped a brush with death in spring 1929, she now monitored her physical and psychological health in her diary. On January 10, she was "dog tired." "Why do I get these fits of sudden fatigue?" she asked. Two weeks later, on her birthday, she noted, "Aetat 72! And I feel exactly as I did 40 years ago!" In early March, she sighed, "What a *weary* year!"[73]

Added to the weariness were the slow sales of *A Backward Glance*, despite a wealth of praiseworthy comments in all the major reviews. Most critics agreed that it was reserved, sensitive, and full of charm, but with a narrative style that some thought too uniform. E. M. Forster, writing for *New Statesman and Nation*, claimed that although prosperity did not spoil Edith Wharton's writing, it did make for "autobiographical monotony." Christopher Morley, in the *Saturday Review of Literature*, complimented her on having overcome social obstacles to become a writer. William Troy wrote in the *Nation,* "If there is any continuous dramatic interest in these pages, it consists in the unbroken persistency of Mrs. Wharton's effort at emancipation—the old battle of the artist with the world." Acknowledging that the memoir left few illusions about the social climate in which Edith Wharton moved, Newton Arvin in the *New Republic* observed that this narrow world had had a straightening effect on her vision. She was a "serious enough writer to look critically at the foibles of her set," but she "never looked any farther inward than that," he said. Her portrait of Henry James was deemed the most memorable set-piece of the book. (Isabel Paterson in the *New York Herald Tribune* declared it a devastating portrait of James as a hypochondriac and "fuss-budget.") Most readers wanted to know even more about the relation of her life to her work and art. In such "sidelights," wrote Amy Loveman, a volume of "picturesque recollections" gained "a significance beyond the memories they unfold." Edith knew her readership wanted the inner view, and she acknowledged their desire only in brief—and carefully edited—glimpses. The more forthright and plain-spoken *Life and I*, an early version of the first chapter of *A Backward Glance*, reveals what was lost through self-censorship.[74]

CHEERED BY THE many friendly letters from friends that greeted *A Backward Glance*, Edith was discouraged by its poor sales. Everything about the "new" America alienated her, yet she needed to stay in touch with it to sustain her literary reputation. She could not afford to lose the economic base her writing provided, not only because she maintained an expansive (and expensive) style of living, but also because she supported more than two dozen dependents—a group that included family members, aged friends, current and former staff members, war and tuberculosis victims. Seeking money anywhere she could find it, she took heart in the news that film companies were suddenly interested in several of her works, and she held Appleton to seeking the highest prices possible—$15,000—even though Jewett reminded her that the movie industry was experiencing financial difficulties.

Two newly organized film companies were interested in *Ethan Frome*. Edith thought this story particularly suitable for filming, and she pressed for news of the negotiations. The tragic, bitter ending of the tale gave the producers pause, and no contract was forthcoming. E. L. Smith, head of the Appleton film department, explained to Edith (through Jewett) that the public wanted light comedies and uplifting stories. When a talking version of *The Age of Innocence*, starring Irene Dunne as Ellen Olenska, opened in October 1934 at Radio City Music Hall in New York, John Williams, president of Appleton, wrote Edith to say that it was reportedly a good film, far better than the 1924 silent version. But it drew little public interest and disappeared immediately. The new film was based on Margaret Ayer Barnes's dramatic version of the novel, which she had prepared some years earlier. Contract money was divided according to the terms of the drama contract; the co-signers were Margaret Barnes, Katharine Cornell, Warner Brothers, and Edith Wharton. Of the $8,500 contract, each received $2,125. In her lifetime, Edith made some $55,000 on the sale of film rights to her works.[75]

Edith's best source of quick money was short stories, and she could as yet command top prices. In spring 1933, Gertrude Lane at the *Woman's Home Companion* purchased "Duration," a satire of changing family mores among upper-class old Boston families, for $3,000. Six months later, she wrote Jewett to say that the magazine could not use the story. Hoping to "salvage" some of the purchase price, Lane sent the manuscript back with the suggestion that Jewett try to place it elsewhere; she conceded that he would probably not sell it for anything

like the price she had paid for it. Edith was "staggered" at the "inso-
lence" of Miss Lane's letter. It was beyond her "capacity," she said, to
"write down to the present standard" of the American pictorials: "If I
could turn out a series of pot-boilers for magazine consumption I
should be only too glad to do so; but I really have difficulty imagining
what they want." He later sent "Duration" to Ellery Sedgwick, editor
of the *Atlantic Monthly* and a longtime friend of Edith's. He, too, rejected it, saying the satire was cutting but not cutting enough. (It needed
to "draw blood.") "Mrs. Wharton's reputation," he wrote Jewett, "is a
real American possession, and in my judgment it would be a mistake
for her to have the story printed in anything like its present form."
Edith withdrew the story from circulation and printed it in a later collection of short stories, *The World Over* (1936).[76]

Eager to patch over the embarrassing moment with Gertrude Lane,
Jewett sent her another Edith Wharton story, "Kouradjine Limited," a
satire involving oil millionaires and movie stars, which she immediately
rejected. He then approached *Hearst's International-Cosmopolitan*, which
bought the story under a new title, "Bread Upon the Waters," for
$5,000—the highest price Edith ever received for a work of this
length. He then sold it for another $5,000 to the movies. The Eastern
Film Company bought it but never made the film; Universal Pictures
produced an adaptation of it, released in 1934 under the title *Strange
Wives*. Minnie Jones signed the movie contract on Edith's behalf: "I
wish the sum had more nearly approached the prices I used to get!"
Edith wrote her.[77]

Harry Payne Burton, editor of *Cosmopolitan*, had not yet decided to
serialize her next novel, *The Buccaneers*. He wanted to see half of it before making an offer. His request pricked Edith's anger. She had mistakenly thought him "very anxious" to take whatever she had to offer,
she wrote Jewett. "I have never before been treated like a beginner, and
I do not like it." In the end, the best Burton could offer was a $1,000
option on the novel, explaining that he could not meet the $50,000 of-
fer Edith had once had from the *Pictorial Review*. That journal had
changed hands several times in the years since its editor, Arthur Vance,
had died, and the new management was unwilling to honor Vance's offer from 1927.[78]

Preoccupied with marketing her work, Edith seemed unaware that
Jewett was unwell. Although rarely absent from his desk, he was experiencing serious eye problems and symptoms of a disturbing heart con-

dition. She apparently had no idea the effect her request to put *The Buccaneers* in the hands of a professional literary agent might have on him. He responded to her letter of May 9 with his usual good grace, saying that he was "only too delighted" to attend such matters himself, adding that "you do not need an agent any more than a duck needs rubbers." Two weeks later, Jewett was very ill, and John Williams, president of Appleton, took over his duties. Writing from Rome, where she was sightseeing with Nicky and Berenson, Edith annnounced to Williams that from now on, she no longer wanted to be published by Appleton's division in England, and asked him to prepare a new book publication contract for *The Buccaneers* that took account of this change. It was an old and familiar complaint, but Williams replied that he could not broach the subject with Jewett in his present condition. He had not dared tell Jewett that his old friend Brand Whitlock had recently died.[79]

A "green mould" was growing over Appleton, Edith observed. She wanted to leave the firm, she told Minnie, but admitted that "on account of Jewett" such a move would be difficult. Saying that "no one could appreciate more sincerely than I do the kindness shown me for many years" by Appleton, and the "many services they have rendered me," Edith restated her desire for a new contract on *The Buccaneers* that would allow her to choose her English publisher. Her letter, sent to John Williams, was answered by D. W. Hiltman, chairman of the board, who said her remarks were "manifestly unfair and unjust." Hiltman compiled a list of earned royalties since her 1912 publication of *The Reef* and began by listing the debit balances on three books that had not yet earned their advances— *The Reef, Summer,* and *The Marne.* This liability amounted to almost $11,000, on which Appleton had made no claim for repayment. On the other twelve books Edith Wharton had thus far published with their firm, she had earned some $200,000 in royalties, another $380,000 in serial contracts, short story sales, and film and dramatic rights. The bulk of this money had come in the thirteen years since *The Age of Innocence,* and all of it, he noted, resulted from Jewett's negotiations of her contracts—on which she had saved almost $58,000 in agent's commissions.[80]

Hiltman's letter was no doubt intended to make her feel ungrateful, but it was also meant to cut short any plans she might have for leaving the firm. Jewett, he added, had suffered a "severe nervous breakdown" caused by conditions resulting from the economic depression, but he was due back in October. Hiltman's strong letter apparently frightened Edith, for she reacted to his implied suggestion that she should repay Appleton the $11,000 unearned advance on the three early books. She noted that several of her books at Scribners had "hung fire" (*Ethan Frome*, for example) before they earned back their advance money, but that Charles Scribner's Sons had never alluded to this fact. "Like every one else in America," she wrote, "I find my income diminishing from day to day, without any means of knowing in advance what the next month will bring, and I am therefore obliged to view my literary work first of all from the point of view of the bread-winner."

Although Jewett partially recovered his health, he never returned to his office nor did he resume an active editorial role. On Christmas Eve, Edith wrote Minnie from Hyères, where her usual holiday group had gathered, asking that she give Jewett her best wishes, adding that she thought his working days were probably over. By the time Minnie received the letter, Jewett had fallen into a coma. He died in January 1935, but in every important way, he had disappeared from Edith's life many months earlier. He had given his best energies to managing her career, and his ill health was due not only to the effects of the current economic crisis on the publishing industry, but also to his efforts to maintain Edith Wharton's earning power and literary prestige. She sent a telegram to Appleton: "Deeply grieved. Warmest sympathy."[81]

Autumn 1934 marked the low point of her literary income, which had been reduced by 70 percent from a few years earlier. It was also the year that an onerous new tax law was instituted in France for the express purpose of obtaining revenue from foreign residents: not only were they liable for property and income taxes, but now the French government could also tax their property held in other countries. Under the new law, her American holdings—most of them on the verge of foreclosure—were also taxable. The drastic reduction in her income meant that she had no money to pay her French property taxes, nor could she openly discuss her situation with representatives of the tax office without risking a full disclosure of her income and property holdings. She sought advice from her attorney, Boccon-Gibod, and from Benjamin Connor, former head of the American Chamber of Commerce in Paris; while they worked on the problem, her French taxes went unpaid.[82]

She had once hoped that movie rights on some of her novels and stories would fill the empty coffers; now, she dreamed of a theatrical success, recalling with pleasure the weekly box office receipts from *The Age of Innocence* in 1928. A dramatic version of *A Son at the Front*, prepared by an unknown Southern California dramatist, proved unsatisfactory. But Edward Sheldon, the blind New York playwright whom Edith knew through Minnie Jones, had read a script of *Ethan Frome* that he thought had potential. Minnie regularly dined with Sheldon on Thursday evenings, and after one of their dinners, she read aloud the latest installment of *The Buccaneers*. The following morning, he dictated a letter to Edith full of praise and practical suggestions. His enthusiasm kept her going on this project during the long periods when ill health prevented her from writing. Visiting the Berensons in November, she read *The Buccaneers* aloud to the "Tattisti," remarking to Mary that "not many authors find such patient ears." Once back at Hyères, she expanded scenes by one-third their original length, commenting to Berenson that she always used this "fattening" process on her "big scenes."[83]

As 1934 came to a close, Edith was working well on *The Buccaneers*. Both *Cosmopolitan* and the *Woman's Home Companion* remained interested in serializing it, although Gertrude Lane of the *Companion* was worried about how Edith would handle the scene in which Nan, now the duchess of Tintagel, escapes from her husband by running off with a lover, Guy Thwarte. "You can understand," she wrote John Williams, "that this situation in itself will be a little difficult for the conservative element among our readers." Although Edith despaired of the American reading public, she spent the next weeks completing a fifty-thousand-word section for consideration by the *Companion*. In November, Edith calculated that the book would be finished within four months. That same month, her story "Roman Fever" appeared in *Liberty* magazine, Jewett having sold it some months earlier for $3,000. It was the last sale he negotiated for her.[84]

One of her most enduring stories, it is a dialogue between two women friends set on the Janiculum Hill above Rome. As the two women talk, an old secret of an illegitimate birth is revealed. Mrs. Ansley and Mrs. Slade had once both loved the same man, the now deceased Delphin Slade. He had had an extramarital affair with Mrs. Ansley, their neighbor on New York's Upper East Side, and she later gave birth to a daughter. Neither Delphin nor his wife knew that Barbara Ansley was actually Slade's daughter. The story rings a change on *The Old Maid*, and on Edith Wharton's own life. When the Christmas group gathered round the fire at Ste. Claire for the holidays, Edith kept them spellbound as she read the dialogue aloud.

Congenial as the holiday gathering was, the village of Hyères showed the worsening effects of the European economic recession and the worrying political scene. With virtually all of the hotels and shops closed, it was a "complete desert." It looked, she had written Berenson on her return from I Tatti in autumn, as if the world were at the end of the "tenth century and preparing our night shirts for the millenium [sic]"—the expression she had used to describe Paris during the first weeks of the war.

Jewett was hardly buried before Edith sent Minnie to see John Williams at Appleton with a new list of complaints about the company. If they wanted to keep her on their list of authors, she said, they would have to do a far better job of advertising her work and secure higher prices for serial rights. Edith had had to delay her Christmas gift money to Minnie (who was now completely dependent on her and Beatrix), but Edith did not reveal to her the gravity of her financial situation. "I must take a new publisher unless they push my books properly, and you can tell Williams that when you see him."[85]

Chapter 10

W

LOYALTIES

THE NEW YEAR BROUGHT GOOD FORTUNE, RELIEVING
Edith of her worst financial worries. Zoë Akins's dramatic
version of *The Old Maid*, starring Helen Menken and Judith
Anderson, and directed by Guthrie McClintic, opened at the Empire
Theater in New York City in January 1935. After a slow start owing
to the post-Christmas lull, the play became a critical and box office
success and in May won the Pulitzer Prize for drama. It brought in
gross receipts of $1,200 on each of seven performances a week; Edith
received a 25 percent share of net, about $350 per week. In September, the company began a two-year road tour, and by spring 1936, an
English company toured Great Britain.[1]

As *The Old Maid* played to enthusiastic audiences, Owen Davis—
whose *Icebound*, a drama of rural New England, won the Pulitzer Prize
in 1923—rewrote the script of *Ethan Frome*. He was assisted by his son
Donald, and Edward Sheldon acted as general supervisor. The production, starring Raymond Massey, Pauline Lord, and Ruth Gordon as
Mattie Silver, would open in New York in spring 1936. Inspired by the
adaptations of her work for the stage, Edith began to write *Kate Spain*,
a play based on the Lizzie Borden case. Although Sheldon praised the
draft of the first act, she rewrote it as a short story, which first appeared under the title "Unconfessed Crime" in *Story-Teller* (March

1936) and later as "Confession" in *Hearst's International Cosmopolitan* (May 1936).[2]

Edith was still hoping to complete the play *Kate Spain* when, on April 11, 1935, she became seriously ill. The attack was similar to the illness she suffered in spring 1929 and that had recurred in May 1934, when she was traveling with Berenson and Nicky in Rome. This time, she temporarily lost the sight in her left eye. Mme Friderich notified Elisina Tyler, who came to stay for several weeks, and in early June, they made their way slowly to Paris in the 1927 secondhand Buick that now served as Edith's touring car. Her progress toward health held steady during the summer, although she could write very little. As she gained strength and recovered the sight in her eye, it appeared that her illness had been caused by overwork and too many houseguests. But this illness was part of a general weakening of her constitution revealed in sudden fits of fatigue, angina attacks, and increased susceptibility to colds, flu, and stomach ailments.[3]

Just before she fell ill in April 1935, Edith received a long letter from Beatrix about the state of Minnie's health. At age eighty-four, she was suffering heart problems and emphysema. Her doctors were not certain that she should take the European trip Edith had offered her—paid for with box office receipts from *The Old Maid*. When Minnie arrived at the Pavillon Colombe in August with Murkett, her venerable lady's maid, the two of them fresh from a rest cure in Aix-les-Bains, Edith found her "more active and enterprising than ever." After a stay of several weeks, Minnie crossed to England in early September. The weather had turned rainy and cold, and she fell ill with laryngitis that turned to pneumonia. She died at Flemings Hotel on September 22. Edith took the boat-train to London to arrange the funeral and burial at Aldbury, Hertfordshire. In a series of letters from the Connaught Hotel, she gave Trix a complete record of events in the hurried days after Minnie's death.[4]

Edith returned from France on the verge of collapse, painfully conscious that she and Beatrix were "alone now." The last representative of Edith's Old New York world, Minnie had personified the strengths and limitations of its culture. The *New York Herald Tribune* portrayed her as a proud and generous woman, a brilliant talker who had held principles as well as prejudices, whose profoundest belief was in the "aristocracy of the intellect." To her fellow residents of Washington Square, she was a "great citizen." In her last days, she organized an effort to preserve that historic area from park commissioner Robert Moses's plans to "reconstruct" the square. Beatrix arranged a memorial service at the Church of the Ascension at Tenth Street and Fifth Avenue on December 12, 1935, Minnie's eighty-fifth birthday. By Christmas 1935, 21 East Eleventh Street, where they had lived for more than fifty years, stood empty. It was soon sold, thereby reducing the financial burden on the Jones family trust. In closing the house, Beatrix made a strange discovery: her mother had been duped by an upper-class British confidence artist, a Mrs. Montague Cecil, who had lived with her for a time in New York (unbeknownst either to Beatrix or Edith) and who "invested" her money on the stock market. Minnie bought risky stocks ("flyers") on margin and at her death owed money to the bank for loans on her stock market speculations. This behavior seemed entirely out of character, explainable only by Minnie's desire to end her dependence on Edith and Beatrix.[5]

After a period of rest, Edith returned to her work on *The Buccaneers* and attended to literary affairs with her usual attention to detail. Sheldon took over Minnie's duties in handling deposits of box office receipts from *The Old Maid* and reported to Edith about plans for the opening of *Ethan Frome* in Philadelphia on January 6 and in New York two weeks later. Produced by Max Gordon, the most successful dramatic impresario of the moment, and directed by Guthrie McClintic with set design by Jo Mielziner (who created a snow hill for the toboggan scene), *Ethan Frome* drew excellent reviews. Edward Sheldon predicted it would not have the popular box office success of the 1935 production of *The Old Maid*, but he was wrong: in Philadelphia, the play accrued gross sales of $10,400 at $2 a seat.[6]

The play's critical and financial success delighted Edith, especially because it refuted supposed American resistance to a stark tragedy like Ethan Frome's story. When she learned of a proposed London production, she commented to John Hugh Smith, "It seems so funny to be blazing along several Great White Ways at a time, and I only wish the tax-collectors of both hemispheres would look the other way."[7]

Although her letters reveal a new note of optimism, she still worried about finances and was troubled by her physical health. She experienced tingling sensations in her left arm and leg (caused by a blockage in her brain that her doctors did not yet know about) and distressing weakness and fainting spells. She was ill enough at Christmas 1935 that Berenson decided to stay at I Tatti, thus reducing Edith's holiday group to Norton and Lapsley. Paul Bourget's house, Les Plantiers, where she had spent many happy hours, now stood empty: he had died several months earlier. Edith wrote an insightful memorial essay about him for the Parisian *Revue Hebdomadaire*.[8]

Despite her unpredictable health, she entertained many visitors in spring 1936, including Berenson and Nicky, who came for two weeks in February and took pleasure in the rain-drenched Ste. Claire gardens, "redolent with violets, so amusing in their variety, some so prim and others so wild," in Berenson's description to his wife. Now an invalid, Mary Berenson had spent the previous summer in Vienna being treated for a tubercular ulcer. The painful radium treatments made her again consider suicide, as she had fifteen years earlier in her despair over her husband's affair with Mme la Caze. But she survived both the disease and its medical therapies and corrected proofs on her second book, *Across the Mediterranean*, a story of the trip she and Berenson made to Syria and Palestine in 1929. She gave Edith a copy of the book as a Christmas gift. "How I envy you this mystic gift of calling up the inner vision, and watch it gradually growing more definite," Edith responded. She still wanted to write the story of her second Aegean cruise, she said, but her "tiresome illnesses" and enforced rest had prevented it.[9]

Edith published one last book before her death, *The World Over*, her tenth short story collection, which appeared in April 1936. She had been preparing it for publication when Minnie visited St. Brice the previous summer, and had probably decided to dedicate it to her even before Minnie's sudden death: "For my dear sister, Mary Cadwalader Jones, who for so many years faithfully revised me in proof and indulgently read me in print." This is Edith's only written reference to Minnie as her "sister," and is all the more endearing because, for the previous forty years, Minnie Jones had not been (legally speaking) even Edith's sister-in-law. In their case, friendship engendered a sense of blood relation. Of the seven tales in the volume, three are Edith Wharton classics—"Pomegranate Seed," "Roman Fever," and "The Looking-Glass," a ghost story. The book jacket carried an appreciation of Edith Wharton by William Lyon Phelps, extracted from his essay in the *Delineator*; the frontispiece listed forty-six books by Edith Wharton—evidence of her prolific and prestigious career. Critics praised her mastery of technique and suspense, and her ability to entertain. *The World Over* sold very well, some twenty-five hundred copies before publication and another seventeen hundred in the next three months.[10]

As the world grew darker, its "shadowland" caused not only by

Edith's weakened health but also by "grim and grimmacing" political developments, she studied art, archaeology, and architecture to escape the rantings of dictators. She had commented to Berenson in late 1933 that rereading Spengler's *Decline of the West* was like listening to Hitler's propaganda on the radio: "all angry screams and accusations of cowardice against everyone who loves peace and beauty better than a general massacre!" She thought Hitler a "frightened man," who was trying to "stand well" among the world's powers. When riots had broken out in Paris in February 1934, triggered by the death of Alexandre Stavisky, a Russian-Jewish émigré who had made a fortune in bonds held against nonexistent credit, Edith stayed close to her "wireless" in Hyères. Casualties from the four-day clash between Communists and Fascists were far higher than officially reported, Boccon-Gibod told her. "The Commune was upon us again," she wrote Minnie, referring to the 1871 Paris riots. "News from Paris tragic," she noted in her diary on February 8, 1934.[11]

The city certainly had not seen such violence since the days of the Commune. The riots threatened to topple the government, which had protected the Stavisky "gang" from prosecution. In Edith's opinion, the "vilest and the best elements were fighting the police together!" But who represented the "vilest" elements? The syntax of her sentence obscures her meaning, but one supposes that she meant the Communists; if so, the "best elements" in this fray were the Action Française, Jeunesses Patriotes, and Solidarité Française—Fascist and near-Fascist organizations. She feared violence and was not alone in thinking that civil war, even revolution, was at hand. Her real reason for not returning to New York to accept the honorary doctorate from Columbia University in 1934, she told Minnie, was fear of civil war. "I would rather stay in France, as I feel about my houses as a crab must about its carapace." She asked Minnie not to "spread about" this idea, "for of course nothing may happen."[12]

The 1936 election of the Left coalition and a Socialist prime minister in Spain affected Edith's health: "I don't think this world-gloom agrees with me," she wrote Elisina. On July 19, Generalissimo Francisco Franco, head of the army in Spanish Morocco, invaded Spain. The civil war had begun, and Edith wrote Berenson that the "smashing" of the country—by which she meant its "archaeological smashing"—was more than she could bear. In 1931, when the monarchy in Spain fell, she agreed with Eric Maclagan, director of the Victoria and Albert Museum in London, who commented, "How entirely I find myself in accord with T. S. Eliot's definition of his attitude as traditionalist in literature, royalist in politics and Anglo-Catholic in religion!"[13]

A traditionalist, she was also an "incorrigible life-lover and life-wanderer and adventurer." In summer 1936, Berenson and Nicky toured the Dalmatian coast as far as Dubrovnik, and Edith took great pleasure in his letters, which recalled to her the *Vanadis* cruise in 1888: "I love to hear from you when you are on your travels." As her world narrowed, she envied his endurance, she said, and his indifference to "heat, cold, long journeys." In July, she made her last annual visit to England, taking in a performance of *Don Giovanni* at Glyndebourne with Kenneth and Jane Clark. She bypassed London, which now "frightened" her, and instead spent a few days with Lady Wemyss at Stanway, where she found her old friend more muddled and forgetful than ever, but still as warmhearted and loving.[14]

Edith was to have one last trip to I Tatti, a memorable sojourn of sunny summer days in which she tried to "drain dry" all the "overflowing hospitality" that the Berensons showered on her. The visit was marred only by a delay in returning to St. Brice caused by her chauffeur having cut his hand. Impatiently waiting for him to recover, she reverted to her old metaphors of violence: "I could tear my hair with rage," she wrote John Hugh Smith.[15]

In December 1936, Madrid was under siege, Italy and Germany giving support to Franco's troops in open defiance of the nonintervention treaty. German troops occupied the Rhineland and the Ruhr. By Christmas Day, Mussolini's army had virtually subjugated Abyssinia. Nazi violence in Austria presaged Germany's annexation of that country. At home, Hitler's government was enforcing the savage Nuremberg laws with unprecedented brutality. Thomas Mann, along with ninety other German citizens, was deprived of citizenship for opposing the Nazi regime that had burned his books. He fled to Switzerland. Taking note of all this, and having inside information about Fascist activities in Italy from his journalist friend Ugo Ogetti, now a liberal senator in the parliament, Berenson could hardly comprehend the "sheer horror" of what he saw. He told himself that even the Nazis could not be "so desperate as to pull the world down about their ears." If it should come to war, he wrote his sister Bessie, "they shall have nothing left but eyes to weep with."[16]

The last meeting of the Ste. Claire Christmas Club, as Edith called her little group, took place in December 1936, and was comprised of Lapsley, Norton, and John Hugh Smith. Berenson passed up her "dear enticing invitation," saying that he had to attend to writing his new book. In recent years, he had found the gatherings stressful. Deaf, John Hugh shouted irritably down the table. Lapsley, self-appointed arbiter of culture, was—in Berenson's opinion—ever more pompous and self-righteous. Edith fidgeted and fussed with the little tea tables and interrupted conversation that had (to Berenson) grown banal to attend to her little dogs. When Alfred White fell briefly but seriously ill over the holidays, Edith realized "how alone I shall be when that wise counsellor is gone." Even from his "death-bed," the stern White had lectured his mistress on her duties and reminded her that she must not forget to renew her French *carte d'identité*.

Gaillard Lapsley believed Edith's serious illness in spring 1929 had caused a "moral dislocation" that weakened the "strong control which she had always exercised over herself." After her 1935 illness, her control again "decreased appreciably with a corresponding increase in restlessness, dislike of sustained conversation and outbreaks of petulance." The last years were "sometimes very trying," he wrote Lubbock in 1938, citing two "horrid" incidents when Edith behaved "unreasonably" at hotels, rejecting rooms and sending food back to the kitchen. These "occasional outbreaks of anger or jealousy without any proportionate offence" seemed to him "an intermittent demoniac possession." Although the "scenes were not numerous and they were never scenes of violence," while they lasted "she spoke like a different woman [,] full of hatred and unreason. I recall cases which shocked and distressed me enormously at the time, but, when I came to consider them, differed only in degree and not kind from what I had observed in earlier years."

Edith's behavior clearly embarrassed Lapsley, a man who cherished social proprieties and kept his own emotions under tight rein. His recollections display a surprising lack of compassion about the problems she faced and the responsibilities she shouldered in her last years. In this period, Lapsley spent long holidays at St. Brice and Hyères, often staying several weeks at a time. Edith sought his advice on a range of personal and professional matters, and apparently had no idea that he found her fussy, temperamental, and impossible or that he detested her "damned Pekingese" and had grown to dislike her favorite rituals—hillside picnics and motorcar excursions.[17]

The first week of 1937 found Edith picnicking on the Mediterranean shores with Robert Norton, entertaining Riviera neighbors (the princesse de Poix and the Charles de Noailles family), and being fitted for new clothes by her Toulon dressmaker. On Sunday, January 24, her seventy-fifth birthday, she motored with Norton under dark skies and rain to lunch with a friend. Beatrix and Max had sent her the *Autobiography of Margery Kempe*, which she had long wanted and read with joy.

Perusing an old diary one afternoon, she discovered a note made on December 10, 1934, about literary composition:

> What is writing a novel like?
> The beginning: A ride through a spring wood.
> The middle: The Gobi desert.
> The end: Going down the Cresta run.

Writing page 166 of *The Buccaneers* that day, she noted: "the middle of the Gobi desert." Setting the novel aside, she wrote a short story ("Weekend," which was never published) and an article entitled "A Little-Girl's New York," a "postscript" to *A Backward Glance*, which was posthumously published in *Harper's*. In March 1937, she began a "Tunisian novel," a project her war duties had forced her to abandon after her return from Morocco in 1914. She awaited Berenson's return from his trip to Cyprus, Rhodes, and North Africa for "fresh documentation" of conditions in that country. "I go with you in imagination every step of the way," she wrote him.[18]

Meanwhile, houseguests came and went, among them Bill and Bettina Tyler with their newborn son, Royall. In honor of "Herc," as Edith called him (short for Hercules), she rented a baby carriage, a Bathinette, and a special bed. When Reginald Nicolson, a British colonial official whom Edith had met during her Aegean voyage in 1926, fell ill while at Ste. Claire, he and his wife prolonged their stay. Molly Nicolson later recalled that Edith, despite her own frailty and frequent relapses into ill health, devoted herself to getting proper medical care for Reginald.

Edith's 1937 daily diary tracks the ups and downs of her health in the months before her death. Two events during that wintry, rainy spring had disastrous consequences for her. First, the death of Linky, her eleven-year-old Pekingese, who was put to sleep on April 15 and buried on the grounds of Pierre Lisse, the house occupied by White and his wife. "Oh, what a troop of ghosts who used to love her (Walter,

Grossie, Elise, and many more) gather about her, where her little ghost waited for me tonight beside my bed. . . ." For days after this event, she noted in her diary the pain of Linky's death. Then, Lady Wemyss came to stay at Ste. Claire as part of her usual spring visit to the Riviera. Frail, she was also quite senile. "The poor inner room seems emptier than ever," Edith wrote Gaillard Lapsley, "and if anything were ever needed to teach me to value the precious gift of the vie intérieure [inner life], it is the old age of some of my English great lady friends, with minds unfurnished by anything less concrete than the Grand National!" When Mary Wemyss departed by the *train bleu* on March 16, it was with the expectation that she would see Edith in England during the summer. Two months later, the news came that Lady Wemyss had died in a nursing home. "A dreadful shock," Edith noted in the diary. This was her last entry until July 28, when she recorded in an almost unreadable script the visit of friends to the Pavillon Colombe.[19]

On June 1, while staying with Ogden Codman at the Château de Grégy southeast of Paris, Edith suffered a heart attack. Elisina Tyler came from Rome, arriving on June 4 at the Pavillon Colombe, where Edith had been transported by ambulance. (Departing in the ambulance, she had quipped to Codman: "This will teach you not to ask decrepit old ladies to stay.") Attended by three physicians, she was very ill, her condition made worse by her financial and tax worries. In March, she had made a new American will, signed before the United States consul at Nice. Making additions to her French will, she named Elisina as residuary legatee. Elisina recorded in her diary of summer 1937 that from the moment Edith handed over these responsibilities, "she seemed at rest, as if her grievous anxiety had fallen from her utterly."

Early June held hope that Edith might recover her health, but by mid-July that hope evaporated. The signs of "mental decay" were tragically evident—her thoughts disconnected and her vision shadowed by a blockage in the brain. By August 5, she was, in Elisina's words, "already visibly a dying woman."[20]

During a most beautiful summer in the Seine and Oise valleys, Edith spent her days stretched out on a chaise longue on the terrace or sitting in the garden in her wheelchair. Elisina sat beside her while she napped or spoke in low tones about the past. The previous summer, a young English writer and naturalist, Vivienne de Watteville, had been a guest at the Pavillon Colombe for a few weeks. She recalled that after her morning's work, Edith would descend to the garden attired in white, wearing gloves and carrying a white parasol with a green silk lining. Seating herself on the stone bench near the reflecting pool, she watched as Vivienne snipped roses, instructing her on the proper method of cutting. The garden was so enchanting that each day they postponed their visit to the Grand Palais in Paris, where an important Cézanne exhibition was in progress. (Edith had donated her own Cézanne landscape, which she inherited from Walter.) They did eventually attend the exhibition, but Vivienne remembered that an afternoon spent viewing individual blossoms from Edith's garden through a powerful magnifying glass offered a more beautiful voyage of discovery than any work of art.

Toward sunset on these days, Edith asked Vivienne to bring from the boudoir a little embroidered bag that held breadcrumbs for the ancient goldfish in the pond. As Edith scattered bread over the pond, she called out in her lighthearted voice, "*Poisse! Poisse!*" She was disconcerted to learn from Vivienne that fish have no aural sense and could not hear her voice. She had always assumed that they knew her voice, because at her approach "golden waves of fish dimpled towards her across the surface" of the water. Ignoring scientific explanations, she continued to call out to the fish, giving pleasure to Vivienne, who loved the sound of Edith's voice. Each evening, she waited for the hour when Edith opened a volume of Montaigne or Robert Browning and began to read aloud.[21]

Vivienne de Watteville was one of several young writers whose work Edith championed, offering both practical assistance and using her prestige as an international literary figure to advance their careers. Recognizing the value of *Out of the Blue*, Vivienne's memoir of a hunting expedition to East Africa, made with her father in 1923, Edith encouraged her to write another book—one in which "nobody wants to kill an animal." Vivienne answered her request by writing *Speak to the Earth* (1935), for which Edith wrote a preface. That same year, Edith pushed Appleton to publish Robert Norton's translation of *Bénédiction*, a novel that won the *Prix Fémina*, written by Philomène de la Forest-Divonne, under the pseudonym Claude Silve. Appleton complied, and the book appeared in 1936 with a foreword by Edith Wharton.[22]

Vivienne and Philomène did not see Edith as the restless and agitated person that the men of her inner circle often described. To them, she was infinitely patient and quiet, someone in tune with the silences of the natural world, whose life organized itself around a center of calm repose. Philomène recalled visiting Edith at St. Brice in that last year, finding her alone. It was a rainy autumn afternoon, the fire was lit, and Edith's face reflected the "hush of the hour": "She forgot to look for the flower to be straightened in its vase, the cushion to be offered you, the little table to be placed at your elbow; even Edith for the time was content to *be*."

That afternoon, Edith brought out the old scrapbook in which Anna Bahlmann many years earlier had pasted photographs, press cuttings, and early reviews. "I would sacrifice many a more eventful day spent in her company," Philomène wrote, "sooner than lose the memory of that hour":

> I realized then, as never before, what Edith might have been for the children she never had. Most striking was the perfect simplicity with which she lingered over the record of the beginnings of her literary fame; she accepted her success without vanity and without false modesty, as a simple fact, as one accepts the heritage of one's race and blood. . . . I still see her pale hand as it turned the leaves of the album; it was like watching the dust of the past, dust with a glint of gold, stream between her fingers from page to page. Her work, her art, her fame, were the gold in it, and as the story grew the gleam absorbed it all. Sitting by her side, in the gracious and orderly room, with the rain beating and the leaves falling outside, I felt the presence of a power at rest, controlled by a lonely and generous spirit.[23]

This vision of Edith Wharton, the most eloquent ever written, also accords with William Tyler's memories of evenings spent with Edith listening to classical music on the phonograph. Such recollections reveal that in her last years—and particularly with young people—Edith found the companionable ease that had eluded her earlier in life.

She spent the last days of her life enclosed by a charmed sylvan beauty in the stillness of her garden. She experienced neither physical pain nor mental distress: "I'm used to invalidism now," she wrote Berenson in the spring, "and find it full of oases and hidden springs." No longer driven to meet publishing deadlines or assume responsibility for household matters, Edith became a guest in her own home. Elisina noted that her reserve seemed to melt away, and she used "astonishing" terms of endearment, calling her friends "dear" and "darling."

Her closest friends made brief visits during these weeks—Norton, Lapsley, John Hugh Smith, Royall Tyler, Bessy Lodge, Kenneth and Jane Clark, Ogden Codman, and Beatrix, who sailed back to New York the very morning Edith was stricken for the last time. On the night of August 7, the doctors decided to "bleed" Edith in an effort to release the pressure on her brain. As they began the procedure, she turned her head toward Elisina, her eyes fearful and shadowed. "Don't be afraid, dearest, I am here," Elisina whispered. A few hours later, Edith suffered a paralytic stroke and fell unconscious, dying four days later in the late afternoon of August 11. It was the hour when the sunlight dropped behind the ancient elms and oaks that encircled the Pavillon Colombe, and as the garden fell into shadow, she could be heard calling, "*Poisse! Poisse!*"[24]

FRIENDS GATHERED TO pay their last respects, mounting the stairs to the second-floor bedroom where her body had been laid in its coffin. Berenson, who could not come to St. Brice, but who grieved perhaps more deeply than any of Edith's men friends, telegraphed a response to Elisina's wire: "Edith takes a large part of our world with her, leaving us impoverished." He then wrote a long letter of condolence to Beatrix, the most precious she was to receive, she said, because it was the only one that mentioned Edith's affection for her and spoke of their shared tastes: "There has been for me a life-long consciousness of her being there, an example and a light to follow, and now the world seems veiled and empty."[25]

On May 23, 1936, during a period of relatively good health, Edith prepared a memorandum for Elisina regarding the funeral and burial. She wanted a "fully choral" memorial service, listing hymns she wished to have sung, and ordering a "*simple hearse, with only two horses*"; friends were "*to meet at the church*"—no long procession through the streets of Paris, as had been done for Walter Berry. The memorial service took place at the Pro-Cathedral on August 21, a week after her burial. The burial went off with only one lapse of decorum. The coffin had been maneuvered up the narrow staircase at the Pavillon Colombe by tilting it. Now that it held Edith's body, it could be removed from the bedroom only by bringing it out the window. Climbing a ladder, the gardener, Emile, eased it through the window by ropes. At mid-morning on August 14, the coffin stood in the entranceway of the

Pavillon Colombe, flanked by seven of the eight pallbearers Edith had chosen—André Boccon-Gibod, Kenneth Clark, Louis Gillet, Gaillard Lapsley, Louis Metman, Robert Norton, and Royall Tyler. John Hugh Smith was unable to attend. An honor guard holding French and American flags formed in the courtyard, representatives of the Mutilés de Guerre (the charity founded by Walter Berry). As the pallbearers hoisted the oak casket with its silver inlaid cross, a bugle sounded. Edith Wharton's body was transported to the Cimetière des Gonards in Versailles, some forty kilometers' distance, where she was buried with all the honors owed a war hero and a chevalier of the Legion of Honor. Dean Frederick W. Beekman of the American Cathedral read the prayers she had selected, a group of some one hundred friends sang a verse of the hymn "O Paradise," and at noon, her body was lowered into the double plot she had purchased near Walter Berry.

In the weeks that followed, Emile made daily trips to the Versailles cemetery in the Peugeot truck she had bequeathed to him, transporting flowers from her garden to her grave.[26]

AFTERWARD

It took more than two years to settle Edith Wharton's French and American estates, to dispose of her properties and personal belongings, and to deal with the many legal problems that ensued on her death. Co-executors of her American will were her cousins Frederic and LeRoy King of New York. Boccon-Gibod and John Hugh Smith served as co-executors of the French will, but as they were each monolingual and unable to communicate directly with one another, the burden of negotiating the obstacles of the Franco-American estate fell to Elisina Tyler. As residuary legatee, she took responsibility for dispensing all bequests, distributing three dozen items of jewelry, furs, paintings, and clothing (including some forty-five dresses of Edith's, which went to her new maid), and the library. Books on art, archaeology, and history went to William Tyler; all the others went to Kenneth Clark, in trust for his son Colin. Elisina sold the Pavillon Colombe and its contents for 1,200,000 francs to Arthur Sachs, an American financier and art collector, and she converted its profits to an endowment for the Maisons de Convalescence at Taverny and Groslay.

Sachs, who hired all Edith's staff members except her maid and her secretary, Mme Friderich (who was unable to find another position), soon found it impossible to maintain the estate. Less than a year after Edith Wharton's death, the property sold again, to the duke of Talleyrand, whose family had once owned the land, for 470,000 francs—a devaluation of more than 50 percent caused by the worsening European economic and political situation. Elisina hurried to settle estate matters, drawing on her own private means to pay property and inheritance taxes. Any delay in tax payments could occasion a government investigation into Edith's estate that would uncover the existence of her American real estate holdings, properties worth very little now but on which the French government could assess back taxes and death duties—the very fear that had haunted Edith in her last years.[27]

By mid-September 1937, Elisina realized the extent to which she had taken on considerable indebtedness in becoming Edith's residuary legatee. Inheritance taxes came to over $60,000, yearly upkeep on Ste. Claire about $3,500. The size and location of the property made it unsalable in the current market (the sales price was $80,000), nor could Elisina herself use it, since she divided her time between Budapest, where Royall Tyler served as a financial adviser for the League of Nations, and her house in Burgundy. Ste. Claire needed a property manager, but there was no money to pay Alfred White to continue in this capacity. Edith had willed to White the contents of Pierre Lisse, the house she built for him in 1926, but she had not left him the house itself. An apparent oversight, its effect on White, now in his late sixties, was devastating. Elisina settled the matter by giving him a life-lease in the house with a nominal rent of 100 francs per year, and she paid the property taxes. She sold Ste. Claire during World War II; later, after White's death, Elisina moved into Pierre Lisse, dying there in 1959.[28]

Relieved at having found solutions to these difficult estate problems, she was unprepared when Beatrix challenged the American will. By November 1937, a venerable New York law firm began to prosecute her action. At issue was the life trust Edith inherited from Lucretia, whose terms Edith had disputed in 1901. She had believed for many years that her agreement with Frederic, reached under threat of a lawsuit, restored her third of Lucretia's estate. In 1931, she learned the money had not been fully restored. Frederic had waived his rights of succession to the trust fund (rights that Lucretia had willed to him), and in practical terms, this presumably meant that at her death, Edith could dispose of her mother's legacy however she wished. Beatrix challenged Edith's right to leave the money outside the family. Her threatened lawsuit occasioned a reexamination of Lucretia Jones's last testament, a document that had not been made hastily or carelessly (as some have suggested), but rather punished Edith for refusing to receive Frederic's "disreputable" second wife. (Edith suspected that Frederic had exerted influence over his mother.) Lucretia's will was designed to keep Rhinelander-Jones wealth within the family as long as possible. Beatrix Farrand now remained the last living "lawful heir" of Lucretia Jones, and the lawyers turned their attention to this phrase.[29]

The letters between Beatrix and Elisina crisscrossing the Atlantic in autumn 1937 betrayed neither Beatrix's bitterness and growing hatred of Elisina nor Elisina's distress at their adversarial legal situation. From Paris, where Royall had joined her for the holidays, she sent Beatrix Christmas greetings and repeated what Edith had told her the previous June—that she intended to leave her godson William Tyler a sum of about $140,000, after deductions of taxes and estate expenses. The residue of George Frederic Jones's legacy went to Beatrix. Dreading an "open conflict," Elisina nonetheless felt obliged to fulfill what she believed were Edith's wishes. (Unbeknownst to Elisina, Beatrix possessed letters dating back to 1920 in which Edith suggested that Beatrix would be sole beneficiary of the Jones family money.) Hoping the issue could be resolved if they were to speak face-to-face, Elisina went to New York in January 1938 and asked that Beatrix meet her. No meeting took place.

To anyone unfamiliar with the history of bitterness, greed, and self-interest in the Jones family, Beatrix's response to the terms of Edith's will would seem unreasonable. Minnie's recent death had recalled to Beatrix all the "cruelty and injustice" Frederic had shown his former wife and daughter. She wrote Edith in May 1936 that he had taken great pains to "make the amount of the trust for Mummy and me as small as possible." Harry Jones showed himself no more generous than his brother, bequeathing to the countess Tekla wealth that rightfully belonged to his sister and niece. The battle for inheritances that were theirs by right formed the common thread in the life stories of Edith Wharton, Minnie Jones, and Beatrix Farrand.[30]

Beatrix no doubt felt that she had won more than a moral victory when, in spring 1938, attorneys interpreted Lucretia Jones's will in her favor. Elisina's only recourse was to question the decision in court, which she refused to do. They eventually came to a compromise settlement that left both women feeling cheated. By this time, an exhausted Elisina was convalescing from a nervous breakdown.

Believing that by her actions Beatrix had betrayed her aunt's wishes, Elisina recorded the events of 1937 and 1938, giving copies to the other executors, including John Hugh Smith. In an accompanying letter, she asked if he would share the costs of placing a tablature stone on the grave. He agreed, and the stone they laid matched the one Edith and Nathalie Alden had chosen for Walter's grave. Inscribed on an embossed cross was the Latin phrase she had chosen for her epitaph: *O Crux Ave Spes Unica*—O Hail Cross, Our Only Hope.[31]

While Elisina coped with real estate and tax problems, Gaillard Lapsley, literary executor of the estate, saw to the disposal of manuscripts and correspondence to the Yale University Library. Certain papers in this huge archive were sealed until thirty years after Edith Wharton's death, by which time all her surviving family and friends would have, in Beatrix Farrand's formula, "disappeared." Lapsley also directed the publication of Edith's posthumous works. *Ghosts*, a collection of reprinted supernatural tales whose page proofs Elisina had corrected as she sat with Edith in the Pavillon Colombe garden during the summer, appeared in October 1937. Obituaries described her as a "great American novelist" and recounted her long list of literary and academic honors. Praise of her literary gifts was matched by tributes to her war work and philanthropy. Among many articles and reevaluations, only the *New York Herald* noted the obstacles that inherited wealth and strict social custom posed to her development as a writer, and suggested that her "eventual fame will be as the first woman to defy the bonds of social custom in the United States and become a first-rank novelist."[32]

One year after Edith's death, in September 1938, *The Buccaneers* appeared. Lapsley appended to this unfinished text the plot summary Edith had sent to John Williams at Appleton in 1935, and he wrote an insightful critical introduction to the volume. Set in Saratoga and London of the 1860s, the story concerns daughters of nouveau riche "invaders" who find a place in New York society by marrying their daughters to sons of the British aristocracy. They come in by the "back door," just as Mrs. Paran Stevens had done in the early 1880s when she wed her beautiful daughter to an English lord. The central figure of the story is Nan St. George, who becomes the wife of the banal and all-too-dutiful duke of Tintagel. Another woman "steals" the tale, however—Laura Testvalley, governess to the St. George daughters. At age forty, she falls in love with the widowed Sir Helmsley Thwarte, an English aristocrat who wants to marry her, but she sacrifices this possibility so that Nan can escape her unhappy marriage and elope with Sir Helmsley's son, Guy. As the character names reveal, *The Buccaneers* is a comedy of manners with a strong moral thrust; it is also arguably the most charming novel Edith Wharton ever wrote.

The book received mixed reviews, as might be expected of a posthumous and incomplete work of fiction. Edith Wharton's literary reputation was already in decline; she was no longer the "great American writer" so lauded in her obituaries. The most negative assessment of *The Buccaneers* came from American poet Louise Bogan, who declared in the *Nation* that for all its "cleverness and skill," the book was "dead at heart." The "essential numbness" of Edith Wharton's literary world, she said, resulted from a sanctioning of decorum and pre–Wall Street merchant respectability over a "rich and free feeling for life." Edmund Wilson countered this view in the *New Republic*. It was fitting, he said, that her last novel pictured a "clever spinster" who, in trading in worldly values, had—like her creator—"given a rebuff to the values of the world." He described Edith Wharton as having followed a "destiny solitary and disciplined," fighting "a campaign" for what in her generation was called "the rights of the heart."[33]

BEATRIX FARRAND OUTLIVED her aunt by twenty-two years. Widowed in 1945 when her husband, Max, died of cancer, she later retired from practice as a landscape gardener and lived on her dwindling inherited income. In the mid-fifties, the town of Bar Harbor refused her request to grant tax-exempt status to Reef Point Gardens, a horticultural project she had designed on her mother's estate. Rather than watch the gardens slowly deteriorate, she dismantled them. In the words of a colleague, Beatrix "was a perfectionist, and she obliterated an important part of her life's work rather than risk its continuation in some form which would not measure up to her standard of excellence." She moved shrubs and trees to other locations, shipped her library and herbarium to the University of California at Berkeley, and tore down the sprawling summer house that Minnie and Frederic built at Reef

Point in the early 1880s, where as a small child, she had watched roads and vistas being cut through the property. According to her niece, Louisa Farrand Wood, this act required greater courage and brought more heartache to Beatrix than anything else in her life.[34]

In this action, she recalled a character in Edith Wharton's fiction—Mrs. Manstey, the eponymous subject of her first published story, "Mrs. Manstey's View," which appeared in the July issue of *Scribner's Magazine* in 1891. When her garden view from a third-floor back room of a New York boardinghouse was threatened by a proposed extension to a neighboring house, Mrs. Manstey attempted to burn down the building site. Her violent act, so out of character, resulted in her death from exposure. Beatrix's story ended on a rather different note. She saved some boards from the wreckage of her mother's house and used them to build an addition to the farmhouse of her former cook, Amy Garland. Mrs. Garland transported some heather from Reef Point and planted it around the two-room extension that Beatrix shared with her ancient French lady's maid, Clémentine. The two women spent their last years sitting by the window looking out on the heather, much as Mrs. Manstey had done in Edith's story.

Beatrix died on February 27, 1959, a few months short of her eighty-seventh birthday. Her last wish was that only her servants attend the funeral and that her ashes be spread on Mount Desert Island. She bought no grave plot and no headstone was erected in her memory. With her death, the George Frederic and Lucretia Rhinelander Jones family passed out of existence. Today, those two unlikely progenitors of genius are remembered only by their daughter and granddaughter—women who answered the summons of their special talents. Beatrix followed her "noble art" with a solemnity and determination appropriate to her character; Edith took up her pen each morning with a glad heart.

"We have lost an incomparable friend," Beatrix wrote to Gaillard Lapsley a few days after Edith's death. "What an example she is of a beautiful construction built around a great gift."[35]

Archives and Abbreviations

W

I. CORRESPONDENTS AND PARTICIPANTS

AB	Anna Bahlmann
BB	Bernard Berenson
MB	Mary Berenson
WB	Walter Berry
STB	Sturgis Bigelow
MBB	Mildred Barnes Bliss
WCB	William Crary Brownell
ELB	Edward L. Burlingame
EC	Elizabeth Sherman Cameron
DC	Margaret (Daisy) Terry Chanler
KC	Kenneth Clark
OC	Ogden Codman, Jr.
SBC	Sarah Bradlee Codman
TC	Thomas Newbold Codman
CC	Charles Cook
HE	Herman Edgar
BF	Beatrix Farrand
FSF	F. Scott Fitzgerald
JDF	Jeanne Duprat Friderich
BMF	Bradford Morton Fullerton

JBF	Julia Ball Fullerton
KF	Katharine Fullerton (Gerould)
RMF	Robert Morton Fullerton
WMF	William Morton Fullerton
MTG	Matilda Travers Gay
LG	Louis Gillet
RG	Robert Grant
HJ	Henry James
RBJ	Rutger Bleecker Jewett
FRJ	Frederic Rhinelander Jones
GFJ	George Frederic Jones
HEJ	Henry Edward Jones
LRJ	Lucretia Stevens Rhinelander Jones
MCJ	Mary (Minnie) Cadwalader Jones
FRK	Frederic R. King
FPK	Francis P. Kinnicutt
GL	Gaillard Lapsley
SL	Sinclair Lewis
PL	Percy Lubbock
SCL	Sybil Cutting Lubbock
CEN	Charles Eliot Norton
LN	Elizabeth (Lily) Gaskell Norton
RN	Robert Norton
SN	Sara (Sally) Norton
TR	Theodore Roosevelt
LAS	Loring A. Schuler
CS	Charles Scribner
ES	Edward Sheldon
JHS	John Hugh Smith
HS	Howard Sturgis
ET	Elisina Tyler
RT	Royall Tyler
WRT	William Royall Tyler
DBU	Daniel Berkeley Updike
ATV	Arthur T. Vance
EWW	Emelyn W. Washburn
EW	Edith Wharton
TW	Edward R. Wharton
NCW	Nancy Craig Wharton
NSW	Nancy Spring Wharton (TW's mother)
WCW	William Craig Wharton
WFW	William F. Wharton ("Billy")
JBW	John Williams

II. PLACES

LE   Land's End
PC   Pavillon Colombe (St. Brice-sous-Forêt)
SC   Ste. Claire le Château (Hyères)

III. TITLES

A. *Primary Texts and Associated Works*

See Chronology for full citations and abbreviations for Edith Wharton titles. Autobiographical works and letters:

ATB   Account Book (royalties)
BG   *A Backward Glance*
CSS   *Collected Short Stories*
CB   Commonplace Book
DD   Daily Diary
LI   "Life and I" (a draft of chapter 1 of *BG*)
LGNY   "A Little Girl's New York"
LD   Love Diary

B. *Secondary Texts*

LE   Leon Edel, ed., *The Letters of Henry James*, 4 vols. (Cambridge, Mass: Harvard University Press, 1974–1984).

SG   Stephen Garrison, ed., *Edith Wharton: A Descriptive Bibliography* (Pittsburgh: University of Pittsburgh Press, 1990).

RWBL   R. W. B. Lewis, *Edith Wharton: A Biography* (New York: Harper and Row, 1975).

LL   R. W. B. Lewis and Nancy Lewis, eds., *The Letters of Edith Wharton* (New York: Scribners, 1988). Bracketed material in citations denotes speculative dating and alternative dating; see A Note on Edith Wharton's Letters to Morton Fullerton.

PEW   Percy Lubbock, *Portrait of Edith Wharton* (London: Jonathan Cape, 1947).

LP   Lyall H. Powers, ed., *Henry James and Edith Wharton: Letters, 1900-1915* (New York: Scribners, 1990).

IV. REFERENCES

Kristen O. Lauer and Margaret P. Murray, eds., *Edith Wharton: An Annotated Secondary Bibliography* (New York: Garland Publishing, 1990).

James W. Tuttleton, Kristen O. Lauer, and Margaret P. Murray, eds., *Edith Wharton: The Contemporary Reviews* (Cambridge: Cambridge University Press, 1992).

V. LITERARY ARCHIVES

1. YCAL: Yale Collection of American Literature, Beinecke Rare Book and Manuscript Library, Yale University. The major archive of Edith Wharton's literary notebooks, manuscripts, professional and personal correspondence, and photographs (fifty thousand items), it includes:

WMF	Morton Fullerton family correspondence
GC	EW's General Correspondence (1917–1937)
GMT	Georges Markow-Totevy Collection
LA	Louis Auchincloss Collection
M	Memoirs gathered from EW's friends by Percy Lubbock for *PEW*

2. LLI: Lilly Library, Indiana University. Archive includes diaries of GFJ, LRJ, and EW, manuscripts, personal and professional correspondence, letters to Royall Tyler family, estate documents, and ET's "Memoir" and "Statement" on EW's last days and disputes over EW's will, and ET's "Report" on the war charities.

3. HRHRC: Harry Ransom Humanities Research Center, University of Texas (Austin). Archive includes more than three hundred letters from EW to WMF, documenting their love affair and friendship; Harry and Caresse Crosby Collection has WB will, obituaries, and funeral register.

4. SA: Scribners Archive in the Firestone Library, Princeton University. Collection includes EW's correspondence with her editors at Scribners between 1891 and 1937. Associated materials include correspondence with *Century* and *Lippincott* magazines, and FSF biographical matter.

5. AC: Amherst College, Robert Frost Library. Archive includes EW's letters to WCB (1901–1921).

6. HL: Houghton Library, Harvard University. Archive includes EW's letters to CEN, LN, and SN, and HJ's letters to WMF, MCJ, GL, and HS.

7. PUL: Pusey Library, Harvard University. Alumni files and class records on: WB, WMF, RG, RT, WFW, and TW.

8. SPNEA: Society for the Preservation of New England Antiquities

(Boston, Massachusetts). In Codman Family Manuscripts Collection, letters from OC to SBC and Thomas Newbold Codman about EW and TW.

9. IT: Villa I Tatti, Harvard Center for Renaissance Studies (Florence, Italy). Archive includes EW and WB letters to BB and MB (1909–1937), letters between BB–MB about EW, and correspondence with KC, GL, PL, SCL, RT, and LG that mention EW.

VI. Newspapers, Magazines, Journals, and Other Resources

AM	*Atlantic Monthly*
BRT	*Berkshire Resort Topics*
BET	*Boston Evening Transcript*
D	*Delineator*
DLB	*Dictionary of Literary Biography* (Detroit, Michigan: Gale Research)
LHJ	*Ladies' Home Journal*
LL	*Lenox Life*
NA	*Nation and Athenaeum* [London]
NDN	*Newport Daily News*
NR	*New Republic*
NS	*New Statesman*
NSN	*New Statesman and Nation*
NYEP	*New York Evening Post*
NYTBR	*New York Times Book Review*
NYW	*New York World*
PR	*Pictorial Review*
PW	*Publisher's Weekly*
SEP	*Saturday Evening Post*
SR	*Saturday Review* [London]
SRL	*Saturday Review of Literature* [New York]
SM	*Scribner's Magazine*
TLS	*Times Literary Supplement* [London]
TT	*Town Topics*
WHC	*Woman's Home Companion*

Chronology of Works by Edith Wharton

〰

Abbreviations: Charles Scribner's Sons (S); D. Appleton and Company (A); Century (C); Medici Society, London (MS); Appleton-Century (AC); University Press of Virginia (UPV); Presses de L'UFR Clerc, Université de Picardie (PP). See guide below to abbreviations of reprints and new editions.

1909   (S)   *Artemis to Actaeon and Other Verses.*
1910   (S)   *Tales of Men and Ghosts*, short stories.
1911   (S)   *Ethan Frome*, novella. (AM, BA, MC, NAD, OR, PN, S)
1912   (A)   *The Reef*, novel. (CO, S)
1913   (S)   *The Custom of the Country*, novel. (BA, NAD, PN, S)
1915   (S)   *Fighting France, from Dunkerque to Belfort.* (GR)
1916   (S)   *Xingu and Other Stories*, short stories.
1916   (S)   *The Book of the Homeless,* ed.
1917   (S)   *Summer*, novel. (BO, CO, HC, MC, SC)
1918   (S)   *The Marne*, novel.
1919   (A)   *French Ways and Their Meaning*, cultural criticism.
1920   (A)   *The Age of Innocence*, novel. (AM, CO, MC, S)
1920   (S)   *In Morocco*, travel.
1922   (A)   *The Glimpses of the Moon*, novel. (S)
1923   (S)   *A Son at the Front*, novel.
1924   (A)   *Old New York: False Dawn, The Old Maid, The Spark, New Year's Day*, novellas. (LA)
1925   (A)   *The Mother's Recompense*, novel. (S)
1925   (S)   *The Writing of Fiction*, criticism.
1926   (A)   *Here and Beyond*, short stories.
1926   (MS)   *Twelve Poems.*
1927   (A)   *Twilight Sleep*, novel.
1928   (A)   *The Children*, novel. (MC, S)
1929   (A)   *Hudson River Bracketed*, novel. (S)
1930   (A)   *Certain People*, short stories.
1932   (A)   *The Gods Arrive*, novel. (S)
1933   (A)   *Human Nature*, short stories.
1934   (A)   *A Backward Glance*, memoir. (S)
1936   (A)   *The World Over*, short stories.
1937   (A)   *Ghosts*, short stories.
1938   (AC)   *The Buccaneers*, unfinished novel. (V, UPV)
1939   (AC)   *Eternal Passion in Poetry*, ed. with Robert Norton and Gaillard Lapsley.
1968   (S)   *The Collected Short Stories*, R. W. B. Lewis, ed.
1973   (S)   *The Ghost Stories of Edith Wharton.*
1977   (UPV)   *Fast and Loose: A Novelette*, by "David Olivieri." Viola Hopkins Winner, ed.
1992   (PP)   *The Cruise of the Vanadis*, travel. Claudine Lesage, ed.
1993   (UPV)   *Fast and Loose and The Buccaneers.* Viola Hopkins Winner, ed.

PUBLISHER DESIGNATIONS

AM	Amereon
AMS	AMS Press
AY	Ayers
BA	Bantam Books
BO	Borgo
CO	Collier
EV	Everyman
GR	Greenwood
HC	HarperCollins
LA	Library of America
MC	Macmillan
NAD	NAL-Dutton
NO	Norton
OR	Orchises
PN	Penguin
SC	Scholarly
UNI	Northern Illinois UP
UPV	University Press of Virginia
V	Viking

Primary Works Cited: Abbreviations

W

Age	The Age of Innocence
AA	Artemis to Actaeon and Other Verses
BG	A Backward Glance
BH	The Book of the Homeless
C	The Children
CI	Crucial Instances
CV	The Cruise of the Vanadis
CC	The Custom of the Country
DH	The Decoration of Houses
EF	Ethan Frome
FD	False Dawn
FF	Fighting France, from Dunkerque to Belfort
FWM	French Ways and Their Meaning
FT	The Fruit of the Tree
GM	The Glimpses of the Moon
GA	The Gods Arrive
GI	The Greater Inclination
HM	The House of Mirth
HRB	Hudson River Bracketed
IB	Italian Backgrounds
IVG	Italian Villas and Their Gardens
JL	The Joy of Living
MT	Madame de Treymes

M	*The Marne*
MR	*The Mother's Recompense*
MFF	*A Motor-Flight Through France*
NYD	*New Year's Day*
ONY	*Old New York*
OM	*The Old Maid*
R	*The Reef*
SF	*A Son at the Front*
S	*Summer*
TMG	*Tales of Men and Ghosts*
TS	*Twilight Sleep*
VD	*The Valley of Decision*

$\mathcal{A}$ $\mathcal{N}$ote on $\mathcal{E}$dith $\mathcal{W}$harton's Letters to $\mathcal{M}$orton $\mathcal{F}$ullerton

W

R. W. B. Lewis's 1975 biography of Edith Wharton appeared five years before the surprise discovery of some three hundred letters from Edith Wharton to Morton Fullerton documenting their friendship, many of the letters belonging to the 1908–1912 period of their love affair. (The Harry Ransom Humanities Research Center at Austin, Texas, purchased the letters in 1980.) In *Edith Wharton*, Lewis conjectured that the couple entered into "physical union" during April and May 1908, when Edith was living at her brother Harry Jones's town house on the place des Etats Unis in Paris, after her husband Teddy Wharton had returned to the United States to take a cure at Hot Springs, Arkansas. On May 3, Edith recorded in her diary the desire to go with Fullerton to some "little inn in the country, in the depth of a green wood." That fantasy was never realized, and Lewis suggested that they instead made love—"(with some regularity, one gathers, and protected by such massive displays of tact by Gross as can only be guessed at)"—in Harry's town house, where Edith felt they were being observed (RWBL, 220–22).

In their 1988 edition of selected *Letters of Edith Wharton*, R. W. B. Lewis and Nancy Lewis suggest that the lovers' intimacy occurred earlier that spring ("soon after the new year [1908], in Paris"), presumably begun when Teddy went south to visit the Ralph Curtises in mid-February. The *Letters* reproduce sixty-eight notes and letters from Edith to Morton, twelve of which appear to verify their progress to sexual intimacy in spring 1908. Of the forty-two missives included in the crucial 1908–1910 period, twenty-eight are without letterhead, watermark, or complete date. Given the secrecy sur-

rounding the relationship, and Edith's fear of discovery, the absence of saluta-
tion and signature in many letters is also not surprising. The *Letters* provide
speculative dates, and in some cases, Edith's diary or other correspondence
supports this dating. But in key instances, no contextual evidence exists to
verify the dating; sometimes, other evidence casts doubt on the speculative
dating. For example, internal evidence in the "[May 1908]" letter (page 144)
suggests that it belongs to autumn 1909, when Fullerton faced losing his
Times job owing to a misunderstanding with his superiors regarding a requested leave of absence to write a book. There are many other such instances, especially for the year 1908. I provide corrective dating in chapter endnotes.

The difficulty of dating the more than three hundred notes and letters
challenges even the most experienced editor, and the problems in speculative
dating that occur in *The Letters of Edith Wharton* are difficult to discuss (much
less solve) without reference to the entire correspondence. We need a complete
and annotated edition of these letters. The primary obstacle to reading them
with a fresh eye, however, is the romantic story of sexual need and early seduction we have known for twenty years. When the letters at the HRHRC
are read as a set, side by side with Edith's diary and in the context of her other
activities in the 1908–1910 period, they plot a new and surprising pattern to
the love affair. Edith's rhetoric of passion outdistances her actions, as it often
did. (She adopted a rhetoric of urgency and self-dramatization with her
friends.) Torn between loyalty to her husband and love for Fullerton, afraid of
losing the respect of her staff, of being subjected to blackmail threats similar
to those Fullerton faced with Mme Mirecourt, and possibly losing her public
reputation, she hesitated in spring 1908. When she finally decided to escape
to the "green wood," it was too late. Presented with a second chance for intimacy a year later, she took it, "no holds barred," as she said. Her poems and
letters of summer 1909 amply record her experiences.

$\mathcal{N}otes$

A NOTE ON THE NOTES

Background texts cited in the text by author's last name; for abbreviations, see Archives and Abbreviations. Quotations are identified by first word/last word. My correspondence and interviews are identified by "SB" and date.

CHAPTER 1

Background texts: Paul M. Angle and Earl Schenck Miers, *Tragic Years: 1860–1865*, vol. 2 (New York: Simon & Schuster, 1960); Louis Auchincloss, *The Vanderbilt Era: Profiles of a Gilded Age* (New York: Scribners, 1989); Bruce Catton, *This Hallowed Ground: The Story of the Union Side of the Civil War* (Garden City: Doubleday, 1956); Margaret Chanler, *Autumn in the Valley* (Boston: Little, Brown, 1936); Shelby Foote, *The Civil War: A Narrative, Fort Sumter to Perryville* (New York: Random House, 1958); Eugenia Kaledin, *The Education of Mrs. Henry Adams* (Philadelphia: Temple University Press, 1981); Charles Lockwood, *Bricks and Brownstone, The New York Row House 1783–1929, An Architectural and Social History* (New York: McGraw-Hill, 1972); Russell Lynes, *The Domesticated Americans* (New York: Harper and Row, 1957); David McCullough, *Mornings on Horseback* (New York: Simon & Schuster, 1981); Lloyd Morris, *Incredible New York: 1830–1850* (New York: Random House, 1951); Allan Nevins and Milton Halsey Thomas, eds., *The Diary of George Templeton Strong: The Civil War* (New York: Macmillan, 1952); Mrs. John King

Van Rensselaer, *The Social Ladder* (New York: Henry Holt and Co., 1924); Dixon Wecter, *The Saga of American Society* (New York: Scribners, 1920); Barrett Wendell, *The France of Today* (New York: Scribners, 1907).

1. chocolate brown, *BG*, 55; *LGNY*: house decoration, "resplendent/cloak," 360–63.

2. Federal Census, 1860, roll 813, p. 501: M. Johnson and G. Watts declared illiterate; Hannah Doyle, listed as New York resident, was either born in the U.S. or naturalized at some earlier date; James Blake's citizenship and age not given; LRJ listed as "Louisa"; Newport property value: *Newport City Directory*, 1868–69; DBU, *M*, quotes EW on LRJ and servants: "I was brought up in a household where there was [no consideration of servants] at all"; "Society/Birth," Van Rennselaer, 108; LRJ "indolent," *LI*, 361.

3. *BG*: "gaunt/black," 59; "script/elegance," 58; "warm/own," 26; lonely childhood, *LGNY*, 362.

4. No EW birth record, New York City Municipal Archives (SB, 16 Sept. 1992); Grace Church baptismal record: Frederic Rhinelander Jones, born 15 Jan. 1846, baptized 13 March 1846, sponsors: Mrs. Rhinelander (LRJ's mother), Mr. Edward Jones (GFJ's brother), and GFJ, vol. 1, 180; Henry Edward Jones, born 29 May 1850, baptized, 4 Oct. 1850, sponsors: Thomas H. Newbold, Frederic F. Rhinelander (probably Frederic W. Rhinelander, LRJ's brother), Elizabeth F. Jones, vol. 1, 193; Edith Newbold Jones, vol. 1, 211; Thomas H. Newbold died 12 March 1869.

5. "sins/society," Van Rensselaer, 48.

6. "illicit/theaters," Nevins, 54.

7. "evil/walking-doll," Nevins, 457.

8. "always/hobgoblin," *BG,* 23–24.

9. *BG*: "incurably prosaic," 21; "extremely/tutor," 49; tutor died with Custer, OC–TC, 24 Aug. 1926.

10. "James Blake," National Archives, Passport Application Register, 1810–1906 (SB, 20 Aug. 1992).

11. List of casualties from battle of Little Big Horn, 25–26 June 1876, National Archives Military Records (SB, 21 May 1992).

12. Marian Mason Bell (Mrs. Gordon Knox Bell), a friend of EW since the early 1900s, told OC the Lord Brougham story, OC–TC, 24 Aug. 1926; LB background, *Debrett's Peerage and Baronetage and Knightage*, 1889, and *Encyclopaedia Britannica*, 11th ed., 652–54. GFJ/LRJ in Paris: Vestry Records, Eglise Américaine, rue Bayard, the former parish church of the American Pro-Cathedral, avenue George V, Paris (SB, 26 April 1993).

13. MTG, DC testimony, see Markow-Totevy papers (YCAL); "image," RWBL, Appendix A, 535–39. Lifelong friends of EW, MTG and DC were intellectual, proper, and deeply religious women, who converted to Ro-

man Catholicism in their late twenties (MTG's family strongly opposed her decision). MTG believed a "shadow" hung over EW's life and that it was her irregular parentage; MTG called EW's fiction the "story of a soul in pain" (ET–FRK, 9 June 1949). FRK first claimed that no one from Edith's "early Newport days" knew the rumor, which he believed began in the 1920s or 1930s (FRK–ET, 21 Aug. [1949], LLI). After speaking with DC, he changed his mind: "I heard from Mrs. Winthrop Chanler that E. W. had talked to her of the legend, had herself believed in it—she (E. W.) had made inquiries in England about the family, etc. So this is pretty conclusive. Of course *I* wouldn't have heard of it from my own family even if they knew [it], which I doubt—since Aunt Lou [LRJ] wasn't disapproved of" (FRK–ET, 10 Sept. [1949], LLI).

14. "niece," BF adoption, disinherited EW and BF, EW–Pendleton Beckley, 29 Jan. 1929, and P. Beckley–EW, 2 Feb. 1929.

15. Background on draft, see Angle and Miers, McCullough; GFJ does not appear on consolidated enrollment lists for Manhattan County, New York (National Archives Military Reference, SB, 31 Aug. 1993).

16. "expression/feeling," ET, "Memoir"; "happy misfortune," *BG*, 44; EW learned of Civil War from EWW, whose parents worked in the Sanitary Commission, EWW–EW, 1 July 1933 (LLI).

17. "Lamp of Psyche," *CSS*, 1: 42–57; GFJ's lack of civic commitment, EWW–ET, 3 Sept. 1937; "secret/citizen," *BG*, 11–14.

18. "safe/monotonous," *BG*, 7; "self-conscious/child," *LI*, 1089.

19. *LGNY*: "much/guarded," 361; "Society/hetaera," yellow brougham, 357; "bumpers/Madeira," Van Rensselaer, 43–44.

20. *BG*: "large/hollow," 2, "wakened/vanity," 3.

21. "poor/girls," *BG*, 18.

22. Rhinelander economic misfortunes, *BG*, 16; mismanagement of EW's trusts, see chapters 8, 10.

23. *BG*: "Miss/Gate," 18, "pretty/roof," 17.

24. *BG*: "avenged," 18; "never/her," 17; LRJ's education, 47–48; GFJ's Columbia degree, Columbiana Collection (SB, 3 March 1993).

25. "very/palace," GFJ *Diary*, 16–19; "inexhaustible memory," *BG*, 17.

26. "too/pleasant," GFJ *Diary*, 22 March [1848]; "certainly/it," GFJ, *Diary*, 25 May [1848].

27. GFJ's grand tour, *BG*, 19.

28. "background/order," *BG*, 44; GFJ's passport application, 17 Nov. 1866, U.S. National Archives, no. 28,808; HEJ's entrance to Cambridge University, Trinity Hall archives, C 79 (SB, 7 Feb. 1992).

29. *BG*: "springy turf," 29; walks with LRJ, 30; Spain trip, 31–32; "quantity/saw," Chanler, 109.

30. "weather/road," *BG*, 31.

31. GFJ at Holy Trinity, Paris: served as Warden (1859), member of finance committee, and (with Hamilton Fish) on committee to name the new church. In 1858, GFJ/LRJ lived at 8 rue Luxembourg; FRJ confirmed, 20 March 1859; in March 1872, LRJ paid 100 francs for pew rental (Vestry Registry, Eglise Américaine, Feb. 1859–June 1873).

32. "making-up," *BG*, 32–33; "secret story-world," *LI*, 1077.

33. "full/dreams," spied on by parents, *BG*, 34–45; mother's bedroom, "devastating/obsession," *LI*, 1076.

34. Halévy play, "rhythmic raptures," *BG*, 36–37.

35. *LI*: "labyrinth," 1077; "normal instinct," games, "so/sun," 1078; "sense/prepense," 1096; parents worried, 1077.

36. "furious/children," *LI*, 1077.

37. *BG*: "I/fancy," 39; "tall/kind," 26; GFJ paralysis, 88; "My/father," finances, *LGNY*, 361.

38. "lonely/unattained," *BG*, 39; *False Dawn* opens with parents' courtship.

39. McNevan, "My Childhood's Hours," LRJ notebook (LLI).

40. *LI*: polite, kind, 1073; "shrivelled/impertinence," LRJ's disapproval, 1072–73; "moral bewilderment," 1084.

41. Doyley's workbasket, "I/still," ET "Memoir" (LLI).

42. *LI*: "absolutely/beings," 1074; "if/life," 1091; "what/about," 1084.

43. *BG*: "primitive/place," typhoid, 40; "bad/manners," 52; "great/produced," 65–66; czar's physician, *LI*, 1079.

44. French child-rearing attitudes, Wendell, 197–212; LRJ monitors EW's reading, *LI*, 1083.

45. "robber/timidity," *LI*, 1079–80.

46. Wyndcliffe, "keeping/Joneses," New York State Conservation Association pamphlet, 157; "ramrod/granite," *BG*, 27.

47. *BG*: "inarticulate/home," 28.

48. "chronic tonsillitis," EW–MBB, 11 April 1926; "I used to have tonsillitis continually when I was young, but I don't think my parents ever changed their plans on that account," EW–JHS, 24 Dec. [year unreadable]; McCullough: "doleful," 93; TR's asthma, 90–108. Asthma, identified as a disease in the mid-1700s and known to attack several family members; Edith and her niece Beatrix both suffered from it; creative animus aligned with dark powers, see chapter 4.

49. "it/terror," *LI*, 1079–80.

50. *LI*: "sociable/pretty," 1089; "meager portion," *LGNY*, 361; *BG*: visored knights, 64; "secret/communion," 69.

51. EW's resentment, *BG*, 52; "intellectual/miseries," *LI*, 1089.

52. "How/depression," *LI*, 1080–81; "when/it," *BG*, 85; 1873 depression, McCullough, 134, 140–41.

53. "scuppers/porgies," *BG*, 45.

54. Eliza Edgar's daughter, Mary Newbold Edgar, drowned at age five; FRJ served as sponsor for her baptism on 1 Nov. 1868, Eglise Américaine, Paris (Vestry Record); FRJ–MCJ married 24 March 1870, Philadelphia City Archives and Episcopal Diocese of Pennsylvania archives; FRJ listed as bookbinder in New York City, marriage certificate, Philadelphia Department of Records, No. 92244; FRJ/MCJ Europe honeymoon, EW–MCJ, 12 Dec. 1930 (LLI); "Pen Craig" (or "Pencraig") and "Pencraig Cottage" not listed in *Newport City Directory* under these names until 1888; prior listings given by address on Harrison Avenue (see years 1872–1881); LRJ's devotion to BF, EWW–ET, 27 Sept. 1937; "friendly gables," *BG*, 44.

55. "shouts/fern," *BG*, 54; *LI*: "vague tremors," 1087; "You're/farther," 1087.

56. "unsympathetic/unsatisfied," AB as tutor, *BG*, 45; "Why/so," EW–Walter Maynard, 9 Nov. 1922 [LA].

57. Ban on Goethe, ordered his works, EWW–ET, 3 Sept. [1938]; "devour," *BG*, 68.

58. *LI*: "struck/spark," 1089; novel reading, "les/twenty," 1083–84; *BG*: LRJ following her mother's orders, 65.

59. *BG*: Belmont lawn, 83; "pagan/forth," 46.

60. LRJ's training, "restless," *BG*, 47; see Kaledin for discussion of educational constraints on women in mid-nineteenth-century America.

61. "queer/nourishment," *LI*, 1085; "nervous child," EWW–ET, 3 Sept. [1938]; EWW/EW friendship, button, EWW–ET, 3 Sept. [1938].

62. Dr. Washburn's intellectual friendships and politics, reading Dante, EWW's studies, EWW–ET, 3 Sept. [1938]; see *LI*, 1085.

63. "I/York," EWW–ET, 3 Sept. [1938].

64. "I/older," nicknames, EWW–ET, 3 Sept. [1938].

65. Writing of "Fast and Loose," EWW–ET, 16 Oct. [1938] (LLI); "Oh/tidy," *BG*, 73. See Viola Hopkins Winner's helpful commentary on this novel in her edition, *Fast and Loose and The Buccaneers* (Charlottesville: University Press of Virginia, 1993), which includes EW's revisions to the novel, ix–xvii.

66. Brugsch Bey poem, publication of *Verses*, EWW–ET, 3 Sept. [1938]; "little booklet," ET, "Memoir."

67. Manuscript pages of *V* are in YCAL.

68. "morbid strain," *LI*, 1091.

69. "She is not dead, but sleepeth," Eleutherian Mills Historical Library, curator John Beverley Riggs to Donald C. Gallup, curator of American Literature Collection, Yale, 2 May 1968, and 10 May 1968 (YCAL); "My/you," EW–Pauline Foster Du Pont, 23 Sept. 1874, LL 29–30.

70. A. T. Rice, friend of HEJ, *LI*, 1092; *Atlantic* poems attributed to EW by Arthur Hobson Quinn and Vito J. Brenni: "The Parting Day," 45 (Feb.

1880), 194; "Areopagus," 45 (March 1880), 335; "A Failure," 45 (April 1880), 464–65; "Patience," 45 (April 1880), 548–49; "Wants," 45 (May 1880), 599; "most/Muses," A. T. Rice–H. W. Longfellow, 12 Aug. 1879 (HL). On 20 Sept. 1879, Rice received a "very kind letter" from Longfellow.

71. "The Last Giustiniani," *Scribner's Magazine* 6 (Oct. 1889), 405–6; "for/more," EWW–ET, 3 Sept. [1938].

72. "alarmed/age," *LI*, 1092; LRJ's worries, "learned/dearly," EWW–ET, 3 Sept. [1938]; "bouncers," "silver gilts," "climbers," Van Rensselaer, 56.

73. Patriarchs and Assembly Balls, Mrs. Vanderbilt waiting, MCJ–EW, Sat., 22 Nov. 1919.

74. house mortgages, EW–BF, 20 Oct. 1935, and OC–TC, 25 Sept. 1918; "the/room," *LGNY*, 361.

75. "my/room," *BG*, 78; L. Morton history, *Dictionary of American Biography*, vol. 7 (New York: Scribners, 1934).

76. "long/misery," *BG*, 78; "pink/me," *LI*, 1093.

77. *LI*: "older/passions," 1093; "charmed circle," *BG*, 79.

78. Background on Stevens family, British aristocracy scandalized by Paget marriage, EWW–ET, 8 Dec. [1938]; M. Stevens's address, *New York City Directory*; obituary, *NYT*, 4 April 1895, section 1, 5; "shadow/her," L. Rutherfurd–M. R. White, quoted in RWBL, 39–40.

79. Death of Dr. Washburn, EWW–ET, 3 Sept. [1938]; "Thy Truth, O Lord" (YCAL); GFJ's death certificate and burial, Mayor's Office, Cannes, France (SB, 2 Nov. 1992), and U.S. Consular Agency, Nice, France (SB, 9 Dec. 1992).

80. Effect of GFJ's death on LRJ, HEJ and FRJ's devotion to LRJ, LRJ's devotion to her children and BF, EWW–ET, 3 Sept. [1938]; West Twenty-fifth Street house, *BG*, 88; West Twenty-third Street house rented, EW–BF, 20 Oct. 1935, and OC–SBC, 25 Sept. 1918; FRJ address, *New York City Directory*, 1883.

81. Books from GFJ, *BG*, 67; "Intense Love's Utterance," 13 Sept. 1881 (YCAL); EW's Riviera activities, *LI*, 1094–95.

82. H. Stevens's comforting presence in Cannes, EWW–ET, 8 Dec. [1938].

83. "wretchedly/one," LRJ–F. Rhinelander, 15 Aug. 1883; "impossible/mother-in-law," EWW–ET, 16 Oct. [1938].

84. EW forced to break engagement, EWW–ET, 8 Dec. [1938]; financial worth of M. Stevens at her death, *TT*, 12 March 1896.

85. "Is/all," Helen Rhinelander–Thomas Rhinelander [1883], LA; LRJ to Paris, *NDN*, 18 Nov. 1883; Margaret Rutherfurd White, see Auchincloss, *Vanderbilt*, 75.

86. Julian White and Patriarchs Ball, W. H. Buckler–GL, 3 Feb. 1928; "inferiority/amusing," *BG*: 88–89.

87. *BG*: "I/me," 88; "You/unreality," 75–76.
88. Power of attorney, 25 Jan. 1883 (LLI); EW's inheritance from GFJ, including investment properties, documents from Cadwalader and Strong, 40 Wall Street, New York City (LLI) and LA notes (YCAL).

CHAPTER 2

Background texts: Louis Auchincloss, *Edith Wharton: A Woman in Her Time* (New York: Viking Press, 1971); Millicent Bell, *Edith Wharton and Henry James: The Story of Their Friendship* (New York: George Braziller, 1965); Paul Bourget, *Outre-mer: Impressions of America* (New York: Charles Scribner's Sons, 1895, no translator listed); Anna Robeson Burr, *Weir Mitchell: His Life and Letters* (New York: Duffield, 1929); Florence Codman, *The Clever Young Boston Architect* (Augusta, Maine, privately printed, 1970); Ernest Earnest, *S. Weir Mitchell: Novelist and Physician* (Philadelphia: University of Pennsylvania Press, 1950); John Foreman and Robbe Pierce Stimson, *The Vanderbilts and the Gilded Age: Architectural Aspirations, 1879–1901* (New York: St. Martin's Press, 1991); Grace Kellogg Griffith, *The Two Lives of Edith Wharton: The Woman and Her Work* (New York: Appleton-Century, 1965); Fred Kaplan: *Henry James: The Imagination of Genius* (New York: Morrow, 1992); Pauline C. Metcalf, ed., *Ogden Codman and the Decoration of Houses* (Boston: The Boston Athenaeum, 1988); S. Weir Mitchell, *Lectures on Diseases of the Nervous System, Especially in Women* (Philadelphia: Lea Brothers and Co., 1885); Edmund Morris, *The Rise of Theodore Roosevelt* (New York: Coward, McCann and Geoghegan, 1979); Frank Luther Mott, *A History of American Magazines, 1885–1905* (Cambridge: Harvard University Press, 1957); Jean Strouse, *Alice James: A Biography* (Boston: Houghton Mifflin, 1980); James Trager, *Park Avenue: Street of Dreams* (New York: Athenaeum, 1990); Richard D. Walter, *S. Weir Mitchell, M.D., Neurologist: A Medical Biography* (Springfield, Ill.: Charles C. Thomas, 1970); Edmund Wilson, *The Wound and the Bow* (New York: Oxford University Press, 1947); Cynthia Griffin Wolff, *A Feast of Words: The Triumph of Edith Wharton* (New York: Oxford University Press, 1977).

1. "love/life," *DD*, 11 Oct. 1927.
2. WB personal and professional history, Harry Crosby materials (HRHRC); obituary, *Le Figaro*, 12 Oct. 1927; Columbiana Collection (SB, 3 March 1993).
3. "dry/manhood," *PEW*, 206–7; "He/world," R. Cortissoz–EW, 22 Oct. 1927; *BG*: "unforgettable/together," 119; "Dearest/W.," WB–EW, 25 Feb. 1923 (YCAL).
4. "communion/otherwise," ET, "Memoir"; "great days," EW–JHS, 15 Oct. 1927, LL 504–05.

5. "forgave," OC–SBC, 16 Oct. 1912; malaria, WB–EW, 16 July 1900; WB "rest cures," WB–EW letters, 1900, passim.

6. TW Pencraig visitor, humor, youthfulness, *BG*, 90; clubman, GL, *M*; "sunshine/house," EWW–ET, 8 Dec. [1938]; detect pretentiousness, "I/either," DBU, *M*.

7. TW at Bar Harbor, summer 1883, EWW–ET, 8 Dec. [1938]; John Wharton, South Ward, Philadelphia City, U.S. Census, 1820, roll 108: 153; 1830 U.S. Census shows no John Wharton in Philadelphia; Massachusetts residency of WCW, U.S. Census, 1850; Nancy Spring's grandfather, OC–TC, 20 June 1937; NSW, 13 Oct. 1820–17 Aug. 1909; WFW, 28 June 1847–20 May 1919; NCW, 7 March 1844–25 Oct. 1921; TW, 3 April 1850–7 Feb. 1928; WCW born [1811], died 22 May 1891, age eighty, Somerville, Mass.; death certificate, vol. 417: 333.

8. TW/WFW student records, PUL; WFW's law career, Massachusetts House of Representatives (1885–88), assistant secretary of state, 1889–93, *Who's Who in New England* (1916), 1136.

9. "winter/T. W," TW–Sarah Perkins Cleveland, Tues., 20 May 1884 (Berg Collection, New York Public Library).

10. No records exist for TW's finances, including the size of his allowance prior to 1909, when NSW's estate was settled. EW/TW stayed with LRJ during winter visits in NYC, EWW–ET, 8 Dec. [1938].

11. LRJ's happiness about marriage, EW in love with TW, EWW–ET, 8 Dec. [1938]; "busy," *BG*, 90.

12. WCW at McLean, OB–SBC, 25 Sept. [1918]; "trial/up," OC–SBC, 2 Sept. 1911; "When/probably," EW–LN, 22 Feb. 1928 (HL); "melancholia," WCW death certificate, Somerville, Massachusetts, 22 May 1891, no. 299.

13. "very/families," *NYT*, 30 April 1885; "Mrs./Avenue," *NDN*, 30 April 1885; wedding invitation, Auchincloss, 46; "The Last Asset," *CSS*, 1: 590–616.

14. "many people expected," *TT*, 7 May 1885; Book of Common Prayer (SB interview with WRT, 29 Oct. 1991).

15. *LI*: "seized/pretend," 1087–88; "all/weeks," 1087; "falsify/misdirect," 1088.

16. Engagement and wedding rings, EW–MCJ, 30 Nov. 1911; wedding breakfast, *NYT*, 30 April 1885. The legend that EW married at Trinity Chapel because her supposed illegitimacy prevented her being married at the high altar at Trinity Church (Broadway and Wall Street) is untrue. She married at the chapel because it was conveniently located and because she had, relatively speaking, a small wedding.

17. Harry Stevens's personal history and death, EWW–ET, 8 Dec. [1938].

18. EW/TW at Pencraig Cottage, 1885–1893, "I/alive," *BG*, 90–91.

19. "no/own," *BG*, 112; CG began employment on 10 Oct. 1884, a date cel-

ebrated in EW's household each year, *DD*, 10 Oct. 1930; AW hired 1888, EW–Benjamin Conner, GC, 17 April 1931; AW held an American passport; RWBL and LL incorrectly refer to AW as "Arthur" White and misspell GC's first name as "Catharine."

20. "Life/Life," *LI*, 1086; *mariage blanc*, OC–SBC, 19 March 1901.
21. *BG*: "watering-place mundanities," 90; TW's dislike of Boston, 96.
22. *BG*: "Awakener/buildings," 91.
23. *BG*: "commonplace," 92–93; "wonder-world/see," 94; "think/better," "Darwinism," E. Winthrop–EW, n.d. (John Work Garrett Library of Evergreen House, Johns Hopkins University).
24. *BG*: "dilettantish leisure," 95; "It/frivolous," 93; "too democratic," GFJ, *D*, 22 March [1848].
25. *BG*: Julian Story (son of William Wetmore Story) portrait, "as/simple," chair, 101; EW thought portrait "not a success," although it hung in the drawing room at 884 and was used on book jacket of *GI*; it was later lost, EW–Emelyn Story Ewer, 20 April 1934 (YCAL).
26. *BG*: "I/Mediterranean," 96; family objections, loan, 97; wealthy fad, "All/then," 98; "crowning/life," EW–BB, 6 Jan. 1925.
27. *CV*: "sea/cloaks," 15; *BG*: EW's archaeological interests, 99; no practical cares, 100; reading Homer, EW–GL, 22 April 1926.
28. Discovery of EW's diary of Aegean voyage, "Editor's Note," *CV*, 7–8.
29. "archaeological ardours," *BG*, 99; *CV*: "greater/poverty," 116; Montenegrin dress, 125–26.
30. *CV*: flora, 34; clothing, 47; "Jewesses/faces," 18; "finely-plaited/gold," 119; EW object of wonder, 67; "local atrocities," 23.
31. Murray's Guide, *BG*, 90; *CV*: surly captain, 137; men scale Athos, treasures, 101–3; "life/Lavra," 103.
32. J. Jones inheritance, "wise economy," *BG*, 100.
33. *BG*: "star," 100–101; Canaries and Azores, 101.
34. "first/houses," *BG*, 109.
35. "one/shanty," EW–OC, 4 May 1896; neighborhood, Trager, 24–32.
36. "clever/architect," *BG*, 106; 884 payment for debt, DBU, *M*; "little shanty," George Baldwin, 32 Nassau Street, rented 884 for EW, EW–OC, 4 May 1896.
37. "ugly/rock," *BG*, 106. OC's account books at SPNEA and the Codman collection at the Metropolitan Museum of Art (New York City) show that he worked on LE in 1892. In 1898, the year EW/TW bought 882 Park Avenue (the adjoining house to 884), they also took out a $50,000 mortgage on LE.
38. R. W. Gilder and *Century*, DLB, vol. 64, 74–76.
39. *BG*: "large/fiction," 107; "authors/editors," visiting card, "senselessly/outlet," 109.

40. wrapping paper, *BG*, 73.

41. "Mrs. Manstey's View," *CSS*, 1: 3–11; "Bunner Sisters," in *Madame de Treymes and Three Novellas* (New York: Macmillan, 1970).

42. "slight sketch," ELB–EW, 26 May 1890; rpt. of "MMV," *Stories From Scribner: Stories of New York* (1893); "admirable/length," ELB–EW, Dec. 1891.

43. "not/average," EW–ELB, 25 Nov. 1893, LL 31–32; "Bunner Sisters," *SM*, Oct.–Nov. 1916.

44. "The Fullness of Life," *CSS*, 1: 12–20.

45. "capital/soulful," ELB–EW, [autumn 1891]; "over-done/purposes," EW–ELB, 26 Aug. 1893.

46. "As/them," EW–ELB, 10 July [1898], LL 36–37; "The Lamp of Psyche," *CSS*, 1: 42–57; "The Journey," *CSS*, 1: 79–87; "gruesome streak," WB–EW, 15 Feb. [1901].

47. WCW's death, Massachusetts State Archives *Death Register*, vol. 419, p. 333, no. 299, 22 May 1891; "queer/irritable," OC–SBC, 19 Dec. 1902; "chief/development," OC–SBC, 10 Aug. 1911; "greatest mistake," OC–SBC, 5 Jan. 1914; "fellow/himself," OC–SBC, 20 Sept. 1910.

48. "Experience," *AA*, 45–46; EW/TW in mourning for WCW, see Auchincloss, *Edith Wharton*.

49. WCW will, Massachusetts State Archives, #87467; NSW will, Suffolk County, #146371, probated by Judge Robert Grant.

50. *BG*: "endlessly/cliffs," 106; "fashionable watering place," 103; *Sensations d'Italie*, "Tanagra Madonna," 104; "brilliant/invisibility," 103–4; PB's background, *Dictionnaire de Biographie Française*, vol. 6 (1954).

51. EW's French, *BG*, 295; "gospel/seriously," Du Bos, *M*; "intellectual/order," *Outre-mer*, 86–106; see RWBL, 69–70.

52. V. Lee, *DLB*, vol. 57, 158–67; *BG*: "best-loved companions," 130; "opalescent/sky," 133; for an excellent discussion of V. Lee's friendship with EW, see Bell, 60–64.

53. "highly/woman," *BG*, 132; EW knew of N. Barney's writing through WB, who sent her in 1900 a gift of *Quelques Portraits—Sonnets de Femmes* (Paris: Ollendorf, 1900), NB's first book of poetry, WB–EW, Mon. [summer 1900].

54. "over-civilized," "archaic/carriage," "A Tuscan Shrine," *IB*, 85–106.

55. "article/public," EW–ELB, 30 July 1894, LL 33–34.

56. "have/counsel," EW–ELB, 26 March [1894], LL 32–33; "waif," "very/work," EW–ELB, 14 Dec. 1895, LL 35–36.

57. "The/it," EW–OC, 5 May 1895.

58. Fire at Breakers, 25 Nov. 1892, Foreman, 248.

59. "pretty/thoroughly," EW–OC, 8 May 1895; "If/veranda," EW "seedy," fourth bout of flu, TW–OC, 24 May 1895.

60. "total/years," RWBL, 74; "not/work," EW–WLB, 14 Dec. 1895.

61. "roads/towns," EW–OC, 17 April 1896; "absurdly/shanty," Stupingi, EW–OC, 8 June 1896.

62. HEJ's Paris address, EW–OC, 24 June 1896.

63. Gossip about the circumstances of the divorce tells the following story: Minnie and her daughter, Beatrix (age twelve), walked up Fifth Avenue on a sunny spring day in 1883 and saw Frederic seated by a window in Delmonico's, lunching with another woman. Minnie pressed her divorce action the very next day (SB interview with Louisa Farrand Wood, niece of Beatrix Jones Farrand, 30 April 1991). The story is not true. Depositions taken in March 1896 suggest that MCJ tried to avoid divorce as long as possible, bringing her case only when the five-year statute of limitations was about to run out.

64. History of FRJ's affair, depositions taken before general counsel, U.S. Embassy, Paris, 13 March 1896; EW/TW in Paris shopping for OC, EW–OC, 23 Feb. 1895.

65. MCJ/BF finances after divorce, BF–EW, 18 May 1936.

66. "disreputable," EW–HE, 5 Aug. 1931. Jones family addresses from New York City and Newport street directories: FRJ/MCJ, East Eighteenth Street, 1880–1884, 21 East Eleventh Street, 1885–; MCJ, 21 East Eleventh Street with "Miss Beatrix," 1891; LRJ and HEJ (Pencraig), Newport, 1895–1899; LRJ ill in Paris, EW–ELB, 19 Oct. 1898; TW seeing to Pencraig furniture, TW–OC, 25 April 1899 and EW–OC, 9 Feb. 1899.

67. McKim's notes on DH, EW–OC, Wed. [Jan. 1897]; OC's fees resented, EW–OC, 20 Nov. 1896, and 24 Nov. 1896; 25 percent reduced to 15 percent, EW–OC, 27 May 1897; "You/box," EW–OC, 7 Jan. 1897.

68. BG: "literally/clear," 107; "excusable/words," 107; OC claimed to have written DH, see William A. Coles, "The Genesis of a Classic," in The Decoration of Houses, ed. John Barrington Bayley and William A. Coles (New York: Norton and Co., 1978), xxiv; see also Florence Codman, 2.

69. MCJ recommended Macmillan, EW–OC, [5 Dec. 1896], and EW–OC, 20 Feb. 1897; Brett and photos, EW–OC, 2 March 1897; new title, EW–OC, 20 Feb. 1897; "with/derision," BG, 108; MCJ reading ms., "I/me," EW–OC, 15 March 1897.

70. LE library, EW–OC, 17 Aug. 1897; EW/TW building lodge for AW at LE, EW–OC, 13 May 1897; NSW/NCW at LE, NSW ill with bronchitis, EW–OC, 9 May 1897, and 13 May 1897; EW gardening, Newport schools, EW–OC, 2 May 1897; EW to add garden chapter, EW–OC, 14 July 1897; TW's sketch for bathhouses, TW–OC, 29 May 1897.

71. "I/once," EW–OC, [1897]; "I/have," EW–OC, [1897 penned in]; "stupid," EW–OC, 11 Sept. 1897.

72. "Anytime/out," EW–OC, Thurs. [June 1897]; photos, EW–OC, 26 July 1897; TW chiding OC, TW–OC, 17 Aug. 1897; "fit/publication," *BG*, 108.

73. "taste-maker," *DLB* 49, 412–19; "most/critic," EW, "William C. Brownell," *SM* 84 (Nov. 1928), 596–602; "grand air," did not suffer fools, *NYT* obituary, 24 July 1928, quoted in *DLB* 71, 44–49.

74. Photograph plates, EW–WCB, 12 Aug. 1897; OC/DBU gossiping about EW, OC–DBU, 27 Feb. 1901; DBU–OC, 31 Jan. 1902, 8 Oct. 1902, and 3 Jan. 1903 (SPNEA); DBU's fondness for her, DBU–EW, 26 May 1913 (YCAL); EW claimed to have designed title page and chosen paper for *DH*, EW–WCB, 3 Sept. 1897.

75. *DH*: "Doors/room," 61; "serviceable feature," 48.

76. *DH* reviews: Anon., *Nation* 65 (16 Dec. 1897), 485; "large/mistreated," W. Berry, *Bookman* 7 (April 1898), 161–63; E. H. Blashfield, *Book Buyer*, 16 March 1898, 129–33; OC being sued, TW–OC, "Bring/you," TW–OC, 11 Nov. 1897.

77. "despair/long," TW–OC, 8 Dec. 1897; EW ill, TW–OC, 13 Dec. 1897; "Intelligent/House," EW–OC, 17 Dec. 1897; "close/prostration," WB–EW, Mon. [1900].

78. "The/trash," C. Shaw to Blackett, 13 Dec. 1897; Chapman and Hall rejection (SA note file, 1897); Batsford sale, SG, 9.

79. "everything/me," ELB–EW, [Oct. 1893]; story volume, ELB–EW, 24 Nov. 1893, and EW–ELB, 25 Nov. 1893. Stories ELB rejected or wanted revised: "Judged" (never published); "Something Exquisite": "I don't like the story as well as any of your others . . . in spite of the excellence (as always) of the execution," ELB–EW, [March 1894]; the story, revised and retitled "Friends," was published in *Youth's Companion*, 23 and 30 Aug. 1900; "April Showers" (ELB rejected July 1893) was published in *Youth's Companion*, 74, 3 (18 Jan. 1900); "A Cup of Cold Water," which ELB thought "too wildly improbable" (ELB–EW, 1894), was revised and appeared in *GI*; "The Valley of Childish Things," which ELB thought too esoteric (ELB–EW, Dec. 1895), was published in *Century Magazine* 52 (July 1896); EW reworked "The Twilight of the God" ("For the first time I do not catch your point," ELB–EW, Jan. 1897) for *GI*. ELB accepted "The Fullness of Life," "That Good May Come," "The Lamp of Psyche," and "The Pelican." Poems ELB accepted: "Experience," *SM* 13 (Jan. 1893); "Chartres," *SM* 14 (Sept. 1893); "Life," *SM* 15 (June 1894); "An Autumn Sunset," *SM* 16 (Oct. 1894); "Phaedra," *SM* 23 (Jan. 1898). EW translations: Edmondo de Amicis, "A Great Day"; Gabriele d'Annunzio, "It Snows"; Enrico Castelnuovo, "College Friends"; all appeared in *Stories by Foreign Authors: Italian* (Scribners 1898). "The Pelican," *CSS*, 1: 88–103; "really/sloppy," EW–ELB, 23 Feb. 1898. For a brief history of EW's working relationship with Charles Scribner's Sons, see Bell, 315–41.

80. "gain," "forlorn/neglected," EW–OC, 5 April 1898; "taken/world," *navrant*, EW–OC, 18 April 1898.

81. "McKinley/eclair," Morris, 610; "War/disgrace," EW–OC, 23 April 1898; HJ on Boston Harbor, Kaplan, 433.

82. "That/composition," EW–OC, 18 April 1898; "one/cloth," EW–DC, 17 May [1902], LL 63–65.

83. "The One Grief," *SM* 24 (July 1898) and *AA* (1909).

84. "irrefutable," EW–ELB, 10 July 1898, LL 36–37. WB's assessment of "A Cup of Cold Water": "You weren't as well as you are now when G.I. [*Greater Inclination*] appeared and I didn't mind saying 'The Cup' was rotten. It just meant that you've covered a lot of ground since then and that you couldn't do that sort of thing any more," WB–EW, Wed. night [1900]. "Edith/writer," EW's health improved in Bar Harbor, EW–OC, 15 Aug. 1898; "crowded out," EW–WCB, 9 Sept. 1898.

85. "ideal/place," EW–OC, 15 Aug. 1898.

86. "The/clay," EW–ELB, 10 July 1898, LL 36–37; "my/going," EW–ELB, 9 Sept. 1898; "uncertain/please," quoted in EW–ELB, 18 Sept. [1898]; "bored/it," EW–WCB, 18 Sept. [1898]; "Since/abroad," EW–WCB, 19 Oct. 1898 (this note contains no reference to a "long rest cure," as RWBL suggests, 82); recalling these events many years later, EW said her heart *flancher* ("gave out"), EW–MCJ, GC, May 1918.

87. Mitchell's neurological research, see Earnest, Walter, and *DLB*, vol. 36: 276.

88. See S. Weir Mitchell, "Rest in the Treatment of Nervous Disease," in E. C. Seguin, ed., *American Clinical Lectures* (New York: G. P. Putnam's Sons, 1875), 1, 4: 83–102; Mitchell, *Lectures*, 265–83; Earnest, 80–86; Walter, 127–40; Strouse, 105–6, 223–24; "Stenton-cure," WB–EW, Sun. [spring 1902]; HJ's cure, Kaplan, 525; Winifred Howells's death, Strouse, 223–24.

89. EW's literary activities, WB–EW, 9 Nov. [1898], 21 Nov. [1898], and EW–WCB, 20 Nov. 1898, 1 Dec. 1898, and 3 Dec. 1898; during these weeks, EW read "specimen pages" of *GI* (EW–WCB, 20 Nov. 1898) and wrote "Portrait"; W. Mitchell's 1898–1899 trip, see Burr, 254, 270; "how/duvets," WB–EW, 7 Dec. 1898.

90. "authentic fact," Wilson, 196. Wilson describes EW's writing as the "desperate product of a pressure of maladjustments" (197) and cites as a contributing factor to the "pressure" TW's mental illness. (The first signs of TW's illness did not appear, however, until 1900.) Griffith takes Wilson's conjecture as fact, saying that those who disliked, envied, and resented EW "made much" of her "famous nervous breakdown," gossiping that she was unable to "adjust to marriage" (82–84). Neither Wilson nor Griffith provides evidence to support their claims. The "maladjustment" argument underwrites most psychological interpretations of EW's life and

work. RWBL, for example, describes her illness as a "severe identity crisis" and speculates that producing enough stories for her first volume "actually helped precipitate the crisis" (76). This "first genuinely creative period [of her work] unsettled her" (81). "There is evidence," he writes, "that she had absorbed into a guilt-ridden corner of her being her society's and her mother's distrust of a person of good family who took seriously to writing" (76); he does not provide the supporting evidence. Agreeing with Lewis's interpretation, C. Woolf argues that EW's "illness" was occasioned by a crisis of commitment to a writing career: EW "started [writing] late and . . . had a very long apprenticeship" (62). She also claims that Mitchell's "treatment appears to have cured her illness" (4). Describing EW's daily life during the Philadelphia weeks, C. Wolff and Lewis (who says that Mitchell "looked in on Mrs. Wharton once or twice"—83) do not draw on EW's own experiences in Philadelphia, which cannot be fully documented, but instead on case histories of other Mitchell patients (RWBL, 82–84; C. Wolff, 85–86).

91. "real devil," heart doing "splendidly," WB–EW, Sun., [8 Jan. 1899]; Mc-Clellan information, archives of Thomas Jefferson University, University of Pennsylvania, and Philadelphia College of Physicians (SB, 2 Feb., 18 March 1993, and 11 May 1993).

92. "Tell/hope," EW–SN, 2 April [1908], LL 139–41; "some/hills," EW–BB, 9 June [1912]; "I/it," EW–WCB, 27 July 1918 (EW was resting in Fleury-en-Bière, having just suffered her third heart attack in eighteen months); "recuperate," NY house rental, EW–Mr. Moody (Charles Scribner's Sons), 5 May 1899; "Luck/please," WB–EW, Sat., 12 p.m. [1898].

CHAPTER 3

Background texts: Millicent Bell, *Edith Wharton and Henry James: The Story of Their Friendship* (New York: George Braziller, 1965); Michael Burns, *Dreyfus: A Family Affair, 1789–1945* (New York: HarperCollins, 1991); Judith Fryer, *Felicitous Space: The Imaginative Structures of Edith Wharton and Willa Cather* (Chapel Hill: University of North Carolina Press, 1986); Norman L. Kneeblatt, ed. *The Dreyfus Affair: Art, Truth, and Justice* (Berkeley: University of California Press, 1987); Blake Nevius, *Edith Wharton: A Study of Her Fiction* (Berkeley: University of California Press, 1953); Sara Norton and M. A. De Wolfe Howe, eds., *Letters of Charles Eliot Norton* (Boston: Houghton Mifflin Co., 1913), vol. 2; Louise Hall Thorp, *Mrs. Jack: A Biography of Isabella Stewart Gardner* (New York: Little, Brown, 1965); Cynthia Griffin Wolff, *A Feast of Words: The Triumph of Edith Wharton* (New York: Oxford University Press, 1977).

1. "very/time," EW–WCB, 25 April 1899, LL 37–38; WB reading proof,

WB–EW, [1899]; second edition in June, EW–Charles Scribner's Sons, 18 Sept. 1899.

2. "distinguished/delightful," Anon., *Academy* 57 (8 July 1899), 40; "A New Writer Who Counts," "We/book," H. T. Peck, *Bookman* 9 (June 1899), 344–46; scrapbook (YCAL); "we/wire," *Brooklyn Eagle*, 2 April 1899; "Style/life," *Baltimore News*, 1 April 1899; affected, *Baltimore Sun*, 1 April 1899.

3. "spoiling/clauses," J. D. Barry, *Boston Literary World*, 1 April 1899, 105–6; "relish/geniuses," J. D. Barry, *Boston Literary World*, 13 May 1899, 152–53.

4. "remarkable/case," SPCA in R.I., *NDN* (June 1899).

5. "clever/nature," *Athenaeum* 3745 (5 Aug. 1899), 189; "scholarly/style," Anon., *SR* 88 (15 July 1899), 82.

6. "This/now," *BG*, 123–24.

7. "rather/orchids," *BG*, 120.

8. *BG*: "vocation/fashionable," 119; "simply/minds," 121–22.

9. "complying/others," 124; society roles, 93; "apathy/letters," 123; "sporting/dissatisfied," 122; "insignificant/known," 113; TW unhappy without clubs, GL, *M.*

10. For Dreyfus affair, see Burns and Kneeblatt.

11. "For/*rôle*," WMF, *Times* (London), 11 Sept. 1899.

12. "domes/region," TW on bicycle, *BG*, 105.

13. *IB*: Giorgione, 27; Cerveno, 30–31; Montagu, 33; "black/socks," 34; Tiepolo and Goldoni, "how/contributes," 35; Brescia, 35–36; "Italian opus," WB–EW, 22 Oct. [1899].

14. "the/perfect," *IB*, 38.

15. "burst/rapture," WB–EW, [autumn 1899]; royalties, EW–Charles Scribner's Sons, 18 Sept. [1899]; other publishers, Newport damp, EW–WCB, 26 Sept. [1899], LL 40.

16. "trembling/bewildered," *BG*, 113; reduced fee, "*engouement*," "Why/Union," WB–EW, 6 Nov. [1899].

17. "don't/time," WB–EW, Wed. [Jan. 1900]; "I/day," R. L. Stevenson–E. L. Burlingame, quoted in WB–EW, Wed. eve. [1899].

18. "sogginess/pudeur," WB–EW, 22 Oct. [1899]; "keep/weller," WB–EW, 6 Nov. [1899]; "altogether delightful," WB–EW, 26 Oct. [1899].

19. *BG*: "within/dimensions," 114; "Don't/telling," "soul," 115.

20. "Dr./back," WB–EW, 1 Nov. [1899]; "I/occasionally," G. Eliot passage, WB–EW, 28 Nov. [1899]; "understood/myself," ET, "Memoir."

21. Fifth printing of *GI* and *Herald* article, WB–EW, Wed. [1899]; "all's/world," WB–EW, Wed. [Jan. 1900]; "travail-pains/badly," WB–EW, 27 Dec. [1899]; "Tight-Rope," "what/884," WB–EW, Thurs. night [Jan. 1900]; boudoir, WB–EW, Wed. night [1900].

22. "great days," EW–JHS, 15 Oct. 1927, LL 504–05; "orgies," WB–EW, Wed. [Jan. 1900]; pool with TW, Sat., 12 p.m. [31 Dec. 1898]; "driven/witchcraft," ET, "Memoir."

23. *CI* title, EW–ELB, 3 Aug. 1900; "sun/hair," WB–EW, 31 May 1900; "just/afterwards," WB–EW, Thurs. eve. [April 1900]; "stretched/forehead," WB–EW, 21 Oct. [1900]; "all yours dear," WB–EW, Wed. eve. [1900].

24. "Wretchedly/me," EW–OC, 5 April 1900; "great/case," WB–EW, 22 May [1900]; Dr. James, Europe trip, WB–EW, 1 May [1900].

25. "almost/drama," R. Le Gallienne, *BET*, 29 Sept. [1900]. "better/possibilities," Anon., *AM* 86 (Sept. 1900), 418–19; "very/America," Anon., *Bookman* 18 (Sept. 1900), 189.

26. Nortons/Whartons in same Boston group, EW meets SN, Elizabeth Gaskell Norton, *M*; background on Norton family (SB interview with James Turner, CEN's biographer, 6 Dec. 1992).

27. "You/approval," EW–SN, 1 March 1900; "fatuous/yesterdays," quoted in WB–EW, Sat. [spring 1900]; "ploughed field," quoted in WB–EW, 27 Feb. 1900; "*baissement*," WB–EW, 30 July [1900]; "bowl/gruel," quoted in WB–EW, Wed. night [May 1900]; "I/all," quoted in WB–EW, 1 May 1900; *T* sales, "boom" to *GI*, EW–WCB, 27 Oct. 1900.

28. Archer, Marbury, WB–EW, 22 May [1900]; NY house by 1900, "ugly/rest," EW–OC, 11 July 1899.

29. *Country Life*, EW–OC, 27 Feb. 1900; LRJ's anger at EW, EW–HE, 5 Aug. 1931; HEJ adopted BF, EW–Pendleton Beckley, 29 Jan. 1929; LRJ estranged from HEJ, FRK–ET, 20 May 1949; "it/dear," WBW–EW, 10 June [1900].

30. LE rented, horse, "never/land," WB–EW, Thurs. eve. [April 1900]; "The/all," EW–OC, 1 Aug. 1900.

31. EW's weight, WB–EW, 24 Oct. 1900; "old/raggedness," WB–EW, 17 July [1900]; WB's birthday, 30 July 1900; "oldman," Thurs. eve. [April 1900].

32. "without/empty," publication schedule, EW–WCB, 7 Nov. 1900, LL 42–43; "great/better," EW–WCB, 27 Oct. 1900.

33. Somerset Hotel, "blowing/guns," EW–OC, 10 Nov. 1900; EW's "new donnée" for Frohman, EW–WB, 21 Nov. 1900, may have been *The Man of Genius*, an English comedy of manners (see LL 44, fn. 4); "crystal/everywhere," EW–WCB, 11 Dec. [1900]; "Mrs./week," AB–WCB, 20 Dec. 1900.

34. offense of "LLR," EW–WCB, 22 Feb. [1904]; "Confessional," EW–WCB, 6 Feb. 1901, and EW–WCB, 27 Feb. 1901.

35. "a/derisive," HJ–EW, 26 Oct. 1900, LE, 4: 170–71, and LP 32–33; "the/Lenox," OC–SBC, 25 Feb. 1901; "fitted/key," WB–EW, Friday eve

[1900]; EW/TW write Sloanes, OC–SBC, 25 Feb. 1901; "glass houses," OC–SBC, 6 Nov. 1901.

36. EW Lenox rest, EW–WCB, Sun., 10 Feb. 1901; "failure/play," OC–SBC, 17 Feb. 1901; Marlowe, WB–EW, 22 Feb. 1901; "monthlies/hard," forty thousand copies, WB–EW [March 1901]; EW withdrew play, WB–EW, Sun. [Feb. 1901].

37. "delicate/colors," Anon., *Independent* 53 (6 June 1901), 1322–23; "rich/fad," Anon., *Munsey's Magazine* 25 (June 1901), 435–36; "at/authority," Anon., *Harper's Monthly* 103 (Oct. 1901), 823–24; *CI* publicity, "best/is," WB–EW, [spring 1901].

38. LL, farm deed of sale, 29 June 1901; "spend," OC–SBC, 17 Feb. 1901; "double/nonsense," OC–SBC, 7 Feb. 1901.

39. "easy/with," OC–SBC, 9 March 1901; EW/TW unpopular, "shut/off," OC–SBC, 25 Oct. 1901.

40. "would/*upset*," OC–SBC, 25 Feb. 1901; "Their/only," OC–SBC, 19 March 1901.

41. "floral tributes," WB–EW, [1901], and OC–SBC, 19 March 1901; "great/friend," EW–OC, 25 March 1901; "disgusting/him," WB–EW, Tues. eve. [spring 1901]; interior, OC–SBC, 10 Jan. 1902.

42. Boston trip, EW–OC, 29 May 1901, and EW–SN, 1 May 1901; "apple/life," EW–SN, Monday, 20 May [1901], LL 46.

43. "There/all," TW to Paris, EW–SN, 3 June 1901; LRJ, age seventy-seven, died at four in the afternoon, 1 June 1901, at 50 avenue du Bois de Boulogne, buried in Jones vault, Cimetière du Grand Jas (letter, Mayor's Office, Cannes, France, to SB, 2 Nov. 1992); LRJ's will, LA.

44. EW threat to break will, WB–EW, 3 Nov. 1901, and Fri., 4 [no month, 1902]; 1931 discovery, EW–HE, 5 Aug. 1931.

45. Architects arrive, *LL*, Sat., 6 July 1901; "The Mount" named "Mount Buonaparte," *BG*, 13; work began, EW–SN, 1 July 1901; "awful/her," Hoppin's complaints, OC–SBC, 1 July 1901.

46. "extremely/plays," *VD* sale, *LL*, Sat., 27 July, 1901; ptomaine, EW–SN, 18 Aug. 1901; "unhinged," EW–SN, 18 Aug. 1901; Belgium trip, "heavy sea," EW's cabin leaking, EW–SN, 16 Oct. 1901.

47. Schopenhauer, EW carrying proofs, EW–SN, 22 Nov. [1901]; "dream-poem," EW–SN, 27 Nov. [1901]; "Uses," *SM*, 31 (Feb. 1902); Christmas, OC–SBC, 24 Dec. 1901.

48. "frighten/impertinence," EW–WCB, 25 Dec. [1901]; *VD* design, DBU, "make-up/length," EW–WCB, 4 Jan. 1902, LL 47–48; "The/last," EW–WCB, 7 Jan. 1902, LL 49.

49. SN and M. Bourget's illnesses, EW–SN, 11 Jan. [1902]; "Don't/service," EW–SN, 24 Jan. [1902], LL 55–56.

50. "calm/insincere," Pendennis [pseudonym], "The Thinking Heart: An Im-

pression of Mrs. Edith Wharton at Close Range," *The Book News Monthly*, 26, 3 (Nov. 1907), 171–73.

51. "The/principality," EW–WCB, 14 Feb. [1902], LL 57–58; "Fulvia/reflected," EW–SN, 13 Feb. [1902], LL 56–57; "convincingly alive," CEN–S. G. Ward, 10 March 1902, *Letters* 2: 329; "it/Decision," E. Lee-Hamilton–EW, 10 June 1902; see C. Wolff, 91–98, 134–35, 143, and Nevius, 41.

52. "carefully wrought," Anon., *Outlook* 71 (24 May 1902), 209; "needed/right," A. Gorren, *Critic* 40 (June 1902), 541–43; "art/audience," H. W. Boynton, *AM* 89 (May 1902), 710–11; "rather/observation," Anon., *Athenaeum* 3894 (14 June 1902), 748–49; "subtlest/it," Anon., *Catholic World* 75 (June 1902), 422–23.

53. *VD* sequel, WB–EW, Wed. [spring 1902]; "Disintegration" planned before *VD*, EW–SN, 10 May [1902]; "egg[ed]," HJ–EW, 26 Oct. 1900, LP 32; "liking," "astonishing," EW–SN, 1 Sept [1902]; "*American subject,*" "Do New York," HJ–EW, 17 Aug. 1902, LP 34.

54. *VD* second edition, EW–SN, 9 March 1902; *BET* review, "The/self," EW–SN, 14 March [1902]; "chorus/demand," EW–SN, 2 April [1902]; March 1903 royalties, $7,963.20, *VD* sold over thirty-five thousand copies; new one-volume format, EW–WCB, 17 March 1903; "It/months," WB–EW, 24 Oct. [1900]; "went/time," WB–EW, Wed. [spring 1902].

55. "sharp attack," EW–SN, 21 Jan. [1902]; TW's influenza, EW–SN, 4 Feb. 1902; "break-down," EW–SN, Sun. [9 March 1902]; "foamed/mouth," OC–SBC, 5 Jan. 1914; "made/anew," EW–SN, 2 April [1902]; "I/aloud," WB–EW, Sun. [March 1902].

56. "very/it," OC–SBC, 3 March 1902; "domesticated/hand," OC–SBC, 24 March 1902; "grimmest look," EW–SN, Mon. [14 April 1902]; train accident, OC–SBC, 14 April 1902.

57. "I/miserable," EW–SN, 10 May [1902].

58. "*Ulysses,*" *Bookman* 15 (April 1902), 168–70; "ethical/severed," "George Eliot," *Bookman* 15 (May 1902), 247–51. "George/time," CS–EW [undated].

59. "unimaginative/colourless," EW–SN, 10 May [1902]; "I/rest," EW–SN, Wed., 21 May [1902]; "off/reel," WB–EW, Wed. [spring 1902].

60. "tonic/plumbing," EW–SN, 7 June [1902], LL 66–67; "at/air," EW–SN, 4 July 1902; Lenox committees, *LL*, 19 July 1902; "I/much," EW–SN, 15 Aug. 1902.

61. "Greek/sky," EW–SN, 29 Aug. [1902], LL 67–68; TR's speech (5 Sept. 1902), "few/bronco-buster," EW–SN, Mon. [Sept. 1902].

62. "Compleat/weather," EW–SN, 30 Sept. [1902].

63. *BRT*, Sat., 10 Sept. 1904; "delicate/Pond," HJ–HS, 17 Oct. 1904, LE, 4:

325–26; England trip, EW–OC, 10 July 1900 (no Belton House listed); "harmonious symmetry," Fryer, 71; "make/alone," EW–MB, 6 July [1918].

64. House design, Scott Marshall, *A History of The Mount: Historic Structure Report* (Lenox, Mass.: Edith Wharton Restoration, 1993); building costs, Richard Guy Wilson, "Edith and Ogden: Writing, Decoration, and Architecture," in Pauline C. Metcalf, ed., *Ogden Codman and the Decoration of Houses* (Boston: Boston Athenaeum, 1988), fn. 87, 181–82; slow paying bills, OC-SBC, 14 Oct. 1905.

65. "torn/over," EW–DC, 27 Sept. 1902; "terrible/stricken," OC–SBC, 8 Oct. 1902.

66. "utter/don't," OC–SBC, 8 Oct. 1902.

67. *JL* rehearsals, EW–DC, 27 Sept. 1902; "great/piano" EW–SN, 24 Jan. [1902], LL 55–56; "most/year," audience members, *New York Mail and Express*, 24 Oct. 1902.

68. "admirably simple," *NYT*, 24 Oct. 1902, reviewer commenting that the play "gripped and held the audience from start to finish"; RWBL (110–11) and LL (72, fn. 3) incorrectly state that *Joy* had only a "brief run." Nineteen hundred and three American tour: January, Chicago, Ill.; March, Detroit, Michigan, and Kansas City, Missouri; April, San Francisco; London production starred Martin Harvey as Beata's lover, Richard. Edith had difficulty rendering the title *Es Lebe das Leben* in English; Mrs. Campbell suggested (and insisted on) *The Joy of Living,* for its ironic effect, see EW–WLB, 12 Sept. 1902, LL 70–72, fn. 3.

69. "Teddy/house," EW–SN, 8 Oct. 1902; "strange/better," OC–SBC, 19 Dec. 1902.

70. Boston trip, no invitation, EW–SN, 30 Dec. 1902; Thorp: "nine/genius," 245; Fenway party, 243–45. EW's comment may have been made about the food on the special train car IG hired to bring New York guests to Boston.

71. Italian translation of *VD* began in *Nuova Antologia*, July 1903, EW–A. Austin, 21 Jan. [1903], LL 76–77, and EW–WCB, 17 March 1903; "summer/blank," cold in Genoa, EW–SN, 30 Jan. 1903; "acuteness," EW-DC, 8 March [1903], LL 77–79.

72. "prodigious," EW–SN, 17 March [1903], LL 80–81; "most/fashion," extra $500, EW–R. W. Gilder, 18 March 1903, LL 82–83; *IVG* terms: $1,000 advance, royalty of 10 percent, $1,500 serial essay, EW–Mr. Scott, 24 Oct. 1902.

73. "garden/landscape," *IVG*, 6. Reviews of *IVG*: Anon., *Nation* 79 (24 Nov. 1904), 423; Anne Benneson McMahan, *Dial* 37 (16 Dec. 1904), 419–21; Anon., *Critic* 46 (Feb. 1905), 166–68; Anon., *International Studio* 25 (April 1905), 179; Anon., *Outlook* 80 (8 July 1905), 643; "almost/appre-

ciation," Anon., *TLS* (7 July 1905), 215; Anon., *Spectator* 95 (30 Sept. 1905), 470–71.

74. "kind/Lourdes," EW–SN, 5 June [1903], LL 84–85; "desperate/bolgia," EW–WCB, 29 April [1903].

75. "bright/pounced," LSC, *M*.

76. "She/voice," LSC, *M*; EW's vision of LSC, EW–GL, [28 Aug. 1933], LL 566–67.

77. "out/patches," EW–SN, 5 June [1903], LL 84–85; leak in house, EW–WCB, 11 June 1903.

78. "accumulated/imagination," EW–SN, 9 Aug. [1903].

79. Fourth of July guests, EW–MCJ, 4 July 1903; WB ill, TW salmon fishing, EW–SN, 12 July [1903]; "The/Italy," EW–ELB, 3 Sept. [1903]; "sank," EW–WCB, 10 Nov. 1903.

80. "*really* conversable," HJ–MCJ, 31 Dec. 1903. EW just missed meeting HJ in August 1883, when he was a guest of MCJ and FRJ at Reef Point. When he arrived for his first stay in Bar Harbor, EW had already left for Newport with LRJ and TW. *BG*: HJ's "rolling/beauty," Roman head, 173–74; first meeting with James, 171–72; "great/epithets," ET, "Memoir"; secondhand, "moderate/dimensions," EW–SN, 24 Jan. [1904].

81. "extraordinary/incalculable," EW–SN, 24 Jan. 1904.

82. "storm-bound/brutal," EW–SN, 13 Feb. [1904]; "Riviera/ailment," EW–SN, 5 May [1904], LL 89–91, and EW–CS, 15 March [1904]; *désoeuvrement*, EW–WCB, 9 March 1904.

83. "glorious chevauchée," EW–WCB, 31 March 1904; "the/home," EW–SN, 5 May 1904, LL 89–91.

84. "quill/eyes," EW–WCB, 10 May 1904; "exquisitely/united," J. R. Pyke, *Bookman* 19 (July 1904), 512–15; "Moral/situation," Anon., *Independent* 56 (9 June 1904), 1334–35; "hints/James," *Athenaeum* 4001 (2 July 1904), 13–14.

85. "I/chic," EW–WCB, 25 June [1904], LL 91–92; "I/novels," EW–*Book-Buyer*, 5 Sept. 1902; "Don't/Dove," EW–WCB, 12 Sept. 1902, LL 70–72.

86. Staff walkout, EW–SN, 5 May [1904]; EW/TW owed F. L. V. Hoppin $1,000, WB–EW, Sun. [autumn 1904]; house party, *BRT*, 4 July 1904.

87. "with/trimmings," *BRT*, 9 July 1904; "best/satisfaction," *BRT*, 30 July 1904; three new motors, EW–SN, 14 June [1905]; trip east, EW–SN, [19 Aug. 1904]; "epic *randonnées*, EW–GL, 29 Nov. 1921.

88. "smartly/voice," GL, *M*; EW's eye cure, EW–SN, Friday [19 Aug. 1904], LL 92–93.

89. HEJ's arrival, EW–SN, 14 Sept. [1904]; EW's joy at seeing HEJ, his plan to buy adjoining estate, EW–SN, 10 Oct. [1904]; "black raiment," EW–SN, 27 Sept. [1904].

90. "every/incarnate," HJ–HS, 17 Oct. 1904, LE, 4: 325–26; "loud-puffing," HJ–Edmund Gosse, 27 Oct. 1904, LE, 4: 331–32.

91. "morning's/wings," HJ–EW, 18 Nov. 1904, LE, 4: 333–35, and LP, 40–41; "black/Mirth," EW–WCB, 7 Oct. 1904; "real/patterns," EW–SN, 3 Jan. [1905].

92. "glacial/hard," EW–SN, 18 Nov. [1904]; "execrable," EW–SN, 2 Dec. [1904]; two years' absence from 884, "rising/such," EW–SN, 3 Dec. [1904]; HJ to Mount, 24–30 June 1905, EW–CEN, 1 July 1905, LL 93–94.

93. Christmas at Biltmore, "sheets/ivy," EW–SN, 26 Dec. [1905], LL 100-101; EW's illness in Washington, EW–SN, 24 March [1905]; Salso, EW–SN, 2 April [1905].

94. Elsie Jones's death, 3 April 1905, buried in family vault, Cimetière du Grand Jas, Cannes (letter, City of Cannes to SB, 2 Nov. 1992); FRJ lost EJ's fortune, OC–SBC, Sun., 7 Dec. 1913; "probable future," EW–CS, 4 April 1905; "incipient/Mirth," EW–CS, 19 May 1905; Bell's history of EW at Scribners assumes that EW received the $8,000 advance she requested on book royalties for *FT*, but the *ABT* shows payments of $10,000 on a serial contract (see Bell, 320–21).

Chapter 4

Background texts: Elisabeth Higgonet-Dugua, *Anna de Noailles: Coeur Innombrable* (Paris: Editions Michel de Maule, 1989); Fred Kaplan, *Henry James: The Imagination of Genius* (New York: William Morrow, 1992); David McCullough, *Mornings on Horseback* (New York: Simon & Schuster, 1981); Francis Steegmuller and Barbara Bray, ed., *Flaubert–Sand: The Correspondence* (New York: Alfred Knopf, 1993).

1. "counted heavily," ELB–EW, 29 July 1904; "discipline/professional," *BG*, 208–9; "fickle/featherheaded," WCB–EW, 6 July 1904.

2. *HM* sales, *Publisher's Weekly*, no. 1761, 28 Oct. 1905, 1094; EW diary (LLI); "I/book," EW–CS, 31 Oct. 1905.

3. "This/death," M. Dix–EW, 1 Dec. 1905; "relation/classes," EW–M. Dix, 5 Dec. 1905, LL 98–100, see fn. 1.

4. "entire/purposes," "Lenox" to *NYT Review of Books*, 24 Nov. 1905; "Newport," 27 Nov. 1905.

5. "appalling/life," Anon., *English Review*, 4 Nov. 1905; "to/to-day," Anon., *TLS*, 1 Dec. 1905; "searching/things," Anon., *Manchester Guardian*, 1 Nov. 1905; "too/force," Anon., *Spectator*, 28 Oct. 1905; "frivolous/ideals," *BG*, 207.

6. French translation, EW–CS, 16 Jan. 1906; "amused/Lily," EW–SN, 8 April 1906.

7. Paris plans, OC–SBC, 8 Jan. 1906; *HM* play, EW–ELB, 12 March

[1906]; "natural/death," EW–SN, 10 Jan. [1906]; SPCA, EW–SN, 25 Jan. [1906]; *HM* drama, EW–CS, 11 Nov. 1905, LL 95–96, and EW–RG, 26 Feb. [1906], LL 103–04. Theatrical agent Elizabeth Marbury convinced Clyde Fitch to dramatize *HM* by telling him that EW was "dying" for him to do it; she convinced EW to collaborate with Fitch by telling her that he was "dying" to do it, OC–SBC, 30 May 1921. EW's reading, EW–SN, 1 March [1906], LL 104–05; WCB essay on Cooper, EW–ELB, 7 March [1906], and EW–SN, 22 April [1906].

8. *Ghosts*, EW–SN, 10 Jan. [1906]; "little/giro," London, EW–SN 6 April [1906]; "trying/today," HJ–W. and A. James, 4 May [1906], LE, 4: 401–02.

9. "breaking/Scribner's," EW–ELB, 10 Aug. [1906]; Howells's earnings, see Susan Edmiston and Linda D. Cirino, *Literary New York* (New York: Gibbs-Smith, 1991), 186.

10. "nameless novel," EW–ELB, 14 June [1906]; "Shadow/Doubt," "theatrical," EW–ELB, 18 June [1906]; Ethel Cram, former owner of LE, DBU, *M*; July 1905 carriage accident, see Scott Marshall, "Edith Wharton, Kate Spencer, and *Ethan Frome*," *Edith Wharton Review* 10, 1 (Spring 1993), 20–21; "If/knot," EW–SN, 7 July [1908], LL 159–60; "Fruit/Tree," EW–ELB, 30 July [1906]; "anxious Parent," EW–ELB, 11 Nov. 1906.

11. "simply/assured," EW–CS, 21 Sept. 1906; fourteen curtain calls, EW–ELB, 26 Sept. 1906; "sad/consequences," *BET*, 17 Nov. 1906, 2, based on interview with C. Fitch; "tragedy/ending," W. D. Howells, quoted in *FWM*, 64, and EW–ES, 14 Dec. 1928.

12. "unaccountably/hat," *Detroit Post*, 17 Nov. 1906.

13. "white/marriage," EW–ELB, 7 Dec. [1906].

14. "rest-curing/comfort," EW–Eunice Maynard, 7 Jan. [1907], LL 110–11; "rested/last," EW–SN, 11 Jan. 1907.

15. "fatigued/thrilling," EW–SN, 25 Jan. 1907.

16. "stored/established," EW–SN, 25 Jan. 1907.

17. Reviews of *MT*: intellect, Hildegarde Hawthorne, *NYT Saturday Review*, 9 March 1907, 137; "only/curiosity," M. Moss, *AM* 97 (1906), 52–53; "entirely/style," M. Moss, *Bookman* 25 (May 1907), 303–4; realistic, Anon., *Nation* 84 (4 April 1907), 313; "eliminations/reserves," Olivia Howard Dunbar, *North American Review* 185 (17 May 1907), 218–21; "never/pen," Anon., *Spectator* 98 (11 May 1907), 764; subtler than James, *Athenaeum* 4149 (4 May 1907), 535; "beautifully/here," HJ–EW (17 Nov. 1906), LP 67; "wretched/earth," EW–SN, 5 Jun [1903], LL 84–85.

18. *Reef* as "Racinian," HJ–EW, 4 [and 9] Dec. 1912, LP 237–42 and LE, 4: 643–46.

19. "mental/refreshment," EW–SN, 1 March [1906], LL 104–5. "restless/im-

possible," EW–SN, Wed., 7 March 1906. EW maintained ties with American animal rights organizations; in 1936, she was reelected honorary vice president of the New York Women's League for Animals, GC, 24 Jan. 1936.

20. "all/Wealth," HJ–MCJ, 18 Nov. 1906; "india/life," HJ–HS, 20 March 1907.

21. "disabled/years," HJ–EW, [2 July 1906], LP 65–66; "Vehicle of Passion," HJ–EW, 17 Nov. 1906, LP 67–68.

22. *MFF*: "The/travel," 1; *Guide Continental*, "blandest/persuasion, 73–74; "burnished/bloom," 78.

23. "piggery/smelliness," HJ–EW, 13 March 1912, LP 215–18, and LE, 4: 602–4; "dark/period," *MFF*, 46; "And/not," *BG*, 308.

24. "image/scale," *MFF* 47; Steegmuller: "Chère maitre," 10; Sand chronology, xv–xix.

25. "dreadfully/it," OC–SBC, 2 Sept. 1911, quoting Rupert Norton (CEN's youngest son).

26. "What/together," HJ–EW, 13 March 1912, LP 215–18, and LE, 4: 602–4; Kaplan: "romancer," 68; "to/imagination," 100, 574, fn. 33; "love/one" (SB trans.), Faquet, *George Sand, Etudes Littéraires, XIV Siècle*; "I'm/scholar," G. Sand–G. Flaubert, 16 Sept. [18]71, Steegmuller, 242–43. Reading the last volume of Karénine's biography of Sand in 1925, EW wrote MB: "George was such a great fountain of life [that] I always rejoice in her. Do you remember what Henry said of her: that she cared only for love and minerology? I wish it had been only love," EW–MB, 25 July 1925.

27. "Never/traveller," EW–SN, 28 March 1907; "a/fear," *MFF*, 106–8.

28. "narrow/yews," *MFF*, 111–12.

29. *MFF*: "France/brick," 117–18; "scars/bronze," 115; "tout/element," 121.

30. *MFF*: arts appeal to eye, 177; "conceive/modifications," 178; BB's restricted aesthetic, EW–MB, 14 Aug. [1913], LL 306–7.

31. *MFF*: "comet-flight," 111; "It/sap," 126; "hermit-haunted," 129; "beset/idling," 132; "the/France," HJ–George and Fanny Prothero, 13 April 1907, LE, 4: 444–45.

32. *MFF*: "lifted/confused," 170–71; Morvan trip, EW–SN, 21 April 1907, LL 112–14.

33. "what/*countenance*," *MFF*, 140–41.

34. "touching/work," EW–SN, 21 April 1907, LL 112–14; history of Port-Royal, *Grande Encyclopedie*, 1892, vol. 27.

35. *MFF*: "victim/passion," 140; "four/Jeanne," 80.

36. "great grief," ET quoted in GL, *M*; "on," EW–RG, [1913].

37. "Resignation," *CB*, 1908.

38. "moral/toil," *MFF*: 177–93.

39. "endless trouble," EW–SN, 1 Nov. 1907; "findable/Christmas," EW–WMF, [1 June 1907].

40. "moment/content," EW–WMF [Feb. 1908], LL 129–30, see fn. 2. EW thought the phrase was from Euripides, but it was from Sophocles's *Trachiniae*. When asked how she recognized Hercules as a god, the captive maiden Iole answered, "Because I was content the moment my eyes fell on him." "Your/mysterious," EW–SN, 21 April 1907, LL 112–14.

41. WMF and HJ in 1890s, M. Brooke, "facilitator-voyeur," "dearest/enfant," Kaplan, 406–9.

42. "delightful/flower," EW–SN, 14 June [1907]; "We/settle," EW–CEN, 15 May 1907, LL 114–15; "oh/it," EW–SN, Sun., 23 [June 1907].

43. "handsome/East," EW–SN, 23 Aug. 1907; "thrilled/impressed," EW–SN, 24 July 1907; readings, *CB*; "A Second Motor-Flight Through France" (Part II of *Motor-Flight*) in *AM*, January–April 1908; EW returned to *MFF* articles in late summer, EW–SN, 23 Aug. 1907.

44. Proust on "Flowerings," Higgonet-Dugua, 133.

45. Background on A. de Noailles, see Higgonet-Dugua, passim.

46. "utterly/language," EW–WCB, 6 Nov. 1907; "grows/her," EW–WCB, 13 Nov. 1907; *CC* begun in Jan.–Feb 1907; taken up again in June–July, then in Oct.–Dec; *CC* "of/order," EW–ELB, 16 Nov. 1907.

47. *FT* sales, SG, 102–3; earnings, *ATB*.

48. "rather/noise," EW–ELB, 15 May 1907; Berkshire Cotton Co., see *Genealogical and Personal Memoirs, Berkshire County Massachusetts*, ed. Rollin Hillyer Cooke (New York: Lewis Publishing Co., 1906), vol. 11.

49. Complaints by industrialists, lawyers, and physicians, letter to editor, *New York Sun* [Nov. 1907]; "It/suffering," qtd. in *Sun* from the *New York Medical Journal*; "controversial," Anon., *Independent* 63 (12 Dec. 1907), 1436–37; "daring/responsibility," William Morton Payne, *Dial* 43 (16 Nov. 1907), 317; "fine/deficiencies," Edward Clark Marsh, *Bookman*, 26 (Nov. 1907), 273–75.

50. "dazzling/amber," TW visited NSW, EW–SN, Sat., 26 Oct. 1907; Teddy Pair (YCAL); HJ called EW "Mrs. Teddy" and the Whartons "The Teddies," HJ–GL, 14 April 1908; "Bear-o," McCullough, 362.

51. "Don't/1st," EW–SN, 1 Nov. 1907; EW kept WMF's letters in a small velvet casket. In 1938, Elisina Tyler told her son William that she planned to burn them, feeling they had no literary value; but she first asked him to read them (SB interview with WRT, 20 May 1992).

52. Success of *Chez les heureux du monde* ("Among the World's Happy Ones"), EW–CS, 18 Dec. [1907]; title was changed from *La Demeure de liesse* (a literal trans. of *HM*) by Louis Ganderax, editor of the *Revue de Paris*, prior to serial publication, Du Bos, M; "I/Capella," EW–SN, 26 Dec. 1907.

53. Giuseppe Tigri (1806–1882), *Canti popolari Toscani: Sono stato all'inferno e*

son tornate;/Misericordia! La gente che c'era./V'era una stanza tutt'illuminate,/ E dentro v'era la speranza mia. (Edvige Giunta provides a literal translation in my text.) EW discovered this quotation in Horatio F. Brown's biography of John Addington Symonds (London: Smith, Elder and Co., 1903), 344. Symonds recorded the line on 27 Nov. 1878 at Davos Platz, a health resort in the Alps where he spent part of each year and to which he eventually retired.

54. *Ame Close*, *LD*, 21 Feb. 1908. Although referred to as the "Herblay Sonnet," the poem is not a sonnet. EW treated a similar theme in her short story "The House of the Dead Hand," *AM* 94 (Aug. 1904), 145–60; "dark/silence," EW–WMF Sun. morn., 9 o.c. [spring 1908]; "a/veil," *LD*.

55. "as/friends," *La Figlia di Iorio* ("The Daughter of Jorio"), EW–WMF, 5 Jan. 1908, LL 127–28 [mistranscribed; misdated as 13 Jan. 1908, the date of the performance]; "simple/dramatic," EW–WMF [Jan. 1908]; written in Italian, the play was performed in "practically unintelligible" Sicilian dialect, EW–SN, 23 Jan. [1908].

56. "That's/about," "sadly," EW–WMF, 26 Aug. [1908], LL 160–62; "amusing," EW–WMF, 31 March [1908]; "fugitive," EW–WMF, Tues. eve. [1908]; "unpack/trunk," EW–WMF, Sat., 10 o.c. [spring 1908].

57. "beautifully played," *DD*, 27 Jan. 1908; *Andromaque*, Jan. 4; "finer/ever," *Electra*, 22 March 1908. EW's open invitation to WMF, letters between 5 and 13 Jan. 1908.

58. *"Ach, Gott, Gott"* ("Oh, God, God"), *DD*, 27 Feb. 1908.

59. TW to R. Curtises, EW–SN, 6 Feb. 1908; "All/Herblay," *LD*, 21 Feb. 1908 (EW's ellipses); "George/hypocrisy," EW–SN, 25 March 1908; Leon Seché, *Hortense Allart de Meritens* (Paris: Société du Mercure de France, 1908); see also *Nouvelles Lettres à Sainte-Beuve*, ed. Lorin A. Uffenbeck (Genève: Librairie Droz, 1965), ix–x.

60. tea gown, *DD*, 22 May 1908; "exquisite/companionship," *LD*, 21 Feb. 1907; "I'm/native," EW–WMF, [early March 1908], LL 134–35; "scruple," EW–WMF, 31 March [1909].

61. "nothing/blur," EW–WMF, [early March 1908], LL 134–35; "I/this," *LD*, 25 April 1908; "A/life," *LD*, 27 April 1908.

62. "I/came," *LD*, 25 April [1908], SB ellipses; "A/life," *LD*, 27 April [1908]; CG's story, GL, *M*; EW being watched, EW–WMF, *LD*, 12 May 1908.

63. "shrine/Hortense," HJ–EW, 3 April 1908, LP, 98; Beauvais, "soaring/choir," *LD*, 1 May 1908.

64. "I/more," *LD*, 3 May 1908; "a/world," "C'est l'aube" [It's dawn], *LD*, 7 May 1908; "Why/once," EW–WMF, 31 March [1908].

65. "O/been," *LD*, 21 May [1908]; "One/longer," *LD*, 27 April [1908].

66. "to/*hélas*," *LD*, 23 May [1908].

67. "Read/it," *"Je n'en peux plus"* (I can't take it any longer), *LD*, 1 June

[1908]; Robert Heath Lock, *The Recent Progress in the Study of Variation, Heredity and Evolution* (London: John Murray, 1906); "*Ici, j'étouffe,*" *DD,* 31 May [1908].

68. "wear/mask," EW–WMF, 5–6 June, LL 147–50.

69. "I/walks," EW–WMF, Fri. and Sat., 5 and 6 June [1908], LL 147–50; "profession/nothing," Kaplan, 388 (HJ–W. James, 29 June 1894); EW asks TW for song, EW–ELB, 4 June [1908].

70. "As/bit," OC–SBC, 8 Aug. 1908.

71. "grind steadily," EW–WMF, Fri. and Sat., 5 and 6 June [1908], LL 147–50; "distinctly/interest," ELB–CS, 4 Aug. 1908.

72. "An/again," *BG,* 183–84.

73. "admonish/*Subject,*" HJ–EW, 17 Aug. 1902, LP 33–35, and LE, 4: 234–36; "diabolical/way," HJ–MCJ, 20 Aug. 1902, LE, 4: 236–38.

74. "I/pace," Bay Lodge to Anna Cabot Mills Lodge, [Sept.] 1908, Massachusetts Historical Society, George Cabot Lodge Papers.

75. "I/you," EW–SN, Sat. [17 Oct. 1908], LL 163; "ever/abandonment," EW–SN, 19 Oct. [1908].

76. suit and veil, EW–SN, Fri. night [24 Oct. 1908]; "complete/conditions," EW–SN, 21 Oct. [1908]; "I/it," EW–CS, 20 Oct. 1908.

77. "Dear/dear," EW–WMF, 26 Aug. [1908], LL 160–62.

78. "When I Am Gone," *DD,* 25 May 1908.

79. "and/tight," HJ–EW, 13 Oct. 1908, LP 101–102, and LE, 4: 494–95.

80. Paris stop, EW–GL, Fri., 6 Nov. 1908; the unpleasantness on the boat is hinted at in a note from EW–Bay Lodge, [Nov. 1908], George Cabot Lodge Papers, Massachusetts Historical Society, Boston.

81. "a/hands," EW–WMF, 19 Dec. 1908, LL 170; "Letters/survives," WMF quoted in EW–WMF, Fri. eve., 31 Dec. [1909].

82. "the/there," EW–SN, 18 Nov. [1908], LL 164–67.

83. "Time/fashion," HJ–WB, 12 Dec. 1908, LE, 4: 505–6; "too/abysmal," HJ–GL, 13 Oct. 1908; "somewhat sulkily," *BG,* 251.

84. "statuesquely/impression," *BG,* 250–54.

85. Dinner for Princess Marie Louise, EW–SN, 23 Dec. 1908; Trevelyan, Goshen, Haldane, "as/letters," *BG,* 215–16; Burne-Jones and Galsworthy, EW–SN, 23 Dec. 1908.

86. "most/radio-active," kisses in literature, *Troilus and Creseide, BG,* 219–20.

87. "I/celebrity," *BG,* 223; EW occasion of Stanway house party, HJ–WB, 12 Dec. 1908, LE, 4: 505–6.

88. Fog, EW–SN, 3 Dec. [1908]; "most/England," EW–SN, 23 Dec. [1908]; "exuberant/endless," JHS, *M;* "you/mean," JHS, *M.*

89. "elopement," EW–JHS, Sat. night [Dec. 1908]; EW to Rye, HJ–EW, Thurs. p.m. [17 Dec. 1908], LP 105.

90. Café de Paris, EW–JHS, 9 Jan. 1909; "frame/steel," HJ–WB, 12 Dec. 1908, LE, 4: 505–6; "general/by," HJ–GL, 4 May 1909.

91. "hell/summer," HJ–EW, Mon., 11 Jan. 1909, LP 105–7 and LE: 4, 509–10; see HJ's letters to WMF: HJ–WMF, 14, 19, 26, and 29 Nov. 1907, LE, 4: 472–80. HJ urged WMF to "break" with her.

92. "immensely/fortified," HJ–EW, 11 Jan. 1909, LP 105–6, and LE, 4: 509–10; chronology of WMF's love affairs, marriage, and divorce drawn from letters in WMF (YCAL).

93. *"hypnotized*/blackmailer," HJ–WMF, 26 Nov. 1907, LE, 4: 477–80; *"estime,"* A. Alfroy–WMF, 12 March 1913 (WMF, YCAL); no record of M. Mirecourt owning 40 bis rue Fabert (letter, Archives de Paris, SB, 11 March 1993); M. Alfroy calls the concierge (who has served in that position for a "very long time") at rue Fabert an "imbecile," A. Alfroy–WMF, 15 March 1913; WMF resident at 40 bis rue Fabert, EW–WMF, 6 Jan. 1909 [postmark]; "profound/affection," quoted in JBF–WMF, 25 May 1 1894 [correct date is 1904].

94. "impertinently/alive," KF–WMF, 9 Jan. 1908.

95. KF's birth, Massachusetts State Archives Birth Register, vol. 311: 266; Charles D. Fullerton, MSA, vol. 305, 299; Elizabeth Prince Fullerton birth/death, MSA, vol. 311, 266; "unforgettable/childhood," KF–WMF, 11 May [1911]; Charles Fullerton cheating BMF (WMF, YCAL).

96. "Of/events," KF–WMF, 11 Sept. [1900].

97. "strange story," KF–WMF, [autumn 1907]; "sacred/me," KF–WMF, 9 Nov. 1907; "quivering/you," KF–WMF, 7 Jan. 1908.

98. "I/all," KF–WMF, [spring 1908]; impulse to suicide, KF–WMF, 7 Jan. 1908 and 10 Jan. 1908.

99. KF wedding plans, KF–WMF, 10 Jan. 1908; "As/her," "Doll"–WMF, [spring 1908]; DW's handwriting identified by SB and D. Wilde's biographer, Sumner H. Peirce III (SHP–SB, 13 March 1993); KF at Convent, KF Gerould–Curtis H. Page, 27 March 1917.

100. "empoisonneuse" [poisoner], EW–JHS, [Jan. 1909]; "frightful crossing," EW–RG, 6 Feb. 1909; "quick `wirelesses,'" EW–JHS, 6 Feb. [1909].

101. "admirable/incoherent," EW–JHS, 2 Feb. [1909], LL 172–74; "enormously/it," EW–JHS, 6 Feb. [1909].

102. "He's/seen," EW–SN, 10 Feb. 1909.

103. "whole/Paris," EW–RG, 6 Feb. [1909].

104. "shabby/dim," EW–JHS, 6 Feb. [1909].

105. "repulsive/it," EW–JHS, 2 Feb. [1909], LL 172–74.

106. HJ's 1908 earnings, Kaplan, 488.

107. "as/again," HJ–EW, 9 May 1909, LE, 4: 521–22, LP 112–13.

108. "I/condition," HJ–GL, 4 May 1909.

CHAPTER 5

Background texts: Joseph Bédier, *The Romance of Tristan and Iseult*, trans. Hilaire Belloc and Paul Rosenfeld (New York: Doubleday, 1955); Michael Burns, *Dreyfus: A Family Affair, 1789–1945* (New York: HarperCollins, 1991); Morris Eksteins, *Rites of Spring: The Great War and the Birth of the Modern Age* (Boston: Houghton Mifflin, 1989); Hanna Kiel, ed., *The Bernard Berenson Treasury* (New York: Simon & Schuster, 1962); J. B. Priestley, *The Edwardians* (London: Thames and Hudson, 1972); Ernest Samuels, *Bernard Berenson: The Making of a Connoisseur* (Cambridge, Mass.: Harvard University Press, 1979, cited as vol. 1 in notes), and Ernest Samuels, *Bernard Berenson: The Making of a Legend* (Cambridge, Mass.: Harvard University Press, 1987, cited as vol. 2 in notes); Barbara Strachey and Jayne Samuels, eds., *Mary Berenson: A Self-Portrait from her Letters and Diaries* (New York: W. W. Norton, 1983); James Trager, *Park Avenue: Street of Dreams* (New York: Atheneum, 1990); Richard D. Walter, *S. Weir Mitchell, M.D.—Neurologist: A Medical Biography* (Springfield, Ill.: Charles C. Thomas, 1970).

1. *AA* more intellectual than emotional, Anon., *New York Saturday Review* 14 (8 May 1909), 330; Anon., *Spectator* 103 (3 July 1909), 20; Brian Hooker, *Bookman* 29 (June 1909), 365–72; "too/heart," W. M. Payne, *Dial* 47 (Aug. 1909), 101; "too/unnatural," Anon., *Independent* 67 (21 Oct. 1909), 934; see "Author's Note," Bédier, 9–10, on his retelling; "Mortal Lease" written by WMF, EW–WMF, Tues. eve. [1909]; "I/takes," EW–WMF, Wed. night [1909]; "Per Te, Sempre per Te" (Latin: For You, Always for You).

2. "stupid/désormais," EW–WMF, Tues. [23 Feb. 1909], LL 176.

3. "triumph/Heaven," KF–WMF, [autumn 1907]; "I/yours," Katharine Fullerton, "Gemma to Beatrice," *SM*, 47 (June 1910), 758–60; "Mr. Fullerton," EW–KF, 3 Feb. [1909].

4. KF's letters to WMF, see RWBL, 287.

5. "long/night," *Terminus* (YCAL).

6. Charing Cross Hotel events, see WMF's note on his copy of "Terminus" (YCAL).

7. "I/tide," EW–WMF, a note accompanying the poem; weekend events, Racine and *AA*, EW–JHS, 8 June 1909; weather, HJ–Arthur Christopher Benson, 5 June 1909, LE, 4: 523; EW thought "Babe" a bore; sexual services, OC–TC, 12 Oct. 1925.

8. "in/want," EW–F. Macmillan, 29 May 1909, LL 180–81.

9. "Studies in Bird Life," Dr. H. Overing (HS), [July 1909], (HL); "the/amelioration," HJ–HS, 16 July 1909, LE, 4: 526–27.

10. "and/westward," EW–JHS, 21 July [1909], LL 187–88; "Your/talking," EW–WMF, Thurs. night, 12 Aug. [1909], LL 189; "Pray/Fullerton,"

HS–EW, 16 July 1909; "dashed/channel," EW–JHS, 21 July [1909], LL 187–88; "high/complain," EW–WMF, Thurs. [July 1909].

11. NSW ill, TW sails, 53 rue de Varenne, EW–JHS, 21 July [1909], LL 187–88; AB arrives, HEJ assistance, EW–Mrs. A. Austin, 28 July 1909 (SA); noisy street, OC–SBC, 10 Nov. 1908.

12. "great/boundless," EW–SN, 7 July 1909, LL 184–87; "very/pendulum," FPK–EW, 13 Dec. [1909] (YCAL); "local/evil," FPK–EW, 14 June [1909] (YCAL).

13. "little/G," HJ–EW, 3 Aug. 1909, LP 117–18, LE, 4: 529–31; illness of WB's mother, HJ–EW, 20 Aug. 1909, LP 120; WMF's Fate, HJ–EW, 29 Oct. 1909, LP 125–26; WB's Fate, HJ–EW, 24 Nov. 1909, LP 127–28; TW's *mauvais moment* (bad moment), HJ–EW, 15 Aug. 1909, LP 118–19.

14. "For/neighbor," "George Cabot Lodge," *SM*, 47 (Feb. 1910), 236–39.

15. "she/ago," Samuels, 2: 95; "worn/nervous," KF–WMF, 1 Nov. 1909; Voisin dinner, Samuels, 2: 95; "combination," EW–BB, Sun. [1909], LL 190.

16. "marriage/adultery," Kiel, 68.

17. BB's motorcar, Samuels, 2: 91; BB's upbringing, Samuels, l: passim; "Paradise/pictures," EW–BB, Wed. [15 Sept. 1909]; "little/toy," EW–BB, [no day] Oct. 1909; "creeping/value," Samuels, 2: 97.

18. "immense/appeal," EW–SN, 20 Oct. [1909], LL 191–92; "I have traced the Journal story—via Blanche to the Pcesse de Polignac," EW–WMF, Wed. [Dec. 1909]; "Mr. Humphrey," editor of *The New American*, told Princess Edmond de Polignac that EW was separating from TW; RFJ speculated that the princess "cooked up" the mystery herself, but EW had revealed something of her marital concerns to J. Blanche, RFJ–WMF, 28 Oct. 1909.

19. flu, EW–SN, 20 Oct. [1909], LL 191–92; "My/amie," EW–WMF [23 Oct. 1909] (misdated in *The Library Chronicle*, N.S. 31: 35, and LL 189–90]); "fragments/uses," EW–WMF, 27 Nov. 1909, LL 193.

20. "seize/proof," WMF–ET, 30 March 1950; "motor-dash/disorder," EW–SN, 2 Dec. [1909], LL 193–95.

21. "indisposed/rococo," EW–SN, 2 Dec. 1909, LL 193–94; "Parting/hard," "other/matter," NCW–EW, 13 Dec. 1909; "Cher/outlet," EW–WMF, [8 Dec. 1909].

22. "My/tonight," EW–WMF, [31 Dec. 1909]; "magnificent," EW–SN, 25 Jan. 1910; 882–884 sold for an undisclosed amount of money.

23. "exasperated/future," EW–WMF, Fri. 9 p.m. [3 Jan. 1910], LL 195–96 [misdated]; "soberly/hard," EW–SN, 25 Jan. 1910; "drivelling/hideous," EW–JHS, 2 March 1910; "It/scenery," EW–SN, [spring 1910]; King Edward's illness and death, Priestley, 180–84.

24. TW's exploits of autumn 1909; Boston property; EW urged to return to Mount, FPK–EW, 9 Feb. [1910].

25. "dreadful/serious," EW–RG, 4 April [1910].
26. "no/grisaille," EW–WCB, 9 April 1910; "very/listless," EW–RG, 4 April 1910; "les ténèbres," EW–WMF, Tuesday [late Feb. 1910].
27. "I/bother," EW–WMF, Fri., 9 p.m. [3 Jan. 1910], LL 195–96 [misdated]; "I/you," EW–WMF, Tues. [late Feb. 1910], LL 196–97 [misdated]; "Equitable friend," EW–WMF, Thurs. [late Feb. 1910]; "What/away," EW–WMF, Sun. night [13 March 1910], LL 197–99 [misdated].
28. HJ ill, Garland's Hotel, EW–WMF, Fri. [18 March 1919], LL 199–201; "cried/door," EW–WMF, Sat. 19, March [1910], LL 201–5; "What/for," EW–WMF, Mon., 21 March 1910, LL 205–6 [misdated]; "rest/`packing,'" HJ–EW, 21 March 1910, LP 154, Kaplan, 525.
29. W. James calls on EW, EW–WMF, [spring 1910].
30. "I/mine," EW–WMF, Fri. [18 March 1910], LL 199–201; "Tu/Terminus," EW–WMF, Tues., 22 March 1910; "Write/change," EW–WMF, Thurs. [30 March 1910], LL 206–7 [misdated]; "I/years," Thurs. eve. [late May] 1910, LL 215–16.
31. "Nay, take my body," dated "15 April 1910" by WMF (YCAL); "met/silence," EW–WMF, Sun. [17 April 1910].
32. "il/vous," invitation list to tea, EW–WMF, Sun. [17 April 1910].
33. "greatly struck," T. Roosevelt–EW, 27 April 1910; "regret/you," EW–WMF, 27 April [1910], LL 212–13; "embassy/impression," see LL, fn. 1, 212–13; "rapidly/worse," EW–WMF, Fri., 29 [April 1910], LL 213–14.
34. "Oh/specialists," EW–BB, 9 May 1910; "day/much," EW–WMF, Tues., 17 May [1910]; "my/d'être," stationery, EW–WMF, Fri. morn. [early June 1910].
35. "I/better," BB–MB [July 1910] (IT); "like/treatment," BB–EW, 15 July 1910; "She/me," BB–MB, 3 Nov. 1910 (IT); "I/friendship," BB–MB [Nov. 1910] (IT); "God's/diggers," WB settles in Paris, WB–BB, 24 April 1910; WB urges EW to break with TW, EW–WMF, Thurs. eve. [May 1910], LL 215–16.
36. "Do/*this*," EW–WMF, Tues. morn. [spring 1910]; TW complaints, L. Binswanger–EW, 11 June 1910; "grand/moral," isolate EW from her family, I. Wall–TW, [June 1910].
37. "open/economies," EW–TW, 6 July [1910]; "impossible," quoted in EW–TW, 28 July [1910]; "explosive/adapt," STB–EW, 16 Aug. 1910.
38. "my/repose," HJ–EW, 9 Sept. 1910, LP 168–70; badly run hotel, EW–SN [Sept. 1910].
39. J. Morton fee, HJ–HS, 18 Oct. 1910, LE, 4: 562–64; Belmont Hotel, Trager, 43; "appalling/despair," EW–BB, 3 Oct. 1910, LL 222–23; "senile/cause," EW–WMF [Oct. 1910].
40. "immensely/was," OC–SBC, 20 Sept. 1910; *TT* gossip, OC–SBC [late 1910].

41. "silver/rags," HJ–HS, 18 Oct. 1910, LE, 4: 562–64; "went/digestion," EW–SN, 10 Nov. [1910].

42. "those/career," HJ–EW, 9 Sept. 1910, LP 168–70; "interior/hope," EW–WMF, Tues., 17 May [1910].

43. "cramping/merit," Anon., *Independent* 69 (17 Nov. 1910), 1089; "deficient/action," Anon., American Library Association *Booklist* 7 (Dec. 1910), 166; "patent," *Nation* 91 (24 Nov. 1910), 496; Anon., *Athenaeum* 4336 (3 Dec. 1910), 700; Anon. *Bookman* [England] 40 (Spring Supplement 1911), 4; "rotten/anecdote," PL, quoted in RWBL, 253. EW admitted the failures of "Legend": "It should have been a novel" (EW–WMF, Sun. night [spring 1910]); she wrote "Blond Beast" at a "bad moment" (EW–JHS, 9 Dec. [1910]).

44. "looked/Medusa," EW–WMF, Sat. 19 March [1910], LL 201–5; "*J'en/point*," EW–WMF, Fri. morning [June 1910].

45. ghost story mentors, "thermometrical/universe," preface *GSEW*, 2–4. On 6 Feb. 1932, EW sent to Mme Charpentier, secretary to the American Chamber of Commerce, a list of celebrated ghost stories: Fitz James O'Brien, "What Was It"; Marion Crawford, "The Upper Berth"; Montague R. James, "Casting the Runes"; W. W. Jacobs, "The Monkey's Paw"; Robert Louis Stevenson, "The Body Snatcher" and "Markheim"; Charles Dickens, "The Signalman"; Sheridan Le Fanu, "Narrative of the Ghost of a Hand" and "Mr. Justice Harbottle" (GC, YCAL).

46. "What/other," EW–Mr. Gray, GC, 19 Jan. 1933.

47. Composition history, "The Writing of *Ethan Frome*," *Colophon*, pt. 11, no. 4 (Sept. 1932), n.p.; "A/accumulation," HJ–EW, 25 Oct. 1911, LP 194–95, LE, 4: 587–89.

48. "volumelet," EW–BB, 16 May [1911], LL 239–41; "sterile pain," *MR*; "It/Varenne," EW–BB, 4 Jan. 1911, LL 232–34.

49. 11 March 1904 sledding accident, *Berkshire Evening Eagle*, 12 March 1904; EW's friendship with K. Spencer, see Scott Marshall, "Edith Wharton, Kate Spencer, and *Ethan Frome*," *Edith Wharton Review* 10, 1 (Spring 1993), 20–21.

50. *EF* serial rights and advance royalty, ATB; French translation of *EF*, Du Bos, *M*; cruel story, EW dramatist passing as novelist, Anon., *NYTBR* (8 Oct. 1911), 603; "great/situations," Anon., *Outlook* 99 (21 Oct. 1911), 405; "don't/is," EW–WMF, 16 Oct. [1911], LL 260–61; "utter remorselessness," F. T. Cooper, *Bookman* 34 (Nov. 1911), 312; "hag-ridden/beauty," Anon., *Nation* 93 (26 Oct. 1911), 396–97; "motive," Anon., *SR* 112 (18 Nov. 1911), 650; "intensely/tragedy," Anon., *Bookman* [England] 41 (Jan. 1912), 216.

51. *EF* sales figures, "pouring/room," EW–CS, 27 Nov. [1911], LL 262–64; "dead/set," ELB–CS, 26 July 1910; "good/wanted," CS–ELB, 26 July 1910; "Mr./infidelity," EW–WMF [June 1912].

52. Duncan, Ballet Russe, EW–BB, 4 Jan. [1911], LL 232–34; "very fine," "pouring/man," EW–BB, 10 March 1911; "really good," EW–BB, 19 March 1911; "*la bande*," EW–BB, 17 Feb. 1911; WMF trans. *Le Tribun*, HJ–EW, 21 July 1911 and 25 Oct. 1911, LP 183–84, 196–99; "deep/country," HJ–HS, 19 April 1911.

53. "material anxiety," EW–E. Gosse, 18 Feb. 1911; "expectedly/ plot," EW–E. Gosse, 17 Nov. 1911.

54. TW return, EW–WMF, 4 March 1911; "I/paper," EW–BB, 21 April 1911; "utter/years," KF–WMF, 5 Jan. 1910; "Courage/love," 19 Feb. 1910.

55. "What/mercantile," EW–WMF, 22 April [1911]; "piggery" paid for by EW's poetry, GL, *M*; EW considers separation from TW, EW–WFW, 23 July 1911, LL 247–49; "I/her," TW–HE, Sun., 8 May 1911; "whether/capital," EW–TW, 30 May 1911.

56. "dry/together," reading list, EW–WMF, 12 May [1911], LL 236–39; "prolong/can," "backyards/scuttled," EW–BB, 16 May [1911], LL 239–41; "interests/done," *CC*, walks, EW–WMF, 15 May 1911, LL 241, see fn. 1; "You/EW," EW–WMF, 24 May 1911.

CHAPTER 6

Background texts: Michael Burns, *Dreyfus: A Family Affair, 1789–1945* (New York: HarperCollins, 1991); Morris Eksteins, *Rites of Spring: The Great War and the Birth of the Modern Age* (Boston: Houghton Mifflin, 1989); John Grigg, *Nancy Astor: A Woman Unashamed* (Boston: Little, Brown, 1980); Barbara Strachey and Jayne Samuels, eds., *Mary Berenson: A Self-Portrait from Her Letters and Diaries* (New York: W. W. Norton, 1983); Christopher Sykes, *Nancy Astor: The Life of Lady Astor* (New York: Harper and Row, 1972).

1. "Decidedly/Mirth," "impenetrable," EW–WMF, 3 July [1911], LL 242–43.

2. "inspired/bolgia," EW–WMF, 5 July [1911]; "mere/story," HJ–HS, 17 Aug. 1911; "completely/fact," EW–JHS, 6 Aug. [1911], LL 253–54.

3. EW/TW with TR, *BG*, 316; "actual/existence," HJ–EW, 19 July 1911, LP 181–83; "childishness/mind," HJ–MCJ, 17 Aug. 1911; "perfectly/be," HJ–HS, 17 Aug. 1911; "about/be," EW–MCJ, 23 Sept. 1911, LL 259–60.

4. TW resigns as trustee, EW–WFW, 22 July 1911, LL 245–47; "cruel/humiliation," 23 July 1911, LL 247–49; "no/weakness," ET, "Memoir."

5. "disregard/me," EW paraphrase of WFW's letter to her, LL 249, fn. 1; *TT* gossip, OC–SBC, 25 Aug. 1911.

6. EW agreed to separation, Mon., 24 July 1911, LL 250–51; "give/trial," quoted in EW–MCJ, 23 Sept. 1911, LL 259–60; "*very*/years," EW–SN,

Sat., 26 Aug. [1911], LL 254–55; "reconcile/terrace," EW–BB, 6 Aug. [1911], LL 251–53.

7. "You/differences," EW–WMF, 30 July [1911]; BMF finances, RMF's indebtedness, JBF–WMF, 20 Sept. [1899].

8. "as/best," EW–WFW, 22 July 1911, LL 245–47; Scott Marshall, *A History of The Mount: Historic Structure Report* (Lenox, Mass.: Edith Wharton Restoration, 1993), 177–78, 202, fn. 16, which corrects RWBL, 313.

9. "Climbing/Florence," EW/WB–HJ, 17 Oct. 1911, LP 359, LL 262.

10. Strachey: "I/people, 68; "deadset/children," 98; "Whenever/untidy," 68.

11. Strachey: "perfection/surroundings," 155; "fashionableness/French," 156; "stimulating/talk," 265; "scenes," 246; "rages," 164.

12. A "bad split" between the "insidious B" and his wife, HJ–MCJ, 6 Nov. 1911; MB and ilex wood, Samuels, 2: 131; "one/her," EW–BB, 9 Nov. 1911.

13. "insisted/well," EW–WMF, 16 Oct. [1911], LL 260–61; TW's psychosis, George D. Kahlo, M.D.–EW, 17 Nov. 1911; "untiring/years," FPK–EW, 1 Dec. 1911; "present/existence," EW–WMF, 16 Oct. [1911], LL 260–61.

14. FRJ's stroke, EW–WMF, 26 Oct. [1911]; EW/HEJ paid FRJ's medical expenses, EW–MCJ, 30 Nov. 1911; "en/dressed," *Outcry*, HJ–EW, 19 Nov. 1911, LP 196–99, LE, 4: 590–93.

15. "world-worn," EW–EWW, 21 March 1919 (LLI); "like/think," English itinerary, EW–WMF, Tues. [Dec. 1911]; Beethoven, TW return, EW–SN, 30 Dec. 1911, LL 264–65.

16. "horrid/demoralized," EW–SN, 26 Jan. 1912; "You'll/bird," HJ–EW, 26 Jan. 1912, LP 209–10.

17. Eagle, HJ–GL, 4 May 1909; "Devastatrix," HJ–HS, 18 Oct. 1910, LE, 4: 562–64; "rode/storm," HJ–MCJ, 1 Sept. 1912; "very/youth, EW–SN, 26 Jan. 1912; "the/shrink," EW–BB, 26 Jan. 1912.

18. "core/imagination," *BG*, 293; earnings, *ATB*.

19. "he/on," HJ–HS, 22 Feb. 1912, LP 214, fn. 2.

20. "Learning/it," EW–WMF, [spring 1912]; "round/plans," EW–BB, 14 March [1912], LL 268–69.

21. TW's indecision, "quick trip," EW–BB, 27 March 1912 (TW did not accompany EW; RWBL, 318, and LP 222, fn. 2 incorrect); "I/possible," EW–WMF, Hotel Ritz, Madrid [April 1912]; EW itinerary, RFJ to Biarritz, postcard from Zaragoza, EW–WMF, 18 April 1912.

22. "dear/George," HJ–EW, 13 March 1912, LP 215–18, LE, 4: 602–4.

23. "The/shade," HJ–EW, 13 March 1912, LP 215–18, LE, 4: 602–4.

24. miners strike, suffragette violence, *Titanic*: Priestley, 207, 217–18, 225–32.

25. "numb/mind," Grigg, 57–58; "full/too," Grigg, 113; "captivated," EW–GL, 9 Aug. [1912], LL 276–77.

26. "entirely/want," Mme Friderich [for EW]–O. Graeve, 12 March 1924.

27. EW, AB, and CG cure, EW–SN, 9 June 1912; "perfect/pomeriggio," EW–BB, 27 May [1912], LL 269.

28. "see/alone," EW–WMF, 10 June [1912].

29. "every/mine," *DD*, 19 May 1908.

30. "No/aid," EW–WMF, 27 June [1912].

31. "Cher/book," EW–WMF, 27 June [1912]; "Mow/vivify," EW–WMF, Sun. [Grand Hotel Portofino, Italy], [20 Oct. 1912], LL 281–82 [misdated], and *Library Chronicle*, N.S., 31: 50 [misdated]; "language/fatigue," EW–WMF, [Nov. 1912], LL 283; WMF's Paris book, EW–WMF, 19 June [1912], LL 270–71; "I/book-maker," HJ–EW, 29 June 1912, LP 224–27.

32. "hanging/coachman," EW–BB, Sat., 29 June 1912, LL 272–74.

33. "I/dog," EW–BB, Wed. evening [July 1912]; "Coming/accueil," HJ–EW, 15 July 1912, LP 227–28; "Reign/talons," HJ–HS, vingt juillet, 1912, LE, 4: 620–21.

34. "monstrous/tiger-cat," HJ–Thomas S. Perry, 26 Sept. 1884, Kaplan, 583, fn. 20; "good/talk," see LE, 3: 403–4, and Kaplan, 316, 372, 393, 588, fn. 45.

35. HJ's angina, EW–GL, 19 Aug. [1912], LL 276–77; "beauty show," Phillips, "positively," EW–WMF, Mon. [12 Aug. 1912], LL 275; "Beauty Queen of England" pageant, *Folkstone Express* [England], Sat., 10 Aug. 1912, and Sat., 17 Aug. 1912; "whirligig," HJ–HS, 20 Aug. 1912, LE, 4: 622–24; "admirable/conquer," HJ–HS, 9 Aug. 1912, LE, 4: 622–24.

36. MCJ visit, HJ–EW, 6 Aug. 1912, LP 229–30; "sunk/villa," Marion Richards, Barante, EW–HJ, 3 Sept [1912], LL 278–80, LP 231–33.

37. Sale of Mount: record of deed, title, and sale, Berkshire County Massachusetts Probate Court, 16 May 1912; chronology of transactions, and record of TW's role, William Derbyshire Curtis, "Daily Reminder," 1911, provided by Berkshire County Historical Society, 25 March 1985, for Edith Wharton Restoration, Lenox, Massachusetts. Purchasing agent for A. R. Shattuck was Albert L. Richardson of Greenwich, Connecticut, who was probably Shattuck's maternal uncle; see Scott Marshall, *A History of The Mount: Historic Structure Report* (Lenox, Mass.: Edith Wharton Restoration, 1993), 202, fn. 22. EW signed agreement before Frank H. Mason, consul general of the United States in Paris, 9 Feb. 1912; "magnificent," quoted in EW–WMF, 22 Sept. [1911], LL 255–58; "Write/still," EW–GL, 19 Aug. [1912], LL 276–77.

38. "settle/suggestion," EW–GL, 19 Aug. [1912], LL 276–77; "female Ulysses," HJ–MCJ, 1 Nov. 1912; "most/America," EW–SN, 18 Sept. 1912.

39. "over-wound/pace," EW–MB, Thurs., 17 Oct. 1912.

40. "paltry/solution," Anon., *Nation* 95 (12 Dec. 1912), 564; "conspicuous

failure," H. I. Brock, *NYTBR*, 24 Nov. 1912, 685; "sordid/life," Anon., [New York] *Sun*, 23 Nov. 1912, 13; "a/subtlest," *Bookman* 43 (Jan. 1913), 224–25; "abnormal/understanding," Anon., *SR* 114 (21 Dec. 1912), 773–74.

41. "poor/worthwhile," EW–BB, 22 Nov. [1912], LL 284 [misdated].

42. "quite/reflection," HJ–EW, 4 [and 9] Dec. 1912, LP 237–42, LE, 4: 643–46; "small/Racine," C. du Bos, *M*.

43. "localised/come," HJ–EW, 4 [and 9] Dec. 1912, LP 237–42, LE, 4: 643–46; "big/weariness," EW–BB, 20 Nov. 1912; "If/mid-current," EW–JHS, 25 Nov. [1912], LL 284–85.

44. AW on TW's condition, EW–BB, Thurs., 7 Nov. 1912; HEJ in London, EW–JHS, 25 Nov. [1912], LL 284–85; FPK warned EW not to live with TW again, quoted in HJ–EW, 10 Dec. 1912, LP 242–43; "gold-garters/affected," HJ–MCJ, 31 Jan. 1913.

45. WB to NYC, EW–BB, 25 Nov. 1912; "That/weather," GL, PL due for holidays, EW–BB, 23 Dec. 1912; "Last/years," *Je vais m'y remettre de suite* (I'll put them back immediately), EW–WMF, Mon. [Dec. 1912].

46. "lined/bloom," EW–DC, 12 Feb. 1913; "really/made," EW in Salle, EW–SN, 2 Feb. 1913.

47. HE in Paris, "perfectly/her," EW–GL, 8 Feb. [1913], LL 285–86; "violent dislike," HEJ adopted BF, later disinherited EW and BF, EW–Pendleton Beckley, 29 Jan. 1929; HEJ on EW, OC–SBC, 7 Dec. 1913; RWBL and LL give "Tecla" for "Tekla," which was not her first name, but her surname, see LL 286, fn. 1.

48. "it's/known," EW–MB, 15 Jan. 1913; "I/arranged," EW–MB, 7 Feb. 1913; "I/anything," W. Chanler–EW, 22 Jan. 1913; "nerve/waste," W. Chanler–EW, 11 April 1913.

49. HE to Monte Carlo, HJ–EW, 31 Jan. 1913, and 3 Feb. 1913, LP 243–47, fn. 7; HJ birthday gift, LL 286–87; "consequent/admiration," March 1913 circular signed by EW and W. D. Howells over names of committee organizers. In England: Edmund Gosse, James Barrie, and Thomas Hardy; in the U.S.: W. D. Howells, Barrett Wendell, and EW (a different letter is reproduced in LL 286; both letters circulated); "Henry fund," EW–GL, 23 March [1913], LL 289.

50. "pinching," HS's surgeries, plans for Egypt, Sicily, EW–GL, Easter, 23 March [1913], LL 289; "horror," HJ–W. James III, cable, 28 March 1913, LE, 4: 652; "You/friends," EW–SN, 12 April 1913, LL 293–95.

51. "A/incredulity," HJ–W. James III, 29 March 1913, LE, 4: 653–54; "My/this," EW–GL, 2 April [1913], LL 290–91.

52. EW returned money, EW–B. Wendell, 12 April 1913, LL 293; "boundless pleasure," 21 April 1913, LE, 4: 664–68; "he/stopped," EW–WMF, 3 May [1913], LL 300–302.

53. Scribners advance to HJ for *Ivory Tower*: "I/away," EW–CS, 29 April [1913], LL 300, fn. 1.

54. "damned/her," OC–SBC, 5 May 1913; "improper/others," "temperament," OC–SBC, 20 Feb. 1913; "anaemic/way," OC–SBC, 24 June 1913; TW/HEJ in Paris restaurants, OC–SBC, 7 Dec. 1913; "could/can," DBU–EW, 26 May 1913; "formal/devotion" B. Wendell–GL, 30 March 1913; "great/me," EW–GL, 14 April [1913], LL 295.

55. "homeless/*autres*," EW–MCJ, 2 Feb. 1912; "Your/annoyances," T. Newbold–EW, 9 April 1913; Wharton name, EW–RG, 29 April 1914.

56. "Ionian," EW–BB, 19 April [1913], LL 296–97; "It's/more," EW–WMF, 3 May [1913], LL 300–30l.

57. "great/sweetness," EW–WMF, 22 April 1913, LL 297–99; "all/world," summer cruise, EW–BB, 19 April [1913], LL 296–97; "It/shore," Soluntum, EW–BB, 28 April [1913]; "fugitive/me," EW–BB, 2 May [1913]; "tremendous/futilities," EW–MB, 20 May [1913], LL 302–3.

58. "extraordinary/sense," *Daphnis*, EW–BB, 14 June [1913]; "magnificent," EW–BB, 10 June [1913]; Diaghilev crying, Eksteins, 15.

59. BB tickets, EW–BB, 5 June, 1913; "truculent/cock," Eksteins, 16.

60. EW did not discuss her opinions, aesthetic theories, GL, *M*; "*scherzo*/shelved," Du Bos, *M*.

61. *CC* galleys, AB–WCB, 27 June 1913; "little/place," EW–BB, 5 June 1913; "squalid little," EW–E. Gosse, Mon., 21 July [1913]; "our/days," HJ–HS, 2 Sept. 1913.

62. "making/ring," EW–WMF, 3 May [1913], LL 300–301.

63. "satire/society," Anon., *NYTBR*, "Hundred Best Books of the Year," 30 Nov. 1913, 664.

64. "mere/vulgarity," H. W.[Boynton], *Nation* 97 (30 Oct. 1913), 404–5.

65. *CC* contract, advance, sales, EW–CS, 26 Jan 1913, and CS–EW, 18 Oct. 1913, 22 Oct. 1913, and 3 Nov. 1913; "languid debut," EW–CS, 6 March 1914; "She/story," Anon., *Athenaeum* 4490 (15 Nov. 1913), 554; parable, Anon., *SR* 116 (22 Nov. 1913), 658–59; incisive, Anon., *Bookman* [England], 45 (March 1914), 30; "decidedly/convince," Edwin Francis Edgett, *BET*, 18 Oct. 1913, pt. 3, p. 8; "It/libel," Anon., ALA *Booklist*, 10 (Dec. 1913), 159; "satiric/together," HJ, "The Younger Generation," *TLS* (2 April 1914), 157–58; "inspired," HJ–EW, 10 Sept. 1913, LP 265–67.

66. "green/chef," EW–BB, Sat., 2 Aug. 1913, LL 303–4; "she/him," BB note added to EW–BB, 5 Aug. [1913] letter, LL 305.

67. "partly/alone," EW–WMF, 13 Aug. [1913]; loan of motor, "alienists," EW–MB, 14 Aug. [1913], LL 306–7.

68. "particularly/country," EW–MB, 14 Aug. [1913], LL 306–7.

69. "cheeky/can," EW–JHS, 4 Sept. [1913], LL 309–11; "Art/her," BB–MB, 26 Aug. 1913, Samuels, 2: 163; "sees/sense," Samuels, 2: 163.

70. "I'm/them," EW substituted "lived" for "suffered" in this sentence, EW–SN, 12 Aug. 1913; "thousand/see," EW–GL, 8 Jan. [1913]; "I/shortcomings," EW–WCB, 2 Nov. 1913.

71. "Edith/look," HJ–CJ, 22 Sept. 1913; "Edith's/possessions," HJ–MCJ, 12 Oct. 1913.

72. "old/lonely," OC–SBC, 2 Oct. 1913; "just/feel," OC–SBC, 25 Oct. 1913; "heart," OC–SBC, 2 Feb. 1910; "less heart," *LI*, 1089.

73. WB and E. Goelet, OC–SBC, 13 Oct. 1913; BF's personality, BF–MF meeting and courtship (SB interview with BF's niece, Louisa Farrand Wood, 26 May 1991).

74. "elephantine," BF–EW, 6 Jan. 1936; EW's Oct. 20–Nov. l England trip, "What/confidence," HJ–MCJ, 31 Oct. 1913; BF's engagement, EW–WMF, Queen's Acre, 30 Oct. [1913].

75. "The/forlorn," OC–SBC, 7 Dec. 1913; "violent/bronchitis," EW–DC, Wed., 31 Dec. 1913.

76. "cracking/waves," EW–DC, Wed. 31 Dec. 1913; "Blessedness/on," emphasis added, EW–BF, 18 Jan. [1914].

77. "blue/vertiginous," EW–MCJ, 20 Jan. 1914; "mad/scrappy," EW–BB, 30 Jan. 1914, LL 312–13.

78. "queer/life," EW–BB, 30 Jan. 1914, LL 312–13; "Edith/coquetry," MB–G. Scott [Jan. 1914] (IT).

79. "People/begin," EW–DC, Wed. 31 Dec. 1913; "maelstrom/hut," EW–SN, 20 Jan. 1914; "village clocher" (clock), "long/evenings," concerts, EW–BB, 30 Jan. 1914, LL 312–13; Theodore Roosevelt, *An Autobiography* (New York: Macmillan, 1913), EW–MCJ, 27 Jan. 1914.

80. Chimney fire, "By/corners," EW–MCJ, 21 Feb. [1914]; "always/is," EW–MCJ, 15 Nov. [1914]; FRJ failing, EW–MCJ, 20 Jan. 1914; HJ's teeth, HJ–EW, 16 Feb. 1914, LP, 275–76; HS's stomach problems, HJ–HS, 12 Jan. 1914; "maniaque/pontifications," EW–BB, 12 March 1914.

81. "I/draughts," EW–BB, 19 Feb. 1914; "tropism," EW–BB, 12 March 1914; PL and Algeria trip, HJ–EW, 16 Feb. 1914, LP, 275–76; "I/Piper," EW–BB, 19 Feb. 1914.

82. "indescribably sinister," EW–BB, 16 April [1914], LL 317–19; "narrow/coast," EW–WMF, 9 April [1914], LL 315–17; "native/savageness," EW–BB, 16 April [1914], LL 317–19; "spicy/desert," EW–BB, 1 May [1914], LL 321–23; RWBL and LL misspell "Duvinck" as "Duvlenck."

83. "motor road," EW–MCJ, 21 April [1914]; "so/shadowy," "'colored' prostitute," EW–GL, 23 April [1914], LL 320–21; "*look*/month," EW–BB, 1 May [1914], LL 321–22; "ugly/Stanhope," EW–WMF, 9 April [1914],

LL 315–17; "stumbling/rose-buds," EW–BB, 23 April [1914]; "incurable nostalgia," EW–BB, Sun., 2 May 1914; "desert magic," "peace/again," EW–SN, 19 May 1914.

84. "critical/afterward," EW–MB, 18 May 1914; "It/enlightened," EW–WMF, 11 May [1914], LL 323–25.

85. "going/longer," EW–WMF, 11 May [1914], LL 323–25.

86. "You/now," EW–WMF, Fri., 20 March 1914; in another letter, she writes, "I would give most things to be able to forget that it was possible for you to say what you did!," EW–WMF. Sat. [March 1914].

87. "like/Chopin," HJ–HS, 4–5 Aug. 1914; WB "Passage to India," "All/Round," WB–BB, 7 Feb. 1914.

88. Balboa cinema, caves, "grassy/it," EW–BB, 26 July [1914], LL 325–26.

89. "exceptionally/dead," *BG*, 336, EW's ellipses.

90. "tranquillizing power," *FF*, 5; EW telescoped the chronology in her two accounts of this period, changing the date of her arrival in Paris to 30 July 1914 in *FF* and 31 July 1914 in *BG*, 338.

91. "millions/other," Burns, 358. Moltke's literary tastes, cultural battle, Eksteins, xv, 89–92; Eksteins comments: "For the Germans this was a war to change the world; for the British this was a war to preserve a world. The Germans were propelled by a vision, the British by a legacy" (119).

92. "new/emotions," *BG*, 336; "The/action," EW–SN, 2 Sept. [1914], LL 335–36; "Les Cloches" [the clocks], Paris flight, "fugitive froussards," "soul-baring/life," EW–JHS, 22 Dec. 1927.

CHAPTER 7

Background texts: Michael Burns, *Dreyfus: A Family Affair, 1789–1945* (New York: HarperCollins, 1991), Morris Eksteins, *The Rites of Spring: The Great War and the Birth of the Modern Age* (Boston: Houghton Mifflin, 1989); Paul Fussell, *The Great War and Modern Memory* (New York: Oxford University Press, 1975); Carlton J. H. Hayes, *A Brief History of the Great War* (New York: Macmillan, 1922); Charles Downer Hazen, *Europe Since 1815* (New York: Henry Holt and Co., 1910, rev. 1923); Fred Kaplan, *The Imagination of Genius* (New York: William Morrow, 1992); Jere Clemens King, *The First World War* (New York: Walker and Co., 1972); Arthur Lubow, *The Reporter Who Would Be King: A Biography of Richard Harding Davis* (New York: Scribners, 1992); Ernest Samuels, *Bernard Berenson: The Making of a Legend* (Cambridge, Mass.: Harvard University Press, 1987, listed as vol. 2 in notes); Barbara Strachey and Jayne Samuels, eds., *Mary Berenson: A Self-Portrait from Her Letters and Diaries* (New York: W. W. Norton, 1983); Barbara W. Tuchman, *The Guns of August* (New York: Macmillan, 1962); Eugen Weber, *France: Fin de Siècle* (Cambridge, Mass.: Harvard University Press, 1986).

1. Nijinsky, "immoral dilettante," Eksteins, 27–28; Jaurès murder, Burns, 358–59; J. Caillaux's politics, Hayes, 292–93; trial, Tuchman, 107, 113; "perfectly/expressionless," EW–MCJ, 19 March 1914. Acquitted, Mme Caillaux, according to Eugen Weber, successfully projected the "traditional image of the helpless woman" (91).

2. EW rented Stocks from July 15 until October 15, EW–GL, 30 June [1914]; to England, EW–BB, 11 Aug. [1914], LL 332–33; "plunge/darkness," HJ–HS, 4 Aug. 1914; "blue-grey softness," *FF*, 18–23; men to front, Eksteins, 98.

3. "cheerful/interesting," EW helpless, HJ–HS, 4 Aug. 1914; "good/interest," EW–BB, 22 Aug. [1914], LL 333–34.

4. WB as banker, EW–BB, 11 Aug. [1914], LL 332–33, fn. 2, incorrectly states that in 1914, WB was already president of American Chamber of Commerce; "decisive battle," *BG*, 343.

5. German advance, Tuchman, 188–325, "fight/retreat," French casualties, 381–82; WB dragon, EW–MB, 20 Dec. [1914], LL 343–45.

6. "Boche beasts," a common epithet for Germans during the war; "infamous violation," HJ–Mrs. Thomas Sargeant Perry, 22 Sept. 1914, LE, 4: 718–19; "butchery/atrocity," HJ–HS, 4–5 Aug. 1914; "playing/trying," EW–RG, 31 Aug. 1914; "the/ever," HJ–EW, 21 Sept. 1914, LP 302–3. EW asked her friend Alfred de Saint-André to translate HJ's letter; it was read to the Académie Française on October 9, and published in the *Journal des Débats* the following day, see LP 303, fn. 1.

7. Bombardment of Rheims, Lubow, 307–8; "glowing/sienna," *FF*, 185–86.

8. HS reaction, HJ–EW, 1 Sept. 1914, LP 296–97; HJ and ambulance corps, HJ–EW, 19 Sept. 1914, LP 301–2; Kaplan, 555.

9. "little aggrieved," EW–SN, 8 July 1914; EW during Battle of Marne, *BG*, 342

10. "die/way," Hayes, 32–33; "taxis/Marne," King, 24.

11. Twenty-two-hour journey, EW–BB, 30 Sept. [1914], LL 341–42; "philanthropic lady," EW–SN, 27 Sept. 1914, and *BG*, 345–46.

12. EW's *ouvroir* and Red Cross, dressmaking sales, EW–SN, 27 Sept. 1914, and *BG*, 342.

13. German prisoners, EW–SN, 27 Sept. 1914; goals of "Foyer Franco-Belge" and "American Hostels," ET "Report," 31 Jan. 1931, 2–3.

14. "miserable/going," money raised, EW, "Story of the Hostels," 15 May 1915; ten thousand meals on 12,000 francs, EW–SN, 26 Nov. 1914; "brazen beggar," EW–MCJ, 15 Nov. [1914].

15. "We/can," EW–MCJ, 25 Nov. 1914; "rather/desperate," EW–MCJ, 15 Nov. [1914]; "I'm/philanthropy," EW–BB, 30 Sept. [1914], LL 341; "fluffy fuzzy," EW–BB, 30 Sept. [1914], LL 341–42.

16. "I/hour," EW–MCJ, 15 Nov. 1914; "on," *BG*, 348; Tyler meeting and marriage (SB interview with WRT, 28 May 1990, 20 May 1992); Tylers married on 26 Nov. 1914 (Thanksgiving Day), ET–MBB, 8 Nov. 1914; see Tyler papers, PUL.

17. ET background (SB interview with WRT, 20 May 1992); "hooked," ET's fear of EW, ET "Memoir."

18. "past/Royall," EW–MCJ, 25 Jan. 1919.

19. "Chief," ET "Report," 31 Jan. 1931; "terrifically/manner," EW–MCJ, 8 May 1919; "sing-song," EW–BB, 17 Dec. 1925; "when/appreciated," EW–DC, 12 April 1928; "indivisible, alas," EW–BB, 14 Nov. 1913.

20. "very/talk," EW–MCJ, 13 Dec. 1914; "beginner/be," EW–MB, 20 Dec. [1914], LL 343–45; "detachment/expense," HJ–EW, 9 Nov. 1914, LP 315–17; "plunge/civilization," HJ–HS, 4–5 Aug. 1914; "It's/relief," WB–BB, 4 Feb. 1915.

21. "living/again," EW–GL, 8 Nov. {1914}, LL 342–43; "It /excuse," EW–SN, 26 Nov. 1914.

22. British recruiting, HJ–EW, 9 Nov. 1914, LP 315–17; Christmas in trenches, Eksteins, 112–13; trench lines, "God /nation," Hayes, 36–39.

23. "form/*generalissima*," PL knitting, HJ–EW, {17} Jan. [1915], LP 320–23; "so visibly," EW–MB, 20 Dec. [1914], LL 343–45; "innate/service," *BG*, 348.

24. "I/activities," EW–MB, 12 Jan. [1915], LL 345–47; "Walter/ dowdy," EW–BB, 27 Jan. 1915; "motionless horror," EW–MCJ, 17 Feb. [1915]; "The/abyss," EW–BB, 10 Feb. 1915; "All/quand même" (just the same), WB–BB, 4 Feb. 1915.

25. "pleasant/August," EW–BB, 10 Feb. 1915.

26. "pen-tied," EW–CS, 14 Nov. 1914; "I/checks," EW–BB, 10 Feb. 1915; 1914 earnings, *ATB*; payment for war articles, EW–R. Bridges, 3 April [1915]; "blood poor," EW–MCJ, 19 April [1915].

27. *FF*: "sunlit silent," 31; "smiling fatalism," 23; "It's/American," EW–MCJ, 17 Feb. 1915; "magnificent/peace," EW–CS, 24 Oct. [1914].

28. "in/sun," EW–MB, 12 Jan. [1915], LL 345–47; "awful/fire," EW–BB, 10 Feb. 1915.

29. WB, N. Astor, MBB, V. Bérard to front with WB/EW, WB–BB, 4 Feb. 1915; "eager/figure," *BG*, 351.

30. De Jouvenel, EW–HJ, 28 Feb. 1915, LL 348–50, LP 323–26.

31. "carved ivory," Anon., *NYTBR*, 5 Dec. 1915, 490; "seeing eye," Florence Finch Kelly, *Bookman* 42 (Dec. 1915), 462–63; "No/up," WB–BB, 5 March 1915; "utterly ravaged," Pompeii, EW–HJ, 28 Feb. 1915, LL 348–50, LP 323–26; "dead/desolate," EW–MB, 13 March 1915; "incredibly destroyed," EW–HJ, 14 May 1915, LL 354–56, LP 339–41; "death-silence," *FF*, 155; cripples, EW–HJ, 11 March [1915], LL 351–53, LP 327–30.

32. "pitch/me," EW–HJ, 11 March [1915], LL 351–53, LP 327–30; "an/Hell," EW–HJ, 14–15 May 1915, LL 354–56, LP 339–41.

33. Du Breuil death, Bessy Lodge, EW–MB, 13 March 1915; "Too/sorrow," EW–DC, 8 June [1915].

34. D'Humières death, "I've/funerals," can't bear weddings, EW–BB, 4 May 1915; "All/spirit," EW–BB, 15 Oct. 1915, LL 361; AB's surgery, EW–MB, 22 July 1915.

35. "picking/dogs," EW, "Children of Flanders Rescue Committee," 15 June 1915 (SA) and 4 April 1917; "immobile/widows," housing and school facilities, ET, "Report," 31 Jan. 1931, 4–7; "Lady/Charge," ET–MBB, 27 April 1915 (PUL).

36. "prettiest/showiest," "Noted," *NYT Magazine*, 28 Nov. [1915], 1–2; "I/strength," *BG*, 350; Kipling refusal, HJ–EW, 26 July 1915, LP 346–48; Parrish refusal, EW–CS, 10 Sept. [1915]; "have/best," Anon., *NYTBR,* 30 Jan. 1916, 37.

37. charity sale, "Find $6,950 War Aid," *NYT,* 26 Jan. 1916; Yvonne Garrick read, *NYT,* 25 Jan. 1916; "doggerel," EW–MCJ, 11 Feb. 1916; Scribners' donation of editorial time came to $1,000, CS–EW, 21 April 1916.

38. "Over/Wharton," International Film Service (SA); EW in Normandy, 14–27 Sept. 1915; HJ invites EW, HJ–EW, 22 Sept. 1915, LP 354–55; "Scotland Yard," EW–ET, 5 Dec. 1915.

39. "It/tragic," EW–B. Wendell, 17 April 1916; "the/nightmare," EW–SN, 27 Oct. 1915.

40. EW work in Oct.-Nov. 1915, problems with AB, "remodelling," EW–MCJ, 10 Nov. 1915 and 25 Nov. 1915.

41. Hostels' operation, Report to Executive Committee, 15 Nov. 1915; "It/Riviera," EW–EC, 26 Nov. 1915, LL 361–63.

42. HJ stroke, T. Bosanquet–EW, [Wed.], 8 Dec. 1915, LP 372-73; "There/still," EW–MCJ, 11 Dec. 1915; Order of Merit, LP 292, Kaplan, 564–65; "Yes/it," "Plus/rien [There is no more left]," EW–GL, 17 Dec. [1915], LL 364–65; "Let/together," EW–GL, 1 March [1916], LL 370.

43. "shattered/break-down," EW–MCJ, 7 Jan. 1916, LL 366–68; "she/secretary," MB–BB, 17 July 1915.

44. Verdun offensive, Hayes, 148–55; "mud/wind," EW–HJ, 11 March [1915], LL 351–53, LP 327–30.

45. "icy/her," Hostels' Report (1 March 1916), 5–8.

46. "every/wards," E. Maynard, *M.*

47. "I/else," EW–Mrs. Winthrop Grenville, 14 Nov. 1917. EW notes that the photo was taken in 1916, "while I was seeing off some 'ambulance motors'"; photo appears in *Heroes of France,* no. 2, 4 Nov. 1918.

48. "wanted/years," EW–CS, 16 Aug. [1916].

49. "she/it," *Le Temps,* 8 Avril 1916; EW cabled news of Legion of Honor to

E. Winthrop, EW–Max Farrand, 12 April [1916]; "Poor/end," EW–MCJ, 17 April 1916, LL 374–75; headstone, EW–BF, 6 July 1916; memorial bed, EW–MCJ, 5 Aug. 1916.

50. "mourning/sides," EW–SN, 9 July 1916; "I/nature," EW–BB, 14 June 1916; "I'm/become," EW–SN, 14 June 1916, LL 379–80; "I/while," EW–MCJ, 29 Aug 1916.

51. "taking/machinery," EW–BB, 4 Sept. 1916; sale of *S*, EW–CS, 15 Jan. 1917; Appleton royalty advance on *S*, D. W. Hiltman–EW, 25 July 1934.

52. "loathing/illness," EW–WMF, 10 Aug. [1916].

53. EW fainted, EW–BB, 10 Nov. 1916; "I/you," EW–GL, 21 Dec. 1916, LL 384–85.

54. "high/fine," ET–RG, 6 Feb. 1938.

55. Lenox minister, *BG,* 294.

56. "old/book," EW–BB, 4 Sept. 1917; artificial, Anon., *Catholic World* 106 (Oct. 1917), 127–28; "foothold/sunshine," H. W. Boynton, *Nation* 105 (29 Nov. 1917), 600; EW's style, Anon., *Bookman* 46 (Sept. 1917), 93–94; unconvincing, Anon., *Literary Digest* 55 (4 Aug. 1917), 37; false note, "slumming/souls," F. H., *NR* 11 (14 July 1917), 311–12.

57. "Anyone/mountain," Anon. [P. Lubbock], *TLS,* 27 Sept. 1917, 464; PL review, EW–MCJ, 14 Nov. 1917; "satirist's/culture," Anon. [T. S. Eliot], *The Egoist* (Jan. 1919), 10; Pittsfield Library, EW–MCJ, 16 Oct. 1917.

58. "It's/own," EW–BB, 4 Sept. 1917, LL 398–99; "bewildered/*beauté,*" J. Conrad–EW, 1 Oct. 1917; "Adam Bede," Edwin Francis Edgett, *BET,* 25 July 1917; "long/advantageous," EW–CS, 15 Jan. 1917.

59. "lovely/Summer," EW–WCB, 20 Aug. 1917; "get away," CS–EW, 21 Sept. 1917.

60. "cheerful/outlook," WB–BB, 4 July 1916; war events, Hayes, 171–82.

61. "French Tuberculous War-Victims" (spring 1916); ET, "Report," 31 Jan. 1931; expanding charity operations, GC, EW–Captain Kipling, 12 May 1917.

62. "overwhelmed," "militarized," EW–MCJ, 13 Sept. 1916; Groslay approved by French War Ministry, offered land at Auteuil, EW–MCJ, 28 Sept. 1916 and 27 Oct. 1916.

63. Eksteins: winter cold, 148; "the Break," David Jones, *In Parenthesis,* 211, 356, fn. 9; Wilfred Owen, "Exposure," 148, 350, fn. 23.

64. "Too/sleep," grand saloon closed, EW–BB, 4 Feb. [1917], LL 389–90; EW's reading, "swim/correspondents," EW–BB, 9 Feb. 1917, LL 391–92; "Sometimes/ loneliness," EW–BB, 17 Feb. 1917, LL 392–94.

65. "The/words," EW–MCJ, 2 Feb. 1917; "It's/last," visit to front, EW–MCJ, 6 April 1917; house search, EW, 15 March 1917 (GC).

66. "fat hauls," EW–MCJ, Feb. (day illegible), 1917; "Red Cross Day," EW–MCJ, 6 April 1917; MCJ bank deposits, EW–MCJ, 12 Jan. 1917.

67. EW–ET about Groslay problems: 17, 21, 22, 25, 28, 29 March 1917; "It/decisions," EW–ET, 28 March 1917.

68. "little/ouvroir," EW–ET, 31 Aug. 1917.

69. "Land/unimaginable," EW–BB, Easter Sun., April 1917; German retreat, Hazen, 704–5.

70. "doing/utmost," EW–ET, Sun., 5 [Aug. 1917]; "get on," EW–MCJ, 11 Dec. 1915; bed rest ordered, GC, 7 May 1917.

71. "party/up," EW–ET, Sun., 5 [Aug. 1917]; "more/climate," OC–SBC, 12 May 1914, quoted Clem March; "*hommage*," Francesca D'Aulby, quoted in KF–WMF, 1 Nov. 1909; "so/survive," EW–ET, Sun., 5 [Aug. 1917].

72. "everything," German prisoners built roads, EW–WCB, 20 Aug. 1917; Rabat fair, Sacrifice of the Sheep, EW–BB, 26 Sept. 1917, LL 399–401; "lovely/minute," EW–BB, 2 Oct. 1917, LL 401–3.

73. "land/vigils," fevered, EW–MCJ, 25 Oct. 1917; personal observations, Anon., *Independent* 104 (13 Nov. 1920), 242; "vivid/aims," Anon., *SR* 130 (23 Oct. 1919), 339.

74. "some/governors," Anon., *Spectator* 125 (23 Oct. 1919), 541; "general/imperialism," Irita Van Doren, *Nation* 111 (27 Oct. 1920), 479–80; "rounded orientalism," Margret Ashmun, *Bookman* 52 (Dec. 1920), 344.

75. Fund-raising, model houses, doctor orders rest, EW–MCJ, 15 Nov. 1917; lost Refugees War Relief money, dependence on Red Cross, EW–MCJ, 29 Nov. 1917; "one/drudge," EW–GL, 28 Dec. 1917.

76. "sordid," Samuels, 2: 231–33; "Russian treachery," EW–CS, 13 April 1918; war events: Hayes, 278–80; Hazen, 700–707.

77. "I/promising," EW–BB, 15 Feb. [1918], LL 403–4; "brilliant/discriminating," EW, *TLS*, 25 June 1914; "rather/friendship," MB–Senda Berenson Abbott, 18 Nov. 1914; "vulgar," MB–G. Scott, 15 Dec. 1913; MB–S. B. Abbott, 7 Jan. 1923; see Strachey, 193, 204, 246.

78. "aspiring/placed," BB–MB, 8 Feb. 1918, Samuels, 2: 230; "profoundly unattainable," BB journal, Samuels, 2: 220; BB recalls lovers' eyes, Strachey, 226; MB suicide attempt, Samuels, 2: 236–37, Strachey, 223.

79. EW reads medical documents, EW–BB, 26 June 1918; "hard/fragments," EW–MB, 6 July 1918; "the/effort," EW–BB, 20 July [1918].

80. Strachey: mental illness in MB's family, 22–23; Pearsall Smith's illness, 299; Karin Costelloe's suicide, 19.

81. H. Adams died 18 March 1918, age eighty; D. Cameron died in his mid-eighties; EC at gravesite, Samuels, 2: 247; "You/dilemma," EW–EC, 22 June 1918, LL 405–06; "There/understanding," E. Hoyt [Lady Lindsay], *M.*

82. "younger/admirable," EW–EC, 22 June 1918, LL 405–6; "madwoman/woman," EW–MCJ, 7 July 1918, LL 406–8; "barbarous/grief," EW–BB, 15 Aug. 1918; "spoilt-child," EW–BB, Sun., 28 July 1918; "vampired," EW–BB, 4 Aug. 1918; "good neurologist," EW–BB, 12 July 1918; "stand it," EW–MCJ, 28 June 1918.

83. "kindergarten," *FWM,* 101; TW bedridden, "nothing/nasty," MCJ and

NCW quoted in OC–SBC, 25 Sept. [1918]; "Teddy's/dear," EW–BB, 4 Aug. 1918; "Incassable," EW–BB, 15 Aug. 1918.

84. FRJ death certificate, Mayor's Office, sixteenth arrondissement, Paris; "hollow/mourning," funeral not announced, financial future for MCJ and BF, EW–MCJ, 7 July 1918, LL 406–8; "cut/ago," EW–EC, 22 June 1918, LL 405–6.

85. "This/murdered," (SB trans. of "*j'ai le coeur meurtri*"), EW–BB, 13 Aug. 1918; "pathetic/fatness," EW–ET, 16 Aug. 1918; "frustrated/being," EW–MCJ, 13 Aug. 1918.

86. "all/others," EW–MCJ, 13 Aug. 1918; "so poor," EW–BB, 11 Sept. 1918; "golden-haired," EW–BB, "late 1918"; EW's search for news of N. Rhinelander, EW–Thomas N. Rhinelander, 31 Oct. 1918, LL 412–13; burial in Murville, France, EW–Colonel Preston, 21 June 1919.

87. "specially/me," R Simmons's mother, EW–SN, 5 Oct. 1918.

88. "weak/children," GC, 11 Dec. 1919; Herrewynn agreement, *DD*, 27 Oct. 1921.

89. "long/dole," EW–ET, 29 July 1918; "devotion/courtesy," advertising, EW–MCJ, 2 Aug. 1918; "When/rhetoric," quoted in Raymond Poincaré, "Rapport sur Les Prix de Vertu," *Académie Française*, 25 Nov. 1920, 16.

90. "ill-timed/hereafter," EW–ET, Mon., 19 Aug. 1918; Lafayette Heroes, EW–ET, 5 Aug. 1918; "that/gang," EW–MCJ, 26 Aug. 1918.

91. "dull thud," EW–ET, 16 July 1918; EW's flirting with RT, EW–ET, 22 July 1918; "stupid/again," EW–ET, Tues., 30 July 1918.

92. EW heart attack, EW–BB, 12 May 1918, GC, 13 May 1918.

93. Appleton advance, J. Sears–EW, 5 April 1918; "reader's/this," Anon., *NYT* (8 Dec. 1918), sec. 8, p. 1; "carved/light," Anon., *TLS* (19 Dec. 1918), 642; "clear-cut/fiction," F. T. Cooper, *PW* 94 (28 Dec. 1918), 2033; "not/adored," Anon., *Nation* 108 (11 Jan. 1919), 56; "significance," Edwin Francis Edgett, *BET* (21 Dec. 1918), pt. 3, p. 8.

94. "crash/triumph," *BG*, 359.

95. *FWM* in U.S. Navy ships' libraries, C. B. Mayo, Commander, USN–Appleton and Co., 14 Oct. 1919; "pioneer people," *FWM*, 113.

96. "highly/other," *FWM*, 113.

97. "intelligent/them," internationalism, Anon., *Nation* [England] 26 (6 Dec. 1919), 368; "Can/defender," Anon., *NR* 20 (24 Sept. 1919), 241; "How/meant," EW–B. Wendell, 19 July 1919, LL 423–25.

CHAPTER 8

Background texts: Matthew J. Bruccoli, *The Life of F. Scott Fitzgerald* (New York: Harcourt Brace, 1981); Daisy Chanler, *Autumn in the Valley* (Boston: Little, Brown and Co., 1936); Kenneth Clark, *Another Part of the Wood: A Self-Por-*

trait (London: John Murray, 1974); Gloria C. Ehrlich, *The Sexual Education of Edith Wharton* (Berkeley: University of California Press, 1992); Hamlin Garland, *My Friendly Contemporaries* (New York: Macmillan, 1932); David Holbrook, *Edith Wharton and the Unsatisfactory Man* (New York: St. Martin's Press, 1991); Sinclair Lewis, *From Main Street to Stockholm: The Letters of Sinclair Lewis, 1919–1930* (New York: Harcourt Brace, 1952); Logan Pearsall Smith, *Unforgotten Years* (Boston: Little, Brown and Co., 1938); W. J. Stuckey, *The Pulitzer Prize Novels: A Critical Backward Glance* (Norman: University of Oklahoma Press, 1981); Andrew Turnbull, *The Letters of F. Scott Fitzgerald* (New York: Scribners, 1963); Barbara White, *Edith Wharton: A Study of Her Short Fiction* (Boston: Twayne, 1991); Cynthia Griffin Wolff, *A Feast of Words: The Triumph of Edith Wharton* (New York: Oxford University Press, 1977).

1. CC ill, EW–ET, 6 Jan. 1919; "frowsty," EW–BB, 15 Feb. 1919; RN's finances, EW–BB, 17 March 1919; "lost/needed," EW–C. Roosevelt, 11 June 1919, LL 422–23.

2. "dithy rambles," EW–BB, 15 Feb. 1919; "bustling/maid," EW–BB, 27 Jan. 1919, LL 421–22; fashion ads from London *Times*, GC, March 1922; two hours writing, EW–MCJ, 19 Feb. 1919; dresses, JDF–M. Noel, 28 Feb. 1919; corset, GC, 7 Nov. 1919; shoes, GC, 4 Feb. 1919.

3. rent for 53 rue de Varenne, EW–Mr. Arthur, 3 Jan. 1919, and EW–ET, 7 Feb. 1919.

4. "pure/background," RN, *M*.

5. ET finds PC, *BG*, 362–63; Allied victory, DBU, *M*; purchase price, EW–MCJ, 1 Aug. 1921, and OC–SBC, 13 June 1920.

6. Colombe sisters, "Mademoiselle Colombe" (a history of the family saved by EW, LLI); history of St. Brice: Jacques Fosse, *"La Seigneurie de Saint-Brice," Bulletin de l'Association des Amis du Vieux Saint-Brice*, 1 (1990), 7, and Guy Vincent, *"De Bossuet au surréalisme," Bulletin*, 1 (1990), 39–41.

7. PC renovation, C. Knight, Allioli, GC, 4 Feb. 1919; move, Widow Noiret–EW, 16 June 1919.

8. "He/manuscripts," RBJ's duties, J. H. Sears–EW, 13 Dec. 1918.

9. "Writing/endless," EW–MCJ, 25 Jan. 1919; income drop, EW–BF, 6 Oct. 1920, and GC, EW–Mr. Hancy, 6 Sept. 1918; "glorious debut," MCJ return to NYC, EW–MCJ, 30 May 1919; *M* sales, J. H. Sears–EW, 11 April 1919.

10. "It/literature," J. H. Sears–EW, 11 April 1919; *SEP* rejected EW's proposed "Victory" essay, F. S. Bigelow–MCJ, 22 Nov. 1918; "somewhat/Mirth," EW–RBJ, 25 July 1919.

11. "like/nigger," EW–MCJ, 11 Sept. 1919; "possess/story," RBJ–EW, 19 Sept. 1919; withdraw royalty advance on *SF*, RBJ–EW, 7 Aug. [1919].

12. "a/propaganda," Anon., *Bookman* [England] 65 (Oct. 1923), 46; "deeply/command," Anon., *Spectator* 131 (13 Oct. 1923), 514; "dull/war,"

Anon., *TLS*, 20 Sept. 1923, 618; sentiment, Maurice Francis Egan, *NYT-BR*, 9 Sept. 1923, 1, 19, 24.

13. Old contract with *PR*, EW–RBJ, 4 Sept. 1919; Vance refused *SF* price, RBJ–EW, 19 Sept. 1919; *Age* proposal, EW–RBJ, 4 Sept. 1919; contract terms, RBJ–EW, 19 Sept. 1919.

14. "Subjects and Notes" (YCAL).

15. "old aunt," MCJ–EW, 10 Dec. 1919; "Society/characters," RBJ–EW, 13 Nov. 1920; "Little/tackled," MCJ–EW, Sat., 22 Nov. 1922.

16. "plunged," EW–MCJ, 11 Oct. 1919; *Age* completed in Hyères, EW–MCJ, 25 March 1920; "work[ing]/over," EW–MCJ, 15 Feb. [1920]; anachronisms, printers' strike, EW–WCB, 21 April 1921; "I/all," RBJ–EW, 13 Nov. 1920; EW's method of quoting poetry and prose, Richard D. Harlan–Arthur Scribner, 28 Jan. 1921.

17. "additional/write," EW–RBJ, 4 Sept. 1919.

18. "great/scored," MCJ–EW, Sat. 22 Nov. 1919; "positively/scene," EW–MCJ, 9 Dec. 1919; EW saw *The Shaughraun* as a girl, *LGNY*, 363.

19. "You/week," MCJ–EW, 19 Dec. 1919; "but/interested," *BG*, 369; "literary/leading," first edition book jacket, *SG*, 229.

20. *Age* sales, Appleton royalty reports; "fillum," EW–MCJ, 16 Oct. 1920; "preposterous price," EW–MCJ, 4 Dec. 1920; incorrect film sale price for *Age* in RWBL, 430; it netted $9,000 after agent's fees, RBJ–EW, 29 Aug. 1922, EW–RBJ, 25 Sept. 1922, and EW–RBJ, 18 Feb. 1923.

21. *PR* contract for *GM*, EW–RBJ, 27 Aug. 1920; "I/grasping," EW–RBJ, 4 Oct. 1920; *SF* serial rights contract, EW–CS, 7 Feb. 1921; *SF* royalty advance, EW–CS, 9 July 1923.

22. "at/suspense," A. Vance quoted in RBJ–EW, 14 Oct. 1920; "I/yard," EW–RBJ, 5 July 1920.

23. "glory," W. L. Phelps, *NYTBR*, 17 Oct. 1920, 1, 11; Phelps's attitudes toward EW, RBJ–EW, 14 Oct. 1920; "articulate," H. S. Canby, *NYEP*, 6 Nov. 1920, 3; "as/them," C. Van Doren, *Nation* 111 (3 Nov. 1920), 510–11; "Does/it," K. Mansfield, *Athenaeum* 4728 (10 Dec. 1920), 810–11.

24. "unintelligent/village," Edwin Francis Edgett, *BET*, 23 Oct. 1920, pt. 4, 4; "declare/novelette," RBJ–EW, 10 Nov. 1920; Pulitzer Prize, RBJ–EW, 16 Nov. 1920.

25. *OM* revisions, EW–MB, 28 April 1921; "vigorous," EW–RBJ, 23 May 1921; "immorality," EW–MB, 19 June 1921.

26. "most/orange-orchards," EW–BB, 21 Feb. 1921; EW discovered the old name for her Hyères property ("what the peasants call it") and renamed it "Ste. Claire le Château," EW–BF, 16 Feb. 1922; leaks, damaged roof, EW–GL, 10 Dec. 1920; "wheeling/constellations," EW–BB, 3 Jan. 1921; "⁵³⁄₁₄," WB–BB, 13 Feb. 1921; "till/first," WB–BB, 20 Jan. [1921].

27. Pulitzer, EW–BB, 6 June [1921], LL 441–43.

28. "dead," R. M. Lovett, "Pulitzer Prize," *NR* 27 (22 June 1921), 114, quoted in Stuckey, 42; "tall/aristocrats," H. Garland diary, quoted in Stuckey, 40, fn. 7; "depressing/vengeful," Garland, *Contemporaries*, 347, see also Stuckey, 41; Stuckey recounts the Pulitzer controversy, 39–41, 58–59.

29. "robbed," Lewis, 203; "He/artist," EW–JHS, 21 March 1925, EW remarking on *Arrowsmith*, which she thought less good than *Babbitt*; "more sparingly," EW–SL, 27 Aug 1922, LL 454–56; Lewis advised EW not to join Authors' League, GC, Jan. 1929; EW did not wish to be part of an organization in whose "administration" she could not participate because she lived away from the U.S., EW–MCJ, 29 Jan. 1929.

30. "uplifting/persons," EW–SL, 6 Aug. 1921, LL 445–46; "best/manhood," quoted in Stuckey, 6; "Virtue/Avarice," EW–MB, 19 June 1921.

31. "For/time," EW–BB, 17 Sept. 1921; "sense/activity," EW–RN, 15 Oct. 1921.

32. *NYD* sale (price was probably $7,500, minus agent's fees), RBJ–EW, 27 April 1922; "profit/publishers," EW–RBJ, 9 May 1922.

33. "top-notch/subscribers," RBJ–EW, 1 June 1922; "trifle/theme," RBJ–EW, 27 April 1922; "victims/editor," RBJ–EW, 29 June 1929.

34. "marsupial/pouch," EW–BB, 5 Aug. [1921].

35. "a/it," EW–BB, 5 July 1921.

36. "finest/truth," *GM* book jacket.

37. "reality/masculine," K. F. Gerould, *NYTBR*, 23 July 1922, 1, 3; "deserved/word," EW–RBJ, 2 Aug 1922; "sharper/simpler," H. S. Canby, *NYEP Lit. Rev.*, 19 Aug. 1922, 883; love reforms morals, C. Van Doren, *Nation* 115 (2 Aug. 1922), 128; "promise/ones," W. Follett, *AM* 130 (Oct. 1922), 10.

38. "supreme/itself," R. West, *NS* 19 (2 Sept. 1922), 588; "In/plot," G. Seldes, *Dial* 73 (Sept. 1922), 343–45; "gaudy/show," R. Hale, *Bookman* 56 (Sept. 1922), 98–99; "the/meet," J. M. Murry, *NA* 32 (28 Oct. 1911), 164–65; "slight/symbols," Anon., *TLS*, 7 Sept. 1922, 566.

39. "the/novel," RBJ–EW, 17 Oct. 1922; "negative realism," H. W. Boynton, *Independent* 109 (19 Aug. 1922), 79–81.

40. planned sequel to *Age* called "Homo Sapiens," EW–RBJ, 9 Nov. 1921, and RBJ–EW, 31 Aug. 1922; *GM* book sales, SG, 246–47; *GM* film sale, RBJ–EW, 29 Aug. 1922; *Age* film sale, RBJ–EW, 25 Sept. 1922; *McCall's* offer, RBJ–EW, 25 Aug. 1922; "I/family," ATV–RBJ, 13 Sept. 1922.

41. "Silence/Approval," *PW* proof copy, Hollywood ads, 26 Aug. [1922]; "Left/hands," RBJ–EW, 29 Aug. 1919.

42. Maugham, RBJ–EW, 14 Sept. 1922; FSF $500 screenplay for *GM*, Bruccoli, 179.

43. "deluded/both," novel subject and delivery date, *FD* plans, EW–RBJ, 25 Sept. 1922.

44. JDF's work routine, GC, 17 Jan. 1920, and Sept. 1925; JDF refuses to come to Hyères in 1919 and EW wants to "sack" her, EW–ET, 16 Jan. 1919, and JDF–EW, 27 Feb. 1920.

45. "the/for," EW–BB, 21 Feb. 1921; N. Herrewynn illness, GC, EW–Reverend Mother, St. Michel Hospice, Poperinghe, Belgium, 11 April 1920, and 19 July 1921; EW wrote Herrewynns weekly, GC, Jan. 1922.

46. "I/unvarying," EW–MCJ, 4 Oct. 1923;; "sadness/youth," EW–BB, 23 Aug. 1922, LL 453–54.

47. MTG comment, see Markow-Totevy papers (YCAL); S. Gray arranged HEJ/EW meeting: "It was all her idea (and utterly useless)," EW–MCJ, 19 June 1921.

48. "My/brother," EW–WMF, Sun. eve. [1920]; "painful/d'or," names HEJ's widow as Anna Julia Caroline Marie Vanherle Tekla Jones, FRK–LA, 21 May 1962 (LA).

49. "enslaved/silenced," EW–BB, 23 Aug. 1922, LL 453–54; "niece," GC, EW–Pendleton Beckley, 5 Feb. 1929.

50. Tekla to NYC, EW–MCJ, 9 Oct. 1922; "pall/me," EW–BF, 1 Dec. 1920; HEJ's widow buried in Cannes, EW/BF to inherit from HEJ, EW–P. Beckley, 29 Jan. 1929.

51. Marian Bell story, OC–TC, 24 Aug. 1926; "realized/sort," notes attached to letter, BF–Wayne Andrews [1958]; DC testimony, RWBL, 535, and FRK–ET, 10 Sept. 1949; "left-over/Egerton," EW–MCJ, 1 March 1921.

52. "unreal," Donald A. Douglas, *NYT*, 8 June 1924, book sec., 21–22; historical authenticity, James L. Ford, *Literature Digest International Book Review* 2 (Oct. 1924), 785–86; "As/subjects," E. Wilson, *NR* 39 (11 June 1924), 77; "staged/in," J. J. Chapman, *AM* 134 (Aug. 1924), 6; "hole/personages," E. F. Edgett, *BET*, 24 May 1924, 4; "affinity/relationship," L. P. Hartley, *Spectator*, 132 (21 June 1924), 1006.

53. "odd," MCJ–EW, 13 Feb. 1921; "I've/resembled," EW–MCJ, 8 March 1921; "stupid," "silly," "idiotic," BF–EW letters, passim; "many/are," EW–MCJ, 24 Jan. 1925.

54. "Beatrice Palmato" plot summary and fragment appear in a notebook dated 1918–1923 (YCAL); JHS, who often provided EW story ideas, may have given her this one. EW mentions an "incest donnée" in a 1935 letter to BB, remarking that it would make similar themes in William Faulkner's *The Sound and the Fury* (1929) and Ferdinand Céline's *Voyage au bout de la nuit* (1932) "look like nursery-rhymes," EW–BB, 14 Aug. 1935, LL 588–89. See C. Wolff, 407–15, for a persuasive theory of the fragment's dating.

55. "incest vision" (referring to a scene in *MR*), EW–JHS, 25 May 1925, LL 479–81; C. Wolff reproduces plot summary and "unpublishable fragment," 301–5.

56. "large/hand," *BG*, 2; "and/cup," "Beatrice Palmato," C. Wolff, 304; Hol-

brook and White claim EW was an incest victim; Ehrlich and C. Wolff read EW's sexual history in relation to her literary creativity.

57. "the/days," EW–BB, 19 May 1923, LL 466–67; "elegant/home," Iris Origo (YCAL).

58. "mediaeval pageant," EW–BB, 1 July 1923, LL 468; ceremony, Phelps's comments on EW, *NYT*, 21 June 1923.

59. "impressive/spectator," EW–James Barbour, GC, July 1923.

60. EW/FSF encounter in CS's office, Bruccoli, 135 [no date for this event is given, but it could only have been 1923]; see also Matthew J. Bruccoli and Scottie Fitzgerald Smith, eds., *Bits of Paradise* (New York: Scribners, 1974). Bruccoli: "no/responsibility," 192; FSF's 1923 earnings, 192, rate on short stories, 193; "strong," 219.

61. Fitzgeralds in Hyères, May 1924, FSF working on *GG*, Bruccoli, 197; "friendly/manufactory," EW–FSF, 8 June 1925, LL 481–82; "generous/Hemisphere," EW–SL, 6 Aug. 1921, LL 445–46.

62. "Will you and Mrs. Fitzgerald come to tea next Sunday? I shall be in at 4—," EW–FSF, 2 July 1925 (FSF Scrapbook 4, Firestone Library, Princeton University); "steady/horrible," *DD*, 5 July 1925; "unyielding/stiffness," T. Chanler–M. Bruccoli, 4 Aug. 1959; GL thought FSF drunk, see Bruccoli, "What Really Happened at the Pavillon Colombe," *Fitzgerald Newsletter* 7 (Fall 1959), 25–26; "ill/condition," EW–ES, GC, 21 April 1934; "I/lousy," FSF–M. Perkins, 27 Dec. 1925, in Turnbull, 193–94. In 1934, FSF sent EW *Tender Is the Night*, which she said appeared to "deal entirely with drunkards and drug-fiends"; in the dedication, FSF "declare[d] that "he is proud that I am of the same race as his,'" EW–ES, GC, 21 April 1934.

63. Influences on FSF, G. Seldes, *Dial* 79 (Aug. 1925), 162–64; "approached/life," L. Bromfield, *NYEP*, 9 May 1925, 3; "whisper[ing]/age," R. M. Lovett, *Edith Wharton* (New York: Robert M. McBride, 1925), quoted in S. P. Sherman, *NYHT*, 17 May 1925, section 5, 1–2.

64. "same/which," EW–DC, 9 June 1925, LL 482–85.

65. "incest-vision," EW–JHS, 25 May 1925, LL 479–81.

66. "well-staged/enlarging," G. Bullett, *SR*, 139 (30 May 1925), 588; "old-fashioned/existed," EW–JHS, 25 May 1925, LL 479–81.

67. "qualified/already," V. Woolf, "American Fiction," *SRL*, 2 (1 Aug. 1925), 1.

68. NIAL gold medal, GC, Jan. 1925; "respectable institution," R. Bridges–EW, 5 Feb. 1925 (YCAL); Nobel Prize, EW–MBB, 15 Jan. 1928, and 11 April 1926; *CC* and Nobel Prize, K. Clark, *Wood*, 204.

69. "managed/men," RG, *M*; "enthusiastic/English," R. Grant, Commemorative Tribute, *American Academy of Arts and Letters* (1939); "supreme/view," A. H. Quinn, *American Fiction* (New York: Appleton-Century, 1936), quoted in Grant; RG and Brand Whitlock facilitated EW's election to the American Academy.

70. "We/balls," RBJ–EW, 5 Jan. 1923.

71. EW's School of Design scholarship, "worthwhile/sentiments," EW–MCJ, 25 April 1923; "I/so," ET "Memoir."

72. Marcel wave, EW–ET, 19 April 1920; tortoise-shell lorgnette, GC, March 1925.

73. "rising/clear," EW–R. Bridges, 12 Nov. 1923; "turgid/drivel," EW–BB, 6 Jan. 1923, LL 461–62; "negative/fiction," Anon., *TLS*, 17 Dec. 1925, 878; "Palates/fare," EW–Dorothy Ward, 13 March 1937.

74. "terrific/Krafft-Ebing," WB–BB, 13 May [1921]; EW on *Sodome et Gomorrhe*, EW–BB, 7 June [1921], LL 441–43; "No/effects," EW–M. Dix, 5 Dec. [1905], LL 98–99.

75. "miracle/parts," EW–MB, 1 Oct. 1925; RN search for yacht, EW–RN, GC, Aug. 1925; JHS interviews Capt. MacLean, GC, EW–J. A. Smith, Nov. 1925; charter costs, GC, May 1926.

76. "crowning/was," EW–BB, 6 Jan. 1925; "depths/beauty," *BG*, 373.

77. "literary/*Lescaut*," EW–GL, 11 April [1926], LL 489–91, fn. 3.

78. *Osprey* provision lists (YCAL), "serene/sunny," *BG*, 372.

79. "most/extravagance," EW–RBJ, 30 March 1926; "keenly interested," RBJ–EW, 7 May 1926; "unbroken bliss," *BG*, 373; "at/time," EW–RBJ, 21 Dec. 1926.

80. "make-up/Society," EW–RBJ, 11 Jan. 1927.

81. "Why/subject," G. Busey, *NYHT*, 27 July 1926, 4.

82. "come/enthusiasm," D. B. Woolsey, *NR* 47 (21 July 1926), 262–63.

83. "bow/ingenuity," envy, RBJ–EW, 26 Jan. 1923; "working/were," EW–RBJ, 9 Dec. 1925; *Delineator* contract, RBJ–EW, 21 Oct. 1926; "modern," EW–RBJ, 2 Nov. 1926.

84. *C* contract, summary and first chapter, RBJ–EW, 15 Feb. 1927; "Have/novel," RBJ–EW, 29 Dec. 1926; five chapters of *C*, EW–RBJ, 21 March 1927.

85. St. Brice property loan, GC, EW–Pendleton Beckley, Dec. 1926; Ste. Claire purchase, GC, Feb.–March 1927; "all/sea," EW–MCJ, 25 Jan. 1927, LL 497–98; "bourgeois/loan," EW–RBJ, 17 May 1927.

86. Spode service, GC, Sept. 1926; Cartier's, GC, Feb. 1927; Vance agreement for *C*; "begged/contention," *LHJ* interest in EW's "fourth novel," RBJ–EW, 7 June 1927; "Do/in," RBJ–EW, 14 June 1927.

CHAPTER 9

Background texts: Caresse Crosby, *The Passionate Years* (New York: Dial Press, 1953); Richard Ellmann, *James Joyce* (New York: Oxford University Press, 1959); Stuart Gilbert, ed. *The Letters of James Joyce* (New York: Viking Press, 1957); Ernest Samuels, *Bernard Berenson: The Making of a Legend* (Cambridge:

Harvard University Press, 1987, listed as vol. 2 in notes); Meryle Secrest, *Kenneth Clark: A Biography* (New York: Holt, Rinehart, Winston, 1984); Logan Pearsall Smith, *Unforgotten Years* (Boston: Little, Brown, 1939); Barbara Strachey and Jayne Samuels, eds. *Mary Berenson: A Self-Portrait from Her Letters and Diaries* (New York: W. W. Norton, 1983); Geoffrey Wolff, *The Black Sun: The Brief Transit and Violent Eclipse of Harry Crosby* (New York: Random House, 1976).

1. "Time/broken," OC–Thomas Codman, Fri., 20 Aug. 1926; "green/know," EW–DC, 11 Aug. 1926, LL 491–93.
2. "nauseating/abyss," EW–GL, 28 Sept. 1926, LL 493–95.
3. "too/type," Anon., *Outlook*, 146 (29 June 1927), 290; "nature/institutions," Isabel Patterson, *NYHT*, 22 May 1927, 1–2; "equal/method," P. Hutchinson, *NYTBR*, 22 May 1927, 1, 27.
4. "devoted services," EW–MCJ, 1 Nov. 1926.
5. "severe/Ritz," EW–GL, 28 Sept. 1926, LL 493–95; Dr. de Martel, EW–MCJ, 14 Nov. 1926; "chocolate/ugly," EW–BB, 30 Nov. 1926; tennis, EW–MCJ, 19 Feb. 1927.
6. "pretty/of," EW–JHS, 13 Jan. 1927; "He/net," EW–MCJ, 25 Jan. 1927, LL 497–98.
7. "hovering over," EW–JHS, Sat., 22 Jan. [1927]; "in/hand," EW–MCJ, 7 Feb. 1927; "Comet/bye," EW–MCJ, 19 Feb. 1927.
8. "very/progress," EW–MB, 8 March 1927; brain specialist, EW–MCJ, 28 Feb. 1927; "dearest/paralytic," WB–EW, 31 March [1927]; WB very depressed, EW–BB, 26 April 1927; "so/lead," EW–GL, 1 April 1927.
9. "experiments," WB dined with EW, EW–MB, 24 Sept. 1927; WB dismissed EW's doctor, EW–JHS, 4 Oct. 1927; dedication from Proust, SB trans.; "anxious/endless," *DD*, 2 Oct. 1927.
10. Modern technology, EW–MB, 26 Oct. 1927; "failing/dear," *DD*, 11 Oct. 1927.
11. "great/humbug," EW–JHS, 15 Oct. 1927, LL 504–5; "so-called/anywhere," WB's will and funeral notes (Crosby Collection, HRHRC).
12. "ghastly hours," *DD*, 13 Oct. 1927; "Slowly/black," *NYHT*, 18 Oct. 1927; "shaken/grief," EW–MB, 26 Oct. 1927.
13. cremation and PC events, Crosby, 212, 217–18, and G. Wolff, 128–29.
14. *Chapelle ardente*, the Pietà (LLI), "The/here," *DD*, 17 Oct. 1927; "The/life," *DD*, 29 Oct. 1927.
15. "mockery," *DD*, 20 Oct. 1927; WB's letters, *DD*, 25 Oct. 1927; "Every/again," EW–GL, 28 Oct. 1927.
16. "advise/unmanageable," EW–GL, 28 Oct. 1927; "half-crazy cad," EW–JHS, Wed. 23 Nov. [1927]; "Grab Act," Crosby, 212; "great many," EW–Benjamin Conner, 6 April 1928; WB's will (HRHRC) lists bequests; death of H. Crosby, see G. Wolff, 127–32, who provides an excellent

analysis of WB's friendship with H. Crosby, 121–23; on WB's library bequest, see G. Wolff, 129–31; H. Crosby giving away books, his death, G. Wolff, 186–88; "murderer," EW–BB, 18 Feb. 1931, LL 534–35.

17. "passion/first," EW–BB, 22 Oct. 1927; "gracious/value," PL, *PEW*, 207–8; "Of/Berry," JHS–PL, 17 Feb. 1938; WB's influence on EW, "ferocious snob," lineage, GL *M*.

18. "beyond measure," EW–ET, 2 Nov. 1927; "one/subject," EW recommends WMF, offers to help him and make WB's letters to her available to him, EW–N. Alden, 23 Sept. 1931; "beloved," *DD* Sun., 2 Nov. 1930.

19. "I/business," EW–BB, 22 Oct. 1927; *C* finished, EW–ET, 19 Jan. 1928; "It/expression," EW–GL, 11 Feb. 1928, LL 514.

20. TW died at his NYC residence, 11 East Sixty-eighth Street; TW's last years, Scott Marshall, "Whatever Happened to Teddy Wharton?" *Vista*, Winter 1987–1988, 4; "You/now," EW–RG, 10 Feb. 1928; "At/on," EW–MB, 11 Jan. 1928.

21. "shades/situations," EW–RBJ, 11 Jan. 1927; "reserved/Children," EW–MB, 25 March 1928; "I/doing," EW–MB, 3 Aug. 1928.

22. *C* earnings, RBJ–EW, 23 July 1928, and 2 Nov. 1928; movie sale, RBJ–EW, 29 Sept. 1928; "artificial," Rachel Annand Taylor, *Spectator* 141 (8 Sept. 1928), 306, 309; "slick," Francis Birrell, *NA* 44 (6 Oct. 1928), 19; "preposterous," [Robert Morss Lovett], *NR* 56 (26 Sept. 1928), 160; "vagaries/caricature," Anon., *TLS*, 20 Sept. 1928, 664; "scarcely credible," Anon., *Independent* 121 (22 Sept. 1928), 285; "still/surprises," C. P. Fadiman, *Nation* 127 (10 Oct. 1928), 370–71; "uncomprehending/vision," EW–R. Cortissoz, 11 Oct. 1928, LL 518–19.

23. "rain/Gothic," "Literature" 1, 2 (YCAL); American landscape architect Thomas Downing defined Hudson River style in 1845, EW–RBJ, 28 June 1927; "unfortunate," RBJ–EW, 29 Aug. 1927.

24. "crude," EW–ET, 1 Jan. 1930, LL 525–26; *LHJ, SEP* offers, RBJ–EW, 24 April 1928; "bad/isolation," RBJ–EW, 6 Jan. 1928; "They/nowadays," EW–RBJ, 19 Jan. 1928.

25. *Age* drama, E. Marbury–EW, 14 Jan. 1921.

26. "brisk/expectation," RBJ–EW, 7 Dec. 1928; "accentuated," literary rather than dramatic, Robert Garland, *New York Telegram*, 28 Nov. 1928; love scenes too long, Robert Littell, *NYEP*, 28 Nov. 1928; Franchot Tone, S. J. Ervine, *NYW*, 29 Nov. 1928; "sad/ vulgar," EW–ES, 14 Dec. 1928; *Age* copy to K. Cornell, GC, Dec. 1928; box office receipts, GC, Jan. 1–15, 1929.

27. "banner year," *R* deficit, RBJ–EW, 2 Nov. 1928 and 18 Dec. 1928; "wing/XIV," EW–MB, 9 Oct. 1928; EW added to WB's art library, EW–MB, 29 Jan. 1929; "lizard-hole," EW–MB, 20 Oct. 1928. G. Wolff says that WB's will had two contradictory codicils regarding number of

books left to EW, but he incorrectly states the number she actually took, 131; "half," EW–BB, 8 Dec. 1928.

28. WB gravestone, maintenance fees, EW visits in Sept. 1928, GC, Oct. 1928; EW bought double plot for herself in 1930, EW–N. Alden, 13 Oct. 1931; "cry/it," EW–BB, 16 Oct. 1928; tuberculosis sanatoria, reconstitute *MC, utilité publique*, EW–MB, 10 Feb. 1928, LL 513–14; French will, GC, 16 March 1928; Fondation Foch, LA.

29. "It/fault," M. Taillandier, *M*; "It/longer," EW–BB, 27 June 1928; "too/fire," EW–GL, 13 Aug. 1928, LL 516–17; "Your/again," EW–DC, 28 Oct. 1928; "How/is," EW–BB, 24 May 1928; "Growing/freer," Strachey, 183–84; "Alas/stone," EW–BB, 16 Oct. 1928.

30. "one/me," EW–CS, 31 July 1928; death of JDF's husband, EW–MB/BB, 22 Dec. 1928; "down/luck," EW–JHS, 20 May 1928; "tiny giro," EW–GL, 18 July 1928; "wild/name," EW–MB, 25 July 1928.

31. "I/1917," EW–GL, 13 Aug. 1928, LL 516–17; *D* serial, EW–RBJ, 31 Jan. 1929; circumstances of serialization, MCJ–ET, 9 April 1929; "I/swing," EW–RBJ, 6 July 1928; "I/more," RBJ–EW, 9 Aug. 1928.

32. "shattered/darkness," EW–MCJ, 3 Dec. 1928; "undeveloped grippe," EW–RBJ, 20 Dec. 1928; "booming," EW–GL, 25 Feb. 1929, LL 519–20; SC freeze, EW–ET, 19 Feb. 1929; "violent/angina," diphtheria, JDF–ET, 11 March 1929.

33. EW cared for by RN and C. de Béhague, weight loss, relapse, JDF–ET, 11 March 1928; more text for *D*, RBJ–EW, 18 Jan. 1929; "hunted," EW–RBJ, 17 Jan. 1929; "The/otherwise," EW–RBJ, 25 Feb. 1929; "mental/editors," RBJ–EW, 15 March 1929.

34. "My/straw," RBJ–EW, 3 July 1929; "When/be," EW–RBJ, 15 July 1929, LL 521.

35. LSC's politics, Samuels, 2: 330; "happy/other," EW–GL, 15 Aug. 1929, LL 522-23; "dazed," "heartbroken," EW, *DD*, 15 Aug. 1929; "uncommonly/her," EW–MB, 15 Aug. [1929]; "I/good," EW–MCJ, 26 Oct. 1929.

36. "Here's/novel," RBJ–EW, 13 Nov. 1929.

37. "nobody/book," EW–MCJ, 13 Nov. 1929; "highest standard," RBJ–EW, 31 July 1929; "very ugly," EW–RBJ, 9 Dec. 1929.

38. Failure, Anon., *Nation* 130, 15 June 1930, 77; "marionettes," Proteus, *NS* 34 (1 March 1930), 669; lacked freshness, G. Seldes, *NR* 61 (29 Jan. 1930), 283; "human sympathy," P. Hutchison, *NYTBR*, 17 Nov. 1929, 4; "most generous," M. Ross, *NYHT*, 17 Nov. 1929, 3; dignity, Anon., *Century* 119 (Autumn 1929), 112–19; painter's canvas, L. P. Hartley, *SR* 149 (1 Feb. 1930), 144–45; "reflection/place," Anon., *TLS*, 16 Jan. 1930, 42; "I/much," EW–BB, 18 Jan. 1930; "fatality," Smith, 268–69.

39. "*tournée*," EW–MCJ, 23 Dec. 1929; SC Christmas, EW–MCJ, 3 Jan. 1930; tuberculosis subscriptions, EW–ET, 9 Jan. 1930; stinginess of rich

friends, EW–ET, 8 Feb. 1930; Gillet translation of *C*, EW–ET, 27 Feb. 1930.

40. R. Doumic and the *RDM*, JJ–Frank Budgen, 17 July 1933, Gilbert, 336–37; "Rue Barbet," EW–LG, 9 April 1928; LG apologizes to Joyce, Gilbert, 231, fn. 1, and Ellmann, 647; EW and Borsch, GC, passim; Joyce and Borsch, Ellmann, 580–86.

41. "I/you," EW–LG, 25 Jan. 1931 (SB trans.); "I/it," EW–LG, 19 July 1925 (SB trans.); "How/French," EW–LG, 13 Dec. 1927 (SB trans.).

42. "enjoyed/process," Du Bos did not translate other EW works, Du Bos, *M*; "*désolée*/simple," EW–A. Gide, 18 Dec. 1916 (SB trans.).

43. Proust translate *CC*, EW–A. Gide, 5 March 1916, LL 371–72; "40/younger," EW–MB, 4 May 1930.

44. "I/did," ET's comments on *HRB*, picnic, EW–ET, 1 Jan. 1930, LL 525–26.

45. *GA* title, EW–RBJ, 6 Jan. 1930.

46. "very/business," EW–RBJ, 12 Feb. 1930; "Yes/demand," RBJ–EW, 25 Nov. 1930.

47. "fine collection," P. Hutchinson, *NYTBR*, 9 Nov. 1930, 7; "happy/contemporaneousness," Anon., *TLS*, 27 Nov. 1930, 1010; "universal appeal," Maxim Liever, *NYW*, 23 Nov. 1930, 3-E; "Didn't/them," EW–BB, 10 Dec. 1930.

48. "fool/cook," EW–JHS, 1 July 1930; Roger death, Romano murder, EW–GL, 15 July 1930, LL 526–27; "old/cycle," EW–JHS, 10 July 1930; second cook's death, EW–GL, 8 Aug. 1930, LL 528–29; Anjou trip, EW–DC, 15 Aug. 1930; "Gloom/distressed," *DD*, 2 July 1930.

49. Schuler on "Pomegranate," RBJ–EW, 17 Jan. 1931, and EW–RBJ, 31 Jan. 1931; story alterations, EW–RBJ, 3 March 1931; story sold to *SEP*, RBJ–EW, 18 March 1931; reader letters on "Pomegranate Seed," RBJ–EW, 22 May 1931; EW ghost story volume, RBJ–EW, 22 May 1931; *CP* sales, RBJ–EW, 5 Dec. 1930.

50. "Her Son" to *SM* for $750, Alfred Dashiell–RBJ, 9 Nov. 1931.

51. "new people," EW–MCJ, Easter Sun. [1931]; "delightful," "pleasant," EW–MCJ, 14 Dec. 1930.

52. "queer/humility," MB diary, 22 June 1934, Strachey, 294; "mistake," Strachey, 258; "complication," MB–L. P. Smith, 4 Jan. 1927, Samuels, 2: 350; Clark marriage, Samuels, 2: 349–50, 362; J. Clark's mental and physical illnesses, drug and alcohol addiction, Secrest, 176, 215.

53. "closed season," EW–MCJ, 12 Aug. 1931; "I/tempo," EW–BB, 26 April 1931; EW glandular deficiency, EW–MCJ, Easter Sun., 1931.

54. "Edith-Matilda" bell, EW–ET, 23 Aug. 1931, OC's gift, EW–MCJ, 20 Sept. 1931; "campanile," EW–MCJ, 14 Oct. 1931.

55. "Beloved," office of the dead, *DD*, 2 Nov. 1930; "liberal/protests,"

O. Graeve–RBJ, 15 May 1931; "What/sermon," RBJ–EW, 22 May 1931; "undoubtedly/wicked," RBJ–EW, 19 June 1931.

56. "work-blind," EW–MCJ, 9 Sept. 1931; "Does/Astor," RBJ–EW, 19 Aug. 1931.

57. "real/mood," NM, *M*.

58. "severely/sphere," NM, *M*; "sensitive/that," GL, *M*.

59. "elect/far," KC, *M*; drive to Beauvais, EW–BB, 21 Oct. 1934.

60. "great/me," EW–MCJ, 24 Jan. 1932; "Economic/Death," BB–William Ivins, 25 Dec. 1931, Samuels, 2: 391; "don't/Mary," MB–Judith Berenson, 25 Feb. 1932, and Strachey, 287; BB lost Duveen retainer and stock portfolio, Samuels, 2: 390–91.

61. "I/people," EW–MCJ, 6 April 1932; "I/Whitsunday," EW, *DD*, 15 May 1932.

62. 737 Broadway foreclosure, BF–EW, 10 July 1932; double mortgages, BF–EW, 20 Oct. 1935; 21 East Eleventh Street, EW–BF, 29 Jan. 1933; "Lantern Slides," BF–JDF, 9 June 1937.

63. "forget/now," EW–MCJ, 1 March 1932; "I/present," EW–ES, 21 March 1932; effect of economic depression on EW's charities, GC, Dec. 1932.

64. *GA* as sequel, EW–RG, GC, Jan. 1932; "half-gods/spirit," "Edith Wharton," *Delineator* 120 (Jan. 1932), 4; "creative mind," EW–B. Lodge, 31 Oct. 1932.

65. M. L. Becker, *SRL* 9 (8 Oct. 1932), 164; frivolously sketched secondary figures, Dorothea Brande, *Bookman* 75 (Oct. 1932), 577, 637–38; "trace/mind," W. L. Phelps, *Delineator* 120 (Feb. 1932), 7; "not/claims," I. Paterson, *NYHT*, 18 Sept. 1932, 3.

66. "in/main," RBJ–EW, 29 Sept. 1932; *BG* title, EW–RBJ, 20 July 1933.

67. "If/look," EW–DC, 6 March 1933; Elise's breakdown due to menopause, "The/Ministers," EW–DC, 4 April 1933; funeral, challenge to inheritance rights, GC, May 1933, EW–Elise Bernard, 2 June 1933.

68. CG's conversion, EW–MCJ, 29 March 1933; CG's death, GC Oct. 1933; "emptier/ever," EW–MCJ, 22 Oct. 1933; "perfect/fidelity," EW–BB, 4 Oct. 1933; "fill/falls," EW–BB, 14 Sept. 1933; "madly/rich," lonely, EW–BB, 20 Oct. 1933; "all/greens," EW–BB, 30 Oct. 1933.

69. "decidedly dull," *BG* cuts, contract fee, L. Schuler–RBJ, 18 April 1933; *LHJ* losing money, RBJ–EW, 19 April 1933.

70. "dull," EW refuses to cut price, MacCarthy and *AM* chapter, EW–RBJ, 29 April 1933, LL 558–60 [LL misspelled Schuler's last name]; "hard/have," EW–RBJ, 8 May 1933; LAS agrees to pay full amount, RBJ–EW, 24 May 1933.

71. "Diagnosis" rejections, Appleton Co.–EW, 14 Nov. 1930; "commanding maturity," A. B., *SR* (London), 155 (29 April 1933), 414; "cool/master," G. Greene, *Spectator* 150 (5 May 1933), 654.

72. "untutored/underling," EW–BB, 30 Oct. 1933; "I/mine," draft version of *BG* (YCAL)), printed in Cynthia Griffin Wolff, ed., *Edith Wharton: Novellas and Other Writings* (New York: Library of America, 1990), 1071–96.

73. "dog/fatigue," *DD*, 10 Jan. 1934; "Aetat/ago," *DD*, 24 Jan. 1934; "What/year," *DD*, 6 March 1934.

74. "autobiographical monotony," E. M. Forster, *NSN* 7 (23 June 1934), 952; social obstacles, C. Morley, *SRL* 10 (2 June 1934), 727; "If/world," W. Troy, *Nation* 138 (23 May 1934), 598; "serious/that," N. Arvin, *NR* 79 (6 June 1934), 107; "fuss-budget," I. Paterson, *NYHT Books*, 29 April 1934, 7; "sidelines," "picturesque/unfold," A. Loveman, *SRL* 10 (28 April 1934), 662.

75. *EF* film rights, E. L. Smith–RBJ, 7 Feb. 1934; *Age* film, JLW–EW, 26 Oct. 1934; sale of rights, RBJ–EW, Tues., 18 July 1933.

76. "salvage," G. Lane–RBJ, quoted in RBJ–EW, 29 Sept. 1933; "staggered/want," EW–RBJ, 26 Oct. 1933, LL 571–73; "draw/form," E. Sedgwick–RBJ, quoted in RBJ–EW, 11 Jan. 1934.

77. "Bread" sold to movies (under title "Charm Incorporated"), RBJ–EW, 20 March 1934; "I/get," EW–MCJ, 10 April 1934.

78. Burton offered option, RBJ–EW, 26 April 1934; *PR* refused to honor old contract, RBJ–EW, 22 March 1934.

79. *B* literary agent, EW–RBJ, 9 May 1934; "only/rubbers," RBJ–EW, 10 May 1934; EW wants English publisher, EW–RBJ, 26 May 1934; RBJ ill, JLW–EW, 24 May 1934.

80. "green/Jewett," EW–MCJ, 8 May 1934; "no/me," EW–JLW, 11 July 1934; "manifestly/unjust," D. W. Hiltman–EW, 25 July 1934, LL 580–82 (fn. 1 incorrectly transcribes Hiltman's first initial and gives wrong date for RBJ's death; he died the third week of January, 1934).

81. "hung/breadwinner," EW–D. Hiltman, 14 Aug. 1934; EW messages to RBJ, EW–MCJ, 24 Dec. 1934; "Deeply/sympathy, EW–Appleton, 27 Jan. [1935].

82. taxes, EW–B. Conner, 17 Dec. 1934, and EW–MCJ, 27 Jan. 1935.

83. ES on *EF* play, EW–ES, 11 Aug. 1934; "Tattisti/ears," EW–MB, 6 Dec. 1934; "fattening/scenes," EW–BB, 17 Dec. 1934.

84. "You/readers," quoted in JLW–EW, 26 Oct. 1934.

85. "completely/millenium [sic]", EW–BB, 17 Dec. 1934; "I/him," EW–MCJ, 8 Feb. 1935.

CHAPTER 10

Background texts: Elisina Tyler, "Memoir," 11 June 1937–11 August 1937, and "Statement Concerning the Circumstances of Mrs. Wharton's Last Will and Testament," May 1939; Edith Wharton's French Will and Bequests (filed 12 August 1937, Montmorency, France), and *Bureau d'Experts sur Questions Fiscales* (30 July 1935) on EW's French tax situation (LLI). Vivienne de Watteville, *Speak to the Earth: Wanderings and Reflections Among Elephants and Mountains*, with preface by Edith Wharton (London: Methuen, 1935); Claude Silve [Philomène de la Forest-Divonne], *Benediction*, trans. Robert Norton, foreword by Edith Wharton (New York: Appleton-Century Co., 1936).

1. *OM* gross receipts, Alice Kauser Dramatists' Agent, 15 June 1935.
2. O. Davis, *EF* and *Icebound*, ES–MCJ, 9 Aug. [1934]; *Kate Spain*, ES–EW, 26 March [1935], and EW–MCJ, 9 March 1935, LL 583–85.
3. EW illness, JDF–BB, 7 May 1935.
4. "more/ever," EW–BB, 4 Aug. 1935; MCJ illness, EW–MCJ, 16 Sept. 1935, and 18 Sept. 1935; MCJ's burial, EW–BF, 25 Sept. 1935.
5. "alone now," BF–EW, 20 Oct. 1935; memorial service, ES–EW, 20 Nov. [1935], and 18 Dec. [1935]; "aristocracy/reconstruct," J. W. Atwood, *NYHT*, 26 Sept. 1935; preservation of Washington Square, Herbert S. Houston to ed., *NYHT*, Oct. 1935; MCJ's stock market dealings, EW–BF, 26 Oct. 1936.
6. *EF* ticket sales, ES–EW, "Ethan Frome" [Feb. 1936].
7. "It/way," EW–JHS, 4 March 1936..
8. EW's weakness, fainting, tingling, EW–ET, 10 Dec. 1935; "*Souvenirs du Bourget d'Outre-mer,*" *Revue Hebdomadaire*, 45 (21 June 1936), 266–86.
9. "redolent/wild," BB–MB, 25 Feb. 1936, Samuels, 2: 422; SC guests, EW–ET, 11 March 1936; MB's Vienna treatment, Samuels, 2: 419; "How/illnesses," EW–MB, 28 Jan. 1936.
10. *WO* sales, SG, 373; EW's mastery of technique: Anon., *TLS*, 25 April 1936, 353; Percy Hutchinson, *NYTBR*, 26 April 1936, 6; Anon., *Time* 37 (4 May 1936), 80; Graham Greene, *Spectator*, 156 (22 May 1936), 950.
11. "shadowland," RBJ–EW, 16 Feb. 1932; "grim/grimmacing," EW–ET, 11 March 1936; "all/well," EW–BB, 30 Nov. 1933; "wireless," Boccon-Gibod's report, "The/again," EW–MCJ, 10 Feb. 1934.
12. "vilest/together," EW–MCJ, 10 Feb. 1934; EW's fear of civil war, "I/happen," EW–MCJ, 10 April 1934, LL 576–78.
13. "I/me," EW–ET, 11 March 1936; "archeological smashing," EW–BB, 7 Aug. 1936; "how/religion," E. Maclagan–EW, 19 April 1931.
14. "incorrigible/adventurer," EW–MB, 11 Oct. 1936, LL 598; "I/travels," EW–BB, 21 July 1936; "heat/journeys," EW–BB, 25 Aug. 1936; "frightened," EW–JHS, 11 May 1936.
15. "drain/hospitality," EW–BB, Tues., 11 Dec. 1936; "I/rage," EW–JHS, 30 Nov. 1936.
16. "sheer/with," BB–Bessie Berenson, 15 Dec. 1936, Samuels, 2: 427.
17. "dear/invitation," BB–EW, 14 Jan. 1937, Samuels, 2: 428; "moral/Pekingese," BB's opinion that "there was no talk in her house at all—only trifling exchange of stories and gossip," GL, *M*; "death-bed," EW–BB, Sun., 3 Jan. 1937.
18. EW's activities, *DD*; "fresh/way," EW–BB, 31 March 1937.

19. "Oh/bed," EW, *DD*, 15 April 1937; "The/National," EW–GL, 2 April 1936, LL 592–94; "dreadful shock," EW, *DD*, 19 May 1937.

20. "this/stay," OC–TC, 5 June 1937; "she/woman," ET, "Memoir."

21. "Poisse," "golden/surface," V. de Watteville, *M*.

22. "nobody/animal," de Watteville, *M*, and EW "Preface," *Speak to the Earth*.

23. "hush/spirit," P. de la Forest-Divonne, *M*.

24. "I'm/springs," EW–BB, 9 April 1937; "astonishing/here," ET–FRK, 9 June 1949.

25. "Edith/impoverished," BB–ET, 12 Aug. 1937; "There/empty," BF–BB, 27 Aug. 1937.

26. "fully/church," hymns included "Lead, Kindly Light" and "Art Thou Weary," see "Instructions after my death," EW–ET, 23 May 1936, LL 594–96; EW's casket, funeral rites, *NYT*, 13 Aug. 1927.

27. PC sale, French tax claims, ET–FRK, 5 Sept. 1937; JDF unemployment, ET–BF, 17 Dec. 1937.

28. Pierre Lisse to AW, ET–BF, 13 Sept. 1937; AW had remarried in June 1929; his bride was a woman half his age, the nursery governess of Philomène de la Forest-Divonne's daughter, EW–BB, 30 June 1929; inheritance taxes and SC upkeep, ET, "Statement," 11.

29. EW's money from LRJ trust, HE–EW, 5 Aug. 1931; ET "Statement": "lawful heir," 11; LRJ deliberately disinherited EW, 14–15.

30. "open conflict," ET–BF, 17 Dec. 1937; BF to receive residue of GJF's estate, EW–BF, 20 June 1920; "cruelty/possible," BF–EW, 18 May 1936.

31. headstone, EW–JHS, 14 Jan. 1939.

32. "disappeared," BF "Notes," BF–Wayne Andrews [1958]; "Great American Novelist": *Times* (London), 14 Aug. 1937; Louis Gillet, "Edith Wharton," *L'Epoque* (Paris), 16 Aug. 1937; Edmond Jaloux, "Edith Wharton," *Le Jour* (Paris), 17 Aug. 1937; Raymond Recouly, "Portrait de Edith Wharton," *Gringoire*, 20 Aug. 1937; "eventual/fame," *NY Herald*, 16 Aug. 1937.

33. "steals," Sean O'Faolain, *London Mercury* 39 (Nov. 1938), 88–89; "cleverness/heart," L. Bogan, *Nation* 147 (22 Oct. 1938), 418; "clever/heart," E. Wilson, *NR* 96 (26 Oct. 1938), 342–43.

34. BF dismantled Reef Point and gardens, "perfectionist/excellence," Robert Patterson, trustee of Reef Point Gardens, quoted in Eleanor M. McPeck, "Beatrix Jones Farrand," *A Biographical Dictionary of Architects in Maine* (Portland, Maine: Maine Citizens for Historic Preservations, 1991), 443; Louisa Farrand Wood comment quoted in Anne Raver, "Beatrix Farrand," *Horticulture*, Feb. 1985, 32–45.

35. BF's last days, Raver, 45; "noble art," Eleanor McPeck, "Beatrix Jones Farrand," in Barbara Sicherman and Carol Hurd Green, eds., *Notable American Women: A Biographical Dictionary* (Cambridge, Mass.: Harvard University Press, 1980), 221; "I/me," EW–MCJ, 1 March 1932; "We/gift," BF–GL, 18 Aug. 1937.

Index

W

Note: *Titles of works are by Wharton unless otherwise identified.*